The Global Economy and Its Economic Systems

Paul R. Gregory
University of Houston
Hoover Institution, Stanford University

Robert C. Stuart
Rutgers University

SOUTH-WESTERN
CENGAGE Learning·

Australia • Brazil • Japan • Korea • Mexico • Singapore • Spain • United Kingdom • United States

SOUTH-WESTERN
CENGAGE Learning·

The Global Economy and Its Economic Systems
Paul R. Gregory,
Robert C. Stuart

Senior Vice President, LRS/ Acquisitions & Solutions Planning: Jack W. Calhoun

Editorial Director, Business & Economics: Erin Joyner

Editor-in-Chief: Joe Sabatino

Acquisitions Editor: Michael Worls

Developmental Editor: Ted Knight

Editorial Assistant: Elizabeth Beiting-Lipps

Marketing Director: Keri Witman

Senior Marketing Communications Manager: Sarah Greber

Marketing Coordinator: Ilyssa Harbatkin

Art and Cover Direction, Production Management, and Composition: PreMediaGlobal

Media Editor: Sharon Morgan

Rights Acquisition Director: Audrey Pettengill

Senior Rights Acquisition Specialist, Text and Image: John Hill

Manufacturing Planner: Kevin Kluck

Cover Image: © Realinemedia/ Shutterstock

Internal Image: © Realinemedia/ Shutterstock

For product information and technology assistance, contact us at **Cengage Learning Customer & Sales Support, 1-800-354-9706**

For permission to use material from this text or product, submit all requests online at **www.cengage.com/permissions**
Further permissions questions can be emailed to **permissionrequest@cengage.com**

Library of Congress Control Number: 2012954799

ISBN-13: 978-1-285-05535-0

ISBN-10: 1-285-05535-7

South-Western
5191 Natorp Boulevard
Mason, OH 45040
USA

Cengage Learning is a leading provider of customized learning solutions with office locations around the globe, including Singapore, the United Kingdom, Australia, Mexico, Brazil, and Japan. Locate your local office at: **www.cengage.com/global**

Cengage Learning products are represented in Canada by Nelson Education, Ltd.

For your course and learning solutions, visit **www.cengage.com**

Purchase any of our products at your local college store or at our preferred online store **www.cengagebrain.com**

Printed in the United States of America
1 2 3 4 5 6 7 17 16 15 14 13

We dedicate this book to our wives, Annemarie and Beverly.

Contents

Preface

Over the past few decades, economists have awakened to the fact that institutions matter. Countries that have "bad" institutions do poorly. Those with good institution generate high per capita incomes and democratic political institutions. Economists also understand the tight link between economics and politics. No matter how well trained or educated the labor force, bad political systems can ruin any chance of economic success. Institutions tend to cluster into combinations that we call economic systems. This book is about the world's economic systems.

Economic systems used to be relatively easy to define and study. The world's economies belonged to capitalist and socialist camps—and just a few in between. With the collapse of the Soviet Union and its Eastern European Empire, the economic systems of the world have become more nuanced. China, the world's fastest growing economy, has abandoned much of its socialist past but has retained its communist one-party system. We now better understand the differences between the economic systems of North America, Europe, and Asia.

The growing trend toward globalization is making us more alike. Companies have become so international that it is difficult to define their nationality. Markets have transformed themselves into global markets that transcend national boundaries. World economies are now connected in ways and in degrees that could not have been imagined in the mid-twentieth century. The result should be an improvement in population well-being, and yet at the same time new trading and financial arrangements present special challenges. As we write this book, Europe is struggling with the challenges posed by a single currency for widely different economies.

Although comparing differing economic systems has a long and rich evolution, there are changes in the twenty-first century that warrant our attention. Economists understand that institutions and economic systems are important determinants of economic performance, but institutions and economic systems defy measurement. They are not particularly amendable to the standard models of micro- and macro-economics. They require knowledge of history. Institutions and economic systems did not arise over night. They are path dependent. Yesterday determines what we are like today.

Comparative economic systems has raised some of the most significant questions of economics: Why do firms exist? Can we plan an economy? What are the most important institutions that determine economic success or failure? How should we organize incentives, rewards, and punishments? What are the information requirements of an economy? What are the tradeoffs between efficiency and equity? Comparative economics raises the ultimate question of which economic system is in some sense the best, or better than other alternatives.

One of the great lessons from the study of comparative economic systems is that the past and present provide us with a wealth of information on institutional arrangements. We have the experiment with planned socialism that began in the Soviet Union in the early 1930s. We have the relatively long European experience with what has come to be called the welfare state. We have economies that, over the past half century, have transformed themselves from backwardness to affluence. Comparative economic systems provides us with natural experiments that enlighten our views on what works and what does not. We have rare cases of countries that have been divided and operated under quite different economic systems and with quite different results. The dramatic collapse of the former command economies and their replacement with varying degrees of market arrangements has provided a vast array of evidence for the purposes of analysis.

This book is organized in five major sections designed to summarize the current state of the field of comparative economic systems. The material is organized to allow instructors to include or exclude topics at their discretion. Frequently, comparative economic systems is taught with special regional emphasis, for example Asia or Europe. This balance can be achieved by selecting the appropriate chapters.

Part I introduces the subject matter of comparative economic systems. What is an economic system, how do economic systems relate to economic outcomes (economic performance), and how have economic systems changed over time? This material provides us with the basics to develop and understand the nature of different models of economic systems.

Part II is devoted to theoretical models of economic systems. Although economic systems differ in fundamental and subtle ways in national (country) settings, they are based on the basic models of the capitalist or socialist (planned and market) economic systems. There is a rich literature that allows us to develop and understand how these basic models function and how their varying components might be combined to create what we often term mixed economic systems.

Part III is devoted to real-world examples of economic systems and the most important cases in national (country) settings. The Anglo-Saxon model is developed and its variants (the United Kingdom and the United States) explained. We next turn to the European model with its more expansive welfare and regulatory systems. The Asian model follows, with its greater emphasis on family ownership and capital formation. We then discuss the Soviet command economy and its collapse, and we end with a chapter on China's "socialism with a Chinese face." In each case, we examine the system's theoretical and ideological foundations and how it allocates resources in capital and labor markets and the role of the state.

Part IV is devoted to system change and perhaps the dominant example of real-world change—the collapse of the Soviet-type command economies of the former USSR and Eastern Europe. The study of this experience has been fundamental for expanding and improving the analysis of different economic systems, and yet it is also important in another dimension, namely, the performance of these new economic system in an increasingly integrated and yet troubled world economy.

Part V examines the performance of world economies and the impact of natural, systemic, social, and other factors on differing economic outcomes. Such comparisons are especially important in an integrated world in which we observe dramatically different economic outcomes, some very positive and some much less so.

Acknowledgments

We must thank the many scholars who have done the painstaking and pathbreaking research on which this book is based. There are too many to single out individually, but both of us feel it appropriate to honor and remember our thesis advisors Abram Bergson of Harvard University and David Granick of the University of Wisconsin—both pioneers in the study of the Soviet command economy. The field of comparative economic systems is so broad that we can hope to capture only a small part of the literature within the finite pages of a text book. We regret that we had to leave out many substantive topics simply due to space considerations.

Co-author Paul Gregory would like to thank the professional librarians at the East-West Center in Honolulu, Hawaii, for their assistance in locating country-specific materials for this book. He would also like to thank his colleagues at the German Institute for Economic Research (DIW) Berlin for their advice and assistance on European subject matter.

We are grateful to Cengage economics editor, Michael Wrols, for seeing us through the challenging creative process of creating a text that captures modern comparative economic systems.

Paul R. Gregory
Robert C. Stuart

PART

I

Introduction, Definition, and Measurement

Economic History and Economic Systems

Economic Systems in Historical Perspective

As we begin the second decade of the third millennium, we must consider what we can learn from the past that informs us about the present. George Santayana's famous saying, "Those who cannot remember the past are condemned to repeat it," applies to economic systems and economic history as well as to conventional history. The past provides us with case studies of economic and political arrangements that have been tried. Some have worked well; others have not. Recent history has taught us that we are able to change dramatically the way societies order their economic and political lives. Countries that were once part of the Soviet Union or fell within its empire have restructured the way they do things, some much more successfully than others. China's economic reforms have changed it from an economic backwater to a world economic and political power. As this book is being written, the Arab world is challenging the existing political and economic system of the Middle East.

We are not bound by the past. The selection of economic and political systems is more important than other more routine matters. These systems determine how we conduct our economic lives on a daily basis: Are we allowed to start up a new business, or must some government official give us permission? Must we stand in line to buy goods, or can we buy what we want at prevailing prices? Do we decide basic economic and political issues at the ballot box, or does a group of "wise men" decide for us? How much economic freedom do we have or should we have?

History provides us examples of arrangements that work and those that do not. We have too many examples of "failed states" so overcome by corruption and bad economic practices that they provide no opportunity for their citizens. We have nations that were once rich (Argentina) that have become relatively poor; and we have countries that were once poor that have become quite wealthy (Hong Kong). We have similar countries that live or lived side by side with a common heritage, where one is an obvious economic failure (North Korea and East Germany) and the other is an economic success (South Korea and West Germany). We easily forget past misadventures: The financial collapses associated with housing bubbles starting in 2007 are fresh in our minds, but few remember the ill-fated rationing of gasoline in the United States in the 1970s. As time passes, only the elderly will remember what is was like to live under Soviet communism. Only an older generation of Americans personally experienced the Great Depression, and only a few living Germans remember the hyperinflations of the 1920s.

Our economic arrangements do not stand still. Prior to the 1980s, there were virtually no hostile takeovers of large companies; now, the practice is widespread throughout the world. Most large companies have mergers and acquisitions departments. Prior to 1976, agricultural production could only take place in large communes in China. Prior to 1987, citizens of the USSR were not allowed to possess foreign currencies. Prior to 2000, the countries of Europe had their own currencies; now, they have a common currency, the Euro. Fifty years ago, most labor union members worked in industry. Now, most work for the public sector. *The most important changes in the way we organize our economic and political systems occur slowly over time.* The changes are not really visible until decades after the fact, but it is these changes that determine how we live and work.

If we look back more than two centuries at out changing economic landscape, we see a world populated by one billion people, most of whom lived in Asia. These one billion people produced a world output well below $1 trillion in today's dollars. At the start of the second decade of the third millennium, more than five billion people populate the globe, producing a GDP of almost $60 trillion dollars.[1] In 1800, the best single measure of the living standard, world per capita GDP, stood at less than $700; by 2011, it had increased to almost $12,000. Over the past two centuries, population increased by more than seven times; production, by more than fifty times; and the standard of living, by almost seventeen times.

These dry statistics point to significant changes in the way we live. Two hundred years ago, most of us worked in agriculture; few had traveled more than fifty miles from where they were born; most subsisted on bread and a few vegetables, and meat was a luxury. The wealthy went to bed cold because of poor heating, and occupants of the most opulent house of Europe, the Palace of Versailles, went for months without baths. In the year 2012, the average citizen of the United States, Europe, or Japan works in a well-heated office, enjoys a wide variety of affordable foods from all over the world, and has traveled to other continents. Residents of countries that were relatively poor three decades ago, such as Taiwan or South Korea, likely own a car, live in an apartment or house with central heating and air conditioning, and face problems of obesity rather than starvation.

The Uneven Distribution of Economic Progress

Economic history teaches us that economic progress has not been evenly shared. If we go even further back in time to 1500, we see that living standards were roughly equal throughout the world, with Asia, Africa, and Europe having about the same per capita GDP (Figure 1.1). We all started with approximately the same standard of living—presumably not much above that required for subsistence. Asia was the dominant producer in 1500, given its much larger population. Europe was relatively small, and North America had just been discovered. By 1820, Europe and the United States had already begun to pull ahead of the rest of the world, and by 1950 the difference between Europe and the United States and other regions was dramatic. At the end of World War II, Western Europe and the United States accounted for most of world output and had per capita GDPs that were large multiples of those of the rest of the world. Asia had been eclipsed, and Africa continued its relative downward spiral. The Soviet Empire accounted for almost 15 percent of world output, thanks to the perceived industrial might of the Soviet Union itself (Figure 1.2). Between 1820 and 1950, Japan was the only Asian nation to achieve affluence.

FIGURE 1.1   Per Capita GDP, 1500, 1820, 1950, 2010

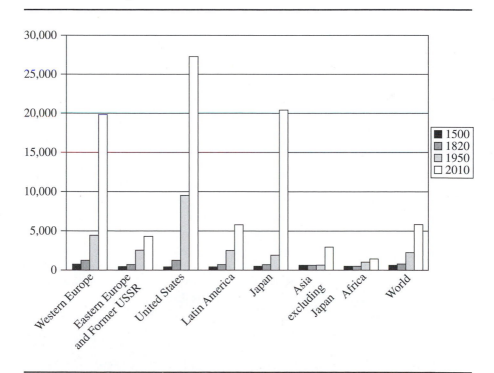

Source: From GREGORY, Comparing Economic Systems in the Twenty-First Century, 7E. © 2004 Cengage Learning.

FIGURE 1.2   Shares of World GDP, 1500, 1820, 1950, 2010

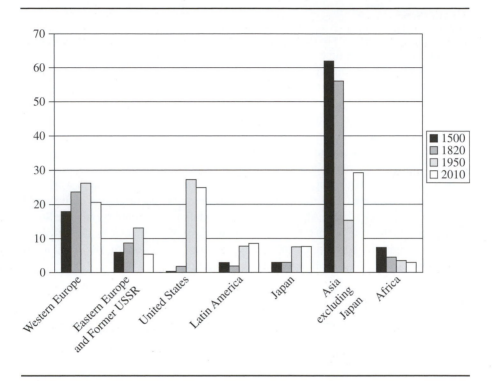

Source: From GREGORY, Comparing Economic Systems in the Twenty-First Century, 7E. © 2004 Cengage Learning.

Around 1800, there began a significant realignment of economic fortunes in favor of a select few countries located largely in western Europe, North America, and parts of Asia. The **Industrial Revolution** *was the dramatic economic rise of Europe and North America in the nineteenth century that began in England and then spread to the European continent and to North America.* The Industrial Revolution was fueled by the rapid growth of science and technology (the steam engine, the cotton spindle, and then electricity); the first transportation and communications revolution (steamships, railroads, and the telegraph); and the creation of institutions that favored economic progress, such as the limited-liability corporation, constitutions that limited the reach of government and protected private property, and stock exchanges that raised capital. Asia was a latecomer to the Industrial Revolution. Japan experienced it in the first half of the nineteenth century; the Four Asian Tigers (Hong Kong, Singapore, Taiwan, and South Korea), after 1960; and the world's most populous countries, China and India, began experiencing rapid growth in the late 1970s and 1990s, respectively.

Other countries or empires had experienced economic progress in the remote past, but this progress was not sustained. The Greek, Roman, and early Chinese and Indian civilizations created high levels of wealth for their eras, but their achievements were later reversed. It was only with the Industrial Revolution that economic progress became irreversible, although, as we have noted, not evenly shared.

The half century from 1950 to the new millennium saw a resurgence of the long-dormant Asia and the dramatic decline of the republics that made up the former Soviet Union as they began their transformations to market economies. Asia's resurgence was largely the consequence of exceptional economic growth in China since the late 1970s. Starting in 1990, India began to grow rapidly, and it appears that its rapid growth will be sustained.

If the world's two most populous countries, China and India, continue on their paths to economic development, the world will be changed forever. China, despite three decades of rapid growth, remains a relatively poor country. India is even poorer. Asia's other economic giant, Japan, virtually ceased growing in the 1990s and shows no signs of recovering its earlier dynamism. Despite some promising starts, Latin America is still a relatively poor region, and much of Africa remains mired in economic and social stagnation.

Europe and the European offshoots in North America and Australasia produce more than half of the world's output but account for less than a quarter of its population. Less than 20 percent of the world's population lives in the affluent countries of Western Europe, North America, Australasia, and Japan (see Figure 1.3A and B). The affluence that most of us take for granted is actually quite rare in today's world. As we began the third millennium, we still had a "third world" that did not share in economic progress.

FIGURE 1.3(A)   Changes in the Distribution of World Population over the Last Two Centuries

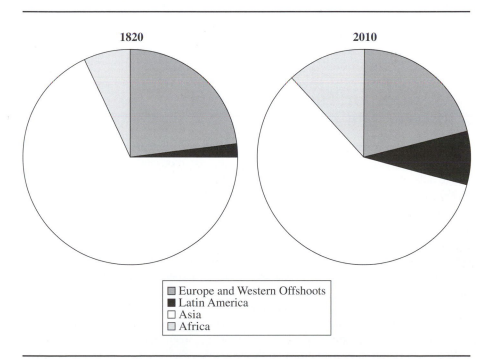

Source: From GREGORY, Comparing Economic Systems in the Twenty-First Century, 7E. © 2004 Cengage Learning.

FIGURE 1.3(B)   Changes in the Distribution of World Output (GDP) over the Last
Two Centuries

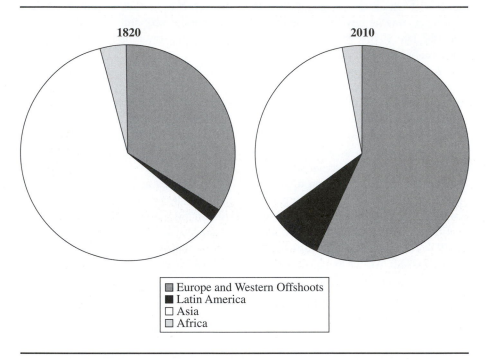

Source: From GREGORY, Comparing Economic Systems in the Twenty-First Century, 7E. © 2004
Cengage Learning.

A Warning for Those Who Want a Simpler Life

Some express a desire for the "simple life" of the past, but the simple life was not as many picture it. Economic progress of the past thousand years has given us, above all, the gift of a longer life. In the first year of the second millennium (1000), the average newborn could expect to live to the ripe old age of 24. Eight hundred years later, life expectancy had not increased much in Asia, Africa, or Latin America, but it had risen to 36 years in the affluent world. By 1950, life expectancies had increased in both rich and poor countries. Newborns in the poor countries of Asia, Africa, and Latin America could expect to live to 44, whereas newborns in the most affluent countries had an expected lifespan of 66 years. Half a century later, newborns in affluent countries could expect to live to 78 years, fourteen years longer than newborns in poor countries (see Figure 1.4). These advances were due to the better nutrition, science, and technology that accompany economic progress. For example, a Green revolution in agriculture spread from rich to poor countries, so that countries that once could not feed themselves can now do so. So although some wish for what they perceive to be the simpler life of, say, the 1950s, they would be sacrificing twelve years of life, according to these figures.

FIGURE 1.4   Life Expectancy in Years, from 1000 to 2010

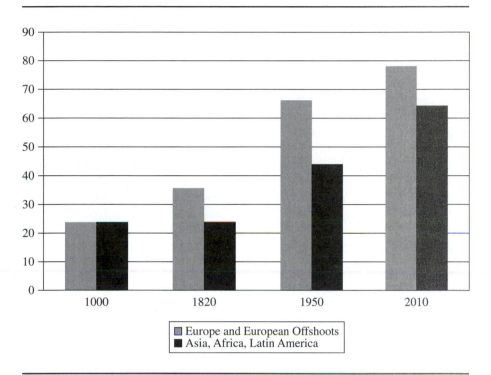

Source: From GREGORY, Comparing Economic Systems in the Twenty-First Century, 7E. © 2004
Cengage Learning.

Economic Institutions and Economic Progress

In the past, economic progress has occurred for different reasons. First, periods of progress occur when opportunities arise to settle empty areas endowed with fertile land and
resources. The settlement of new areas was the source of growth for the Roman Empire
and explains the relatively high level of Chinese living standards in the eighth century.
The European settlement of North America after Christopher Columbus's discovery of
the New World in 1492 explains the rising affluence of western Europe and of North
America itself. The rapid economic growth of the United States over a protracted period
of time was due in part to the settlement of the vast areas of land in the West.

Second, rising prosperity is associated with opportunities to increase trade and
the movement of capital among countries. The rising wealth of Venice between
1000 and 1500 is explained by the Venetian opening of trade routes to China and
India. Portugal's rise after 1500 is attributable to its opening of trade, navigation,
and settlement of the Atlantic islands, Africa, Japan, and China by sea routes. The
rapid economic growth of the affluent world in the late nineteenth century and after
World War II is largely due to the rapid growth of international trade as new transportation and communications systems emerged and barriers to trade fell.

Third, economic progress is associated with technological innovation. The
Industrial Revolution saw the first systematic application of scientific discoveries

to industrial and agricultural technology as new sources of mechanical power were applied to transportation and manufacturing. The rapid growth of the period 1980 to 2007 was associated with advances in telecommunications and information processing. Future waves of economic growth will be spurred by technologies that we cannot even conceive of today. History teaches us that we have been consistently too pessimistic about technological change. At various points in time, experts have proclaimed that everything that can be discovered has already been discovered, only to be taken off guard by an entirely new technology.

This book is about the fourth source of economic growth and prosperity: the economic system that we use to take advantage of trading opportunities, to settle new areas, and to use new technologies to economic advantage. Economic progress depends on having the right constellation of economic institutions. ***Economic institutions*** *reflect the way we organize our economic activities. They cover a broad range of economic, social, and political activities: how we govern ourselves, our laws concerning internal and external trade, how property is owned, how economic activity is organized into various business forms, and our formal and informal practices.* We discuss these institutions and how they are measured in the next chapter.

Some Themes for the Twenty-First Century

History can be a guide for the future. It allows us to understand long-term trends and, hopefully, to avoid repeating past mistakes. It is a guide to organizing our economic and political institutions. If history teaches that the expansion of trade and capital flows has created prosperity in the past, we should organize institutions that promote an outward view of the world economy. If history teaches that new science and technology are created by societies that are open to new ideas and that do not protect the status quo, we should create institutions that promote the development and dissemination of new ideas.

We begin the second decade of the new millennium with a number of unresolved issues on our plate. How they are resolved in the next decades and half century will dictate our future.

Has History Ended, and What Do We Do Now?

History purportedly "ended" more than two decades ago as the Soviet Union and its satellites in Eastern Europe rejected communism. The Cold War was over, and the West had won! Was this, as Francis Fukuyama proclaimed in his September 1989 article, "The End of History"? *The **End of History** is Fukuyama's idea that Western liberalism had triumphed over socialism, leaving no competing alternatives.* Fukuyama wrote: "The triumph of the West, of the Western idea, is evident first of all in the total exhaustion of viable systematic alternatives to Western liberalism."[2] The communist system of a state owned and operated economy had been defeated in Russia, central Asia, and Eastern and southeastern Europe. The largest remaining Communist country—China—had a decade and a half earlier abandoned its communist economic system in favor of globalization and market reforms, while keeping its monopoly of the Chinese Communist Party.

Fukuyama's End of History was centuries in coming. In February 1848, Karl Marx and Friedrich Engels issued their *Communist Manifesto*. *The* **Communist Manifesto** *invited the "workers of the world to unite" against their capitalist oppressors; they "have nothing to lose but their chains."* Technically coauthored, Engels credited the main ideas to Marx, who issued the manifesto in the expectation that a socialist revolution was imminent. Abortive communist revolutions in Paris, Berlin, and elsewhere failed. It was not until the Bolshevik Revolution in Russia in October 1917 that the "workers of the world" had their first chance to build a communist state. As noted British economist John Maynard Keynes remarked, "In the long run, we are all dead." This epithet applied to Marx: He was dead by the time of the Bolshevik Revolution.

The early Russian Bolsheviks put their hopes in their Communist International to spread their workers' revolution to Europe and Asia, but in the end they had to be content to build socialism only in one country (the USSR). In this endeavor, the workers and peasants were ruled, willingly or unwillingly, by the elite of the communist party, first under Vladimir Lenin, then Joseph Stalin, and then a collective leadership after Stalin's death in March 1953. The result was far from the workers' paradise Marx promised.

Marxists in Europe, to the chagrin of Soviet leaders, chose a different path to the workers' paradise. They rejected violent revolution and opted to work within the existing political system to gain power. From this were born the social democratic and labor parties of Europe, which came to alternate in power with Christian democrat, conservative, and Tory parties on the European continent and in Great Britain. Although they continued to have their Marxist fringes, social democrats understood they had to become a part of democratic politics if they wished to succeed. Although parties that call themselves "socialist" currently rule in Spain and Portugal and have ruled in France, they are a far cry from the socialist parties Marx envisioned.

After the defeat of Germany and Japan in World War II, the Soviet Empire expanded under the auspices of the Red Army into Eastern and southeastern Europe. It spread throughout China, Vietnam, and North Korea as a consequence of the victories of the Chinese Communists in the bloody Chinese civil war and of the Vietnamese Communists over French and then American forces. Whether imposed by force or won by victory, the communist model was on the move. At its peak, some one-third of the world's population lived in communist states.

Communism's collapse from this peak was precipitous: It began in Poland, Hungary, and Czechoslovakia in the late 1980s as these countries sought out alternatives to communist rule. The communist regime of East Germany collapsed in 1989; the USSR ended as a political entity in December of 1991. By the early 1990s, only Cuba and North Korea remained true to the classical Soviet model. China kept the monopoly of its communist party but operated an economic system that bore little resemblance to its earlier Soviet manifestation.

As the twentieth century wound down, Fukuyama's End of History continued to hold. East Germany became a part of the Federal Republic of Germany. Some thirty or so newly independent states embarked on a transition that would create new economic and political systems far removed from their Soviet past. China had experienced rapid growth for more than two decades under its market reforms, although the Chinese leadership rejected democratization after suppressing demonstrations at Tiananmen Square in June of 1989. The U.S. economy was among the fastest growing of the

industrialized countries. It was creating at a fast pace new technologies for the information revolution, its stock markets were soaring, and American methods of business—
the American model—were held up as models for the world. Although Europe was
completing the integration of its European Union (EU), it was suffering from anemic
growth and high unemployment, and it had to confront the task of integrating the new
and poorer countries of the "New Europe" into its fold. The nations of "Old Europe"
began to question whether the welfare states they had created were the cause of their
stagnation and whether they could learn from the Americans.

The 1980s witnessed the beginnings of repudiation of social democracy in the
form of an overbearing welfare state. This decade was dominated by Reaganism in
the United States and by Thatcherism in England—both movements committed to
reducing "big government." In Germany, the conservative Christian Democratic
Party exercised power over German politics at the expense of the Social Democratic
Party until the late 1990s. Reaganism and Thatcherism set in motion policies to reduce
the role of government and to shift existing government functions from federal to state
and local levels. Tax reductions were used to improve incentives, welfare programs
were cut, and privatization was encouraged in Great Britain, Germany, and France.
Even Sweden, long a symbol of the welfare state run amuck, experienced a voter
backlash against excessive social expenditures and high tax rates.

The 1990s yielded few major changes for the industrialized West. Bill Clinton
governed the United States as a centrist "New Democrat." Tony Blair did the same
in the United Kingdom under the rubric of "New Labor." Social Democrat Gerhard
Schroeder replaced Christian Democrat Helmut Kohl in Germany, but he did not
refute Kohl's policies. A major economic event of the 1980s and 1990s was the
shattering of the myth of Japanese invincibility. Japan's growth rates tapered off,
and Japan bogged down in one recession after the other. Although Japan's trade
performance remained strong, its poor economic performance raised questions
about the wisdom of Japan's touted industrial policy and its practice of lifetime
employment.

The reluctance of the leaders of the world's major countries to change economic policies despite changes in leadership is explained by economic success.
From the mid-1980s to well into the new millennium, economic growth was strong
and economic downturns were avoided. In fact, this period has been called the
"Great Moderation." *The **Great Moderation** is the period from the 1980s to 2007
noted for its economic growth and economic stability.*

Questioning the American Model and the Rise of State Capitalism

Just when we think everything has been resolved, we learn that this is far from the
truth. In the first five years of the new millennium, it appeared that the American
model had won the day, but this consensus broke apart quickly.

In December 2007, the U.S. economy entered into a recession and financial
crisis that had alarmists predicting a replay of the Great Depression of the 1930s.
Particularly alarming was the collapse of housing prices, which tore apart the home
mortgage market with actual and threatened defaults. Despite government bailouts

of financial firms and automobile producers and huge government stimulus spending programs, the U.S. unemployment rate rose to near 10 percent and showed few signs of improvement; economic growth remained too sluggish to push down unemployment. The resulting surge in the federal deficit raised alarms about the safety of the U.S. dollar both at home and abroad. The U.S. recession's spread throughout the world was uneven; it hit Latin America and Europe hard, but Asia and in particular China appeared to be spared its worst excesses.

The first reaction to the protracted U.S. recession was to question the victory of Fukuyama's "Western liberalism" as best embodied by the American economic model of private enterprise, private ownership, and more limited government intervention. Critics argued that free markets were to blame for the economic collapse and that the role of the state should be increased to tame its excesses. Wise government regulators would have seen the warning signs and prevented this disaster, it was said.

The new Obama administration reacted by expanding the role of government and by, in effect, taking temporary control of troubled banks and General Motors and Chrysler. Headlines in major newspapers posed the question: "Is Capitalism Dead?" Pundits on the left claimed "we seem to have entered the death spiral where rising unemployment leads to reduced consumption and hence to greater unemployment. Any schadenfreude we might be tempted to feel as executives lose their corporate jets and the erstwhile Masters of the Universe wipe egg from their faces is quickly dashed by the ever more vivid suffering around us." They decried "the religion of market fundamentalism and the approaching collapse of capitalism."

Critics of the American model, however, had to offer an alternative. The collapse of the Soviet model did not recommend it. Instead, they looked to another model: state capitalism. *State capitalism is an economic model in which the state exercises considerable influence over the economy through its control of large enterprises and extensive regulation.* So critics held up China as an example. By exercising its muscle over private enterprise and directly controlling large state enterprises and banks, the "wise" Chinese Communist Party, it was said, guided China through the world downturn without a loss of growth or dynamism. Perhaps an enlightened dictatorship—even one that denies civil rights and electoral freedom—is superior to the chaos of unfettered private enterprise?

The world's largest country—Russia—under its president, prime minister and again president, Vladimir Putin, also opted for state capitalism with much less success. Russia's large enterprises, most of which had been privatized to private oligarchs, were returned to state control either through deprivatization or by placing them in the hands of Kremlin-friendly oligarchs. Putin argued that the state should control "national champion" companies. They must serve the interests of the state. In 2005, Russia's largest private oil company, Yukos, was divided among state companies. Yukos would be the first of many companies returned to state control.

Whereas China's state capitalism projected an image of success, Russia's projected an image of stagnation, corruption, and decline. Only Russia's vast energy resources kept it going—an industry subject to wild swings as energy prices fluctuated. In fact, the Russian version of state capitalism even appears more extreme than that of China. Some observers substitute "crony capitalism" for "state capitalism" as more appropriate for countries like contemporary Russia. *Crony capitalism is an economic system in which the nation's wealth is siphoned off by insiders close to those in power and by those in power themselves.*

In a number of cases, kleptocracy emerged as another extreme form of state capitalism. **Kleptocracy** *is the widespread theft of society's resources by the nation's rulers.* Contemporary Russia, Ukraine, Kazakhstan, Zaire, Haiti, Zimbabwe, and many other countries are cited as examples of kleptocracies (see Table 1.1).

TABLE **1.1** The World's Kleptocrats

Part A: Kleptocrats Ranked by Absolute Wealth

Ruler (ranked top to bottom)	Year	Wealth (bl. 2010 $)
Putin (Russia)	2011	40
Suharto (Indonesia)	1998	25
Nazarbaev (Kazakhstan)	2011	20
Marcos (Philippines)	1986	7.5
Aliev (Azerbaijan)	2011	10
Mobutu (Congo, Zaire)	1997	5
Mubarak (Egypt)	2011	5
Abacha (Nigeria)	1998	3.5
Milosevich (Serbia)	2000	1
Duvalier (Haiti)	1986	0.55
Fujimori (Peru)	2000	0.6
Alemain (Nicaragua)	2002	0.1
Estrada (Philippines)	2001	0.08

Part B: Kleptocrats Ranked as a percent of GDP

Mobutu (Congo, Zaire)	1997	0.4202
Aliev (Azerbaijan)	2011	0.1111
Nazarbaev (Kazakhstan)	2011	0.1036
Duvalier (Haiti)	1986	0.1000
Marcos (Philippines)	1986	0.0429
Suharto (Indonesia)	1998	0.0331
Putin (Russia)	2011	0.0180
Milosevich (Serbia)	2000	0.0165
Abacha (Nigeria)	1998	0.0127
Mubarak (Egypt)	2011	0.0100
Alemain (Nicaragua)	2002	0.0073
Fujimori (Peru)	2000	0.0029
Estrada (Philippines)	2001	0.0003

Source: From Blog What Paul Gregory is Writing About, "Kleptocrats, Oligarchs, and Billionare Entrepreneurs (In this game Mubarak is a Piker)," Sunday, Februrary, 13, 2011 (http://paulgregorysblog.blogspot.com/2011_02_01_archive.html).

Democracy versus Dictatorship

Democracy, the boldest idea of Western liberalism, also seemed to be on the rise as the twentieth century came to an end. Dictatorships in the former Soviet bloc were replaced by democracies or near democracies in central Europe, southeastern Europe, and the Baltic states. According to the authoritative Freedom House surveys, the number of "free countries" (as measured by civil liberties and electoral rights) rose from 72 in 1993 (after the creation of the newly independent states) to 86 in 2000, while the number of "not free" countries fell from 55 to 48 (see Table 1.2). The Bush administration, which took office in 2000, embarked on a risky experiment in democratization, betting that states with no history of democracy would be willing to embrace it if given the chance, and support of the United States.

The march to democracy has not been even. The first decade of the third millennium saw disappointing reversals in Russia and Venezuela. To quote from the 2010 edition of Freedom House's *Freedom of the World*:

> In a year of intensified repression against human rights defenders and democratic activists by many of the world's most powerful authoritarian regimes, Freedom House found a continued erosion of freedom worldwide, with setbacks in Latin America, Africa, the former Soviet Union, and the Middle East. For the fourth consecutive year, declines have trumped gains. This represents the longest continuous period of deterioration in the nearly 40-year history of *Freedom in the World*, Freedom House's annual assessment of the state of political rights and civil liberties in every country in the world.
>
> In 2009, declines for freedom were registered in 40 countries, representing 20 percent of the world's polities. In 22 of those countries, the problems were significant enough to merit downgrades in the numerical ratings for political rights or civil liberties.[3]

History does not move linearly. At the beginning of 2011, spontaneous protests broke out in the Middle East, a region characterized as not free by Freedom House. These protests swept long-ruling dictators from power in Egypt, Libya, and Tunisia and placed others under attack, such as in Syria. Other dictatorial and autocratic regimes either began to examine reforms to make their countries more democratic (such as in Jordan) or cracked down with extreme political repression (such as in Iran).

TABLE 1.2 Freedom House Classification (Civil Liberties and Electoral Freedom)

Number of Countries	1993	2000	2011
"Free"	72	86	88
"Not Free"	55	48	47

Source: Statistics complied from various editions of Freedom House's "Freedom in the World Series," http://www.freedomhouse.org/template.cfm?page=445.

We do not know whether the ongoing regime changes will produce more democracy or revert to one dictator simply replacing another, but optimists can hope that this will be a new wave of democracy.

A Clash of Civilizations

History has not ended but has taken new, unexpected, and, in some cases, unwelcome directions. In the summer of 1993, Samuel Huntington, in an article entitled "The Clash of Civilizations," concluded that "history is not dead." Western liberalism still had plenty of competition. *Huntington's **clash of civilizations** predicted that the fundamental sources of future conflict will not be based on ideology or economics but on clashes of culture.* Huntington wrote:

> Nation states will remain the most powerful actors in world affairs, but the principal conflicts of global politics will occur between nations and groups of different civilizations. The clash of civilizations will dominate global politics. The fault lines between civilizations will be the battle lines of the future…. The world will be shaped in large measure by the interactions among seven or eight major civilizations. These include Western, Confucian, Japanese, Islamic, Hindu, Slavic-Orthodox, Latin American and possibly African civilization. The most important conflicts of the future will occur along the cultural fault lines separating these civilizations from one another.

Political scientists indeed have determined that the world can be divided into a number of different cultures and civilizations that are based on separate histories, norms, and life events. Figure 1.5 shows one such classification.

Huntington emphasized the clash between the "civilized world" and Islam. He cited a Muslim scholar's warning that "the West's next confrontation is definitely going to come from the Muslim world. It is in the sweep of the Islamic nations from the Meghreb to Pakistan that the struggle for a new world order will begin."[4]

The Cold War was an ideological clash between Western liberalism and Marxism, but, according to Huntington, differences in social and religious norms can cause nations to clash just as violently or more violently than ideology can. Moreover, the outcome of this new clash of civilizations will not be judged by economic success or failure but by each nation's ability to win hearts and minds of followers.

Indeed, the clash of Islamic and Western civilizations has dominated world politics since the fall of communism. One fifth of the world's population shares Islam as an ethical tradition; Muslims are the dominant population group in fifty-seven countries. Several major countries, such as Pakistan and Iran, label themselves as "Islamic Republics." Six countries officially use Sharia law—legal rules based on the Koran—as the foundation of their legal system. Sharia law itself requires specific economic practices; for example, it prohibits charging interest, and it enforces the charging of "fair" prices.

The clash of Islamic and Western civilizations has focused not on economic competition but on a clash of values. Although this clash has resulted at times in armed conflicts, such as between Muslim and Christians in Bosnia, Indonesia, and other

FIGURE 1.5   Cultural Map of the World

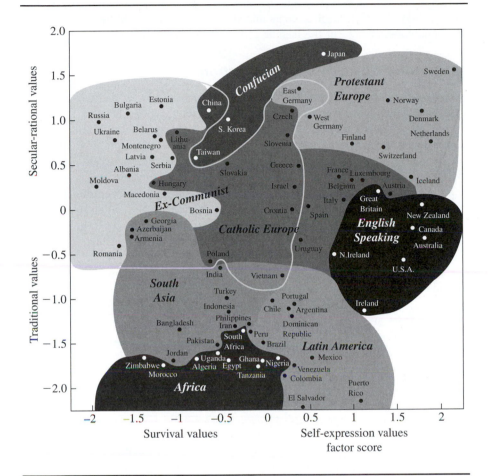

Source: R. Inglehart and C. Welzel, *Modernization, Cultural Change, and Democracy. The Human Development Sequence* (Cambridge: Cambridge University Press, 2006).

locations, its most stark manifestation has been in the form of international terrorism by Muslim extremists against Western targets (New York City on September 11, 2001; Madrid in 2004; and London subways, July 2005, among others).

The most striking aspect of Huntington's clash of civilizations is that it is not necessarily a conflict among nations. Rather he noted that the goals of Islam transcend international borders. Islam, some supporters teach, must be an international religion that transcends and even eliminates national boundaries. In its more extremist forms, Islam sets the goal of establishing Sharia law throughout the world unfettered by national borders.

On the economic front, the Islamic model does offer an alternative to American capitalism or state capitalism. Islamic economists propose a world of "fair prices," of Islamic banks that do not charge interest rates, rules on charitable giving, and business organization. The Islamic world has operated with these rules, to a lesser or greater extent depending on the country, but no Islamic country has so far achieved a high level of economic success. We must therefore consider the economic consequences of the Islamic economic model as we go forward.

Multinationalism and Globalization

Globalization continued its march forward in the last decades of the twentieth century as transportation costs fell, international communications became incredibly cheap, and countries lowered their trade barriers. Between 1970 and 2008, world exports increased almost sevenfold, and world production increased threefold.[5]

Globalization has created an increasingly interdependent world economy. Highly skilled people find employment in any number of countries, not just in their own. Young people attend universities outside their own countries and then seek jobs in a "world" job market. A slight change in U.S. interest rates can cause billions of dollars to flow from Hong Kong, Zurich, and Toronto to New York. Transactions between Venezuela and Austria are conducted in U.S. dollars. China has become the largest owner of U.S. government debt.

The period since 1970 has seen a strong expansion of economic internationalism and an expanding role for multinational corporations. Europe established a European Union and created a single currency, the euro. The European Union expanded from six core states in the heart of Europe to twenty-seven members from the south and east. Its expansion has not ceased. The EU is considering the accession of Turkey as its first "non-European" nation. The United States, Canada, and Mexico established a barrier-free North American market (North American Free Trade Agreement, NAFTA) in 1994. The United States is currently debating additional free trade agreements with South Korea and Columbia.

These decisive moves toward economic integration have raised the issue of multinationalism versus national sovereignty—a divisive issue that must be resolved in the twenty-first century. Multinationalism threatens national identity and weakens sovereign control over economic destiny. How much autonomy should supranational European economic organizations enjoy? How will the European central bank administer its common monetary policy and a common European currency? Must nations that belong to a common market follow a common political policy? Will the European Union truly become a "United States of Europe"?

The movement toward economic multinationalism has been accompanied by a deeper and more gradual trend: the increased integration of the world economies. The major industrial firms of the West are no longer constrained by national boundaries. In fact, they are no longer national companies; rather, they have become multinational corporations.

A **multinational corporation** *is a corporation that manages and delivers production and services in a number of countries and employs managers and employees from a number of countries.* For example, the IBMs, Siemens, and Sonys of the world are now equally at home in New York, Mexico City, Montreal, London, or Singapore. An oil venture in Indonesia may be carried out by a consortium of BP, Royal Dutch Shell, and Exxon/Mobil and may be financed by the Bank of Tokyo and Deutsche Bank. Countries have become increasingly confused as to the national identity of companies operating on their territory and even do not know in which political jurisdiction they should be taxed.

The Choice of Economic Systems in the Twenty-First Century

The dramatic events of the last two decades of the twentieth century—the end of the Cold War, German reunification, the fall of communist political systems in Eastern Europe, and the dissolution of the Soviet Union—surprised most observers. The fall of some of the world's most durable dictatorships in the Middle East in 2011 similarly caught the pundits off guard. The rise of China has become an undeniable fact of the past three decades and could change the economic and political landscape of the twenty-first century. These changes, unimaginable before they happened, raise new and challenging issues for the study of comparative economic systems.

Only decades ago, we could frame the study of comparative economic systems as the choice between two quite different economic systems: market capitalism (or simply "market economies") and planned socialism. Market capitalism was practiced in North America, Western Europe, Australasia, and Japan. Planned socialism was practiced throughout the Soviet Empire. Now, in the twenty-first century, planned socialism has become an endangered species practiced by two maverick countries, and most of the other countries of the world are market economies of one type or another. In fact, in the summer of 2002, the EU officially declared Russia, the most populous country of Europe, a market economy.

The fact that the struggle between capitalism and socialism is over for the time being does not mean that economic systems no longer matter. How a society organizes its economic institutions continues to matter a great deal, only now the differences are more subtle. The Four Southeast Asian Tigers experienced phenomenal growth because they chose the proper institutional arrangements—export orientation, high saving rates, and heavy investments in education. Pakistan and Bangladesh have stagnated because they have traditionally chosen institutions that do not create economic growth, such as protection from imports. There can be no economic progress in failed states that are so corrupt and chaotic that commerce cannot grow. The superior economic performance of the Untied States over Europe in the past two decades is attributed to its more efficient capital market and its more flexible labor market. The deep recession that began in 2007 has caused some to question the U.S. model. Japan's economic decline is attributed to its inert political system, inflexible labor markets, and inefficient capital market.

In the twenty-first century, we must study a large number of differences in economic institutions—differences that affect economic performance in significant ways yet are not as recognizable as the differences between capitalism and socialism.

History shows that we do have a choice of economic systems. The former Soviet Union and the countries of Eastern Europe have transitioned to new economic systems. The industrialized West has operated with fairly stable economic systems for decades if not centuries, but even these societies must make continuous and often subtle choices concerning the shape of their economic systems. The United States is currently grappling with fundamental reform of its health care system and debating how large its welfare system should be. Europe is confronting the limits of its extensive welfare state and worrying about its inflexible labor markets. China must determine whether it can become an affluent country while retaining the monopoly of the Chinese Communist Party. The emerging worlds of Asia and Latin America must make crucial choices concerning the economic systems that will bring them to an appropriate level of affluence. Africa must develop institutions that can create economic progress.

If choosing among economic systems were not possible, the study of comparative economic systems would be less compelling. Insofar as people, through the ballot box and through their private and public lives, make choices that affect the economic system, it is important to stay informed about the strengths and weaknesses of alternative economic systems. We have made a number of such choices in the past, such as the first full-fledged, conscious creation of an economic system in the Soviet Union in the late 1920s, a decade after the October Revolution of 1917. In the 1930s, the contrast between the Depression-ridden West and the industrializing Soviet Union cast doubt on the superiority of capitalism. The weaknesses of the capitalist system were all too evident, whereas the flaws of the Soviet system were hidden behind a veil of official secrecy and claims of extraordinary successes. The gap between the economic performance of the East and that of the West became pronounced in the 1980s. The West experienced a sustained recovery from the oil shocks of the 1970s and began a long business expansion. The contrast between the affluence of the West and the stagnation of the East set the stage for the collapse of communism.

Just as individuals learn from the examples of others, countries learn from the successes and failures of other countries. The ultimate goal of the study of comparative economic systems is to learn what works and in what settings.

Summary

- We study history to learn from the past. We study economic systems to learn from their past successes and failures.
- Economic progress has been uneven, starting with the diverging underperformance of Asia and the rise of Europe and its offshoots. Economic systems and institutions are presumed to explain such things.
- Economic institutions make up the economic system and they affect economic performance.
- The collapse of communism caused some to proclaim an end to history. The end of communism was long in coming, starting with Marx's predictions of capitalist collapse.
- The economic crisis that began in 2007 raised doubts about the market capitalist model and proposed in its place state capitalism, such as is practiced in China.
- State capitalism can transform into crony capitalism and kleptocracy.
- The type of government—democracy versus non-democracy—is an important ingredient in the study of economic systems. The rise of democracy worldwide seems to have slowed.

- Globalism and multinational corporations affect the way we conduct our economic lives.
- Societies do have a choice of economic systems.

Key Terms

clash of civilizations—The fundamental sources of future conflict will not be based on ideology or economics but on clashes of culture (Huntington).

Communist Manifesto—Invited the "workers of the world to unite" against their capitalist oppressors; they "have nothing to lose but their chains" (Marx and Engels).

crony capitalism—An economic system in which the nation's wealth is siphoned off by insiders close to those in power and by those in power themselves.

economic institutions—The way we organize our economic activities, covering a broad range of economic, social, and political activities.

End of History—Fukuyama's idea that Western liberalism had triumphed over socialism, leaving no competing alternatives.

Great Moderation—The period from the 1980s to 2007 noted for its economic growth and economic stability.

Industrial Revolution—This was the dramatic economic rise of Europe and North America in the nineteenth century that began in England and then spread to the European continent and to North America.

kleptocracy—The widespread theft of society's resources by the nation's rulers.

multinational corporation—A corporation that manages and delivers production and services in a number of countries and employs managers and employees from a number of countries.

state capitalism—An economic model in which the state exercises considerable influence over the economy through its control of large enterprises and extensive regulation.

Notes

1. "Gross Domestic Product," last updated November 9, 2011, http://www.google.com/pub licdata?ds=wb-wdi&met=ny_gdp_mktp_cd&tdim=true&dl=en&hl=en&q=world+gdp.
2. Francis Fukuyama, "The End of History," *The National Interest*, Summer 1989.
3. http://www.freedomhouse.org/template.cfm?page=130&year=2010.
4. Samuel Huntington, "The Clash of Civilizations," *Foreign Affairs*, Summer 1993.
5. World Trade Organization, "Appendix Tables," http://www.wto.org/english/res_e/ statis_e/its2010_e/its10_appendix_e.htm.

Recommended Readings

Anders Aslund, *How Capitalism Was Built: The Transformation of Central and Eastern Europe, Russia, and Central Asia* (New York: Cambridge University Press, 2007).

Erik Berglof and Gerard Roland (eds.), *The Economics of Transition: The Fifth Nobel Symposium in Economics* (New York: Macmillan, 2007).

Eric Brousseau and Jean-Michael Glachant, *New Institutional Economics* (New York: Cambridge University Press, 2008).

F. A. Hayek, *Studies in Philosophy, Politics, and Economics* (New York: Norton, 1969).

Angus Maddison, *The World Economy: A Millennial Perspective* (Paris: OECD, 2001).

E. Wayne Nafziger, *Economic Development* (New York: Cambridge University Press, 2005).

Frederic L. Pryor, *Capitalism Reassessed* (New York: Cambridge University Press, 2010).

———, *The Future of U.S. Capitalism* (New York: Cambridge University Press, 2002).

David Remnick, *Lenin's Tomb: The Last Days of the Soviet Empire* (New York: Random House, 1993).

Joseph E. Stiglitz, *Whither Socialism?* (Cambridge, Mass.: MIT Press, 1994).

Gale Stokes, *The Walls Came Tumbling Down: The Collapse of Communism in Eastern Europe* (New York: Oxford University Press, 1993).

Daniel Treisman, *The Return: Russia's Journey From Gorbachev to Medvedev* (New York: The Free Press, 2011).

World Bank, *From Market to Plan: World Development Report 1996* (Washington, D.C.; World Bank, 1996).

CHAPTER
2

Definition and Classification of Economic Systems

Comparative economics was once described as "a field in search of a definition."[1] This search began more than two decades ago when we realized that we can no longer neatly divide the world into capitalist and socialist economies. Although the socialist system will always be a core component in the study of economic systems, we now have a much broader and nuanced field to survey.

The economic system has long been part of economics. Standard textbook definitions of economics typically include reference to the economic system, such as **economics** *is the study of how economic agents (households, firms, and governments) allocate scarce resources (land, labor, and capital) among competing ends according to the prevailing economic system.* In most of economics, the last part of this definition plays a minor role. We study micro, macro, and international economics in a given economic setting. This approach allows us to study the behavior of consumers and firms, monetary and fiscal policy, and exchange rates without having to concern ourselves with changes in the underlying institutional setting.

The development of the field of political economy, however, has taught us that the way we organize our political lives has a profound impact on economic outcomes and performance. **Political economy** *applies economic analysis to the study of how we organize our political system and how politics impacts economic behavior and outcomes.* Some nations have organized their political institutions in such a way as to produce good economic outcomes. Others are kleptocracies or even failed states that yield miserable economic outcomes for their citizens because of poor political systems. Even democracies in affluent nations must worry about their political economy. Lobbyists, vested interests, and corruption can harm economic performance and welfare. Political economists have taught us that how we organize our political systems has such a large impact that this should be a central focus of economics—not something peripheral that we hold constant while examining other phenomena.

The greater use of comparative economic data has also impacted the way we study economics. Three to four decades ago, economists primarily used data from one country (usually their own) to engage in applied economic analysis. If we wanted to study household behavior, we studied household surveys of one country or looked at how household behavior changed over time. If we wanted to study fiscal policy, we examined the state budget and tax policies of a specific country.

One of the most important advances in economic analysis in recent decades has been the creation and development of international databases for large numbers of countries over long periods of time. These international databases have been a valuable contribution of international organizations such as the World Bank, the International Monetary Fund, the United Nations, and the Asian Development Bank.

Comparative economists can now study the determinants of poverty, fertility, household behavior, and many other topics across countries and over time simultaneously. **Comparative economics** *is the use of international data across countries and across time to study economic phenomena.*

Comparative economic analysis differs from the study of comparative economic systems, although the two are closely related. Comparative economic analysis does not directly address the core economic system that underlies each country in the international sample, but it does recognize that each of these countries is organized in its own way and that these organizational differences must be held constant in applied analysis. It is for this reason that most empirical studies that use international databases use country fixed effects to not confuse the effects of economic variables with those of the underlying economic system. **Country fixed effects** *use dummy variables assigned to each country to hold, in effect, constant the impact of the economic system so as to allow proper analysis of other variables.*

Economic science, like any other scientific discipline, does not stand still. It advances along a number of fronts, and its various branches cross-fertilize. The study of comparative economic systems has been cross-fertilized particularly by advances in political economy and in comparative economic analysis. As comparative economic systems advances, it cross-fertilizes its ideas back to political economy and comparative economic analysis.

Economic Systems:
Definition and Classification

Comparative economists face similar problems to comparative economists, but our problems are more difficult to solve. Whereas comparative economists seek to hold constant the effect of the economic system to isolate the effects of conventional economic variables on economic outcomes, we wish to study directly the economic system's effect on economic outcomes.

Our definition of economics already tells us that economic outcomes are determined by how households, business, and governments allocate land, labor, and capital among competing ends according to the economic system. The economic system is only one of many determinants of economic outcomes. Unlike many other determinants, the economic system does not lend itself easily to quantification, such as hours of work or dollars of capital.

Economic systems are difficult to measure because they are, by their very nature, multidimensional. The definition of the economic system Assar Lindbeck proposed emphasizes the multidimensionality of the economic system.[2] *An* **economic system** *is a set of institutions for decision making and for the implementation of decisions concerning production, income, and consumption within a given geographic area.* According to this definition, the economic system consists of, among other things, mechanisms, conventions, organizational arrangements, customs, and decision-making rules. An economic system can vary in any of its dimensions, particularly in its structure, its operation, and its adaptability to change over time. It "includes all those institutions, organizations, laws and rules, traditions, beliefs, attitudes, values, taboos, and the resulting behavior patterns that directly or indirectly affect economic behavior and outcomes."[3]

The *multidimensional* nature of economic systems can be formalized in the following manner:

$$ES = f(I_1, I_2, ..., I_n) \tag{2.1}$$

As equation 2.1 indicates, the economic system (ES) is defined by its institutions (*Ii*), where there are *n* such attributes. An economic system is defined only partially by a single institution such as property ownership; rather, a more complete set of institutions must be known before ES is specified.

Defining the economic systems by its many institutions shows the inadequacy of the traditional "isms"—feudalism, capitalism, socialism, and communism. This classification identified a system in terms of one characteristic, in this case ownership of the means of production. We must classify economic systems not by one but by a number of institutional features.

Insofar as we define the economic systems in terms of its institutions, we need a definition of institutions. Intuition tells us that institutions encompass a broad range of things: the legal system, business organization, customs, conventions, norms, informal practices, and other things too numerous to list here. They vary in complexity and in measurability. There is no universally accepted definition of the term **institutions**, but most definitions focus on their serving as the "rules of the game" under which economic decisions are made.[4] Nobel laureate Douglass North provides such a definition: *"Institutions are the rules of the game of a society or, more fundamentally, are the humanly devised constraints that shape human interaction. In consequence, they structure incentives in human exchange whether political, social, or economic."*[5] According to North's definition, political, social, and economic institutions are broadly interpreted to include customs, voting procedures, legislation, organizations such as trade unions and corporations, or any other political, social, and economic rules that affect the way people deal with each other in the exchange of private or public goods.

Enforcement Mechanisms

If institutions define society's "rules of the game," society must have institutions to enforce these rules. Institutions consist not only of the rules themselves but also of the means of their enforcement. Five types of rules and their enforcement

TABLE 2.1   Societal Institutions: The Rules of the Game[6]

Type of Rule	Means of Enforcement
Convention	Self-enforcing
Ethical rule	Self-commitment
Customs	Informal social control
Private rule	Organized private enforcement
State law	Organized state enforcement
Anarchy	No rules at all

Source: Stefan Voigt and Hella Engerer, "Institutions and Transformation—Possible Policy Implications of the New Institutional Economics," in Klaus Zimmerman (ed.), Frontiers in Economics, p. 131. Copyright © 2002 Springer-Verlag with permission of Springer Science+Business Media.

mechanisms are given in Table 2.1. The sixth, anarchy, is a system of no rules and hence no enforcement.

Rules can be enforced by the state or by private institutions. Conventions are generally accepted practices, such as the unwritten rule that physicians not charge for referrals. Ethical rules, such as the practice of not selling customers defective or dangerous goods, are self-enforced, in this case by the commitment of merchants to accepted codes of behavior. Customs are enforced through informal social control. The practice that officers of a corporation act in the interest of the corporation rather than in their own private interest—called exercising their fiduciary responsibility—is enforced by the threat of firing or salary reduction by the owners of the corporation. Private rules, such as the rules that govern the behavior of dealers in stock exchanges, can be enforced by private enforcement bodies. Violators of private rules are punished by private bodies, such as the NASDAQ stock exchange. We are more accustomed to rules issued by the state (by which we mean any governing body, state or federal) as laws and regulations. The state may rule, for example, that two competitors may not formally agree on their prices. If they violate this rule, they can be investigated by a government enforcement agency, such as a justice department, and can then be punished through the court system by fines or imprisonment. State law can also regulate exchanges in which conventions or customs apply. For example, a state may pass consumer protection laws to shield buyers from shoddy or dangerous goods, thereby transferring enforcement from private actors to the state.

Organizations

Economic and political activity is ultimately carried out by individuals working in economic and political organizations. *An **organization** is an administrative or functional structure formed for a particular purpose.* In comparative economic systems, we are interested primarily in organizations that produce goods and services, participate in political decision making, or organize exchange of the factors of production, such as labor unions or capital markets. Some organizations are simple (a chess club); others are complex. The organization of a giant multinational corporation is more complex than that of a family business, but in parts of Asia family-owned business can be huge. Organizations are not only business organizations. Political parties bring together groups and individuals sharing common political beliefs or goals. Organizations also include nonprofit bodies, such as churches, charities, and clubs.

An organization implies the participation of more than one person. The more complicated and large the organization, the more complicated its hierarchy. A **hierarchy** *is the division of an organization into superior and subordinate levels. The person in charge of a higher level in the organization is superior to subordinates at lower levels.*

Organizational hierarchies are of particular interest to comparative economic systems. Different systems use different institutions to organize hierarchies and to encourage subordinates to faithfully carry out the instructions of superiors. We are particularly interested in how businesses are organized to conduct private economic activity and how governments are organized to conduct public economic activity. In particular, we are interested in how government makes public choices. **Public choice** *studies how the political system is organized to tax citizens and to spend public resources.*

All organizations can be described in terms of certain characteristics, such as how they deal with information, their behavior rules, their decision-making arrangements, and their ownership structure. But we are interested in more than taxonomies of organizations. We must study why they exist and whether they are carrying out in an effective way the tasks for which they were formed.

Institutional Economics versus Comparative Economic Systems

An economic system is defined by its institutions, which may be many and varied (*n* may be very large). We may be interested in the effect of each institution on economic decision making. For example, we may want to know how the choice of the legal system affects the ownership of companies or how the provision of health care affects the distribution and quality of medicine. These two topics alone are of considerable interest and worthy of study. They are important to policy decisions. We can make better policy if we know how policy actions affect economic outcomes. An example is the current debate over President Obama's proposed changes in the provision of health care in the United States. We would like to know whether it is good or bad policy.

Yet the economic system (*ES*) is comprised not only of its legal system or how it provides health care. It is defined by a large number of other institutions. In fact, seen in this light, a virtually infinite number of economic systems are possible depending on the constellations of the multitude of institutions. We cannot study a virtually infinite number of economic systems. We can only examine a few. Therefore, we must determine whether there is a clustering of institutions, such that we deal with a relatively limited number of economic systems.

Frederic Pryor suggests that we resolve the problem of a potentially infinite number of economic systems by determining whether they cluster into a manageable number of groups.[7] As an illustration, say we define *ES* in terms of only two institutions (I_1 and I_2). The two institutions can be measured quantitatively (such as the percentage of private ownership or the share of health care provided by the state).

FIGURE 2.1   Institutional Economics versus Comparative Economic Systems

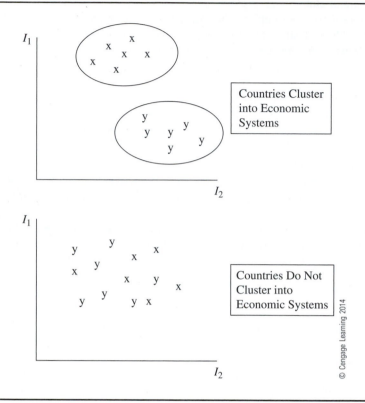

We then take twelve hypothetical countries and plot I_1 and I_2, with two possible outcomes as shown in Figure 2.1.

A clustering of economies according to institutions means that we can study "economic systems" of countries that share, albeit imperfectly, common characteristics. *If the countries do not* **cluster** *according to their institutions, we can still study the effects of institutions but we cannot treat them as economic systems.*

Indeed, in his analysis of countries as classified by a large number of measureable institutions, Pryor finds that the economies of the world (with the exception of those in transition) do cluster into distinctive groups, which we can classify as economic systems.

Five Types of Institutions

According to our definition, economic systems can be characterized by hundreds or thousands of institutions. It is beyond our analytical capacities to deal with more than a few; so we must single out the most important institutions that really determine the character of the economic system. Although we have moved well beyond the "isms" approach, the terms, "capitalism, communism, socialism, and kindred terms, whatever system traits they may in actuality represent, have a life of their own. They live as symbols or clusters of symbols in the minds of participants in all modern systems …, and they may have a profound influence on the way actual systems change or on the reasons why they fail to change."[8]

Capitalism, communism, and socialism are defined largely in terms of ownership. How property rights are organized remains a key institution in identifying different economic systems. In addition to property, we must include other core institutions that define how societies make political and economic decisions, how they gather and process information, and how they incentivize people.

We consider the following five general types of institutions ($n = 5$) as critical in differentiating economic systems:

1. Property rights
2. Decision-making arrangements
3. Market Versus Plan: Institutions for the provision of information and for coordination
4. Incentive mechanisms for setting goals and for inducing people to meet these goals
5. Procedures for making public choices

We chose these five characteristics because economic systems differ along these dimensions. They have also been chosen because they affect economic outcomes. We do not list features that are relatively uniform across systems—for example, the organization of production in factory units.

Characteristics of Economic Systems

Each of the five characteristics explains why economic outcomes differ. Initially, the characteristics appear to have little in common with characterizations of economic systems as capitalist or socialist. But later in this chapter, we will bring them together to formulate definitions of capitalism and socialism based on the nature of organizational arrangements.

Property Rights: Control and Income

Institutions differ according to how property is owned. **Ownership** *is "an amalgam of rights that individuals may have over objects or claims on objects or services" and "these rights may affect an object's disposition or its utilization."*[9]

Ownership confers property rights, which can be complete or partial. Property rights are divided into three categories. First is the right to dispose of property—the transfer of ownership rights to others, as in the selling of an automobile. Second, property rights include the right to utilization, whereby owners can use the property as they wish. Third, property rights give owners the right to receive the income generated by the property. **Full ownership** *(or full property rights) requires the owner to have the right to dispose of the property, use the property, and receive the income the property generates.*

Owners of property in zoned communities cannot use their property in violation of zoning regulations. Families that have leases to live in homes owned by landlords have utilization rights (for the life of the lease) but lack the two other property rights. If the state imposes a 100 percent tax on enterprise profits, owners lose the right to the income from their property.

De jure ownership rights may differ significantly from de facto rights. For example, although members of Soviet collective farms (*kolkhoz*) and Chinese communes "owned" the assets of the farm, departing members could not sell their share of these assets, nor could they decide how to use farm assets.

There are three broad forms of property ownership—private, public, and collective (cooperative). *Under* **private ownership**, *the three ownership rights ultimately belong to individuals, subject to limitations on disposition, use, and earnings. Under* **public ownership**, *these rights belong to the state. With* **collective ownership**, *property rights belong to the members of the collective.*

In many countries and cities, families own their own homes and apartments, but they do not own the land on which the property sits, such as in China, parts of Hawaii, and London. Corporations are owned by private shareholders, but the company's executives may be limited in their ability to sell their shares. In some countries, farmland is owned by families that have passed the farm from one generation to another; in others, the state owns farm land. In many countries, the gas and electric works are owned by the municipal or state government. In the majority of oil-rich countries, underground resources are owned by the state. The private ownership of underground energy resources in the United States and Canada is the exception rather than the rule.

Most countries have all three forms of property ownership. The collective ownership form is the rarest. In most countries, there are restrictions on property rights. Totally unrestricted property rights in all three dimensions are increasingly rare.

Ownership also varies in the security of property rights. In some countries, the legal system protects private property rights; in other countries, there is no rule of law and property rights are insecure. Even in "secure" property rights countries, such as the United States, owners can lose all or part of their property rights if the "public interest" appears to require this. In Russia today, the property rights of owners of large companies can be taken away by the political elite using arbitrary courts. In Egypt, a recent study found that only 10 percent of property rights are secure from arbitrary seizure.[10]

Differences in ownership rights affect economic outcomes. Consider an economy in which all three ownership rights belong to individuals. As the owners seek to maximize their lifetime incomes, they disburse capital to gain the highest rate of return commensurate with the risk. If capital is owned by the state, greater attention may be paid to long-term social rates of return or capital may be allocated simply to political friends. The distribution of income will differ according to private or state ownership: Property income will accrue to private owners in the one case and to the state, or to the state's favorites, in the other.

The security of property rights also affects economic outcomes. If owners know their property can be taken away without reasonable compensation, there is little need to improve it. If owners of companies understand that they could lose their ownership rights at any time, they will strip the company of its assets and pay little attention to raising its value.

Clearly, ownership arrangements and ownership rights are important in the classification of economic systems. In the traditional "ism" classification, ownership arrangements are the distinguishing characteristic.

Most economic systems are, in fact, a mixture of private and public ownership, but we can measure the extent of private, state, and collective ownership and distinguish among them rather clearly. Formal ownership rights do not tell the complete story. For that, we need to know the extent to which formal owners possess all three property rights and the security of their ownership rights.

The Organization of Decision Making

We know much more about decision making in the private sector than in the state sector.[11] The nature of decision making and of its impact on resource allocation in a state enterprise or a state bureaucracy is much less well understood in both theory and practice.

Most economic and political activity is carried out in organizations. Individuals, consultants, and sole proprietors engage in business by themselves, but they account for a minor share of economic activity. Nobel laureate Herbert Simon defines an **organization** as *"the complex pattern of communications and other relations in a group of human beings."*[12] J. M. Montias offers a similar definition: *"An* **organization** *consists of a set of participants (members) regularly interacting in the process of carrying on one or more activities."*[13]

Both definitions emphasize that organizations bring various participants together to communicate among themselves and to carry out a common activity. Organizations are not characterized by dry organization charts but by human beings working together presumably toward a common goal. Organized behavior has advantages over unorganized behavior. In an organization, goals exist, information is created, and assumptions and attitudes are formed, all of which play a part in the making of decisions.

According to organization theory, individuals participate in organized behavior, pursuing self-interest constrained by bounded rationality.[10] **Bounded rationality** *means that decision makers have limited information and other constraints that force them to use rules of thumb.* Economic theory usually assumes that we make rational decisions, armed with perfect information. If we lack perfect information and outcomes are uncertain, we cannot rationally weigh every decision to find the maximizing outcome. Rather, in such a situation, we turn to the use of rules or guidelines. Therefore in an organization, such as a corporation, rules replace a complex series of profit-maximizing choices. The corporation may set general hiring rules, guidelines on minimum rate of return, or travel rules—standards that may not be optimal in all instances but that work under conditions of imperfect information and uncertainty. Self-interest may be construed as the maximization of some utility function constrained by a broad range of human limitations, such as the ability to generate, process, and utilize information.

These characteristics lead to two major classes of organizational problems. **Technical–administrative problems** *derive from our limited ability to make decisions because of incomplete information.* **Agency–managerial problems** *arise* *when self-interested members of the organization pursue objectives that differ from the organization's objectives.*

If we knew everything, we would not have to use rules in organizations. Every decision could be made in such a way as to yield optimal results. However, in the real world, information is costly. Organizations are faced with **transaction costs** *associated with searching for information, bargaining, policing, and enforcement.* When transactions costs are high, the organization is inclined to use rules to solve technical–administrative and agency–managerial problems instead of making individual decisions in each case.

The organization's rules determine how the activities of the organization are carried out. The two extreme organizational structures are hierarchy and association. In a **hierarchy**, *superiors (principals) establish objectives and issue orders to subordinates (agents) who are supposed to carry out assigned tasks to achieve organizational objectives.* Examples of hierarchical organizations are corporations, government agencies, and the military. In an **association**, *members make decisions in the absence of a superior–subordinate relationship.* Examples would be a law partnership, church assembly, or a dairy cooperative. Hierarchical organizations are more prevalent and account for most economic activity.

Except in the case of associations or very simple organizations (such as an owner-operated company with no employees), a hierarchy is present. There can be substantial differences in the number of levels in the hierarchy, the allocation of tasks among these levels, and the span of control or the number of subordinates directed by a superior.

There are reasons for hierarchy in organizations. Roy Radner argues that hierarchical structures allow a specific breed of actors—managers—to control decentralized information processing in a setting in which it is impossible for single persons to know and manage all relevant information.[14] Simple economic intuition suggests that business organizations must be divided into managers (owners) and employees. Some individuals are risk takers, whereas others avoid risk. Employees agree to work for an owner and to obey the owner's instructions. The owner reaps the rewards of profits if the business succeeds but also risks losses if the business fails.

Raaj Sah and Nobel Laureate Joseph Stiglitz consider well-devised hierarchies as ways to minimize the accumulation of mistakes made by the various members of an organization.[15] Armen Alchian and Harold Demsetz claim that hierarchies exist because technology requires members of the organization (say, a firm) to work together in "team production." With team effort, it is difficult to assess each individual's contribution. Such a setting may cause some to slacken work effort unless a superior monitors work and relates rewards to effort.[16]

Whatever the reasons, most economic and political activity is carried out in hierarchies. Hierarchies are characterized by superior–subordinate relationships whereby the actors are classified as principals or agents.

Principal–Agent Problems   An organization is characterized by the levels at which resource-allocation decisions are made and executed. *In a* **decentralized** *organization, decisions are made primarily at low levels of the organization. In a* **centralized** *organization, most decisions are made at high levels.* Decision-making levels reflect the organization's structure, how it generates and utilizes information, and, finally, the way it allocates authority and responsibility making among the levels of the organization.[17]

A superior–subordinate (or principal–agent) relationship implies that agents are organized as groups, subunits, or smaller organizations. An enterprise may be a branch of a larger company that is itself owned by a conglomerate. A government enterprise may be subordinate to a government department that in turn is subordinate to a ministry. The hierarchy of the Roman Catholic Church consists of the pope, archbishops, cardinals, metropolitans, and bishops.

Participants in a hierarchy act either as a principal or as an agent. *A **principal** is a party that has controlling authority and that engages an agent to act subject to the principal's control and instruction. An **agent** is a party that acts for, on behalf of, or as a representative of a principal.*[18]

Firm X is a principal when it enters into a contract with Firm Y whereby Firm Y (the agent) will supply Firm X with specified amounts of a product at specified prices over a specified period of time. Firm X is also a principal when it signs a contract with an employee (the agent) that calls for the employee to perform specific services at a specified wage for a specified period of time.

Once an agency relationship is established, the principal is responsible for monitoring performance. When both the principal and the agent are motivated to achieve the same goal, or when the performance of the agent can be easily monitored, conflicts between principal and agent are unlikely. However, when the parties have different goals and when monitoring is difficult, principal–agent problems are expected.

A **principal–agent problem** *exists when the agent has a different goal from the principal and when the agent has more information than the principal.* If principals and agents share the same goal, the principal can rely on the agent to work in the principal's interests. In a corporation, if the hired management team (the agent) shares the shareholders' (principal's) goal of a higher stock price, there should be no conflict. If, in a communist state, state managers share the political elite's goal of the "building of socialism," there should be no conflict among them. In the same cases, if the principal has perfect information about the activities of the agent, agents would be caught if they acted against the interests of the principal.

Opportunistic behavior *occurs when agents act contrary to the goals of the principal.* Much of the study of alternative economic systems deals with how to resolve principal–agent problems that lead to opportunistic behavior.

Figure 2.2 illustrates the principal–agent relationships in a hierarchical command economy in which a political authority (such as a communist party) works with planners to issue instructions to its agents, the industrial ministries. The industrial ministries then issue instructions to their agents, the enterprises subordinated to them. When we study the Soviet planned economy, we will delve into the principal–agents problems of such a hierarchical arrangement.

Figure 2.3 spells out the stylized hierarchical structure of a corporation. It places the principal (the shareholders) at the top. The shareholders elect a board of directors to represent them, which selects the management team (the agent). The branch divisions are agents of the corporate headquarters management. As the diagram illustrates, there are many opportunities for principal–agent problems

FIGURE 2.2   The Hierarchical Command Economy: Principals and Agents

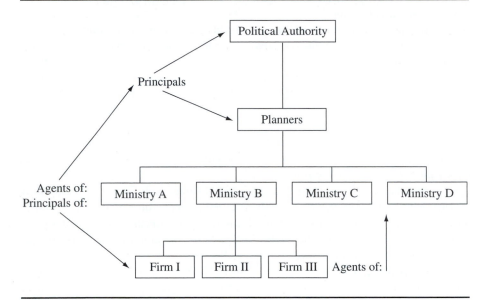

Source: From GREGORY, Comparing Economic Systems in the Twenty-First Century, 7E. © 2004 Cengage Learning.

FIGURE 2.3   The Hierarchy of a Corporation

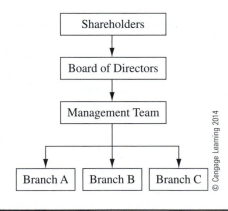

within a corporation. Much of our later discussion of the corporation in different institutional settings will focus on how it deals with principal–agent problems.

Information Problems   Hierarchal organizations make decisions based on the information at their disposal. No organization has (or could process) all the information relevant to the organization. As noted, limitations on information lead organizations to use rules of thumb in recognition that they do not know everything. Imperfect information also contributes to principal–agent problems. If principals knew everything about their agents, they could monitor them to rule out opportunistic behavior. But in virtually all organizations, agents possess more local information about what is going on in their immediate vicinity than their principals.

In a perfectly centralized organization, the authority to make decisions rests in a single central command that issues orders to lower units in the organization. The perfectly decentralized case would be a structure wherein all decision-making authority rests with the lowest subunits (households and individual firms), independent of superior authorities. In the real world, authority is typically spread through various levels in the hierarchy.

The level of decision making depends not only on the hierarchical structure of the organization. It also depends on how it manages information. **Perfect centralization of information** *means that a single decision maker possesses all information about all participants, their actions, and their environment and transmits only limited pieces of information to subunits.* Perfect centralization of information is rarely possible. Principals possess less than complete information; their agents have information they do not have. Therefore most organizations are informationally decentralized. **Informationally decentralized systems** *generate, process, and utilize information at the lower levels in the organization that is not exchanged with higher levels.* In such a decentralized system, information is exchanged among lower units and is passed up to superiors on a limited basis.

Opportunistic behavior can take two forms: moral hazard and adverse selection.[19] **Moral hazard** *occurs when the agent exploits an information advantage to alter its behavior after entering into an agreement with the principal.* For example, a buyer may promise a supplier steady purchases at fixed prices if that supplier acquires specialized equipment suited only to that buyer's product. Then, after the equipment has been installed, the sole buyer reduces its purchases or the price it will pay. In a command economy (such as in Figure 2.2) the state enterprise may agree to produce 100,000 meters of high-quality cloth, but it fulfills the plan by reducing quality.

Adverse selection *occurs when agents conceal information from principals, making it impossible for their superiors to distinguish among them.* For example, all enterprises may claim that they cannot adopt a new technology proposed by the ministry. Some can and others cannot, but those that can adopt it conceal this fact from the ministry. The ministry therefore may be forced into inefficient decision making, such as requiring all firms to adopt the technology. Adverse selection is a problem long noted by insurance companies. They find it difficult to offer guaranteed health insurance because only those with serious health problems will apply.

Market versus Plan: Institutions for the Provision of Information and for Coordination

The **market** and the **plan** are the two major mechanisms for providing information and for coordinating decisions in and among organizations. Centralization is commonly identified with planning and decentralization with market, but there is no simple relationship between the two. Some economies combine considerable concentration of decision-making authority and information in a few large corporations with substantial state involvement and yet have no system of planning as such. Economies that have national planning have also varied but tend to follow a more common pattern.

Markets or Plan?   **Coase Market** *refers to activities that are coordinated by the buying and selling of goods and services among organizations*, whereas **plan** *refers to activities that are carried out entirely within the organization without the use of market transactions with other organizations.*

Nobel Laureate Ronald Coase posed the question of why some activities are carried out through markets, whereas others are carried out by administrative directives (plan) within enterprises.[20] Coase concluded that activities are carried out by directives whenever the transaction costs of using markets are too high. The coordination of decision-making activities in markets has costs. The participants in market-coordinated activities must develop appropriate contracts based on market-generated information and must bear the legal and financial consequences of unfulfilled contracts. Business firms can limit the costs of market coordination by producing within the firm.

The task of building a new generation of commercial aircraft illustrates the two choices: European Aeronautic Defence and Space Company (EADS) and Boeing Company are currently competing to market instead of produce a new generation of commercial aircraft. In EADS's case, it is the double-decker Airbus 380; in Boeing's case, it is the 787 Dreamliner. Both companies encountered significant and costly delays. EADs has chosen the market path. The mainframe and components are organized through multiple market contracts involving hundreds of contractors. EADS feels that it can develop its Airbus 380 better through market subcontracting. Boeing (while using more market contracts than usual) has chosen to build its 787 Dreamliner in-house by issuing administrative directives to its various divisions. In both cases, they are acquiring the engines through market contracting.

Although both companies are building a similar product and use similar economic calculus, they have come to different conclusions about the cost of organizing activity inside the firm versus the cost of organizing that activity using markets.

Figure 2.4 illustrates the choice of market or plan by firms, government entities, and households. The boxes show activities carried out within the organization, be it a household, government, or business. The lines from the boxes to the product and factor markets show activities that are coordinated by markets. The figure shows that firms can acquire goods through the product market or produce them within the firm. For example, an auto manufacturer can either produce tires or buy them from other producers. The firm can use its own employees or hire outside consultants through the factor market. Similarly, the government can produce its own weapons with its own employees or acquire them through markets. In all cases, whether to produce within the box and using markets depends, as Coase taught, on the relative costs of using administrative directives versus the market.

Coase applied his theory of transaction costs to explain why economies organize themselves into business organizations. His ideas apply on a grander level to explain why some organizations, such as economic systems, carry out their

FIGURE 2.4   Market versus Plan

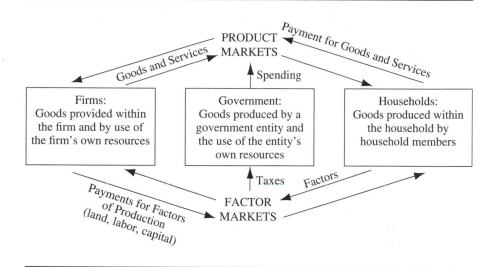

Source: From GREGORY, Comparing Economic Systems in the Twenty-First Century, 7E. © 2004 Cengage Learning.

transactions by directive or command and not use markets at all. If the system's directors conclude that the transaction costs of using markets are everywhere too high, they conclude that a planned economy is better than a market economy.

Planned versus Market Economies   *In a* **planned economy**, *agents throughout the economy are coordinated by specific instructions or directives formulated by a superior agency (a planning board) and disseminated through a plan document (sometimes termed* **directive planning***).* Agents are induced to carry out the directives via incentives or threats designed by the planning authorities. The specifics differ, but in a planned economy, economic activity is guided by instructions of higher units and subsequently transmitted to lower units. Rewards depend on the achievement of plan directives. A planned economy and a market economy are mutually exclusive: In the former, resources are allocated in accordance with the instructions of planners, who thereby usurp the role of the market as allocator of resources. There may remain room for the market in peripheral or informal activities, but resource allocation is dominated by the plan.

In a **market economy**, *the market—through the forces of supply and demand—provides signals that trigger organizations to make decisions on resource utilization. The market thereby coordinates the activities of decision-making units.*

Households earn income by providing land, labor, and capital, and with this income they buy the goods that firms supply. Firms and households respond to the market. Other mechanisms for information or coordination play secondary roles, and decision-making authority is vested at the lower level of the economic system.

More common forms of planning are intended to nudge market allocation in a direction desired by the state. In indicative planning, the market serves as the principal instrument for resource allocation, but a plan is prepared to guide decision making. *An* **indicative plan** *is one in which planners seek to project aggregate or sectoral trends and to provide information beyond that normally supplied by the market.* An indicative plan is *not* broken down into directives or instructions for individual production units; enterprises are free to apply the information in the indicative plan as they see fit, although indirect means are often used to influence economic activity. We have few examples of indicative plans today, but they were used in countries in the early postwar period, such as France.

A more common form of planning is industrial policy. **Industrial policy** *is a set of instruments whereby the state attempts to preferentially promote and develop industries and branches that are particularly worthy or deemed important to growth and development.* Industrial policy does not hand down administrative orders but it provides tax preferences, subsidies, and other encouragements for the favored economic activity. The pioneer in industrial policy was Japan in the early postwar period. In Japan, a government ministry worked closely with banks and companies to pick "winners" and "national champions" and to provide them with favorable financing and other support. Currently, a number of countries, including Russia and China, have active industrial policies to promote companies and industries favored by state authorities.

The ultimate decision makers are different in planned and market economies. In a market economy, the consumer can "vote" in the marketplace and exercise consumer sovereignty. *With* **consumer sovereignty**, *consumers in the marketplace dominate the basic decision of what to produce.* In a planned economy, on the other hand, decisions are made by the planners, and hence planners' preferences prevail. *With* **planners' preferences**, *planners make the basic decision of what to produce.*

Figure 2.5 illustrates the differences between a planned and a market economy. It depicts the production and allocation of a particular industrial commodity such as pig iron, denoted by X. The demand curve D shows the quantity of X demanded by the various potential users at different "prices" of X. The price could be the official price or some more comprehensive price, which captures the resources costs that potential users must pay to acquire X. The supply curve S shows the various quantities of X supplied by its producers at different prices. If this were a market economy (diagram on the left), the market would determine how much of X is produced and which potential users would get the available supply. All those willing to pay the market price (P') would get X'. The basic feature of an administrative-command economy (diagram on the right) is that the dictator decides both how much X is produced and who gets X. The market (diagram on the left) is driven by an invisible hand that does not distinguish among buyers. Anyone who can pay the price will get the good. The planner, on the other hand, can use his or her "visible hand" of allocative power to reward and punish either buyers or producers for economic or political ends. In the diagram, the planner sets the production of X at X^* and its price at P^*. At this price, the producer is supposed to sell the entire output (X^*) to authorized buyers at the official price P^*. The planner decides who gets X^* among all those willing to pay the official price, P^*. Note that buyers wish to buy more than is available (X^{**}). Planners allocate the available supply among a larger number of willing buyers. If subordinates obey orders, only those designated to receive X will actually get it.

FIGURE 2.5   Market Economy versus Planned Economy

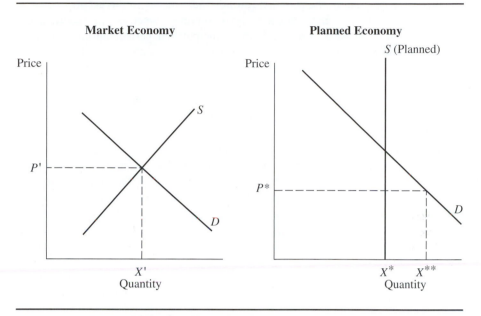

Source: From GREGORY, Comparing Economic Systems in the Twenty-First Century, 7E. © 2004 Cengage Learning.

According to this diagram, there is a basic equilibrium in a market economy and a basic disequilibrium in a planned economy. In the market economy, all those willing to pay the market price will get the product. Buyers are prepared to buy the same amount as sellers are prepared to sell. All others who "want" the good are excluded from the market because they are not prepared to pay its market price. In the planned economy, buyers want to buy more of the good than is available at the price. It is the planner, not the price, that determines who gets the product. This contrast reveals potential sources of conflict between the principal (the planner) and agents (the buyers of the product). Those who are prepared to pay the going price but are excluded by the planner may seek to strike a side deal with the producer to get the good in place of those designated by the planner. We shall discuss this conflict in greater detail in a later chapter.

Incentive Mechanisms

An organization can also be characterized in terms of the incentives that motivate people. "Goals and incentives are ... vital links in understanding the transformation of property rights and informational inputs into effective actions."[21]

Incentive mechanisms should induce participants at lower levels (agents) to fulfill the directives of those at higher levels (principals). An effective mechanism must fulfill three conditions.[22] First, the agent who is to receive the reward must be able to influence the outcomes for which the reward is given. Second, the agent's principal must be able to check on the subordinate to see whether tasks have been executed properly. Third, the potential rewards must matter to the agent.

In a hierarchy in which superiors issue binding directives to subordinates, incentives would be easy to devise if the principal had perfect information. The principal would automatically know whether the agent was carrying out tasks properly and could issue an appropriate reward or punishment. In complex organizations, however, principals typically lack perfect information. The subordinate knows much more about local circumstances than the superior, and the superior cannot issue perfectly detailed instructions. The subordinate must be left with some discretion. Because of the imperfect information of the principal, the agent gains local decision-making authority in a number of realms. The principal needs to devise an incentive system that will induce the agent to act in the interests of the superior when the subordinate makes such local decisions. If the principal's incentive system is flawed, then the agent will not act in the interest of the superior.

The information disadvantage of superior organizations affects the way the system is organized. If it is not possible to devise incentive systems that cause agents spontaneously to work in the interests of superior organizations, a more centralized solution may be required. If incentive systems do not elicit necessary information, the superior organization may impose decisions on the subordinate organization without consultation. If private insurance companies cannot elicit information on disabilities or on driving habits in a cost-effective way, then government agencies, rather than private markets, may have to provide such insurance. Information disadvantages explain why governments instead of private markets handle unemployment and poverty insurance.

The superior can devise and use either material or moral incentives to motivate the subordinate. Material incentives have typically dominated modern economic systems, yet some systems have attempted to emphasize moral rewards. **Material incentives** *promote desirable behavior by giving the recipient a greater claim over material goods.* **Moral incentives** *reward desirable behavior by appealing to the recipient's responsibility to society (or the company) and accordingly raising the recipient's social stature within the community.* Moral incentives do not give recipients greater command over material goods. In simpler terms, the difference between material and moral incentives is the difference between a cash bonus and bestowing a medal.

It is rare in democratic societies for punishment to be used in the incentive system. Carl Shapiro and Joseph Stiglitz maintain that equilibrium unemployment is used in market economies to punish workers for shirking and shoddy work,[23] but such punishment is mild compared to historical examples of extreme punishment for managerial mistakes and poor work performance. The Soviet Union, under Joseph Stalin, instituted a vast network of prison camps for common criminals and for those whose bad economic performance made them "an enemy of the state." At its peak, the Gulag imprisoned 2.5 percent of the adult population.[24]

Models of Public Choice

Societies must have arrangements for making public choices, for example, the political decisions that societies make on taxation and government expenditures.

The government normally provides public goods: roads must be built, children must be educated, and provision must be made for national defense and police protection. Even in market economies, **public goods** must be provided by the state because **free riders, or nonpayers,** *cannot be prevented from using them, and one person's use does not prevent any other person from using them.* Decisions on public choices can be made according to different political institutional arrangements. At one extreme—dictatorship—public choices are made by a person or small group of persons. Citizens are not consulted via the ballot box, and the dictator may make political decisions that are strongly opposed by the population. Stalin's Russia was such an example. The current Chinese dictatorship, however, appears to pay closer attention to public opinion, although it is the final arbiter.

At the other extreme is democracy. *In a* **democracy**, *public choices are put to a majority vote.* Pure democracy is rare because it is difficult to vote on every public choice, although referendums are often used for specific issues. Of the world's democracies, Switzerland may be the closest example to a democracy that directly votes on a large number of issues. Most democracies are **representative democracies** *in which the voters elect representatives to make their public choices for them.* Elected representatives gather in legislatures or parliaments, and power is usually divided among executive, legislative, and judicial branches.

Dictatorships are usually associated with planned economies or with industrial policy. In fact, Nobel Laureate Friedrich Hayek argued that planning inevitably leads down a "Road to Serfdom" to political dictatorship.[25] Hayek saw little difference between Adolf Hitler's Germany and Stalin's Russia. Domination of political life inevitably meant the domination of economic life. Hugo Chávez of Venezuela and Vladimir Putin of Russia have both increased the state's intervention in economic affairs. In a rare counterexample, Augusto Pinochet, the military dictator of Chile in the 1970s and 1980s, relied on a market economy with limited state intervention.

A Threefold Classification

We examined the attributes that characterize economic systems. Figure 2.6A summarizes the alternative options available for each attribute. We use the five criteria for distinguishing among economic systems. Although additional criteria could have been introduced, we feel that these five are the most important. They yield a threefold classification of economic systems: *capitalism, market socialism,* and *planned socialism.* As Figure 2.6B shows, each system is characterized multidimensionally in terms of the five criteria.

Capitalism *is characterized by private ownership of the factors of production. Decision making is decentralized and rests with the owners of the factors of production. Their decision making is coordinated by the market, which provides the necessary information. Material incentives are used to motivate participants. Public choices are made by democratic political institutions.*

Market socialism *is characterized by public ownership of the factors of production. Decision making is decentralized and is coordinated by the market mechanism. Both material and moral incentives are used to motivate participants.*

Figure 2.6(A)   Attributes of Economic Systems

ATTRIBUTE	CONTINUUM OF OPTIONS
Organization of Decision Making	Centralization ◄──────► Decentralization
Provision of Information and Coordination	Plan ◄──────────► Market
Property Rights	Public ◄───► Cooperative ◄───► Private
Incentive System	Moral ◄──────────► Material
Organization of Public Choices	Dictatorship ◄────────► Democracy

Source: From GREGORY, Comparing Economic Systems in the Twenty-First Century, 7E. © 2004 Cengage Learning.

Planned socialism *is characterized by public ownership of the factors of production. Decision making is centralized and is coordinated by a central plan, which issues binding directives to the system's participants. Both material and moral incentives are used to motivate participants. Public choices are made by a dictator.*

These definitions raise as many questions as they answer. They merely state the most important characteristics of "core" economic systems. They do not tell us how and how well each system solves the economic problem of resource allocation. Under capitalism, how do the owners of the factors of production actually allocate their resources, according to what rules, and with what results? Under market socialism, how can public ownership be made compatible with market coordination? In fact, is public ownership *ever* compatible with market coordination? Under planned socialism, how is information gathered and processed to allocate resources effectively? How is it possible to ensure that the system's participants will follow the center's directives?

We call these three economic systems "core" economic systems. They are easily distinguished, one from the other. One of the core systems is scarcely practiced in the world today. It virtually disappeared with the collapse of the Soviet Union. We are hard pressed to identify examples of market socialism, Although modern China may come fairly close. Most of the world's economies fall, often very

FIGURE 2.6(B)   The Pure Systems

	CAPITALISM	MARKET SOCIALISM	PLANNED SOCIALISM
Decision-making Structure	Primarily Decentralized	Primarily Decentralized	Primarily Centralized
Mechanisms for Information and Coordination	Primarily Market	Primarily Market	Primarily Plan
Property Rights	Primarily Private Ownership	State and/or Collective Ownership	Primarily State Ownership
Incentives	Primarily Market	Material and Moral	Material and Moral
Public Choice	Democracy	?	Dictatorship

Source: From GREGORY, Comparing Economic Systems in the Twenty-First Century, 7E. © 2004 Cengage Learning.

imperfectly, under the rubric of capitalism. There is private ownership (perhaps much owned by the political elite). There is market allocation, although with cases of significant state interference. Incentives are primarily material. More countries do not meet the democracy criterion. In fact, noted Hungarian economist János Kornai argues that we should use "government friendly to private ownership and market allocation" in place of democracy.[26]

Perceptional Measures: Freedom, Corruption, Governance

International organizations and non-governmental organizations have led the way in exploring entirely new ways to measure various aspects of the economic system.[27] Agencies, both public and private, produce ratings of countries on metrics of institutional development. Some seek to capture metrics of interest to international businesses and investors, such as indicators of business risk (International Country Risk Guide, ICRG) or country competitiveness (The World

Competitiveness report). Others look directly at institutions, such as perceptions of corruption (Transparency International) or economic and political freedom indexes. Freedom House has published annually its *Survey of Freedom* for 191 countries since 1974. The Heritage Foundation has assembled its economic freedom index, broken down according to political freedom or democracy, economic freedom or openness, legal framework effectiveness or property rights protection, for 148 countries since 1995. The European Bank for Reconstruction and Development (EBRD) has published its Transition Report for twenty-five transition countries since 1994. The World Bank published in 1998 a survey on the institutional environment in a large number of countries for its World Development Report. The survey covered areas such as government predictability regarding laws and policies, property rights, the quality of the government–business relationship, bureaucratic red tape, and efficiency of the government in providing services.

These indexes of economic institutions are based on perceptions of experts. Transparency International, for example, asks officials and businesspersons familiar with the country their perceptions of how honest or corrupt a country is. The Heritage Foundation's Economic Freedom index is compiled from the answers to checklists of questions by teams of in-house experts, country experts, and scholars. The EBRD's transition indicator scores reflect the judgments of the office of the chief economist as to progress in large- and small-scale privatization, the removal of soft budgets, and price and foreign-trade liberalization.

Perceptional measures of the economic system such as Transparency International's corruption index, Freedom House's political freedom index, the EBRD, and the Heritage Foundation's economic freedom index have revolutionized the study of comparative economic systems. **Perceptional measures** *use quantitative measures of aspects of the economic system to study the performance of economic systems.*

We now have a substantial empirical literature that examines the effects of institutions on economic performance using these different measures of the institutions of economic systems.[28]

Summary

- Comparative economic systems studies the effect of the economic system on economic behavior and performance. Other branches of economics hold the economic system constant.
- Political economy and comparative economic analysis have contributed to modern economic systems.
- An economic system is a set of institutions for decision making and for the implementation of decisions concerning production, income, and consumption within a given geographic area.
- The economic system is comprised of institutions that determine the rules of the game and the means of their enforcement.
- Economics systems studies organizations and their hierarchies of principals and agents. Much of comparative economic analysis is about how the system deals with information and principal–agent problems.

- Comparative economic systems are distinctive clusters of economies with similar institutions.
- The most important institutions are the organization of property rights, organization of decision-making arrangements, market versus plan, institutions for the provision of information and for coordination, incentive mechanisms, and procedures for making public choices.
- Full property rights require the rights to dispose, use, and receive the income of the property. Property rights can also be defined by private, state, and collective ownership.
- Economic activity is carried out by organizations that maximize their objectives subject to constraints. Bounded rationality requires the use of rules of thumb. Whether organizations use market or plan is determined by transaction costs.
- Economists explain why economic activity is carried out by businesses and why some transactions occur through administrative commands rather than through the market.
- A principal–agent problem exists when the agent has a different goal from the principal and when the agent has more information. Opportunistic behavior occurs when agents act contrary to the goals of the principal. Economic systems study how to resolve principal–agent problems.
- Economic systems can also be differentiated by how they handle information and deal with the information problems of adverse selection and moral hazard.
- A planned economy is one wherein agents are coordinated by specific instructions or directives formulated by a superior agency.
- A market economy provides signals that trigger organizations to make decisions on resource utilization. The market coordinates the activities of decision-making units.
- Economic systems studies how economic agents are incentivized either through material rewards or punishments or social incentives.
- Public choice is the study of how economic systems make choices of taxation and public spending. The polar models are democracy and dictatorship.
- We divide economic systems into three major types: capitalist, or market economies; planned socialism; and market socialism.
- We now have various indexes of attributes of economic systems that make possible empirical analysis of the impact of the economic systems on economic outcomes.

Key Terms

adverse selection—Agents conceal information from principals, making it impossible for their superiors to distinguish among them.

agency–managerial problems—Members of the organization pursue objectives differing from those established for the organization.

agent—Acts for, on behalf of, or as a representative of a principal.

Association—*Members make decisions in the absence of a superior–subordinate relationship.*

bounded rationality—Decision makers have limited information and other constraints that force them to use rules of thumb.

capitalism—Private ownership of the factors of production, decentralized decision making, coordinated by the market, material incentives, and public choices are made by democratic political institutions.

centralized—Most decisions are made at high levels.

cluster—If countries do not cluster according to their institutions, they cannot be treated as economic systems.

collective ownership—Property rights belong to the members of the collective.

comparative economics—The use of international data across countries and across time to study economic phenomena.

consumer sovereignty—The basic decision of what to produce is dominated by consumers in the marketplace.

country fixed effects—The use of dummy variables assigned to each country to hold constant the impact of the economic system so as to allow proper analysis of other variables.

decentralized—Decisions made primarily at low levels of the organization.

democracy—Public choices are put to a majority vote.

economic system—A set of institutions for decision making and for the implementation of decisions concerning production, income, and consumption within a given geographic area.

economics—The study of how economic agents (households, firms, and governments) allocate scarce resources (land, labor, and capital) among competing ends according to the prevailing economic system.

free riders, or nonpayers—*Cannot be prevented from using a good, and one person's use does not prevent any other person from using the good.*

full ownership (or full property rights)—Owner has the right to dispose of the property, use the property, and receive the income the property generates.

hierarchy1—Superiors (principals) establish objectives and issue orders to subordinates (agents) who are supposed to carry out assigned tasks to achieve organizational objectives.

hierarchy2—The division of an organization into superior and subordinate levels. The person in charge of a higher level in the organization is superior to subordinates at lower levels.

indicative plan—Planners project aggregate or sectoral trends and provide information beyond that normally supplied by the market.

industrial policy—State attempts to preferentially promote and develop industries and branches that are particularly worthy or deemed important to growth and development.

informationally decentralized systems—These systems generate, process, and utilize information at the lower levels in the organization that is not exchanged with higher levels in the organization.

institutions—The rules of the game of a society that shape economic decisions, or, more fundamentally, the humanly devised constraints that shape human interaction.

market—Activities that are coordinated by the buying and selling of goods and services among organizations.

market economy—Market provides signals that trigger organizations to make decisions on resource utilization and coordinates the activities of decision-making units.

market socialism—Public ownership; decentralized decision making; coordinated by the market; both material and moral incentives.

material incentives—Promote desirable behavior by giving the recipient a greater claim over material goods.

moral hazard—Agent exploits an information advantage to alter its behavior after entering into an agreement with the principal.

moral incentives—Reward desirable behavior by appealing to the recipient's responsibility to society (or the company) and accordingly raising the recipient's social stature within the community.

opportunistic behavior—Agents act contrary to the goals of the principal.

organization—The complex pattern of communications and other relations in a group of human beings. Or, organization consists of a set of participants (members) regularly interacting in the process of carrying on one or more activities.

ownership—Amalgam of rights that individuals may have over objects or claims on objects or services; these rights may affect an object's disposition or its utilization.

perceptional measures—Measure quantitative measures of aspects of the economic system to study the performance of economic systems.

perfect centralization of information—Single decision maker possesses all information about all participants, their actions, and their environment and transmits only limited pieces of information to subunits.

plan—Activities that are carried out entirely within the organization without the use of market transactions with other organizations.

planned economy—Agents throughout the economy are coordinated by specific instructions or directives formulated by a superior agency (a planning board) and disseminated through a plan document.

planned socialism—Public ownership of the factors of production; centralized decision making; coordinated by a central plan; issuing binding directives; both material and moral incentives; public choices are made by a dictator.

planners' preferences—The basic decision of what to produce is made by planners.

political economy—Applies economic analysis to the study of how we organize our political system and how politics impacts economic behavior and outcomes.

principal—Party having controlling authority and engaging an agent to act subject to the principal's control and instruction.

principal–agent problem—Exists when the agent has a different goal from the principal and when the agent has more information than the principal.

private ownership—Ownership rights ultimately belongs to individuals, subject to limitations on disposition, use, and earnings.

public choice—The study of how the political system is organized to tax citizens and to spend public resources.

public goods—Must be provided by the state because nonpayers, or free riders, cannot be prevented from using them, and one person's use does not prevent any other person from using them.

public ownership—Ownership rights belong to the state.

representative democracy—Voters elect representatives to make their public choices for them.

technical–administrative problems—Limits on decision making because of, for example, incomplete information.

transaction costs—Costs associated with searching for information, bargaining, and policing and enforcement.

Notes

1. Alexander Eckstein, "Introduction," in Alexander Eckstein, ed., *Comparison of Economic Systems: Theoretical and Methodological Approaches* (Berkeley: University of California Press, 1971), p. 1; John Michael Montias, *The Structure of Economic Systems* (New Haven: Yale University Press, 1976).

2. Assar Lindbeck, *The Political Economy of the New Left: An Outsider's View*, 2nd ed. (New York: Harper & Row, 1977), p. 214.

3. Frederic Pryor, *Property and Industrial Organization in Communist and Capitalist Nations* (Bloomington: Indiana University Press, 1973), p. 337; T. C. Koopmans and J. M. Montias, "On the Description and Comparison of Economic Systems," in Eckstein, *Comparison of Economic Systems*, pp. 27–28.

4. Stefan Voigt and Hella Engerer, "Institutions and Transformation—Possible Policy Implications of the New Institutional Economics," in Klaus Zimmerman (ed.), *Frontiers in Economics* (Berlin: Springer-Verlag, 2002), p. 132.

5. Douglass North, *Institutions, Institutional Change and Economic Performance* (Cambridge: Cambridge University Press, 1990), p. 3.

6. Voigt and Engerer, "Institutions and Transformation," p. 131.

7. Frederic Pryor, "Market Economic Systems," *Journal of Comparative Economics* 33, no. 1 (March 2005), 25–47.

8. Montias, *The Structure of Economic Systems*, p. 8.

9. Montias, *The Structure of Economic Systems*, p. 116. For a survey of the literature, see Erik Furubotn and Svetozar Pejovich, "Property Rights and Economic Theory: A Survey of Recent Literature," *Journal of Economic Literature* 10 (December 1972), 1137–1162. For a discussion in the comparative context, see Pryor, *Property and Industrial Organization*; Alan Ryan, "Property," in John Eatwell, Murray Milgate, and Peter Newman, eds., *The New Palgrave: Dictionary of Economics* (New York: Stockton Press, 1987), pp. 1029–1031; Louis Putterman, "Ownership and the Nature of the Firm," *Journal of Comparative Economics* 17 (1993), 243–263; John P. Bonin, Derek C. Jones, and Louis Putterman, "Theoretical and Empirical Research on Producers' Cooperatives: Will Ever the Twain Meet?" *Journal of Economic Literature* 31 (September 1993), 1290–1320.

10. Hernando DeSoto, "Egypt's Economic Apartheid," *Wall Street Journal*, February 3, 2011.

11. For a discussion of decision making in the public sector, see V. V. Ramanadham, *Public Enterprise: Studies in Organizational Structure* (London: Frank Cass, 1986). For a

discussion of nonprofit organizations, see Avner Ben-Ner and Theresa Van Hoomissen, "Nonprofit Organizations in the Mixed Economy: A Demand and Supply Analysis," *Annals of the Public and Cooperative Economy* 62, no. 4 (October–December, 1991), 519–550; Susan Rose-Ackerman, ed., *The Economics of Nonprofit Institutions: Studies in Structure and Policy* (New York: Oxford University Press, 1986); Burton A. Weisbrod, *The Nonprofit Economy* (Cambridge, Mass.: Harvard University Press, 1988); Jean-Jacques Laffont and Jean Tirole, "Privatization and Incentives," *Journal of Law, Economics & Public Organization* 7 (1991) Special Issue, 84–105.

12. Herbert A. Simon, *Administrative Behavior*, 2nd ed. (New York: Free Press, 1966), p. xvi.

13. Montias, *The Structure of Economic Systems*, p. 8.

14. Roy Radner, "Hierarchy: The Economics of Managing," *Journal of Economic Literature* 30 (September 1992), 1382–1415.

15. Raaj Kumar Sah and Joseph E. Stiglitz, "The Architecture of Economic Systems: Hierarchies and Polyarchies," *American Economic Review* 76, no. 4 (September 1986), 716–727.

16. A. A. Alchian and H. Demsetz, "Production, Information, Costs and Economic Organizations," *American Economic Review* 62 (December 1972), 777–795.

17. There is a large body of literature concerned with issues of centralization and decentralization. For early contributions, see Leonid Hurwicz, "Centralization and Decentralization in Economic Processes," in Eckstein, *Comparison of Economic Systems*, pp. 79–102; Leonid Hurwicz, "Conditions for Economic Efficiency of Centralized and Decentralized Structures," in Gregory Grossman, ed., *Value and Plan* (Berkeley: University of California Press, 1960), pp. 162–183; Thomas Marschak, "Centralization and Decentralization in Economic Organizations," *Econometrica* 27 (1959), 399–430. A summary of different meanings can be found in Pryor, *Property and Industrial Organization*, Ch. 8. For a recent discussion of the issues, see Robert G. Lynch, "Centralization and Decentralization Redefined," *Journal of Comparative Economics* 13 (March 1989), 1–14; Donald Chisholm, *Coordination Without Hierarchy* (Berkeley: University of California Press, 1989).

18. Principal–agent relationships are discussed in Stephen A. Ross, "The Economic Theory of Agency: The Principal's Problem," *American Economic Review Papers and Proceedings* (May 1973); Glen MacDonald, "New Directions in the Economic Theory of Agency," *Canadian Journal of Economics* 17 (1984), 415–440; George Baker, Michael Jensen, and Kevin Murphy, "Compensation and Incentives: Practice vs. Theory," *Journal of Finance* 43 (1988), 593–616; Bengt Holmstrom and Paul Milgrom, "Multitask Principal–Agent Analyses: Incentive Contracts, Asset Ownership, and Job Design," *Journal of Law, Economics, & Organization* 7 (1991), Special Issue, 34–52; John Pratt and Richard Zeckhauser, eds., *Principals and Agents: The Structure of Business* (Cambridge, Mass.: Harvard Business School, 1985).

19. See David Conn, ed., "The Theory of Incentives," *Journal of Comparative Economics* 3 (September 1979). For a discussion of incentives in simple cases, see Bernard Caillaud, Roger Guesnerie, Patrick Rey, and Jean Tirole, "Government Intervention in Production and Incentives Theory: A Review of Recent Contributions," *Rand Journal of Economics* 19 (1988), 1–26; Nahum D. Melumad and Stefan Reichelstein, "Value of Communication in Agencies," *Journal of Economic Theory* 47 (1989), 334–368; David E. M. Sappington, "Incentives in Principal–Agent Relationships," *Journal of Economic Perspectives* 5 (Spring 1991). For a discussion of incentive arrangements under adverse selection and moral hazard, see Liang Zou, "Threat-Based Incentive

Mechanisms Under Moral Hazard and Adverse Selection," *Journal of Comparative Economics* 16 (March 1992), 47–74.

20. Ronald H. Coase, "The Nature of the Firm," *Economica*, vol. 4 (1937), 386–405. Reprinted in George Stigler and Kenneth Boulding, eds., *Readings in Price Theory* (Homewood, Ill.: Irwin, 1952).
21. Pryor, *Property and Industrial Organization*, p. 338.
22. Montias, *The Structure of Economic Systems*, Ch. 13.
23. Carl Shapiro and Joseph Stiglitz, "Equilibrium Unemployment and as Worker Discipline Device," *American Economic Review* 74, no. 3 (June 1984), 433–444.
24. Paul Gregory and Valery Lazarev (eds.), *The Economics of Forced Labor* (Stanford, Ca.: Hoover, 2004).
25. F. A. Hayek, *The Road to Serfdom* (Chicago: University of Chicago Press, 1944).
26. János Kornai, "What the Change of System from Socialism to Capitalism Does and Does Not Mean," *The Journal of Economic Perspectives* 14, no. 1 (Winter 2000), 27–42.
27. Oleh Havrylyshyn and Ron van Rooden, "Institutions Matter in Transition, But So Do Policies," *Comparative Economic Studies* 45 (2003), pp. 2–24.
28. Hernando De Soto, "The Missing Ingredient," *The Economist*, 1998; Robert Barro and X. Sala-i-Martin, *Economic Growth* (New York: Mc-Graw Hill, 1994); V. Tanzi, and H. Davoodi, "*Corruption, public investment and growth*," IMF Working Paper, WP/97/139, Washington, 1997; P. Mauro, "The Effects of Corruption on Growth, Investment and Government Expenditure: A Cross-Country Analysis," in K. A. Elliot, ed., *Corruption and the Global Economy* (Washington, D. C.: Institute of International Economics, 1997); S. Knack and P. Keefer, "Institutions and Economic Performance: Cross-Country Tests Using Alternative Institutional Measures," *Economics and Politics* 7 (1995), pp. 207–227.

Recommended Readings

Comparative Systems: General

A. A. Alchian and H. Demsetz, "Production, Information, Costs and Economic Organizations," *American Economic Review* 62 (December 1972), 777–795.

David Conn, ed., "The Theory of Incentives," *Journal of Comparative Economics* 3 (September 1979).

H. Demsetz, "Toward a Theory of Property Rights," *American Economic Review* 57 (May 1967), 347–359.

Alexander Eckstein, ed., *Comparison of Economic Systems: Theoretical and Methodological Approaches* (Berkeley: University of California Press, 1971).

Erik Furobotn and Svetozar Pejovich, "Property Rights and Economic Theory: A Survey of Recent Literature," *Journal of Economic Literature* 10 (December 1972), 1137–1162.

John Montias, *The Structure of Economic Systems* (New Haven: Yale University Press, 1976).

Frederic Pryor, *Property and Industrial Organization in Communist and Capitalist Nations* (Bloomington: Indiana University Press, 1973).

———, *A Guidebook to the Study of Economic Systems* (Englewood Cliffs, N.J.: Prentice-Hall, 1985).

Herbert Simon, *Administrative Behavior*, 2nd ed. (New York: Free Press, 1966).

P. J. D. Wiles, *Economic Institutions Compared* (New York: Halsted, 1977).

———, "What Is Comparative Economics?" *Comparative Economic Studies* 31 (Fall 1989), 1–32.

Oliver Williamson, *Markets and Hierarchies* (New York: Free Press, 1975).

Organizations

Armen Alchian and Susan Woodward, "The Firm Is Dead; Long Live the Firm: A Review of Oliver E. Williamson's 'The Economic Institutions of Capitalism,'" *Journal of Economic Literature* 26 (March 1988), 65–79.

Avner Ben-Ner, John Michael Montias, and Egon Neuberger, "Basic Issues in Organizations: A Comparative Perspective," *Journal of Comparative Economics* 17 (1993), 207–242.

Alred Chandler, "Organizational Capabilities and the Economic History of the Industrial Enterprise," *Journal of Economic Perspectives* 6 (Summer 1992), 79–100.

James Coleman, "Constructed Organization: First Principles," *Journal of Law, Economics, & Organization* 7 (1991), Special Issue, 7–23.

Paul Milgrom and John Roberts, *Economics, Organization and Management* (Englewood Cliffs, N.J.: Prentice-Hall, 1992).

R. R. Nelson and S. G. Winter, *An Evolutionary Theory of Economic Change* (Cambridge, Mass.: Harvard University Press, 1982).

Douglass North, *Institutions, Institutional Change and Economic Performance* (Cambridge: Cambridge University Press, 1990).

Frederic Pryor, "Corporatism as an Economic System: A Review Essay," *Journal of Comparative Economics* 12 (September 1988), 317–344.

Oliver Williamson, *The Economic Institutions of Capitalism: Firms, Markets, Relational Contracting* (New York: Free Press, 1985).

———, ed., *Organization Theory: From Chester Barnard to the Present and Beyond.* (Oxford: Oxford University Press, 1990).

The Structure of Organizations

Sanford Grossman and Oliver Hart, "The Costs and Benefits of Ownership: A Theory of Vertical and Lateral Integration," *Journal of Political Economy* 94 (August 1986), 691–719.

Paul Milgrom, "Employment Contracts, Influence Activities and Efficient Organizational Design," *Journal of Political Economy* 96 (February 1988), 42–60.

Raj Kumar Sah and Joseph E. Stiglitz, "The Architecture of Economic Systems: Hierarchies and Polyarchies," *American Economic Review* 76 (September 1986), 716–727.

Herbert Simon, "Organizations and Markets," *Journal of Economic Perspectives* 5 (Spring 1991), 25–44.

Joseph Stiglitz, "Symposium on Organizations and Economics," *Journal of Economic Perspectives* 5 (Spring 1991), 15–24.

Principal–Agent Relationships

Joseph Farrell, "Information and the Coase Theorem," *Journal of Economic Perspectives* 1 (Fall 1987), 113–129.

Bengt Holmstrom and Paul Milgrom, "Multitask Principal–Agent Analyses: Incentive Contracts, Asset Ownership and Job Design," *Journal of Law, Economics, & Organization* 7 (1991), Special Issue, 34–52.

Glen MacDonald, "New Directions in the Economic Theory of Agency," *Canadian Journal of Economics* 17 (1984), 415–440.

John Pratt and Richard Zeckhauser, eds., *Principals and Agents: The Structure of Business* (Cambridge, Mass.: Harvard Business School, 1985).

Incentive Arrangements

David Conn, "Effort, Efficiency, and Incentives in Economic Organizations," *Journal of Comparative Economics* 6 (September 1982), 223–234.

Jean-Jacques Laffont and Eric Maskin, "The Theory of Incentives: An Overview," in Werner Hildenbrand, ed., *Advances in Economic Theory* (Cambridge: Cambridge University Press, 1982).

Louis Putterman and Gil Skillman, "The Incentive Effects of Monitoring Under Alternate Compensation Schemes," *International Journal of Industrial Organization* 6 (March 1988), 109–120.

Yingyi Qian, "Equity, Efficiency, and Incentives in a Large Economy," *Journal of Comparative Economics* 16 (March 1992), 27–46.

David E. M. Sappington, "Incentives in Principal–Agent Relationships," *Journal of Economic Perspectives* 5 (Spring 1991), 45–66.

Liang Zou, "Threat-Based Incentive Mechanisms Under Moral Hazard and Adverse Selection," *Journal of Comparative Economics* 16 (March 1992), 47–74.

Property Rights

H. Demsetz and K. Lehn, "The Structure of Corporate Ownership: Causes and Consequences," *Journal of Political Economy* 93 (December 1985), 1155–1177.

Louis Putterman, "Ownership and the Nature of the Firm," *Journal of Comparative Economics* 17 (1993), 243–263.

Alan Ryan, "Property," in John Eatwell, Murray Milgate, and Peter Newman, eds., *The New Palgrave: Dictionary of Economics* (New York: Stockton Press, 1987), pp. 1029–1031.

Xiaoki Yang and Ian Wills, "A Model Formalizing the Theory of Property Rights," *Journal of Comparative Economics* 14 (June 1990), 177–198.

The Theory of Cooperatives

John Bonin, Derek C. Jones, and Louis Putterman, "Theoretical and Empirical Research on Producers' Cooperatives: Will the Twain Ever Meet?" *Journal of Economic Literature* 31 (September 1993), 1290–1320.

Nonprofit Organizations

Walter Powell, ed., *The Nonprofit Sector: A Research Handbook* (New Haven: Yale University Press, 1987).

Susan Rose-Ackerman, ed., *The Economics of Nonprofit Institutions: Studies in Structure and Policy* (New York: Oxford University Press, 1986).

Burton Weisbrod, *The Nonprofit Economy* (Cambridge, Mass.: Harvard University Press, 1988).

The Public Sector

Abram Bergson, "Managerial Risks and Rewards in Public Enterprises," *Journal of Comparative Economics* 2 (September 1978), 211–225.

A. Boardman and A. Vining, "Ownership and Performance in Competitive Environments: A Comparison of the Performance of Private, Mixed, and State-Owned Enterprises," *Journal of Law and Economics* 32 (1989), 1–33.

Estelle James, Egon Neuberger, and Robert Willis, "On Managerial Rewards and Self-Selection: Risk Taking in Public Enterprises," *Journal of Comparative Economics* 3 (December 1979), 395–406.

Jean-Jacques Laffont and Jean Tirole, "Privatization and Incentives," *Journal of Law, Economics, & Organization* 7 (1991), Special Issue, 84–105.

Economic Systems and Economic Outcomes

If economic systems did not affect economic performance, economists would have little interest in them. This chapter shows that a country's economic performance depends on its economic institutions (that is, its economic system), on the environment in which it operates, and on the policies that its leaders select.

There is no dispute that the economic system affects economic performance. We know that "bad" economic systems laden with corruption, lack of rule of law, and rampant rent seeking produce poor economic outcomes. Countries with good institutions, like a stable government or rule or law, produce better economic performance. Few dispute Douglass North's contention: "I wish to assert a much more fundamental role for institutions in society; they are the underlying determinant of the long-run performance of economies."[1] If "bad" economic institutions hamper and "good" institutions promote economic performance, societies are challenged to change "bad" into "good" institutions. Countries that are otherwise rich in economic resources can be made poor by the unwise choice of economic institutions. Any number of countries in Africa, Latin America, Central Asia, and the Middle East have been impoverished by bad economic institutions.

The Forces Influencing Economic Outcomes

The **economic system (ES)** *is multidimensional and is defined in terms of its many institutions, such as its organizational structure, its provision for property rights, how it manages information, and how it makes public choices.* **Economic outcomes (O)** *describe the performance of the economy as measured by criteria such as economic growth, living standards, employment, and other measures that are deemed important.* Economic outcomes are determined by factors other than the economic system, such as environmental factors and policy.

Environmental factors (ENV) *represent the economic setting in which the economic system operates.* They include natural resource endowments, the level of economic development, human and physical capital accumulation, education, random events, and initial conditions.

Economic outcomes also depend on the policies that the policy makers choose. **Policy (POL)** *refers to trade policy, macroeconomic decision making, the regulatory setting, and other actions that can be changed without changing the economic system itself.* As an example, a country can increase its openness to international trade without changing the fundamental institutions that constitute its economic system. If the country chooses to change from 100 percent state ownership to 100 percent private ownership, however, this is a change in ES, not in policy.

These concepts can be formalized as follows:

$$O = f(\text{ES}, \text{ENV}, \text{POL}) \tag{3.1}$$

where

O	denotes economic outcomes
ES	denotes the economic system
ENV	denotes environmental factors
POL	denotes policies pursued by the economic system

Equation 3.1 and Figure 3.1 highlight the ceteris paribus problem of determining the impact of the economic system (ES) on observed outcomes (O). **Ceteris paribus** *is a Latin term meaning all other things being equal.* Insofar as outcomes depend on factors in addition to the economic system, we cannot isolate the impact of the system without first controlling for, or holding constant, the influence of the environmental (ENV) factors and the policy variables (POL). If we wish to

FIGURE 3.1   Forces Influencing Economic Outcome

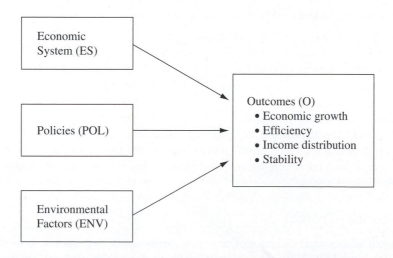

Source: From GREGORY, Comparing Economic Systems in the Twenty-First Century, 7E. © 2004 Cengage Learning.

Table 3.1 The Ceteris Paribus Problem

Economic System	Natural resources	Trade Policy	Outcome
Type A, Country 1	rich	open	good
Type A, Country 2	poor	open	good
Type B, Country 3	poor	closed	bad
Type B, Country 4	rich	closed	bad

© Cengage Learning 2014

determine the impact of two different types of economic systems on outcomes, we must adjust for the fact that the countries we use to represent the economic systems may differ in terms of ENV and POL.

Table 3.1 illustrates the ceteris paribus problem. We have a sample of four countries, two having economic system Type A and two having economic system Type B. The last column indicates that the Type A countries have good outcomes and the Type B have bad outcomes. We cannot conclude from this information alone that the Type A system performs better than the Type B system. The well-performing countries have open trade policies; the poorly performing countries have closed trade policies. We therefore do not know whether the better performance is due to ES or POL. What we might conclude is that the better performance is not due to differences in ENV because both sets of countries have both rich and poor natural resources.

There is a whole branch of economics that offers statistical tools to solve the ceteris paribus problem. This branch of economics is called econometrics. In the case of Table 3.1, we do not have enough information to pinpoint the effect of the economic system on the observed outcome. We need many more observations before we can draw solid conclusions.

Performance Criteria

Just as there are any number of economic institutions, so are there many measures of economic performance—the O in Equation 3.1. We cannot consider all of them; we can only consider a limited number that we deem particularly important. We limit ourselves here to five performance criteria that are generally applied to assess economic outcomes. Our list may omit some criteria (military power, for instance, or environmental quality) that are important, but we cannot include everything. For some, we are leaving out the most important performance indicators. Many parliamentary democracies have "green" parties, such as the European Union parliament. Members of such parties regard environmental quality as more important than other performance indicators.

Economic Growth

The most widely used indicator of economic performance is **economic growth**, *the increase in real GDP or real GDP per capita over a period of time.* We are interested in the growth of economic output because material well-being or welfare can be approximated by the volume of goods and services per capita. A growing economy means growing jobs and opportunities. A growing economy means a greater ability to provide for defense, welfare, or other needs. A growing economy raises prestige and visibility, such as the attention China recently received upon becoming the world's second largest economy.

Growth in output per capita brings about increases in the material welfare of the population. The level of economic well-being—the living standard—is the consequence of cumulated past growth of per capita GDP. Countries with low living standards have had little economic growth per capita. Therefore, per capita income itself is a possible measure of the performance on an economic system.

Because economic growth is so widely employed as a performance indicator, it is useful to spell out some complications. Measurement problems arise in assessing economic growth, especially when different economic systems are compared. When East Germany became part of a united Germany, German statistical authorities decided not to reconstruct East German growth statistics. The East German economy produced such different products at such different costs than in West Germany that reconstructed growth rates would be like comparing apples and oranges.

Growth rates are also affected by initial conditions. **Initial conditions** *refer to the starting point from which the growth and development of an economy begins.* Initial conditions include past history (such as a colonial past), infrastructure, development of the legal system, and other factors that constitute the environmental factors initially on hand. For example, the Chinese reforms that set off rapid growth in the late 1970s started from the initial condition of recent private ownership in agriculture. The Russian agrarian reforms under Mikhail Gorbachev began from the initial condition of a half century of collective agriculture. The African continent began its postwar development with the artificial boundaries left behind by the colonial powers.

Economic growth does not bring about a proportional growth of happiness. In fact, **happiness research** *is a fairly young branch of economics that uses national and international surveys of households probing how content residents of different countries are with their lives.* Presumably the ultimate goal of any economic and political system (at least one that allows citizen participation in political decision making) is to provide the economic goods and services—food, transportation, and medical care—without which people could not be content. Indeed, if an economic system provides only the bare minimums, or threatens periodically to fall below the minimum, people cannot be happy. Even dictators, other things being equal, prefer a materially contented population. A people with food in their stomachs are less likely to rebel.

We are less certain as to the extent to which continued economic growth in affluent countries raises national happiness. Once we have "enough" (whatever that means), it is not clear how much our happiness rises when we get more. What we do know is that measures of happiness correlate strongly with per capita income. Figure 3.2 is a scatter diagram showing the strong positive correlation between a country's per capita income and happiness rankings. The correlation is far from perfect, meaning that factors other than the standard of living determine happiness.

FIGURE 3.2   Scatter Diagram: Happiness vs. Per Capita Income

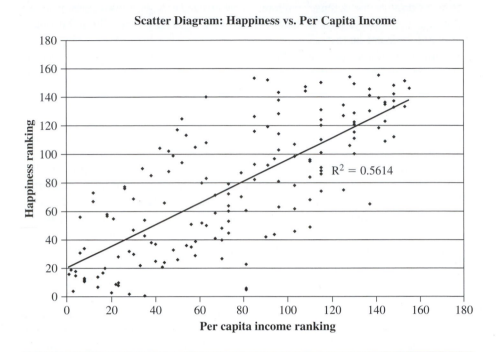

Source: Gallup Poll organization and World Bank.

Efficiency

Our second measure of system performance is economic efficiency. The strict economic definition is as follows: **efficiency** *is the effectiveness with which a system utilizes its available resources (including knowledge) at a particular time (static efficiency) or through time (dynamic efficiency).* Static and dynamic efficiency are interrelated, and both depend on a variety of factors.

The concept of efficiency can be conveniently illustrated by the production possibilities frontier shown in Figure 3.3. The initial production possibilities schedule *(AB)* illustrates all feasible combinations of producer and consumer goods that a particular economic system is capable of producing at a particular time using all available resources at maximal efficiency. The production possibilities schedule shows that, given its existing resources, the system has a menu of production choices open to it. Economic systems must choose where to locate on the schedule. In capitalist societies, the consumer–voter dominates this choice. In planned socialist societies, planners make the decision.

The *shape* of the production possibilities frontier is not accidental. The fact that it is a curve convex from the origin illustrates a basic fact of economic life: As we attempt to produce increasing amounts of, say, consumer goods, we have to give up ever larger amounts of producer goods to obtain identical increases in

FIGURE 3.3 The Production Possibilities Frontier: An Economic System's Menu of Choices

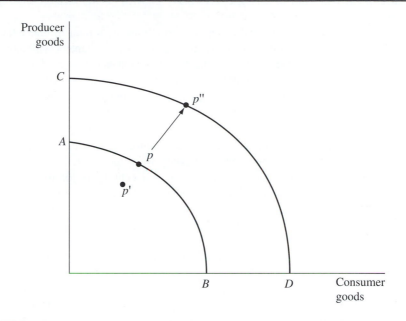

Source: From GREGORY, Comparing Economic Systems in the Twenty-First Century, 7E. © 2004 Cengage Learning.

consumer goods. In more technical terms, there is a diminishing marginal rate of technical substitution between the production of consumer goods and the production of producer goods.

The production possibilities schedule illustrates the concept of efficiency. We have already indicated that *AB* represents the capacity of a particular economy at a particular time. **Static efficiency** *requires an economy to be operating on its production possibilities frontier*—for example, at point *p*. Output combinations beyond *AB* are impossible at that time; combinations inside *AB* are feasible but inefficient. An economy that has the capacity *AB* but is producing at point *p'* is statically inefficient because it could move to point *p* and produce *more of both* goods with no increase in available resources.

Dynamic efficiency *is the ability of an economic system to enhance its capacity to produce goods and services over time without an increase in capital and labor inputs.* Dynamic efficiency is indicated by movement of the frontier outward from *AB* to *CD* from *p* to *p'* (without an underlying increase in resources); the distance of this movement indicates the change in efficiency. Static and dynamic efficiency are subject to measurement problems. The basic approach to measuring static efficiency is to make productivity calculations, as measured by the ratio of output to inputs. Dynamic efficiency is measured by the ratio of the growth of output to the growth of inputs.

Economic growth and dynamic efficiency are not the same. Economies may grow by increasing efficiency (finding better ways of doing things with the same resources) or by expanding the amount of, say, labor but using that labor at a constant rate of effectiveness. **Intensive growth** *is growth that occurs through the increase in efficiency of resource use.* **Extensive growth** *occurs through the expansion of inputs.*

The concepts of intensive and extensive growth are important in understanding the growth experiences of different economic systems. Later chapters will show that the former planned socialist systems of the Soviet Union and Eastern Europe grew more rapidly in their early years and then experienced continuing slowdowns in their later years. The early rapid growth has been widely attributed to a strategy of extensive growth—a growth-oriented policy designed to expand inputs rapidly. As economies reach higher levels of economic development, growth in output is increasingly derived from intensive economic growth. Mature economies no longer experience the increases in population and saving rates necessary for extensive economic growth.

One of the major questions of the twenty-first century is for how long will China's rapid economic growth continue. If it continues only for a few years, China will level off as a large but relatively poor economy. If China's rapid growth continues for decades, China will be both a large and affluent economy—truly deserving of the designation of a super power. If past history is a guide, China must make the transition from extensive to intensive growth if its rapid growth is to persist over a long period of time.

The rightward shift of the production possibilities schedule from *AB* to *CD* could have three causes. First, it could be due to dynamic efficiency. Dynamic efficiency is usually attributed to technological progress, broadly defined. With dynamic efficiency, output increases without any change in inputs or in the economic system—the phenomenon of intensive growth. Second, output could increase because capital or labor inputs grow—the phenomenon of extensive growth. Third, "negative" institutions that inhibit output (such as trade barriers, corruption, excessive regulation, or insecure property rights) might be improved, allowing output to expand without any increase in inputs or technology.

An economic system operating at points inside the production possibilities frontier is wasting resources. It is producing less than it could have, and, in economics, more is always better than less. When an economy operates at a point inside the production possibilities frontier, it is said to be incurring a deadweight loss. **Deadweight loss** *is a measure of inefficiency caused by a variety of distortions that cause the economy to operate below its potential.* These distortions can arise from imperfections in the market, such as monopoly power or distortive taxes. It can also be caused by inefficient political decision making, such as the political allocation of investment at rates of return below other more promising projects. Deadweight loss could also be used to describe theft of resources by politicians, dictators, and their favored oligarchs.

Income Distribution

How "fairly" an economic system distributes income among households is the third criterion for assessing economic performance. Technically, income distribution is measured by the Lorenz curve or Gini coefficient, as shown in Figure 3.4.

FIGURE 3.4   Measuring Income Inequality: The Lorenz Curve

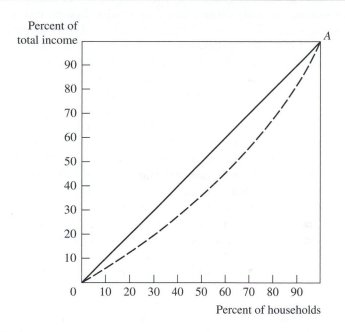

Explanation: Percent of households is measured on the horizontal axis, percent of income on the vertical axis. Perfect equality would be, for example, where 10 percent of households received 10 percent of all income. This would be illustrated by a 45-degree line between the origin (0) and point A. Inequality can be illustrated by the dashed line. The further the dashed line bows away from the 45-degree line, the further from equal the distribution of income. In the diagram, for example, the bottom 20 percent of households receive 10 percent of the income. A comprehensive measure known as the *Gini coefficient* is typically used to measure income inequality. The Gini coefficient is the area between the 45-degree line and the dashed line divided by the entire area under the 45-degree line.

Source: From GREGORY, Comparing Economic Systems in the Twenty-First Century, 7E. © 2004 Cengage Learning.

The Gini coefficient *is a numerical measure of the degree of inequality in the distribution of income or wealth. Its value ranges from zero, if everyone has the same income or wealth, to one, if one person has all the income or wealth.*

What constitutes a "good" or "fair" distribution of income? There may be substantial agreement on the definition of "bad" income distributions (for example, where 1 percent of the population receives 95 percent of all income); judgments about intermediate cases are more difficult to make.

What constitutes an equitable distribution of income? Equity involves fairness, although perceptions of what is fair differ dramatically from person to person or from country to country, One criterion of fairness might involve rewards according to contribution to the production process. In a capitalist society, personal income is determined by the human and physical capital one owns and by their prices as determined by factor markets. Income differences reflect differences in effort (provision of labor services), differences in frugality (provision of capital), inheritance of physical and human capital, luck, and so on. The market distribution of income may be modified by the tax system and by the provision of social services. The extent to which government redistributive action is justified on equity grounds is a matter of continuing controversy in capitalist societies. Under socialism, the factors of production are, with the exception of labor, publicly owned. Capital and land are both socially owned in a socialist society; hence their remuneration belongs to the state, not directly to individuals.

There will always be debate about the distribution of income. Resort to "class warfare" is seductive in political campaigns anywhere from the United States to Venezuela. Both dictators and democratic politicians can blame all that is going wrong on the "rich." On the other hand, the distribution of income can indeed become too skewed in favor of the rich. Debates about the distribution of income are far from theoretical. All societies can "correct" the distribution of income by progressive taxes and the provision of public services. There appear to be prominent differences in public opinion in Europe, the United States, and Asia as to the state's role in making such corrections. In Asia, it is the extended family's responsibility to handle poverty. Europeans welcome a greater role of the state than do Americans. No consensus will ever be reached on this subject.

Stability

The fourth criterion is economic stability. *By* **stability** *we mean the absence of significant fluctuations in growth rates, the maintenance of relatively low rates of unemployment, and the avoidance of excessive inflation.* Economic stability is a desirable objective for two reasons. The first is that various segments of the population are damaged by instability. Individuals on fixed incomes are hurt by unanticipated inflation; the poorly trained are hurt by unemployment. Second, cyclical instability can lead to losses of potential output, making the economic system operate inside its production possibilities schedule.

Capitalist economies have historically been subject to fluctuations in the level of economic activity—in other words, to business cycles.[2] In planned socialist economies, aggregate economic activity (including investment) is subject to the control of planners. Although cyclical activity did occur in planned socialist economics—through planning errors or transmission through the foreign sector— the socialist society was less likely to suffer large cyclical fluctuations.

Instability is compounded during periods of extreme booms and busts, where the boom period is characterized by a "bubble" of some sort. The bubble can manifest itself as overinvestment in high-tech industries or in housing. The bubble is followed by a burst of the bubble as investment values decline or housing prices fall below their purchase prices.

The more state controlled economy of China avoided the extremes of the housing bubble that preceded the recession starting in 2007. This fact is currently being used to support the superiority of China's state capitalism versus the more freewheeling capitalism of the United States. As we write, however, China appears headed for its own housing bubble.

Stability of economic growth is of practical importance. Potential lost at any particular time is lost forever. A system that, because of cyclical instability, does not reach its potential cannot be expected to achieve its potential rate of growth through time. Therefore, the matter of cyclical instability, the length and the severity of cycles, and the forms in which they find expression can be indicators of the relative success of economic systems.

Inflation, a second manifestation of instability, may appear in open form as a general rise in the price level, or it may occur in repressed form as lengthening lines for goods and services or as regional and sectoral shortages. In capitalist economies, inflation typically occurs in the first form; in the planned socialist economies (where planners set prices), it historically manifested itself in repressed form. In much of the Middle East today, basic consumer goods, such as bread and fuel, are supplied by the state. Consumers want more of the good than the state makes available at established prices. The result is either long lines or corruption.

In either case, excessive inflation is viewed as an undesirable phenomenon; it can distort economic calculation (where relative prices are used as sources of information), cause increased use of barter, and alter the income distribution.

Excessive unemployment is also undesirable. It implies, along with the personal hardships of those unemployed, less than full utilization of resources. The planned socialist economies did not maintain records on unemployment (which was said to have been "liquidated"). Moreover, the standard definition of unemployment (the unemployed are those seeking employment but unable to find jobs) leaves room for differences in interpretation. There are different types of unemployment, ranging from unemployment associated with the normal changing of jobs to chronic, hard-core unemployment.

These definitions, however, fail to account for the more subtle concept of **underemployment**, *or the employment of individuals on a full-time basis at work in which they utilize their skills at well under their full potential.* Underemployment (which was common in the Soviet Union) is less visible than unemployment, but it can have a similarly adverse effect on capacity utilization. It typically takes the form of overstaffing, a situation in which ten people are employed for a job that could be done just as well by five.

If the state operates a system of guaranteed jobs, virtually everyone will be employed but will not work efficiently. *In a* **jobs rights economy**, *everyone is guaranteed a job; there are no incentives to change jobs, and there are few incentives to work hard.*[3] On the surface, a job rights economy appears to avoid the loss of output associated with unemployment, but the lack of incentives and poor work discipline may result in more output being lost than with outright unemployment. Job rights economic systems exist in partial form throughout the world. In large Japanese corporations, workers and employees are guaranteed lifetime jobs. In tenured jobs, teachers and civil servants have considerable job rights that protect them from unemployment.

Viability

The ultimate test of an economic system is its long-term viability. The basic premise of Marxian economics was that over the course of history, "superior" economic systems replace "inferior" ones. In the Marxian scheme, capitalism replaces feudal-ism, and then socialism replaces capitalism. Inferior systems are beset by internal contradictions that make it impossible for them to survive over the long term. Karl Marx depicted capitalism as unstable, suffering from a number of insurmountable internal contradictions. These internal contradictions, he believed, ensured the eventual demise of capitalism and its replacement by the "superior" system of socialism.

Since the beginning of the Soviet experiment with planned socialism (and its later expansion to one-third of the world's population), discussion had focused on the *relative* economic performance of planned socialism. Most experts felt that planned socialism, although inefficient, would be able to muddle along—to survive at relatively low levels of efficiency and consumer welfare.

Events of the late 1980s highlighted the problem of the long-term viability of planned socialism. The leaders of the former Soviet Union and in Eastern Europe transformed their planned economic systems into something resembling market econ-omies. The rejection of planned socialism casts serious doubt on its ability to deliver an economic performance strong enough to ensure its continued existence.

Among the other basic performance criteria—economic growth, efficiency, income distribution, and stability—the long-term viability of the economic system stands out as the dominant test of performance. If an economic system cannot sur-vive, it has clearly proved itself inferior.

It may be premature to declare the planned socialist system dead. The move away from socialism in the former Soviet Union and in Eastern Europe could be reversed. Socialism continues to have appeal in China, which is combining com-munist dictatorship with market reform and the opening up of the economy to inter-national trade and investment. It also continues to have a strong emotional appeal because of its promises of equity and stability. Many still believe that an economy run by planners and bureaucrats will function better than one dictated by the chaos of markets. Many respond to socialism's appeal for fairness as a way to improve a society they see as dominated by rich Wall Street bankers and greedy CEOs.

Evaluating Performance: What Determines Success?

From the beginning of the postwar era to the collapse of the Soviet Union, there was a protracted debate about the superiority of economic systems. In the heady 1950s, after the USSR launched the first rocket into space and recorded rapid rates of growth, Soviet premier Nikita Khrushchev announced that he would "bury" the United States. There was no longer a need for war, he said; the Soviet Union need only demonstrate its economic superiority to the rest of the world. In this time period, the poorer countries of the globe, in fact, looked to the Soviet Union for guidance.

USSR–USA comparisons raised, probably for the first time, practical issues of how to evaluate an economic system's performance. When we compare economic outcomes of different economic systems, we wish to determine which economic system performs "better." But there is no clear and simple way to decide which outcome is "better" unless one economic system outperforms the other with respect to all possible outcomes.

Weights

To evaluate outcomes, we must decide the importance of each of the performance criteria: growth, efficiency, equity, and stability. We must add different results together by assigning *weights* to produce a single index of achievement.

The **weights** *attached to economic outcomes measure how important each performance indicator is.* Clearly, the weights determine the value of the index of achievement, O, but they are themselves subjective.[4] Some might argue that economic growth is most important. Others might say that guaranteed jobs or a pervasive social safety net are more important, even if that means lower growth.

There is another question: Whose weights do we use in evaluating outcomes? In the Soviet Union and contemporary China, the preferences of communist political authorities appear to count most, although the Chinese Communist Party leadership appears to pay attention to what the people want. In a volatile world, ignoring the people has its consequences, as events in the Middle East in early 2011 showed. In market economies, what is produced and for whom is decided largely by the market, although the state is left with producing public goods and providing social welfare. In dictatorships, the dictator's preferences dominate. In democracies, the will of voters counts most. The will of voters can be distorted by lobbying, political corruption, and influence peddling, but by and large the people ultimately decide.

Social Norms

Different societies have different cultures, norms, and customs. According to stereotypes, Asian cultures value working together collectively and are more respectful of authority, whereas the U.S. "frontier society" values rugged individualism. The Europeans are said to value leisure more than their North American counterparts. In some societies, losing face can be a personal tragedy, whereas other societies shrug such things off as something to be forgotten quickly or even exploited (such as the press attention devoted to disgraced Hollywood stars).

With differing norms, different societies will place different weights on performance indicators. If the European–American stereotypes are accurate, Europeans will value outcomes that provide more leisure; Americans will value outcomes that raise labor productivity.

Figure 3.5 focuses on just one dimension of differences in norms among different societies: support for democracy (where a higher number indicates greater support). It shows that citizens of sub-Saharan Africa and of Orthodox Islamic states have little support for democracy. Catholic European, Confucian, and Latin American citizens offer intermediate levels of support. English-speaking citizens and Protestant Europeans have the highest levels of support for democracy.

The stability of any economic system depends on whether the next generation is in agreement with its basic characteristics. The Gallup organization carried out a

FIGURE 3.5   Support for Democracy by Culture

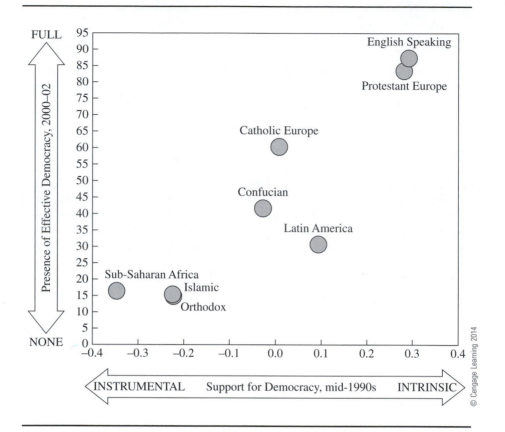

poll of young people aged 19 to 24 to determine with what institutions young people are dissatisfied, which tells us which institutions they would like to change. Figure 3.6 shows that young citizens of different cultures have different evaluations of the system of institutions they face in their daily lives. American and Australian youth share fairly equal concerns about social welfare for the poor and the environment. French, Indian, and Philippine youth are most concerned about differences between the rich and poor, although the French distribution of income is much more equal than in the other two countries. Indian youth are almost as concerned about the laxity of law, order, and morality as they are about the distribution of income.

Tradeoffs   If various goals are laudable, why not pursue all of them? In many cases, specific goals can often be achieved only by sacrificing other, less important goals. The necessity of choosing to pursue some goals at the expense of others is a consequence of the fundamental scarcity of resources, which prevents every economic system from producing unlimited quantities of goods and services. Instead, choices must be made among goals.

FIGURE 3.6   National Priorities Differ

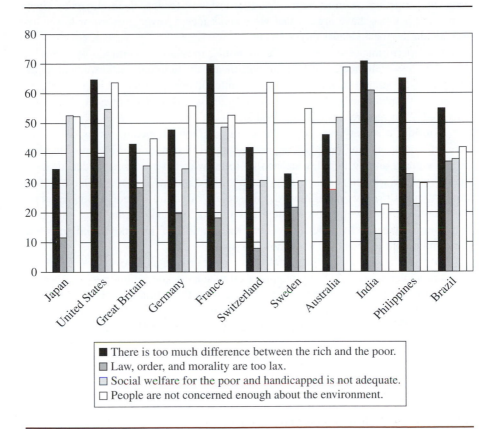

Source: From GREGORY, Comparing Economic Systems in the Twenty-First Century, 7E. © 2004 Cengage Learning. (Data from George Gallup, The International Gallup Polls, Public Opinion 1978 (Wilmington, Del.: Scholarly Resources, 1980).)

The nature of these sacrifices is often subject to dispute. Can unemployment be lowered without increasing inflation? Is sustained economic growth compatible with a cleaner environment? Can affluent economies maintain generous welfare and benefits programs without sacrificing economic growth? Can China maintain an open economy *and* the political dictatorship its leaders desire? Tradeoffs matter in at least two ways. First, we cannot assess the performance of economic systems without understanding their tradeoffs among alternatives. Second, when one goal must be sacrificed to achieve another, we should not criticize a system for not achieving a goal that it has, in effect, decided not to pursue.

In the contemporary world, there is agreement that economic growth, good employment opportunities, price stability, technological innovation, economic security, clean environment, and a good distribution of income (different people define "good" differently) are desirable. But there is disagreement on tradeoffs. **Tradeoffs** *refer to the sacrifice of one thing (such as one economic goal) for another.* One of the most basic lessons of economics is that there is no such thing as a free lunch.

We understand tradeoffs only imperfectly. Macroeconomists have debated, for a long time, whether we must trade off higher inflation for low unemployment. Environmental activists have argued that we should accept lower growth, or lower living standards, for a cleaner environment.

If all performance criteria were compatible, measuring economic performance would be less complicated. If high growth meant the automatic achievement of the other goals, countries would need only to aim for one goal and expect to achieve the others spontaneously. This is not the way the world works, however. Achieving one goal often requires sacrificing another.

Consider a society that sets a "fair" distribution of income as its overriding economic goal, where "fairness" requires an equal distribution of income. Dividing output equally among families means that those who have worked harder, or more effectively, or who have taken risks receive the same as those who have not. If unequal effort receives equal reward, this society offers no incentives to encourage hard and effective work, risk taking, and innovation, and in the long run these activities will cease to occur. An equal distribution of income would therefore undermine both efficiency and economic growth.

Consider next a society that establishes rapid growth as its overriding goal and seeks to achieve this growth by requiring all teenagers and retired persons to work and by forcing households to save more for capital formation than they wish. Such policies would create economic growth through extensive means (growth through expansion of inputs), but they would probably reduce static efficiency and dynamic efficiency. The capital and labor employed at the margin would not be effective; the loss of household production might make people work less effectively.

Consider finally a society that wishes to guarantee employment to all those able and willing to work. This guarantee is made in the form of an implicit job rights contract that declares that the state will, as a last resort, provide a job and an income to all. Such a job rights contract would mean that workers have a job no matter how ineffectively and unconscientiously they work. Under such an arrangement, effort would slacken, absenteeism would rise, and employee discipline would fall. These events would depress economic efficiency and cause the society to produce below its production possibilities.

Maximizing According to Constraints

Despite differing values and norms, which lead us to weigh economic outcomes differently, we all share the common objective of getting the most out of what we have. All societies should share the objective of achieving the maximal value of its economic outcome (O), subject to the constraints imposed by the economic system (ES), policies (POL), and environmental factors (ENV), which include technology and resource constraints. The objective, then, is to

$$\text{Maximize: O} \qquad \qquad \text{(3.2)}$$
$$\text{Subject to (ES, ENV, POL)}$$

This formula suggests how to evaluate the effect of ES on O. After adjusting for differences in environment and policy (solving the ceteris paribus problem), we can conceptually determine which system achieved the higher economic outcome. As noted, the economic outcome (O) is a combination of performance indicators, which are weighted differently by different societies:

$$O = \sum_{j=1}^{k} a_j o_j \qquad \text{(3.3)}$$

where

o_j = desirable (or undesirable if negative) economic outcomes
a_j = the relative importance of the various outcomes

In sum, to capture the impact of the economic system on outcomes, we must know a great deal. We must be able somehow to "measure" the economic system, which is itself comprised of a number of institutions. We must be able to hold ENV and POL constant, and we must know the weights that society uses to value the various performance indicators.

Measuring the Impact of the Economic System on Performance: Applications

As a result of the USSR's superpower status, years of serious research went into comparing Soviet economic outcomes with its rival superpower, the United States. We knew that the United States and the Soviet Union had quite different economic systems—one a planned socialist economy, the other a market capitalist country. One could offer theoretical arguments in favor of the superiority of either system. Those who believed in "scientific planning" could argue that expert planners could produce a better result than the market. Those who understood the enormous complexity of national planning could argue such an economic system would be impossible in practice.

There were measureable performance differences in Soviet–American comparisons: The USSR's measured growth rate was initially higher than the U.S. rate, although it was steadily declining after the mid-1960s. However, the USSR was a latecomer to growth and had a lot of catching up to do. Both countries fielded powerful militaries, despite the USSR's lower per capita output. The Soviet economy offered guaranteed employment; there were periods of high unemployment in the United States. The USSR published no unemployment statistics, claiming there was none. The United States was clearly doing a better job in technological innovation as measured by landmark inventions and innovations. The USSR had a more equal distribution of income but a less equal distribution of political power, which was concentrated in the hands of a few members of the monopoly communist party.

Although the answer to the "superiority" question later became obvious with the collapse of the Soviet system, researchers had great difficulty coming up with a definitive answer because each system outperformed the other in one or more areas. Which system was "better" therefore depended on the weights attached to each performance measure. If economic growth was deemed most important, the Soviet economy (throughout much of its history) outperformed the U. S. economy. If technological innovation was more important, the United States was the clear winner. If stability of employment dominated, the USSR was the winner. The end of the Soviet Union in December of 1991 ended discussion of this issue.

Natural Experiments

To capture the impact of the economic system on economic outcomes, we must "hold constant" the economic system. This is easier said than done. There are imperfect statistical procedures, such as lumping together countries that we think have the same system characteristic, and then comparing differences in outcomes.

The economies that were part of the Soviet empire adopted pretty much the same economic system. For this reason, they could be lumped together so that average growth rates or labor productivity could be compared with groups of countries of the industrialized West. Differences in group averages might be informative, but factors other than the Soviet system could explain them.

Going to a slightly higher level of statistical sophistication, other factors (such as country size or resource endowments) could be held constant using statistical procedures to better capture the effect of the economic system on the outcomes, such as growth or productivity. In fact, early studies revealed a distinctive "soviet" model of industrial structure.[5] Yet even the most authoritative studies of Soviet growth and productivity found it difficult to reach decisive conclusions.[6]

In a few rare cases, we were able to compare countries that were alike in most respects other than the economic system. In such cases, we can study natural experiments. **Natural experiments** *in economics are serendipitous situations in which persons, groups, or countries are assigned randomly to a treatment and a control group, and outcomes are analyzed for the purposes of testing hypotheses.*[7] The "treatment" in this case would be, say, the Soviet economic system (versus the control group of capitalist market economies).

We have the notable natural experiments of two countries that were once united and were split by the vagaries of geopolitics at the end of wars into different countries with quite different economic and political systems. Countries that were once one, therefore, have a common ENV and we can more easily attribute performance differences to the economic system they adopted.

Korea   Korea was split between North and South Korea at the end of World War II. Korea remained split after the Korean War (1950–1953), which ended in a stalemate. North Korea adopted a peculiar version of the Soviet system, with a personalized dictatorship, or "cult of personality," first of Kim Jong Il and then his son Kim Il Sung. The North Korean leadership rejected private ownership in industry, trade, and agriculture. Economic and political life was dominated by a monopoly party under the Kims.

In contrast, South Korea began as a military dictatorship but evolved into a democracy. From the beginning, South Korea was characterized by private ownership and market allocation. At the time of the split into two countries, the North and South were equally prosperous. In fact, the North was historically more developed than the South.

Today, the contrast between North and South could not be more striking. The North Koreans live near subsistence and suffer from periodic famines. They are kept afloat by generous aid from South Korea and from China. The citizens of the North have no political freedoms and are punished with imprisonment or execution if they cross the regime. In contrast, South Koreans have joined the exclusive club of wealthy nations. The average South Korean has a car, an apartment, and does not have to worry about food. Also, South Koreans are free to criticize the government without fear of reprisal. The South Korean government is chosen by raucous political elections.

North Korea–South Korea comparisons offer a rare case of virtually universal agreement. Without doubt, the South Korean economic system has outperformed the North Korean system.

East and West Germany There would also be agreement that the West German economy outperformed that of East Germany before the latter's collapse in 1989 and incorporation into a united Germany in 1990. Despite equal starting points at the end of World War II, the West German economy grew more rapidly than the East; living standards (even with imperfect measures) were considerably higher in the West. The comparison of the pitiful East German Trabi with gleaming German BMWs and Mercedes captured the higher West's achievement better than any dry and imperfect statistics. Indeed, all performance indicators, with the exception of Gini coefficients, showed that the West German economy outperformed that of the East. The West German economy grew faster; it produced a much higher standard of living, and it operated at a much higher level of economic efficiency. In fact, the performance differentials calculated before the collapse of East Germany probably presented the East in a more favorable light than it deserved.

In a telling anecdote, West Germans visiting the residence of the East German leaders in the Niederschönhausen district of Pankow after German reunification discovered that the communist elite did not live better than a typical middle-class German.

Cuba versus Latin America Despite alternating democracies and military dictatorships, Cuba's GDP per capita was about equal to Greece's and the Latin American average in 1957 as Fidel Castro launched his Cuban revolution. By 2004, Cuba had fallen to less than half of the Latin American average. Over the fifty years of Castro's communist rule, Cuba went from being among the most prosperous countries in Latin America to being among its poorest.[8] When Castro victoriously entered Havana in 1959, Cuba had some of the highest consumption rates in Latin America and a vibrant middle class, and Havana was the world's fourth most expensive city. Despite its small size, Cuba had fifty-eight newspapers and one of the highest numbers of doctors per capita.

Apologists for Castro's Cuba cite its low rates of infant mortality and its high life expectancies, but they do not mention its high rates of imprisonment of journalists and political dissidents. The right to use the Internet is granted only to a few selected people, and illegal Internet use carries with it a prison sentence.[9]

Cuba is located in a part of the world that has lagged behind the rest of the world, but Cuba has lagged behind even that lagging geographic region in terms of economic performance.[10]

These three natural experiments yield rather conclusive results: In cases where we can hold most other things constant, Cuba being the least satisfactory case, planned socialist systems grossly underperformed their market capitalist counterparts. Moreover, they combine poor economic performance with political repression. Although some statistics can be cited in their favor (such as Cuba's health outcomes), most would agree that they do not compensate for the negative features of the system.

Evaluating System Performance without Natural Experiments

Natural experiments are rare. In other cases, we must somehow sort out the impact of the economic system on economic outcome from the effects of environmental and policy factors. Moreover, after the collapse of communism, we have to deal with less striking contrasts, such as differences between the capitalism of the United States and of Europe, or between the industrial policy of Japan, Russia, and China.

One avenue is to examine the performance of economic systems after significant changes have been put in place. In countries where growth accelerated, such as China, India, and Chile, we could look for institutional changes that would have accelerated growth. In the case of China, we would look to the decisions beginning in 1977 and 1978 to reform China's planned socialist economy. In Chile, we might look at the privatization of its pension system, which promoted increased capital formation. In the case of India, we might look at its market-oriented reforms begun in 1990 and continued to the present day.

In the 1980s and 1990s, the United States' economy grew more rapidly than Europe's. During this period of time, the United States changed its tax system and passed welfare reform, but it also saw the spread of personal computers and the Internet into business and households. Was the higher U.S. growth the result of changes in institutions or the result of the "environmental" factor (the country's reaping the benefits of the computer and the information revolution)?

The sorting out of economic system, environmental effects, and policy effects typically requires statistical or econometric analysis. If we related just one factor to an economic outcome, we might falsely conclude that one had caused the other. Only by examining the effects of all three factors simultaneously can we isolate the effect of the economic system on economic outcomes.

Perceptional Measures:
Freedom, Corruption, Governance

International organizations and non-governmental organizations have led the way in exploring entirely new ways to measure various aspects of the economic system.[11] Agencies, both public and private, produce ratings of countries on metrics of institutional development. Some seek to capture metrics of interest to international businesses and investors such as indicators of business risk (International Country Risk Guide, ICRG) or country competitiveness (The World Competitiveness report). Others look directly at institutions, such as perceptions of corruption (Transparency International) or economic and political freedom indexes.

These indexes of economic institutions are based on perceptions of experts. Transparency International, for example, asks officials and businesspersons familiar with the country their perceptions of how honest or corrupt a country is. Others provide further detail of institutional development by categories.[12]

The "Index of Economic Freedom" is published by the Heritage Foundation and the *Wall Street Journal*, starting with data for 1994, although coverage for the full set of transition countries is only done as of 1997. There is an overall index that is based on the evaluation by outside experts of ten specific institutional factors or areas that are considered to be relevant for economic freedom. These are trade, taxation, government intervention, monetary policy, foreign investment, banking, wages and prices, property rights, regulation, and black market.[13] It is very thorough and looks reasonable, but it is still fundamentally subjective.

The *Nations in Transit* reports from Freedom House provide a second source of institutional indicators, in addition to Freedom House's annual *Survey of Freedom*. Both are again based on expert outside opinion. Useful measures are democratic and economic freedom, which are based on subindicators for political process, civil society, independent media, rule of law, government and public administration, privatization, and the economy. Other valuable indicators are subindices for rule of law and governance and public administration and indices for political and civil rights.

A third set of measures are the EBRD's transition indicators. These are also based on an evaluation by outside experts. In particular, the EBRD's legal reform index, measuring the de jure extensiveness and the de facto effectiveness of the legal systems of countries, is especially useful and has been compiled since 1995.

A fourth source of system measurement is the survey conducted in 1998 by the World Bank on the institutional environment in a large number of countries for its World Development Report. The survey was divided into five sections: (i) government predictability regarding laws and policies; (ii) property rights; (iii) the quality of the government–business relationship; (iv) bureaucratic red tape; and (v) efficiency of the government in providing services. The survey reflects the situation in 1997 as perceived by a sample of firms located in these countries. We used the average of the responses to those questions that best captured institutional factors (WB).

Finally, the country risk ratings published by "Euromoney," which go back to 1992 and are based on the assessments of country-risk experts, can be used as institutional measures. Of particular value is political risk rating.

The availability of these measures of institutions has generated a large and rich literature of the effect of the economic system on economic outcomes. We shall examine this literature in later chapters.[14]

Summary

- Outcomes are influenced by the prevailing economic system (ES) as well as by environmental factors (ENV) and policy factors (POL).
- We must solve the ceteris paribus problem in order to capture the effect of the economic system on economic outcomes.
- We use five economic performance criteria—economic growth, efficiency, income distribution, stability, and viability—to evaluate the performance of economic systems.
- Economic growth consists of increases in the output of goods and services and/or increases in output per capita.
- Efficiency is the effectiveness with which a system uses its resources at a given time (static efficiency) or through time (dynamic efficiency). It can be further related to extensive economic growth and intensive economic growth.
- Income distribution is inherently subjective, although it is related to the effectiveness with which participants pursue system objectives. The income distribution is measured by the Gini coefficient.
- To obtain an aggregate measure of performance, we must use weights that are influenced by social norms to add the various measures together.
- We cannot seek to maximize all performance measures simultaneously because of tradeoffs.
- A society should maximize its objectives subject to its economic system, environment, and policy.
- To hold the economic system constant, we can either use econometric methods or natural experiments such as East and West Germany, North and South Korea, and Cuba versus Latin America.
- Various international organizations publish measures of economic institutions, such as corruption or economic freedom, based on perceptions of experts.

Key Terms

ceteris paribus—A Latin term meaning all other things being equal.

deadweight loss—A measure of inefficiency caused by a variety of distortions that cause the economy to operate below its potential.

dynamic efficiency—The ability of an economic system to enhance its capacity to produce goods and services over time without an increase in capital and labor inputs.

economic growth—The increase in real GDP or real GDP per capita over a period of time.

economic outcomes (O)—The performance of the economy as measured by criteria such as economic growth, living standards, employment, and other measure that are deemed important.

economic system (ES)—This is multidimensional and is defined in terms of its many institutions, such as how it manages information, its organizational structure, its provision for property rights, and how it makes public choices.

efficiency—The effectiveness with which a system utilizes its available resources (including knowledge) at a particular time (static efficiency) or through time (dynamic efficiency).

environmental factors (ENV)—The economic setting in which the economic system operates.

extensive growth—Growth through the expansion of inputs.

Gini coefficient—A numerical measure of the degree of inequality in the distribution of income or wealth. Its value ranges from zero, if everyone has the same income or wealth, to one, if one person has all the income or wealth.

happiness research—A fairly young branch of economics that uses national and international surveys of households probing how content residents of different countries are with their lives.

initial conditions—The starting point from which the growth and development of an economy begins.

intensive growth—Growth that occurs through the increase in efficiency of resource use.

jobs rights economy—Everyone guaranteed a job; no incentives to change jobs, and few incentives to work hard.

natural experiments—Serendipitous situations in which persons, groups, or countries are assigned randomly to a treatment and a control group, and outcomes are analyzed for the purposes of testing hypotheses.

policy (POL)—Trade policy, macroeconomic decision making, the regulatory setting, and other actions that can be changed without changing the economic system itself.

stability—The absence of significant fluctuations in growth rates, the maintenance of relatively low rates of unemployment, and the avoidance of excessive inflation.

static efficiency—An economy operating on its production possibilities frontier.

tradeoffs—The sacrifice of one thing (such as one economic goal) for another.

underemployment—The employment of individuals on a full-time basis at work in which they utilize their skills at well under their full potential.

weights—These measure how important each performance indicator is.

Notes

1. Douglass North, *Institutions, Institutional Change, and Economic Performance* (New York: Cambridge University Press, 1990), p. 107.
2. For the basic theory of business cycles, see Andrew W. Abel and Ben S. Bernanke, *Macroeconomics* (Reading, Mass.: Addison-Wesley, 1992), Ch. 11. There has been a

great deal of interest in the issue of cycles in the formerly planned socialist economic systems. For a summary, see Paul R. Gregory and Robert C. Stuart, *Soviet and Post-Soviet Economic Structure and Performance*, 6th ed. (New York: Addison Wesley Longman, 1997), Ch. 11.

3. David Granick, *Job Rights in the Soviet Union: Their Consequences* (Cambridge: Cambridge University Press, 1987).

4. See Tjalling C. Koopmans and John Michael Montias, "On the Description and Comparison of Economic Systems," in Alexander Eckstein, ed., *Comparison of Economy Systems: Theoretical and Methodological Approaches* (Berkeley: University of California Press, 1971), pp. 27–78.

5. Gur Ofer, *The Service Sector in Soviet Economic Growth* (Cambridge: Harvard University Press, 1973); Paul Gregory, *Socialist and Non-Socialist Industrialization Patterns* (New York: Praeger, 1970).

6. Abram Bergson, *Productivity and the Social System—The USSR and the West* (Cambridge, Mass.: Harvard University Press, 1978).

7. This definition is adapted from J. Dinardo, "Natural Experiments and Quasi-Natural Experiments," *The New Palgrave Dictionary of Economics*, 2nd ed. (Basingstoke: Palgrave, 2008).

8. "Angus Maddison," http://www.ggdc.net/MADDISON/oriindex.htm.

9. "Cuba," http://arabia.reporters-sans-frontieres.org/article.php3?id_article=10611.

10. See Carmelo Mesa-Lago, *Market Socialist and Mixed Economies: Comparative Performance, Chile, Cuba and Costa Rica* (Baltimore: John Hopkins University Press, 2000).

11. Oleh Havrylyshyn and Ron van Rooden, "Institutions Matter in Transition, But So Do Policies," *Comparative Economic Studies*, vol. 45, 2003, pp. 2–24.

12. A. Brunetti, G. Kisunko, and B. Weder, "Institutional Obstacles to Doing Business," World Bank Policy Research Working Paper, No. 1759, Washington, 1997.

13. K. R. Holmes, B. T. Johnson, and M. Kirkpatrick, *1995–1998: Index of Economic Freedom*. The Heritage Foundation and the *Wall Street Journal*: Washington.

14. See, for example, Hernando De Soto, "The Missing Ingredient," *The Economist* (September 1993); R. J. Barro and X. Sala-i-Martin, *Economic Growth* (New York: McGraw Hill, 1994); V. Tanzi and H. Davoodi, *"Corruption, Public Investment and Growth,"* IMF Working Paper, WP/97/139, Washington, 1997; P. Mauro, "The Effects of Corruption on Growth, Investment and Government Expenditure: A Cross-Country Analysis," in K. A. Elliot, ed., *Corruption and the Global Economy* (Washington, D.C.: Institute of International Economics, 1997); S. Knack and P. Keefer, "Institutions and Economic Performance: Cross-Country Tests using Alternative Institutional Measures," *Economics and Politics* 7 (1995), 207–227.

Recommended Readings

Traditional Sources

Kenneth Arrow, *Social Choice and Individual Values*, 2nd ed. (New York: Wiley, 1963).
Trevor Buck, *Comparative Industrial Systems* (New York: St. Martins, 1982).
Edward F. Denison, *Why Growth Rates Differ* (Washington, D.C.: Brookings Institution, 1967).
———, *Accounting for Slower Economic Growth* (Washington, D.C.: Brookings Institution, 1979).
John W. Kendrick, *Understanding Productivity* (Baltimore: Johns Hopkins University Press, 1977).

Etienne S. Kirschen and Lucien Morrisens, "The Objectives and Instruments of Economic Policy," in Morris Bornstein, ed., *Comparative Economic Systems: Models and Cases*, 7th ed. (Homewood, Ill.: Irwin, 1994), 49–66.

Simon Kuznets, *Modern Economic Growth: Rate, Structure and Spread* (New Haven: Yale University Press, 1966).

John Michael Montias, *The Structure of Economic Systems* (New Haven: Yale University Press, 1977).

P. J. D. Wiles, *Distribution of Income: East and West* (Amsterdam: North-Holland, 1974).

Economic Growth and Productivity

Robert J. Barro, "Economic Growth in a Cross Section of Countries," *Quarterly Journal of Economics* 106 (May 1991), 407–444.

Y. Mundlak, "Empirical Evidence in Economic Growth Theory," *American Economic Review: Papers and Proceedings* 83, no. 2 (May 1993), 415–430.

Malcolm Gillis, Dwight H. Perkins, Michael Roemer, and Donald R. Snodgrass, *Economics of Development*, 3rd ed. (New York: Norton, 1992), Chs. 2–3.

Bruce Herrick and Charles P. Kindleberger, *Economic Development*, 4th ed. (New York: McGraw-Hill, 1985).

Ross Levine and David Renelt, "A Sensitivity Analysis of Cross-Country Growth Regression," *American Economic Review* 82, no. 4 (September 1992), 942–963.

Angus Maddison, "Growth and Slowdown in Advanced Capitalist Economics," *Journal of Economic Literature* 25, no. 2 (June 1987), 649–698.

E. Wayne Nafziger, *The Economics of Developing Countries*, 2nd ed. (Englewood Cliffs, N.J.: Prentice-Hall, 1990), Ch. 3.

Robert Summers and Alan Heston, "A New Set of International Comparisons of Real Product and Price Levels: Estimates for 130 Countries, 1950–1985," *Review of Income and Wealth* 34 (March 1988), 1–25.

Income Distribution

Anthony B. Atkinson and John Micklewright, *Economic Transformation in Eastern Europe and the Distribution of Income* (Cambridge: Cambridge University Press, 1992).

Malcolm Gillis, Dwight H. Perkins, Michael Roemer, and Donald R. Snodgrass, *Economics of Development*, 3rd ed. (New York: Norton, 1992), Ch. 5.

Margaret E. Grosh and E. Wayne Nafziger, "The Computation of World Income Distribution," *Economic Development and Cultural Change* 34 (January 1986).

Jacques Lecaillon, Felix Paukert, Christian Morrison, and Dimitri Germidis, *Income Distribution and Economic Development: An Analytical Survey* (Geneva: International Labor Office, 1984).

E. Wayne Nafziger, *The Economics of Developing Countries*, 2nd ed. (Englewood Cliffs, N.J.: Prentice-Hall, 1990), Ch. 6.

Barry W. Poulson, *Economic Development* (New York: West, 1994), Ch. 7.

Cyclical Stability

Morris Bornstein, "Unemployment in Capitalist Regulated Market Economies and Socialist Centrally Planned Economies," in Morris Bornstein, ed., *Comparative Economic Systems: Models and Cases*, 7th ed. (Homewood, Ill.: Irwin, 1994), 597–605.

Carlo Frateschi, ed., *Fluctuations and Cycles in Socialist Economies* (Brookfield, Vt.: Avebury Publishers, 1989).

David Granick, *Job Rights in the Soviet Union: Their Consequences* (Cambridge: Cambridge University Press, 1987).

Paul R. Gregory and Robert C. Stuart, *Soviet and Post-Soviet Economic Structure and Performance*, 6th ed. (New York: Addison Wesley Longman, 1997), Ch. 11.

Barry W. Ickes, "Cyclical Fluctuations in Centrally Planned Economies: A Critique of the Literature," *Soviet Studies* 38, no. 1 (January 1986), 36–52.

CHAPTER

4

How Economic Systems Change

The economic system, the environment in which the system operates, and economic policies all influence economic outcomes. As these influencing forces change, so does economic performance. This chapter is about how economic systems change over time.

The New Institutional Economics was pioneered by Oliver Williamson, Douglass North, Gordon Tullock, Ronald Coase, Mancur Olson, and others. Three of these (Coase, North, and Williamson) received Nobel prizes for their work.[1] *The* **New Institutional Economics** *teaches that we can explain the evolution of institutions and their effect on economic life by using the logic of economic rationality as reflected in the pursuit of self-interest.* Specifically, we can explain major changes in the course of economic history by examining, among other things, property rights, transaction costs, and rent-seeking opportunities.[2]

There are many examples of this approach. Among them are the following: the increase in agricultural output and the urbanization of Britain during the Industrial Revolution were made possible by changes in property rights in the English countryside, as changes in laws and customs reduced the transaction costs of enclosing agricultural land into separate estates. England's greater economic progress than France during the nineteenth century is explained by the creation of stable financial markets as a consequence of parliamentary restraints on arbitrary royal spending. England's long-term decline in the twentieth century may be due to its social and political stability, which allowed vested interests to form and dominate. Imperfect capital markets explain the persistence of sharecropping in the American South along with high information costs. Economists use risk avoidance and the natural insurance of subsistence crops to account for French peasant resistance to cash crops in the nineteenth century.[3]

According to the New Institutional Economics, market institutions—corporations, futures markets, contract law, cartels, commercial banks—arose because they happened to be economically rational given the circumstances of time and place.

If economic conditions change—if something happens to lower transaction costs, raise information costs, or change property rights—then our economic institutions change accordingly.

Whereas Karl Marx viewed institutional change as inevitable and as following a predetermined path, the New Institutional Economics views institutional change as dictated by economic variables, whose course of change cannot be predicted in advance. Nor does this course of change follow an inevitable path, but instead it depends on the starting point and institutional factors. The course of change is path-dependent. It depends on the initial conditions from which progress begins. **Path dependence** *states that technology and institutional arrangements are not predetermined but depend on initial conditions.* Path dependence teaches that "history matters" in the sense that the eventual outcome depends on the starting point.

The principle of path dependence has been applied to the development of technology and market structure. For example, the "qwerty" keyboard layout of the modern typewriter/computer was originally designed to prevent keys from jamming on mechanical typewriters. Its head start caused it to be adopted in subsequent applications where another system may have been better. Similarly Microsoft's Windows became the industry standard not due to its superiority over other alternatives but due to favorable initial conditions.[4]

In his early writings, F. A. Hayek also considered how economic institutions evolve over time. Hayek argued that economic institutions arise according to *a* **spontaneous order** *in which new organizations, laws, regulations, and customs are tested by daily economic life.* Arrangements that "work" are retained by society; those that do not fall by the wayside, losers in a Darwinian struggle. The corporation arose as a way of raising capital and sharing risk in medieval times. It survived because it served a useful economic function. Worker guilds also arose during the medieval period; they later evolved into craft unions. They served their purpose for a long time, but they can disappear if they outlive their usefulness.

According to Hayek, the institutions of economic life exist in the form of written and unwritten information that is passed from one generation to the next. They are the result of **human action**, not of **human design**. *Institutions that change by* **human action** *do so spontaneously, not as the result of deliberate, planned, or legislative activity.* They do not have to be codified into law or written into charters or contracts. They evolve in bits and pieces, so no single person or entity knows them in their entirety. Rather, these bits and pieces are known and understood by those who require specialized knowledge in order to conduct their economic lives. An example is money. All economies use money, but no one created money. Because money is something that fills a void, it resulted from spontaneous human actions.[5]

Other changes in economic institutions do so by human design. *Institutions that change by* **human design** *are the result of deliberate decision making by governments or organized groups of individuals.* Examples of human design would be the passage of sweeping health care reform in the United States under Barack Obama in 2010, the introduction of the first social welfare acts in Otto von Bismarck's Germany in November of 1881, or the creation of the European Union after World War II.

Reform versus Transition

For our purposes, we can differentiate between two types of change by human design. *We define **economic reform** as an attempt to modify an existing system. We define **transition** as the shift from one system to another*. It is sometimes difficult to draw the line between reform and transition. Some would argue that the introduction of cradle-to-grave welfare reforms in Western Europe created a new and different economic system—the European Welfare State. Others would maintain that these changes, albeit extensive, have not altered the basic nature of the European economic system.

Changes in the institutions of the countries of the former Soviet Union and Eastern Europe after 1989 have indeed transformed them from one type of economic system to another. These changes go far beyond "reform." It is for this reason that we refer to the study of the economic change in the countries that were once part of the Soviet Empire as transition economics. ***Transition economics*** *studies the process of transforming the countries of the former Soviet Union and Eastern Europe from planned socialist economies into entirely different economic systems*.

Economic change occurs differently in capitalist and socialist economic systems. Economic change in capitalist systems is generally evolutionary in nature, gradual in pace, and, to a significant degree, introduced on a decentralized basis through market-type or democratic institutions. In socialist systems, however, change has been abrupt and introduced by a central authority. It was largely the communist parties of Eastern Europe and the Soviet Union that initiated at least the earliest course of reform. China's move toward modernization was introduced by its communist leaders, albeit after spontaneous reform from below. The characterization of change in capitalist market economies as evolutionary does not deny the fact that a number of significant changes, such as social security or regulatory reforms, are brought about by state legislative or bureaucratic action. But, over the long sweep of history, the most significant changes have been the evolutionary result of change by Hayek's "human action."

The forced introduction of command planning and collectivized agriculture in the Soviet Union at the end of the 1920s and the subsequent transmission of such arrangements into Eastern Europe and China after World War II are further examples of fundamental and rapid changes in economic systems brought about by the "human design" of the system's leaders. In these cases, decision-making arrangements were centralized, the market was replaced by the plan, state ownership supplanted private ownership, and moral incentives and punishments became increasingly important. The replacement of command planning by worker-managed socialism in the former Yugoslavia in the 1950s is another case of "human design" of the Yugoslav Communist Party under Marshall Tito. Mikhail Gorbachev's "radical reforms" of 1987 and 1988 also brought about abrupt and dramatic change in the way the Soviet economy functioned.

If economic reforms in socialist economic systems are "packages" introduced by a central authority, the reforms of capitalist systems are more difficult to characterize. Today's market economies operate differently from those of one hundred years ago. Changes have occurred gradually, without clear milestones. When resources are allocated through markets, changes in allocation procedures are less visible than when a central authority makes sweeping changes by fiat.

Some milestones can be identified. Britain's passage of the Corn Laws in 1846 turned the English economy into the world's first open economy. Bismarck's introduction of labor legislation in 1881 changed Germany's economic system, as did the passage of Social Security laws in the United States in 1935 during the Great Depression. Further examples include privatization during the Thatcher years in Great Britain, the passage of Great Society legislation under Lyndon Johnson in 1965, New Zealand's liberalization reforms conducted between 1985 and 1995, Chile's macroeconomic and privatization reforms under Augusto Pinochet, Singapore's creation of a forced saving program starting in 1955, and European privatizations of the 1990s. It is still too early to characterize the effects of the passage of universal health insurance coverage under Obama in the United States in 2010.

Marx's Theory of Change

How we view systemic change is influenced by the models we use. The classical economists of the nineteenth century, most particularly David Ricardo (1772–1823) and Thomas Malthus (1766–1834), had a pessimistic view of the economic future. Ricardo and Malthus paid little attention to economic institutions. They analyzed what was primarily an agricultural economy of landowners and small farmers. Ricardo concluded that such an economy had distinct limits to growth. Because of diminishing returns, an upper limit on output would be reached. Malthus argued that population would expand geometrically unless restrained by famine, war, and pestilence. The two notions combined to yield a classical stationary state in which output was stagnant, and the population lived at subsistence. The pessimistic writings of Ricardo and Malthus gave the economics of the nineteenth century the label of the "dismal science."

Karl Marx (1818–1883) wrote in the classical tradition of Ricardo and Malthus, but instead of technical issues like diminishing returns and fertility rates, he focused directly on economic systems and their institutions. He sought to demonstrate the inevitability of the transformation of one system into another. In so doing, he formulated the most famous theory of economic system change. Whether Marx's approach is used as a framework to interpret change or to understand the foundations of socialism, his effect on the course of world history has been profound.

Marx concluded in his famous three-volume *Capital* (*Das Kapital* in German) that capitalism is an unstable economic system whose lifespan is inevitably limited.[6] Marx's theory of capitalism is based on his materialist conception of history. *The **materialist conception of history** states that economic forces (called **productive forces**) determine how production relations, markets, and society itself (the **superstructure**) are organized.*[7] Weak productive forces (underdeveloped human and capital resources) result in one arrangement for producing goods and services (**production relations**), and strong productive forces lead to more advanced production arrangements. A society with underdeveloped economic resources has underdeveloped production relations and superstructure (manifested in barter exchange, serf labor, a rigid social hierarchy, and religious biases against commerce). As the productive forces improve, new economic and social relationships emerge (such as hired rather than serf labor and monetary rather than natural exchange). These new arrangements are not compatible with the old economic, cultural, and social relationships. When they come into contact, tensions and conflicts mount.

Eventually, incompatibilities become so great that a qualitative change produces new production relations and a new superstructure, compatible with the new productive forces that replace the old order. *Qualitative changes are abrupt and violent changes caused by the conflict between old and new productive forces that create a new superstructure.* The most important qualitative change is the world socialist revolution that overthrows capitalism.

In effect, Marx's "superstructure" is what we call the "economic system." Qualitative changes are inevitable because societies are destined to evolve from a lower to a higher order. The engine of change is the conflict between old and new, primarily in the form of class struggle (the emerging capitalist class versus the landed gentry in feudal societies, the worker versus the capitalist in capitalist societies). *Marx's theory of **dialectical materialism** describes the process of evolutionary and inevitable qualitative change through the competition of opposing forces (**thesis versus antithesis**).* Marx derived his views on dialectical change from the writings of the German philosophers George Wilhelm Hegel and Ludwig Feuerbach.

The upshot of Marx's materialist conception of history is that societies evolve according to an inevitable pattern of social and economic change in which lower systems are replaced by more advanced systems. In this manner, feudalism is bound to replace slavery, capitalism inevitably displaces feudalism, and socialism eventually replaces capitalism.

Table 4.1 describes the inevitable stages of evolution of society from one set of productive forces and superstructures to another.

The victory of capitalism over feudalism represented a qualitative step forward for society. A highly efficient productive machine, capitalism, replaced an inefficient one, feudalism, based on semi-servile labor and governed by traditional

TABLE **4.1** Marx's Stages of Economic Systems

Primitive Society
Slave Society
Feudal Society
Capitalist Society
Imperialism (added by V. I. Lenin)
Lower Stage of Socialism
Higher Stage of Socialism (Communism)

© Cengage Learning 2014

landed interests. Two landmarks signaled the emergence of capitalism. The first was the initial accumulation of capital by the emerging capitalist class—a process Marx called primitive accumulation of capital. ***Primitive (or original) accumulation of capital*** *was the process whereby the capitalist class gained a monopoly over the means of production.* The second indicator was the formation of a "free" labor force at the disposal of capitalist employers. Laborers were separated from control over land, tools, and livestock and were left with only their own labor to sell. At this point, the capitalist, who now controlled the means of production, hired this free labor, and capitalist factories were established. In this manner, the basic class conflict of capitalism was created—the conflict between the working class and the capitalist, who "owns" the labor services of the worker.

The feature that distinguishes labor from the other factors of production is that the employer can compel workers to produce a value that exceeds the value that workers need to maintain themselves. However, the employer is not required to pay workers the full value of their production—only enough to allow them to subsist. One worker may have to work eight hours to produce a value sufficient to meet subsistence needs, yet the employer can force the worker to create a surplus by working twelve hours, for example, which is four hours more than required for subsistence.

The exploitation of labor is the source of capitalist profits, which Marx called surplus value. ***Surplus value*** *was Marx's term for profit and is created by the exploitation of labor.* Marx pictured capitalism, in its early stages, as a world of cut-throat competition. The capitalist was driven to maximize profits (surplus value) and to accumulate more capital out of profits. Capitalists, operating in intensely competitive markets, are forced to introduce cost-saving innovations lest their competitors do so first and drive them out of business. One capitalist introduces a new labor-saving technology, attracts competitors' customers through lower prices, and experiences a temporary increase in profits above "normal" levels. The profits are short-lived, however, because competitors respond by introducing the same cost-saving techniques, and new competitors enter the market in response to windfall profits. Excess industry profits are eliminated, and no capitalist ends up better off.

But when fixed capital is substituted for labor, the profit rate declines. There is an inherent tendency to substitute capital for labor, even though labor is the sole source of surplus value. Marx predicted that the profit rate would fall, with disastrous consequences for capitalism. *Marx's* ***law of the declining rate of profit*** *stated that the profit rate of capitalists must inevitably fall and contribute to the general crisis of capitalism.*

As the profit rate falls, capitalism's internal contradictions and weaknesses become apparent. In an effort to halt the decline in profits, capitalists increase the exploitation of their workers, and alienation and exploitation intensify. The declining profit rate leads to the failure of marginal businesses, and bankrupt capitalists now swell the ranks of the unemployed. Those fortunate enough to be employed are exploited and alienated; the unemployed fare even worse. A more ominous phenomenon is overproduction. Workers are kept at subsistence wages by high unemployment. Capitalists, driven by the desire to accumulate capital, are not willing to increase their spending on luxury goods. Moreover, the ranks of the capitalists are thinning, as monopolies drive out smaller capitalists. Yet all the while, the productive capacity of the economy is growing because of rising capital intensity. Aggregate demand falls chronically short of aggregate supply; recessions and then depressions occur, and worldwide crises become commonplace. The declining profit rate leads to declines in investment spending and to further shortfalls in aggregate demand.

Marx described only generally *the final stages of capitalism called the **capitalist breakdown***. Overproduction, underconsumption, disproportions, and the exploitation and alienation of workers combine to create the conditions necessary for the violent overthrow of capitalism. Workers unite against the weakened capitalist class and, through a violent *world* revolution, establish a new socialist order.

Marx had little to say about this new order. Implicit in Marx's writings on the final stage of capitalism is that contradictions will be more intense in the most advanced capitalist countries. The socialist revolution would be initiated there.

Marxism after Marx

Marx's writings influenced generations of economists, philosophers, politicians, and revolutionaries. The Soviet Union and its satellites in Eastern Europe, China, Cuba, and Vietnam all recognized, at one time, Marxism as the foundation of their economic and political systems. As time passed, the role of Marxist ideology was diluted by practical experience, but historically Marxism was the core belief of such countries.

After Marx's death, Marxism split broadly into two camps. In Russia, the Russian Social Democratic Labor Party, which split between Vladimir Lenin's Bolsheviks and the Mensheviks at Lenin's insistence in 1903, followed Marx's call for socialist revolution. Russian Marxists were revolutionaries who aimed to overthrow the capitalist system in Russia and throughout the world via a violent socialist revolution. ***Lenin's Bolshevik Party*** *was a small party of professional underground revolutionaries bent on a violent socialist revolution.* Through their willingness to use brutal force, Lenin's Bolsheviks gained control of Russia in the October 1917 revolution and remained in control until the collapse of the Soviet Union in December of 1991. Lenin's immediate successor was Joseph Stalin, who introduced a reign of terror over his own people and those of Eastern Europe after World War II.

The European Marxists, under Eduard Bernstein and Karl Kautsky, took a revisionist approach to Marx's writings.[8] Confronted with the reality that the capitalist breakdown was not imminent, they chose to work within the political system to reform capitalism. *The **European Marxist reformers** abandoned the goal of socialist revolution and chose to work within the political system to reform capitalism to make it better for workers.*

The European Marxist reform movement morphed into the social democratic, socialist, or labor parties that today contend against Christian democratic, conservative, or Tory parties throughout Europe for parliamentary majorities. In Germany, the Social Democratic Party of Germany (SPD) alternates in power with the Christian democrats; in France, the socialist party alternates in power with a coalition of rightist parties.

The appeal of Marxism remains strong among intellectuals, college professors, and young radicals throughout the world. They are drawn to its charges of oppression of the working class and of third-world countries by greedy capitalists and imperialists. According to surveys, the highest proportion of Marxist academics (26 percent) in U.S. universities can be found in departments of sociology. In the humanities, about a quarter of professors consider themselves radicals or activists.[9] In Europe and Latin America, the percentages are likely higher.

Almost daily, a new Marxist organization of some sort is formed and sets up its own website. These contemporary Marxists are unfazed by the collapse of Soviet socialism, arguing that the Soviets made too many mistakes and deviated from the true teachings of Marxist revolution. Their energies are not directed at world socialist revolution but to anti-capitalist, anti-imperialist demonstrations against globalization and environmental damage. They admire different and purer Marxists, such as Che Guevara, Leon Trotsky, and MIT linguist, Noam Chomsky.

Schumpeter: The Evolution of Capitalism

An Austrian economist transplanted to Harvard, Joseph Schumpeter (1883–1950) described the dynamics of capitalism much differently from Marx.[10] Although Schumpeter was also pessimistic about the survival of capitalism and predicted its eventual replacement by socialism, he viewed the causes of this demise much differently from Marx.

Schumpeter argued that the capitalist economy cannot be understood within the framework of static economic analysis—that is, the pursuit of objectives by existing institutions. Capitalism, he argued, is fundamentally dynamic and can be understood only through the forces of change. The important issues, therefore, are not how an organization functions at a point in time but, rather, how that organization comes into being and how it evolves over time as a mechanism to generate economic growth.

The driving force of the capitalist system, according to Schumpeter, is innovation: the development and implementation of new products, new ideas, and new ways of doing things. Innovation is carried out by entrepreneurs, who are driven by and rewarded through profits. The result of the development of new ideas broadly defined is creative destruction. *Schumpeter's* **creative destruction** *describes how new capitalist enterprises outcompete and replace established firms only to be replaced themselves by more effective newcomers in the long run.*

According to Schumpeter, the life cycle of a capitalist enterprise is one of struggle. By having a better idea, a superior innovation, or a new product, the young enterprise drives more mature rivals from the field. However, its competitive advantage is transitory. Eventually, every business must face creative destruction, even monopolists and giant concerns. Business rivals are constantly in search of better production techniques and better products. Yesterday's dominant firm (the railroad, cable TV) becomes today's dinosaur as better products (trucking and air freight, the Internet) are introduced. Yesterday's secure monopoly (such as the Bell system in the 1970s) becomes today's competitive battlefield (the multitude of providers of telecommunications services).

Schumpeter viewed the capitalist economy not in terms of the competitive ideal but rather as characterized by the concentration of large businesses. Concentration would eventually lead to the routinization of the entrepreneurial spirit and a lack of social willingness to reward risk takers. In brief, yesterday's winners become fat, lazy, and bureaucratic. The decline in entrepreneurial activity will be a fundamental reason for the eventual decline of capitalism. As capitalism declines, it is replaced by socialism.

Schumpeter has withstood the test of time. "Creative destruction" has become a buzzword on Wall Street and within the business community. It explains why few businesses maintain their dominance over long periods of time, why yesterday's giants, such as Blockbuster Videos or AOL, are today's candidates for the bankruptcy courts. Schumpeter's warnings about the unwillingness to reward risk takers foretell today's complaints about controlling the greedy rich. Schumpeter's creative destruction also sheds light on contemporary political practice. If previously thriving companies eventually face being outcompeted by new rivals with better technology and products, their natural reaction is to seek protection from the state. Schumpeter's creative destruction can easily be expanded to explain the vast amount of lobbying, political contributions, and outright corruption that arises as declining industries vie for protection by friendly politicians.

Hayek's Road to Serfdom

F. A. Hayek proposed a dynamic of the economic system that leads from an individualistic democratic market economy to a non-democratic collectivist state. He argued in his best-selling *Road to Serfdom* that "good intentions" will have the unintended consequence of creating a collectivist state.[11] The basic proposition of his best-selling and influential treatise is that personal and political freedom cannot exist without economic freedom, but there are strong forces pushing us in the direction of state control of economic affairs.

At the time Hayek was writing, it was clear that the centralized planning and control of the Soviet Union was inconsistent with individual and political freedom. The Soviet planned-socialist state forced its citizens to bow to the planners' will under the justification that the Communist Party was omniscient and knew what was best for society. Hayek concluded that Soviet Russia was not the only example of loss of personal economic freedom to the state. There was, in reality, little difference between Stalin's socialism and Adolf Hitler and Benito Mussolini's fascism. Both were collectivist states that imposed their will on citizens and deprived them of individual liberty. In Stalin's Russia, it was the planner that ordered economic actors what to do. In Hitler's Germany, it was leaders of the Nazi Party.

In 1944, as Hayek wrote, the dangers of Stalinist communism and Hitler's fascism were obvious, but Hayek's concern was that collectivist thinking would triumph in England and the United States and lead both countries down a similar Road to Serfdom. Their loss of economic and personal freedom would be less obvious and would be justified as necessary for the good of the community. As the end of the war approached, there was growing sentiment for increased state intervention. Before the war, the British economy had been in the long slump of the Great Depression. The militarization of the British war economy had introduced a form of centralized planning that was enjoying increasing support. There were calls to not return to the prewar chaos of the market economy and appeals for the state to take a more active role in assuring the health and welfare of the population.

A collectivized economy of central planning, Hayek countered, imposes the will of a small minority (of government officials) on the people. It destroys the rule of law because collectivized planners have the authority to take property and order around citizens in their private economic activity. With increased collectivism, the individual would more than ever become a mere means to be used by the state in the services of abstractions as the "social welfare," where government officials define social welfare. Hayek warned that "the last resort of the competitive economy is the bailiff, but the ultimate sanction of a planned economy is the hangman." (At this time, Stalin was executing large numbers of managers, engineers, and workers for economic crimes!)

Hayek feared that England and the United States would not heed his warnings. The "siren song" of a rational state that can better solve economic issues than hundreds of thousands of businesses or millions of consumers will win out. We will progressively shy away from competitive markets in favor of state intervention to provide economic security and order. But to abandon freedom in economic affairs is to lose personal and political freedom.

The Austrian School of Mises and Hayek: The Socialist Critique

Whereas Marx and others believed in the inherent instability of capitalism, a number of critics argued the exact opposite: that socialism is the inherently unstable economic system. Hayek warned in his *Road to Serfdom* against socialist experiments on the grounds that once started, they might be difficult to stop. At a more fundamental level, Hayek and his colleagues argued that if a socialist economy was indeed established, it would be destined either to collapse or to operate at very low levels of efficiency.

*The **Austrian School of Economics** emphasized the importance of individualism and free markets to create the information and incentives needed to manage the complex interactions of an economy. It warned against planning and state intervention as threats to individual liberty and to economic efficiency.* Its most prominent proponents were two Austrians, F. A. Hayek (1899–1992) and Ludwig von Mises (1881–1973).

Mises was an early critic of socialism. In his classic article, "Economic Calculation in the Socialist Commonwealth," published in 1922, Mises anticipated most of the modern problems of socialism. He argued that socialist economies would lack market exchange and would hence lack the vital information provided by the price system.[12] Without relative prices, socialist managers would not have enough information to make rational economic decisions. Moreover, lacking property rights, socialist managers would not behave in an economically rational manner but rather would overdemand and waste scarce resources.

According to both Hayek and Mises, socialism lacked the informational basis for rational economic calculation. Its institutions were created by "human design" and could not withstand the test of spontaneous order. The socialist experiment, they felt, was bound to fail.

Experiments with socialism, such as those that took place in Russia after the Bolshevik Revolution of 1917, created an economic system of planned socialism that contained a number of internal contradictions. Mises and Hayek felt that a socialist economy would be too complex to plan from the center and would require more information on technology, prices, quantities, and assortments than a central planning board could gather and digest. Moreover, they felt that the task of planning and management could not be effectively decentralized because in the absence of private property, even the best-intentioned managers of state enterprises could not make economically correct decisions.

For these reasons, Mises and Hayek felt that socialist experiments such as those in the Soviet Union would eventually be abandoned. In this sense, the theories of Mises and Hayek are models of the change of socialism back to capitalism on the grounds of socialism's inferiority as an economic system.

The Mises-Hayek prediction of the collapse of the Soviet system came true, but almost three quarters of a century after they first leveled their critique. Indeed, one of the central issues in studying the Soviet socialist planned economy is why it lasted so long in the face of the pathologies Mises and Hayek identified.

Kornai: The Economics of Shortage

The Hungarian economist János Kornai also argued that socialism was inherently unstable because of its natural tendency to generate shortage.[13] As a young economist studying the Hungarian socialist economy in the 1960s, Kornai formulated his theories based on firsthand observation. He better than others understood how planned socialism worked and would later write the most detailed retrospective of the socialist system.[14]

Kornai characterized the planned socialist economy as *an economy of shortage in which shortage is systemic, perpetual, and self-reproducing*. Others had argued earlier that persistent shortages or excess demand in the socialist system are functions of identifiable, although not necessarily easily corrected, forces. Consumer goods are simply not a high priority and are supplanted by producer goods and military production. Errors in planning, inadequate incentives, and other system shortfalls lead to continuing shortages. If only these "mistakes" could be corrected, shortages would go away.

From a very different perspective, Kornai argued that the economy of shortages arises from the nature of the enterprise in the planned socialist system. The socialist enterprise operates under fundamentally different rules. The capitalist enterprise is motivated to maximize profits. It makes its input and output decisions on the basis of prices established in markets. As a profit maximizer, the capitalist enterprise has little incentive to overdemand resources. If it employs more resources than technology requires, its profits suffer. The capitalist enterprise operates under a ***hard budget constraint***, *whereby the capitalist enterprise must cover its costs while earning an acceptable rate of return on invested capital.* If it fails to meet its budget constraint, the capitalist firm will fail in the long run. The capitalist firm must live within its means. The hard budget constraint "polices" capitalist enterprises and effectively eliminates excess demand for inputs.

The socialist firm operates in a supply-constrained economy. Socialist planners have as their objective the expansion of outputs, and they judge the performance of socialist enterprises on that basis. The manner in which socialist enterprises select inputs to meet their output objectives is of less importance than the output targets themselves. Although socialist enterprises face prices for inputs and outputs, their resource-allocation decisions are aimed at meeting output targets. Relative prices play only a minor role. High prices do not discourage enterprises from buying.

The capitalist enterprise that fails to live within its means is punished by bankruptcy. The socialist enterprise that fails to cover costs plus a rate of return on the state's invested capital does not suffer the same consequences. Socialist planners value enterprises for their outputs; socialist enterprises that make losses remain in business by virtue of state subsidies. Accordingly, socialist enterprises face *a **soft budget constraint*** *whereby socialist enterprises can live beyond their means over the long run through automatic bailouts by superior organizations.*

The hard budget constraint forces capitalist enterprises to limit their demands for inputs. The soft budget constraint on socialist enterprises fails to reward them for restricting their input demands. Hence the socialist system generates continuous excess demands for inputs. The supply of inputs falls chronically short of the demand for inputs, and persistent shortages or imbalances result.

Kornai explains the soft budget constraint through political negotiation. Loss-making enterprises bargain with superiors or banks to bail them out. Others deduce the soft budget constraint from the formal rules and incentives arising from specific institutions. Mathias Dewatripont and Eric Maskin contend that large sunk costs (which authorities are reluctant to abandon) and centralized financing are institutions that result in soft budgets.[15] Mark Schaffer emphasizes the problem of dynamic commitment in which the state does not intend to support loss-making ventures but is unable to commit itself not to after the event, and those responsible for the losses anticipate this beforehand.[16]

Economic systems must allocate resources in an orderly fashion. Persistent imbalances and chronic shortages detract from the orderly allocation of resources. With imbalances, those who obtain resources may not be those who will put them to their best and highest use. Kornai's analysis of socialism is related to the complexity and motivation issues raised by Mises and Hayek. Kornai's conclusion is that the socialist motivation system and inattention to relative prices disrupt the orderly allocation of resources under socialism. Accordingly, socialism will not be an efficient economic system. This lack of efficiency and coherence would eventually lead to an economic system that simply "muddled along" or one that would eventually fail.

Kornai's soft budgets have implications beyond the classical socialist economy. Recent historical experience shows that they apply to enterprises that for political or other reasons are deemed "too big to fail." It has become common practice in Europe for the state to rescue large enterprises from insolvency because their loss would harm the general welfare. Even in the United States, large manufacturers (Chrysler, 1979 and 2009; General Motors, 2009) and financial institutions (AIG, Citigroup, Bank of America, 2009) were rescued by the federal government for fear of the impact on the economy of their failure. These soft-budget cases remain limited and have not created Kornai-like shortages throughout the economy, but they do have potential significance for the efficiency of operations.

Olson and Murrell: Critique of Socialism

Public choice economists, in particular Mancur Olson and Peter Murrell, argue that the process of change in socialist economies will be dictated by the extent to which the system's directors (say, a monolithic communist party spearheaded by a small elite) can prevent distributional coalitions from emerging.[17] A ***distributional coalition*** *is a vested-interest coalition that uses the political process to gain monopoly profits or other forms of economic rents for itself.* As long as the socialist system is rigidly controlled by the system's dictator, that dictator will strive to allocate resources toward growth. It will be in the dictator's interest, as the beneficiary of economic growth, to create high savings rates, new technologies, and managerial behavior that elicits maximal enterprise capacity. By imposing terror or other coercive policies, the dictator can force agents throughout the economy to work toward the goal of economic growth.

As time passes, however, the power of the dictator weakens. Dedication to the goal of "overtaking the West" may diminish. Various interest groups (such as a military lobby or a heavy-industry pressure group) emerge, and the primary interest of every such group is promoting its particular branch or enterprise at the expense of others. These coalitions find ways to insulate themselves from the pressure of the dictator, such as concealing information from the center or appropriating resources that could have been used more productively by others. They develop ways to promote their own interests at the expense of the interests of the economy as a whole.

As the power of separate interest groups increases, the center finds it more difficult to impose discipline on the periphery. Power is devolved from the center to lower levels. Interest groups form into coalitions to promote their own interests. Instead of resources being devoted to generating the highest possible growth rates, resources are dissipated among distributional coalitions, which evade central controls and use resources for their own benefit.

The net result of the rising power of interest groups is that growth rates decline and efficiency of resource use drops. The dictator cannot maintain a strong hand forever, but the system works well *only* under a strong hand. As growth rates decline, distributional coalitions become bolder. They begin to engage in outright corruption and theft. No one considers the interest of society as a whole; attention is paid only to the narrow interests of vested-interest groups.[18] Moreover, given that each distributional coalition has vested interests to protect (such as special access to scarce goods and the opportunity to buy at below-equilibrium prices), there is no support for reform, which means that the system will not be able to take corrective action.

Conclusions

For almost two centuries, the best minds in economic science have pondered how economic institutions are formed, which of them survive, and how the collection of economic institutions we call the "economic system" change. Although modern comparative economists have left behind the capitalism versus socialism paradigm, intellectual thought of the last century and a half has been dominated by this dichotomy. Hence the major thinkers in economics have had to address the issue of how capitalist and socialist economies change and whether one will be "victorious" over the other.

Marx issued the first challenge: Capitalism is doomed; socialism is the economic system of the future. History, Marx argued, is on my side. The effect of Marx's challenge on history was profound. Intellectuals of the last two decades of the nineteenth century and the first three decades of the twentieth century tended to accept Marx's proposition of socialism's superiority and the necessity of socialist revolution, either violent or evolutionary. In the entrenched monarchies of Europe, Marxist revolution seemed the only alternative. Few economic philosophers stood up to defend the status quo capitalist system, especially after it sank into a deep depression in the 1920s and 1930s. Socialism, it was argued, would save the day. The Austrian economists were a rare voice in the wilderness, explaining to all who would listen that socialism's internal contradictions would lead to its doom. Even when glimpses of the brutality and inhumanity of Stalin's Russia filtered through the Iron Curtain, socialism's many well-wishers chose to ignore them.

Even two of the most prominent scholars of capitalism, Schumpeter and Hayek, expressed pessimism about capitalism's future. Schumpeter feared a reaction against capitalism's very strength—the dynamism of creative destruction. Hayek feared the lure of collectivist action, which would prove irreversible.

We should not conclude that the capitalism-socialism debate as over. The appeal of Marxism remains potent. It is easy to see the many apparent problems of capitalism: unemployment, cycles, bubbles, inequality. It is not difficult for the advocates of socialism to complain about the failure of capitalism and to promise that the great Soviet experiment with socialism was run by the wrong people who lost their Marxist bearings. Such arguments are particularly appealing in the course of yet another capitalist "crisis."

Hayek in his *Road to Serfdom* described the perennial struggle, to use his words, between collectivism and individualism. He warned that if the pendulum swings too far in the direction of collectivism, we will find ourselves in a "stealth" world of socialism, not by plan but as an unintended consequence. Societies face the choice of collectivism versus individualism on a regular basis in the form of legislative initiatives, government bailouts, health care programs, and government debt. How such routine decisions are decided determines the shape of economic systems to come. Appeals for government intervention are more attractive when individualistic markets appear to have flaws—recessions or speculation that is deemed excessive. When market capitalism is running smoothly with high growth, low inflation, and rising living standards, the public is less receptive to calls for intervention. If, as Hayek warns, collectivism is difficult to reverse, then the long-run prognosis is for increased collectivism, perhaps much more than we would want.

Summary

- The New Institutional Economics teaches that we can explain the evolution of institutions using economic rationality. Path dependence teaches that "history matters."
- Institutions can change by human action and by human design.
- Economic reform aims to improve an economic system. Transition is the replacement of one economic system with another.
- Marx used dialectical materialism to explain why socialism will replace capitalism as an inevitable product of class struggle. Marxism divided after Marx's death into a Russian revolutionary party under Lenin and a social democratic party in Europe.
- Schumpeter's dynamic model of capitalism explains why new firms displace old in the process of creative destruction.
- Hayek warned that increasing collectivism will lead us on a Road to Serfdom.
- Mises and Hayek (the Austrian school) explained why socialism will fail because of the absence of price signals and incentives. Planning will be too complex, and decentralization of decision will not be possible.
- Kornai explained why shortage and soft budgets are inevitable features of socialism.

Key Terms

Austrian School of Economics—The importance of individualism and free markets to create the information and incentives needed to manage the complex interactions of an economy.

capitalist breakdown—Conditions occurring in the final stages of capitalism— overproduction, underconsumption, disproportions, and the alienation of the working class.

creative destruction—The driving force of capitalism according to Schumpeter in which innovation ensures the replacement of the old by the new.

dialectical materialism—The philosophical foundations of change in the Marxian vision of change based on the writings of Hegel and Feuerbach.

distributional coalition—A component of contemporary public choice theory—a vested-interest coalition that uses the political process to gain monopoly profits.

economic reform—An attempt to modify an existing system.

economy of shortage—A cornerstone of socialist economic systems according to Kornai, characterized by shortage as a perpetual and self-reproducing condition.

European Marxist reformers—People who abandoned the goal of socialist revolution to work within the political system to reform capitalism to make it better for workers.

hard budget constraint—Under capitalism, enterprises must cover costs or eventually be replaced, according to Kornai.

human action—Spontaneous institutional change not the result of human action.

human design—Institutional changes resulting from *deliberate, planned, or legislative activity.*

law of the declining rate of profit—The profit rate of capitalists must inevitably fall and contribute to the general crisis of capitalism.

Lenin's Bolshevik Party—A small party of professional underground revolutionaries, the Bolsheviks, bent on a violent socialist revolution.

Materialist conception of history—Economic forces (called productive forces) determine how production relations, markets, and society itself (the superstructure) are organized.

New Institutional Economics—The evolution of institutions and their effect on economic life as explained by economic rationality and self-interest.

path dependence—Technology and institutional arrangements are not predetermined but depend on initial conditions.

primitive accumulation of capital—Initial capital accumulation by the emerging capitalist class.

production relations—The arrangements for producing goods and services in an economic system.

productive forces—The basic economic forces, for example labor and capital resources, of an economic system.

qualitative changes—Abrupt and violent changes caused by the conflict between old and new productive forces that create a new superstructure.

reform—Systemic changes designed to make the existing system work better.

soft budget constraint—Enterprises in socialist economic systems can live beyond their means because they are automatically bailed out by a higher authority.

spontaneous order—Spontaneous process in which institutions that "work" are sustained and improved while those that do not "work" are replaced.

superstructure—The organizational arrangements through which resources (productive forces) will be organized and utilized.

surplus value—Profits under capitalism derived from the exploitation of labor.

Thesis versus antithesis—Evolutionary and inevitable qualitative change that occurs through the competition of opposing forces.

transition—The replacement of one economic system by a fundamentally different economic system.

transition economics—Study of the process of converting the countries of the former Soviet Union and Eastern Europe from planned socialist economies into entirely different economic systems.

Notes

1. Douglass North, "Economic Performance Through Time," *American Economic Review* 84, no. 3 (June 1994), 359–368; Douglass North and Barry Weingast, "Constitutions and Commitment: The Evolution of Institutions Governing Public Choice in 17th Century England," *Journal of Economic History* 49, no. 4 (December 1989), 803–832; Mancur Olson, *The Rise and Decline of Nations* (New Haven: Yale University Press, 1982).
2. Oliver E. Williamson, *Markets and Hierarchies, Analysis and Antitrust Implications: A Study in the Economics of Internal Organization* (New York: Free Press, 1975); Ronald Coase, "The New Institutional Economics," *American Economic Review* 88, no. 2 (1998), 72–74.
3. Jon Cohen, in Thomas Rawski, ed., *Economics and the Historian* (Berkeley: University of California Press, 1996), pp. 60–84.
4. Paul David, "Path Dependence, its Critics and the Quest for 'historical economics,'" in P. Garrouste and S. Ioannides (eds), *Evolution and Path Dependence in Economic Ideas: Past and Present* (Cheltenham, England: Edward Elgar Publishing, 2000).
5. Friederick von Hayek, *Studies in Philosophy, Politics, and Economics* (New York: Norton, 1969).
6. Karl Marx, *Capital*, Vols. I–III, (Chicago: Charles Kerr and Company, 1906, 1909).
7. Our discussion of the economic theories of Marx and Friedrich Engels is based primarily on the following sources: Murray Wolfson, *A Reappraisal of Marxian Economics* (New York: Columbia University Press, 1966); Alexander Balinky, *Marx's Economics: Origin and Development* (Lexington, Mass.: Heath, 1970); John Gurley, *Challengers to Capitalism: Marx, Lenin, Mao* (San Francisco: San Francisco Book Company, 1976); William Baumol, Paul Samuelson, and Michio Morishima, "On Marx, the Transformation Problem, and Opacity—A Colloquium," *Journal of Economic Literature* 12 (March 1974), 51–77; *Grundlagen des Marxismus–Leninismus: Lehrbuch*, German translation of the 4th Russian edition (Berlin: Dietz Verlag, 1964); Karl Marx and Friedrich Engels, *The Communist Manifesto*, in Arthur Mendel, ed., *Essential Works of Marxism* (New York: Bantam Books, 1965), pp. 13–44; Paul Samuelson, "Understanding the Marxian Notion of Exploitation: A Summary of the So-called Transformation Problem Between Marxian Values and Competitive Prices," *Journal of Economic Literature* 9 (June 1971), 399–431.
8. According to Paul Sweezy, *The Theory of Capitalist Development* (New York: Monthly Review Press, 1968), Ch. 11, the Marx–Engels description of the end of capitalism and the coming of socialism was scattered and sketchy. Their failure to deal more thoroughly with the breakdown of capitalism led to the breakdown controversy among socialist writers—Eduard Bernstein, M. Tugan-Baranovsky, Karl Kautsky, Rosa Luxemburg, and others. The central issue of this controversy was whether a violent overthrow of capitalism was obviated by reform of the capitalist system and the capitalist government. For Lenin's view of Kautsky and "revisionism," see V. I. Lenin, *State*

and Revolution, in Mendel, *Essential Works of Marxism*, pp. 103–198; and V. I. Lenin, *Izbrannye proizvedeniia, Tom I* (Moscow: Gospolitizdat, 1960), pp. 56–63 ("Marxism and Revisionism").

 9. Neil Gross and Solon Simmons, "The Social and Political Views of American Professors," Working Paper, September 24, 2007, Harvard University, http://www.wjh.harvard.edu/~ngross/lounsbery_9-25.pdf.

10. The basic works are Joseph Schumpeter, *Capitalism, Socialism, and Democracy*, 3rd ed. (New York: Harper, 1950); and Joseph Schumpeter, *The Theory of Economic Development* (Cambridge, Mass.: Harvard University Press, 1934).

11. F. A. Hayek, *The Road to Serfdom* (Chicago: University of Chicago Press, 1944).

12. Ludwig von Mises, "Economic Calculation in Socialism," in Morris Bornstein, ed., *Comparative Economic Systems*, rev. ed. (Homewood, Ill.: Irwin, 1969), pp. 61–68.

13. See János Kornai, *Economics of Shortage*, Vols. A and B (New York: North-Holland, 1980); "Resource Constrained versus Demand Constrained Systems," *Econometrica* 47 (July 1979), 801–819; *Anti-Equilibrium: On Economic Systems Theory and the Tasks of Research* (Amsterdam: North-Holland, 1971); *Rush versus Harmonic Growth* (Amsterdam: North-Holland, 1972); *Overcentralization in Economic Administration* (London: Oxford University Press, 1959); *Growth, Shortage, and Efficiency: A Macrodynamic Model of the Socialist Economy* (Berkeley: University of California Press, 1983).

14. János Kornai, *The Socialist System*: The Political Economy of Communism (Princeton: Princeton University Press, 1992); John Bonin, "Janos Kornai, From Socialism to Capitalism: Eight Essays," *Journal of Economic Literature* 47, no. 3 (2009), 853.

15. Mathias Dewatripont and Eric Maskin, "Credit and Efficiency in Centralized and Decentralized Economies," *Review of Economic Studies* 62, no. 4 (1995), 541–555.

16. Mark Schaffer, "The Credible-Commitment Problem in the Center-Enterprise Relationship," *Journal of Comparative Economics* 13, no. 3 (1989), 80–103.

17. See Peter Murrell and Mancur Olson, "The Devolution of Centrally Planned Economies," *Journal of Comparative Economics* 15, no. 2 (June 1991), 239–266.

18. For descriptions of how these interest groups engage in rent-seeking behavior, see Josef Brada, "The Political Economy of Communist Foreign Trade Institutions and Policies," Michael Mandler and Randi Ryterman, "A Detour on the Road to the Market Coordination, Queues, and the Distribution of Income," and Michael Alexeev, "If Market Clearings Are So Good Then Why Doesn't (Almost) Anybody Want Them?" all in *Journal of Comparative Economics* 15, no. 2 (June 1991).

Recommended Readings

Marxism

Paul Baran, *The Political Economy of Growth* (New York: Monthly Review Press, 1957).

William Baumol, Paul Samuelson, and Michio Morishima, "On Marx, the Transformation Problem, and Opacity—A Colloquium," *Journal of Economic Literature* 12 (March 1974), 51–77.

John Gurley, *Challengers to Capitalism: Marx, Lenin, Mao* (San Francisco: San Francisco Book Company, 1976).

Oskar Lange, "Marxian Economics and Modern Economic Theory," *Review of Economic Studies* 2 (June 1935).

Earnest Mandel, *Marxist Economic Theory* (New York: Monthly Review Press, 1970).

Karl Marx, *Capital* (Chicago: Charles Kerr and Company), Vol. I, 1906; Vols. II and III, 1909.

Joan Robinson, *An Essay on Marxian Economics* (New York: Macmillan, 1966).

Paul Samuelson, "Understanding the Marxian Notion of Exploitation: A Summary of the
   So-called Transformation Problem Between Marxian Values and Competitive Prices,"
   Journal of Economic Literature 9 (June 1971), 399–431.
Leon Smolinsky, "Karl Marx and Mathematical Economics," *Journal of Political Economy*
   81 (September–October 1973), 1189–1204.
Paul Sweezy, *The Theory of Capitalist Development* (New York: Monthly Review Press,
   1968).
Murray Wolfson, *A Reappraisal of Marxian Economics* (New York: Columbia University
   Press, 1966).

Creative Destruction, Austrian Economics, New Institutional Economics

Ronald Coase, "The New Institutional Economics," *American Economic Review* 88, no. 2
   (1998), 72–74.
Paul David, "Path Dependence, its Critics and the Quest for 'Historical Economics,'" in
   P. Garrouste and S. Ioannides (eds.), *Evolution and Path Dependence in Economic
   Ideas: Past and Present* (Cheltenham, England: Edward Elgar Publishing, 2000).
F. A. Hayek, *Studies in Philosophy, Politics, and Economics* (New York: Norton, 1969).
Douglass North, "Economic Performance Through Time," *American Economic Review* 84,
   no. 3 (June 1994), 359–368.
Douglass North and Barry Weingast, "Constitutions and Commitment: The Evolution of
   Institutions Governing Public Choice in 17th Century England," *Journal of Economic
   History* 49, no. 4 (December 1989), 803–832.
Mancur Olson, *The Rise and Decline of Nations* (New Haven: Yale University Press, 1982).
Joseph Schumpeter, *Capitalism, Socialism and Democracy*, 3rd ed. (New York: Harper,
   1950).
———, *The Theory of Economic Development* (Cambridge, Mass.: Harvard University
   Press, 1934).
Oliver E. Williamson, *Markets and Hierarchies, Analysis and Antitrust Implications: A
   Study in the Economics of Internal Organization* (New York: Free Press, 1975).

Socialist Changes

Mathias Dewatripont and Eric Maskin, "Credit and Efficiency in Centralized and Decentra-
   lized Economies," *Review of Economic Studies* 62, no. 4 (1995), 541–555.
János Kornai, *Anti-Equilibrium: On Economic Systems Theory and the Tasks of Research*
   (Amsterdam: North-Holland, 1971).
———, *Economics of Shortage*, Vols. A and B (New York: North-Holland, 1980).
———, *Growth, Shortage, and Efficiency: A Macrodynamic Model of the Socialist Econ-
   omy* (Berkeley: University of California Press, 1983).
———, "Resource Constrained versus Demand Constrained Systems," *Econometrica* 47
   (July 1979), 801–819.
———, *Rush versus Harmonic Growth* (Amsterdam: North-Holland, 1972).
———, *The Road to a Free Economy* (New York: Norton, 1990).
———, *The Socialist System: The Political Economy of Communism* (Princeton, N.J.:
   Princeton University Press, 1992).
Richard Nelson and Sidney G. Winter, *An Evolutionary Theory of Economic Change*
   (Cambridge, Mass.: Harvard University Press, 1982).

CHAPTER

5

The Setting of Economic Systems

We are studying comparative economic systems from the vantage point of the beginning years of the second decade of the twenty-first century. We hope that what we learn will give us insights into things that are to come: What will be the constellations of economic systems as we reach the half century mark? Will the institutional arrangements that we know today be less recognizable forty years from now? Will socialism enjoy resurgence? Will we be dominated by the Chinese model of state capitalism, as some think?

Presumably, the economic system that is deemed to be the "best" in some sense will prevail. That constellation of arrangements that produces the best economic outcomes, it would seem, would "outcompete" others. Or are there disfunctionalities that will push us toward "inferior" economic systems as Friedrich Hayek warned in his *Road to Serfdom*?

Often the best prediction of the future is the past. In this chapter, we look back to describe the road to the present. What did the institutions that make up the economic system look like in the past, and how much change have they experienced? If the institutions of economic systems are changing rapidly, our study of present arrangements may yield a snapshot of something that will not be around tomorrow. If, however, institutions are changing slowly or have attained some "institutional equilibrium," then study of current economic systems makes more sense.

Our examination of the recent past focuses separately on changes in capitalist and socialist systems. We have already noted that change in capitalist systems tends to occur slowly, often imperceptibly. A time traveler who managed a large transportation corporation eighty years ago would not have much trouble understanding how such a corporation works in 2012. The basics of accounting, profits, and marketing would remain essentially the same. Change occurs more rapidly in planned socialist economies or, to use Hayek's term, collectivist economies, where change can be ordered from above. A manager of the Moscow Hammer and Cycle factory in the 1930s would not be able to comprehend how his old factory was being operated in 2012. Instead of plans and centrally allocated supplies, he would have to worry about markets, competition, prices, and profits, all of which were irrelevant eighty years earlier. A Chinese manager from 1975 would be challenged as well in understanding Chinese enterprise operations in 2012.

Changes in the Economic Environment

The environment (ENV) is a catchall term for factors that affect economic outcomes other than policies (POL) and the economic system (ES) itself. With such a broad definition, it is difficult to single out a few environmental factors whose change has been most notable and impactful over the past sixty years. There is, however, one singular environmental factor that has clearly changed the world in which we live: *An **information, telecommunications, and transportation revolution** has created a smaller, interconnected, and more competitive world.*

Young people today would be hard pressed to recognize the world in which we (the authors) spent our youth. Then, even middle-class families had one telephone (or shared a party line with another family); there was one family car, which teenagers had to beg to use. Telephone numbers had to be patiently dialed on rotary phones. Long-distance calls were considered a luxury. Most travel was by cars, trains, or buses; air travel was for the wealthy. A trip to Europe was a luxury for the superrich. The main forms of written communication were letter or telegram. We would have considered the Internet as something only a science fiction writer could dream up. Calculators were reserved for businesses and banks and weighed twenty pounds or more. There were virtually no imported cars other than luxury Jaguars or MGs until the Volkswagen entered our markets in the 1950s. The United States produced all of its own oil. The production potential of the Middle East was just being discovered.

In those years, Ronald Coase was just formulating his famous theorems, one of which pointed out the importance of information and transactions costs. With the information, telecommunications, and transportation revolution, information and transactions costs plummeted. Transactions whose costs earlier would have been prohibitive now became affordable. American consumers now had choices between cars produced in Detroit and cars produced in Germany and Japan. Corporations could now do business worldwide. International branches could communicate with each other in real time at virtually no cost. The lower middle class could now fly to distant destinations. Even Europe or Asia was not out of financial reach.

Globalization

The shrinking of the world increased the degree of competition. Local florists now had to compete with Internet sellers promising same-day delivery to any city or town. The local bank had to compete with national and international banks. Recruiters for engineers and scientists could make their pitches to graduates not only of American colleges and universities but also to graduates of Indian or British institutions of higher education, among others. Detroit automobile manufacturers had to compete not only among themselves but also with their counterparts in the rest of the world, many of which set up manufacturing facilities in the American South. Reservation and help-line services could answer questions 24/7 from remote locations in India, Poland, and South America.

Globalization is the increasing interlocking of the world's economies via expanding trade in goods, services, and capital. Globalization affects economic performance and the way we organize our economic institutions. With rising globalization, consumers can buy a wider assortment of goods and services at lower prices than if they had been confined to local markets. Businesses face more competition and must become more efficient and innovative to stay ahead of competitors. Legal institutions must adapt to the needs of international commerce. Contracts must be valid in the various jurisdictions in which the business operates. Businesses are no longer confined to raising capital in their own countries. They can issue new shares of capital in New York, Frankfurt, London, or even Beijing or borrow from Japanese or French banks. Executives of international businesses must understand how different cultures work if they are to be effective at their jobs.

Figure 5.1 shows the remarkable amount of globalization since the 1950s. Although the world economy has grown, word trade has grown much faster. The volume of imports plus exports has risen to equal about half of world GDP.

A remarkable by-product of the information revolution has been to turn national capital markets into a single world capital market. The Chinese government and other Asian investors buy U.S. government treasury bills. Fractional changes in interest rates in Japan cause billions of dollars to shift from Europe to

FIGURE 5.1   Globalization of the World Economy

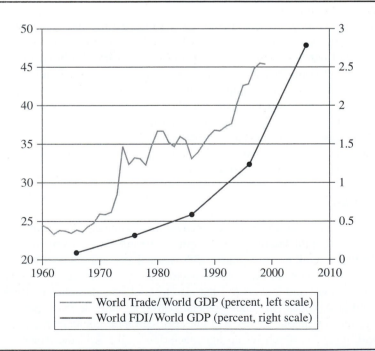

Source: Charles Jones and Paul Romer, "The New Kaldor Facts: Ideas, Institutions, Population, and Human Capital" (with Paul Romer) American Economic Journal: Macroeconomics, January 2010, Vol. 2 (1), pp. 224–245.

Australia in a fraction of a second. The stocks of Russian, European, and Asian companies are listed on the New York Stock Exchange. International investment houses such as Goldman Sachs arrange for the initial public offerings of stock in Russian, Chinese, and Indonesian companies.

This world capital market is huge. The market capitalization of all the world's stock markets combined is currently in the vicinity of $50 trillion. Even more remarkable is the huge flow of foreign direct investment among countries. *Foreign direct investment (FDI) is investment by investors in one country in companies in other countries by which the investors gain significant management control.* For much of this period, the country that attracted the most FDI has been China.

Rising Living Standards

Improvements in technology, like those of the information, telecommunications, and transportation revolution, helped elevate living standards. In fact, technological advances are the major explanation of increases in per capita GDP, the best single measure of living standards. The increase in world living standards, albeit not evenly spread across the globe, is another major change of the environment in which economic systems function.

Figure 5.2 shows the dramatic increase in world per capita GDP over the past sixty years. In 1950, the average person had a per capita income of less

FIGURE 5.2   Rising Per Capita GDP

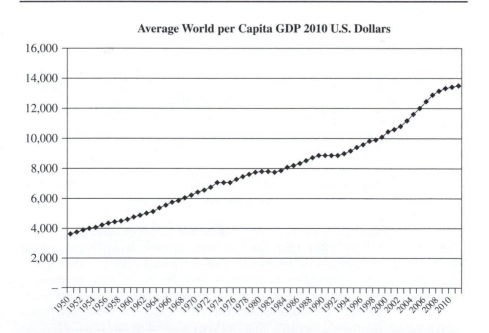

Average World per Capita GDP 2010 U.S. Dollars

Source: Complied from Angus Maddison Historical Statistics, http://www.ggdc.net/MADDISON/oriindex.htm.

than $4,000. In 2011, per capita GDP exceeded $13,000. Affluence can affect institutions just as institutions affect the economic growth that produces affluence.

Economist Henry Rowen has noted that all countries that had attained a GDP per capita of at least $8,000 per year ranked no worse than "partly free" in the ratings of political rights and civil liberties published by Freedom House. With the exception of oil-rich and population-poor Middle Eastern states, all affluent nations were ranked as "free."[1] In applying this standard to China and assuming continued rapid growth, China should become at least "partially free" within a few decades. According to this argument, democracy is a good that is increasing in demand along with affluence. It is only the poor countries that are "unfree" in the long run.

Although economic growth has not been even among the regions of the world (Africa, in particular, has experienced much less), new technology and innovation have made life better throughout the world. Due to the spread of cheap modern medicines, life expectancy in the Middle East, North Africa, South Asia, and Latin America has soared in the past three decades.[2]

Policy and System Change

We defined policy (POL) as changes in legislation, state policy, and regulation that affect economic outcomes but do not change the economic system. In subsequent chapters, we shall have a lot to say about policy. At this juncture, we wish to say a few words about significant policies that have altered economic outcomes.

Globalization and Competition

We just discussed the globalization that has so changed the ways we live our lives. This globalization is the result not only of the lowering of information and transportation costs. Policy makers who wish to hold back globalization—as perhaps harming domestic businesses—can do so through their command of policies. Indeed, constituencies and coalitions of manufacturers and trade unions are potent voices against globalization.

Globalization shows the intertwining of ENV and POL. One factor behind globalization is the environmental factor of declining information and transportation costs. Another factor is the adoption of policies that promote or retard globalization.

There is strong evidence that those countries that have welcomed globalization have prospered. Those that have tried to hold it back have lagged behind. The fastest-growing countries are export-oriented Asian countries. Although an export-oriented country could try to protect its own businesses from international competition, they can do so only at the risk of losing markets in the longer run. It is difficult to promote globalization and exports on the one hand and restrict imports on the other, even though China has been accused of this practice.

That economies should be open to international trade and finance and should reduce their barriers to trade enjoys a consensus (but not unanimity) among economists. ***Trade barriers** are tariffs, export subsidies, and other non-tariff barriers that are designed to reduce imports*. Trade barriers sprout up like weeds because they favor specific interest groups that stand to lose from free trade, whereas the benefits of free trade are spread over many that little notice that they are being hurt. In the United States, for example, few know that they are paying higher prices for sugar and other protected goods, while a few sugar producers earn substantial benefits from protection. Those customers who enjoy Walmart's low prices do not recognize that they are there thanks to free trade. American shoe, umbrella, and blender manufacturers certainly know how much they have lost.

The costs of trade protection are most obvious when tariffs and other forms of protection become so onerous that they stifle world economic development and growth. Such was the case with the passage of the disastrous Smoot-Hawley Tariff Act in the United States in June 1930, which caused world trade to shrivel and the Great Depression to worsen. In fact, some scholars assign Smoot-Hawley a major role in creating and prolonging the Depression. In the 1950s and 1960s, the United Nations UNCTAD organization under the misguided leadership of the Argentinean economist, Paul Prebisch, preached that poor countries should protect themselves from free trade under a policy of import substitution. ***Import substitution** is the protection of the domestic economy from foreign competition by tariff barriers so as to reserve the domestic economy for domestic producers*. Pakistan, India, Chile, and many other countries were held back for many years because of trade protection of their domestic industries.

Figure 5.3 shows that Smoot-Hawley raised import tariffs to 60 percent, meaning that the prices of imports were raised by about the same amount. It would be hard to imagine the globalization of the postwar period as being possible with such high tariffs.

Figure 5.3 also shows a rather consistent worldwide policy of tariff reductions from the peak rates in the Great Depression to the present, where average import duties are less than 10 percent.

*The consistent policy of trading countries to **lower trade barriers** throughout the postwar period contributed to the globalization of the world economy*. One of the best-documented trends of the past sixty years is the reduction of international trade barriers. The industrialized capitalist countries created international arrangements for dismantling the restrictive trade barriers that were erected during the Great Depression, and there is little doubt that the degree of international competition expanded rapidly throughout the postwar period. Europe has become one common market virtually free of trade barriers within its boundaries. The United States, Canada, and Mexico have signed the North American Free Trade Agreement (NAFTA), despite considerable political opposition in the United States. The United States under President Obama has a number of free trade agreements pending (such as with South Korea and Colombia), but Obama still faces considerable political opposition from within his own party.

FIGURE **5.3**   Average U.S. Import Duties, 1900–Present

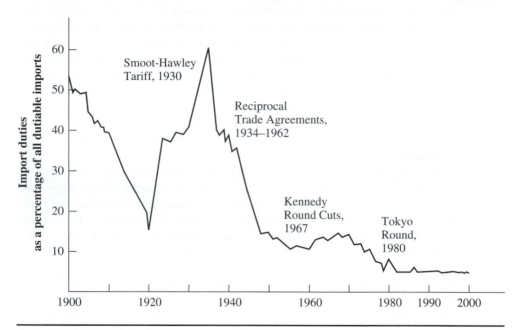

Sources: From GREGORY, Comparing Economic Systems in the Twenty-First Century, 7E. © 2004 Cengage Learning; Historical Statistics of the United States; Statistical Abstract of the United States.

Deregulation

There is no single measure of the degree of competition present in an economy. Clearly, the globalization of the world economy has made individual economies more competitive, but competition can also be affected by policies toward competition, such as the deregulation of potentially competitive industries. *Deregulation is the removal of state regulation of companies and industries, allowing them freedom in price setting and product quality.* Deregulation is intertwined with the economic system. One of the characteristics of an economic system is at what level and by whom economic decisions are made. If businesses are heavily regulated by government, this means a transfer of decision-making power to a higher authority. Therefore today's economic system is partially a product of past policy decisions on whether to regulate or deregulate.

Throughout the past three centuries, there has been a great deal of state regulation. However, regulation may have reached its peak during the seventeenth century, when labor markets and product markets were strictly regulated and controlled by state institutions under the philosophy of mercantilism. *Mercantilism was the notion that the state must strictly regulate all forms of economic activity to limit the flow of imports and grounds of political and economic security.* Although few economists encourage mercantilism, it was the dominant political-economic policy throughout Europe, especially in France, in the seventeenth century. It was

England that first broke with mercantilism when it reduced agricultural tariffs in 1804.

There are legitimate reasons for regulation in cases of monopoly producers or products, such as food and medicine, whose quality must be protected. However, custom and mercantilist thinking resulted in a number of companies and industries being regulated despite the fact that they were potentially competitive. In the United States, for example, brokerage fees, bank interest rates, trucking prices, and air fares were set by regulatory agencies prior to the 1980s. There was even more regulation of potentially competitive markets in Europe.

The trend toward deregulation started in the United States in the late 1970s, and it spread from North America to Western Europe and Japan in the 1980s. Deregulation has been most prominent in transportation, communications, and banking, but it remains to be seen whether other capitalist countries will deregulate to the extent of the United States and whether the deregulation experiment will continue well into the twenty-first century. The example of U.S. deregulation has clearly been spreading. The European Union has deregulated passenger airline traffic, telecommunications, and financial services as part of Europe's move to a single market.

An important perspective on deregulation in the American economy is provided by the major changes in airlines, telecommunications, trucking, and other important sectors of the economy during the 1980s.[3] According to a survey of the outcomes of this deregulation, fully regulated industries produced 17 percent of gross national product in 1977; by 1988, this share had decreased to 6.6 percent. Although the results of this deregulation experience have often been controversial, economic analysis suggests that the benefits have outweighed the costs, resulting in significant net gains for the American public.

The combination of globalization and deregulation has increased the amount of competition throughout much of the world. Telecommunication giants, such as AT&T and Deutsche Telekom compete for customers around the world. Europe's Airbus and the United States' Boeing Company compete ferociously for orders among Asian, American, and European airlines. Even bulky products like metallic coal can be shipped at economical costs to steel manufacturers in Asia from Australia and the Appalachian region of the United States. This means that American coal miners in West Virginia compete against their counterparts in Moranbah, Australia.

William Shepherd attempted to measure the changing degree of competition in the U.S. economy from the late 1930s to 1980. He concluded that the American economy became more competitive after 1960 as a consequence of growing international competition and deregulation. According to Shepherd, the share of the U.S. economy that was effectively competitive remained fairly stable at 52 to 54 percent between 1939 and 1958 but rose to 77 percent by 1980.[4] Similar studies have not been conducted for the other industrialized capitalist countries, so we do not know whether the American experience is representative. However, because virtually all industrialized capitalist countries have been subject to growing international competition, the impact of this development should be equally strong in other capitalist countries.

Trends in economic policy are reversible. A number of experts consider that the financial crisis that began in 2007 was caused by the too aggressive deregulation of financial services. They argue that we need to return to the days of stricter state regulation, when financial firms were prevented from taking on too much risk. Such advocates claim that government regulators could better have foreseen the systemic risks of lending for the housing market. Others argue that the financial crisis was instead the product of misguided regulation, in particular the U.S. government policy of encouraging mortgage lending to families with low incomes.

Whatever the case, the degree of competition that businesses face affects how they order their institutions and economic systems. It also affects their performance. China operates in a world market in which lower-wage countries are quite willing to steal their customers if they lag in efficiency. Competition is a threat that does not allow even state-owned companies to relax. In contrast, Soviet enterprises were isolated from world markets and from competition. There was no threat of a competitor to keep them honest and efficient. If a country whose economy must compete in a competitive world economy has "bad" economic institutions, it will lose out in the competitive struggle and lag behind.

Private versus Public Ownership

Property ownership is a distinguishing characteristic of economic systems. Marx used it as his most important criterion. Capitalism began, according to Marx, when the capitalist class monopolized the ownership of capital in the course of original capital accumulation.

Significant changes in the shares of public and private ownership of property alter the nature of the economic system. Indeed, if the state owns a major share of existing property, we would no longer classify the system as capitalist. At its peak, the Soviet state owned 99 percent of transportation, construction, and manufacturing.

Philosophers raised the issue long ago as to whether the state grants property rights or whether property belongs among the natural rights, along with life, liberty, and the pursuit of happiness. Marx felt that whoever was in charge of the state, be it landowners or capitalists, controlled property rights. The natural rights philosophers, most prominently John Locke (1632–1704), contended that private property is a right given by God and not by the state, when he wrote:

> Every man has a *property* in his own *person:* this no body has any right to but himself. The *labour* of his body, and the *work* of his hands, we may say, are properly his…. for this *labour* being the unquestionable property of the labourer, no man but he can have a right to what that is once joined to, at least where there is enough, and as good, left in common for others.[5]

For this reason, Locke advised that government's principal role should be the protection of private property.

All societies must confront how property is to be owned. Locke himself agreed that some property should be held commonly for the general welfare. Nations must decide whether their underground mineral resources are to be the property of the state or of the surface landowners. With respect to oil reserves, most nations have opted for state ownership. But there are many choices to be made: Should the schools be private or public? Should garbage be collected by public employees or private firms? Should health care be insured by the state or by private carriers?

Real-world capitalist systems are mixed, some having higher shares of public ownership than others. The mix changes when privatization or nationalization occurs. *Privatization is when property that had been state-owned is transferred to private owners. Nationalization occurs when privately owned property becomes publicly owned.* The shares of public ownership can be increased either by government investment that creates new government-owned capital (such as the U.S. government's Tennessee Valley Authority initiated during the Great Depression) or by direct government buying of existing facilities. The Russian government under president and then prime minister Vladimir Putin renationalized Russian oil and mineral companies. By selling their shares of British Air and Lufthansa, the British and German governments privatized what had been state companies by increasing the share of private ownership. Most of China's large companies are owned by the state, often with minority private ownership.

Public sentiment in favor of public ownership was high in the United States during the Great Depression, when many concluded that capitalism had failed. In the United States, government shares of structures and land have not changed noticeably since the early 1930s, nor has the share of output produced by government enterprises changed. After a rise in public ownership in the early 1930s, the share of government ownership remained fairly stable.

In the United Kingdom, the elections of Labor governments in the 1940s and 1950s provided political support for nationalization, whereas the lengthy tenure of a Conservative government from the mid- to late 1970s through the mid-1990s increased support for privatization. Alternating socialist and conservative governments in France also reflect rising and falling sentiment for privatization or nationalization. In Germany, both socialist and conservative governments have consistently favored privatization since the end of World War II. The German government has sold its shares of major corporations to private owners throughout the postwar era. One of the largest such privatization was the sale of what had been the German telephone monopoly, Deutsche Telekom. In Japan, one of the most heated political issues of the last two decades has been the privatization of its state-owned postal saving banks.

Table 5.1 shows the government shares of fixed capital in 1970, 1980, and 1997 in seven industrialized capitalist countries including Greece as the poorest. The differences in ownership shares partially result from different accounting procedures, but even so, substantial changes in government ownership shares within each country cannot be observed from these figures. In some countries, government ownership shares have fallen since 1980 (Canada, Australia, Belgium, and Greece). In others, they have risen (United Kingdom, Finland, and Sweden). In the majority of countries, government shares of capital have been stable over the twenty-five-year period.

TABLE **5.1**   Share of Government Ownership of Fixed Capital, Capitalist
Countries (percentages of total)

	1970	1980	1997
Australia	17	18	14
Belgium	15	15	13
Canada	20	24	19
Finland	16	16	20
Germany	8	8	8
Greece	2	1	1
Italy	—	15	15
Norway	—	17	18
Sweden	—	13	12
United Kingdom	5	6	7

Source: OECD, *Flows and Stocks of Fixed Capital* (Paris: OECD, various years).

In Germany and Italy, government ownership shares either were unchanged or changed only slightly.

Figure 5.4 shows that the production of government enterprises as a percent of GDP varied considerably among industrialized countries. At its peak, government enterprises produced some 15 percent of GDP in Austria and 12–13 percent in France. These figures are somewhat dated, and we imagine that more recent government enterprise shares are lower. But Figure 5.4 shows no strong trend over the thirty-year period from 1950 to 1980. In no industrialized country does state enterprise account for more than a relatively small share of output.

Figure 5.5 shows what branches of the economy tend to be dominated by government enterprises in different countries around the globe. It is more common for transportation and utilities (like electricity, gas, and water) to be produced by public enterprises. Agriculture and commerce are dominated, as one might expect, by private enterprise.

The share of public and private enterprise is a prime characteristic of the economic system. This distribution should affect economic performance. Locke pointed out in 1690 that few would have the incentive to use their effort to develop and improve property unless their rights to that property were protected. Hayek and Ludwig von Mises argued that even honest and patriotic managers of state enterprises would be hard pressed to operate public enterprises efficiently. In fact, in Stalin's Russia, there was an "honest manager's dilemma," whereby even uncorrupted managers did not know how to properly fulfill their state plans.[6]

Overall, there has been little change in private and public ownership shares in capitalist countries, which suggests that these countries have reached a basic consensus on the distribution of public and private ownership. Changes in governments over the years have not notably altered this consensus.

Gone, for now at least, are the days when government enterprise was seen as the engine of the future and as a means of ensuring fairness in the business sector. During the early postwar period, the British Labor Party favored the nationalization

FIGURE 5.4   Public Enterprise Share of GDP (selected industrialized countries)

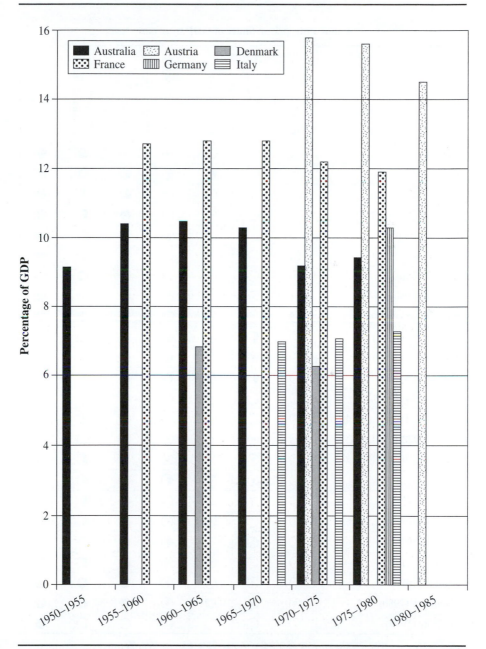

Source: From "The Role of Public Enterprises: An International Statistical Comparison," in Robert Floyd, Clive Gray, and Robert Short, eds., *Public Enterprise in Mixed Economies* (Washington, D.C.: IMF, 1984), pp. 110–196. Reprinted by permission of the International Monetary Fund.

FIGURE 5.5   Distribution of State Enterprises By Economic Branch

Public Enterprises' Share of GDP by Sector

	Agriculture	Commerce Personal Services	Construction	Manufacturing	Mining	Transport Communication	Electricity, Gas and Water
Austria (1970–75)	○	○	○	◉	◉	●	●
France (1971)	○	○	◐	◐	◐	◕	●
Italy (1975)	○	○	○	◉	◐	◐	●
United Kingdom (1975)	○	○	○	○	●	◐	●
Congo (1980)	○	○	◉	◉	○	◐	●
Ivory Coast (1979)	○	○	◉	○	◉	◐	●
Kenya (1980)	○	○	○	○	○	◕	●
Senegal (1980)	○	◉	○	○	●	○	●
Sierra Leone (1979)	○	○	○	○	◉	◕	●
Tanzania (1980–81)	○	◐	◉	◐	●	○	◐
Bangladesh (1980)	○	◉	○	◐	●	○	●
Burma (1980)	○	◐	●	◕	●	◐	●
India (1978)	○	○	◉	○	●	◐	●
Republic of Korea (1974–77)	○	○	○	○	◉	◐	●
Nepal (1978–79)	○	◉		◉	○	○	◉
Pakistan (1980)	○	◉	○	◉	◉	◐	●
Sri Lanka (1974)	○	◉	◉	◐	○	◐	●
Greece (1979)	○			○	●	◐	◐
Portugal (1976)	○	○	○	◉	○	◐	◐
Tunisia (1976)	○	○		◐	◐	◕	●
Argentina (1980)	○	○	◉	◉	◐	◐	◐
Mexico (1980)	○	◉	○	◉	●	◕	●
Nicaragua (1980)	◉	◉	◕	◉	●	◕	●
Uruguay (1979)	○	○	○	○	○	○	●

Note: < 5% ○; 5%~25% ◉; 25%~50% ◐; 50%~75% ◕; >75% ●.

Source: UNIDO; World Bank (1983); Peter Short (1984). Adapted from Yair Aharoni (1986, figure 1.2)

of whole industries, often those that were in the most trouble. The trend in England at the time was for a Labor government to nationalize and the next Conservative government to undo their work. Nationalization appears to have been dropped from the British Labor Party's agenda, especially with the coming of a "new labor party" under Tony Blair, who was British Prime Minister from 1997 to 2007. In only a few countries are there trends toward more state enterprise. In China, the Communist Party has argued for continued state ownership of the most important companies, called "national champions." Hugo Chávez in Venezuela has nationalized foreign companies in the name of "the poor." Vladimir Putin in Russia has raised state ownership (or control) of oil, pipeline, and mineral companies, reversing earlier privatizations.

Regulation and Corruption

The Heritage Foundation's Economic Freedom indexes provide measures of "business freedom, which captures the amount of intervention by various levels of government in business affairs, such as regulations, licensing, and inspections." It also provides a corruption index, which measures how corrupt government officials are in their dealings.

Figure 5.6 shows a strong positive correlation between business freedom and lack of corruption. (Note that a high figure means less corruption.) In effect, the more state intervention in the affairs of businesses, the greater the opportunities for official corruption. In many countries around the globe, health and fire inspectors have to be bribed. Agencies that issue business licenses or export licenses have to be paid under the table. Regulation is a way for corrupt officials to enrich themselves. The less the regulation, the fewer such opportunities for giving and accepting bribes.

The Role of Government: Share of Output and Income Redistribution

Although government production and shares of capital show no clear trend throughout the world, the government's claim on output has increased in almost all countries over the long run. Government has not increased its share of output or capital in the long run, but its expenditures on goods and services and transfers have risen over time.

Figure 5.7 shows a distinct pattern: Most European countries have a GDP share of government expenditure of 50 percent or above. The United States and Canada in North America, Japan and South Korea in Asia, and Australia in the South Pacific have kept their ratios below 50 percent. Figure 5.7 also reveals that countries whose governments grow "too large" have been able to reverse the trend toward bigger government, examples being Sweden and the Netherlands, which have reduced the government expenditure share.

Figure 5.8 provides a long-run historical perspective on government spending in the United States. It shows the inexorable rise in the government's share of output, beginning at well below 10 percent at the turn of the previous century and

FIGURE **5.6**   The Correlation between Business Freedom and Corruption

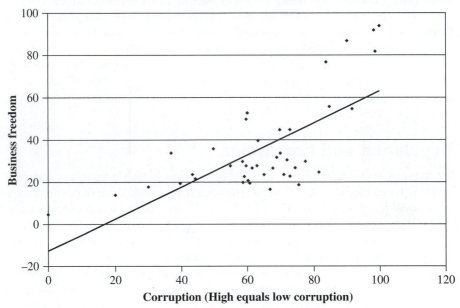

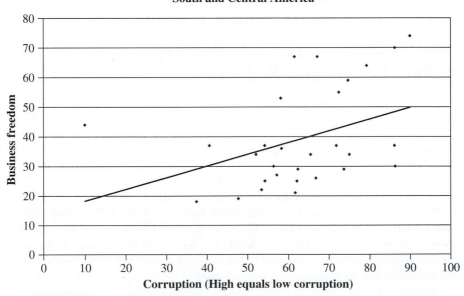

Source: Based on data from The Heritage Foundation, http://www.heritage.org/index/explore.

FIGURE 5.7   Government Expenditure as a Percentage of GDP

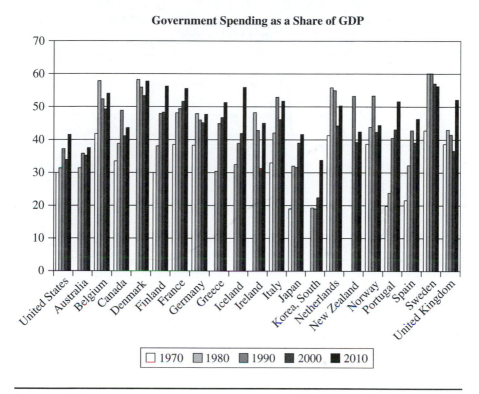

Government Spending as a Share of GDP

□ 1970   ■ 1980   ■ 1990   ■ 2000   ■ 2010

Source: Statistical Abstract of the United States.

spiking to contemporary levels only during periods of world war. The spending levels that used to be the result of war have become "normal" in our contemporary world.

Taxes and Redistribution

Capitalism uses material incentives to motivate economic behavior, and a move away from material incentives would signal a fundamental change in the capitalist economic system. If a capitalist state altered the distribution of income earned in factor markets, wages and profits would become less decisive in determining command over resources. For example, if the tax system equalized the distribution of income after taxes, material rewards would cease to guide economic decision making. Changes in tax policy can indeed change the nature of the capitalist economic system.

For a tax system to have a large impact on the reward system, taxes must make up a large share of income, and the tax system must redistribute income. Income is

Figure **5.8**   U.S. Government Spending: A Century Perspective

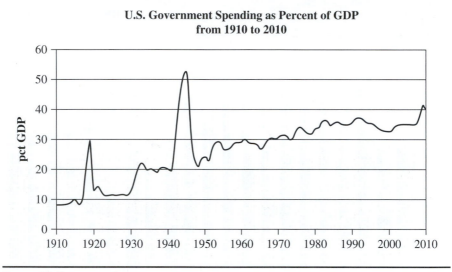

Source: US Government Data.

redistributed via either a progressive tax (which redistributes proportionally away from high-income earners) or a *regressive tax* (which redistributes proportionally away from low-income earners). *In a **progressive tax system**, the tax's share of income rises with income. In a **regressive system**, the tax's share of income falls with rising income.* In order to redistribute income away from high-income earners, the tax system must take up a large share of income earned and must be progressive.

Taxes and Social Expenditures

Figure 5.9 shows that in almost all industrialized countries, taxes rose as a percentage of GDP over the long run, but not as much as expenditures. Because 2009 (the end year in the figure) was a year of recession, tax revenues as a percent of GDP actually fell relative to 1995. The highest taxed countries tend to be in the heart of Europe and in Scandinavia. The United States, Australia, Japan, and Korea are among those with lower shares of taxes to GDP.

The shares of taxes on income and profits, labor, and goods in Table 5.2 provide indirect information on the redistributive role of the tax system. Taxes on income and profits tend to be progressive, whereas taxes on goods and services are regressive. Taxes on labor, such as payroll taxes, are usually regressive because they apply to wages and salaries usually levied up to an upper limit.

Assuming no significant changes in income tax rates by income bracket, the tax system would become more progressive as a whole when the share of income taxes rose. The tax system would become more regressive as a whole when the shares of taxes on goods and labor rise.

FIGURE 5.9   Taxes as a Percent of GDP

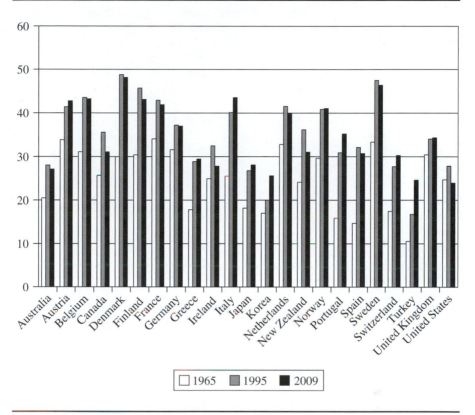

Source: Based on data from OECD Tax Database.

Table 5.2 shows that the mature European nations typically tax labor (social security contributions) and goods and services (value added taxes) about equally, at around one third of all taxes. Taxes on income and profits account for a smaller share. The shares of social security taxes have been high throughout the period. Countries that began with low shares of taxes on labor, such as the United States, Canada, and Korea, experienced substantial increases in the share of social security taxes. Japan went from being below European levels to high by European standards. Relatively few economies rely primarily on income taxes, as the United States does.

What have governments done with the increasing tax share of GDP? Figure 5.10 shows the gradual rise in public social spending as a percent of national income in Europe, in the top 30 industrialized countries (OECD-30) and in the United States, Japan, and Mexico. The pattern is for very high public social expenditures in Europe at currently between 30 and 35 percent of national income. (Sweden even reached near 45 percent in the early 1990s.) The U.S. share rose from about 15 to 18 percent

TABLE 5.2   Distribution of Taxes by Type, 1965–2008

	1965	1995	2008
Austria			
Social security	24.9	36.0	33.5
Goods and services	37.4	28.6	27.1
Income and profits	25.5	26.3	30.7
Belgium			
Social security	31.4	32.9	31.5
Goods and services	37.2	25.7	24.5
Income and profits	27.6	38.1	38.0
Canada			
Social security	5.6	14.0	14.7
Goods and services	40.5	25.4	23.6
Income and profits	38.6	46.4	49.1
France			
Social security	34.2	42.9	37.2
Goods and services	38.4	27.6	24.5
Income and profits	15.9	16.3	24.1
Germany			
Social security	26.8	39.0	37.6
Goods and services	33.0	28.0	28.5
Income and profits	33.8	30.3	31.1
Greece			
Social security	31.6	32.4	37.6
Goods and services	48.8	41.3	34.9
Income and profits	9.1	22.3	22.5
Ireland			
Social security	6.5	14.4	17.7
Goods and services	52.6	40.7	37.1
Income and profits	25.7	39.1	37.6
Italy			
Social security	34.2	31.5	31.2
Goods and services	39.5	27.3	24.5
Income and profits	17.8	35.3	34.4
Japan			
Social security	21.8	33.5	38.6
Goods and services	26.2	15.8	18.0
Income and profits	43.9	38.3	33.7
Korea			
Social security	0.7	12.1	21.8
Goods and services	62.0	40.7	31.6
Income and profits	23.0	30.1	31.0

TABLE 5.2   Distribution of Taxes by Type, 1965–2008 (cont.)

	1965	1995	2008
Netherlands			
Social security	30.8	41.9	37.0
Goods and services	28.6	27.2	30.3
Income and profits	35.8	26.3	27.2
Norway			
Social security	11.9	23.5	20.9
Goods and services	41.1	38.6	25.6
Income and profits	43.4	35.1	50.8
Portugal			
Social security	21.8	30.5	32.7
Goods and services	47.6	40.9	36.6
Income and profits	24.6	24.9	26.3
Spain			
Social security	28.3	36.2	36.4
Goods and services	40.8	28.6	25.1
Income and profits	24.5	29.2	30.9
Sweden			
Social security	12.1	27.6	24.8
Goods and services	31.2	28.1	27.7
Income and profits	54.9	39.3	36.3
United Kingdom			
Social security	15.4	17.8	19.0
Goods and services	33.1	35.3	28.8
Income and profits	37.0	36.9	40.0
United States			
Social security	13.3	24.9	25.1
Goods and services	22.8	18.0	17.6
Income and profits	48.1	46.0	45.2

Source: OECD Tax Data Base.

and has since risen even more. Japan rose the most, from 13 to near 25 percent. Countries with less generous public benefits like Korea and Japan have seen rising benefits, but they remain under 10 percent of national income.

How is this rising share of public social expenditures financed? The European budget data presented in the tables and figures included in this chapter show that state expenditures are about half of GDP. Social security taxes (which are levied to cover public social expenditures) are some third of total taxation, which means that they are roughly 15 percent of GDP. Yet public expenditures are about one third of GDP. About half of public social expenditures must be covered out of other revenue sources. In the United States, social security taxes account for less than 10 percent of GDP, whereas spending for social purposes is slightly over 15 percent. As in Europe, a significant share of social public spending must be financed from other budget sources.

FIGURE **5.10**   Public Social Spending as a Percent of Net National Income

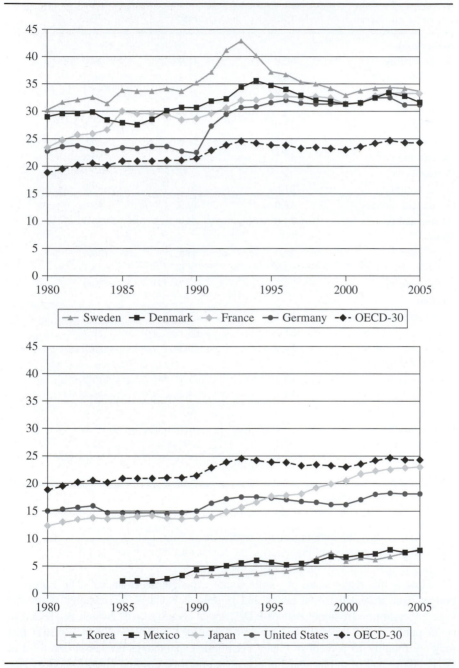

Source: OECD (2008), Social Expenditure Database, 1980–2005, http://www.oecd.org/els/social/
expenditure.

Taxes and Income Redistribution

We can draw only cautious conclusions about the degree of progressivity or regressivity in the tax system. The figures in this chapter show there has been a substantial increase in the share of taxes in the industrialized countries, but there has not been a substantial shift in the form of taxation. The slight drift away from taxes on goods and toward taxes on income (which should increase progressivity) has been relatively minor. The overall conclusion is that the redistributive role of the tax system has not changed much in capitalist economies, even though the share of taxes has been rising.

The evidence that has been collected for the United States shows that the U.S. tax system as a whole (federal, state, and local taxes) is slightly progressive and did not change much between the 1970s and the present.[7] Studies for the United States show that the tax system does not materially alter the distribution of income, but the distribution of transfers does.[8] The major instrument of income redistribution in the United States is the distribution of transfer payments to low-income recipients and the elderly. Note that the two groups are not the same. A high percentage of the elderly belongs to the top income brackets. In 2004, government spending equaled $22,000 per elderly person, whereas expenditures on children equaled $9,000 per child.[9] If we include the value of goods and services received, particularly by the elderly, the U.S. distribution is more equal by almost 20 percent.[10]

Change in Socialist Economies

Although change in the capitalist West may appear to be significant, it has been mild compared to change in the socialist economies of the former Soviet Union, Eastern Europe, and Asia. With the minor exceptions of Cuba and North Korea, planned socialist economies either have been dramatically changed through the process of reform or have been abandoned through the process of transition.

We reiterate that reform is the process of changing (improving) an existing system. Transition is the movement from one economic system (planned socialism) to another (capitalism). In all cases, reform and transition have been motivated by economic performance. In the cases of the former Soviet Union and Eastern Europe, the decision to begin transition was motivated by declining growth rates, the failure to find ways to grow through intensive growth (rather than extensive growth), rising consumer dissatisfaction, and the general sense of being left behind by the other world economies.

Many reasons have been advanced to explain the general slackening of their economic performance, but the fact remains that the planned socialist economies found the transformation from extensive to intensive growth very difficult. The basic Stalinist model, although draconian and costly, had served to bring idle and underused resources into the production process in the early decades. However, the luxury of idle resources was, for many socialist systems, over by the late 1960s.

We shall later explore why intensification in socialist systems proved so difficult. Clearly there were consumer pressures in these systems, and clearly they grew more complex over time. Advances in planning methods did not keep pace with the demands on the planning system. The diffusion of technology was inadequate. These systems were not demand-driven, and enterprise rules generally did not stimulate growth in productivity and cost reduction. Efficiency was simply not a hallmark of the Stalinist command economy. Moreover, in contrast to the cyclical nature of productivity problems in market systems, socialist systems seemed to experience long, steady declines in productivity growth through the 1980s.

Interest in socialist reform began in the 1960s and grew in the 1980s and 1990s. By the mid-1980s, performance in most socialist systems had slipped alarmingly. With inadequate incentives, there appeared to be little hope for improved productivity. Moreover, most socialist countries had not been able to compete well enough in export markets to afford significant imports of consumer products. Seen in this perspective, the imperative of reform was evident, although the sudden spread of radical change in the late 1980s caught most observers by surprise.

Backdrop of Reform

The Soviet experiment with planned socialism began in earnest in the late 1920s with the introduction of command planning to industry and of forced collectivization to agriculture. The economic system that Stalin created in the late 1920s and early 1930s proved durable. It was introduced into Eastern Europe by Soviet troops at the end of World War II, and it found its way into China with the victory of communist forces there.

Prior to the early 1960s, reform of the Stalinist economic system was not possible. According to Stalinist dogma, the system was perfect. Any failures encountered were the result of human error or sabotage. Such thinking did not provide fertile ground for reform. The death of Stalin and the ensuing mild liberation allowed discussion of reform to begin. The problems of the planned socialist economy were apparent, and it was natural to consider improving the system.

The Soviet Communist Party officially approved such discussion when the official communist newspaper, *Pravda*, published the reform proposals of an obscure economist, Evsei Liberman, in 1962. In this fashion, reform discussion was initiated in the Soviet Union and Eastern Europe. Although official reforms in the Soviet Union were modest, reforms in Eastern Europe were more substantial. Hungary, for example, initiated a long and careful reform process designed to orient its economy more toward the consumer. None of these reforms, either in thought or in content, was designed to replace the planned socialist economy with a market capitalist economy.

China, after experiencing cataclysmic political upheavals in the 1950s and 1960s, embarked on its own reform program in the late 1970s. The Chinese path to reform focused on unleashing private initiative in agriculture and small business and on opening the Chinese economy to world capital and product markets. China's suppression of student revolts in June 1989 signaled that China was not prepared to combine economic reform with democracy. China's example stands out as a reform that has generated rapid economic growth under a political dictatorship.

Socialist Reform Models

Reform of planned socialist economic systems focused on changes in some or all of the system components. However, prior to the dramatic changes of the late 1980s and 1990s, most reform in socialist systems was very modest and was characterized as an attempt, by means of very limited changes, to make the existing system work better.

Socialist economic reform has focused on reform models that differ in intensity. We characterize socialist economic reform in terms of three basic variants: making planning work better, changes in organizational arrangements, and decentralization of decision making.

Improving the Planning Mechanism   Improving planning is a weak alternative— one that signals unwillingness to make serious changes in the economic system. The arguments in support of this alternative are that problems of economic performance arise largely because planning had not been perfected and that planning can be improved through the application of more sophisticated computer technology. To the extent that enterprise managers make bad decisions because they lack information, ready access to accurate information through an advanced computer network would alleviate the problem. It is assumed that better planning methods, better information channels, and more attention to incentive compatibility could perfect the planning system and improve economic performance. The 1970s were devoted to a number of attempts to improve planning both in the Soviet Union and in Eastern Europe. Each experiment was introduced with fanfare and then forgotten as it proved impotent.

Organizational Reform   Changing the organizational arrangements of the existing plan structure represents a second reform alternative. *An **organizational reform** is the introduction of intermediate organizations into the organizational hierarchy.* Ministries, it was argued, are too distant from the enterprises they supervise. Moreover, each ministry supervises enterprises that produce too diverse an array of products. Ministries cannot keep in touch with enterprises and do not truly understand their problems. Thus an intermediate agency or association should be inserted between the ministries and groups of enterprises that produce similar products. The intermediate association, it is argued, could understand and manage a particular group of firms more successfully.

Another way to implement organizational reform would be to shift the emphasis from sectoral to regional planning. An economy planned on a sectoral basis may place the interests of the branch above national interests. A shift to regional planning might loosen the grip of an entrenched bureaucracy and encourage a better flow of information among units in the economy. It was this type of reform that Nikita Khrushchev tried, without success, in the Soviet Union of the late 1950s and early 1960s. Most—although not all—past reform attempts in socialist systems have been organizational in nature.

Decentralization   Decentralization is the third broad category of socialist economic reform. ***Decentralization*** *is a shifting of decision-making authority and responsibility from upper to lower levels.* Decentralization is often viewed as "real" reform that can fundamentally change the nature of economic systems and, especially, reduce the role of central planning.

Decentralization implies that decisions about resource allocation can be shifted downward in the economic hierarchy. Most important, in a decentralized economy, decisions are not made by planners but are reached at lower levels by means of market-like signals. ***Economic levers*** *are prices, profits, and rates of return that can guide socialist managers in their decision making.* Decentralization of decision making entails both the devolution of decision-making authority and responsibility *and* the use of different decision-making tools in the process. To put it another way, although planning still exists, decentralization implies that local decision makers pay less attention to planners and more attention to market signals.

This type of economic reform was characterized as real reform or significant reform to distinguish it from organizational change. Taken to its limits, it might be called radical reform. Its existence raises new and difficult questions about the development of markets—and thus market signals—in systems previously dominated by planners, by state ownership of property, and by an absence of market signals.

Record of Socialist Reform

China has recorded rapid economic growth since the introduction of its reforms in the late 1970s, but the other attempts to reform the planned socialist economies through organizational change, improvements in planning, and decentralization failed. China is firmly on a path of transition from what was once a planned socialist to an open market economy. However, much of Chinese heavy industry is owned and controlled by the state, and remnants of central planning persist in the form of heavy-handed industrial policy managed by the monopoly Communist Party.

The failure of reform in the Soviet Union and Eastern Europe had far-reaching consequences culminating in the decision to abandon the planned socialist system and to move to a market capitalist system. As the dominant force in the former Soviet bloc, the Soviet Union is where the actions that made this move possible originated.

Declining economic performance in the Soviet Union and Eastern Europe, despite repeated reform efforts in the 1970s and early 1980s, convinced the leaders of the Soviet Communist Party that radical change was necessary. They appointed a relatively young and vigorous general secretary, Mikhail Gorbachev, to lead this reform effort, which Gorbachev immediately described as radical to distinguish it from the modest reforms of the past. Internationally, Gorbachev relaxed Soviet political control over Eastern Europe. As a result, these countries gained their political independence and their freedom to experiment with reform and transition. The collapse of the Soviet Union in December 1991 allowed an additional fifteen former republics of the Soviet Union to select their economic systems freely.

The Collapse of Communism: Contemporary Transition

Following the emergence of communist economist system in Russia in the early 1930s, very little systemic change occurred. For the most part, economic reform was limited, inconsequential, and had little or no impact on performance. This picture changed in major ways in the late 1980s and early 1990s when the Soviet Empire, its politics and its economics, collapsed. This collapse introduced the era of transition, or the replacement of one economic system by another. Market economic systems generally replaced command or planned economic systems. We shall devote a great deal of attention to transition in later chapters. Although there has been a measure of normalization in the transition economies, the transition paths have been quite different among the transition economies.

The economies of Eastern Europe and the Soviet Union began their transitions in the late 1980s (Eastern Europe) and in late 1991 or early 1992 (the former Soviet Union). Hence we now have some twenty years of experience with transition successes and failures. We have a number of transition successes (Poland, Hungary, the Czech Republic, Slovenia, and the Baltic states). But we also have transition failures in those economies that sought to continue the Soviet model in Belarus and Central Asia. No transition economy, even the most successful, experienced a smooth introduction of market forces.

The transition economies have entered a new era with respect to the reformulation of their economic systems. If we take the case of Russia, there has been a fundamental restructuring of property rights—one of the fundamental institutions of an economic system. In Figure 5.11(A) we see the degree to which property rights changed from state to nonstate ownership just a few years after transition began in Russia. Figure 5.11(B) shows the significant shift of the Russian labor force away from the state sector and toward the nonstate sector. A similar conclusion can be derived from Figure 5.11(C), which shows the movement away from state-owned housing and toward private housing.

These changes are very significant, and even though observers argue that the Putin-Medvedev "tandem" has expanded the role of the Russian state, these fundamental changes in property rights cannot be reversed.

Such major changes have taken place in a relatively modest span of time, and they have not been without significant costs, both political and economic. Each country undergoing transition experienced substantial declines in output, dramatic changes in the distribution of income, and rampant inflation. These costs have created political backlashes that have returned to power those who favor the old system, but even sympathizers with the old regime have not reverted to it.

Finally, the combination of transition and a young democracy has proved to be difficult. Politicians in newly democratic countries must somehow enact transition policies that are costly in terms of lost political support. This difficult combination has created considerable interest in the Chinese reform model, which has combined market-oriented reforms with Communist Party dictatorship. The Chinese model, as we will observe, is different from many other transition economies and has been applied in a unique setting.

FIGURE 5.11(A)   Nonstate Shares of Capital (Russia)

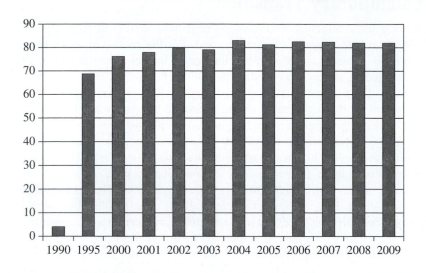

Source: Based on *Natsional'nye scheta Rossii v 1989–1994 gg.* (Moscow: Goskomstat, 1995), p. 71; *Sotsial'naia sfera Rossii* (Moscow: Goskomstat, 1995), p. 26; http://www.gks.ru/bgd/regl/b08_12/Iss WWW.exe/stg/d02/24-03.htm; http://www.gks.ru/bgd/regl/b10_12/IssWWW.exe/stg/d02/24-03.htm.

FIGURE 5.11(B)   Distribution of Russian Labor Force (type of enterprise)

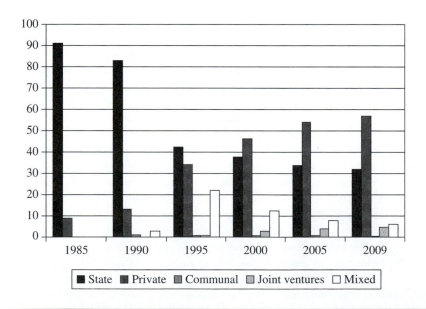

Source: Based on *Natsional'nye scheta Rossii v 1989–1994 gg.* (Moscow: Goskomstat, 1995), p. 71; *Sotsial'naia sfera Rossii* (Moscow: Goskomstat, 1995), p. 26; http://www.gks.ru/bgd/regl/b08_12/Iss WWW.exe/stg/ d02/24-03.htm; http://www.gks.ru/bgd/regl/b10_12/IssWWW.exe/stg/d02/24-03.htm.

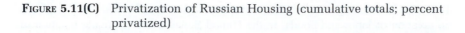

FIGURE 5.11(C)   Privatization of Russian Housing (cumulative totals; percent privatized)

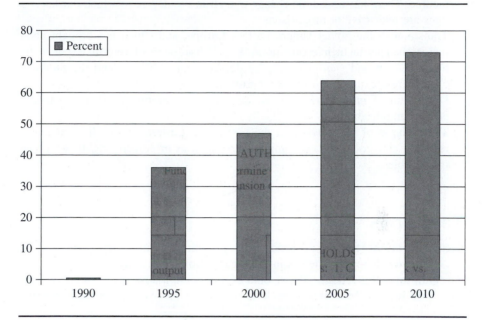

Source: Based on *Natsional'nye scheta Rossii v 1989–1994 gg.* (Moscow: Goskomstat, 1995), p. 71; *Sotsial'naia sfera Rossii* (Moscow: Goskomstat, 1995), p. 26; http://www.gks.ru/bgd/regl/b08_12/Iss WWW.exe/stg/d02/24-03.htm; http://www.gks.ru/bgd/regl/b10_12/IssWWW.exe/stg/d02/24-03.htm.

Although the final outcomes of transition are not fully known, the former Soviet Union and Eastern Europe have taken the first steps of dismantling the power structure on which their planned economic systems were based. The planned socialist economy no longer exists, although the nature of the market-type replacement has changed and will continue to change over time.

Summary

- A key change in the environment of economic systems has been the information, telecommunications, and transportation revolution, which lowered transactions cost and promoted competition, globalization, and rising per capita income.
- Globalization was also promoted by policies that reduced trade barriers. Deregulation has also increased competition.
- Property rights and ownership are affected by nationalization and privatization. The shares of state ownership and production have not changed much over the past decades.
- Government shares of output have increased over time with the highest shares in Europe. Taxes as a percent of GDP have also increased significantly.

- Taxes are levied on goods, labor, and income. In Europe, there is more emphasis on taxation of labor and goods. In the United States, there is greater taxation of income. There has been little change overall in the degree to which our tax systems are regressive or progressive.
- Transition in the Soviet Union, Eastern Europe, and China has brought about major changes in their economic systems. Discussion of reform began in the Soviet Union and was motivated by declining growth rates and the failure to change from extensive to intensive growth.
- Discussion of reform centered on organizational reform, improving planning, and decentralization.
- The collapse of communism in the USSR and Eastern Europe has led to far-reaching changes in the economic system, such as in property rights, which are irreversible.

Key Terms

decentralization—Shifting decision-making authority and responsibility from higher levels to lower levels in the organizational hierarchy.

deregulation—Reduction in the amount of regulation a business or industry faces.

economic levers—Mechanisms such as prices and profits used to guide socialist managers.

foreign direct investment (FDI)—Investment by investors in one country in companies in other countries by which the investors gain significant management control.

globalization—Increasing interlocking of the world's economies via expanding trade in goods, services, and capital.

import substitution—Protection of the domestic economy from foreign competition by tariff barriers so as to reserve the domestic economy for domestic producers.

information, telecommunications, and transportation revolution—Technological changes that lower transactions costs in domestic and international trade.

mercantilism—Notion that the state must strictly regulate all forms of economic activity to limit the flow of imports and grounds of political and economic security.

nationalization—When privately owned property becomes publicly owned.

organizational reform—Changes in organizational arrangements that comprise an economic system.

privatization—Property that had been state-owned is transferred to private owners.

progressive tax—Higher income earners pay a larger share of their incomes in taxation.

regressive tax—Higher income earners pay a smaller share of their incomes in taxation.

trade barriers—Tariffs, export subsidies, and other non-tariff barriers that are designed to reduce imports.

Notes

1. Henry Rowen, "When Will the Chinese People Be Free?" *Journal of Democracy* 18, no. 3 (2007), 38.
2. Charles Kenny, *Getting Better: How Global Development is Succeeding—and How We Can Improve the World Even More* (New York: Basic Books, 2011).
3. Clifford Winston, "Economic Deregulation: Days of Reckoning for Microeconomists," *Journal of Economic Literature* 31, no. 3 (September 1993), 1263–1289.
4. William G. Shepherd, "Causes of Increased Competition in the U.S. Economy, 1939–1980," *Review of Economics and Statistics* (November 1982), 613–626.
5. John Locke, *Two Treatises of Government* (1690), Chapter 6: On Property.
6. Eugenia Belova, "Economic Crime and Punishment," in Paul Gregory (ed.), *Behind the Façade of Stalin's Command Economy* (Stanford: Hoover Institution Press, 2001), chap. 7.
7. Brian Roach, "Progressive and Regressive Taxation in the United States: Who's Really Paying (and Not Paying) their Fair Share?" Global Development and Environment Institute, Working Paper No. 02-10, October 2003.
8. Edgar K. Browning, "The Trend Toward Equality in the Distribution of Net Income," *Southern Economic Journal* 43 (July 1976), 914.
9. Julia B. Isaacs, "Spending on Children and the Elderly," The Brookings Center on Children and Families, November 2009.
10. U.S. Census Bureau, "The Effect of Taxes and Transfers on Income and Poverty in the United States: 2005," *Current Population Reports*, March 2007, P60–232.

Recommended Readings

Change of Capitalist Economies

Richard R. Nelson and Sidney G. Winter, *An Evolutionary Theory of Economic Change* (Cambridge, Mass.: Harvard University Press, 1982).

R. D. Norton, "Industrial Policy and American Renewal," *Journal of Economic Literature* 24, no. 1 (March 1986), 1–40.

Nitin Nohria and Robert G. Eccles, eds., *Networks and Organizations: Structure, Form, and Action* (Boston: Harvard Business School Press, 1993).

Richard B. Freeman, "Unionism Comes to the Public Sector," *Journal of Economic Literature* 24, no. 1 (March 1986), pp. 41–86.

William G. Shepherd, "Causes of Increased Competition in the U.S. Economy, 1939–1980," *Review of Economics and Statistics* (November 1982), 613–626.

Grahame Thompson, Jennifer Frances, Rosalind Levacic, and Jeremy Mitchell, eds., *Markets Hierarchies and Networks: The Coordination of Social Life* (London: Sage Publications, 1991).

Michael L. Vasu, Debra W. Stewart, and S. David Garson, *Organizational Behavior and Public Management*, 2nd ed., revised and expanded (New York: Marcel Dekker, 1990).

Leonard W. Weiss and Michael W. Klass, eds., *Regulatory Reform: What Actually Happened* (Boston: Little, Brown, 1986).

Oliver E. Williamson and Sidney G. Winter, eds., *The Nature of the Firm: Origins, Evolution and Development* (Oxford: Oxford University Press, 1991).

Clifford Winston, "Economic Deregulation: Days of Reckoning for Microeconomists," *Journal of Economic Literature* 31, no. 3 (September 1993), 1263–1289.

The Socialist Economy: Reform and Transition

Anders Aslund, *Building Capitalism: The Transformation of the Former Soviet Bloc* (New York: Cambridge University Press, 2001).

Robert W. Campbell, *The Socialist Economies in Transition: A Primer on Semi-Reformed Systems* (Bloomington: Indiana University Press, 1991).

Christopher Clague and Gorden Rausser, *The Emergence of Market Economies in Eastern Europe* (Cambridge: Blackwell, 1992).

Sebastian Edwards, "The Sequencing of Economic Reform: Analytical Issues and Lessons from the Latin American Experience," *World Economy* 1 (1990).

Paul R. Gregory and Robert C. Stuart, *Russian and Soviet Economic Performance and Structure*, 7th ed. (Reading, Mass: Addison Wesley Longman, 2001), chap. 12.

Edward P. Lazear, *Economic Transition in Eastern Europe and Russia* (Stanford: Hoover Institution, 1995).

Peter Murrell, "Public Choice and the Transformation of Socialism," *Journal of Comparative Economics* 14 (June 1991), 203–210.

Daniel Treisman, *The Return: Russia's Journey From Gorbachev to Medvedev* (New York: Free Press, 2011).

Economic Systems in Theory

CHAPTER
6

Theory of Capitalism

This chapter is about the *theory* of capitalism. Subsequent chapters discuss capitalism in practice in its various manifestations. We identify three models of capitalism that differ in institutions and practice: the Anglo-Saxon, the European, and the Asian models.

This chapter asks *how* and *how well* capitalist market economies should *in theory* solve the problem of allocating scarce resources among competing ends. This issue needs to be raised for two reasons. First, theories of economic systems offer hypotheses concerning performance, which we hope can be tested against real-world experience. Second, theoretical models tell us something about the performance of economic systems under *ideal conditions*. Because actual economies diverge from the theoretical ideal, they do not reveal the system's performance if it operated under conditions associated with a theoretical ideal.[1]

The confrontation of the socialist model with its real-world manifestations has proven disappointing. In contemporary debates in Europe and the United States, some use economic theory to advocate market-oriented solutions with limited government and worry that real-world economies have strayed too far from this ideal. Others doubt market-based solutions and favor more state intervention. They fear that we rely too much on markets and that there is too little state intervention.

Economics, unlike some other social sciences, has a core theory that is accepted by all parties in economic debates. There remain substantive differences, such as the efficacy of Keynesian economics, but there is general agreement on consumer choice, the competitive firm, and supply and demand. There is also agreement that there can be market imperfections, such as monopoly, and market failures. Disagreements arise because of different emphases, such as whether market failures are harmful enough to warrant government intervention or regulation.

Moral Philosophers: Thomas Hobbes, John Locke, and Adam Smith

The giants of political economics, writing in England in the seventeenth and eighteenth centuries, did not call themselves economists. Rather, they described themselves as moral philosophers, dedicated to answering fundamental questions about how humans organize themselves in a society. These "worldly philosophers" considered how we produce, consume, and regulate our everyday economic and political lives.[2] They wanted to know whether we are naturally cooperative and require limited government, or naturally uncooperative and belligerent, such that society can exist only with a strong state.

Thomas Hobbes: The Leviathan State

Thomas Hobbes's (1588–1679) masterwork, *The Leviathan*, was published in England in 1660, as the power of the king was under heated debate. Hobbes, often accused of being an apologist for the divine right of kings, argued in his *Leviathan* that competition is deeply rooted in human nature. Competition makes men "invade for gain" and "use violence to make themselves masters of other men's possessions." A "condition of nature" would be tantamount to a "condition of war of every man against every man." ***The Leviathan** is the term Hobbes used to describe the all-powerful state that he advocated.*

In the condition of nature, contracts and covenants are "void upon any reasonable suspicion" by either of the contracting parties. In such a dog-eat-dog world, people can reach and honor agreements only "if there be a common power set over them both, with right and force sufficient to compel performance.... For he that performs first has no assurance the other will perform after, without the fear of some coercive power."

A powerful government is the only way to make order out of this natural state of conflict, violence, and war against each other:

> But in a civil estate, the only way to erect such a common power is to appoint one man, or assembly of men, to bear their person; and ... therein to submit their wills, every one to his will, and their judgments to his judgment.... For by this authority, given him by every particular man in the Commonwealth, he hath the use of so much power and strength conferred on him that, by terror thereof, he is enabled to form the wills of them all.[3]

In other words, Hobbes argued that societies require a powerful sovereign to control the natural tendency of people to feud, violate agreements, and steal. This Leviathan, as Hobbes called it, must have sufficient authority to cowe its subjects into submission to its judgments and will. In turn, the Leviathan's subjects should accept the "peace and defense" that state power to "terrorize" brings about.

John Locke: The Social Contract

John Locke (1632–1704) was an English philosopher and physician, called the father of liberalism. He published anonymously his *Two Treatises of Government* in 1689.[4]

In these books, Locke enunciated a philosophy of natural rights in which individuals' rights to private property derive from their effort. We create property through our own labor, such as a farmer clearing and irrigating fields. It is our work or perhaps the work of forefathers that has created this property; therefore, it is our right to own it. Such property rights should be secure and protected by the state.

According to Locke, "legitimate government is instituted by the explicit consent of those governed. Those who make this agreement, transfer to the government their right of executing the law of nature and judging their own case. These are the powers which they give to the central government, and this is what makes the justice system of governments a legitimate function of such governments."

Locke proposed a form of government based on a social contract between the government and the governed. *Locke's **social contract** states that the people contract together consensually to establish a limited government. Only such a government is legitimate.* To quote Locke:

> And thus every man, by consenting with others to make one body politic under one government, puts himself under an obligation to every one of that society to submit to the determination of the majority, and to be concluded by it; or else this original compact, whereby he with others incorporates into one society, would signify nothing …

The power of the government should be limited; citizens have no obligation to obey the government if it violates the social contract:

> The people cannot delegate to government the power to do anything which would be unlawful for them to do themselves.… whenever the Legislators endeavor to take away, and destroy the property of the people, or to reduce them to slavery under arbitrary power, they put themselves into a state of war with the people, who are thereupon absolved from any farther obedience.

If the government exceeds the power delegated to it, citizens have the right to dissolve that government and return to their "original liberty":

> Whenever therefore the legislative shall transgress this fundamental rule of society, and either by ambition, fear, folly or corruption, endeavor to grasp themselves, or put into the hands of any other an absolute power over the lives, liberties, and estates of the people; by this breach of trust they forfeit the power the people had put into their hands, for quite contrary ends, and it devolves to the people, who have a right to resume their original liberty.

In sum, Locke, contrary to Hobbes, favored a government "of the people, by the people and for the people." He favored a government whose power is strictly limited to the powers that the people themselves have given it. That government cannot take away natural rights, such as the right to property. If it exceeds the bounds of the social contract, the government becomes null and void, and the people need no longer obey it.

Adam Smith: The Invisible Hand

The pioneering analysis of free-market capitalism is Adam Smith's *The Wealth of Nations*, published in 1776. Smith (1723–1790) was a Scottish philosopher, aptly called the father of economics. His classic *Wealth of Nations* was written as an attack on the prevailing system of pervasive state controls of the economy, called mercantilism.[5] Mercantilists maintained that economies must be heavily regulated by the state to prevent a loss of resources to rival nations. Mercantilism was practiced throughout western Europe, including England, but it was particularly strong in France, where intrusive state regulation was comparable to the later Soviet planned economy.[6]

Smith turned Hobbes's notion of destructive competition on its head. Smith concluded that the very competition that Hobbes condemned, surprisingly, causes individuals to serve the general welfare by pursuing their selfish aims. In such a setting, a strong state's intervention in individual affairs is more likely to cause harm than good.

An invisible hand of markets causes selfish individuals to promote the public interest by voluntarily producing and exchanging goods in the marketplace. *Smith's invisible hand states that a highly efficient and harmonious economic system is the result if competitive markets function freely without government intervention.* To quote Smith:

> Every individual … generally, indeed, neither intends to promote the public interest, nor knows how much he is promoting it. By preferring the support of domestic to that of foreign industry he intends only his own security; and by directing that industry in such a manner as its produce may be of the greatest value, he intends only his own gain, and he is in this, as in many other cases, led by an *invisible hand* to promote an end which was no part of his intention.

Smith wrote further on the invisible hand using this memorable phrase: "It is not from the benevolence of the butcher, the brewer, or the baker that we expect our dinner, but from their regard to their own interest."

Smith's most striking insight was that any intervention of the state in the economic dealings among self-interested persons is more likely to do harm than good. He argued that,

> It is the highest impertinence and presumption, therefore, in kings and ministers, to pretend to watch over the economy of private people, and to restrain their expense.… They are themselves always, and without any exception, the greatest spendthrifts in the society. Let them look well after their own expense, and they may safely trust private people with theirs. If their own extravagance does not ruin the state, that of their subjects never will.

Smith's policy prescription—the state should leave the private economy alone—is encapsulated in the term laissez-faire. *Laissez-faire (French for "let it be") is a policy that says that the state should not intervene in private economic transactions except in strictly limited cases.*

In sum, Smith argued that if individuals were given free rein to pursue their own selfish interests, the invisible hand of competitive markets would cause them to behave in a socially responsible manner. Products desired by consumers would be produced in the appropriate assortments and quantities, and the most efficient means of production would be used. No government or social action would be required. Individuals acting in their own interests could be counted on to do the right thing. In fact, government action would probably interfere with this natural process, so government should be limited to providing those essential public services that private enterprise could not produce on its own.

Smith's notion of a natural tendency toward an efficient economic equilibrium was the foundation of the liberal economic thought of the nineteenth century, which is now the free-market ideology of the twenty-first century. In the words of one authority, Smith's most important triumph was that "he put into the center of economics the systematic analysis of the behavior of individuals pursuing their self-interest under conditions of competition," and this remains "the foundation of the theory of resource allocation."[7] Most of the later theorizing aimed at a further elaboration of Smith's vision of market capitalism.

How Markets Work

The theory of capitalism, first formulated by Smith, focuses on demand and supply determining prices for factors such as labor (factor markets) and products such as consumer goods (product markets). *A **market** is any organizational arrangement that brings buyers and sellers together.* Markets provide the institutional mechanism for harmonizing consumers' desires with producers' ability to satisfy these desires.

Market Equilibrium

Smith's description of markets was left to modern economists to complete. Partial equilibrium assumes that two motivating forces drive market capitalism: the desire of producers to maximize profits and the desire of consumers to maximize their own welfare (utility) subject to the constraint of limited income.[8] Under competitive conditions, producers supply larger quantities at higher prices, while combining inputs to minimize costs. Consumers, seeking to maximize their welfare, will purchase less at higher prices. The producer and consumer meet in the marketplace, where their conflicting objectives are brought into equilibrium. If the quantity demanded exceeds the quantity supplied at the prevailing price, the price automatically rises, squeezing out some demand and evoking a larger supply until all those willing to buy and all those willing to sell at the prevailing price can do so. At this point, an equilibrium price is established, the market clears, and there is no tendency to depart from the equilibrium unless it is disrupted by some exogenous change (see Figure 6.1).

All other things being equal, an increase in consumer demand disrupts the established equilibrium, and the price starts to rise. As the price rises, producers

FIGURE 6.1   Market Equilibrium in a Competitive Economy

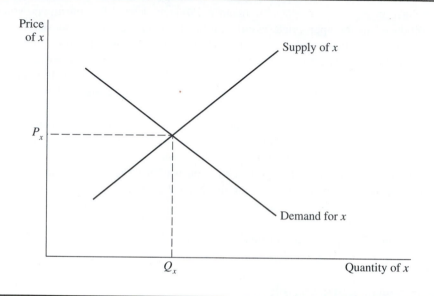

Explanation: In a competitive market economy, the price at which *x* sells will be P_x. If the price were *below* this level, the quantity demanded would exceed the quantity supplied. The *shortage* of *x* then would cause the price of *x* to rise. If the price were *above* P_x, the quantity supplied would exceed the quantity demanded. The surplus of *x* then would cause the price of *x* to fall. Only at P_x is the quantity supplied equal to the quantity demanded (Q_x).

Source: From GREGORY, Comparing Economic Systems in the Twenty-First Century, 7E. © 2004 Cengage Learning.

find it in their interest to supply larger quantities. If larger profits can be obtained at the new price, additional producers enter the market. On the demand side, the rise in the price causes substitution of now less expensive commodities and income effects, thereby reducing the quantity demanded (see Figure 6.2). The increase in demand causes resources to be shifted automatically to the product in greater demand, and the wants of the consuming public are met without intervention from outside forces. Consumers are said to be sovereign because the economy responds to changes in their demand.

Efficiency of Market Allocation

There are two arguments for the efficiency of market allocation. *Efficiency measures how effectively the factors of production are combined to produce output using available technology.*

With perfectly competitive markets, production will take place at the point where the marginal cost of society's resources equals the marginal benefit to consumers. Firms that operate in competitive markets produce the level of output that equates price and marginal cost, and that price is set in the marketplace. When costs and benefits are not equal at the margin, society can gain by producing

FIGURE **6.2**   Consumer Sovereignty in a Competitive Economy

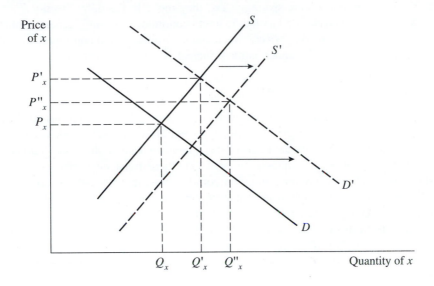

Explanation: We begin with the market for *x* in equilibrium at price P_x and quantity Q_x. *There is an increase in consumer demand from D to D'.* As a consequence, the price of *x* rises to P'_x and the equilibrium quantity *rises* to Q'_x. If economic profits are being made at this new price, new firms will enter the market and the supply curve will eventually shift to S'. Now a new long-run equilibrium is established at price P''_x and quantity Q''_x. An increase in consumer demand *automatically* leads to an increase in the quantity produced. The long-run effect on market prices depends on the entry of new firms at the higher price.

Source: From GREGORY, Comparing Economic Systems in the Twenty-First Century, 7E. © 2004 Cengage Learning.

more or less of the product. For example, if price exceeds marginal cost, the product yields more benefits than costs, and society can gain by producing more. If marginal costs exceed price, too much of the product has been produced, and production should be reduced.

F. A. Hayek emphasized a second proefficiency property of markets: their ability to generate information in an efficient manner.[9] *Hayek's information economics analyzes how markets cause specialization in the generation and utilization of information.*

Hayek wrote that the principal economic problem is not how to allocate resources but "how to secure the best use of resources known to any member of society, for ends whose relative importance only these individuals know. Or, to put it briefly, it is a problem of the utilization of knowledge not given to anyone in its totality."[10] Consumers and producers specialize in information about prices, products, and location that is relevant to them in their daily lives. Economic agents need not know all prices, products, and locations to behave efficiently in the marketplace.

Hayek wrote to illustrate that "The marvel is that in a case like that of a scarcity of one raw material, without any order being issued, without more than perhaps a handful of people knowing the cause, tens of thousands of people whose identity could not be ascertained by months of investigation, are made to use the material or its products more sparingly; i.e., they move in the right direction."

According to Hayek, the fact that market economies efficiently generate information in the form of market prices, which enable producers and consumers to plan their actions in a rational manner, is the principal advantage of capitalism.

Markets and Institutions

The invisible hand of markets works within a framework of institutions. If these institutions are absent, markets work poorly or not at all. Markets work when parties to transactions abide by the terms of the agreement; that is, they enter into contracts that they obey. If contracts are violated, there must be public or private institutions, such as courts or arbitration commissions, that resolve the dispute. It is also necessary that people respect private property and that illegal violations of private property rights be punished.

These legal institutions are termed the rule of law. *A **rule of law** prevails when participants in the economy agree on the legal rules concerning social and economic behavior, adhere to these rules, and are punished when they violate the rule of law.*

Economies must also have established arrangements for monetary and fiscal policy. ***Monetary policy** is conducted by a central bank, which determines the quantity of money and credit conditions.* ***Fiscal policy** is how the state collects taxes and spends revenue.*

Economic transactions are carried out in money, which serves as a medium of exchange, unit of account, and standard of deferred payment. If the money supply is not under control, hyperinflation can result, and transactions are carried out in barter rather than money terms. If the state does not have a predictable system for collecting taxes and spending revenues, businesses will not be able to calculate their tax burden and hence cannot make informed economic decisions. If the state can confiscate private property via excessive taxes, property rights are not protected.

Market economies require financial intermediaries, such as banks. ***Financial intermediaries** link savers and borrowers in financial markets that include banks and other bank-like institutions.* Savers and investors are brought together by financial intermediaries, who attract the savings of individuals and then make loans to businesses that require credit. Financial intermediaries cannot operate without a rule of law and without reasonable monetary policy. Savers will not deposit their funds if they cannot trust banks; banks would find it difficult to attract deposits if there is a fear of hyperinflation.

In a number of countries, the basic rule of law is set out in a constitution. *A **constitution** establishes the basic political, economic, and social rules of the game for a society.* For example, a constitution might spell out the degree to which private property is protected, the basic rights of citizens, and the cases in which the state can intervene in private economic activity. The United States and modern Germany and Japan are examples of market economies based on formal constitutions.

Other countries, such as the United Kingdom and France, have basic rules of the game that evolved over relatively long periods of time and cannot be traced to one single event, such as the ratification of a constitution. Constitutions are not immutable; they can be amended, but the process of amendment is usually difficult and time-consuming.

Capitalist economies consist of a wide variety of markets. Some are simple and others complex. **Simple markets** *are markets that do not require sophisticated institutions.* Examples of simple markets would be a farmers' market in rural Bolivia or cash-and-carry trade where the merchants pay in cash and carry away the goods themselves to sell. In contrast, **complex markets** *require sophisticated institutional infrastructure that often deal in nonhomogeneous goods and services that may be bought in one period of time and sold in another period of time or that involve a series of payments over time.*[11]

A farmer selling vegetables at a roadside stand does not require sophisticated legal and business institutions. A bank making a twenty-year mortgage loan or a trader in futures markets for commodities needs sophisticated business and legal institutions, such as contract enforcement mechanisms, stable monetary policy, and common understanding of ethical business behavior in order to carry out transactions.[12]

Rationale for State Intervention

Critics of the harmonious model of capitalism argue that we need state intervention to deal with monopoly power, externalities, public goods, and income-distribution problems. They also stress the inherent cyclical instability of capitalism and the problems of making rational public choices.[13] The question we consider here is in what instances state intervention may be necessary to correct deficiencies in market allocation.

Monopoly

The costs of monopoly were known even before publication of *The Wealth of Nations.* Smith warned that "People of the same trade seldom meet together, even for merriment and diversion, but the conversation ends in a conspiracy against the public, or in some contrivance to raise prices."[14] A **monopolist** *is the sole producer of a product for which there are no good substitutes. The monopolist has power to set the price of the product.*

The crux of the monopoly problem is the monopolist's inclination to hold output below the competitive level.[15] Monopolists underproduce and overcharge relative to competitive producers. Monopoly causes a "deadweight loss" in that the gains of the monopolist are less than the losses to consumers. Figure 6.3 demonstrates that monopolies produce less and charge higher prices than competitive markets.

Economic theory suggests four approaches to the control of monopoly, three of which require state intervention. The first is to use the state's authority to *tax and subsidize* to induce the monopolist to expand output to the competitive level, while at the same time producing a social tax dividend for society. The obvious difficulty

FIGURE 6.3   The Competitive and Monopolistic Models

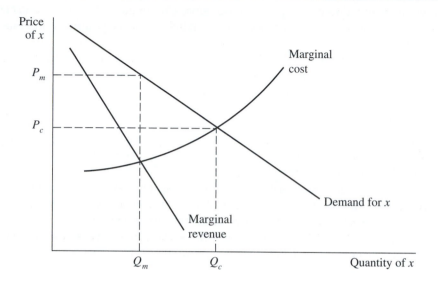

Explanation: This diagram presents the models of price and output determination under conditions of perfect competition and monopoly.

Let us suppose that industry X could be organized either as a monopoly (with a single producer) or as a competitive industry (with a large number of producers). The marginal costs are the same whether the industry is a monopoly or is perfectly competitive. The industry demand schedule and the industry marginal-cost schedule are given in the diagram. The latter is the marginal-cost schedule of the monopolist (in the case of the monopolistic industry) or the sum of the individual marginal-cost schedules of producers (in the case of the competitive industry). Because the demand schedule is negatively sloped, the monopolist's marginal revenue is less than the product price. To maximize profits, the monopolist produces that output (Q_m) at which marginal cost and marginal revenue are equated and sells this output at the price dictated by the market (P_m). Competitive producers produce output levels at which the product price and marginal costs are equal; therefore, the supply schedule of the competitive industry is the industry marginal-cost schedule. The competitively organized industry produces Q_c, and the product sells for P_c.

The monopoly produces less than the competitive industry and charges a higher price. The monopolist charges a price greater than the marginal costs of production, whereas the competitive industry equates price and marginal cost. Because price and marginal revenue are not equal, an economy made up of monopolies is not efficient.

Source: From GREGORY, Comparing Economic Systems in the Twenty-First Century, 7E. © 2004 Cengage Learning.

is that tax authorities must make quite sophisticated calculations and be able to enforce their orders. In the real world, this is more difficult than it is on paper.

Regulation is a second form of state intervention. ***Regulation** is the setting of prices and product quality by an agency of the state.* Theoretically, state regulatory authorities could force the monopolist to charge a regulated price equal to marginal costs. However, the monopoly could inflate its costs to obtain a higher regulated price. Marginal-cost pricing would probably force the monopolist to operate at a loss and require subsidization.

In virtually all cases, regulators eventually allow regulated monopolies to charge prices that cover their costs plus a guaranteed rate of return. Therefore, monopolies have little incentive to economize on costs, and they overspend on investment in order to obtain more profits through the guaranteed rate of return.[16]

Regulatory capture provides a final reason for skepticism. ***Regulatory capture refers to the fact that regulators favor the interests of the monopolist rather than the interests of the public***. Regulated industries are said to "capture" their regulators because of their lobbying power. The benefits of lax regulation to the producer are large, and the costs to consumers are diffused. Regulators end up "working" in the interests of those they regulate rather than the public they are supposed to serve.[17]

Antitrust legislation is a third form of intervention. In the case of antitrust legislation, the state may break up a monopoly or it may prevent mergers from taking place. In these cases, it hopes to transform the industry from monopolistic to competitive.

The fourth proposal is to simply leave monopolies alone. Milton Friedman argued that an unregulated monopoly performs better than a regulated monopoly.[18] Monopolists face Joseph Schumpeter's creative destruction and cannot get by indefinitely with an inefficient use of resources. The unregulated monopoly must keep its costs down and innovate if it wishes to avoid competition. Regulated monopolies are protected by regulators and are not under pressure to hold down costs and introduce new products and technologies.

External Effects and Collective Action

In cases where businesses impose costs and benefits on others not reflected in their own costs, the price system fails to reflect true costs and benefits. ***Externalities occur where the actions of one producer or consumer directly affect the costs or utilities of others outside of the price system***.[19] Examples of externalities are the dumping of wastes into a river by one producer, requiring a downstream producer to increase costs by installing water purification equipment or a neighbor with a rundown house who lowers the property values of neighbors.

When externalities are present, the allocation of resources is not optimal, even if the economy is competitive. Producers do not take the external impact of their actions into account. Rather, they seek to maximize their private profit on the basis of their private costs, not on the basis of social costs. ***Social costs*** *equal the private cost plus the unpriced cost of the externality*. The producer of an external harmful effect therefore produces an output level in excess of the optimum, for the private producer tends to underestimate the true social costs of production (Figure 6.4).

Economic theory suggests remedies for externalities. One is internalization. ***Internalization*** *is an action that makes the cost of the externality a private cost*. An example of internalization would be merging the enterprises producing external effects and those being affected by them. Consider the example of the waste-dumping factory. If it merged with the downstream factory, the water purification costs would become private costs for the combined enterprise, and waste dumping would be limited as a natural consequence of profit maximization.

FIGURE 6.4   The Inefficiency of External Costs

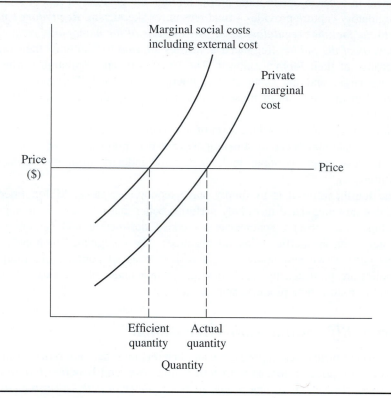

Explanation: When externalities are present, enterprises base their decisions on private marginal costs. This perfectly competitive firm produces where *P* = private marginal cost, not where *P* = full marginal cost. Therefore externalities cause competitive firms to produce more than the optimal quantity.

Source: From GREGORY, Comparing Economic Systems in the Twenty-First Century, 7E. © 2004 Cengage Learning.

In the absence of internalization, remedies may require state action, such as taxation and subsidies, to equate private and social costs. If appropriate taxes and subsidies cannot be levied, another alternative is regulation. In theory, regulators could order producers to supply the optimal output, but it is unclear how to do this in practice. In addition, those producing the externalities may have a strong political lobby.

Ronald Coase suggested voluntary agreements as a third solution.[20] Coase contends that whenever harmful externalities exist, the affected parties have opportunities for gains from trade by striking deals. The shared gains from an agreement must exceed the costs of transacting the agreement in order for this to work. If the transaction costs of agreement are low, voluntary agreements can correct the misallocation of resources caused by external effects.

When a small number of parties are involved, voluntary agreements are feasible. When the agreement must be ratified by a large number of parties, some of whom have relatively small stakes in the matter, the probability of reaching a mutually acceptable agreement is small.

Problems of Public Choice

Capitalism is associated with democratic political institutions. The political scientist, Seymore Lipset, argued that democracy is strongest and most durable in affluent economies,[21] a proposition that has considerable empirical support. Robert Barro, for example, shows the fragility of democracy in poor countries and its durability in affluent countries.[22]

Public-choice economics studies the efficiency of public decision making in democratic societies. In particular, public-choice economists study whether choices with respect to public goods will be efficient. ***Public goods*** *are goods where non-payers (called free riders) cannot be prevented from enjoying the benefits of the public good, and one person's use of the good does not generally prevent others from using it.* Both of these features make it difficult for the private sector to produce national defense, police protection, a legal system, dams, flood control projects, and the like, in efficient quantities.

Political scientists typically assumed that democracy would ensure "good" public choices. If a government spending project were bad for society, a majority (or their elected representatives) would vote against it. Public-choice theorists, such as Nobel Laureate James Buchanan, concluded, however, that certain factors prevent efficient public choices in a democratic society.[23]

Efficiency requires, at a minimum, that the marginal benefits of the public good equal or exceed its marginal costs. Public-choice theory outlines a number of potential problems. First, majority voting fails to consider the intensity of preferences among voters. A number of voters may have intense feelings about a specific public-expenditure decision, whereas others may be virtually indifferent. Yet each person's vote counts equally, and changes in preferences typically do not change the voting outcome.

In a majority-rule system, the median voter decides the outcome. ***The median voter*** *separates the lower half of the voting population from the higher half.* In a majority election, the candidate who wins will have a policy position closest to that of the median voter. This means that there will be little diversity in political platforms because the chances of winning are greatest when each candidate tries to get as close to the median voter as possible.

Democracies engage in vote trading and logrolling. A group that favors one public-expenditure program may offer its support for the program of a second group if that group will form a majority coalition. Through such logrolling, public-expenditure programs may be enacted where marginal costs exceed marginal benefits.

Politicians are in the business of getting reelected and are likely to serve special-interest groups that finance elections. The voter, on the other hand, does not have a great incentive to be well informed about public-choice issues. Individual voters are aware that their single vote is unlikely to change any outcome, and the costs of gathering information on technically detailed government programs are high. It is therefore in the voter's economic interest to remain "rationally ignorant."

Logrolling, vote trading, and rational ignorance cause governments to authorize public programs that are not economically efficient.

Income Distribution

In a capitalist market economy, people who own resources that command a high price have higher incomes than those who own resources that command low prices. How equally or unequally should income be distributed? To what extent should the state redistribute income?

The marginal productivity theory of income distribution says that the private owners of labor, land, and capital are paid the marginal revenue products. If the factor market is perfectly competitive, the owner receives the value of the marginal product of the factor. The first great American economist, John Bates Clark (1847–1938), proposed that a distribution of income based on marginal productivity was "just" because factor owners receive a reward that is equal to the factor's marginal contribution to society's output.[24] *Bate's advocacy of an income distribution based on marginal productivity is known as the **natural justice** view of income distribution.*

Bestowing rewards according to marginal productivity encourages the owners to raise the productivity of their factors. If the state alters this distribution, there would be less incentive to be productive. There would be less investment in human capital and less risk taking, and society's output would accordingly be less.

Critics of natural justice point out that the marginal productivity depends on the presence of cooperating factors. An American coal miner may work with millions of dollars of capital equipment, whereas the Indian coal miner works just as hard with only a pick and shovel. The marginal productivity of the American coal miner is therefore many times that of the Indian coal miner. Moreover, marginal productivity is affected by human capital investment, and not everyone has equal access to education.

There are a number of arguments in favor of a redistributive role for the state. First, people are not indifferent to the welfare of others, and their own welfare is diminished by poverty around them. Yet despite altruistic motives, we cannot count on private charity to solve income distribution problems. No single donor can make a real difference. Therefore it makes sense to be a free-rider; that is, it is better to contribute nothing and hope that others will. Private contributions are unlikely to be great.

Government income redistribution eliminates the free-rider problem of private charity. Only the state is in a position to alter the distribution of income.

The Harvard philosopher John Rawls advanced another argument in favor of redistribution.[25] Rawls argued that we have an unequal distribution of income because those who benefit from income inequality are unwilling to accept changes that favor the poor. People are unwilling to agree to redistribution because those who will be rich know fairly early in life their chances of being rich. For this reason, a social consensus can never be formed whereby the rich agree to redistribute income to the poor.

Rawls asked how people would behave if they did not know in advance their lifetime endowment of resources. How would they react if they operated behind a veil of ignorance? *John Rawls's **veil of ignorance** refers to a hypothetical situation in which people would be born without any clue of the advantages or disadvantages that lay before them in life.* With a veil of ignorance, people would naturally act to minimize the risks of being poor. They would therefore reach a social consensus in favor of a fairly equal distribution of income. If people, operating behind a veil of ignorance, would naturally favor an equal distribution of income, then society should have an equal distribution of income.

There are two related distributions of material well-being: the distribution of income and the distribution of wealth. Income derives from wages and salaries, rents, dividends, and profits. *Net wealth is the accumulation of assets in excess of debts or other liabilities*. The major source of wealth is from profits. Wealth is distributed more unequally than income.

The fact that wealth derives largely from profits requires us to consider the sources of profits. Marx argued that profits accrue from the exploitation of labor. According to him, profits are unearned and stolen from the working class. The modern political Left largely accepts this Marxist interpretation of profits as the result of domestic exploitation and colonial exploitation.

Frank Knight, a University of Chicago economist, provided the most thoughtful analysis of profits. He regarded profit as a reward to risk taking. There is no such thing as a profit opportunity without risk and uncertainty. Some people are willing to take risks; others are not.[26] Those who take risks become entrepreneurs and business owners; those with a lower tolerance for risk become wage earners and salaried employees. The income and wealth distribution, therefore, is populated by the successful risk takers at the top and the unsuccessful risk takers and wage and salary earners in the bottom.

If there were no opportunity for profit, there would be no reason for anyone to risk their time, savings, and even their home to start a business or to invent a new product. Moreover, profits tend to be transitory. Once an entrepreneur takes advantage of a profit opportunity, others will follow and any exceptional profit will disappear.

There is probably no more controversial issue in politics and economics than redistribution by the state. The Left always feels that the "rich" get too much of the income. The Right retorts that the amount of income for all falls if there is too much redistribution. Like Goldilocks, there is a perennial debate over what is "too hot, too cold, or just right."

Prominent economist and policy advisor Arthur Okun favored wealth transfers by taxation from the relatively rich to the relatively poor. But, as a reasonable economist, he recognized that redistribution causes a loss of output and efficiency. Okun wrote: "The money must be carried from the rich to the poor in a leaky bucket. Some of it will simply disappear in transit, so the poor will not receive all the money that is taken from the rich."[27] All societies must deal with Okun's "leaky bucket" to decide how much income to redistribute and the economic costs of such redistribution.

Macroeconomic Instability

A major challenge to Adam Smith's vision of laissez-faire capitalism was mounted by John Maynard Keynes (1883–1946) in *The General Theory of Employment, Interest, and Money*, published in 1936 against the global backdrop of the Depression.[28] The Depression, which began in Europe slightly earlier and in 1929 in the United States, seemed to deny neoclassical notions of an automatic tendency toward equilibrium over time. Keynes asserted that activist government action was required to stabilize capitalist economics. *The **Keynesian revolution** is the general acceptance of Keynes's proposition that governments must actively counter economic downturns.*

Keynes   Keynes disputed the mainstay of classical equilibrium theory, Say's Law, named after the French economist, J. B. Say (1767–1832).[29] ***Say's Law** asserts that there can be no lasting deficiency of aggregate demand because the act of producing a given value of output creates an equivalent amount of income.* According to Say's logic, if income were not spent directly on consumer goods, it would be saved. The savings would end up being spent on investment, as interest rates adjusted. If we were only patient, eventually prices and wages would adjust to bring about equilibrium at full employment. Unemployment exists because workers are unwilling to accept the lower real wages required for labor market equilibrium. As long as prices and wages are flexible, there will be an automatic adjustment mechanism to restore full employment.

Keynes argued that there is no assurance that equilibrium will occur at full employment or that the automatic adjustment mechanism will work with reasonable speed. Thus—and this is the foundation of the Keynesian revolution—it is the responsibility of government to raise or lower spending and taxes (**fiscal policy**) or control investment spending (through **monetary policy**) to ensure full employment.

After World War II, Keynes's advocacy of discretionary monetary and fiscal policy became widely accepted by economists and public officials, who felt justified in abandoning the traditional hands-off policies favored by the neoclassical school. Federal budgets could be openly in deficit in order to stimulate the economy. In the United States, for example, tax cuts and tax increases were passed for the expressed purpose of manipulating aggregate demand. The practice of demand management became standard procedure in Western Europe, Japan, and Canada. Monetary policy also became an instrument of macroeconomic regulation. At the height of optimism in the mid-1960s, there was talk of being able to "fine-tune" the economy, and the business cycle was declared dead.

In 2009 and 2010, a huge fiscal stimulus package passed Congress to combat the recession that began in 2008 in response to a world financial crisis. It will take years and thousands of policy reports and scholarly debates to determine the effect of this stimulus program, but its initial results have been disappointing to say the least.

Self-Correcting Capitalism: Monetarism and Rational Expectations

Keynes advocated policy activism. ***Policy activism** is the discretionary use of monetary and fiscal policy to try to prevent or ameliorate the business cycle.* The monetarists, under the intellectual leadership of Milton Friedman, and the rational expectations economists, led by Robert Lucas, argue against the use of activist policy.[30] They argue that the Great Depression was an aberration caused by economic-policy blunders. The capitalist economy has a built-in self-correcting mechanism that will restore it to full employment.

Monetarists *argue that the money supply should be expanded at a fairly constant rate rather than being manipulated to combat the business cycle*. Monetarists maintain that activist monetary policy is as likely to do harm as good. Lengthy and indeterminate lags separate recognition of a macroeconomic problem, the taking of necessary monetary action, and realization of the effect of that action on the economy. An anti-inflationary policy adopted during a period of rising prices may begin to affect the economy at the very time that an expansionary monetary policy is required. Rather than running the risk of policy mistakes, the monetarists favor a fixed-monetary-growth rule, which would bind monetary authorities to expand the money supply by a fixed rate each year (roughly equal to the real growth of the economy) regardless of the state of the economy.

Advocates of the rational-expectations theory also argue against activist policy. *Rational-expectations theory* *states that people and businesses tend to use all available information to try to anticipate the future, in particular the rate of inflation*. Proponents of rational expectations maintain that activist policy will have the desired effect on the economy only if the policy catches people off guard. If taxes are lowered for the purpose of stimulating employment, and people know from experience that lower taxes raise inflation, then people will take actions to defeat the policy. If monetary authorities expand the money supply to raise employment, and workers and employees know that more monetary growth means more inflation, then the higher wages and prices will not raise employment or real output.

Growth and State Policy

Schumpeter's creative destruction is an apt description of what we see around us. No company or industry seems able to maintain a dominant position over the long run. The railroads were dominant in the nineteenth century; now they face tough competition from superior technologies, such as truck and air transport. IBM dominated computer production until new technologies enabled smaller, more efficient companies to grab most of IBM's market share. Google earned huge profits by being the first to dominate the search-engine market, but even Google is being challenged by newcomers.

Although Schumpeter would argue that market economies can be trusted to select growth industries, some economists and policy makers believe we need industrial policy to manage and promote growth. *Industrial policy* *uses the state to promote, subsidize, and generally manage the economic growth of a country*.

The proponents of industrial policy argue that private markets cannot effectively produce growth. Returns from research and development are insufficient to encourage private-sector financing. The state must therefore fund R&D, perhaps in partnership with private industry. Private industries are not farsighted; they are unable to identify the growth industries of the future. Therefore government must find, support, and subsidize the growth industries of the future. The real-world model for industrial policy has been Japan, which used industrial policy to promote its automobile and electronics industries in the early postwar period but has not been able to identify growth industries since the 1980s.

Countries that lack a formal industrial policy use the tax system to promote certain industries. The Obama administration has used tax preferences and government-business partnerships to promote favored companies and industries, producing things like green energy and electric automobiles. Although the goal seems noble, tax-administered growth policy runs into the same public-choice problems as regulation and management of externalities. Companies and industries tend to be picked on the basis of lobbying power, not on the basis of growth potential. Also, as has been the case in Europe, many of the subsidized businesses are those that require government bailouts or support just to survive. They are not poster boys for growth.

The Performance of Capitalist Economic Systems: Hypotheses

Chapter 3 discussed criteria by which to judge the performance of economic systems: efficiency, stability, income distribution, economic growth, and viability. What hypotheses, if any, follow from the theory of capitalism in each of these areas?

One of the primary lessons of economics is that "everything is relative." A $3.50 per gallon price of gas has no meaning in itself. It only has meaning compared to other prices (gas is cheap if bread costs $10 a loaf). The same is true of economic performance. There is no such thing as a perfectly performing economic system. We can only judge relative to some alternative.

Before the collapse of communism, the task of formulating hypotheses concerning the performance of the capitalist economic system was easier because we had a ready alternative: the planned economies of the Soviet Union and its satellites. Now, we have different types of capitalist economies that have institutional differences. But we must examine their nuanced differences rather than the mammoth differences between capitalism and planned socialism.

Table 6.1 takes us back in time to where we indeed had the alternative of planned socialist economic systems and could draw some comparisons of performance hypotheses.

TABLE **6.1**   Hypothesis on the Performance of Capitalist Economic Systems

Criterion	Performance
Efficiency	Better
Stability	Potentially poor; debate over government role
Income distribution	Unequal in the absence of state action
Economic growth	No clear a priori hypothesis; greater efficiency versus potentially lower capital formation
Viability	Has existed for centuries; is viable

Efficiency

Capitalism should provide a higher level of efficiency than planned socialism, especially in the static case. The more competitive the economy, the more efficient the economy. The producer's desire to maximize profits and the consumer's desire to maximize utility lead to a maximal output from available resources under conditions of perfect competition. Imperfect competition and external effects reduce this efficiency. Another point promoting static efficiency is capitalism's ability to process and utilize information more effectively than an economic system in which the market is lacking. Probably the most important point is that profit maximization, under all market arrangements, strongly encourages the efficient (least-cost) combination of resources to produce output.

Stability

Stability is the ability of an economic system to grow without undue fluctuations in the rate of growth and without excessive inflation and unemployment. Of course, it is a subjective judgment what *undue* and *excessive* mean in such a context. (We shall later show that even the planned socialist economies had their share of instability.) Keynes argued that capitalist economies are not stable, at least in terms of short-run automatic equilibrating forces. Monetarists and rational-expectations theorists believe that capitalist economies are (or could be) inherently more stable if left to their own devices, so there is considerable disagreement on this point. However, capitalism continues to suffer periodic bouts of inflation, unemployment, and growth fluctuations, which the general public regards as troubling. The sustained and pronounced economic downturn that began in 2007 provides a reminder of our susceptibility to economic downturns and to the fact that, despite advances in economic knowledge, we still do not know how to prevent and then cure economic crises.

Income Distribution

The theory of capitalism cannot make definitive judgments about equity and how resources should be divided among the members of capitalist societies. Only value judgments can provide answers. We lack a consensus about "fairness," and without an agreed-upon definition it is difficult to arrive at hypotheses. Instead, we can only consider empirical measures of income distribution and make statements such as the following: Income is distributed more nearly equally in society X than in society Y. It is difficult to proceed further and say that income is distributed "better" ("more fairly") in X or in Y.

The theory of capitalism, however, does suggest the likelihood of significant inequalities in the distribution of income. The factors of production are owned predominantly by private individuals, and the relative value of these factors is determined by the market. Insofar as human and physical capital and natural ability are not likely to be evenly distributed, especially when such things can be passed from one generation to another, private ownership of the factors of production raises the likelihood of an uneven distribution of income and wealth among the members of capitalist societies. Exactly how unevenly income and wealth are distributed will depend on the distribution of human and physical capital and also on the redistributive role of the state.

Economic Growth

One of the supposed advantages of planned socialist economies was supposed to be their ability to direct resources to specific goals, such as economic growth and military power. To a greater extent than capitalist economies, they can marshal resources for economic growth, if they so desire, by controlling the investment rate and the growth rate of the labor force. Although capitalist governments can and do affect the investment rate, the amount saved is largely a matter of individual choice, and it is likely that individual choice will result in lower savings rates than will a planned socialist economy. Thus if the growth of factor inputs is left to individuals, one would hypothesize a slower rate of growth of factor inputs and hence of economic growth, *ceteris paribus*, under capitalism.

A counterbalancing factor must be considered: the hypothesized efficiency of capitalist economies. Static efficiency means that a maximal output is produced from available resources and (with a given savings rate) a greater volume of savings is available relative to less efficient production methods. Moreover, there is the unresolved matter of the dynamic efficiency of capitalist economic systems. Up to this point, capitalist theory has had relatively little to say about dynamic efficiency. It is conceivable that the greater static and dynamic efficiency of capitalism can compensate for its lesser control over the growth of productive resources.

Viability of the Capitalist System

The viability of capitalism has been demonstrated by both theory and historical experience. Capitalist theory points to its inherent tendencies toward equilibrium. Historical experience shows that capitalism has survived several centuries and that there are no signs of impending collapse.

Two Different Visions of Market Capitalism

Marx, Hobbes, Locke, and Smith initiated a debate that will never end. Marx disliked the capitalist economic system and wanted it overthrown to be replaced by socialism. Hobbes doubted that society could function without a strong invasive government to control base human emotions. Locke preached the doctrine of limited government, and Smith taught us that markets and profits will lead us to cooperative and efficient outcomes without any help form government. State intrusion in our private economic lives would only make matters worse.

The contemporary heirs of Marx and Hobbes continue to argue in favor of a strong intrusive state that protects workers from exploitation and corrects the natural deficiencies of free markets. They tend to support regulation, taxation, and subsidies to promote economic and social goals, industrial policy, and substantive income redistribution by the state. Unlike Smith, they favor a large state that does much more than the tasks Smith enumerated.

The contemporary heirs of Locke and Smith fear a Leviathan state; they believe in the natural self-corrective forces of markets; they worry that too much income redistribution will dampen efficiency and incentives. They understand that few legislative decisions are based on "what is good for the country"; rather, they are determined by lobbyists, logrolling, and outright corruption.

As we said, this debate will never end. It has never been a polite discussion suited to polite drawing rooms. These issues bring violent anti-globalist and anti-capitalist demonstrators to the streets when world leaders meet to discuss global economic issues. They lead to bitter clashes between union members and Tea Party activists and to mudslinging political contests. Those who wonder "why we cannot just all get along" are naïve. Given that people tend to view the world in two quite different lights, we will never be able to "just get along," nor should we.

Summary

- The moral philosophers—Hobbes, Locke, and Smith—differed in their views of the state. Hobbes argued for a strong intrusive state; Locke and Smith favored a limited state.
- The traditional neoclassical model maintains that capitalist economies have a strong tendency to equilibrium and that they generate and process information efficiently.
- Market capitalism promotes consumer sovereignty, which enables consumers to determine what will be produced.
- In the perfectly competitive market capitalist economy, government would play a very limited role.
- There are a number of reasons for state intervention: monopoly, externalities, public goods, income distribution, and macroeconomic instability.
- There are no clear and easy ways for the state to correct the deficiencies of a market economy.
- Public choice economics teaches that government decisions are often made in an economically inefficient manner.
- Keynes demonstrated that economies could establish a stable macroeconomic equilibrium at less than (or greater than) full employment. He believed that it was the responsibility of government, through fiscal and monetary policy, to bring about full employment.
- The monetarist view of the market economy argues that activist macroeconomic policy is not stabilizing and can make things worse.
- Market capitalism tends to result in an efficient allocation of resources but that economic activity remains unstable or cyclical. The distribution of income will be less even in a market capitalist system than in those systems where greater degrees of social ownership or government intervention are present.

Key Terms

complex markets—Require sophisticated institutional infrastructure that often deal in nonhomogeneous goods and services that may be bought in one period of time and sold in another period of time or that involve a series of payments over time.

constitution—Establishes the basic political, economic, and social rules of the game for a society.

efficiency—Measures how effectively the factors of production are combined to produce output using available technology.

externalities—The actions of one producer or consumer directly affect the costs or utilities of others outside of the price system.

financial intermediaries—Link savers and borrowers in financial markets that include banks and other bank-like institutions.

fiscal policy—How the state collects taxes and spends revenue.

information economics—How markets cause specialization in the generation and utilization of information.

internalization—An action that makes the cost of the externality a private cost.

invisible hand—A highly efficient and harmonious economic system is the result if competitive markets were left to function freely without government intervention (Smith).

Keynesian revolution—The general acceptance of Keynes's proposition that governments must actively counter economic downturns.

laissez-faire (French for "let it be")—A policy that says that the state should not intervene in private economic transactions except in strictly limited cases (Smith).

Leviathan—Hobbes's term to describe the all-powerful state that he advocated.

market—Any organizational arrangement that brings buyers and sellers together.

median voter—Separates the lower half of the voting population from the higher half.

monetarists—The money supply should be expanded at a fairly constant rate rather than being manipulated to combat the business cycle.

monetary policy—Conducted by a central bank, which determines the quantity of money and credit conditions.

monopolist—The sole producer of a product for which there are no good substitutes. This gives the monopolist some power to set the price of the product.

natural justice—An income distribution based on marginal productivity.

net wealth—The accumulation of assets in excess of debts or other liabilities.

policy activism—The discretionary use of monetary and fiscal policy to try to prevent or ameliorate the business cycle.

public goods—Nonpayers (called free riders) cannot be prevented from enjoying the benefits of the public good, and one person's use of the good does not generally prevent others from using it.

public-choice economics—Studies the efficiency of public decision making in democratic societies.

rational-expectations theory—People and businesses tend to use all available information to try to anticipate the future, in particular the rate of inflation.

real business cycle—The business cycle is caused by random shocks and cannot be controlled by factors other than the self-correcting mechanism.

regulation—The setting of prices and product quality by an agency of the state.

regulatory capture—Regulators favor the interests of the monopolist rather than the interests of the public.

rule of law—Participants in society and the economy agree on the legal rules concerning social and economic behavior; they behave according to these rules, and there is a punishment mechanism when the rule of law is violated.

Say's Law—There can be no lasting deficiency of aggregate demand because the act of producing a given value of output creates an equivalent amount of income.

simple markets—Markets that do not require sophisticated institutions.

social contract—People contract together consensually to establish a limited government. Only such a government is legitimate (Locke).

social costs—Equal the private cost plus the unpriced cost of the externality.

veil of ignorance—A hypothetical situation in which people would be born without any clue of the advantages or disadvantages that lay before them in life.

Notes

1. Examples of how the latter approach has been applied are found in Abram Bergson, *The Economics of Soviet Planning* (New Haven: Yale University Press, 1964); Jaroslav Vanek, *The Participatory Economy* (Ithaca, N.Y.: Cornell University Press, 1971), Chs. 2 and 3; and Benjamin Ward, *The Socialist Economy* (New York: Random House, 1967), Chs. 8 and 9.
2. Robert Heilbroner, *The Worldly Philosophers* (New York: Simon & Schuster, 1953).
3. This and other quotes are from Thomas Hobbes, *The Leviathan*, 1660, http://oregon state.edu/instruct/phl302/texts/hobbes/leviathan-contents.html.
4. John Locke, *Two Treatises of Government In the Former, The False Principles and Foundation of Sir Robert Filmer, and His Followers, Are Detected and Overthrown: The Latter, Is an Essay Concerning the Original, Extent, and End, of Civil Government*, http://socserv.mcmaster.ca/~econ/ugcm/3ll3/locke/government.pdf.
5. Adam Smith, *The Wealth of Nations,* ed. Edwin Cannan (New York: Modern Library, 1937).
6. Peter Boettke and G. Anderson, "Soviet Venality: A Rent-Seeking Model of the Communist State," *Public Choice* 93 (1997).
7. George Stigler, "The Successes and Failures of Professor Smith," *Journal of Political Economy* 84 (December 1976), 1199–1214.
8. It is difficult to single out a few individuals and claim that they are the major contributors to partial-equilibrium analysis, but these three would appear on most lists: Alfred Marshall, *Principles of Economics,* 8th ed. (New York: Macmillan, 1948); J. R. Hicks, *Value and Capital,* 2nd ed. (Oxford, England: Oxford University Press, 1946); and Paul Samuelson, *Foundations of Economic Analysis* (Cambridge, Mass.: Harvard University Press, 1948).
9. Friederick Hayek, "The Price System as a Mechanism for Using Knowledge," *American Economic Review* 35 (September 1945), 519–530; and Ludwig von Mises, *Socialism: An Economic and Sociological Analysis* (New Haven: Yale University Press, 1951).

10. F. A. Hayek, "The Use of Knowledge in Society," *American Economic Review* 35, no. 4 (September 1945), 519–530, http://www.princetonphilosophy.com/background/Hayek.pdf.

11. This definition is crafted from Joseph Stiglitz, "Whither Reform: Ten Years of Transformation," Annual World Bank Conference on Development Economics, Washington, D.C., April 1999.

12. A. Denzau and D. North, "Shared Mental Models: Ideologies and Institutions," *Kyklos* 47 (1994), 3–31.

13. Paul Samuelson, "The Pure Theory of Public Expenditure," *Review of Economics and Statistics* 36 (November 1954), 26–30.

14. Thinkexist.com, "Adam Smith Quotes," http://thinkexist.com/quotation/people_of_the_same_trade_seldom_meet_together/145519.html.

15. George Stigler, *The Theory of Price,* rev. ed. (New York: Macmillan, 1952), pp. 204–222.

16. The tendency of regulated monopolies to use too much capital was discovered by H. Averich and L. L. Johnson, "Behavior of the Firm Under Regulatory Constraint," *American Economic Review* 52, no. 5 (December 1962), 1052–1069.

17. George Stigler, "The Theory of Economic Regulation," *Bell Journal of Economics and Management*, 2 (Spring, 1971), 3–21; S. Peltzman, 'Toward a More General Theory of Regulation', *Journal of Law and Economics*, 14 (August 1976), pp. 109–48.

18. Milton Friedman, "Monopoly and Social Responsibility of Business and Labor," in Edwin Mansfield, ed., *Monopoly Power and Economic Performance,* 3rd ed. (New York: Norton, 1974), pp. 57–68; and George J. Stigler, "The Government of the Economy," in Paul Samuelson, ed., *Readings in Economics,* 7th ed. (New York: McGraw-Hill, 1973), pp. 73–77.

19. The discussion of externalities is based on the following sources: E. J. Mishan, "The Postwar Literature on Externalities: An Interpretive Essay," *Journal of Economic Literature* 9 (March 1971), 1–28; George Daly, "The Coase Theorem: Assumptions, Applications, and Ambiguities," *Economic Inquiry* 12 (June 1974), 203–213; and Erik Furobotin and Svetozar Pejovich, "Property Rights and Economic Theory: A Survey of Recent Literature," *Journal of Economic Literature* 12 (December 1972), 1137–1162.

20. R. H. Coase, "The Problem of Social Costs," *Journal of Law and Economics* 3 (October 1960), 1–44.

21. Seymore Lipset, "Some Social Requisites of Democracy: Economic Development and Political Legitimacy," *American Political Science Review* 53 (1959), 69–105.

22. Robert Barro, *Determinants of Economic Growth* (Cambridge, Mass.: MIT Press, 1997), Ch. 2.

23. James Buchanan and Gordon Tullock, *The Calculus of Consent* (Ann Arbor: University of Michigan Press, 1974); Kenneth Arrow, *Social Choice and Individual Values* (New Haven: Yale University Press, 1976). For a discussion of differing views of the state, see Barry W. Poulson, *Economic Development: Private and Public Choice* (New York: West, 1994).

24. John Bates Clark, *The Distribution of Wealth: A Theory of Wages, Interest and Profits* (New York Macmillan, 1899).

25. John Rawls, *Theory of Justice* (Oxford, England: Clarendon Press, 1976).

26. Frank Knight, *Risk, Uncertainty, and Profit* (New York: Harper, 1957).

27. Arthur Okun, *Equality and Efficiency: The Big Tradeoff* (Washington, D.C.: Brookings Institution, 1975).

28. John Maynard Keynes, *The General Theory of Employment, Interest, and Money* (New York: Harcourt, 1936). The most important early work to interpret Keynes's general

theory for nonspecialists was Alvin Hansen, *A Guide to Keynes* (New York: McGraw-Hill, 1953).

29. There is considerable controversy over what Keynes actually meant to say in *The General Theory*, and some authorities argue that the more popular interpretations of Keynes are incorrect. For discussion of this controversy, see Don Patinkin, *Money, Interest, and Prices*, 2nd ed. (New York: Harper & Row, 1965); Axel Leijonhufvud, *On Keynesian Economics and the Economics of Keynes* (New York: Oxford University Press, 1968); Herschel Grossman, "Was Keynes a 'Keynesian'? A Review Article," *Journal of Economic Literature* 10 (March 1972), 26–30; and Alan Coddington, "Keynesian Economics: The Search for First Principles," *Journal of Economic Literature* 14 (December 1976), 1258–1338. For an historical perspective on the Keynesian revolution, see Alan Sweezy et al., "The Keynesian Revolution and Its Pioneers," *American Economic Review, Papers and Proceedings* 62 (May 1972), 116–141.

30. The discussion of the monetarist school is based on the following sources: Milton Friedman, ed., *Studies in the Quantity Theory of Money* (Chicago: University of Chicago Press, 1956); Milton Friedman and A. J. Schwartz, *A Monetary History of the United States* (Princeton, N.J.: Princeton University Press, 1963); Milton Friedman, *Dollars and Deficits* (Englewood Cliffs, N.J.: Prentice-Hall, 1968); Franco Modigliani, "The Monetarist Controversy, or, Should We Forsake Stabilization Policies?" *American Economic Review* 67 (March 1977), 13; Edmund Phelps, *Microeconomic Foundations of Employment and Inflation Theory* (London: Macmillan, 1974); and Milton Friedman, "Inflation and Unemployment," *Journal of Political Economy* 85 (June 1977), 451–472.

Recommended Readings

History of Economic Thought

Robert Heilbroner, *The Worldly Philosophers* (New York: Simon & Schuster, 1953).

Thomas Hobbes, *The Leviathan*, 1660, http://oregonstate.edu/instruct/phl302/texts/hobbes/leviathan-contents.html.

John Locke, *Two Treatises of Government In the Former, The False Principles and Foundation of Sir Robert Filmer, and His Followers, Are Detected and Overthrown: The Latter, Is an Essay Concerning the Original, Extent, and End, of Civil Government*, http://socserv.mcmaster.ca/~econ/ugcm/3ll3/locke/government.pdf.

Sylvia Nasar, *Gran Pursuit: The Story of Economic Genius* (New York: Simon& Shuster, 2011).

Microeconomics of Capitalism

F. M. Bator, "The Simple Analytics of Welfare Maximization," *American Economic Review* 47 (March 1957), 22–59.

Abram Bergson, "A Reformulation of Certain Aspects of Welfare Economics," *Quarterly Journal of Economics* 52 (February 1938), 310–334; reprinted in R. V. Clemence, ed., *Readings in Economic Analysis* (Reading, Mass.: Addison-Wesley, 1950), Vol. I, pp. 61–85.

Edward Chamberlin, *The Theory of Monopolistic Competition,* 6th ed. (Cambridge, Mass.: Harvard University Press, 1948).

J. R. Hicks, *Value and Capital,* 2nd ed. (Oxford, England: Oxford University Press, 1946).

Joan Robinson, *The Economics of Imperfect Competition* (London: Macmillan, 1959).

Externalities and Public Goods

R. H. Coase, "The Problem of Social Costs," *Journal of Law and Economics* 3 (October 1960), 1–44.

J. de V. Graaff, *Theoretical Welfare Economics* (London: Cambridge University Press, 1957).

E. J. Mishan, "The Postwar Literature on Externalities: An Interpretive Essay," *Journal of Economic Literature* 9 (March 1971), 1–28.

A. C. Pigou, *The Economics of Welfare,* 4th ed. (London: Macmillan, 1946).

Paul Samuelson, "The Pure Theory of Public Expenditure," *Review of Economics and Statistics* 36 (November 1954), 26–30.

Tibor Scitovsky, *Welfare and Competition,* rev. ed. (Homewood, Ill.: Irwin, 1971), Chs. 20 and 21.

Income Distribution and Regulation

Dennis W. Carlton and Jeffrey M. Perloff, *Modern Industrial Organization* (New York: HarperCollins, 1990).

John Bates Clark, *The Distribution of Wealth: A Theory of Wages, Interest and Profits* (New York: MacMillan, 1899).

Douglas F. Greer, *Business, Government, and Society,* 2nd ed. (New York: Macmillan, 1987).

Frank Knight, *Risk, Uncertainty, and Profit* (New York: Harper, 1957).

R. D. Norton, "Industrial Policy and American Renewal," *Journal of Economic Literature* 24 (March 1986), 1–40.

Arthur Okun, *Equality and Efficiency: The Big Tradeoff* (Washington, D.C.: Brookings Institution, 1975).

Barry W. Poulson, *Economic Development: Private and Public Choice* (New York: West, 1994).

John Rawls, *Theory of Justice* (Oxford, England: Clarendon Press, 1976).

F. M. Sherer and David Ross, *Industrial Market Structure and Economic Performance,* 3rd ed. (Boston: Houghton Mifflin, 1990).

Leonard W. Weiss and Michael W. Klass, eds., *Regulatory Reform: What Actually Happened* (Boston: Little, Brown, 1986).

Clifford Winston, "Economic Deregulation: Days of Reckoning for Microeconomists," *Journal of Economic Literature* 31 (September 1993), 1263–1289.

Public Choice

James Buchanan and Robert Tollison, eds., *Theory of Public Choice: Political Applications of Economics* (Ann Arbor: University of Michigan Press, 1972).

James Buchanan and Gordon Tullock, *The Calculus of Consent* (Ann Arbor: University of Michigan Press, 1974).

Macroeconomics

Alan Coddington, "Keynesian Economics: The Search for First Principles," *Journal of Economic Literature* 14 (December 1976), 1258–1338.

A. S. Eicher and J. A. Kregel, "An Essay on Post-Keynesian Theory: A New Paradigm in Economics," *Journal of Economic Literature* 13 (December 1975), 1293–1314.

Milton Friedman, *Dollars and Deficits* (Englewood Cliffs, N.J.: Prentice-Hall, 1968).

————, ed., *Studies in the Quantity Theory of Money* (Chicago: University of Chicago Press, 1956).

Robert J. Gordon, "What Is the New Keynesian Economics?" *Journal of Economic Literature* 28 (September 1990), 15–71.

Herschel Grossman, "Was Keynes a 'Keynesian'? A Review Article," *Journal of Economic Literature* 10 (March 1972), 26–30.

John Maynard Keynes, *The General Theory of Employment, Interest, and Money* (New York: Harcourt, 1936).

Axel Leijonhufvud, *On Keynesian Economics and the Economics of Keynes* (New York: Oxford University Press, 1968).

Franco Modigliani, "The Monetarist Controversy, or, Should We Forsake Stabilization Policies?" *American Economic Review* 67 (March 1977), 1–19.

Paul M. Romer et al., "New Growth Theory," *Journal of Economic Perspectives* 8 (Winter 1994), 3–72.

Adam Smith, *The Wealth of Nations*, ed. Edwin Cannan (New York: Modern Library, 1937).

CHAPTER

7

Theory of Planned Socialism

Chapter 2 introduced two variants of the socialist economy: planned socialism and market socialism. The dictionary definition of socialism captures two essential aspects: collective or state *ownership* and collective or state *control* of the means of production. The three Merriam-Webster definitions, for example, read as follows: (1) Socialism is any of various economic and political theories advocating collective or governmental *ownership* and *administration* of the means of production and distribution of goods, (2) Socialism is a system or condition of society in which the means of production are *owned* and *controlled* by the state, (3) Socialism is a system of society or group living in which there is *no private property*.[1]

According to these definitions, socialism can be a theoretical or political idea that advocates a particular way of organizing economic and political life. It can be an actual economic system in which the state owns and controls resources, or it can be a system of collective or group ownership of property.

In Chapter 2, our definition focused on state ownership and control. But, as the Merriam-Webster definition suggests, there can be an entirely different socialism characterized by group ownership. If property is owned by groups of individuals or families, there must be a means of coordinating their activities, which could be either markets or plans. Collective ownership could be consistent with either market or planned allocation.

Therefore, we appear to have two options for socialism: one in which the state owns and controls; the other in which groups own property, and the interactions among groups is coordinated in some fashion. The most likely coordination option is the market, yielding us a model of decentralized socialism. We could call it "cooperative" or "market" socialism.

Early socialist writers were split over whether to define socialism by cooperative or group ownership or by state ownership and control. The appeal of collective ownership is as old as the ages. The Pilgrims who came to America to establish the Plymouth Colony agreed to place in a common stock for all to share "all profits and benefits that are got by trade, working, fishing, or any other means."[2] Socialist writers of the nineteenth century proposed socialist arrangements for sharing as a response to the inequality and poverty of the industrial revolution. English socialist Robert Owen proposed that ownership and production take place in cooperatives, where all members shared equally. French socialist Henri Saint-Simon proposed to the contrary: socialism meant solving economic problems by means of state administration and planning, and taking advantage of new advances in science.

When Vladimir Lenin and the Bolsheviks gained power in 1917, they were also faced with a choice between the two types of socialism. The "Soviets" (from which the Soviet Union eventually derived its name) were revolutionary councils of workers or soldiers who provided the firepower for the Bolshevik victory. They advocated cooperative socialism in which the workers owned and managed the enterprises. Lenin decided on something else: centralized "democratic" socialism, in which the Communist Party represented the workers in owning and managing the economy.

This chapter is about the first type of socialism—the planned socialism of Chapter 2. The next chapter is about market socialism.

Socialism: The Search for Basic Principles

Our definition of a planned socialist economy in Chapter 2 focused on decision-making procedures, property rights, and incentive arrangements. These arrangements, along with different policies and a one-party dictatorship, mean an economic system quite different from capitalism. Unlike the market capitalist economy, however, no widely accepted theoretical paradigm of the socialist economy exists.[3]

In order to qualify as a "theory" of socialism, we must be able to explain how it resolves the four fundamental tasks of any economic system—what to produce, how to produce, who gets the product, and how to provide for the future. On a strictly intuitive level, we would expect a number of differences between socialism and capitalism. First, although "what to produce" could in theory be the same in capitalist and socialist systems, such an outcome is unlikely. If the socialist economy is directed by the state, its socialist leaders would most likely want economic outcomes that are different from those generated by consumer sovereignty. We would expect the socialist state to favor public goods, defense, and the socialization of consumption as compared to a market capitalist economy. If socialism produces the same economic outcomes as market capitalism, we could legitimately ask why it is necessary.

Second, if "how to produce" is also decided by the state, there should be profound differences between capitalism and socialism. Instead of enterprises acquiring inputs through factor markets and selling in wholesale markets, they will get their inputs through state channels and they will sell to state trading companies. In such an undertaking, prices would play a secondary role. It is the state that is making these decisions, not the marketplace.

Friedrich Hayek and Ludwig von Mises emphasized the complexity of decision making in markets and the crucial role of prices in providing information. If input and output decisions are made by the state, it will likely be done by assuming simple technologies of production. The mix of factor inputs is determined as by engineering recipes. In such a setting, there are fewer requirements for information, and engineers rather than business managers decide how to combine inputs.

Third, state ownership should have fundamental implications for "who gets what." In a socialist economy, the primary source of household income is labor. Private income from capital is absent, although the state can allocate some of the socialist capital return to its citizens as a dividend. The main source of income under socialism, however, will be wages and salaries and, with the state in control of education and presumably discouraging inheritance, income from labor should be more equally distributed.

If one of the system's core goals is to make things "fairer," one way to accomplish this is through the socialization of consumption. Instead of private apartments or homes, citizens live in communal apartments and eat together in factory cafeterias, not around their own dinner table. With "fairness" as the objective, we expect a more even distribution of income. The most relevant measure of material welfare is consumption, not income. Insofar as a socialist state considers that human needs are fairly homogeneous, communally consumed goods would be distributed fairly evenly. (A differentiated pattern would be difficult to accomplish anyway.) All of these considerations should yield a more egalitarian distribution of income.

Finally, the way socialist economies provide for the future should differ. Capitalist market economies base investment decisions on the market interest rate. If it is high, future returns will be heavily discounted, and less investment will be undertaken. The socialist state is free to establish its own discount rate, independently of conditions in credit markets. If socialist discount rates are lower, there will be a greater amount of investment. In other words, socialist states may place a higher value on the future than would a capitalist economy. If so, socialist economies would choose to expand savings to offset individual shortsightedness.

Its advocates view socialism as an economic system that can offset the perceived deficiencies of the market capitalist economy. The socialist economy places greater emphasis on economic equality and socialization and, in doing so, would be expected to use a variety of state controls and policies to offset the problems of unemployment, inflation, and slow economic growth, which are perceived as inevitable under capitalism.

It is difficult to compare the paradigm of the market with that of the socialist economy because there is no single socialist paradigm. Karl Marx himself analyzed capitalism, and, in doing so, he envisioned socialism (and ultimately communism) as an inevitable outcome of the process of social change. Marx had relatively little advice for the framers of the first socialist state, which was established in Russia in October of 1917. Although he spent most of his time explaining why capitalism would fail, he did provide certain hints for those who followed him.

Marx and Lenin: The New Socialist State

*Marx's **dialectical materialism** explains the pending triumph of socialism over capitalism.* For Marx, historical evolution, from primitive societies to communism, was inevitable. Capitalism, because of its exploitation of workers and its internal contradictions, would be replaced by socialism. Capitalism would inevitably replace feudalism. Under capitalism, capital accumulation would raise the productive capacity of the economy, but only the capitalists would benefit. Socialism would inherit this productive capacity and would use it for the benefit of the working class. (Marx's views were discussed in Chapter 4.)

Dictatorship of the Proletariat

According to Marx, as Lenin later elaborated, socialism would evolve in two stages. The first stage, socialism, would be a transition step to the final stage of communism. *Socialism is an intermediate and transitory stage during which scarcity still exists and a strong state would be required.* As the worker state increases its productive capacity, communism would eventually be attained. *Communism, the highest stage of social development, is characterized by the absence of markets and money, abundance, and the withering away of the state.*

Under socialism, vestiges of capitalism would continue and some familiar institutions, such as money and market exchange, would remain. The state would be transformed. Instead of representing the interests of the capitalists, it would be a dictatorship that represented the interests of the workers. *A **dictatorship of the proletariat** would govern in the first stage of socialism and would directly represent the interests of the proletariat.*

Marx (and his collaborator Friedrich Engels) emphasized that this government of the working class must be a dictatorship. Lenin continued this theme in his writings:

> When the workers replace the dictatorship of the bourgeoisie, by their revolutionary dictatorship ... to break down the resistance of the bourgeoisie ... the workers invest the state with a revolutionary and transitional form.... Therefore, the state is only a transitional institution, which is used in the struggle, in the revolution, to hold down one's adversaries by force. It is sheer nonsense to talk of a "free people's state"; so long as the proletariat still needs the state, it does not need it in the interests of freedom, but in order to hold down its adversaries, and, as soon as it becomes possible to speak of freedom, the state, as such, ceases to exist.[4]

Lenin, in his *State and Revolution*, written on the eve of the October 1917 revolution, agreed with Marx on the need for force "to hold down adversaries." He rejected democracy, as a "liberal" concept.[5]

After the revolution, Lenin warned that the defeated capitalist class would still have wealth and money, connections, greater military experience, and better education and training. Without mincing words, Lenin argued that the dictatorship of the proletariat should use unrestrained violence against its opponents:

> The revolutionary dictatorship of the proletariat is as a rule won, and maintained, by the use of violence, by the proletariat, against the bourgeoisie, a rule that is unrestricted by any laws.... Why do we need a dictatorship when we have a majority? And Marx and Engels explain: to break down the resistance

of the bourgeoisie; to inspire the reactionaries with fear; to maintain the authority of the armed people against the bourgeoisie; that the proletariat may forcibly hold down its adversaries.[6]

One of Lenin's first acts was to unleash the "Red Terror" of his secret police on political opponents and class enemies. The role of the state could then diminish after the foes of socialism had been dispatched by the dictatorship. The state could perhaps even "wither away."

It was left to Lenin's successor, Joseph Stalin, to explain why the power of the socialist state should increase rather than wither away. Stalin, as the head of the Central Committee of the Communist Party, argued that it represented the working classes; therefore, his own decisions were actually those of the working class. Anyone who questioned him was questioning the will of the people.

The USSR, which Stalin ruled, was surrounded by enemies both within and without. They could not be eradicated "once and for all time" despite his killing and imprisonment of millions. Instead of diminishing, Stalin concluded that the class struggle was intensifying. He had to conclude, with feigned regret, that the dictatorship must grow stronger and use even more draconian forms of terror.[7]

Distribution of Income: Socialism and Communism

The socialism-communism stages, according to Marx (and subsequently elaborated by Lenin), also differ according to the distribution of income among the working class. During the higher stage—communism—distribution would be according to need:

> In a higher phase of communist society, after the enslaving subordination of the individual to the division of labor, and therewith also the antithesis between mental and physical labor has vanished; after labor has become not only a means of life but life's prime want; after the productive forces have also increased with the all-around development of the individual, and co-operative wealth flows more abundantly—only then can ... society inscribe on its banners: From each according to his ability, to each according to his needs![8]

After the stage of absolute abundance has been attained, people will work for the joy of labor; there is more than enough to go around, and people will take from society's production what they need—a kind of material paradise on earth.

During the lower phase of socialist development, however, the reward system must resemble the old one in certain respects. The working class will be rewarded according to productivity. Even though property is now owned by society rather than individuals and hence production belongs to society as a whole, people should continue to be rewarded according to their contribution, under the principle that "he who does not work does not eat."

The actual scheme that Lenin proposed was to give certificates based on the amount of work performed. Workers redeem these certificates with a comparable quantity of goods from public warehouses. Under this arrangement, workers receive from society what they have contributed to society. Lenin recognized that some unjust differences will result, but the "exploitation of man by man" will no longer exist because the state rather than individuals own the means of production.

The motto "To each according to his contribution" proved to be a lasting formula for distribution. In the Soviet economy, wages continued to be differentiated according to indicators of productivity, such as education and type of work performed. In fact, the one area where the Soviet planned economy had a capitalist-style market was its labor market.[9]

Primitive Accumulation

Marx's theory of primitive accumulation provided another operational instruction for later leaders of socialist states. According to Marx, *primitive accumulation was the means by which the capitalist class gained a monopoly ownership of capital.*

Marx's interpretation differed dramatically from the established view that capital accumulation is the result of patience, saving, and frugality. Marx denied that capital accumulation is explained by the outmoded "anecdote of two sorts of people; one, the diligent, intelligent, and, above all, frugal elite; the other, lazy rascals, spending their substance, and more, in riotous living…. Thus it came to pass that the former sort accumulated wealth…. Such insipid childishness is every day preached to us in the defense of property."

Marx also rejected the notion of the righteous saver: "In actual history it is notorious that conquest, enslavement, robbery, murder, briefly force, play the great part…. As a matter of fact, the methods of primitive accumulation are anything but idyllic." According to Marx, capitalists came to control the means of production by violence, theft, and war. They then used their monopoly over capital to enslave the working class who had "at last nothing to sell except their own skins."[10] With such a view of capital accumulation, Marx welcomed with open arms the expropriation of capitalists after the socialist revolution.

In Marx's framework, it should be noted, capital accumulation is what creates growth. Marx's condition for growth is that the output of capital goods must exceed the depreciation requirements of the economy. In other words, economies grow when they produce more capital than they use up. Hence, the greater the capital accumulation, the higher the growth. (The early Soviet economists developed growth models of the economy based on this principle, which were influential in arguing for high rates of capital accumulation.[11])

Marx's primitive accumulation raised a vital question for the early leaders of the Soviet state: If the capitalists gained a monopoly over capital by methods "anything but idyllic," should not the new socialist state also gain a monopoly over society's capital, even if it requires doing so by force?

Insofar as Marx's guidelines concerning nationalization of industry were clear: There was to be state ownership in industry, the only remaining nonstate capital was in agriculture. Should the dictatorship of the proletariat use force to gain control over capital still in the hands of the peasant population?[12] The prospect was appealing because the state could use its control of agricultural capital to force peasants to deliver a "surplus" to finance industrialization. In fact, there was a remarkable debate in the mid-1920s in the Soviet Union over this issue, which Stalin resolved in late 1929 with the forced collectivization of agriculture.[13]

The appeal of primitive socialist accumulation was not limited to the early years of the Soviet Union. Mao used the same idea during his disastrous Great Leap Forward, starting in 1958. Mao, like Stalin, hoped that he could make Chinese peasant agriculture "pay" for China's industrialization. In both cases, they guessed wrong.[14]

How to Plan? The ABCs of Communism

Lenin, the first leader of the Soviet Union, suffered his first stroke in May 1922. He suffered a second stroke in December of that year and largely withdrew from public life. During his short time of active leadership, Lenin headed both the Communist Party and the government. In both capacities, he had to oversee the management of the world's first socialist economy. He tried two experiments: The first, War Communism, has been interpreted by many as a botched attempt to skip to the higher stage of socialism immediately. *War Communism is the Soviet economic system that existed from 1918 to March 1921 in which virtually all enterprises were nationalized, private trade and money were outlawed, and peasant crops were confiscated.*

In March 1921, Lenin replaced War Communism with the New Economic Policy. *The* **New Economic Policy** *(March 1921 to 1928) restored private trade in agricultural goods, and denationalized smaller enterprises but kept larger enterprises under state ownership and control.*

As Lenin and his government tried to manage the new socialist economy under these two different regimes, two prominent, young, and idealistic "Left Communists" published a blueprint mapping out how to manage a planned economy. One of the authors was Nikolai Bukharin, who would later provide the last opposition to Stalin's collectivization and forced industrialization. His book (co-authored with Evgeny Preobrazhensky), *The ABC of Communism* published in 1921, described a planned and administered economy managed by newly trained specialists—not professional bureaucrats—drawn from the ranks of workers. These worker-administrators would return to their workplaces after their stint as administrators was completed. They would work together with workers' councils running factories to plan and manage the economy. Everyone should be involved in this glorious process: "It is absolutely indispensable that every member of a Soviet play some definite part in the work of state administration. It is incumbent upon every member, not merely to pass opinions upon the matters that come up for discussion, but to take part in the common task, in his own person to fill some social office."

Bukharin and Preobrazhensky admitted that such an administration would be far from perfect: "Naturally, therefore, the workers, having risen to power, will, while learning by experience, make a great many mistakes. By these mistakes they learn, but inevitably they make them."

The task of the state would be immense. All larger enterprises would be owned and administered by worker-administrators. Private trade would be abolished;

distribution of goods would be in the hands of the state. According to Bukharin and Preobrazhensky, "The main task of Soviet power has been and remains the unification of all economic activities into a national plan. Such a plan ... eliminates the anarchy of capitalism.... The construction of communist society requires a considerable amount of time, but its foundation is an integrated national plan."

The main conclusion of *the ABC of Communism* was the need for a national economic plan. *A **national economic plan** is one that directs resource allocation for all (or the most important) sectors of the economy.* National planning begins with a survey of what is available—the plants and enterprises, raw materials, fuels, the relationships among enterprises, and the like. The plan starts at the bottom with plans of managers of enterprises approved by the factory trade union. These managers report to local economic councils, which report to central administrative boards for different branches of industry. The heads of these industry boards should be approved by a national economic council. Bukharin and Preobrazhensky admitted: "Needless to say, the streamlining and planning of the economy is far from perfect. Instead, it is characterized by chaos and confusion." This stage is transitory, though, as everyone moves forward in a united front.

The task will be made simpler by "comradely" labor discipline, which will be the most important means of organizing production. "This does not mean that workers have to wait for orders from above and show no initiative; on the contrary, they should promote improvement in production and find new ways of organizing work." The working class will understand that they are now "the masters of their lives."[15]

The Socialist Controversy: The Feasibility of Socialism

The 1921 *ABC of Communism* was long on idealism and hope but short on details. As the first guide to planned socialist resource allocation, it expressed hope that workers and administrators (who were one and the same) would work together harmoniously and cooperatively. It spelled out that there was to be a unified national plan and that planning would be by industry, but that is about all. It admitted that a large number of mistakes would be made, but it avoided the toughest questions of all: Exactly how would the hundreds of thousands of enterprises and the millions of products be planned? How would producers and consumers behave? Would the information on which the national plan was to be based be accurate and reliable?

The problems of resource allocation under socialism have been widely discussed over the past century, and this discussion has been loosely termed the socialist controversy. *The **socialist controversy** asks whether a planned socialist economy can work at all, and, if yes, can it work at a reasonable level of efficiency.*

Socialist economic theory must explain how resources are to be allocated under socialism. If the socialist economy is planned, how will planners make rational decisions about the use of scarce resources? Is private ownership necessary for the proper functioning of markets?

Barone: A Theoretical Framework

The first consistent theoretical framework of resource allocation under socialism was developed by the Italian economist Enrico Barone. In 1907, Barone published "The Ministry of Production in the Collectivist State."[16] He argued, although in a limited and purely theoretical way, that prices, understood as relative valuations, are not bound to the market. *Barone's relative valuations meant that calculated ratios of equivalence could substitute for market prices.* These ratios of equivalence could be set by a central planning board (CPB), according to Barone.

Barone's model consisted of simultaneous equations relating inputs and outputs to the ratios of equivalence. When solved (Barone admitted that a real-world solution would be impossible), the equations could provide the appropriate relative valuations of resources required to balance demands and supplies. A CPB armed with perfect computation techniques would require perfect knowledge of all relevant variables, specifically (1) individual demand schedules, (2) enterprise production functions, and (3) existing stocks of both producer and consumer goods. Barone's principal conclusion was that the CPB's computed resource allocation would be similar to that of competitive capitalism. In fact, he saw no reason for substantial differences.

The impracticality of this approach, both at the time Barone was writing and with today's supercomputers, is obvious. Modern economies have hundreds of thousands or millions of enterprises producing almost an infinite number of goods and services for billions of people (if we take the world market). Barone's was a purely theoretical enterprise. Nevertheless, it demonstrated that the relative valuations of resources essential for rational resource allocation could, in theory, be discovered by solving equations rather than through the particular institutional arrangements of the market.

Economic Planning: Can the Barone Problem Be Solved?

In the 1950s and 1960s, Western economists began to work seriously on solving the "Barone problem." They asked: Can we use equations and computers to plan an entire economy in some optimal fashion? At the time, there was experimentation in Europe, especially in France, with "Planification" or indicative planning. *Indicative planning sets nonbinding targets for industries or sectors to provide information about the future to businesses.* In practice, these plans were not entirely indicative; the state promoted the fulfillment of these plans by credit assistance and subsidies.

Indicative planning differs from directive planning. In the case of *directive planning, targets are set by planners to directly determine outcomes because plan targets are legally binding on enterprises.* A popular expression in the Soviet Union was that "the plan is law." There was to be no choice: The plan had to be fulfilled.

The *ABC of Communism* and Barone provided no real operational instructions for producing a national plan, be it indicative or directive. But as French planners and advisors to developing economies, such as India, became interested in planning, they began to consider real-world solutions to the planning problem.

The theory of economic planning focuses on achieving an *optimal* balance. It shows how, again in theory, we could plan an economy so that it produces the optimal combinations of outputs, subject to the constraints of limited land, labor, and capital resources. Despite the optimism of the 1950s and 1960s, the outcome was not that hoped for by would-be planners. No contemporary economy actually came to allocate resources by using administrative planning techniques that selected detailed optimal combinations of outputs. Although the solution to such a planning problem is evident in theory, in practice it is elusive.

The planning problem can be expressed in the following manner:

$$\text{Maximize } U = U(X_1, X_2, ..., X_n) \qquad i = 1, ..., n \tag{7.1}$$

Here X_i are products that are produced subject to existing technology:

$$X_i = f(u_1, u_2, ..., u_m) \tag{7.2}$$

where u_j are resources (land, labor, materials, and others) and are subject to

$$u_j \le b_j \qquad j = 1, ..., m \tag{7.3}$$

where b_j represents resource availabilities, and u_j represents the total amount of resource j used by all producers. Moreover, resources are employed at zero or positive levels:

$$u_j \ge 0 \tag{7.4}$$

The goal of planning is to achieve the maximal value of Equation 7.1, which is termed the objective function. *The **objective function** summarizes the planners' economic objectives.* It defines the utility derived by society (U) from the outputs of different amounts of goods and services (X_i). The magnitude of goods and services available is limited by resource availabilities (u_j) with given technology. Resources cannot be used beyond their available supplies (b_j), either in the aggregate or for any individual resource.

In theory, if planners know the objective function, the production technologies, and the resource constraints, they could solve a system of equations that would tell them what and how to produce. Intuition tells us why such optimal planning is virtually impossible in practice.

First, an economy produces millions of distinct products and factor inputs. Even with powerful computers, it is not possible to solve the millions of simultaneous equations for the optimal combinations of inputs and outputs. To reduce the computational problem to manageable proportions, planners would have to work with aggregations of distinct commodities (such as tons of steel or square meters of textiles). Real-world economies do not operate with aggregated commodities. Factories make steel of specific grades and qualities. To go from a planning solution based on aggregate inputs or outputs to real production and distribution processes is an unsolvable problem.

Second, even if planners could gather the necessary information and make the complicated calculations, it is still not clear how to get enterprises actually to produce the planned commodities using the optimal combinations of inputs. Incentives must be created to encourage firms to implement the optimal production and distribution computed by planners.

Third, planning requires an almost infinite amount of information from enterprises and suppliers. The suppliers of information might be tempted to "game" the information they pass up to the planners. They control the local information, and planners cannot know if their information is accurate or falsified. Planners might find it difficult to elicit accurate information from enterprises, whose success or failure might hinge on these statistical reports.

A fourth problem is obtaining agreement on the objective function of society. How can planners know what goods and services are more important than others? Presumably, planners would have some insights on this issue, but the more complex the economy becomes, the more difficult it is to determine the relative social valuations of different goods and services. In a complex economy, planners must know whether industrial plastics are more important than stainless steel or ceramics, which might serve similar functions as substitutes.

When we examine modern planning theory, therefore, we come to the same conclusion as we did for the original Barone model: Planning is conceivable conceptually but cannot be implemented in practice. This conclusion applies to a national economic plan. It does not deny that businesses can use these methods to solve particular resource allocation problems within the firm. Only when we try to apply these techniques to an entire economy do we conclude that an "optimal" national plan is impossible.

The Challenge of Mises and Hayek

The discussion of the feasibility of socialism went little further until the 1920s and 1930s, when three important developments took place. First, Mises and Hayek mounted a formidable and now famous attack against the case for rational resource allocation under socialism.[17] Second, a number of Soviet economists made significant contributions to the theory of planning, then in its formative stages. Third, the noted Polish economist, Oskar Lange, set forth his famous model of market socialism, to be discussed in the next chapter.[18]

Hayek and Mises's challenge was directed at the problem of allocating producer goods in a socialist economic system, a task presumably in the hands of the state (with the allocation of consumer goods left to the market). Mises argued that, for a state to direct available resources rationally toward the achievement of given ends, knowledge of relative prices would be essential. The only way to establish these valuations would be through the market, which is absent in such a socialist system. In effect, Mises was making a very simple point: If enterprise managers do not know what is "cheap" and what is "expensive," how can they make rational economic decisions? They would be like a ship's captain sailing in the pitch dark with no stars visible and without a compass.

If prices are the vehicle by which relative scarcities are reflected, why not artificially simulate prices via a system of equations as proposed by Barone? Hayek argued that it would be difficult if not impossible to separate the allocation function from the workings of the market. Both, he suggested, are tied together through the profit motive and private property.

Mises argued that rational resources allocation depends on private property and the profit motives, both of which would be lacking in the socialist economy.

Instead, enterprises would be managed by state officials, who have no personal stake in profits. Mises argued that individuals are motivated by the urge for material self-betterment, which translates into utility and profit maximization. It is the search for profits that motivates enterprises operating in markets to produce goods and services as efficiently as possible. This drive for achievement cannot be socialized; it cannot be translated from the individual to the group. If resources are owned by the state, profits accrue to the state, not to individuals. Thus, the motivation for utilizing available resources in the most efficient way is lost.

Mises and Hayek's **socialist critique** *maintained that socialism would not work because relative scarcities cannot be known without market prices and individuals will not be motivated without private property.*

There have been two interpretations of Mises and Hayek. The first is that they concluded that socialism could not "work" in the sense that resource allocation would be impossible in the absence of markets. The socialist system would collapse under its own internal contradictions. The second and more common interpretation is that they were claiming that socialism cannot work *efficiently*. We now know in hindsight that the Soviet planned economy survived more than a half century. We also know that it operated at a relatively low level of efficiency. For these reasons, the subsequent cold-war debate over the relative merits of socialism and capitalism turned to questions of relative efficiency.[19]

In fact, few experts, either within or outside of the USSR, predicted that the system would collapse in the late 1980s, confirming Mises's and Hayek's assessments made seventy to eighty years earlier.

Solving Motivation Problems: The New Soviet Person

The *ABC of Communism* spoke of "comradely" labor discipline and "loyal" administrators working enthusiastically toward a common goal. Such idealists are working to "build socialism." The prospect of contributing to this noble effort will be a motivation that is lacking under capitalism, where workers are exploited.

Hayek and Mises discussed the motivation problems that would be present in the socialist system under the best of circumstances. They did not assume that socialist managers would be crooked or disloyal or that workers would shirk. Rather they described socialist managers with the best of intentions, who simply did not know what to do in the absence of price signals. They did not worry about corruption, preferential treatment of friends and relatives, or other forms of rent seeking.

The planned socialist economy is clearly complicated enough without having to worry about worker and managerial misbehavior. This is why official Soviet ideology predicted that a "New Soviet Man"—a *Homo soveticus*—would replace the capitalist *Homo economicus*.

Lenin expressed this new relationship to work: "For the first time after centuries of working for others, of working in subjection for the exploiter, it has become possible to work for oneself, and moreover to employ all the achievements of modern technique and culture in one's work."[20] Socialism will therefore create a "New Socialist Person" whose behavior will be honest, comradely, and heroic. As expressed by the official

Soviet *Political Economy, A Textbook*: "Socialism transforms labor into a matter of honor, valor, and heroism and imparts to it an increasingly creative character. In socialist society the working man, if he works well and displays initiative in improving production, is surrounded with honor and glory. All this gives rise to new social incentives to labor that are unknown under capitalism."[21]

*The **New Soviet Person** is a new breed of worker, expert, and manager who shares the idealistic goal of building socialism and will work unselfishly for that goal.* The *Textbook* goes on to mention that the New Soviet Person will be imperfect until communism is reached. Therefore, the state must still use "distribution according to contribution" as an incentive to work hard and well. But as the stage of communism approaches, the New Soviet Person will work for the joy of working and for the satisfaction of building communism.

Hopes for a New Soviet Person were dashed rather quickly. Managers, it was quickly learned, looked after their own interests. Workers worked poorly, especially when they could not buy the goods they wanted with the income they earned. There were indeed socialist idealists and activists who made enormous sacrifices for the goal of socialism, especially in the early years. Jubilant youths disembarked to build new factories in remote areas. Activists ventured into a hostile countryside to enforce the state's will on a hostile peasantry. But as time passed, the ranks of such idealists thinned.

Note the importance of the creation of a New Soviet Person to the feasibility of planned socialism. If we introduce an uncooperative and "selfish" labor and managerial force on top of the other immense complexities and problems of the system, the system would become even more unworkable.

Stalin combined the assumption of the New Soviet Person with party infallibility to justify purges of workers, experts, and managers. In May 1935, he declared in an address to the Red Army Academy that "cadres decide all."[22] Stalin used his "cadres decide all" slogan to place the blame for economic failures on deliberate sabotage by "enemies of the people." If the system itself was infallible and created a New Soviet Person, then all failures must be planned and executed by those who wished to destroy Soviet power. The end result was the imprisonment and execution of some two million Soviet citizens between 1935 and November 1938 alone.[23]

Resource Allocation under Planned Socialism

The leaders of the new Soviet socialist state had no choice but to come up with a practical solution to the planning problem. They did not have the luxury of debating theoretical solutions. They had immediate decisions to make: How much steel should they produce? Who should get it? Who was to write the plan? How was plan enforcement to be assured? The decision in favor of state ownership had already been made. After Stalin's ascendancy, it was decided that even agriculture and retail trade were to follow a plan rather than the market. These additions made the task of planners even more complicated.

By trial and error, the Soviet economic leadership searched for ways to develop and implement a unified national plan that would be "scientific" in nature. As the official Soviet textbook put it:

> Socialist planning is built up on a strictly scientific basis…. Socialist planning is based upon strict scientific foundations; it demands the continuous generalization of the practical experience of the construction of Communism as well as the utilization of the accomplishments of science and technology.[24]

The actual result was not pretty; it was an ad hoc system that was anything but "scientific planning."

Origins: The Soviet Union in the 1920s

The 1920s were "a golden age of Soviet mathematical economics and economic theorizing."[25] There was relatively open discussion, including debate about the appropriate path and mechanisms for economic growth under socialism.[26] The emphasis was on formulating a socialist path of development, guided by Marxist-Leninist ideological principles. Leading economists were given relatively free reign to explore different solutions as they sought to devise a national plan.

The calculation of balances of the national economy provided the starting point for what later would become the core feature of national economic planning. ***Balances of the national economy** were tallies of the availability and uses of commodities, such as grain or electricity.* From the first days of Soviet power, economic officials compiled grain balances, in which supplies were matched against proposed uses of grain. Grain was considered of such importance to feed the military and workers in the cities that its distribution should not be left to chance, much less to the market. As more and more commodities became critically short in supply, additional balances, such as sugar and cooking oil, and then of coal and metals, were compiled. In each case, the job of the balance was to check supplies against demands.[27]

As a planning routine emerged, balances of the national economy became the core of the national economic plan. The national plan was made up of a series of material balances for different products or sectors of the economy. *A **material balance** is a comparison of the planned supply of a particular product with the planned uses of that product.* These material balances summarize the demands and supplies for basic industrial, transport, and agricultural products and called for planners to bring them into balance without relying on market forces. They became the core of planning not only in the Soviet Union but also in Eastern European satellites and China.

Material Balances in Practice

Material-balance planning works as follows: A planning commission (based on instructions from political authorities) specifies a list of goods and services that are to be produced in the forthcoming plan period. The planning commission bases its work on a series of technical coefficients. ***Technical coefficients*** *measure the inputs (land, labor, capital, and intermediate products) needed to produce one unit of output.* They are based on historical relationships between inputs and outputs. Using these technical coefficients, planners draw up a list of inputs necessary to produce the planned outputs. The availability of inputs limits how much can be produced given available technology.

The planning commission task is to ensure a balance between outputs and inputs. For each factor input and intermediate good, the amount needed to produce the output (the demand) must be equated with the amount available (the supply). If a balance between the two sides does not exist, administrative steps must be taken to reduce demand and/or expand supply. A balance must exist for each item in order for the plan to be in balance. *A **balanced plan** is one in which the availabilities of each good or service match its planned uses.*

On the supply side, there are three main sources of inputs: production, stocks on hand, and imports. On the demand side, there are two main elements: ***interindustry demand***, *where the output of one industry (for example, coal) is used as the input for another industry (for example, steel)*, and ***final demand***, *which consists of output that will be invested, consumed by households, or exported.* If there are imbalances between demand and supply sides, planners can make adjustments on either side to bring the two into balance.

Note that adjustments are made by administrative interventions. Prices do not play a role. If there is too much demand for steel relative to its supply, the price of steel would not be raised. Rather a planner will cut the demand somewhere or raise the supply somewhere else.

The problem of balancing supply and demand can be conveniently formalized in the following manner:

$$
\begin{array}{cc}
\text{Sources} & \text{Uses}
\end{array}
$$

$$
\begin{aligned}
X_1 + V_1 + M_1 &= X_{11} + X_{12} + \cdots + X_{1n} + Y_1 \\
X_2 + V_2 + M_2 &= X_{21} + X_{22} + \cdots + X_{2n} + Y_2 \\
&\vdots \\
X_n + V_n + M_n &= X_{n1} + X_{n2} + \cdots + X_{nn} + Y_n
\end{aligned}
\tag{7.5}
$$

where n items are included in the balance, and

X_i = planned output of commodity i
V_i = existing stocks of commodity i
M_i = planned imports of commodity i
X_{ij} = interindustry demand; that is, the amount of commodity i required to produce the planned amount of commodity j
Y_i = the final demand for commodity i; that is, for investment, household consumption, or export

Table 7.1 depicts a simplified material balance. Note that for each commodity a balance exists. In the case of steel, there are three sources on the supply side: production of 2,000 tons, no stocks on hand, and imports of 20 tons, for a total supply of 2,020 tons. On the demand side, there are six users of steel: the coal

TABLE 7.1 Sample Material Balance

	Sources			Intermediate Inputs Required by				Final Uses	
	Output	Stocks	Imports	Coal Industry	Steel Industry	Machinery Industry	Consumer Goods Industry	Exports	Domestic Uses
Coal (tons)	1,000	10	0	100	500	50	50	100	210
Steel (tons)	2,000	0	20	200	400	1,000	300	100	20
Machinery (units)	100	5	5	20	40	10	20	10	10
Consumer goods (units)	400	10	20	0	0	0	100	100	230

Demonstration that a balance exists:

Sources of coal: 1,010 tons   = uses of coal: 1,010 tons
Sources of steel: 2,020 tons   = uses of steel: 2,020 tons
Sources of machinery: 110 units   = uses of machinery: 110 units
Sources of consumer goods: 430 units   = uses of consumer goods: 430 units

industry using 200 tons, the steel industry using 400 tons, the machinery industry using 1,000 tons, the consumer goods industry using 300 tons, exports of 100 tons, and domestic use of 20 tons, for a total demand of 2,020 tons. In this example, supply and demand are balanced at 2,020 tons.

For any planned economy, maintaining an appropriate balance between the supplies and demands for all products is an enormous task, a point emphasized by Hayek and Mises. Clearly, it would have been beyond the technical capacity of the early planning commissions to construct balances for thousands or tens of thousands of products. They were hard pressed to manage less than a hundred.

The early Soviet planners reduced the material-balance problem to more manageable proportions by applying one of Lenin's concepts. *Lenin's **Commanding Heights** was the notion that the entire economy could be controlled by centralized control of only its most important industries.* According to the commanding heights principle, the center needed to plan only the most important inputs and outputs. Others could be handled on a more decentralized basis, such as by regional authorities. Although only a portion of total output is under the control of planners, it is nevertheless sufficient to exert a major degree of influence over economic outcomes.

Indeed, actual planning practice limited centrally planned targets to a relatively small number, which grew over time as the sophistication of planning improved. Even this major simplification did not do away with a number of problems that the planners faced.

First, the determination of how much of each input ($X_{ij}s$) will be necessary to produce a unit of output turned out to be an extremely difficult problem. The technical coefficients relating input to output were typically derived from the previous year's plan and adjusted somewhat to allow for investment and productivity improvements.

If the technical coefficients are based on past history, there is no real attempt to ask whether they are optimal, in the sense that they represent the least amount of input required to produce a unit of output. If production in the past was inefficient, this inefficiency simply carries over into future plans. There is little that the planners can do about this. In the early years, they brought in engineering experts to evaluate the efficiency of blast furnaces, but this could be done only in a very limited number of cases.[28]

Second, it proved impractical to continuously update the technical coefficients. Technological advances change the relationships between outputs and inputs, but collecting such information from enterprises, many of which were not particularly cooperative, was a mammoth task. Planners therefore took the easy way out: They simply assumed that the technical coefficients remained the same, aside from some minor tinkering.

Third, the interrelatedness of economic sectors locked planners into the same patterns of inputs and outputs. To illustrate the problem: If more steel is needed, more coal will also be needed for the production of the steel. But to produce more coal, more electricity is needed, and on, and on, and on. These second-round effects reverberate throughout the economic system. *Second-round effects in material balance planning are the effects of changing one output or input on other inputs and outputs elsewhere in the balance.* Second-round effects mean that changes in one part of the material balance set off changes throughout the entire balance. One significant change means that the whole balance has to be recalculated.

The planners' response to second-round effects was to make as few changes as possible in their plans, even though technology and tastes changed in the meantime. Even if a new technology meant that chemical fertilizers should be substituted for traditional fertilizers, to insert a new sector (chemical fertilizers) into the balance would disrupt all the other balances.

To prevent the disruption of balances, planners adopted the strategy of planning from the achieved level. ***Planning from the achieved level*** *means that planners will make few changes in their plans and will repeat historical patterns to avoid major disruptions of the material balances.*

The practice of planning from the achieved level deprived the planned economy of dynamism by locking into place a fixed pattern of resource allocation. An example is the fact that Soviet lathes produced in 1970 were almost exactly the same as the ones produced in 1935—a practice scarcely heard of in market capitalist economies, where products are constantly changing.

Fourth, the goal of planners was to produce a consistent plan, not an optimal plan. *A **consistent plan** is one in which the supplies and demands for the various planned commodities are in balance.*

The balancing of demands with supplies is the essence of material balance planning, but the discovery of a consistent plan does not mean it is an optimal plan. *An **optimal plan** is that plan from all the possible consistent plans that maximizes the planners' objectives.*

Although it might be possible with advanced computers and programming to select an optimal plan from among a number of consistent plans, in practice, planners only were able to prepare two or three consistent variants at best, and there was no reason to suspect that the selected variants was the optimal one.

Powell's Nonmarket Signals

When we examine Soviet planning in practice in a later chapter, we shall have a chance to consider further aspects of material balance planning. At this juncture, let us simply observe that material balance planning worked, although at a low level of efficiency. Furthermore, it enabled the planners to select key areas on which pressure could be applied to seek rapid expansion, regional economic growth, or some other goal. However, it was cumbersome, and achieving a balance frequently required buffer or low-priority sectors (typically consumer goods) to absorb planning mistakes.

Raymond Powell examined how economies that operate through material balance planning were able to survive and grow.[29] Powell explained that material balance planning does not prevent managers, ministers, and planners from responding to nonprice scarcity indicators. Imbalances between output targets and the inputs allocated to produce these targets will prompt managers to generate alternative indicators of scarcity.

Managers will recognize that some materials are harder to acquire than others or that some materials held by the enterprise are scarcer than others. Ministries will receive warnings from their enterprises concerning production shortfalls and material shortages and will have to assess the reliability of this information.

On the basis of this nonprice information, resources will be reallocated within and among firms according to perceived indicators of relative scarcity. *Nonprice information constitutes signals of scarcity and priority that agents in the planned economy send out that are unrelated to prices.*

Managers may allocate internal resources (personnel and trucks) to seek out and transport scarce materials. Ministries and central planners will reallocate materials to enterprises that, according to the scarcity indicators, have legitimate emergencies. According to Powell, these natural responses to scarcity indicators introduce into material balance planning the workability that allows it to function and survive.

Horizontal Transactions and Opportunism

When orders are issued by administrative superiors to subordinates, we say that activities are organized as vertical transactions. *A vertical transaction is occasioned by an order from an administrative superior that is binding on the subordinate who is obligated to fulfill it.* In a vertical planning structure, subordinates are not supposed to deal directly with one another in horizontal transactions. *A horizontal transaction is one concluded by subordinates at the same level of the administrative structure without the approval of administrative superiors.* In a planned socialist economy, presumably, the goal of the dictator (the Communist Party or the Council of Ministers) is to ensure that the planned economy runs according to vertical orders and not according to "unplanned" horizontal transactions. *If most transactions are horizontal, it is unclear whether the economy is a planned economy at all.*

Early writers on the administrative-command economy, such as Hayek and Mises, paid little attention to the manner in which the dictatorship organized its bureaucratic staff to manage producers. Mises and Hayek spoke vaguely of a central planning board that would deal directly with enterprises. Students of dictatorship also simplified by assuming "costless coercion"—that the dictator could effectively persuade subordinates to do his bidding.[30] The dictator actively discourages horizontal relations among industrial ministries, regional authorities, or factories, because such alliances weaken control, particularly when they become powerful interest groups. Yet despite the dictator's opposition, informal "horizontal" structures inevitably emerge and weaken the center.

Figure 7.1 shows the source of conflict between vertical and horizontal transactions. It depicts the production and allocation of a particular industrial commodity such as pig iron, denoted by X. The demand curve D shows the quantity of X demanded by various potential users at different "prices" of X. The price could be the official price or some more comprehensive price that captures the resources costs of potential users to acquire X. The supply curve S shows the various quantities of X supplied by its producers at different prices.

FIGURE 7.1   Vertical versus Horizontal Structures

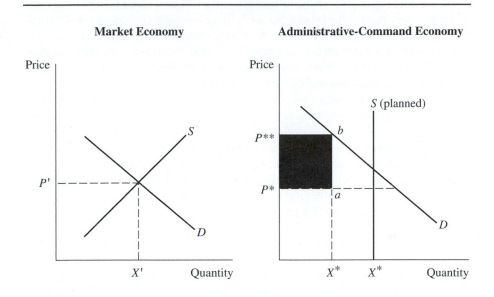

Market Economy   **Administrative-Command Economy**

Source: From GREGORY, Comparing Economic Systems in the Twenty-First Century, 7E. © 2004 Cengage Learning.

If this were a market economy (see the figure on the left), the market would determine how much of X would be produced and which potential users would get the available supply. All those willing to pay the market price (P') would get X'. The basic feature of an administrative-command economy (see the figure on the right) is that the dictator decides both how much X is produced and who gets X. The competitive market (on the left) is driven by an invisible hand that does not distinguish among buyers. Anyone who can pay the price will get the good. The dictator, on the other hand, can use his "visible hand" of allocative power to reward and punish for either economic or political ends. In the diagram, the dictator sets the production of X at X^* and its price at P^*. At this price, the producer is supposed to sell the entire output (X^*) to authorized buyers at the official price P^*. In a pure vertical system, the dictator decides who gets X^* among all those willing to pay the official price, P^*.

How agents respond to vertical orders depends on the degree of vertical trust. *Vertical trust is present when subordinates obey orders given them by superiors.* In this case, vertical trust means that only those designated to receive X will actually get X in the designated amounts from the producers.

Figure 7.1 illustrates why horizontal transactions inevitably compete with vertical orders. The producer of X realizes that it is producing a valuable commodity. In fact, a number of buyers are prepared to pay a "price" well in excess of the official price. Buyers are prepared to buy X^{**} at P^{**}. If the producer of X sells X^{**} to unauthorized buyers at P^{**}, the producer gains a "rent" denoted by the shaded area of the rectangle P^*abP^{**}. Those who are prepared to pay more may also be those who supply the producer of X with another valuable commodity, Y. The producer of Y also realizes that it is producing a valuable commodity for which a large number of buyers are prepared to pay more than the official price. If producers of X and Y follow vertical orders, they receive the official price $P*$. They have not violated any orders, and they will receive rewards from the dictator. On the other hand, both have passed up the opportunity to sell above the official price. They could obtain monetary bribes in addition to the official price, maintain good relations with their own best customers, or receive preferential treatment if the buyer happens to be a supplier.

In order for horizontal transactions to trump vertical transactions, there must be horizontal trust. *Horizontal trust is present when parties to horizontal transactions trust each other sufficiently to engage in transactions not sanctioned by superiors.*

If the reward from the horizontal transaction (the rent) exceeds the reward for vertical loyalty, the producer will engage in "illegal" or "unplanned" horizontal transactions. In extreme cases, horizontal transactions dominate vertical transactions. The dictator loses effective control of transactions and serves instead as a kind of referee, who must organize and control the rents of various competing interest groups.[31] The effective loss of control to interest groups leads to the kind of "red sclerosis" described by political economists, such as Mancur Olson.[32]

Various studies of the Soviet planned economy uncovered a seething current of horizontal transactions that ran counter to higher directives. Stalin himself raged at his own subordinates for acting in their own interests.[33] Studies of Soviet managers introduced the term "the pusher" (*tolkach*)—the traveling enterprise agent whose job it was to arrange illegal horizontal transactions.[34] The real *Homo soveticus* proved far removed from the New Soviet Person Soviet propaganda heralded.

The Performance of Planned Socialism: Hypotheses

Chapter 6 put forth several hypotheses concerning the expected performance of capitalist economic systems in terms of the performance criteria of income distribution, efficiency, economic growth, and stability. We shall now attempt to do the same for socialist economic systems.

Because we have no single paradigm of socialist economic systems, the formulation of hypotheses is especially difficult. Moreover, it is difficult to formulate hypotheses independently of the performance of real-world socialism. We now know a great deal about the efficiency problems of planned socialism in practice and about the collapse of the Soviet Union. Real-world experience is hard to ignore.

Income Distribution

The first hypothesis is obvious. Income should be more evenly distributed under planned socialism than under capitalism. The state (society) owns capital and land, and the returns on these assets go to the state. If the state chose to distribute a social dividend from capital, that would be distributed fairly equally as well. Presumably, authorities in planned socialist economies attach considerable importance to the "fair" distribution of income. We therefore expect income to be distributed relatively equally in a planned socialist economy.

Efficiency

The critics of planned socialism wrote that planned socialist economies have difficulty in efficiently allocating resources. Planners, they argued, would have great difficulty in processing information, constructing a plan, and motivating participants. Moreover, the planned socialist economy would not automatically generate relative prices that would enable participants to make good use of resources. These theoretical difficulties suggest that planned socialist economies operate at relatively low levels of efficiency. Planning techniques that aim at optimality are lacking, and planned socialist economies have had to use material balance planning procedures that are unlikely to place them on their production possibilities frontier. In fact, the aim of material balance planning is consistency, not optimality. Therefore, the hypothesis that the planned socialist economies do not perform well in terms of both dynamic and static efficiency appears to be a fairly safe one.

Economic Growth

In planned socialism, the state is able to exercise greater control over investment and savings rates than under capitalism. This is true because virtually all nonlabor income accrues to the state. One would therefore expect a higher savings rate under socialism, because the socialist state is likely to adopt rapid growth as a priority objective (the building of socialism).

In the planned socialist economies, rapid growth can be promoted both by the high savings rate and by the planners' direction of resources into growth-maximizing pursuits. At first glance, therefore, it would appear that one should hypothesize a higher growth rate for the planned socialist economies. The complicating factor, however, is the hypothesized lower efficiency of the planned socialist economies. Thus we must again refrain from stating a strong hypothesis about the relative growth of planned socialism, an issue that must be investigated empirically.

Stability

We hypothesize that the planned socialist economies will be more protected from the business cycle and unemployment than their capitalist counterparts. In making this statement, we do not deny that significant concealed instabilities (repressed inflation, underemployment) will be present in the planned socialist economies. We base our hypothesis of greater stability on the following considerations. First, investment spending will be subject to the control of planners and will probably be maintained at a fairly stable rate. Thus fluctuations in investment spending (a major source of instability in capitalist economies) will probably be small. Second, material balance planning will lead to an approximate balance of labor supplies and demands. Third, supplies and demands for consumer goods will be subject to a great deal of state control. Fourth, firms operating under pressure to meet output targets will provide workers with guaranteed jobs.

Viability

The capitalist economic system has existed for centuries. It shows no sign of disappearing, although some fear that it is being threatened by excessive state intervention and challenges to private property rights. With the exception of a few small and peculiar countries (such as Cuba and North Korea), there are no planned socialist economies left. Has planned socialism failed the viability test? Most would answer yes, but a few would argue that planned socialism failed because it was not run by the right people. Too many mistakes were made. They argue that if we could do it again, it would work magnificently.

Summary

- Socialist thinkers identified two types of socialism: planned versus market (or cooperative) socialism.
- The socialist planned economy must solve the what, how, and for whom problems. It is likely to solve them differently than a capitalist economy would.
- Marx and Lenin developed the theory of the new socialist state, which would be run by a dictatorship of the proletariat and which would go through a socialist and a communist stage.
- In the socialist stage, distribution would be according to contribution. Under communism, distribution would be according to need.
- Marx's notion of primitive capital accumulation raised the issue of whether the socialist state should also accumulate capital at the expense of another class, namely the peasants.
- The text *ABC of Communism* spelled out the principles of a national economic plan directed by worker-specialists.
- Mises and Hayek argued in the socialist controversy that socialism would be either unworkable or highly inefficient.
- Barone gave a theoretical framework for a national economic plan but one that was unworkable.
- Soviet leaders hoped that a New Soviet Person would emerge motivated by the desire to assist in building socialism.
- The Soviets' practical solution to the planning problem was the material balance system.
- The goal of Soviet planning is a balance. The need for administrative balance made Soviet planners reluctant to move away from the status quo.
- Powell used to concept of nonprice signals to explain the durability of the Soviet planning system.
- Agents in the Soviet economy are torn between horizontal and vertical transactions. The more horizontal transactions are used, the less planned the economy.
- Horizontal transactions encourage opportunistic behavior.
- The planned socialist economy should have a more equal distribution of income, lower efficiency, perhaps higher growth, and greater stability.

Key Terms

balanced plan—Availabilities of each good or service matches its planned uses.

balances of the national economy—Tallies of the availability and uses of commodities, such as grain or electricity.

Commanding Heights—Notion that the entire economy could be controlled by centralized control of only its most important industries (Lenin).

communism—The highest stage of social development, characterized by the absence of markets and money, abundance, and the withering away of the state.

consistent plan—Supplies and demands for the various planned commodities are in balance.

dialectical materialism—Marx's explanation of the pending triumph of socialism over capitalism.

dictatorship of the proletariat—Governs in the first stage of socialism and directly represents the interests of the proletariat.

directive planning—Targets set by planners to directly determine outcomes; plan targets legally binding on enterprises.

final demand—Output invested, consumed by households, or exported.

horizontal transaction—Concluded by subordinates at the same level of the administrative structure without the approval of administrative superiors.

horizontal trust—Parties to horizontal transactions trust each other sufficiently to engage in unsanctioned transactions by superiors.

indicative planning—Sets nonbinding targets for industries or sectors to provide information about the future to businesses.

interindustry demand—The output of one industry (for example, coal) used as the input for another industry (for example, steel).

material balance—Comparison of the planned supply of a particular product with the planned uses of that product.

national economic plan—Directs resource allocation for all (or the most important) sectors of the economy.

New Economic Policy—Restored private trade in agricultural goods, denationalized smaller enterprises, and kept larger enterprises under state ownership and control (March 1921 to 1928).

New Soviet Person—New breed of worker, expert, and manager sharing the idealistic goal of building socialism.

nonprice information—Signals of scarcity and priority that agents in the planned economy send out that are unrelated to prices.

objective function—Summarizes the planners' economic objectives.

optimal plan—That plan from all the possible consistent plans that maximizes the planners' objectives.

planning from the achieved level—Planners make few changes in their plans and repeat historical patterns to avoid major disruptions of the material balances.

primitive accumulation—Means by which the capitalist class gained a monopoly ownership of capital.

relative valuations—Calculated ratios of equivalence substituting for market prices (Barone).

second-round effects—Effects of changing one output or input on other inputs and outputs elsewhere in the balance.

socialism—An intermediate and transitory stage during which scarcity still exists and a strong state would be required.

socialist controversy—Whether a planned socialist economy can work at all, and, if yes, whether it can work at a reasonable level of efficiency.

socialist critique—Socialism would not work because relative scarcities cannot be known without market prices and individuals not motivated without private property (Mises and Hayek).

technical coefficients—The inputs needed to produce one unit of output.

vertical transaction—An order from an administrative superior that is binding on the subordinate.

vertical trust—Subordinates obey orders given them by superiors.

War Communism—The Soviet economic system that existed from 1918 to March 1921; virtually all enterprises nationalized, private trade and money outlawed, and peasant crops confiscated.

Notes

1. Merriam-Webster, "Socialism," http://www.merriam-webster.com/dictionary/socialism. Emphasis added.
2. Free Republic, "The Pilgrims, A Study in Socialism vs. Capitalism," http://www.free republic.com/focus/f-news/1730530/posts.
3. For efforts to define such a theory, see A. C. Pigou, *Socialism Versus Capitalism* (New York: St. Martin's, 1960), Ch. 1; Benjamin N. Ward, *The Socialist Economy* (New York: Random House, 1967), Ch. 1; J. Wilczynski, *The Economics of Socialism* (London: Unwin Hyman, 1970), Ch. 1; and Tom Bottomore, *The Socialist Economy: Theory and Practice* (New York: Harvester Wheatsheaf, 1990).
4. V. I. Lenin, *State and Revolution: The Marxist Theory of the State and the Task of the Proletariat in the Revolution*, written August–September, 1917, first published 1918. Source: V. I. Lenin, *Collected Works*, Volume 25, pp. 381–492.
5. V. I. Lenin, *State and Revolution*, http://www.cym.ie/documents/State_Rev.pdf.
6. V. I. Lenin, "The Proletarian Revolution and the Renegade Kautsky: Can There Be Equality Between the Exploited and the Exploiter?" *Lenin's Collected Works* (Moscow: Progress Publishers, 1974), vol. 28, pp. 227–325.
7. J. V. Stalin, Political Report of the Central Committee to the Sixteenth Congress of the C.P.S.U.(B.), June 27, 1930. First published: *Pravda* 177 (June 29, 1930). Source: J. V. Stalin, *Works* (Moscow: Foreign Languages Publishing House, 1955), vol. 12, pp. 242–385, http://www.marxists.org/reference/archive/stalin/works/1930/aug/27.htm.
8. Karl Marx, "Part I." *Critique of the Gotha Program*. First published in 1875. Reproduced in, http://www.marxists.org/archive/marx/works/download/Marx_Critque_of_the_ Gotha_Programme.pdf
9. Abram Bergson, *The Economics of Soviet Planning* (New Haven: Yale University Press, 1964), chap. 6.
10. Karl Marx, *Capital*, Vol. 1, Chapter 26 (Primitive accumulation). Reproduced in, http://www.marxists.org/archive/marx/works/1867-c1/ch26.htm.
11. Evsey Domar, "A Soviet Model of Growth," in *Essays in the Theory of Economic Growth* (New York: Oxford University Press, 1957), pp. 223–261.

12. James Millar, "A Note on Primitive Accumulation in Marx and Preobrazhensky," *Soviet Studies* 30, no. 3 (July 1978), 384–393.

13. Alexander Erlich, *The Soviet Industrialization Debate, 1924–1928* (Cambridge, Mass.: Harvard University Press, 1960); E. A. Preobrazhensky, *The New Economics*, Brain Pierce, transl. (Oxford: Oxford University Press, 1964); Nicolai Spulber, *Foundations of Soviet Strategy for Economic Growth* (Bloomington: Indiana University Press, 1964); Arvyn Vyas, "Primary Accumulation in the USSR Revisited," *Cambridge Journal of Economics* 3, no. 2 (1979), 119–130; Michael Ellman, "Did Agriculture Provide the Resources for the Increase in Investment in the USSR During the First Five Year Plan?" *The Economic Journal* 85, no. 340 (December 1975), 844–863.

14. Paul Gregory, "The Agricultural Surplus: A Retrospective," *Europe-Asia Studies* 61, no. 4 (2009), 669–683.

15. These quotations are from Bukharin and Preobrazhensky, *The ABC of Communism*, written in 1920. An English translation was published as Nikolai Bukharin and Evgeny Preobrazhensky *The ABC of Communism* (New York: Penguin Books, 1969). These quotes are from the original Russian (chaps. 6 and 12), reproduced in, http://www.marxists.org/russkij/bukharin/azbuka/azbuka_kommunizma.htm.

16. The key articles on this debate can be found in F. A. Hayek, ed., *Collectivist Economic Planning*, 6th ed. (London: Routledge and Kegan Paul, 1963).

17. See Ludwig von Mises, "Economic Calculation in Socialism," in Morris Bornstein, ed., *Comparative Economic Systems*, rev. ed. (Homewood, Ill.: Irwin, 1969), pp. 61–68.

18. The best source for the original article by Oskar Lange and related discussion is Benjamin Lippincott, ed., *On the Economic Theory of Socialism* (Minneapolis: University of Minnesota Press, 1938), reprinted by McGraw-Hill in 1964.

19. Abram Bergson, *Essays in Normative Economics* (Cambridge, Mass.: Harvard University Press, 1966), Ch. 9; also see Abram Bergson, "Market Socialism Revisited," *Journal of Political Economy* 75 (October 1967), 663–675. For contemporary views, see Don Lavoie, *Rivalry and Central Planning: The Socialist Calculation Debate Reconsidered* (New York: Cambridge University Press, 1985); Peter Murrell, "Did the Theory of Market Socialism Answer the Challenge of Ludwig von Mises? A Reinterpretation of the Socialist Controversy," *History of Political Economy* 15 (September 1981), 261–276.

20. V. I. Lenin, "How to Organize Competition," *Selected Works*, 1950; English edition, Vol. II, Part I, p. 368.

21. Institute of Economics of the Academy of Sciences of the USSR, *Political Economy, A Textbook* (London: Lawrence & Wisehart, 1957), chap. 31. Reproduced in, http://revolutionarydemocracy.org/archive/PoliticalEconomy.pdf.

22. J. V. Stalin, Address to the Graduates of the Red Army Academies, Kremlin, May 4, 1935. http://www.marxists.org/reference/archive/stalin/works/1935/05/04.htm.

23. Paul Gregory, *Terror by Quota* (New Haven: Yale University Press, 2009), chap. 7.

24. *Political Economy*, chap. 30, http://revolutionarydemocracy.org/archive/PoliticalEconomy.pdf.

25. Leon Smolinski, "The Origins of Soviet Mathematical Economics," in Franz-Lothar Altmann, ed., *Jahrbuch der Wirtschaft Osteuropas* [Yearbook of East European Economics], Band 2 (Munich: Gunter Olzog Verlag, 1971), pp. 137–154.

26. The most famous Soviet growth model is by P. A. Feldman and is discussed in Evsey Domar, *Essays in the Theory of Economic Growth* (New York: Oxford University Press, 1957), pp. 233–261. The classic work on the Soviet industrialization debate is Alexander Erlich, *The Soviet Industrialization Debate, 1924–1928* (Cambridge, Mass.: Harvard University Press, 1962).

27. R. W. Davies and S. G. Wheatcroft, eds., *Materials for a Balance of the National Economy 1928/29* (Cambridge, England: Cambridge University Press, 1985).
28. R. W. Davies, *The Soviet Economy in Turmoil, 1929–1930* (Cambridge, Mass.: Harvard University Press, 1989), 188–191.
29. Raymond Powell, "Plan Execution and the Workability of Soviet Planning," *Journal of Comparative Economics* 1 (March 1977), 51–76.
30. Ronald Wintrobe, *The Political Economy of Dictatorship* (Cambridge and New York: Cambridge University Press, 1998).
31. P. Boettke, *Calculation and Coordination* (London and New York: Routledge, 2001).
32. Mancur Olson, "The Devolution of Power in Post-Communist Societies," in Robert Skidelsky, ed., *Russia's Stormy Path to Reform* (London: Social Market Foundation, 1995), pp. 9–42.
33. Paul Gregory, *Political Economy of Stalinism* (Cambridge: Cambridge University Press, 2004), chap. 6.
34. Joseph Berliner, *Factory and Manager in the USSR* (Cambridge, Mass: Harvard University Press, 1957).

Recommended Readings

Socialist Principles: Founding Documents and Commentary

Michael Ellman, "Did Agriculture Provide the Resources for the Increase in Investment in the USSR During the First Five Year Plan?" *The Economic Journal* 85, no. 340 (December 1975), 844–863.

Alexander Erlich, *The Soviet Industrialization Debate, 1924–1928* (Cambridge, Mass.: Harvard University Press, 1960).

V. I. Lenin, "The Proletarian Revolution and the Renegade Kautsky: Can There Be Equality Between the Exploited and the Exploiter?" *Lenin's Collected Works* (Moscow: Progress Publishers, 1974), vol. 28.

V. I. Lenin, *State and Revolution: The Marxist Theory of the State and the Task of the Proletariat in the Revolution*, written, August–September 1917; first published 1918, Source: Collected Works, Volume 25.

Karl Marx, "Part I," *Critique of the Gotha Program*. First published in 1875, http://www.marxists.org/archive/marx/works/1875/gotha/ch01.htm.

James Millar, "A Note on Primitive Accumulation in Marx and Preobrazhensky," *Soviet Studies* 30, no. 3 (July 1978), 384–393.

E. A. Preobrazhensky, *The New Economics*, Brain Pierce, transl. (Oxford: Oxford University Press, 1964).

Nicolal Spulber, *Foundations of Soviet Strategy for Economic Growth* (Bloomington: Indiana University Press, 1964).

Arvyn Vyas, "Primary Accumulation in the USSR Revisited," *Cambridge Journal of Economics* 3, no. 2 (1979), 119–130.

The Socialist Economy: General Readings

Abram Bergson, "Socialist Economics," in Howard Ellis, ed., *A Survey of Contemporary Economics* (Philadelphia: Blakiston, 1948).

———, "Market Socialism Revisited," *Journal of Political Economy* 75 (October 1967), 655–673.

R. N. Carew-Hunt, *The Theory and Practice of Communism* (Harmondsworth, England: Penguin, 1963).

G. D. H. Cole, *Socialist Economics* (London: Gollancz, 1950).

Maurice Dobb, *Welfare Economics and the Economics of Socialism* (Cambridge, England: Cambridge University Press, 1969).

F. A. Hayek, ed., *Collectivist Economic Planning*, 6th ed. (London: Routledge and Kegan Paul, 1963).

Michael P. Todaro, *Development Planning: Models and Methods* (Nairobi: Oxford University Press, 1971).

Benjamin N. Ward, *The Socialist Economy* (New York: Random House, 1967).

The Socialist Economy

Pranab K. Bardhan and John E. Roemer, eds., *Market Socialism: The Current Debate* (New York: Oxford University Press, 1993).

Tom Bottomore, *The Socialist Economy: Theory and Practice* (New York: Harvester Wheatsheaf, 1990).

Bernard Crick, *Socialism* (Minneapolis: University of Minnesota Press, 1987).

Don Lavoie, *Rivalry and Central Planning: The Socialist Calculation Debate Reconsidered* (New York: Cambridge University Press, 1985).

Andrew Levine, *Arguing for Socialism: Theoretical Considerations* (London: Routledge and Kegan Paul, 1984).

Peter Murrell, "Did the Theory of Market Socialism Answer the Challenge of Ludwig von Mises? A Reinterpretation of the Socialist Controversy," *History of Political Economy* 15 (September 1984), 261–276.

———, "Incentives and Income Under Market Socialism," *Journal of Comparative Economics* 8 (September 1984), 261–276.

Alec Nove, *The Economics of Feasible Socialism* (Winchester, Mass.: Unwin Hyman, 1983).

S. Pejovich, *Socialism: Institutional, Philosophical, and Economic Issues* (Norwell, Mass.: Kluwer Academic Publishers, 1987).

James A. Yunker, *Socialism Revised and Modernized: The Case for Pragmatic Market Socialism* (New York: Praeger, 1992).

Economic Planning

John Bennett, *The Economic Theory of Central Planning* (Cambridge: Blackwell, 1989).

Morris Bornstein, ed., *Economic Planning, East and West* (Oxford: Ballinger, 1975).

Roger A. Bowles and David K. Whynes, *Macroeconomic Planning* (London: Unwin Hyman, 1979).

Phillip J. Bryson, *Scarcity and Control in Socialism* (Lexington, Mass.: Heath, 1976).

Parkash Chander and Ashok Pavikh, "Theory and Practice of Decentralized Planning Procedures," *Journal of Economic Surveys* 4 (1990), 19–58.

Pawel H. Dembinski, *The Logic of the Planned Economy* (Oxford: Clarendon Press, 1991).

G. M. Heal, *The Theory of Economic Planning* (New York: American Elsevier, 1973).

Don Lavoie, *National Economic Planning: What Is Left?* (Oxford: Ballinger, 1985).

Abdul Qayum, *Techniques of National Economic Planning* (Bloomington: Indiana University Press, 1975).

Gerald Sirkin, *The Visible Hand: The Fundamentals of Economic Planning* (New York: McGraw-Hill, 1968).

Nicolas Spulber and Ira Horowitz, *Quantitative Economic Policy and Planning* (New York: Norton, 1976).

CHAPTER
8

Theory and Practice of Market Socialism

Market socialism is a hybrid of market and state ownership. *Market socialism is an economic system that combines social ownership with market allocation.* As such, it offers the potential of combining the "fairness" of socialism with the efficiency associated with market allocation. The state (or cooperative groups) owns the means of production, and returns to capital accrue to the state or the cooperative. Because resources are allocated primarily by markets, many of the problems of planned socialism—the administrative and computational burdens of planning and the problem of valuing resources—appear to be avoided.

This chapter presents the theory of market socialism. Unlike the perfectly competitive model of capitalism, there is no single paradigm of market socialism. Instead, there are alternative visions of market socialism, one characterized by state ownership of the means of production, the other by worker ownership and management. Both visions rely on markets (or at least artificial markets) to do the job of resource allocation.

Whereas we can study the actual workings of both market capitalism and planned socialism on a large scale, the world has little practical experience with market socialism. The amount of real-world experience depends on the definition of market socialism.

In the third amendment to its constitution (March 1999), the People's Republic of China, "under the people's democratic dictatorship," will among other things "persist in reform" and "develop a "socialist market economy."[1] China's self-classification as a socialist market economy rests on the "leading role" of its Communist Party and on extensive state ownership in industry, transport, and finance. China is an open economy, a major beneficiary of globalization, and has no binding national economic plan. Resources are clearly being allocated, for the most part, by the market.

A second real-world experience was the decision of the former Yugoslavia, under Marshall Tito and the Yugoslav Communist Party, to reject Soviet-style planning for a form of worker-managed socialism in which enterprises were to be owned by the workers, who shared profits among themselves. It was the Yugoslav experiment that brought forth the formal theories of labor-managed economies discussed in this chapter. The Yugoslav experience, however, remains inadequately studied despite widespread scholarly interest. In addition, Yugoslavia no longer exists.

Third, we have experience with producer cooperatives in which employee-owners join together to manage the company jointly and share in profits. ***Producer cooperatives** are defined by three characteristics: worker control, profit sharing, and employee ownership.*[2] Producer cooperatives are located around the globe, but they remain a relatively small share of employment. Italy has the largest producer-cooperative employment at 2.5 percent of the nonagricultural labor force.[3] Although they have grown recently in the European Union, producer-cooperative numbers remain quite small.

The state of Israel has its own form of worker-managed firm, the kibbutz. *The **kibbutz** is characterized by equal (or more equal) sharing in the distribution of income: no private property, a noncash economy, high provision of local public goods for use by kibbutz members, and separate residences for children.*[4] Currently, the kibbutz population exceeds one hundred thousand in a country of more than seven million.

Partial employee ownership is another possible and more sizable form of labor-managed enterprises. In a number of U.S. companies, employees "own" the majority shares in the company through Employee Stock Ownership Plans. At one time, the then-largest U.S. airline, United Airlines, had majority employee ownership.[5] However, employee-owned companies should not be classified as producer cooperatives because the employees do not have management control.

In Japan, employees of corporations receive bonuses based on the company's performance. Martin Weitzman has labeled such arrangements as a share economy.[6] *A **share economy** is one in which employee compensation is tied to company performance through profit sharing.* Such a share economy is not a producer cooperative (labor-managed firm) because again the employees do not have management control.

A final possible example of a worker-managed firm is the Soviet/Chinese collective farm. *The **Soviet/Chinese collective farm** delivered to the state obligatory agricultural products at prices set by the state, sharing what was left over after deliveries and without ownership rights.* Insofar as most of the Soviet and Chinese farm populations were at one time or another members of collective farms (or communes as they were called under Mao Zedong), they accounted for a substantial share of national employment. They fail the definition of labor-managed concerns on two grounds: collective-farm households had no management rights, and they had no real ownership rights. Moreover, they operated in a nonmarket setting. We save discussion of them for later chapters.

The collapse of planned socialism in the late 1980s and 1990s has made market socialism the major alternative to capitalism. If you want socialism and it is clear that centralized planning does not work, the solution lies in socialist ownership within the setting of a market economy.

The demise of communism in Eastern Europe does not mean the demise of socialist thought and of democratic variants of socialism. The latter will continue to have appeal under the concept of radical economic democracy in which factories are owned and managed by workers and supplied with capital by public banks or some other "socialist" arrangement.[7] Such proposals, however, must answer the question of how to carry out such ideas in practice, not just in appealing theory.

Market Socialism: Theoretical Foundations

The problems of optimal planning—computational difficulty and motivation—make the concept of market socialism appealing. Permitting the market to direct most resource-allocation decisions reduces the burden on planners. The theorists of market socialism used **central planning board (CPB)** *as a catchall phrase for the political and administrative committees in charge of resource allocation.*

Another appealing feature of market socialism is that, by allowing individual participants to respond to market incentives, agents would have greater incentives to combine resources efficiently at the local level.

Advocates of market socialism had to answer two questions raised by Hayek and Mises (see Chapter 7). If the means of production are owned by society, what assurances are there that capital will be used efficiently? And will the social ownership of capital distort incentives or lead to perverse economic behavior?

The Lange Model

The most famous theoretical model of market socialism among economists is that proposed by the Polish economist Oskar Lange.[8] This model focuses on the use of a general equilibrium framework (emphasized in the writings of Barone, Vilfredo Pareto, and Leon Walras) that approaches a "solution" through a number of sequential stages (emphasized by Walras).

Other economists (most notably H. D. Dickinson and Abba Lerner) contributed to the Lange model, and a number of variants of the model exist.[9] Furthermore, the Lange model of market socialism differs from our definition of market socialism in that Lange envisioned only indirect usage of the market.

The Lange model posits three levels of decision making (see Figure 8.1). At the lowest level are firms and households; at the intermediate level, industrial authorities; and at the highest level, a CPB. The means of production, with the exception of labor, are state-owned. Consumer goods are allocated by the market.

The CPB would set the prices of producer goods. Producing firms would be informed of these prices and would be instructed to produce in accordance with two rules. **Lange's two rules** *are (1) to produce the level of output at which price is equal to marginal cost and (2) to minimize the cost of production at that output.* Households could make their own decisions about how much labor to supply and what to buy.

FIGURE 8.1   The Organization of Market Socialism in the Lange Framework

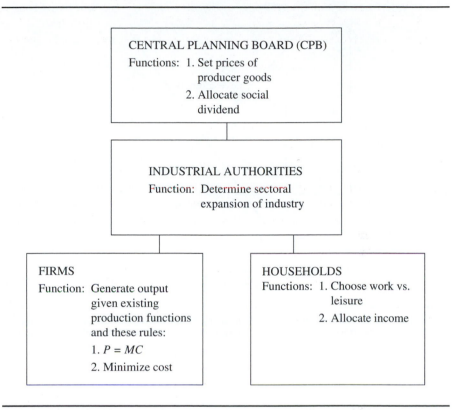

Source: From GREGORY, Comparing Economic Systems in the Twenty-First Century, 7E. © 2004 Cengage Learning.

The CPB would set price by trial and error. ***Lange's trial and error pricing*** *requires that the CPB sets prices arbitrarily and then adjusts them based on shortages and surpluses until equilibrium prices are reached.* According to this scheme, firms would demand and supply goods based on the CPB's prices. At first, there would be no reason to expect prices to equate supplies and demand, but these prices could be adjusted after observing whether shortages or surpluses exist until the CPB settles on a set of equilibrium prices.

Thus, in a sequential trial and error process, the CPB adjusts prices until they were at the "right" levels, where supply and demand were balanced.

In addition to setting prices, the CPB would also allocate the social dividend (rents and profits) earned from the use of productive resources owned by the state. This dividend could be distributed in the form of public services or investment, the latter decision being made in conjunction with the intermediate industrial authorities.

The state would have a substantial degree of power because it could determine both the magnitude and the direction of investment, although Lange argued that investment funds should be generally allocated to equalize marginal rates of return

FIGURE 8.2   Lange's Trial and Error Pricing

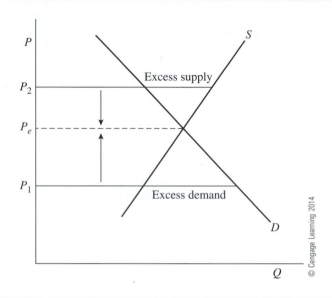

Explanation: The CPB first sets the price at P_1. It observes that there is excess demand at this price and raises it to P_2, where there is an excess supply. It then lowers the price to P_e. It continues to adjust until it finds the equilibrium price.

in different applications. Considerable central control over the economic system would be maintained by the CPB. At the same time, prices would be used for decision making to relieve the CPB of a substantial administrative task.

Let us examine some of the proposed advantages of the Lange model. Lange envisioned that, with the means of production owned by the state, both the *rate* and the *direction* of economic activity would be determined in large part by the state. Therefore, the returns from and the influence of private ownership would be removed. Accordingly, the distribution of income would be substantially more equal than under capitalism. Furthermore, the mix of output would be different, and insofar as the investment ratio would be largely state-determined. Both these features of the Lange model (a more even distribution of income and state control over investment) are presumed advantages. Lange further presumed that state control over savings and investment would reduce cyclical instability, a mainstay in the socialist critique of capitalism.

Lange argued that externalities could be better dealt with because the state could manipulate resource prices. Other economists—for example, Jan Tinbergen and Maurice Dobb—had argued that, in general, decisions made at higher levels rather than lower levels are likely to be "better" in terms of preventing undesirable environmental effects.[10]

Real-world market systems depart from the perfectly competitive model. Simulation of the market, argued Lange, would utilize the positive aspects of the market while eliminating its negative characteristics. In this context, it is ironic that Lange said little about difficulties of entry, economies of scale, and changes in technology. These forces are crucial in determining the degree of competition in a capitalist economic system. Might not some of these problems arise in the real-world operation of a Lange-type model?

Critics of the Lange Model

The Lange model captured the fancy of many, but it has not been dismissed by others as unworkable and lacking in substance. Critics ask, Why simulate market prices when you can have them naturally? The Lange model has never been tried, which tells us something about its feasibility. Even if the CPB limited price setting to intermediate goods, it would have to find balances for hundreds of thousands of millions of products.

Lange himself recognized that the many tasks assigned to the CPB could lead to a large bureaucracy, long considered a negative feature of socialism. The most outspoken critic on this score was F. A. Hayek. Hayek suggested that although the task set for the CPB might be manageable in theory, it would probably be unmanageable in practice.[11]

Abram Bergson and others have pointed to the problem of managerial motivation.[12] How would the intermediate authorities, and especially enterprise managers, be motivated to follow Lange's rules of conduct even if they knew marginal costs? The problem of establishing a workable incentive structure has been a major theme in modern socialist economic systems. The Lange model must also answer this question.

Bergson also emphasized the possibility of monopolistic behavior in the Lange framework—if not at the enterprise level, then at the intermediate level. This problem and the matter of relating one level to another are substantially neglected in the original formulation of the Lange model.

Although the Lange model uses features of capitalism, it also has elements normally associated with socialism. The debate, therefore, focused on whether the Lange model can operate in reality and, if so, how effectively. The Lange model also sparked interest because the USSR and other planned socialist economies used a crude form of trial and error for the setting of consumer prices. Although the process of price change was slow and cumbersome, prices were eventually adjusted to take into consideration the degree of excess demand as evidenced by queues and other visible signs of shortage.

The most telling critique of the Lange trial-and-error model is Kornai's theory of socialism as a scarcity economy (Chapter 4). It will be recalled that Kornai viewed scarcity as inherent to socialism. Because of soft budgets and other reasons, the demands for products would be almost unlimited. In such a setting, Lange's CPB would in vain search for higher and higher prices to achieve equilibrium only to find that no equilibrium existed. Although Lange felt that such excessive demanding of goods could be controlled by his two managerial rules, Kornai was convinced, based on actual experience, that managers would be driven into demanding more than they needed.

Market Socialism:
The Cooperative Variant

The second variant of market socialism is the labor-managed or cooperative economy. The *producer cooperative* and the *kibbutz* are two manifestations of cooperation and labor management. Recall that labor-managed firms or producer cooperatives are defined by the three characteristics of worker control, profit sharing, and employee ownership.

As noted at the start of the chapter, we can find real-world examples of labor-managed firms, but we have no examples of an economy in which the majority of firms operate according to labor management or cooperation. Cooperative and labor-managed firms have operated within a market economy in which they constitute a very small share. Therefore, such firms do not have to worry about setting prices because prices are set in the economy at large. Although they set the compensation for cooperative members, wages elsewhere in the economy serve as benchmarks whereby members gauge their own rewards from belonging to the cooperative.

Jaroslav Vanek, an enthusiastic advocate of the **participatory economy**, maintained that people should participate in making the decisions that affect their well-being:

> The quest of men to participate in the determination and decision-making of the activities in which they are personally and directly involved is one of the most important sociopolitical phenomena of our times. It is very likely to be the dominant force of social evolution in the last third of the twentieth century.[13]

Vanek proposed that, in theory, participation could be applied to an entire economy and offered five characteristics to identify the participatory economy. The **participatory economy** *is defined as one in which:*

1. *Firms will be managed in participatory fashion by workers.*
2. *Income sharing will be on the basis of equality for labor of equal intensity and quality, using a democratically agreed-upon income-distribution schedule assigning to each job its relative claim on income.*
3. *Workers enjoy the fruits of the operation, but they do not own, and must pay for the use of, productive resources.*
4. *The economy is a market economy. Economic planning may be used indirectly, but "never through a direct order to a firm or group of firms."*
5. *There is freedom of choice in employment.*[14]

In essence, resources are state-owned but are managed by the workers in the enterprises, whose objective is to create a maximal dividend per worker. Cooperative socialism belongs to the more general category of market socialism because there is state ownership of the means of production but also an exchange of goods and services in the market without intervention by central planners. Producer goods would use market prices, as opposed to prices manipulated by the CPB in the Lange framework.

The cooperative form of socialism has been viewed as an important and path-breaking addition to socialist thinking, especially by those who would identify with democratic socialism as a political system.

The theory of the cooperative model dates from a path-breaking article by Benjamin Ward published in 1958. It was then elaborated by Vanek and thereafter by other authors.[15] In this model, resources (with the exception of labor) are owned by the state and will be used by each firm, for which a fee will be paid to the state. Prices for both producer goods and consumer goods will be determined by supply and demand in markets. Enterprises will be managed by the workers (who may hire a professional manager responsible to them), who will maximize the dividend per worker (net income per worker) in the enterprise.

The objective of the labor-managed enterprise is to maximize net income per worker, where net income equals revenue minus costs including taxes. With this objective, management must decide on input and output combinations.

In addition to charging for the use of capital assets and for land, the state will administer the public sector and levy taxes to finance cultural and industrial development. In this environment, how will the cooperative firm behave? Let us examine two cases: first, the short run, where there is a variable supply of labor but capital is fixed; second, the long run, where both labor and capital are variable.

The cooperative model assumes that the enterprise manager maximizes net earnings per worker (Y/L) and that output (Q) is solely a function of the labor input (L) in the short run. The output can be sold on the market at a price (P) dictated by *market* forces. The firm must pay a fixed tax (T) on its capital. In the short-run variant, capital is fixed; so is the tax. Under these conditions, the firm will seek to maximize the following expression:

$$Y/L = \frac{PQ - T}{L} \qquad (8.1)$$

where

$$Y/L = \text{net income per worker}$$
$$P = \text{price of the product}$$
$$Q = \text{quantity produced}$$
$$T = \text{fixed tax levied on capital}$$
$$L = \text{labor input}$$

Maximum net income per worker in Equation 8.1 will be achieved when the amount of labor hired (L) is such that the value of the marginal product of the last worker hired is the same as the average net earnings per worker, or, in terms of the notation of Equation 8.1, when the following balance is achieved:

$$P \cdot MP_L = \frac{(PQ - T)}{L} \qquad (8.2)$$

where

$$MP_L = \text{marginal product of labor}$$

The logic of this solution is quite simple. If the enterprise can increase average net revenue by hiring another worker—that is, if the marginal product of the last worker hired is greater than average net revenue—then the worker should be hired, and average net revenue can be increased. The addition of workers should continue until the value of the marginal product of the last person hired and the average net revenue are the same. If the manager were to hire, at the margin, a worker the value of whose marginal product was less than the average net revenue per worker, then the net income of the remaining workers would fall.

In the *long run*, the cooperative must select its optimal capital stock (K), on which it will pay a rental charge (r) per unit of capital used. The firm now seeks to maximize its average net revenue as given by the following expression:

$$Y/L = \frac{PQ - rK}{L} \tag{8.3}$$

where

$$K = \text{amount of capital}$$
$$r = \text{charge per unit of capital}$$

The maximal value of this expression (average net revenue per worker) will be achieved in a manner similar to that of the short-run case. As long as the value of the marginal product of capital $(P \cdot MP_K)$ is greater than the rental rate (r) paid on capital, more capital should be hired and utilized until the return and the cost are equalized $(P \cdot MP_K = r)$. This rule applies to the perfectly competitive capitalist firm and the Lange-type firm as well. The same rule as for Equation 8.3 would apply for the hiring of labor, except that the charge for variable capital would have to be deducted as follows:

$$P \cdot MP_L = \frac{PQ - rK}{L} \tag{8.4}$$

These two cases, the short run and the long run, are both simple variants of the cooperative model. The short-run case is elaborated diagrammatically in Figure 8.3. Note that the model assumes that both product and factor markets are perfectly competitive and that there is no interference by the state.

The cooperative model works through product and factor markets. Households supply labor services as a consequence of maximizing household utility in the choice of work versus leisure. Labor supply schedules are determined in this way, as are demand schedules for consumer goods. Firms maximize net revenue per worker and in so doing supply goods and services at various prices and, at the same time, purchase inputs at various prices.

There is a close relationship between the cooperative model and the competitive capitalist and Lange models. In essence, the cooperative model captures some of the efficiency features of both. In the Lange model, the firm follows two rules, equating price and marginal cost and minimizing average cost of production. In the cooperative model, these two rules are replaced by a single rule (in the short run represented by Equation 8.2). In the case of the capitalist market economy, the firm follows the rule of equating marginal cost and marginal revenue, which in the case

FIGURE 8.3   The Cooperative Model

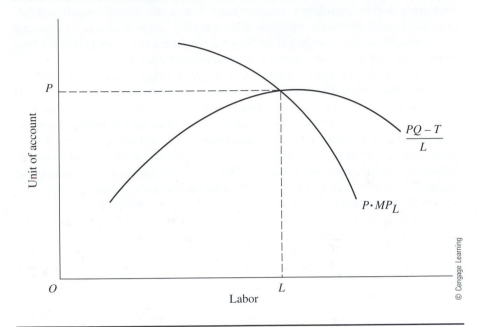

Explanation:

$$\frac{PQ-T}{L} = net \text{ receipts per worker}$$

$$P \cdot MP_L = \text{marginal value product of labor}$$

If the cooperative wishes to maximize the value of net receipts per worker, it should hire labor until the value of the marginal product of the last worker hired is the same as the net receipts per worker. In the diagram, the cooperative would hire *OL* labor, and each worker would receive *OP*.

of perfect competition reduces to the Lange rule; so here too, the cooperative variant simply replaces this rule with Equation 8.2.

There is now a considerable body of literature on the cooperative model and its variants. Many pertinent issues have been raised by the model's critics as well as by its admirers.

Criticism of the Cooperative Model

The cooperative model has been analyzed in detail by its pioneer Benjamin Ward. Ward noted that the two key features of the model are "individual material self-interest as the dominant human motivation" and "the resort to markets as the means of allocating resources."[16]

Ward devoted considerable attention to analyzing the response of the cooperative to various changes in capital charges, taxes, input prices, and product prices. For the capitalist and the Lange-type firm, an increase in price induces an increase in output (that is, a positively sloped supply curve). Ward demonstrated that the cooperative supply curve may well be negatively sloped (that is, an increase in price generates a *decrease* in output), especially in the short run.[17] If true, this would certainly be a perverse and undesirable result, especially in an economy where resources are allocated by the market. Such a result might (although it would not necessarily) threaten both the existence and the stability of equilibrium in product markets.

Ward also argued that if two cooperatives producing an identical product use different technologies, there will be a misallocation of labor and capital that would not occur if the two were capitalist firms.[17] In the case of the capitalist firms, both would hire labor until the wage was equal to the value of the marginal product ($W = P \cdot MP_L$), for both would face the same market-determined wage (W) and hence would settle at the same value of marginal product. In the case of the cooperative, however, unless the production functions are identical, the average net revenue per worker will differ between the two cooperatives. Although each cooperative equates average net revenue per worker with the marginal product of the last worker hired, overall output could be increased by moving workers to the cooperatives where the value of the marginal product is higher. In other words, the cooperative may be inefficient.

The cooperative is **inefficient** *if in equilibrium two cooperative have different productivities. This result is inefficient because output could be increased by redistributing labor between the two firms.*

Ward also argued that the cooperative might be undesirable if it existed in a noncompetitive environment. Specifically, he contended that the monopolistic cooperative would be less efficient than either its competitive twin or its monopolistic capitalist twin. The monopolistic cooperative would hire less labor, produce less output, and charge a higher price than either the competitive cooperative or the monopolistic capitalist firm.

Critics of the Lange model raised the issue of how to ensure appropriate managerial motivation. To the extent that the cooperative utilizes hired professional management, the problem of how to motivate and regulate managers will exist. Ward noted that in some cases the cooperative would have the incentive to expand, although in the absence of private property, it is not clear who the entrepreneur would be. It is possible that the state would play an important role in capital expansion questions through its ownership of the economy's capital.

Advantages of the Cooperative Model

Strong support for the cooperative model came from Vanek, who argued that the participatory economy is an element of social evolution that will be especially important in future years.[18] In addition to prescribing the participatory economy for present-day economies, Vanek argues that it is also the best alternative for developing economies.

Vanek does not agree with Ward's criticisms. He argues that if two cooperative firms have access to identical technology, and if there is free entry and exit, the input–output decisions of the cooperatives will be identical to those of capitalist firms operating under the same conditions. Moreover, Vanek argues, the result will be much more desirable socially because in the capitalist case the workers are rewarded according to the value of the marginal products, whereas under the cooperative case, workers are rewarded according to the decision of the collective, which they themselves control.

Vanek also maintains that under certain likely cases, the supply curve of the cooperative firm will not be negatively sloped as Ward suggests. Vanek shows that if the cooperative is a multiproduct firm, or if it faces an external constraint (for example, a limited supply of labor), the firm's supply curve will be positively sloped.

Vanek argues that the imperfectly competitive cooperative firm will be superior to the imperfectly competitive capitalist firm because it will have no incentive to grow extremely large and hence to dominate a particular market. Further, the cooperative will have no incentive to act in a socially wasteful manner—to create artificial demand for a product through advertising. Finally, Vanek maintains that both the demand for investment and the supply of savings will tend to be greater in the cooperative than in the competitive capitalist environment.

Many of the issues surrounding the comparative performance of cooperative and capitalist firms seem highly abstract and theoretical. They are, however, of basic importance to the efficiency of each system. The response of the cooperative firm to market signals determines the extent to which it can meet consumer goals and, in the long run, the extent to which an appropriate industrial structure is established in line with long-term development goals and aspirations.

Many of the supporters of the cooperative model, especially Vanek, argue that beyond these specific performance characteristics, the crucial features of the cooperative would be its "special dimensions." Among the most important is elimination of the capitalist dichotomy between management and labor. It is also argued that there would be greater social justice in the distribution of rewards.

The Cooperative Model: Empirical Studies

The pioneering work of Benjamin Ward in the late 1950s and the subsequent elaboration by Jaroslav Vanek in the late 1960s spawned a large and ever-growing body of literature devoted to labor management and, more specifically, to producer cooperatives as a means of organizing production in an economy.[19] A survey by John Bonin, Derek Jones, and Louis Putterman covers the theoretical and empirical literature on the subject in considerable detail. We can only highlight a few findings here.[20]

The participatory economy raises a number of empirical issues: Why does cooperation remain such a small share of economic activity? How do real-world cooperatives solve problems (not especially emphasized in the theoretical literature) of shirking within the collective? If we compare cooperative producers with their noncooperative counterparts, can we substantiate the theoretical predictions of the model, such as restrictions on entry by high-dividend cooperatives or low responsiveness to price?

Empirical research on these issues is difficult because of the small numbers of cooperatives and the problem of matching pairs of cooperative and noncooperative firms. There is some support (based on the U.S. plywood industry and Swedish and Danish producer cooperatives) that the cooperative model does not create inefficiencies in terms of differences in marginal products or negatively sloped supply curves. The available research also fails to find cooperative members shirking or supplying suboptimal effort, while admitting that such things are hard to measure. In the Israeli kibbutz, shirking is reduced by in-depth interviews of potential new members, the shunning of shirkers, and the acquisition of human capital that is specific to the kibbutz.[21] Although results are mixed, there is some evidence from studies of European producer cooperatives that they have a positive effect on productivity in the majority of cases.[22]

There is also the question of how cooperatives finance themselves. Do they self-finance through member contributions, or do they raise funds in capital markets? Intuition suggests that members will be reluctant to risk their own capital if they cannot sell their share upon exiting. Such considerations raise the issue of whether cooperatives underinvest relative to their market counterparts. This is an almost impossible question to answer empirically, but there does seem to be evidence that cooperatives are limited to self-financing in the absence of lenders sympathetic to their cause.[23]

There is one striking stylized fact concerning cooperatives: They remain a modest share of employment wherever they have been tried. The explanation is likely quite simple: Cooperatives require active management by members. If the cooperative becomes large, the link between membership and management is broken. Just like partnerships, the scale of cooperatives must be kept within limits to where individual members feel they are responsible for the company. Another factor is the known inability of cooperatives to obtain external funding. Lenders will want to know who is liable in the case of default. Are all members personally liable? If so, members would be reluctant to borrow in external markets if they have to risk their personal capital. Also, the larger the membership and the looser the tie between individual performance and the eventual dividend, the more likely there is shirking.

Democratic Socialism?

Proponents of socialism have been reluctant to give up on its feasibility after the collapse of communism in the Soviet Union and Eastern Europe. They specifically cling to socialism's perceived advantages: a more even distribution of income and a greater willingness, as a consequence of state ownership and control, to deal with externalities and monopolies. Lange's market socialism model seems to offer prospects for feasible socialism in that it uses markets to allocate resources while retaining the feature of socialism its proponents admire most, state ownership, but its proposed use of trial and error pricing does not seem possible in today's modern economies.

Specifically, market socialism's contemporary supporters argue that planned socialism failed because it was based on totalitarianism rather than democracy and that it failed to create rules for the efficient operation of state enterprises. The failure of a specific type of socialist economic system does not mean that other types would not work. Such systems could provide social justice and democracy. A form of democratic socialism should take their place. ***Democratic socialism*** *is state ownership of the means of production combined with a democratic state.* Democratic socialism has been proposed in a number of variants.

Pranab Bardhan and John Roemer maintain that socialist economies in the Soviet Union and elsewhere failed because of the mistakes in the way they were constituted: their noncompetitive and nondemocratic politics and their command/administrative allocation of resources and commodities.[24] A form of "competitive socialism" that rejects dictatorship and command allocation could work and could prove superior.

State-owned firms are not that different from large corporations in market economies, whose managers are separated from their owners. Just as market economies use
incentives to ensure that managers work in the interests of the owners, so can socialist
economies use similar incentives to motivate state managers. Bardhan and Roemer
reserve a key role for the state in the democratic socialist undertaking. State-owned
banks can represent the state's interest as insider monitors. State banks would make
sure that enterprise managers were operating the firm in society's interests and would
hold them politically accountable. Although it might not be easy, society must find
ways to make state-owned enterprises, managed by professional managers, work efficiently and in the society's interests. Managers would not be expected to be autom-
atons following Lange's two rules or selfless, they would have to be monitored and
be guided by appropriate incentives. But the difference between the managers of
large widely held corporations and state-owned companies is not that substantial and
can be bridged by appropriate monitoring and incentives.

James Yunker advocates what he terms "pragmatic socialism" based on public
ownership and a bureau of public ownership "to enforce upon the executives who
manage the publicly owned business corporations a strong profit motivation."[25]
The objectives of the publicly owned and privately owned company would be the
same. Socialist managers would be encouraged, just as capitalist managers are, to
maximize profits. The difference, however, is that dividends from profits are distributed to society at large rather than to private shareholders. In this fashion, the
unequal distribution of wealth will be equalized. The social "board of directors"
would ensure that the social dividend is disbursed in an egalitarian manner.

One of the most practical problems of this "pragmatic" socialism is how to get
from the current system of private ownership to state ownership. How is the nationalization of private property to be effected? How are private shareholders to be
compensated? How much force must be applied, and can the transition be carried
out within a democratic society? If a great deal of coercion is required, would this
be consistent with the democratic ideal?

The pillar of democratic socialism is its combination of state ownership
with democratic government. In his 1944 *The Road to Serfdom* (see Chapter 4),
F. A. Hayek wrote that state ownership will eventually lead to political
totalitarianism.[26] Ownership by the state will automatically lead to demands for planning and to intrusion into economic decision making by politicians. Hayek maintained that administrative resource allocation necessarily leads to authoritarianism;
socialist economies can never be democratically organized. Resources cannot be
administratively allocated without the exercise of extreme political power. Administrative orders to subordinates must be backed by the threat of punishment and the use
of coercion. Only those with skill in exercising political power will advance in the
political apparatus. Such a system requires a talent for unscrupulous and uninhibited
moral behavior. As Hayek wrote, "Totalitarianism is a logical consequence of the
attempt to centrally plan an economy. Although there may be no original intent to
exercise political power over people, the exercise of arbitrary power is the consequence of the desire to plan the economy scientifically." And furthermore, in order
to "achieve their end, collectivists must create power—power over men wielded by
other men—of a magnitude never before known, and ... their success will depend on
the extent to which they achieve such power."[27]

Even if we grant that socialist economies can be democratically organized, a number of other strictly economic problems must be solved. Andrei Shleifer and Robert Vishny make the case that, for a number of reasons, even a democratically organized market socialist economy will not work.[28]

First, with state ownership, state enterprises will be run to achieve political objectives, such as ensuring employment or buying the loyalty of supporters. If the state owners decided to use the most common economic criterion—profit maximization—they would divide the country's enterprises into monopolies because monopolies yield more cumulative profits than competitive firms. Past experience with socialism shows that socialist economies have indeed been organized into monopolies and cartels.[29]

Second, Shleifer and Vishny argue that public choice decisions will be more inefficient under democratic socialism than under market democracy. Like other forms of democracy, democratic socialist governments are prone to exploit the minority for the benefit of the majority or be dominated by interest groups. However, because state ownership is pervasive, these abuses will have more profound effects in socialist economies.

Third, no matter how hard the democratic socialist economy attempts to avoid it, the management of state-owned firms will become bureaucratized. Criteria like cost economies or technological innovation will be ignored, and state enterprises will be run for the convenience of their bureaucratic managers. Moreover, it will be difficult to monitor bureaucratic management. Even if state-owned banks are used as major shareholders in state enterprises to ensure that they are run in a businesslike fashion, the state remains the ultimate owner. As such, there is no way to avoid the politicization of the running of the enterprise.

These ongoing discussions send several messages. First, the demise of socialist economic systems in the former Soviet Union and the countries of Eastern Europe did not end discussions about socialism in general and market socialism in particular. Second, much of the discussion now focuses on the nature of the state in a socialist system and on how agency and incentive problems can be resolved if ownership is public. Finally, the promise of a more egalitarian distribution of income has had and continues to have strong emotional and political appeal.

State ownership of the means of production is not a new idea. Nationalization was a standard feature of the British Labor Party's program until the 1970s. France had the largest shares of state ownership in Europe in the early postwar period. Yet the share of state ownership has shrunk throughout the world in reaction to their inefficient and politicized operations. Instead of increasing state ownership, the trend of the last three decades has been the privatization of formerly state-owned companies. Most national airlines, state utilities, and manufacturing companies have switched from government to private hands. If privatization were not perceived as a superior result, it would not be taking place so broadly.

Although oil companies may have features not shared by other enterprises, it is one sector in which we can make crude efficiency comparisons, based on utilization of reserves, employees per barrel of production, and so on. Figure 8.4 shows the rankings of the world's oil producers by their measured productivity. It shows that the most efficient oil companies are private and the least efficient are state owned.

FIGURE 8.4   The Relative Efficiency of State and Private Energy Companies

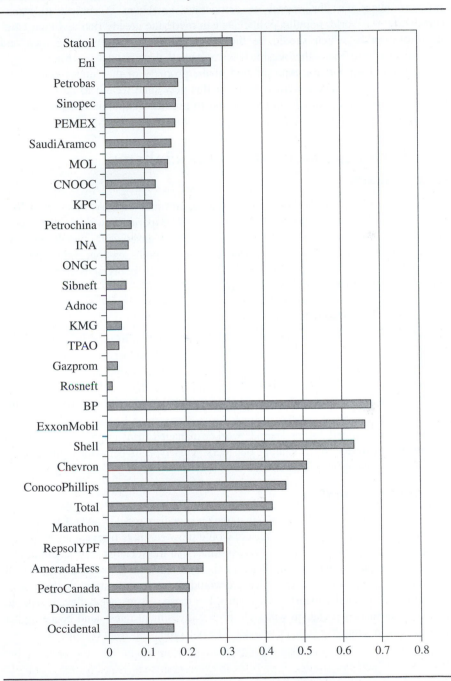

Source: Data from James Baker III Institute for Public Policy Rice University, "Empirical Evidence on the Operational Efficiency of National Oil Companies," Stacy Eller, Peter Hartley, and Kenneth Medlock III, March 2007. http://www-local.bakerinstitute.org/programs/energy-forum/publications/docs/NOCs/Papers/NOC_Empirical.pdf

The idea of democratic socialism is far from dead. Although conceived with idealistic intentions, the appeal of democratic socialism is subject to abuse. Throughout the world, populist politicians can revile the greedy rich and their command of wealth, which should be the property of the hard-working men and women on whose backs this wealth was created. If their appeal is strong enough, they can build support for expropriation of the property of the "undeserving rich" to the poor masses. The pattern is then for this new state wealth to be misused to rewards cronies and political supporters and to provide economic rents for current employees to ensure their loyalty.

The Performance of Market Socialism: Hypotheses

With the exception of the former Yugoslavia, a small country beset by ethnic problems that led to its demise, we lack real-world experience with market socialism of either the Lange or the worker-managed type. Consequently, we do not have the advantage of long historical experience to test hypotheses concerning the economic performance of market socialism. The following paragraphs represent our best analytical—though somewhat speculative—efforts.

Income Distribution

The easiest hypothesis to formulate concerns the distribution of income under market socialism. Inasmuch as capital continues to belong to society, we would expect income to be distributed more nearly equally under market socialism than under capitalism. Even in the case of worker-managed enterprises, the state must be paid a fee for the use of capital, and the state would presumably divide such income among the population on a fairly equal basis. Some reservations must be expressed, however. As critics have pointed out, prosperous worker-managed firms might protect extraordinarily high earnings by excluding outsiders. This type of behavior could lead to significant inequality in wage income.

Economic Growth

Proponents of market socialism claim that market socialism would yield relatively high rates of growth, primarily because society would plow earnings from capital back into the economy. This conclusion, however, assumes that the socialist state would not be pressured into putting the "social dividend" into current consumption in the form of subsidies and social services. Such pressure would be particularly strong in the case of democratically elected socialist governments. For these reasons, we believe it risky to presume that market socialism will yield higher investment rates—and hence higher rates of growth—than the capitalist model. The outcome is far from certain.

Efficiency

The theory of market socialism does not yield strong propositions concerning economic efficiency. Arguing that market socialism can indeed be more efficient than capitalism, its advocates cite the lack of monopoly, the greater attention to externalities, and individual participation in decision making. Its critics, however, mount equally convincing arguments about the inefficiency of market socialism: motivation problems, perverse supply curves, and the difficulty of finding equilibrium prices. Accordingly, we cannot venture any hypotheses about the relative efficiency of market socialism.

Stability

Advocates of market socialism make the following case for greater economic stability: The state will have greater control over the investment rate, so sharp fluctuations in investment can be avoided. Counterarguments exist, however. If market socialist economies (we are using the Lange model) have trouble adjusting prices to equilibrium, macroeconomic instabilities associated with nonequilibrium prices might be experienced. Moreover, democratically elected officials will be under strong pressure to pursue "popular" economic policies (the political business cycle), while feeling less pressure from market forces to tighten the reins on economic policy. Again, we cannot propose any strong hypotheses concerning the relative stability of market socialism.

Summary

- The appeal of market socialism is its attempt to combine the efficiency of markets (capitalism) with the more equitable distribution of income (socialism).
- The Lange model combines public ownership and trial and error to set output at equilibrium. Enterprise managers minimize cost and produce where price equal to marginal cost, according to Lange's rules.
- Critics of the Lange model argue that it is computationally inefficient, lacks in managerial motivation, and is potentially subject to monopoly problems.
- The cooperative model of socialism requires worker ownership, management by workers, and distribution of profits to worker-owners.
- The cooperative (or labor-managed) variant of market socialism substitutes maximization of the per-worker dividend for profit maximization. The cooperative will add new members as long as their marginal product exceeds the average product.
- The cooperative model suggests certain inefficiencies such as negative sloped supply curves and differences in productivity among cooperatives. Empirical research on the small share of cooperatives in the real world does not provide much support for these propositions, but results are mixed.
- Democratic socialism aims to combine political democracy with state ownership. The advocates and critics of democratic socialism debate whether state enterprises can be run efficiently.

Key Terms

central planning board (CPB)—Catchall phrase for the political and administrative committees in charge of planned resource allocation.

democratic socialism—State ownership of the means of production combined with a democratic state.

inefficient cooperatives—This occurs if two cooperative in equilibrium have different productivities. This result is inefficient because output could be increased by redistributing labor between the two firms.

kibbutz—Characterized by equal (or more equal) sharing in the distribution of income: no private property, a noncash economy, high provision of local public goods for use by kibbutz members, and separate residences for children.

Lange's two rules—(1) Produce the level of output at which price is equal to marginal cost and (2) minimize the cost of production at that output.

market socialism—An economic system that combines social ownership of capital with market allocation.

objective of the labor-managed enterprise—Maximize net income per worker, where net income equals revenue minus costs including taxes.

participatory economy—Firms managed in participatory fashion, income sharing equal for labor of equal intensity and quality, capital owned by the state, and market allocation and freedom of choice of occupation (Vanek).

producer cooperatives—Defined by three characteristics: worker control, profit sharing, and employee ownership.

share economy—Employee compensation is tied to company performance through profit sharing (Weitzman).

Soviet/Chinese collective farm—Delivers to the state obligatory agricultural products at prices set by the state, sharing what was left over after deliveries and without ownership rights.

trial and error pricing—The CPB sets prices arbitrarily and then adjusts them based on shortages and surpluses until equilibrium prices are reached (Lange).

Notes

1. Constitution of the People's Republic of China, Amendment Three (Approved on March 15, 1999, by the 9th National Party Congress at its 2nd Session), http://chinese culture.about.com/library/china/basic/blconstitution198314.htm.
2. John Bonin, Derek Jones, and Louis Putterman, "Theoretical and Empirical Studies of Producer Cooperatives: Will Ever the Twain Meet?" *Journal of Economic Literature* 31 (September 1993), 1290–1320.
3. Avner Ben Ner, "Comparative Empirical Observations of Worker-Owned and Capitalist Firms," *International Journal of Industrial Organization* 8, no. 3 (September 1984), 7–31.
4. Ran Abramitzky, "Lessons from the Kibbutz on the Equality–Incentives Trade-off," *Journal of Economic Perspectives* 25, no. 1 (Winter 2011), 185–208.
5. Avner Ben Ner, "Comparative Empirical Observations of Worker-Owned and Capitalist Firms," *International Journal of Industrial Organization* 8, no. 3 (September 1984), 7–31.
6. Martin Weitzman, *The Share Economy: Conquering Stagflation* (Cambridge, Mass.: Harvard University Press, 1984).
7. David Schweickart, *After Capitalism* (Landham: Rowman & Littlefield, 2002).
8. Benjamin Lippincott, ed., *On the Economic Theory of Socialism* (Minneapolis: University of Minnesota Press, 1938).
9. See, for example, F. M. Taylor, "The Guidance of Production in a Socialist State," *American Economic Review* 19 (March 1929), reprinted in Lippincott, *On the Economic*

Theory of Socialism, pp. 39–54; H. D. Dickinson, *Economics of Socialism* (London: Oxford University Press, 1939); and Abba P. Lerner, *The Economics of Control* (New York: Macmillan, 1944).

10. Maurice Dobb, *The Welfare Economics and the Economics of Socialism* (Cambridge: Cambridge University Press, 1969), p. 133.

11. F. A. Hayek, "Socialist Calculation: The Competitive Solution," *Economica* 7 (May 1940), 125–149, reprinted in Bornstein, *Comparative Economic Systems*, pp. 77–97.

12. Abram Bergson, *Essays in Normative Economics* (Cambridge, Mass.: Harvard University Press, 1966), Ch. 9.

13. Jaroslav Vanek, *The Participatory Economy* (Ithaca, N.Y.: Cornell University Press, 1971), 1–4.

14. Jaroslav Vanek, *The Participatory Economy* (Ithaca, N.Y.: Cornell University Press, 1971), 1–4.

15. For Ward's original contribution, see Benjamin Ward, "The Firm in Illyria: Market Syndicalism," *American Economic Review* 48 (September 1958), 566–589. See also E. Domar, "The Soviet Collective Farm as a Producer Cooperative," *American Economic Review* 56 (September 1966), 734–757; and Walter Y. Oi and Elizabeth M. Clayton, "A Peasant's View of a Soviet Collective Farm," *American Economic Review* 58 (March 1968), 37–59. For a general treatment of Vanek's argument, see Vanek, *The Participatory Economy*. For a survey, see John P. Bonin and Louis Putterman, *Economics of Cooperation and the Labor-Managed Economy* (New York: Harwood Academic Publishers, 1987).

16. Benjamin Ward, *The Socialist Economy* (New York: Random House, 1967), 183.

17. Benjamin Ward, *The Socialist Economy* (New York: Random House, 1967), 191–192.

18. Jaroslav Vanek, *The General Theory of Labor-Managed Market Economies* (Ithaca, N.Y.: Cornell University Press, 1970).

19. For more literature on participatory socialism, see Ellen Turkish Comisso, *Worker's Control Under Plan and Market* (New Haven: Yale University Press, 1979), chaps. 1 and 2; Hans Dieter Seibel and Ukandi G. Damachi, *Self-Management in Yugoslavia and the Third World* (New York: St. Martin's, 1982); Howard M. Wachtel, *Workers' Management and Workers' Wages in Yugoslavia* (Ithaca, N.Y.: Cornell University Press, 1973), chap. 2.

20. The literature on producer cooperatives is surveyed in John P. Bonin, Derek C. Jones, and Louis Putterman, "Theoretical and Empirical Studies of Producer Cooperatives: Will the Twain Ever Meet?" *Journal of Economic Literature* 31 (September 1993), 1290–1320.

21. Ran Abramitzky, "Lessons from the Kibbutz on the Equality–Incentives Trade-off," *Journal of Economic Perspectives* 25, no. 1 (Winter 2011), 192–194.

22. Bonin, Jones, and Putterman, "Theoretical and Empirical Studies of Producer Cooperatives," 1300–1305.

23. Bonin, Jones, and Putterman, "Theoretical and Empirical Studies of Producer Cooperatives," 1309–1311.

24. Pranab Bardhan and John E. Roemer, "Market Socialism: A Case for Rejuvenation," *Journal of Economic Perspectives* 6 (Summer 1992), 101–116.

25. James A. Yunker, *Socialism Revised and Modernized: The Case for Pragmatic Market Socialism* (New York: Praeger, 1992), p. 38.

26. F. A. Hayek, *The Road to Serfdom* (Chicago: University of Chicago Press, 1994).

27. Hayek, *Road to Serfdom*, 144.

28. Andrei Shleifer and Robert Vishny, "The Politics of Market Socialism," *Journal of Economic Perspectives* 8, no. 2 (Spring 1994), 165–176.

29. Peter Boettke, *Calculation and Coordination: Essays on Socialism and Transitional Political Economy* (London: Routlege, 2001), pp. 52–56.

Recommended Readings

Traditional Sources

H. D. Dickinson, *The Economics of Socialism* (London: Oxford University Press, 1938).

Abba P. Lerner, *The Economics of Control* (New York: Macmillan, 1944).

Benjamin Lippincott, ed., *On the Economic Theory of Socialism* (New York: McGraw-Hill, 1964).

Jaroslav Vanek, *The General Theory of Labor-Managed Economies* (Ithaca, N.Y.: Cornell University Press, 1970).

————, *The Labor-Managed Economy* (Ithaca, N.Y.: Cornell University Press, 1971).

————, *The Participatory Economy* (Ithaca, N.Y.: Cornell University Press, 1971).

Benjamin N. Ward, "The Firm in Illyria: Market Syndicalism," *American Economic Review* 48 (September 1958), 566–589.

————, *The Socialist Economy* (New York: Random House, 1967).

The Lange Model

Abram Bergson, "Market Socialism Revisited," *Journal of Political Economy* 75 (October 1967), 663–675.

Benjamin Lippincott, ed., *On the Economic Theory of Socialism* (New York: McGraw-Hill, 1964).

Market Socialism: The Labor-Managed Variant

Katrina V. Berman, "An Empirical Test of the Theory of the Labor-Managed Firm," *Journal of Comparative Economics* 13 (June 1989), 281–300.

John P. Bonin, Derek C. Jones, and Louis Putterman, "Theoretical and Empirical Studies of Producer Cooperatives: Will the Twain Ever Meet?" *Journal of Economic Literature* 31 (September 1993), 1290–1320.

John P. Bonin and Louis Putterman, *Economics of Cooperation and the Labor-Managed Economy* (New York: Harwood Academic Publishers, 1987).

Saul Estrin, "Some Reflections on Self-Management, Social Choice and Reform in Eastern Europe," *Journal of Comparative Economics* 15 (June 1991), 349–361.

Derek C. Jones and Jan Svenjar, eds., *Advances in the Economic Analysis of Participatory and Labor Managed Firms,* Vols. 1–4 (Greenwich: JAI Press, various years).

Kathryn Nantz, "The Labor-Managed Firm Under Imperfect Monitoring: Employment and Work Effort Responses," *Journal of Comparative Economics* 14 (March 1990), 33–50.

Hugh Neary, "The Comparative Statics of the Ward–Domar Labor-Managed Firm: A Profit–Function Approach," *Journal of Comparative Economics* 12 (June 1988), 159–181.

V. Russell and R. Russell, eds., *International Handbook of Participation in Organization* (New York: Oxford University Press, 1989).

Fernando B. Saldanha, "Fixprice Analysis of Labor-Managed Economies," *Journal of Comparative Economics* 13 (June 1989), 227–253.

Feasible Socialism: Contemporary Views

Pranab Bardhan and John E. Roemer, "Market Socialism: A Case for Rejuvenation," *Journal of Economic Perspectives* 6 (Summer 1992), 101–116.

————, eds., *Market Socialism: The Current Debate* (New York: Oxford University Press, 1993).

————, "On the Workability of Market Socialism," *Journal of Economic Perspectives* 8 (Spring 1994), 177–181.

Alec Nove, *The Economics of Feasible Socialism* (Winchester, Mass.: Unwin Hyman, 1983).

S. Pejovich, *Socialism: Institutional, Philosophical and Economic Issues* (Norwell, Mass.: Kluwer Academic Publishers, 1987).

Andrei Schleifer and Robert W. Vishny, "The Politics of Market Socialism," *Journal of Economic Perspectives* 8 (Spring 1994), 165–176.

James A. Yunker, *Socialism Revised and Modernized: The Case for Pragmatic Market Socialism* (New York: Praeger, 1992).

PART

III

Economic Systems in Practice

CHAPTER

9

Introducing the Anglo-Saxon, European, and Asian Models

Three Models of Capitalism

Chapter 6 related the theory of capitalism. The theory of capitalism shows how an economy uses the invisible hand of markets to allocate resources in an efficient manner, assuming that markets are competitive, that externalities are not overwhelming, and that reasonable macroeconomic stability is maintained. In practice, capitalist market economies organize themselves in different ways while still hewing to this generic description. In fact, each capitalist country of the globe differs from others in a number of respects, such as geography, culture, and history.

The next three chapters describe three different models of capitalism, dubbed the Anglo-Saxon model, the European model, and the Asian model. *The Anglo-Saxon model has its historical origins in Great Britain and is patterned after the classical liberal ideas of Adam Smith and the constitutional precepts of classical liberalism.* The Anglo-Saxon model uses common law, which operates with lay judges, juries, broader legal principles, oral arguments, and precedents and contends that government intervention in the economy should be limited. Although the U.S. economy diverges in any number of respects from this ideal model, it is the best real-world example we have.

The European model uses economic ideas enunciated in France and Germany in the nineteenth century that place less faith in the invisible hand and call for more state intervention in economic affairs. Its legal foundation is based on what James Buchanan terms "the constitutional order of socialism."[1] The European model accords the state a higher level of activity in the economy, pays relatively more attention to the "common good" as opposed to individual property rights, and provides for more regulation of private economic activity. The European model operates on civil (or Roman) law, which uses professional judges, legal codes, and written records. Real-world examples of the European model, among others, are France, Germany, and Sweden.

The **Asian model** *focuses on high rates of capital formation and on other devices, often supported by the state, to overcome relative backwardness in as short a time as possible.* The Asian model, as a relative latecomer, exists in a variety of forms and involves a considerable amount of experimentation, but its best real-world examples are Japan, South Korea, and Taiwan. Japan pioneered the Asian model in the nineteenth century and went on to become one of the most affluent of the world's economies. Contemporary Japan has lost many of the features of the Asian model, but we must include it.

The three chapters that follow explain the characteristics of these three models—in particular, how they differ in terms of the functioning of the labor and capital markets, the role of the state, and the legal system.

The black-and-white days of studying comparative economic systems disappeared with the collapse of the Soviet Union. We must now deal with nuanced differences that do not apply universally to all so-called members of a particular economic system. Germans consider their economic system as quite different from that of France and vice versa. The Taiwanese and South Koreans might object to being lumped together with Japan in one model. Nevertheless, the common features are strong enough to warrant our use of the three models we have outlined.

Our division of the capitalist world into three models is consistent with a general understanding that the Americans and Australians do things differently from the Belgians and the Norwegians or the Koreans and the Malaysians. Europeans talk, often disparagingly, about the "American way of doing business." U.S. executives must be trained to understand differences in the way of doing business before being shipped off to Tokyo. The Japanese executive must go through the same preparation before a posting to the United States. Moreover, nations that belong within one of these systems may look quite different from one another, especially in the case of the Asian model where "rich" countries like Japan and Singapore are bunched together with poor countries like Indonesia and Philippines. Moreover, the two most prosperous Asian countries, Hong Kong and Singapore, are really island-cities with strategic locations that they have utilized to create enormous wealth and affluence.

Our three models of capitalism leave out much of the world, most specifically Latin America, the Middle East, and Africa. We shall deal with these regions in later chapters, but, at this point in time, it is difficult to develop a framework in which we can identify them as distinctive economic systems.

Characteristics of the Three Models

In Chapter 2, we introduced the notion of using clusters to identify economic systems. If real-world economies cluster together according to measurable institutions, we have different economic systems. If there is no clustering, we end up with a large number of economies comprised of complex sets of institutions that defy analysis.

Economies identified as belonging to the Anglo-Saxon, European, or Asian models clearly will not be perfect fits. Insofar as the economic system is defined

TABLE 9.1 Clusters of Countries According to Economic Systems

Anglo-Saxon Cluster	European Cluster (North)	European Cluster (South)	Asian Cluster (From other developing countries)
United States	Germany	Spain	Thailand
United Kingdom	Sweden	Portugal	Taiwan
Switzerland	Norway	Italy	S. Korea
New Zealand	Netherlands	Greece	Malaysia
Japan	France		Non-Asian in cluster: Chile
Ireland	Finland		and S. Africa
Canada	Denmark		
Australia	Belgium		
	Austria		

Sources: Frederic Pryor, "Market Economic Systems," *Journal of Comparative Economics*, 33, no. 1 (March 2005): 25–47; Pryor, "Economic Systems of Developing Nations," *Comparative Economic Studies*, 48 (2006), 77–99 (Table 1).

in terms of a large number of institutions, we cannot expect any one economy to match the characteristics of its "parent" economic system in all respects. Rather, we must look at a number of real-world economies to see if we can identify shared or common characteristics that seem to hold in most cases.

Table 9.1 shows that industrialized countries and medium-income countries cluster into groups that roughly coincide with our three models of capitalism. The United States, United Kingdom, Canada, Switzerland, New Zealand, Ireland, and Australia form one "Anglo-Saxon" cluster. (Japan, as an Asian country, falls within this group as well.) Germany, France and other Northern European economies fall in a "European" cluster, whereas the poorer economies of South Europe appear to form their own group. Taiwan, South Korea, Thailand, and Malaysia cluster into an Asian group. We can also divide the Asian countries into two groups: the Four Tigers and the Mini Dragons.

The **Four Tigers** *are Hong Kong, Singapore, South Korea, and Taiwan, which have grown rapidly since the 1970s and are now relatively affluent. The* **Mini Dragons** *are Asian countries like Thailand, Indonesia, Malaysia, and the Philippines that have begun to grow rapidly but remain relatively poor.*

We take guidance from these groupings to determine the extent to which the institutions within each group differ from those outside the group.

In this chapter, we shall limit ourselves to five basic characteristics: ownership, the raising of capital, the size of the state, the degree of economic freedom, and the legal system. As we study each system in subsequent chapters, we ask the following common set of questions about each one:

1. What is the pattern of ownership, especially of corporations that account for the bulk of output?
2. How are corporations governed?
3. How is capital raised?

4. How do labor markets function?
5. What is the extent of government involvement via taxation, spending, and regulation?
6. How is income distributed and redistributed and with what results?
7. What is the prevailing legal system, and how does it affect other institutions and economic performance?

If all societies answer these questions in the same way, we really do not have much reason for studying economic systems. We use the term *comparative* economic systems because that is what we are interested in. We want to know how and why the economic systems of the world differ and how these differences affect economic performance.

Ownership

In Figure 9.1, we show three groups of countries that we have chosen to represent the Anglo-Saxon, European, and Asian models. In our descriptions and in later

FIGURE **9.1(A)**   Ownership Patterns: Anglo-Saxon, European, and Asian Model Countries (percent of total)

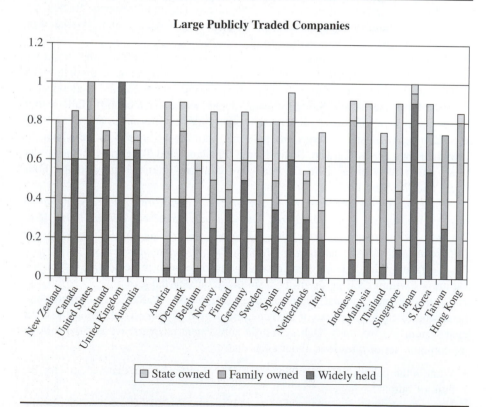

Large Publicly Traded Companies

☐ State owned   ▨ Family owned   ■ Widely held

Source: Rafael La Porta, F. Lopez-de-Silanes, and A. Schleifer, "Corporate Ownership Around the World," *Journal of Finance* 54, no. 2 (April 1999), 444; S. Claessens, S. Djankov, and L. Lang, "The Separation of Ownership and Control in East Asian Corporations," *Journal of Financial Economics* 58 (2000), 103

FIGURE **9.1(B)**   Ownership Patterns: Anglo-Saxon, European, and Asian Model
Countries (percent of total) (cont.)

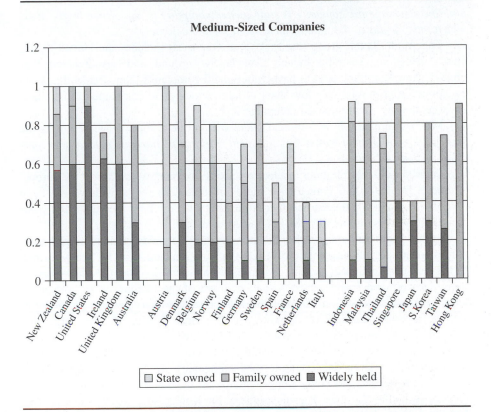

Medium-Sized Companies

☐ State owned   ▨ Family owned   ■ Widely held

Sources: Rafael La Porta, F. Lopez-de-Silanes, and A. Schleifer, "Corporate Ownership Around the World," *Journal of Finance* 54, (2) (April 1999), 444; S. Claessens, S. Djankov, and L. Lang, "The Separation of Ownership and Control in East Asian Corporations," *Journal of Financial Economics*, 58 (2000), 103.

The figures apply to medium-sized traded companies except for Indonesia, Malaysia, and Thailand, which are drawn from general surveys of businesses. Therefore, we use the same numbers for large and medium-sized businesses for these countries.

chapters, we focus on particular countries that come as close as possible to mani-festing the ideal form of the system, even if we have to go back in history. For the Anglo-Saxon model, we will single out the United States and England during its Industrial Revolution. For the European model, we use France and Germany and to a lesser extent Sweden. For the Asian model, we use South Korea and Taiwan and some of the Mini Dragons in this capacity.

In Figure 9.1, the three main ownership options are widely held companies, family owned companies, and state-owned companies. Figure 9.1 includes only companies traded on stock exchanges; we omit small establishments, almost all of which will be privately owned. There are other forms of ownership, such as coop-eratives and closely held small corporations, which are not shown in the figure.

The three main ownerships can be defined as follows: *A **widely held company** is one in which there are a large number of owners (shareholders), none of which own a controlling interest. A **family-owned company** is one in which families own and likely manage the company. A **state-owned company** is one owned by the state, which must organize the management team for the company.*

The Anglo-Saxon group (the first seven countries) includes the United States, United Kingdom, Australia, Ireland, Canada, Switzerland, and New Zealand. Figure 9.1 shows that they tend to have widely held companies. New Zealand is as an exception; it has a relatively low share of large widely held companies. Australia is an exception for medium-sized companies.

When a company is widely held, there will not be a control owner among the shareholders. *A **control owner** has sufficient ownership shares to control the operation of the company.*

Widely held corporations traded on stock exchanges are rarer in Europe. Although Denmark and France have more substantial shares of widely held large corporations, none of the European countries have widely held medium-sized companies, such as is common in the Anglo-Saxon model.

In the Anglo-Saxon countries, the sum of family owned and state-owned companies constitute a distinct minority (except in New Zealand, with its family farms). In the European countries, family-owned plus state-owned companies dominate. In both Germany and France, close to half or more of the medium-sized companies are owned by families. In Austria, the state is the primary owned of medium-sized companies. Particularly striking are the large shares of both large and medium-sized companies owned by the state in Europe.

The Asian economies tell a strikingly different story. With the exception of Japan, Asian large and medium-sized companies are owned by families. In Indonesia, Malaysia, and Hong Kong, virtually all large and medium-sized companies are owned by families. The stereotype of the Korean soap opera is indeed true: Families, often dynastic in their composition, own companies, both large and medium sized. There are even names for this type of family. In Korea, they are called *Chaebols*. The Li Ka-Shing (Hong Kong), Stanley Ho (Hong Kong),

TABLE **9.2** Number of Asian Billionaires, Specific Countries, 2011

Hong Kong	25
Japan	22
Indonesia	22
Taiwan	18
Malaysia	9
Philippine	5
Singapore	4
Thailand	3

Source: Based on data from *Forbes* Magazine, The World's Billionaires, http://www.forbes.com

Suharto (Indonesia), Henry Ty (Philippines), and Lee Kun Hee (Korea) families share the list of the world's billionaire families with American, Chinese, and European families.

Raising Capital: Issue Stock or Borrow?

Capitalist economic systems also differ in the way they raise capital. Small companies raise capital in the same way the world over. They save their own money to invest in their businesses. They borrow from relatives. After they are established, they borrow from banks.

Different economic systems deal differently with the financing of new businesses that need more capital than the owners can raise themselves. Some economic systems have organized venture capital markets to supply such capital; others are sorely lacking in markets for venture capital.

Venture capital is capital invested in new businesses in which there is a considerable amount of risk. California's vaunted Silicon Valley is an example of a vibrant venture capital market, largely lacking in other countries.

Corporations are distinguished from other legal forms of businesses by their ability to raise capital, often huge amounts in the billions of dollars. Corporations, unlike proprietorships and partnerships, raise capital by issuing stock and bonds in stock and bond market exchanges and by borrowing from lending institutions, most specifically from banks.

Figure 9.2 provides some insights into how the Anglo-Saxon, European, and Asian models use different approaches to raise capital. The best single indicator of the extent to which corporations raise capital by issuing new shares of stock is market capitalization. *Market capitalization is the market value of outstanding shares.* If XYZ Company has one million shares outstanding trading at $10 per share, its market capitalization is $10 million. Economies that have high market capitalizations (as a percent of GDP) tend to raise capital by selling new shares of stock. Those with low market capitalizations raise capital by other means.

Figure 9.2 shows that, again with the exception of New Zealand, the Anglo-Saxon countries have market capitalizations in excess of GDP. Switzerland has the highest market capitalization because it is a small country with huge banks and pharmaceutical companies. European countries (with the exception of Netherlands and its Royal Dutch Shell) have market capitalizations well below their GDPs. Asian countries (with the exception of the two city-states of Hong Kong and Singapore, which host giant multinational corporations and have huge market capitalizations) have capitalization rates even lower than Europe.

Corporations can also raise money by issuing bonds. *Corporate bonds require the corporation to pay interest over the life of the bond and then return the principal at maturity.* The value of outstanding corporate bond debt is a measure of the reliance of corporations on raising capital by issuing debt. It should be noted that corporate bonds account for a relatively small share of a nation's bond debt. Other forms of bonds tend to dominate, such as mortgage debt or the debt of federal, state, and local governments, which for a number of countries is approaching or exceeding the value of GDP.

FIGURE 9.2   Stock Market Capitalization as a Percent of GDP

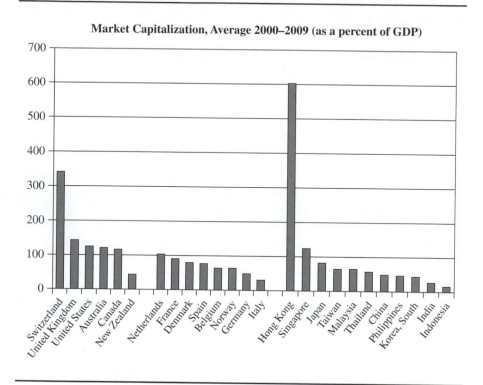

Market Capitalization, Average 2000–2009 (as a percent of GDP)

Sources: Standard and Poor's, New York, NY, Standard & Poor's Global Stock Markets Factbook 2010 (copyright). For more information, see http://www.standardandpoors.com, Internet release date 12/15/2010. GDP figures are from *Statistical Abstract of the United States, 2011* http://www.census. gov/compendia/statab/.

Figure 9.3 does not reveal strong patterns among the three prototype economic systems, although the Asian countries, with the exception of Singapore, raise relatively small amounts of capital (relative to GDP) by issuing corporate debt. We will later explore why Asian countries, especially the poorer ones, do not raise much capital in stock and bond markets, despite the supposed lure of investing in emerging markets. For now, we can say that considerable trust in the corporate governance and management of a corporation is required to entice investors to buy stocks and bonds, especially in foreign countries, whose business practices may be unknown and suspect.

Companies that raise their capital through stock and bond exchanges must satisfy an impersonal capital market. *An **impersonal capital market** is one in which the capital is supplied by entities outside of and unrelated to the enterprise on the basis of economic criteria.* In such a market, family or political relations count for little, if anything at all. If the deal is a bad one for the suppliers of capital, they will reject it.

FIGURE 9.3   Corporate Debt as a Percent of GDP

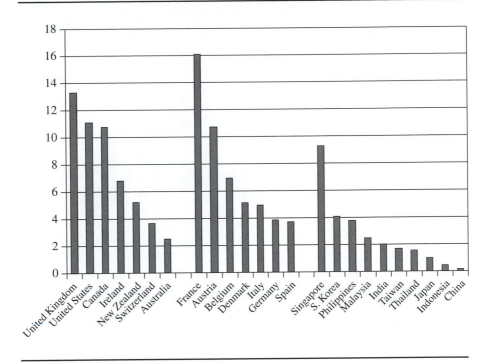

Source: Bank for International Settlements, http://www.bis.org/publ/qtrpdf/r_qa1103.pdf#page=106.

Banks, especially those that operate within the country and have local ties to management, should have a better sense of who is creditworthy and who is not. They may also make decisions based on personal or political relations or the intertwining of the bank with the borrower. Banks, as recipients of deposits, are positioned to channel these deposits for consumer loans, home mortgages, or business loans. U.S. banks, for example, make the majority of their loans to consumers and home buyers. (Their over-lending was a prime factor in the credit crisis that began in late 2007.) As of January 2011, of the $9.2 trillion in U.S. commercial bank credits, only $1.2 trillion went for commercial and industrial loans.[2] The largest Dutch bank (ABN AMRO), on the other hand, devoted some 40 percent of its loan portfolio to business lending.[3] Unfortunately, an exhaustive study would be required to break down bank lending between business lending and other forms of lending (such as mortgages and consumer lending).

Figure 9.4 shows that Asian economies are more dependent on bank credit than their European or Anglo-Saxon counterparts. The two exceptional bases of limited dependence on bank credit are the United States and Canada, both countries in which the banking sector focuses more on real estate and consumer loans than on business lending.

FIGURE **9.4**   Bank Loans as a Percent of GDP

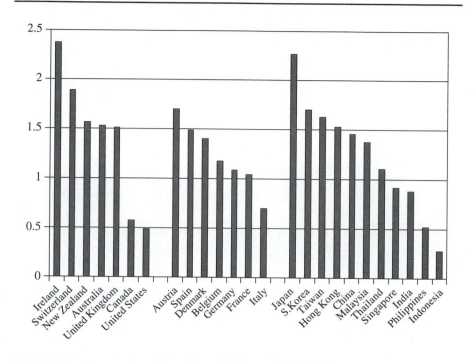

Sources: National Bank of Switzerland, "Swiss Financial Accounts, 2009," http://www.snb.ch/en/iabout/ stat/statpub/finacc/stats/frch; Federal Reserve Bank of St. Louis, "Total Loans and Leases of Commercial Banks," http://research.stlouisfed.org/fred2/series/TOTLL?cid=49; Asian Development Bank, "Country Tables," http://www.adb.org/Documents/Books/Key_Indicators/2010/Country.asp; European Central Bank, "Consolidated Banking Data," http://www.ecb.int/stats/money/consolidated/html/index.en.html.

The Role of Government

The size and impact of government are key institutions that determine the workings and performance of economic systems. The size of government is measured by its spending and taxation. The impact of government can be distinct from its size. Through regulation of unfunded mandates, the state can impose costs on businesses that do not depend on its size. A government that spends little of society's resources or imposes smaller tax burdens could still impose a heavy regulatory burden. However, usually the size and impact of government are strongly correlated.

Figure 9.5 captures the size of government as the ratio of government spending to GDP. Government spending is the better measure of the role of the state as a user of resources that could have been used in private activities.

With respect to the role of government, the countries divide rather neatly into three groups: The Asian countries have relatively small shares of government with the exception of Japan. The European countries have uniformly high shares of the

FIGURE 9.5 Government Spending as a Percent of GDP (2000–2009 Average)

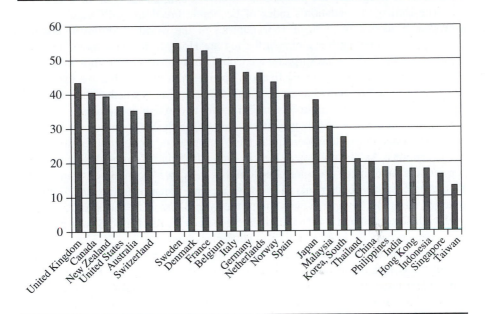

Source: Statistical Abstract of the United States, 2011; Asian Development Bank, Country Tables.
Note: Asian countries other than Japan and South Korea are for the year 2008.

state in overall economic activity. The average European shares for the first decade of the twenty-first century are all between 40 and 50 percent. By the end of the decade, only three remained below 50 percent. The Anglo-Saxon state shares were between 30 and 40 percent with only Canada and the United Kingdom reaching 50 percent or above in 2011.

The Asian countries, except Japan, tell an entirely different story. They fall between 15 and 30 percent of GDP. In the Asian countries, the state takes a much more modest share of output than in Europe. The United States represents a bellwether for the rise in government. Currently, the share of government spending is in excess of 40 percent. The debate in the United States is about whether to move to European levels—to fund a European-style welfare state or return to the lower rates of the past.

Economic Freedom

Economic freedom measures the degree to which participants in the economy are free to make economic decisions unconstrained by state intervention or corruption. Are businesses free to invest as they wish? Are they overburdened by taxes? Must they pay off corrupt officials? Are their property rights secure? Are they free to choose their jobs and are employers free to fire them? Some of these concepts can be measured, such as the fiscal burden or tariff rates. Others, such as corruption, must be gauged by the perceptions of those doing business in the country.

The Heritage Foundation's Index of Economic Freedom (see Chapter 2) measures the economic freedom of 183 countries of the world according to fourteen indicators of economic freedom.[4] At the top are Hong Kong, Singapore, and New Zealand. At the bottom (no surprise) are Cuba, Zimbabwe, and North Korea. These and other measures of economic freedom are far from perfect, but we expect that they capture real differences among nations. Our question is whether they yield distinct differences among Anglo-Saxon, European, and Asian economies.

Figure 9.6 reveals a striking pattern: The Anglo-Saxon countries tend to have stronger economic freedom scores than their European or Asian counterparts. There are exceptions: As already noted, the city-states of Hong Kong and Singapore are top ranking in terms of economic freedom, but the other Asian nations rank below their Anglo-Saxon counterparts. The lower income Asian countries have rankings that are quite low compared with either the Anglo-Saxon or European countries. Although Denmark and the Netherlands compete with the Anglo-Saxon rankings, the others, especially France and Italy, fall well behind.

The three sub-indexes of economic freedom in Figure 9.7 yield similar results for all three models for trade freedom. It seems that all the countries in Figure 9.7 have equal trade freedom, even the poorest country. The Anglo-Saxon, the European (except Spain and Italy), and the more affluent Asian nations have about the same levels of business freedom. The poorer Asian countries have much less. There are differences in freedom from corruption. There is more corruption among the poorer Asian nations than elsewhere. Among the Anglo-Saxon and European

FIGURE 9.6   Index of Economic Freedom (Comprehensive Total)

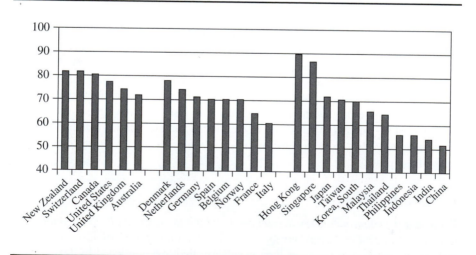

Source: Based on data from "2012 Index of Economic Freedom," The Heritage Foundation, http://www.heritage.org/index/

FIGURE 9.7   Economic Freedom: Sub-Indexes

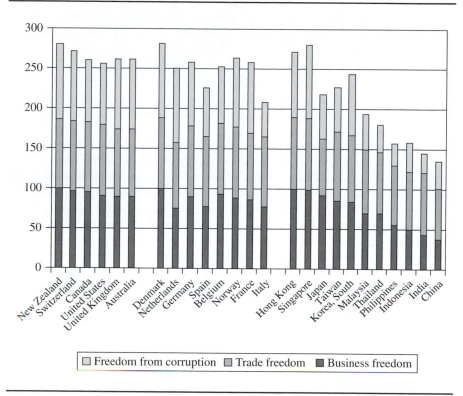

Source: Based on data from "2012 Index of Economic Freedom," The Heritage Foundation, http://www.heritage.org/index/

countries, the levels of corruption are relatively uniform except for Italy, which has an "Asian-style" level of corruption.

The Legal System

In an earlier chapter, we said that the institutions that constitute the economic system determine the "rules of the game" by which the system operates. Societies that have no rules of the game operate on an ad hoc basis. Usually the strongest and the cruelest win with no rules.

The legal system is the institution that spells out the formal rules of the game. It is comprised not only of the laws themselves but also the mechanisms by which they are enforced. Nations have a choice of legal systems. Usually the legal system was decided on in the distant past. English law began to form in the fifteenth century or even earlier. The legal systems that prevail in much of Europe draw from that of ancient Rome. Other countries were relative newcomers. The German and Japanese legal codes were adopted after World War II. The new Russian legal system was put in place in 1993, and Egypt will shortly begin considering a new legal system.

There are three basic types of legal systems: common law, civil law, and religious law, primarily Islamic Sharia law. ***Common law*** *is a legal system based on custom and precedents rather than a written legal code.* Common law originated in medieval England and spread into English offshoots in North America and then to English colonies. ***Civil law*** *is a legal system in which laws are written and codified and are not determined by judges based on custom or precedent.* ***Islamic (Sharia) law*** *is religious law based directly on the teachings of the Koran as interpreted by senior religious figures.*

Nations can have mixtures of two or three of the above "pure" forms of law. Table 9.3 lists the Anglo-Saxon, European, and Asian countries according to their legal systems. The implications of the choice of legal system will be explored in later chapters. For now, we note that Anglo-Saxon countries have common law legal systems (with the exception of Switzerland), the European economies uniformly use civil law, and the Asian economies have all three types of legal systems, even mixing them together.

We add in Table 9.3 a new category of countries that have adopted Islamic Sharia law either in its pure form or as a mixture with another legal system. In cases where the population is of mixed religions, Islamic laws apply to the Muslim population and another legal system applies to the rest of the population.

Origins of Civil Law   Civil law owes its origins to imperial conquests and to competition between the king and feudal lords. The two major historical exercises in written and codified law were motivated by imperial conquest.

In Roman times, the emperor needed a uniform set of laws to govern his far-reaching empire, which extended from northern Africa to England and to Constantinople at its peak. His governors needed a written law that would bring some uniformity to the legal system throughout the empire. Emperor Justinian ordered that Roman laws be collected into a clear system of laws, and the Justinian Code was completed in 534 AD.

The Napoleonic Code was drafted on the orders of Napoleon Bonaparte in 1804 to provide a uniform legal system for his territorial conquests that included much of Europe. The Napoleonic Code spread throughout this territory and supplanted the patchwork of feudal laws in effect throughout most of Europe.

Civil law proved particularly suited to countries, such as France and Germany, where feudal princedoms competed for power with the king. Each fiefdom or barony had its own rules, which meant that laws were unevenly applied across regions. The Napoleonic Code was intentionally written in clear and concise language so that it could be uniformly applied in each territory.[5]

Civil codes could not be enforced by local juries or judges as was the case with common law. Rather, civil law was enforced by professional judges, trained in central institutions and appointed by the central government.

We shall show in later chapters that the legal system affects the choice of other institutions and also economic performance. The choice of legal system is also part and parcel of Huntington's "clash of civilizations" (see Chapter 1). In geopolitical

TABLE 9.3   Legal Systems

Anglo-Saxon Economies	
New Zealand	common
Switzerland	civil
Canada	common
United States	common
United Kingdom	common
Australia	common
European Economies	
Denmark	civil
Netherlands	civil
Germany	civil
Spain	civil
Belgium	civil
Norway	civil
France	civil
Italy	civil
Asian	
Hong Kong	common
Singapore	common
Japan	civil
Taiwan	civil
Korea, South	civil
Malaysia	common and Islamic
Thailand	civil, common, Islamic
Philippines	mixed civil and common
Indonesia	mixed civil and Islamic
India	common
China	civil
Religious	
Afghanistan	Islamic (Sharia)
Iran	Islamic
Libya	Islamic
Nigeria	Islamic
Yemen	Islamic
Saudi Arabia	Islamic
Egypt	Islamic and civil
Syria	Islamic and civil

Source: Based on data from "List of Country Legal Systems," http://en.wikipedia.org/wiki/List_of_
country_legal_systems.

battles, such as in Iran or Afghanistan, wars have been fought and revolutions waged over the introduction of Islamic law. In many countries today that have sub-stantial Muslim populations, there is political debate over whether Islamic law can be applied separately to the Muslim population.

Conclusions

In this chapter, we examined some of the key institutions of Anglo-Saxon, European, and Asian clusters of economic systems. We examined who owns companies, how they raise capital, the size of government, their economic freedom, and their legal system. We find some distinctive differences: In the Anglo-Saxon countries, companies that are traded in stock exchanges have more widely held ownership and less family and state ownership. In the Asian group, family ownership dominates, but there is also more significant state ownership. The Anglo-Saxon and European models have different legal systems. The Anglo-Saxon countries have common law, whereas the European countries have civil law. The Asian countries have mixtures of civil, common, and religious law.

The most distinctive pattern emerges for the size of government, which is not a perfect measure of the role of government. The share of government spending is highest in Europe and lowest in the Asian countries, with the Anglo-Saxon countries generally in the middle ranges.

With a few exceptions—the two city-states of Asia (Singapore and Hong Kong) and Denmark and Netherlands in Europe—the measures of economic freedom are higher in the Anglo-Saxon countries. If we look at only three sub-indexes, business freedom, trade freedom, and freedom from corruption, the major differences are the greater degree of corruption in the middle-income and poorer Asian countries. It appears that all countries pursue about the same degree of trade freedom. This is an expected result: In today's global economy, countries must be open to trade or else they lose out.

As we study each of the models, we will go into more details. For now, we can say that there appears to be sufficient evidence to proceed with the three basic models of capitalism: the Anglo-Saxon, the European, and the Asian models. We do not have time to study a large number of economies for each economic system. If we did, this book would be without end. In the case of the Anglo-Saxon model, we study the United States in some detail. Because the European nations now belong to the European Union and share a large number of common features, we shall look at Europe more broadly, highlighting a number of countries. In Asia, we must deal separately with China, but we spend time on both the Four Tigers and the Mini Dragons. Although our charts show that Japan has more in common with the Anglo-Saxon model than the Asian model, we must include it in the Asian group as the pioneer of the Asian model.

Summary

- Countries form into clusters of economic systems.
- Three capitalist economic systems are the Anglo-Saxon, the European, and the Asian models.
- These models differ in terms of ownership, the raising of capital, the role of the state, and economic freedom.
- The Anglo-Saxon model has widely held corporate ownership. The Asian model has family ownership. The European model has little widely held ownership and more family and state ownership.

- The Anglo-Saxon model raises capital more through the stock market. Other models rely on other forms of raising capital.
- The size of the state relative to GDP is largest in the European countries and the smallest in the Asian countries.
- The Anglo-Saxon, European, and Asian models differ according to the legal system.

Key Terms

Anglo-Saxon model—Historical origins in Great Britain; patterned after the classical liberal ideas of Adam Smith and the constitutional precepts of classical liberalism.

Asian model—High rates of capital formation and on other devices, often supported by the state, to overcome relative backwardness in as short a time as possible.

civil law—A legal system in which laws are written and codified and are not determined by judges based on custom or precedent.

common law—A legal system based on custom and precedents rather than a written legal code.

control owner—Sufficient ownership shares to control the operation of the company.

corporate bonds—Corporation pays interest over the life of the bond and returns the principal at maturity.

economic freedom—The degree to which participants in the economy are free to make economic decisions unconstrained by state intervention or corruption.

European model—Economic ideas enunciated in France and Germany in the nineteenth century that place less faith in the invisible hand and call for more state intervention in economic affairs.

family-owned company—Families own and likely manage the company.

Four Tigers—Hong Kong, Singapore, South Korea, and Taiwan, which have grown rapidly since the 1970s and are now relatively affluent.

impersonal capital market—Capital is supplied by entities outside of and unrelated to the enterprise on the basis of economic criteria.

Islamic (Sharia) law—Religious law based directly on the teachings of the Koran as interpreted by senior religious figures.

market capitalization—The market value of outstanding shares.

Mini Dragons—Countries like Thailand, Indonesia, Malaysia and the Philippine that have begun to grow rapidly but remain relatively poor.

state-owned company—Owned by the state, which must organize the management team for the company.

venture capital—Capital invested in new businesses in which there is a considerable amount of risk.

widely held company—A large number of owners (shareholders), none of which own a controlling interest.

Notes

1. James Buchanan, Notes on the Liberal Constitution, *Cato Journal* 14, no. 1, http://www.cato.org/pubs/journal/cj14n1-1.html.
2. "Assets and Liabilities of Commercial Banks in the United States," http://www.federal reserve.gov/releases/h8/20110304/.
3. "Financial Disclosures," http://www.abnamro.com/en/investor-relations/financial-disclosures/index.html.
4. Business freedom, trade freedom, fiscal freedom, government spending, monetary freedom, investment freedom, financial freedom, property rights, freedom from corruption, labor freedom, tariff rate, income tax rate, corporate tax rate, and taxes as a percent of GDP.
5. Edward Glaeser and Andrei Shleifer, "Legal Origins," NBER Working Paper 8272, May 2001.

Recommended Readings

S. Claessens, S. Djankov, and L. Lang, "The Separation of Ownership and Control in East Asian Corporations," *Journal of Financial Economics* 58 (2000), 103.

E. Glaeser and Andrei Shleifer, "Legal Origins," NBER Working Paper 8272, May 2011.

Heritage Foundation, *2011 Index of Economic Freedom.* A product of the Heritage Foundation and the *Wall Street Journal.*

Rafael La Porta, F. Lopez-de-Silanes, and A. Schleifer, "Corporate Ownership Around the World," *Journal of Finance* 54, no. 2 (April 1999).

R. La Porta, F. Lopez-de-Silanes, A. Shleifer, and R. Vishny, "Law and Finance," *Journal of Political Economy*, 106, no. 6 (December 1998), 1113–1155.

F. Pryor, "Economic Systems of Developing Nations," *Comparative Economic Studies* 48 (2006), 77–99.

_____, "Market Economic Systems," *Journal of Comparative Economics* 33, no. 1 (March 2005), 25–47.

The Anglo-Saxon Model: England during the Industrial Revolution

The Anglo-Saxon model of capitalism originated in England during the Industrial Revolution. Its most complete incarnation was as the U.S. model of free-enterprise capitalism that had its roots in the common law inherited from England and the U.S. Constitution.

In the previous chapter, we cited empirical differences among countries that belong to the Anglo-Saxon, European, and Asian models. In the next two chapters, we examine more closely two countries to learn more about the Anglo-Saxon model: England in the period of the Industrial Revolution and the United States from its foundation to the present.

Intellectual Foundations of the Anglo-Saxon Model

The intellectual foundations of the Anglo-Saxon model go back to the Natural Law philosophers of the nineteenth century. The most influential thinkers of this tradition were John Locke and Adam Smith (Chapter 3), both of whom argued for limited government. English common law, another pillar of the Anglo-Saxon model, has roots in the twelfth century.

English common law is applied by judges, who use precedent and common sense to create a legal system of predictable outcomes. *The **principle of judicial** **precedents** means that court decisions should be consistent with past decisions.* Because cases were tried in courts across the country, separate rules of law threatened to evolve in different parts of the country. As time passed, a system of superior or appellate courts emerged that bound lower courts to their rulings. Because English common law was based on precedent, it defied codification into a uniform legal code as was the practice in the continental legal systems.

The English Industrial Revolution

The United Kingdom was home to the first Industrial Revolution (Chapter 1). The English Industrial Revolution was superimposed on preindustrial social, legal, and political traditions.

On the eve of the Industrial Revolution, the English countryside was transforming from feudal to modern agriculture. Manufacturing was carried out by a cottage industry of craftspeople and their families. Artisans formed craft guilds that regulated trade and were part of local government. These state-chartered guilds set norms, standards, and trademarks and restricted competition from outside the guild. Corporations were chartered by the crown or by noble families. Only much later could corporations, or joint stock companies as they were called, incorporate without a charter from the crown or state.

The English state followed mercantilist trade policies, such as the Navigation Acts, which forced colonies to trade only with the mother country. At times, the English state had to raise large sums to wage wars (such as against Napoleon Bonaparte) and finance campaigns against restive colonies (The American War of Independence).

The high degree of state intervention was the subject of Adam Smith's wrath as he wrote his *Wealth of Nations*. The English Industrial Revolution had to be superimposed onto an interventionist state.

The Industrial Revolution began in England in the late eighteenth century. New sources of mechanical power were harnessed to run textile mills and metallurgical industries. Science was systematically applied to create the new technologies that drove the Industrial Revolution. New sources of power (the steam engine and then electricity) and transportation (the railroad and steamship) made it possible to locate factories away from the rivers that had powered mills and transport goods to faraway markets. The result was the first sustained growth of real GDP in excess of population, which also began to expand. There had been episodes of growth of per capita GDP before, but they could not be sustained.

The Industrial Revolution spread from England to the European continent and to the European offshoots in North America and Australia. It remained limited to Europe and areas of European settlement until Japan joined the group of industrialized nations at the beginning of the twentieth century.

Figure 10.1 shows the effects of the Industrial Revolution on the United Kingdom and then later on its two European rivals: France and Germany. In 1700, the United Kingdom had a smaller economic output than France or Germany (almost half of France's output). By 1850, the United Kingdom had a larger GDP than either France or Germany. By 1900, the United Kingdom had a substantial advantage over France, which Germany had overtaken. Germany and France both benefited from their own industrial revolutions but could not keep up with England.

England began the Industrial Revolution with a per capita GDP above that of France and Germany, and widened its advantage by 1850. By 1900, Germany had gained the advantage over France, but both had fallen even further behind the United Kingdom. In 1900, England was the richest country in the world. It had

Figure 10.1   United Kingdom, France, and Germany: Divergence of the Industrial Revolution

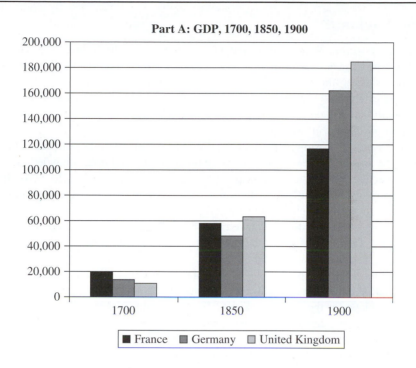

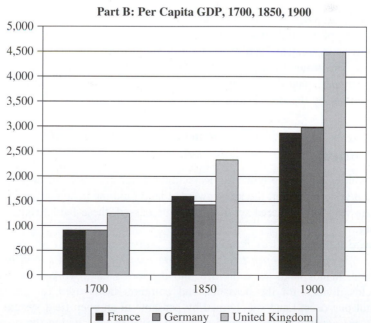

Source: Based on data from Angus Maddison home page, http://www.ggdc.net/MADDISON/oriindex.htm

almost quadrupled its standard of living since 1700. The latecomers, France and Germany, had more than tripled their affluence.

Why England?

Economic historian Walt Rostow sought to explain why the Industrial Revolution occurred in England and not in a continental country like Holland, which had shown earlier promise.[1] Rostow concluded that England, over a long period of time, had established preconditions for a takeoff into sustained growth. *The **takeoff** into sustained growth was the initial spurt of industrial growth from the first effects of the Industrial Revolution.*

According to Rostow, a country must have in place a number of preconditions before the Industrial Revolution could begin. His preconditions included, among others, secular education, a transportation infrastructure, a middle class from which entrepreneurs can be drawn, and a stable banking system. Preconditions do not come about overnight. Countries have to go through the necessary steps to establish preconditions. Rostow stated that one of the empirical signals of takeoff would be a doubling of the investment rate; therefore, the Industrial Revolution required a "revolution" in capital formation.

Rostow did not emphasize legal and other institutional preconditions. Edward Glaeser and Andrei Shleifer, however, showed that English common law provided a key advantage for the English takeoff.[2] English common law established a rule of law for contracts, dispute settlement, and the protection of private property. It placed restrictions on the power of the monarch to engage in fiscally ruinous wars and ventures. The power of the English king had been tamed by the start of the Industrial Revolution. The laws of the land were made by Parliament.

The corporation, whose legal foundations had been established centuries earlier (the colleges of Oxford and Cambridge were first organized as corporations), offered investors limited liability and raised large amounts of capital in stock exchanges. The American colonies were first settled by corporations, such as the Virginia Company and the Plymouth Company, while British colonization in Asia was carried out by the British East India Company.

Enclosures of Agriculture and the Development of Factories

In the centuries before the Industrial Revolution, English agriculture was organized as a feudal system. Earlier, the king rewarded land (and the people on it) to knights and others who had rendered services. As time passed, these feudal rights became hereditary.

***Feudal agriculture** was based on large estates, or manors, where peasants farmed strips of land in open fields and worked on the landlord's land in return.* In England, manor lands were divided into the lord's land, worked by the serfs; open fields divided for the peasants; and common lands used for grazing and other joint purposes. Land was farmed by peasants in an open field system, where different peasant households farmed scattered strips of land within the open field.

These strips could be periodically redistributed, destroying any sense of private ownership.

Feudal agriculture was notably inefficient because of strip farming and lack of peasant effort on the landlord's land. The inefficient use of common property is known as the tragedy of the commons. *The **tragedy of the commons** is the misuse and eventual destruction by individuals, acting in their own interests, of a commonly held asset.*[3] In the case of feudal agriculture, the common lands used by all for grazing or wood fuel were collectively overused, despite the collective interest in the common property.

The English solved the low productivity of feudal agriculture by consolidating land holdings in larger units and assigning property rights to the commons through enclosures. ***Enclosure** meant that lands that had been tilled in open fields or used in common were assigned to specific users, such as the manor owner or more prosperous peasant families.*

For more than two centuries, manor lands were enclosed, but at a slow pace. In some case, serfs resisted violently to enclosures. Around the time of the Industrial Revolution, enclosures accelerated as parliament passed a series of enclosure acts. In some cases, peasants were compensated for their losses; in others, they were not. In any case, rural dwellers increasingly left agriculture for textile mills and coal mines. Enclosures facilitated the thriving English woolens industry by allowing sheep farmers to rationally organize grazing lands. Although there is some dispute about the magnitude of the increase, agricultural productivity improved after enclosures.[4]

Social critics, including Karl Marx, viewed enclosures as a way to displace the agricultural population from the land to the cities. Whatever the facts, the general public paid more attention to Oliver Goldsmith's sorrowful poem the "Deserted Village" (1770) than the dry population censuses that showed the agricultural population did not decline during the Industrial Revolution. Rather, its share of the total fell as people swarmed to towns and cities.

Charles Dickens, in *Oliver Twist*, decried the miserable urban living conditions, especially of the impoverished youth, who worked in "dark satanic mills." Indeed, some 15 percent of workers in mining and textile mills in the 1850s were 15 years or younger.[5] Living conditions in the cities were miserable by twentieth-century standards, but life in the countryside or in cottage industries had not been much better.

Prior to the Industrial Revolution, there were no real factories. England's wool and textile products were processed by a cottage industry, whereby merchants "put out" the raw material to cottage manufacturers and picked up finished products for sale. The whole family, including small children, scraped out subsistence with long hours of tedious work.

The population lived in small towns and villages. Cities were dangerous, breeding disease and pestilence. In 1650, the metropolis of London had a population of between 350,000 and 400,000. Labor for the farms and cottage industries was supplied by the family, including children. In cottage industry, apprentices were taken in and were paid in training rather than with wages.

In the towns and cities, merchants and craftspeople were organized into guilds that gave them monopolies. These guilds of merchants, bakers, butchers, iron makers and so on were established by charters of the city or the king, and only the "masters" were members of the guild. They were the "freemen" of the city, and the various guilds were responsible for local government and for the welfare of their fellow guild members and the town's residents. Different towns and cities became known for the quality of certain products. Sheffield became known for its steel products, for example; other towns became noted for their wool tweeds.

Production facilities, such as mills or mechanized spinning facilities, first had to be located where rivers and streams could power waterwheels. With the development of the Watt steam engine in the mid-1760s, factories and shops moved to towns and cities, where ready labor was available. As factories and companies moved to towns and cities, the corporation replaced unincorporated associations and partnerships. Corporations raised capital by selling shares to investors, who were not liable for the debts of the company. Shareholders received dividends and could sell their shares to others in stock exchanges, like the London Exchange. Through sales of shares, there could be turnover of ownership without disrupting the business of the corporation.

The Joint Stock Company Act of 1844 made it possible to incorporate companies without specific legislation but without limited liability. *Limited liability meant that the shareholders of a joint stock company (corporation) were not responsible for the debts of the company if it went bankrupt.* The Joint Stock Company Act of 1856 allowed for limited liability of shareholders as long as the company's name included the word "limited." In a landmark court ruling of 1897, the corporation was acknowledged as a legal person.[6] *Legal personhood* meant *that the corporation could enter into contracts and do business in its own name.*

In the 1850s, corporations raised about a quarter of their capital on the London Exchange. By 1913, they were raising one third. Figure 10.2 shows that London markets were particularly good at raising capital for the railroads, which were financed privately. This was different from continental Europe, where the state played a major role in financing railroads. Comparative statistics confirm that stock-market financing characterized capital formation in the United Kingdom and the United States, whereas bank financing was used in Europe.[7]

Figure 10.2 also shows competition between government debt and corporate financing. Until 1883, there was more government debt traded on the London market than private shares. Jeffrey Williamson refers to this phenomenon as the crowding out of private investment by public debt issue, especially during the French wars, which he gives as a reason why British growth was not higher during the Industrial Revolution. This is one reason why Adam Smith warned about a spendthrift state.[8]

The Role of Government

The role of the state in the British Industrial Revolution was more than the "night watchman state" Adam Smith advocated. The British state taxed its subjects more heavily than France and Germany did, largely to finance its wars and colonies. It had a plethora of economic regulations, and the protections of private property were not ideal.[9] During the Industrial Revolution, the British state accumulated a

FIGURE **10.2** London Stock Exchange, Quoted Securities

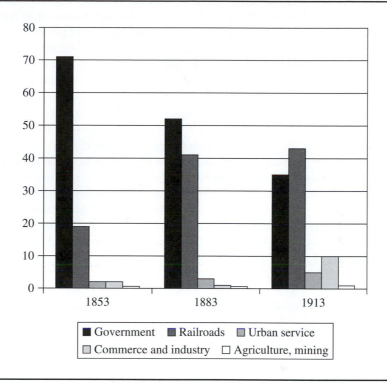

Source: R. Michie, *The London and New York Stock Exchanges, 1850–1913* (London: Allen Unwin, 1987), 54.

substantial national debt to finance the military ventures that made it the world's dominant power. The British state, however, was not indifferent to its poor, young, and helpless. Its Poor Laws required parishes to provide public support through local taxes. Although far from today's welfare states, substantial resources were provided through these transfer programs, even in the early years. Each parish was responsible only for its own poor and had to finance relief from its own sources. In 1696 the Poor Laws relieved only 4 percent of its five million population, but by 1803 it relieved 15 percent of its nine million population.

Mercantilist statutes in place at the start of the Industrial Revolution included laws regulating production (notably in the woolen sector), labor (the Statute of Artificers), the movement of people (the Poor Laws), shipping (the Navigation Acts), usury laws, and laws regulating joint-stock companies. Much of this regulation fell by the wayside in the first half of the nineteenth century, but new regulations were added, such as the Factory Act of 1833, the Joint-Stock Companies Act of 1844, and the Railway Act of 1844. The state's capacity to enforce regulatory and tax regulations improved over time. So we do not know whether there was more or less state regulation as the Industrial Revolution proceeded.

According to Douglass North and Barry Weingast, England performed the role of defining and protecting private property rights better than its European counterparts.[10] They argue that when Parliament effectively limited the power of the king during the Glorious Revolution of 1688, England was freed from the risk of a king taking private property by means of excessive taxation. Property free from appropriation and limited state expenditures made possible an orderly market for government debt. The private share market piggy-backed on this public debt market, thereby creating a stock market for the sale of corporate shares to public investors.

English common law protected private property from others, but it did not protect private property from the state. The English Bill of Rights (1689) provided freedom from royal interference in the law, freedom to petition, freedom of speech, the right to bear arms, and no taxation without the consent of parliament. It did not limit the government's ability to confiscate property and did not require just compensation.

Whereas the later American Constitution limited the ability of state to expropriate property, the English laws did not. The dominant characteristic of the English political and constitutional system, both before and after 1689, was the sovereignty of Parliament. This meant that Parliament had the right to make or unmake laws with few restrictions.

Summary

- The intellectual origins of the English Anglo-Saxon model were natural law philosophy and English common law.
- The Industrial Revolution began in the United Kingdom and then spread to the European continent and then to the United States. Economic growth of output exceeded population, and the United Kingdom became the world's dominant economic and political power.
- The Industrial Revolution was made possible by the application of science and engineering to the economy.
- Rostow described the preconditions necessary for the industrialization takeoff.
- English agriculture developed because it used enclosures to consolidate agricultural land and remove the tragedy of the commons.
- Towns and cities followed mercantilist practice of guilds.
- The Industrial Revolution was made possible by the limited liability corporation that attracted capital.
- The role of government in the United Kingdom was substantial, but taxation and spending was put in the hands of Parliament.

Key Terms

enclosure—Lands that had been tilled in open fields or used in common were assigned to specific users, such as the manor owner or more prosperous peasant families.

feudal agriculture—Large estates, or manors, where peasants farmed strips of land in open fields and worked on the landlord's land in return.

legal personhood—Corporation could enter into contracts and do business in its own name.

limited liability—Shareholders of a joint stock company (corporation) were not responsible for the debts of the company if it went bankrupt.

principle of judicial precedents—Court decisions should be consistent with past decisions.

takeoff into sustained growth—Initial spurt of industrial growth from the first effects of the Industrial Revolution (Rostow).

tragedy of the commons—The misuse and eventual destruction by individuals, acting in their own interests, of a commonly held asset.

Notes

1. W. W. Rostow, *The Stages of Economic Growth: A Non-Communist Manifesto* (Cambridge: Cambridge University Press, 1960).
2. Edward Glaeser and Andrei Shleifer, "Legal Origins," NBER Working Paper 8272, May 2001.
3. Garrett Hardin, "The Tragedy of the Commons," *Science* 162, no. 3859 (December 13, 1968), 1243–1248.
4. D. N. McCloskey, "The Enclosure of Open Fields: Preface to a Study of Its Impact on the Efficiency of English Agriculture in the Eighteenth Century," *Journal of Economic History* 33 (March 1972); Robert Allen, *Enclosure and the Yeoman* (Oxford: Clarendon Press, 1992).
5. Carolyn Tuttle, "Child Labor during the British Industrial Revolution," http://eh.net/encyclopedia/article/tuttle.labor.child.britain.
6. Ron Harris, "Government and the Economy, 1688–1850," http://jenni.uchicago.edu/WJP/papers/Harris_govt_and_econ.pdf.
7. R. Michie, *The London and New York Stock Exchanges, 1850–1913* (London: Allen Unwin, 1987), 54; C. Mayer, "New Issues in Corporate Finance," *European Economic Review* 32 (1988), 1180.
8. Jeffrey Williamson, "Why Was British Growth So Slow During the Industrial Revolution?" *Journal of Economic History* 44, no. 3 (September 1984).
9. This section is based on Ron Harris, "Government and the Economy, 1688–1850," *The Cambridge Economic History of Britain since 1700, Volume I, 1700–1850*, ed. Roderick Floud and Paul Johnson (New York: Cambridge University Press, 2004), 204–237. Available at: http://works.bepress.com/ron_harris/3Ron Harris, Government and the economy, 1688–1850.
10. Douglass North and Barry Weingast, "Constitutions and Commitment: The Evolution of Institutions Governing Public Choice in Seventeenth-Century England," *Journal of Economic History* 49 (1989), 803–832.

Recommended Readings

Derek H. Aldcroft and Simon P. Ville, eds., *The European Economy, 1750–1914: A Thematic Approach* (Manchester: Manchester University Press, 1994).

Robert Allen and Cormac O'Grada, "On the Road Again with Arthur Young," *Journal of Economic History* 38 (1988), 93–116.

Paul Bairoch, "Agriculture and the Industrial Revolution 1700–1914," *Fontana Economic History of Europe* vol. 3.

Jan de Vries, *The Economy of Europe in an Age of Crisis* (Cambridge: Cambridge University Press, 1976).

Roderick Floud and Deirdre N. McCloskey, *The Economic History of Britain since 1700* (Cambridge: Cambridge University Press, 1981).

Garrett Hardin, "The Tragedy of the Commons," *Science* 162, no. 3859 (December 13, 1968), 1243–1248.

Ron Harris, "Government and the Economy, 1688–1850," *The Cambridge Economic History of Britain since 1700, Volume I, 1700–1850*, ed. Roderick Floud and Paul Johnson (New York: Cambridge University Press, 2004), pp. 204–237.

David Landes, *The Unbound Prometheus* (Cambridge: Cambridge University Press, 1969).

Joel Mokyr, *The Economics of the Industrial Revolution* (Totowa, N.J.: Rowmann and Allenheld, 1985).

W. H. Newell, "The Agricultural Revolution in Nineteenth Century France," *Journal of Economic History* 33, no. 4 (December 1973).

Douglass North and Barry Weingast, "Constitutions and Commitment: The Evolution of Institutions Governing Public Choice in Seventeenth-Century England," *Journal of Economic History* 49 (1989), 803–832.

P. K. O'Brien, "Agriculture and the Industrial Revolution," *Economic History Review* 2nd. series 30, no. 1 (February 1977), 166–181.

W. W. Rostow, *The Stages of Economic Growth: A Non-Communist Manifesto* (Cambridge: Cambridge University Press, 1960).

Jeffrey Williamson, "Why Was British Growth So Slow During the Industrial Revolution?" *Journal of Economic History* 44, no. 3 (September 1984).

The Anglo-Saxon Model: The U.S. Economy

The American economy is large and wealthy and has enjoyed considerable success. It is the world's only superpower, perhaps to be joined soon by China. It relies predominantly on market allocation, with less government intervention than in most other capitalist economies. It is also the most technologically advanced economy, and many experiments, such as deregulation and privatization, originated in the United States. The legal foundations of the U.S. economy are made up of the common law inherited from England and the U.S. Constitution, the original intent of which was to limit the power of the federal government.

The circumstances under which the U.S. political and economic model was created provide the basis of claims of U.S. exceptionalism. *U.S. exceptionalism is the notion that the United States is a unique social, economic, and political experiment made possible by a unique confluence of events in the late eighteenth century.* The exceptional nature of the United States is welcomed by some with pride and belittled by others who contend that the United States is no different from any other affluent country.

The exceptional confluence of events in the late eighteenth century refers to the fact that the United States is a large nation with huge potential that has been led by exceptional political thinkers such as Thomas Jefferson, John Adams, James Madison, and Alexander Hamilton. These thinkers crafted a political and economic system from the ideas of the moral philosophers of the era. The system that they constructed proved remarkably successful and durable.

The Rise of the United States

Until its victory in the War of Independence (1775–1783), the thirteen American colonies were subjects of Great Britain and to its laws and regulations. Among other causes, the American colonies revolted because of excessive taxation without representation imposed by the British parliament, and the Navigation Acts, which restricted their freedom of trade.

After achieving independence, the colonies determined to draft a Constitution that would define their political relationships. A Constitutional Convention was called in Philadelphia. It began in May 1787, and the Constitution was signed in September. The Constitution was ratified by the states in September of 1788 after a protracted debate. The framers of the Constitution published a series of papers, the *Federalist Papers*, which made the case to the various states to ratify the new Constitution.

At the time the U.S. Constitution was signed, there were thirteen colonies, with a combined population of almost four million. The United States expanded westward and to the South with the Louisiana Purchase from the French. By 1900, there were forty-five states with a population of 76 million, a substantial portion of whom had not been born in the United States. The United States had become a "melting pot" of immigrants. In between the founding and the turn of the twentieth century, the United States fought a bloody civil war from 1861 to 1865 over slavery and the rights of states in the South to secede from the union.

Figure 11.1 tells the story of U.S. economic success and growing dominance. In 1870, the U.S. economy was larger than France or Germany and almost equal to the United Kingdom, the world's largest. In per capita terms, it was well above France and Germany but below the United Kingdom. By 1900, the United States produced the world's largest GDP and was only slightly below the United Kingdom (the world's most affluent country) in per capita GDP. By 1950, after two world wars and the Great Depression, U.S. GDP was some four times that of the United Kingdom (the world's second largest economy) and the U.S. had a per capita GDP some 30 percent higher than its nearest competitor.

Constitutional Foundations of the U.S. Economy

The U.S. Constitution was heavily influenced by the classical liberal thinking of the turn of the nineteenth century. James Madison can rightly be called the father of the U.S. Constitution, which bears his indelible imprint and rejects the "stronger federal government" notions of his rival Alexander Hamilton. At the time of the Constitutional Convention, Thomas Jefferson, who drafted the Declaration of Independence, was ambassador to France and could not participate directly.

Following classical liberalism's belief that a strong state poses a danger to its polity, Madison argued that the Constitution's task was to limit the powers of government. He wrote in the *Federalist Paper* (51):

> It may be a reflection on human nature, that such devices should be necessary to control the abuses of government. But what is government itself, but the greatest of all reflections on human nature? If men were angels, no government would be necessary. If angels were to govern men, neither external nor internal controls

FIGURE 11.1   GDP and Per Capita GDP, United States and Other Countries,
1820 to 1950

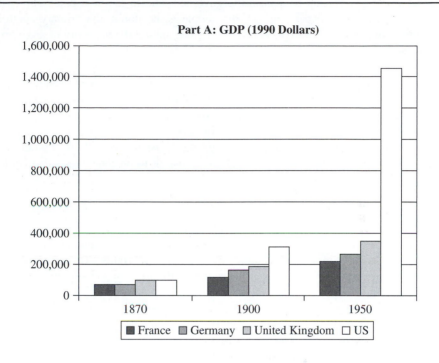

Part A: GDP (1990 Dollars)

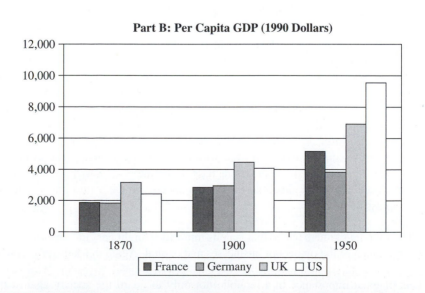

Part B: Per Capita GDP (1990 Dollars)

Source: Based on Angus Maddison Home Page, http://www.ggdc.net/MADDISON/oriindex.htm.

on government would be necessary. In framing a government which is to be administered by men over men, the great difficulty lies in this: you must first enable the government to control the governed; and in the next place oblige it to control itself. A dependence on the people is, no doubt, the primary control on the government; but experience has taught mankind the necessity of auxiliary precautions.[1]

Madison argued that the best way to limit the power of government was the separation of powers. The Constitution created three branches of government—the executive, legislative, and judicial—which could check each other and thus prevent abuse by any one branch of government. Not only would the executive and judicial branches check the legislative branch but also the legislative branch itself would be divided into two houses—the Senate and the House of Representatives—that could check each other. In Madison's words,

We see it particularly displayed in all the subordinate distributions of power, where the constant aim is to divide and arrange the several offices in such a manner as that each may be a check on the other—that the private interest of every individual may be a sentinel over the public rights. These inventions of prudence cannot be less requisite in the distribution of the supreme powers of the State.

The founders worried that, with majority rule, a majority might pass laws that discriminated against minorities—in particular against owners of property for the purpose of "more fairly" distributing wealth. In Madison's words,

Measures are too often decided, not according to the rules of justice and the rights of the minor party, but by the superior force of an interested and overbearing majority. However anxiously we may wish that these complaints had no foundation, the evidence of known facts will not permit us to deny that they are in some degree true. The diversity in the faculties of men, from which the rights of property originate, is not less an insuperable obstacle to a uniformity of interests. The protection of these faculties is the first object of government. From the protection of different and unequal faculties of acquiring property, the possession of different degrees and kinds of property immediately results; and from the influence of these on the sentiments and views of the respective proprietors, ensures a division of the society into different interests and parties. The majority, having such coexistent passion or interest, must be rendered, by their number and local situation, unable to concert and carry into effect schemes of oppression.[2]

The founding fathers feared that jealous minorities might pass unfair laws against minorities, such as the owners of businesses and capital. Again in Madison's words,

It is of great importance in a republic not only to guard the society against the oppression of its rulers, but to guard one part of the society against the injustice of the other part. Different interests necessarily exist in different classes of citizens. If a majority be united by a common interest, the rights of the minority will be insecure.[3]

Douglass North wrote that the political structure of the United States "was explicitly oriented to preventing domination by factions." He [Madison] wished "to make it unprofitable for groups in society to devote their efforts toward redistributing wealth and income through the political process. The tripartite system of government ... was designed to make efforts at restructuring property rights to redistribute wealth and income very difficult."[4]

By limiting the power and scope of government, the Constitution embraced the idea of strict restraints on government interventions that would reduce the liberties of private individuals in their economic activities.[5]

The Fifth Amendment states, among other things, that no person can "be deprived of life, liberty, or property, without due process of law; nor shall private property be taken for public use, without just compensation."[6] This amendment protected private businesses from government intervention and regulation, with exceptions such as the recognized right of government to take property through the right of eminent domain, the obligation of private persons to pay taxes, and the power of the state to regulate through police power for purposes of public safety and welfare.

Whereas the English Bill of Rights did not explicitly protect private property from the state, the Fifth Amendment of the U.S. Constitution did. Many court battles have subsequently been fought over the interpretation of the "due process" clause of the Fifth Amendment.

Common Law and Economic Efficiency

As Chapter 9 pointed out, the United States operates on a system of common law. Other economic systems use civil law or even Shariah law. As an instrument of the state, civil law tends to allot more rights to the state than does common law, which gives greater weight to the rights of private property and of private contract and less to the rights of the state.

Legal scholars have argued that common law rules as applied by English and American judges provide a superior business environment than civil law does. One simple explanation is that American judges are more likely to have practiced law and are more knowledgeable of business practices than the career civil-servant judges of civil law.

Legal theorists, such as Richard Posner and F. A. Hayek, approach the issue of the economic efficiency of legal systems from another perspective.[7] They point out that common law is "judge-made law," whereas civil law is "government made law."

Common law uses the principle of precedent, whereby current judgments must be consistent with past rulings. The use of precedent provides greater certainty than state-made laws, which can be changed on the whim of the state. This principle goes back to 1345, when an English lawyer argued to the court: "I think you will do as others have done in the same case, or else we do not know what the law is."[8]

In the U.S. legal system, superior appeals courts ensure that common law produces consistent laws even though different judges may rule differently in their own jurisdictions. A ruling by a local judge can be appealed to higher courts to determine whether the lower-court ruling is consistent with the law. The superior court examines the appeal and overturns it if the ruling of the lower-court judge is deemed inconsistent with established legal practice. Even the Supreme Court of the United States uses the principle of precedent, which it applies unless it must rule on a completely new issue for which no precedent exists.

What ensures that precedent will yield legal rules that are economically efficient? Hayek argued the role of the judge is not to find economically efficient solutions to particular problems, but rather to ensure that the ruling conforms to previously established legal principles. According to Hayek's notion of spontaneous order (Chapter 4), if a legal principle leads to inefficient economic outcomes, it will disappear over time as more efficient rules show it to be inferior.

Common law does appear to produce logically economically efficient results, an example being the Hand Formula, named after noted justice Learned Hand.[9] According to the Hand Formula, a company should be held liable for an accident if the cost of preventing it is less than the expected cost of the accident. If a company could have prevented a $1 million accident at a cost of $10,000, the company should bear the liability as the party better able to prevent or minimize the damage. As noted by one international legal expert: "The superiority of common law would therefore be based on its assumed superiority in finding efficient solutions to some of the main questions involved in the development of private law."[10]

The Private Sector versus the Public Sector

The American economy, like all economies, consists of a private sector and a public sector. The economic role of government in the United States is more limited than in most other industrialized economies, but it has been growing since the 1930s.

The ***private sector*** *is the business sector in which private ownership prevails and government regulation or intervention is limited.* If a private business is so tightly regulated that it cannot make its own decisions, it may not be appropriate to call it "private." Milton Friedman estimated that roughly 25 percent of economic activity was government operated or government supervised in 1939; the remaining 75 percent was private.[11] Frederic Scherer estimated that in 1965, the government-regulated sector accounted for 11 percent of GDP and that the government-operated sector accounted for another 12 percent, a total close to Friedman's figure for 1939.[12] Clifford Winston estimated that in 1977, 17 percent of the U.S. GDP "was produced by fully regulated industries," whereas by 1988, this share had fallen to 7 percent.[13] Although we have no authoritative study to back this up, we suspect that the U.S. private sector today amounts to well over 80 percent of the American economy.

Figure 11.2 shows the changing size and role of government. At the turn of the twentieth century, government accounted for some 4 percent of employment, owned 7 percent of structures (buildings and plants), and owned about one-quarter of the land (much of which was wasteland of little value). By 1950, the government's share of structures reached 21 percent, and it owned a little more than a quarter of all land. Its share of the labor force had risen from 4 to about 8 percent. Since 1950, its share of employment increased to more than 15 percent. Government purchases of goods and services increased from 8 percent of GDP in 1950 to 22 percent in 2011.

The government's contribution to GDP (in effect the production by government) has been rising steadily over the last one hundred years. The increase in the federal government's share has been more substantial than that of state and local government.

FIGURE 11.2   Government (Federal, State, and Local) Shares of Land, Structures, Employment, and Purchases (1900–2010)

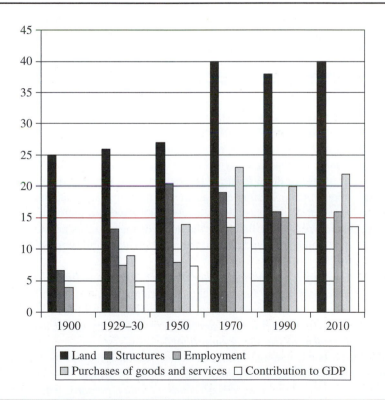

Source: Historical Statistics of the United States, Statistical Abstract of the United States http://www. ers.usda.gov/publications/arei/eib16/Chapter1/1.3/. Volume Title: Solomon Fabricant, "Government-owned and Non-Military Capital Assets Since 1900," Studies in Income and Wealth, Conference on Research in Income and Wealth, 1950.
Volume URL: http://www.nber.org/books/unkn50-1 p. 535.

Since 1929, business's share of national output has fallen from 91 to 81 percent at the expense of the government.

Figure 9.2 showed that the scope of the public sector in the United States is below the average of the industrialized European countries and above the average for the industrialized Asian economies. The rising share of U.S. government output, expenditure, and employment follows worldwide patterns of rising government.

We now have an economy in which federal, state, and local government accounts for between 15 and 20 percent of employment, purchases, and output. In Europe, the numbers are higher; in Asia, they are lower. These figures do not include the extent to which government redistributes income by means of transfer payments. We shall show later in the chapter that this has been the fastest-growing government activity in the last half century.

Business Organization

Private businesses vary by type of ownership (private, cooperative, or state), by their legal form of organization, and by the degree of competition in the markets in which they operate.

Legal Forms of Business

Business enterprises are divided into three categories on the basis of legal organization: sole proprietorships, partnerships, and corporations. *The **sole proprietorship** is owned by one individual who makes all the business decisions and absorbs the profits (or losses) that the business earns. A **partnership** is owned by two or more partners who make all the business decisions and share in the profits and losses.* The major advantages of these forms of business organization are their relative simplicity (the proprietorship is simpler than the partnership) and that, under existing U.S. tax law, their profits are taxed only once. They have two major disadvantages: (1) The owners are personally liable for the debts of the business and (2) the ability to raise capital is limited, dependent as it is on the owners' ability to borrow against personal assets.

The **corporation** *is owned by its stockholders, who have limited liability and can act as a legal person.* In England, the corporation is called a joint stock company. On the European continent it is called a "society with limited liability." *The **board of directors** is elected by the stockholders, makes its major decisions, and appoints management to run the corporation.*

Each of the board members has a fiduciary responsibility to the shareholders. *A **fiduciary responsibility** refers to a relationship in which one person has a responsibility to care for the assets or rights of other persons. The term "fiduciary" is derived from the Latin term for "faith" or "trust."*

Board members must make decisions in the interests of all shareholders. They cannot act in their interests alone or, say, in the interests of large shareholders. In the United States, board members take their fiduciary responsibilities seriously. If board members favor large over small shareholders, small shareholders can file a class action lawsuit. Most board members carry director's insurance in case of claims against them.

The board's legal fiduciary responsibility to all shareholders gives shareholders, especially small, or minority shareholders, confidence to buy shares. It is a factor that explains why the ownership of U.S. corporations is broad and liquid.

A *broad and liquid stock market means that there are a large number of shareholders, none of whom hold significant shares, and shareholders can sell their shares readily without affecting the share price.* The previous chapter showed that the United States is an exception with its broad and liquid markets for corporate shares. Much of this is due to the protections that minority shareholders enjoy in the United States. In other parts of the world, they enjoy less protection.

The advantages of the corporation are (1) that its owners (the stockholders) are not personally liable for the debts of the corporation (limited liability), (2) that its management can be changed if necessary without changing the owners, and (3) that it has more options for raising capital through the sale of bonds and additional stock. A major disadvantage of the U.S. corporation is that its income is taxed a second time when corporate earnings are distributed to stockholders as dividends. Double taxation gives American corporations an incentive to reinvest earnings rather than pay out dividends.

These three forms of business organization are supplemented by innovative mixed legal arrangements, such as limited-liability partnerships, that circumvent a variety of problems, yet the threefold classification remains valid.

Figure 11.3 shows the distribution of U.S. enterprises according to the legal form of business organization. Although sole proprietorships account for most (72 percent) businesses, they account for only 4 percent of business revenues. Corporations, although few in number (about 18 percent of the total), account for 82 percent of business revenues. The larger size of the corporation is explained by limited liability and its strength in raising capital. The sole proprietorship is important in agriculture, retail trade, and services; the partnership is more frequently used in finance, insurance, real estate, and services; the corporation is the dominant form in other sectors.

Competition and Businesses

If businesses face little competition, they have market power. *Market power is present when the business can affect the price at which it buys or sells.* The less market power it has, the more competitive its environment.

The degree of competition in the U.S. economy is hard to measure. Most empirical studies focus on manufacturing, which accounts for less than one-fifth of national output. Many industries that produce raw materials, such as agriculture, forest products, and coal, are organized competitively. Retail stores and most services used to operate in local markets, but today huge retailers like Walmart and Target operate throughout the United States. With electronic shopping and the Internet, businesses are faced daily with new competition, almost unlimited by geographic boundaries.

FIGURE **11.3**   Proprietorships, Partnerships, and Corporations, 2010

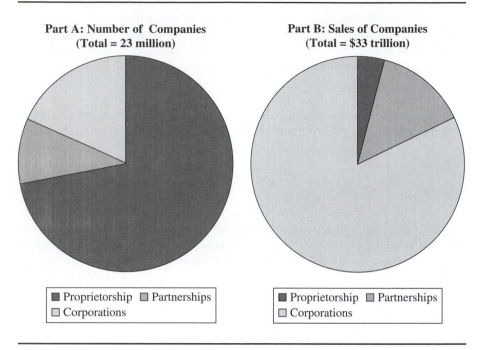

Part A: Number of Companies
(Total = 23 million)

Part B: Sales of Companies
(Total = $33 trillion)

■ Proprietorship   ■ Partnerships
☐ Corporations

■ Proprietorship   ■ Partnerships
☐ Corporations

Source: Statistical Abstract of the United States.

Estimates of the overall level of competitiveness are few and far between. Milton Friedman calculated that the private sector was between 15 and 25 percent "monopolistic" and between 75 and 85 percent "competitive" in 1939.[14] A study from the 1980s found that competition increased for the economy as a whole from the 1960s through the 1980s.[15] If anything, U.S. firms operate in markets that are becoming increasingly competitive, especially with rising globalization.

The surprising feature of U.S. manufacturing, a sector for which we have long-run data, is that the degree of concentration appears to have changed little since the turn of the century (see Table 11.1). The top one hundred firms have accounted for about the same percentages of output for about a century. (Of course, the firms are different, but the shares of the largest have remained about the same.)[16]

We tend to be overwhelmed by the huge size of businesses. In 1950, U.S. automobile manufacturers made fewer than 200,000 cars and trucks. Today, they manufacture more than 7 million. Companies have become much larger, but that does not mean that they face less competition. We should not confuse growing size with a reduction in competition. We learn from experience that competition does not necessarily depend on the number of producers. Coke and Pepsi are fierce competitors, although the two of them dominate the world market. Boeing and Airbus fight tooth and nail for customers although there are only two of them.

TABLE 11.1   Trends in Concentration in American Manufacturing: Percentage of Output of 100 Largest Firms

1895–1904	33
1947	23
1954	30
1958	32
1972	33
1977	33
1982	33
1997	31
2002	33

Source: G. Warren Nutter, *The Extent of Enterprise Monopoly in the United States, 1899–1939* (Chicago: University of Chicago Press, 1951), pp. 35–48, 112–140; F. M. Scherer, *Industrial Market Structure and Economic Performance* (Boston: Houghton Mifflin, 1980), pp. 68–69; *Concentration Ratios in Manufacturing, 1977 Census of Manufacturing,* MC77-SR-9; 1982 Census of Manufacturers, MC82-S-7. http://www.census.gov/prod/ec97/m31s-cr.pdf.   http://www.census.gov/prod/ec02/ec0231sr1.pdf. (The 1895–1904 figure is obtained by extrapolating from Nutter's figure on four-firm concentration ratios.)

Corporate Governance

Large corporations everywhere are characterized by a separation of ownership and management. The managers of large U.S. corporations own only a small fraction of outstanding shares. The bulk of shares are owned by individuals either directly or through private pension and retirement funds. Some 50 percent of Americans own stock—a figure that may be the highest in the world.[17]

The separation of corporation ownership and management, first studied in 1932 by Adolf Berle and Gardiner Means, suggests a potential problem of corporate governance.[18] *Corporate governance decides in whose interests a corporation, in which owners are not managers, will be run.* In theory, corporations can be run in the interests of their shareholders, their stakeholders, or the community. *Stakeholders are those who participate in the operation of the corporation as managers, employees, workers, suppliers, or buyers, but not as owners.*

The U.S. corporation tends to be run in the interests of shareholders more than in other countries. Their managers therefore have the job of maximizing shareholder value. *Shareholder value is the value of the corporation in stock markets as measured by its **market capitalization**.* The **market capitalization** is the number of shares outstanding times the stock price in the stock market where it is listed, such as the New York Stock Exchange, the American Stock Exchange, or NASDAQ.

Insofar as the stock price reflects the anticipated value of future profits, managers committed to maximizing shareholder value sacrifice stakeholder interests to improve the profit performance. If a manufacturing corporation whose goal is creating shareholder value is suffering a slump in profits, management would be expected to downsize the labor force, announce layoffs, or seek lower-cost suppliers. Similarly, an airline would be expected to cease service to a low-yielding community, despite the harm to that community.

After Berle and Means focused attention on the separation of ownership from management, economists began to consider **principal–agent problems** and their solution. If managers are not owners, will they not run the corporation in their own interests or pay too much attention to employees, rather than making the hard decisions required to maximize profits?

Two typically U.S. approaches to aligning the interests of managers and shareholders were apparent by the 1980s: a market for corporate control and incentive systems for managers that would cause them to maximize shareholder value.

The Market for Corporate Control

A market for corporate control forces management to focus on long-run profits.[19] *A **market for corporate control** exists when a rival management team has the opportunity to buy control of the corporation from its share owners.* Prior to the 1980s, there were relatively few changes of management in large corporations, even in cases where the management did not live up to the company's profit potential. With a large number of shareholders, the largest owning only a small percentage, it was too difficult for shareholders to organize "hostile" takeovers.

Two developments changed this situation. First, as ordinary citizens began investing in private pension funds and in mutual stock funds, these funds acquired significant shares of large corporations. Today, institutional investors own more than 50 percent of all listed corporate stock and more than 60 percent of the listed stock of the 1,000 largest corporations.[20] Fidelity, Vanguard, and CREF Teachers Retirement Fund each have hundreds of billions of dollars invested in stocks.

Second, a new breed of ***corporate raiders*** (individuals such as Carl Icahn, Michael Milken, and Warren Buffett or investment banks such as Goldman Sachs) mobilized substantial funds to mount hostile takeovers against underperforming corporations. Corporate raiders develop business plans showing how the corporation could earn higher profits under a different management. The corporate raider would then offer a price high enough above the current stock price to shareholders to acquire enough shares to replace the current management with a "better" management team.

The U.S. market for corporate control really began in the early 1980s. Figure 11.4 shows how it took off. It was less active during the two recessions of the period. The market for corporate control became quite complex and effective in the 1980s and 1990s, using exotic instruments such as the purchase of one company with shares of another or issuing junk bonds to raise funds to buy the targeted company. At its peak level of activity in 2005-6, the market for corporate control arranged the purchase of corporations worth $2.5 trillion.

The market for corporate control has become institutionalized in the United States and has spread throughout the world. Industrial and financial corporations now routinely have mergers and acquisitions (M&A) departments. ***Mergers and acquisitions*** *refer to the buying, selling, and merger of one company with another.* The merger or acquisition can be friendly or hostile. *A **hostile merger or acquisition** is one in which the targeted company actively opposes the takeover.* Table 11.2 shows the largest worldwide deals to date.

FIGURE 11.4   The Market For Corporate Control: North American Mergers and
Acquisitions

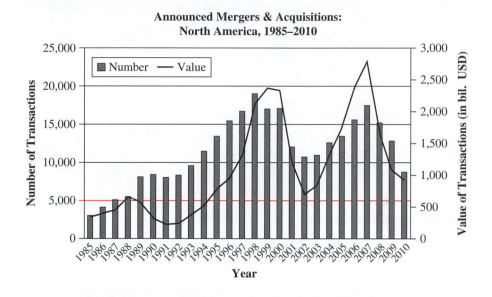

**Announced Mergers & Acquisitions:
North America, 1985–2010**

Source: Announced Mergers & Acquisitions: North America, 1985–2011, Institute of Mergers, Acquisitions and Alliances (IMAA), http://www.imaa-institute.org/images/figure_announced%20mergers%20&%20acquisitions%20(north%20america).jpg.

TABLE 11.2   The Top Deals (Largest M&A Transactions)

Rank	Year	Acquiror	Target	Transaction Value (in billions USD)
1	1999	Vodafone AirTouch PLC	Mannesmann AG	202.8
2	2000	America Online Inc	Time Warner	164.7
3	2007	Shareholders	Philip Morris Intl Inc	107.6
4	2007	RFS Holdings BV	ABN-AMRO Holding NV	98.2
5	1999	Pfizer Inc	Warner-Lambert Co	89.2
6	1998	Exxon Corp	Mobil Corp	78.9
7	2000	Glaxo Wellcome PLC	SmithKline Beecham PLC	76.0
8	2004	Royal Dutch Petroleum Co	Shell Transport & Trading Co	74.6
9	2006	AT&T Inc	BellSouth Corp	72.7
10	1998	Travelers Group Inc	Citicorp	72.6

Source: Institute of Mergers, Acquisitions and Alliances, http://www.imaa-institute.org/statistics-mergers-acquisitions.html#TopMergersAcquisitions_Worldwide.

Although mergers and acquisitions are no longer an exclusively American phenomenon, they are considered to typify American shareholder capitalism. Opponents argue that takeovers force draconic cost savings, personnel reductions, and asset sales on the new acquisition. Loyal employees are let go and established supply relationships are broken. Lawrence Summers, academic economist and former secretary of the treasury in both the Clinton and Obama administrations, argued in his academic work that hostile takeovers constitute "breaches of trust." Any gains of shareholders are at the expense of wealth losses by stakeholders, such as employees and suppliers, and this will undermine the trust that is necessary for the effective functioning of business.[21]

Advocates of the market for corporate control counter that they improve corporate efficiency and restructure the acquired company to compete in the dog-eat-dog world economy. The world market is unforgiving. Only the most efficient survive. The market for corporate control forces even a reluctant manager to become more efficient.

Corporate Incentives

Corporations use incentives to align the interests of management with those of owners. Traditionally, U.S. executives receive a fixed salary plus a bonus based on the performance of the corporation, such as its profitability. In the 1980s and 1990s, corporations began introducing different incentives to ensure that corporate executives and even middle managers were motivated to maximize shareholder value.

The most prominent such instrument was the stock option. *A **stock option** grants executives the right to buy a designated number of shares of the company at a specified price (often the stock price on the day the stock options were granted).* Stock options, therefore, give executives the incentive to maximize the stock price so they can "cash in" their stock options at a profit. In theory, the stock price should reflect the long-term, not short-term, profitability of the company. Hence stock options should direct executives to think about the company's long-term performance.

Other incentive devices involve matching employee contributions to their 401K retirement accounts invested in the corporation's own stock. Although employees can acquire the stocks of other corporations, the offer of one "free" share for every share purchased can be enticing. If both upper and middle levels of management own shares of the company, they have a personal interest in the stock price.

A final incentive feature is the golden parachute. *A **golden parachute** is a provision for a limited number of top executives to receive generous severance bonuses if their company is taken over.* Its purpose is to prevent the existing management from resisting corporate takeovers that, in theory, will install a better management with a better business plan and, in the process, drive up the stock price for shareholders.

Some fear that maximizing shareholder value distorts the flow of information. This criticism argues that top executives will be tempted (as in the 2001–2002 scandals involving Enron, Arthur Andersen, and WorldCom) to withhold negative information, such as sinking profits or other bad news. When information is distorted, stock prices are not properly valued and provide misleading information.

In the aftermath of the corporate scandals of 2001 and 2002, there was alarm that many companies were providing false information to raise the share price. Investigations revealed that such practices were rare. It made no real sense for management to lie because they understood that they would eventually be found out. Gains from false information would be transitory, and the personal risks would be huge.

Capital Markets

The manner in which capital markets function varies with the type of capitalist economic system. *The **capital market** is the market in which businesses raise investment finance through the issue of stocks and bonds and bank borrowing.*

A capital market can be either a primary or a secondary market. *In the **primary market**, the corporation sells (issues) new shares of stocks or bonds to buyers. Such sales of new shares are called **initial public offerings** (IPOs).* The secondary market is a "secondhand" market in which shares of stock or bonds that have already been issued are traded by one owner to another. It is in the primary market that investment financing is created.

The American (Anglo-Saxon) capital market is one in which new shares are sold to private investors by underwriters. ***Underwriters** organize the initial sale of shares, sometimes buying stakes in the company themselves.* It is a "public offering" in the sense that, theoretically, any buyer willing to buy at the offering price can be accommodated.

In U.S. stock markets, shares are issued on the various organized stock exchanges, such as the New York Stock Exchange, the American Stock Exchange, the NASDAQ Exchange, or numerous smaller exchanges. The listing of shares of stock in the large exchanges must follow the rules of the Securities and Exchange Commission and of the exchange itself. The stock exchanges are private organizations that have established operating rules and punish underwriters, brokers, or companies that violate their rules.

Full Disclosure

Full disclosure is the operating principle in the major U.S. stock exchanges. ***Full disclosure** is the principle that the corporation listing stock must make available to potential buyers all relevant information, good and bad, about the* *company.* Neither the exchange nor the Securities and Exchange Commission issues a ruling on the merit of the company. Rather, their task is to ensure that potential buyers have full information about the company, such as a list of its officers, the use to which the funds will be put, any outstanding lawsuits, and potential conflicts of interest. The offer to sell new shares will be contained in a prospectus, which contains obligatory accounting information prepared by a recognized accounting firm according to standard accounting procedures (generally accepted accounting procedure, GAAP). The accounting statement also includes a statement from the accounting firm as to whether the firm can continue to exist as a "going concern."

As long as all relevant information is disclosed and other requirements specific to the exchange are met (such as reaching a minimal capitalization), the underwriter is free to sell the new shares to buyers. Once these new shares are in the hands of owners, they trade in the secondary market.

Unlike Europe (as we shall see in the next chapter), more investment is financed by the issue of stocks and bonds than through bank financing. Table 11.3 shows the financing of U.S. investment in a typical year (1993). This table, which covers all net investment, both corporate and noncorporate, shows that the issue of new stocks and bonds through equity markets accounted for almost 60 percent of all net investment and that retained corporate earnings accounting for another 25 percent. This left virtually nothing for bank financing, especially considering that much noncorporate investment is financed by other means entirely. In Europe, on the other hand, banks finance two-thirds of business needs.[22]

The financing of investment through stock markets, which is a characteristic feature of the Anglo-Saxon model, means a separation of those who finance corporations from those who manage corporations. In the European and Asian models, which rely heavily on bank financing, the bank can be associated with the corporation and would be reluctant to withhold financing from a closely related company.

TABLE 11.3   The Financing of Investment, U.S. Economy, 1993 (billions of dollars)

Net private domestic investment	474 (100%)
New security issues, corporations	
Stocks	154 (33%)
Bonds	114 (24%)
Total	268 (57%)
Undistributed corporate profits	121 (26%)
Other	75 (17%)

Source: Statistical Abstract of the United States.

The separation of the financing from management in the Anglo-Saxon model has the advantage that a generally impartial judgment will be made about whether a particular company deserves additional financing. If the corporation cannot make, in its prospectus, a convincing case to potential investors that the investment funds will yield sufficient returns, investors will not buy the stock or bond issue.

There is also another way in which the capital market influences who gets capital. If a company is mismanaged or otherwise falls on hard times, its stock price will fall. Buyers of stocks in the secondary model decide on their own that the corporation's future profits will be small. Now, in order to raise new capital, the corporation must sell new shares at a low price. Earlier, if the stock price was $100, the company could raise $100 million by selling 1 million new shares. If the stock price falls to $25, the company must now sell 4 million shares to raise the same amount of investment finance. Under these circumstances, the corporation will probably decide not to issue new stock and will not obtain more investment financing. Thus the stock market punishes companies that are performing poorly with a low stock price and denies them access to new capital.

Opponents of the Anglo-Saxon model of investment finance argue that stock markets are too volatile and are dominated by emotion. They believe it is better to have knowledgeable bankers deciding who should get investment financing. A disadvantage of bank financing, as we have said, is that the bank tends to get too closely linked to the corporation to make impartial investment decisions.

Venture Capital Markets and Dynamism

In Chapter 3, we discussed Joseph Schumpeter's **creative destruction**. The U.S. capital market promotes dynamic change by moving capital around quickly. If one sector develops a new technology and another sector's technology lags, the capital market will automatically direct capital to develop the new technology. If consumer tastes change, new capital will flow to the sector with rising consumer demand. New businesses cannot develop without financing.

Entirely new business concepts tend to come from new business start-ups. Economies that can raise venture capital for risky business start-ups will therefore prove more dynamic. *Venture capital is financing through purchases of shares or loans to start up businesses.*

The United States has the world's most sophisticated system of venture capital, the prime example of which is the high-tech companies of Silicon Valley, which receive their initial capital from venture capital firms located in the area. *A venture capital fund provides start-up capital to new firms and takes a stake in them in return.* It then shepherds the firm through various stages of financing and development until it is ready for an IPO. If the venture capital fund takes a 50 percent stake in a company that later goes public for $5 billion, its share is worth $2.5 billion. Table 11.4 shows the size of the U.S. venture capital market from 1995 to 2010.

TABLE 11.4   Venture Capital Investments ($)

Industry	1995 Total	2000 Total	2005 Total	2010 Total
Biotechnology	745,722,600	3,938,682,000	3,780,714,700	3,765,089,000
Business Products and Services	154,900,500	4,404,360,800	345,983,700	425,601,600
Computers and Peripherals	298,268,100	1,516,940,000	534,261,500	436,038,700
Consumer Products and Services	430,822,100	3,009,387,600	318,769,700	596,149,600
Electronics/ Instrumentation	119,166,100	716,554,400	447,757,800	437,888,600
Financial Services	177,776,000	4,008,226,300	913,076,300	563,923,900
Healthcare Services	450,330,600	1,302,344,300	373,724,900	312,080,800
Industrial/Energy	467,359,600	2,501,654,000	832,804,500	3,502,349,400
IT Services	164,339,700	8,589,914,700	1,107,298,700	1,890,915,100
Media and Entertainment	938,535,500	9,908,040,800	1,135,951,500	1,680,519,200
Medical Devices and Equipment	581,981,700	2,255,533,800	2,180,277,800	2,394,042,600
Networking and Equipment	354,790,300	11,224,303,100	1,483,392,500	656,154,500
Other	32,989,900	57,933,900	57,099,000	28,133,000
Retailing/Distribution	312,199,400	2,994,355,900	187,329,100	236,441,100
Semiconductors	189,067,400	3,392,839,200	1,869,843,400	1,044,285,500
Software	1,081,242,800	23,315,071,800	4,887,683,300	4,308,998,500
Telecommunications	813,910,400	16,087,548,100	2,233,873,600	984,318,400
Grand Total	7,313,402,700	99,223,690,700	22,689,842,000	23,262,929,500

Source: PricewaterhouseCoopers/National Venture Capital Association MoneyTree™ Report, Data: Thomson Reuters Investments by Industry Q1 1995 - Q1 2011, http://www.nvca.org/. Reprinted with permission.

Top venture capital firms—such as Kleiner, Perkins, Caulfied & Byers; New Enterprise Associates; First Round Capital; and Sequoia Capital—are hardly household names. They provide, by world standards, huge amounts of venture capital. In 1995, venture capital firms invested some $7 billion. In one of their peak years (2000), they supplied $100 billion to young firms before settling back to annual investment in the low $20 billions. (See Table 11.4 for the total amounts of venture capital).

Critics of venture capital complain that they make investments that are too risky; they are accused of creating investment bubbles. Indeed, venture capitalists invested too much in high tech in 2000 and the immediate years before, leading to a bubble that burst in 2001. Venture capitalists, however, perform a vital function. They provide capital to new firms that otherwise would not qualify for bank loans. They give high-risk entrepreneurs a chance. Many fail; few succeed, but venture capitalists provide a hothouse for innovation. Of course, one of

Exhibit 11.1   Timeline: The Story of Apple Computer

Summer 1971: Steve Jobs and Steve Wozniak meet.

Fall 1971: Jobs and Wozniak sell illegal "blue boxes" enabling free phone calls.

February 1973: Wozniak starts work in HP's Advanced Products Division.

1973: Jobs starts work at Atari. Wozniak helps Jobs design the game Breakout during Jobs' night shifts.

March 1975: The first meeting of the Amateur Computer Users Group. (Homebrew Computer Club) is held in a Menlo Park.

March 1976: Wozniak builds the Apple I. Wozniak pitches his bosses at HP. Jobs pitches his bosses at Atari. Both are denied.

April 1976: Jobs recruits his Atari co-worker, Ronald Wayne, and Jobs, Wayne, and Wozniak found Apple Computer. Wayne sells his 10% share in Apple less than two weeks later for $800.

May 1976: Wozniak is granted a release by HP to produce Apple I. Production begins in a bedroom in Jobs' parents' home. Eventually, production moves to the garage.

October 1976: Commodore considers but declines buying a company that operates out of a garage. Wozniak quits his job at HP, at Jobs' insistence.

January 1977: Apple Computer is incorporated.

January 1978: Apple moves to an office building in Cupertino, CA.

December 1980: Apple's IPO.

February 1985: Wozniak and Jobs receive the National Technology Medal from President Reagan at the White House.

Source: "The Story of Apple Computer" in Pino G. Audia and Christopher I. Rider, "A Garage and an Idea: What More Does an Entrepreneur Need?" in *California Management Review* vol. 48, no. 1 (Fall 2005), pp. 6–28. © 2005 by the Regents of the University of California. Reprinted by permission of the University of California Press.

the great stories of entrepreneurship is that of Apple Computer as shown in Exhibit 11.1:

In other countries that rely on bank finance, entrepreneurs with a vision would be hard-pressed to convince a staid banker to lend them money. Without venture capital, economies cannot experiment with doing new things, whether they are crazy or brilliant ideas.

One way to gauge dynamism is to compare the rankings of the largest U.S. corporations over time. Table 11.5 shows the dramatic changes in ranking over a relatively short two-decade period. In each period, different companies occupied the top ranks. Dow Chemical disappeared from the top fifteen after 1985. Enron and WorldCom, ranked seventh and thirtieth in 2000, no longer exist. IBM, once accused of monopolizing the computer market, fell from the top ranks after 2000.

The U.S. capital market punishes, with great decisiveness and speed, corporations that fail in their business plans. It rewards those who succeed with new infusions of capital to allow them to grow.

TABLE 11.5   Ranking of Largest U.S. Corporations (by sales)

1985	2000	2012
ExxonMobil	ExxonMobil	Exxon Mobile
General Motors	Walmart	Walmart
Ford	General Motors	General Motors
IBM	Ford	General Electric
AT&T	General Electric	Berkshire Hathaway
DuPont	Enron	Ford Motors
General Motors	IBM	Hewlett-Packard
U.S. Steel	AT&T	AT&T
United Technologies	Verizon	Bank of America
Boeing	Philip Morris	McKessen
Procter & Gamble	JPMorgan Chase	Verizon
Beatrice	Bank of America	JPMorgan Chase
Philip Morris	SBC Corporation	Apple
Dow Chemical	Boeing	CUS Caremark
		IBM

Note: Because of energy mergers and name changes, energy companies other than ExxonMobil have been omitted.

Source: Based on *Fortune Magazine*, http://money.cnn.com

Regulation

The Constitution's Fifth Amendment's due process clause states that the government cannot take private property without due process and just compensation. The actual "taking" of private property by the state is rare, but the state can restrict property rights and make private property less valuable by regulating it. If you own property along a busy highway, and the state declares that it cannot be used for commercial purposes, your property, in effect, has been taken.

The due process clause creates a dilemma: What should the state do to protect the general welfare from the misuse of property by private owners? The Constitution did not intend for government to refrain from all action affecting property rights. The state's right to tax owners of property is clear, and the Constitution allowed eminent domain. **Eminent domain** *is the right of the state to take property under certain conditions in the public interest (such as buying land for the construction of railways or making way for an interstate highway).*

In early American history, eminent domain was used to build railroads, highways, and government buildings. Although there were reluctant property owners, the state asserted its right to the land without much public outcry. The broader interpretations of eminent domain in recent years have caused considerable public disapproval. In 2005, the Supreme Court affirmed a lower court decision (*Kelo* v. *New London, Connecticut*) by which private property was transferred under eminent domain to a private property developer. The argument was that the developer would improve the property and the community would benefit through higher property taxes. This logic was subsequently applied to the private development of a sports stadium in New Jersey.

From the Constitution's adoption to the 1930s, the right of the federal government to regulate private businesses was strictly limited. Under John Marshall, Chief Justice from 1801 to 1835, the U.S. Supreme Court consistently ruled that the Constitution's contract clause protected the right of contracts from state laws. Marshall himself was a delegate to the Virginia ratifying convention and was the justice most knowledgeable about the original intent of the contract clause.[23] Marshall himself viewed courts as "tribunals which are established for the security of property and to decide human rights." Following Marshall's lead, the Supreme Court consistently ruled that state laws that challenged the right of contract, such as state laws that prohibited the buying of insurance from out-of-state companies or established minimum wage laws, were unconstitutional.

Constitutional protection of private property began to break down starting in 1877 when the courts ruled in *Munn* v. *Illinois* that businesses "affected with the public interest" were subject to regulation and control by the state of Illinois.[24] A decade later, the Interstate Commerce Commission was set up to regulate the railroads; the Pure Food and Drug Administration was established in 1906, followed by the Federal Trade Commission in 1914. Constitutional protection of private property rights was further weakened during Roosevelt's New Deal when the Supreme Court in 1934 declared that the economic emergency justified a state law affecting private mortgage debt obligations.[25] Such decisions opened the door for increased government regulation. Of the almost thirty major federal departments and agencies in existence today, more than half have significant regulatory functions, such as the Environmental Protection Agency, Labor, Occupational Safety and Health Administration (OSHA), Commerce, Health and Human Services, and Transportation.

The levels and rates of growth of federal regulation cannot be captured with one or two statistics. All new federal regulations and amendments must be published in the *Federal Register*.[26] The *Register*'s number of pages is therefore a rough proxy for the volume of new regulations.

Figure 11.5 shows the huge growth in federal regulations, starting in the 1970s and peaking in 1980. After slight rollbacks in the 1980s, the number of pages remains in excess of 80,000 per year. According to the Office of the Federal Register, in 1998 the *Code of Federal Regulations* (CFR), the official listing of all regulations in effect, contained a total of 134,723 pages in 201 volumes that claimed 19 feet of shelf space. In 1970, the CFR totaled only 54,834 pages. The Government Accountability Office (GAO) reported that in the four fiscal years from 1996 to 1999, a total of 15,286 new federal regulations went into effect. Of these, 222 were classified as "major" rules, each one having an annual effect on the economy of at least $100 million.[27]

Table 11.6 lists just some of the major regulatory acts passed during a period of rapid expansion of regulatory agencies and their functions.

Government regulation is either social or economic.[28] *Social regulation is regulation of health, safety, and environment.* Examples include consumer

FIGURE 11.5   Number of pages in the federal register, 1936–2010

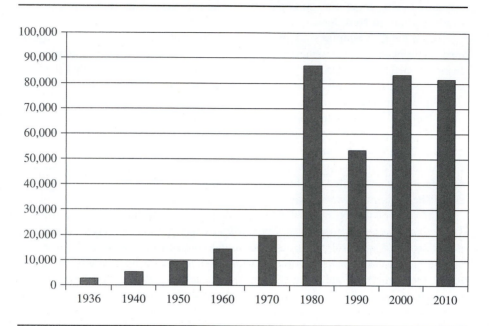

Source: Based on Clyde Crews, Jr., *Ten Thousand Commandments* (Competitive Enterprise Institute, 2009).

TABLE 11.6   Increasing Government Regulation of Business, 1962–1978

Year of Enactment	Name of Law	Purpose and Function
1962	Food and Drug Amendments	Requires pretesting of drugs for safety and effectiveness and labeling of drugs by generic names
1962	Air Pollution Control Act	Provides first modern ecology statute
1963	Equal Pay Act	Eliminates wage differentials based on sex
1964	Civil Rights Act	Creates Equal Employment Opportunity Commission (EEOC) to investigate charges of job discrimination
1965	Water Quality Act	Extends environmental concern to water
1965	Cigarette Labeling and Advertising Act	Requires labels on hazards of smoking
1966	Fair Packaging and Labeling Act	Requires producers to state what a package contains, how much it contains, and who made the product
1966	Child Protection Act	Bans sale of hazardous toys and articles
1966	Traffic Safety Act	Provides for a coordinated national safety program, including safety standards for motor vehicles

TABLE 11.6   Increasing Government Regulation of Business, 1962–1978 (cont.)

Year of Enactment	Name of Law	Purpose and Function
1966	Coal Mine Safety Amendments	Tightens controls on working conditions
1967	Flammable Fabrics Act	Broadens federal authority to set safety standards for inflammable fabrics, including clothing and household products
1967	Age Discrimination in Employment Act	Prohibits job discrimination against individuals aged 40 to 65
1968	Consumer Credit Protection Act (Truth-in-Lending)	Requires full disclosure of terms and conditions of finance charges in credit transactions
1968	Interstate Land Sales Full Disclosure Act	Provides safeguards against unscrupulous practices in interstate land sales
1969	National Environmental Policy Act	Requires environmental impact statements for federal agencies and projects
1970	Amendments to Federal Deposit Insurance Act	Prohibits issuance of unsolicited credit cards. Limits customer's liability in case of loss or theft to $50. Regulates credit bureaus and provides consumers access to files
1970	Securities Investor Protection Act	Provides greater protection for customers of brokers and dealers and members of national securities exchanges. Establishes a Securities Investor Protection Corporation, financed by fees on brokerage houses
1970	Poison Prevention Packaging Act	Authorizes standards for child-resistant packaging of hazardous substances
1970	Clean Air Act Amendments	Provides for setting air quality standards
1970	Occupational Safety and Health Act	Establishes safety and health standards that must be met by employers
1972	Consumer Product Safety Act	Establishes a commission to set safety standards for consumer products and bans products that sent undue risk of injury
1972	Federal Water Pollution Control Act	Declares an end to the discharge of pollutants into navigable waters by 1985 as a national goal
1972	Noise Pollution and Control Act	Regulates noise limits of products and transportation vehicles
1972	Equal Employment Opportunity Act	Gives EEOC the right to sue employers
1973	Vocational Rehabilitation Act	Requires federal contractors to take affirmative action on hiring the handicapped
1973	Highway Speed Limit Reduction	Limits vehicles to speeds of 55 miles an hour
1973	Safe Drinking Water Act	Requires EPA to set national drinking water regulations

(continued)

TABLE **11.6**   Increasing Government Regulation of Business, 1962–1978 (cont.)

Year of Enactment	Name of Law	Purpose and Function
1974	Campaign Finance Amendments	Restricts amounts of political contributions
1974	Employee Retirement Income Security Act	Sets new federal standards for employee pension program
1974	Hazardous Materials Transportation Act	Requires standards for the transportation of hazardous materials
1974	Magnuson–Moss Warranty Improvement Act	Establishes federal standards for written consumer product warranties
1975	Energy Policy and Conservation Act	Authorizes greater controls over domestic energy supplies and demands
1976	Hart–Scott–Rodino Antitrust Amendments	Provides for class action suits by state attorneys general; requires large companies to notify the Department of Justice of planned mergers and acquisitions
1976	Toxic Substances Control Act	Requires advance testing and restrictions on use of chemical substances
1977	Department of Energy Organization Act	Establishes a permanent department to regulate energy on a continuing basis
1977	Surface Mining Control and Reclamation Act	Regulates strip mining and the reclamation of abandoned mines
1977	Fair Labor Standards Amendments	Increases the minimum wage in three steps
1977	Export Administration Act	Imposes restrictions on complying with the Arab boycott
1977	Business Payments Abroad Act	Provides for up to $1 million penalties for bribing foreign officials
1977	Saccharin Study and Labeling Act	Requires warning labels on products containing saccharin
1978	Fair Debt Collection Practices Act	Provides for the first nationwide control of collection agencies
1978	Age Discrimination in Employment Act Amendments	Raises the permissible mandatory retirement age from 65 to 70 for most employees

Source: WEIDENBAUM, BUSINESS GOVERNMENT AND THE PUBLIC, 2nd Edition, © 1981. Reprinted by permission of Pearson Education, Inc., Upper Saddle River, NJ.

product safety rules, environmental protection, and automobile safety and gasoline mileage requirements. ***Economic regulation** is government involvement in markets, such as setting prices, restricting corporate decision making, and controlling competition.* Examples include regulation of utility rates and market structures and the setting of local taxi rates. Much economic regulation is done at the state and local level.

U.S. businesses are regulated in the interest of protecting the public good. Government regulations impose costs on businesses. Presumably when Congress debates regulatory measures or when regulatory agencies pass new regulations, it considers both the costs and benefits. On September 30, 1993, President Bill Clinton issued Executive Order 12866, "Regulatory Planning and Review," requiring each agency to assess the costs and benefits of regulatory alternatives, including the alternative of no regulation and to tailor regulations to impose the least possible burden on society.

That regulations should yield benefits in excess of costs makes sense, but they are difficult to estimate, especially the benefits of social regulation. The various estimates of regulatory costs and benefits in Table 11.7 show that the costs of regulation have been increasing (measured as a percent of GDP) and that even the lowest estimates (3.3 percent of GDP, or $1,635 for every man, woman, and child) yield significant costs. The higher-end estimates (8.5 percent of GDP, or $4,149 per capita) represent huge costs of regulation. Table 11.7 also shows we are not able to measure the benefits with any degree of accuracy. Therefore, we are not able to make public policy based on real numbers.

The substantial fixed costs of paperwork and compliance hits small companies proportionally harder than large companies. Small manufacturing companies pay over $15,000 per employee to meet regulations, while larger companies pay less than $10,000.[29]

Supporters of regulation point to its significant benefits. Over the past thirty years, the United States has made substantial progress in cleaning up air, water, and land; reducing automobile emissions; reducing lead pollution; and improving

TABLE 11.7   Estimates of Costs and Benefits of Federal Regulation

	Percent GDP	Per Capita (as a percent of 2010 GDP)
Federal Reserve Bank of Dallas (Costs)		
1976	3.5	$1,709
1979	4.0	$1,953
1992	8.0	$3,900
Office of Management and Budget (Costs)		
1997	3.3	$1,635
Hopkins		
1997	8.5	$4,149
Hahn and Hird (Benefits)		
1997	Range: .6–2.9	$322–$1,395

Source: Thomas D. Hopkins, "Regulatory Costs in Profile," Policy Study No. 132, Center for the Study of American Business (August 1996). Report to Congress on the Costs and Benefits of Federal Regulations, Office of Management and Budget, Estimates of the Total Annual Costs and Benefits of Federal Regulatory Programs, http://www.whitehouse.gov/omb/inforeg_chap2; Robert Hahn and John Hird, "The Costs and Benefits of Regulation," *Yale Journal of Regulation* 8, no. 1 (1991), 233–78; Federal Reserve Bank of Dallas, *America's Economic Regulation Burden* (Fall 1996), 1–6.

safety and design in airbags and infant safety seats. Regulation, however, cannot be evaluated only in terms of its benefits. ***Economically rational regulation*** *should yield benefits in excess of its costs.*

There are two complications in applying this principle: First, it is very difficult to quantify the benefits of regulation. Second, we lack counterfactual information for such an analysis.

Counterfactual information *indicates what would have happened in the absence of a particular event.* It is presumed that improvements in automobile safety, gasoline mileage, and seat belt technology, as well as safer foods and drugs and the like, are due to government regulation and would not have occurred in its absence. But private businesses might have been motivated by profit maximization to produce a similar result without regulation. Automobile manufacturers might produce a more fuel-efficient or safer car because it would be easier to market and would command a higher price.

Given the costs of regulation, federal government agencies have had to entertain new regulatory ideas, such as the greater use of "economic" regulation of the environment. In particular, regulatory agencies have used trading in "rights to pollute." In a particular industry, for example, the Environmental Protection Agency (EPA) sets limits and issues "licenses to pollute" that keep emissions within the caps. Such programs are called "cap and trade." The companies receiving these licenses can sell them. Companies that can reduce their emissions at low cost then sell their pollution rights to companies who can only reduce their emissions at high costs. There is active trading in acid rain pollution rights under the Clean Air Act. In an April 2011 auction, the 125,000 emission rights of the EPA were purchased by electrical power companies for $351,000.[30] Notably, the prices of emission rights have been falling steadily, driven down by new pollution abatement technologies. Although "cap and trade" for CO_2 emissions was a legislative priority for the Obama administration, the program did not receive Congressional approval.

Once Congress establishes regulatory agencies, they can exercise their regulatory powers to impinge on the legislative authority of Congress. A case in point was the controversial January 2011 decision of the EPA to regulate greenhouse gases emissions after Congress failed to pass "carbon tax cap and trade" legislation New EPA rules require electrical utilities to apply for state permits to open new facilities. Congress has fought this EPA action on the grounds that it requires legislative action, which has not been forthcoming.

Chief Justice John Marshall stated that "the power to tax is the power to destroy." We are learning that "the power to regulate is the power to destroy," if carried to the extreme. Regulation also threatens the delineation of the separation of power established by the Constitution. In April 2011, the U.S. Supreme Court took up a lawsuit by several states and the city of New York seeking court-imposed limits on greenhouse gases emitted by five major power companies. With this suit, all three branches of government have become involved in greenhouse gas emissions. We imagine the framers of the Constitution would not welcome this confusion over the separation of power.

Deregulation

In the 1960s and 1970s, the high costs and inefficiencies of regulation prompted a movement toward deregulation. ***Deregulation*** *is the reduction of government regulation and the return of decision making back to the private business.* Deregulation was promoted by stories of trucks required by regulations to return empty from long hauls, airlines forced to serve communities with few customers, and rail freight required to charge the same rates as truckers. Deregulation advocates promised that if decisions were returned to the businesses themselves, customers would benefit from lower prices and better service.[31] The opponents of deregulation warned of deteriorating service, pricing wars, and general instability in deregulated industries.

Deregulation began in the late 1970s. The Airline Deregulation Act, signed in October 1978, allowed the airlines rather than the Civil Aeronautics Board (which remarkably went out of existence in 1984) to set fares and choose routes.[32] In 1980, the Motor Carrier Act curbed the role of the Interstate Commerce Commission in interstate trucking. Also in 1980, the Staggers Rail Act led to major changes in railroad transport, and the Depository Institution Deregulation and the Monetary Control acts significantly liberalized banking. The AT&T Settlement of 1982 and the Cable Television Deregulation Act of 1984 brought major changes in the telecommunications and cable television industries, respectively. With new technology and a national grid system of high-voltage cables, a market in electricity was created. Electrical utilities were broken up into common carriers and marketers, who sold electricity purchased in electricity trading markets. There were market failures, particularly in California, which froze the retail price, while wholesale prices were set in the electricity market. As energy prices (and electricity prices) rose unexpectedly in world markets, California's retail prices did not cover wholesale prices, and state had to cover the price differential from its budget.[33] As in other cases, deregulation was blamed for the mistakes of others.

The United States' thirty-year experience has shown that deregulation leads to lower prices for most—but not all—consumers. Deregulation has increased the diversity of services and consumers have more freedom of choice. Firms that had been protected by regulation lowered their costs substantially and passed the savings on to their customers in the form of lower prices. Deregulation has also had its losers. Firms that could not meet competitive pressures have gone out of business or have been acquired by more successful firms. Employees of formerly regulated businesses, such as flight attendants and pilots, have seen their earnings fall as cost cutting occurred.

The pattern of finger-pointing is now well established. When things go wrong, it is the fault of deregulation, even if this may not be the case. The most spectacular case was the financial crisis of 2007–2009, which originated in the collapse of the home mortgage market. Financial deregulation had made it possible for financial firms of all sorts to be involved directly or indirectly in home mortgages. U.S. government policy, backed by lending from government mortgage insurers (such as Fanny Mae) aggressively promoted private home ownership. Mortgage lenders were encouraged to lend (and even assigned quotas) to unqualified borrowers under the assumption that home prices would continue to rise. These mortgage loans were then insured by government mortgage insurers. Deregulated financial institutions, such as large commercial banks, then bundled these mortgages into packages, which were sold to other financial institutions around the world. When inflated home prices collapsed, a large proportion of mortgages were "under water" (the loan balance was worth more than the loan), and defaults accelerated, creating a worldwide financial crisis. Financial institutions experienced huge losses. Some failed. Others were bailed out by the government. Was this a failure of deregulation, or was it a failure of policy? Deregulation allowed large financial institutions to speculate with bundles of mortgages (which proved to be worth little), but government policy encouraged risky lending to unqualified mortgage borrowers.

The Labor Market

Labor markets are flexible or inflexible. *Flexible labor markets give employers freedom to hire and fire employees and change conditions of work and pay with few restrictions.* *Inflexible labor markets require employers to follow strict rules and procedures in hiring and firing employees.* We shall explore these differences when we study the European model in the next chapter. For now, it suffices to say that the United States has one of the most flexible labor markets in the industrialized world. It could be called a *hire and fire labor market, which is a market in which workers and employees can be fired or laid off with few limits placed on it by the state.*

The greater flexibility of the U.S. labor market is no surprise. The U.S. corporation maximizes shareholder value, not stakeholder value. The interests of managers, employees, and workers are regarded as less important than shareholders. Hence, there should be less job security in the American labor market than in the European labor market, where stakeholder rights are greater.[34] In the United States, worker rights are usually the result of custom and practice, not state regulation. One such factor is the degree to which workers are organized into labor or trade unions.

Unions

A *labor or trade union is an organization of employees and workers of a company, occupation, or branch that comes together for the purpose of affecting conditions of work and pay.* Currently, 11.7 percent of the U.S. labor force belongs to labor unions, a figure that is exceptionally low by European standards. Most of these are in public-sector unions (such as state employees or school teachers). Among private-sector workers, only 7 percent belong to unions. The percentage is 36 percent for public workers. In the 1930s, union members accounted for 6 to 7 percent of the labor force. Union membership rose in the 1940s and peaked at 25 percent in the mid-1950s. Since then, the percentage has declined—despite the notable increase among public employees.

American trade unions are more decentralized than their counterparts in Europe. More authority rests with local unions, and unions failed to produce their own political party. U.S. labor unions generally do not bargain at a national level, as do the German unions, where the metal workers and public-sector employees set wage patterns for the entire labor force. Also, there is less cohesion among U.S. labor unions, so it would be difficult to organize a general strike that would paralyze the entire economy. The American unions consist of loose federations of local unions banded into national unions. More American unions are associated with the AFL-CIO (American Federation of Labor–Congress of Industrial Organizations) than with any other umbrella organization. The AFL-CIO accounts for almost 80 percent of all union members.

As Table 11.8 shows, the largest unions now represent public workers or service employees. With the relative decline of manufacturing, industrial unions have lost membership.

The rising heft of public sector unions threatens to change the face of collective bargaining. Industrial unions bargain with private employers, who have to worry about the bottom line of the business. If they are too generous, profits fall and the business is threatened. Public sector unions, however, bargain with municipal and state governments, which represent taxpayers. These local and state politicians are tempted to take the easy way out and grant pay and benefits increases even during trying economic times. Increases in retirement benefits are particularly appealing because they will be paid by future taxpayers. Moreover, public sector unions can make generous political contributions to the very politicians who decide their wages and benefits.

This problem became apparent as state and local revenues collapsed in 2010 and 2011 in the aftermath of the worldwide recession. Some state and local governments, faced with massive deficits, decided that past arrangements were not working and sought to put in place legislation that restricted collective bargaining for

TABLE 11.8   The Largest U.S. Labor Organizations

Members	Union
2,731,419	National Education Association of the United States
1,505,100	Service Employees International Union
1,459,511	American Federation of State, County, and Municipal Employees
1,396,174	International Brotherhood of Teamsters
1,311,548	United Food and Commercial Workers International Union
828,512	American Federation of Teachers
754,978	United Steelworkers of America
704,794	International Brotherhood of Electrical Workers
669,772	Laborers' International Union of North America
653,781	International Association of Machinists and Aerospace Workers
557,099	International Union, United Automobile, Aerospace, and Agricultural Implement Workers of America
545,638	Communications Workers of America

Source: National Labor Organizations with Membership over 10,000 © 2000–2012 Pearson Education, publishing as InfoPlease. All Rights Reserved.

public unions, especially collective bargaining for benefits. These unions have mounted a counterattack, and we will not know the results until the presidential election of 2012.

Government Regulation of the Labor Market

Although U.S. employers feel that they are subject to extensive regulation, such regulation is relatively minor compared to the major European labor markets in Germany, France, and Italy, as will be explained in the next chapter. U.S. employers are regulated by several acts.

The *National Labor Relations Act of 1935* (NLRA, also called the Wagner Act) has been called the union "bill of rights." It provides a framework for workers to organize unions through elections at their workplace; it investigates charges of unfair labor practices and can issue formal complaints against employers. The NLRA is adjudicated by a National Labor Relations Board (NLRB) whose five members are appointed by the president and confirmed by Congress. NLRB judgments are subject to appeal in the federal courts.

The NLRB can, on occasion, flex its muscle against employers. In 2011, the NLRB ruled against Boeing Company's building of a production facility in South Carolina on the grounds that its investment was in retaliation for strikes at its Washington State plant. Boeing Company has taken this matter to the federal appeals court, arguing that unions do not have the right to dictate its expansion decisions.

The *Fair Labor Standards Act of 1938* establishes standards for minimum wages, overtime pay, record keeping, and child labor. The act covers enterprises with $500,000 or more in annual dollar sales—less if they are engaged in interstate commerce. The act requires employers to pay a minimum wage set by Congress and to keep records on wages, hours, and other information as set forth in the Department of Labor's regulations. The act also prohibits the shipment, in interstate commerce, of goods that were produced in violation of the minimum wage, overtime pay, child labor, or special minimum wage provisions. Willful violators may be prosecuted criminally and fined. A second conviction may result in imprisonment.

The Transfer Economy

Figure 11.6 illustrates the rising role of transfer payments in government spending. *Transfer payments are payments by the state out of revenues from taxpayers to recipients who have not provided a service in return.* Examples would be unemployment insurance, Social Security retirement checks, or aid to families with dependent children. The state pays recipients from taxes collected (or increasingly from borrowed funds) and pays recipients, who qualify by meeting eligibility requirements. To receive unemployment insurance, for example, the recipient must have lost a job and not have drawn payments for more than the eligibility period.

FIGURE 11.6   Government Transfers, 1962 to 2009

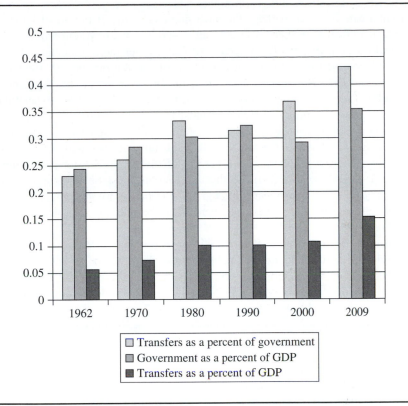

Legend:
☐ Transfers as a percent of government
▨ Government as a percent of GDP
■ Transfers as a percent of GDP

Source: Economic Report of the President.

*Transfer programs are called entitlements. An **entitlement program** is one in which recipients are entitled to receive payments once they qualify under the rules of the program.* Unemployed persons cannot be denied payment if they meet all the eligibility requirements. Retired persons who qualify cannot be denied payment.

Figure 11.6 shows that as late as 1962, transfer payments accounted for less than a quarter of government spending and for about 5 percent of GDP. By 2009, transfers were approaching 45 percent of government spending and had reached 15 percent of GDP. These figures illustrate not only the general rise of government (as a percent of GDP) but also the increasingly redistributive role of the state in the U.S. economy. Whereas once the government played virtually no role in redistributing income, now about 15 percent of economic activity is redistributed by the state.

Prior to the 1930s, nearly all retirement, health, and unemployment insurance was organized privately; in 1929, only 10 percent of personal health expenditures was funded by government. Although public school education has dominated, the government share of support for higher education has increased substantially over the last fifty years. During that time, public universities supplanted private universities as the dominant institutions in higher education.

Health care has seen perhaps the most dramatic shift, as Figure 11.10 shows. In 1950, more than 80 percent of health care costs were paid by households. At that time, health care accounted for 4 percent of GDP. After the introduction of Medicare and Medicaid (and subsequent expansion of these programs) in 1964 under President Johnson, the balance began to shift in favor of public payment. By 2010, public expenditures on health care were nearly equal to private expenditures, while health care spending had risen to almost 18 percent of GDP. In March 2010, the Obama administration proposed and Congress passed (against strong Republican opposition) a major expansion of public health care that will further reduce private payments for health care as a percent of the total. A major component of the reform package was a mandate that all persons must buy health insurance. In March 2011, the Republicans offered an alternative to the Obama program that replaces, in part, the "designated benefit" plan with subsidies to buy health insurance.

The future of American health care will probably be decided in the 2012 presidential election. If the Republican candidate wins, there will be no universal health insurance mandate and health care will likely be paid for with private insurance programs subsidized by the state. If Obama is reelected, health care will be paid for more directly by the state, and citizens will be "guaranteed" medical services, at least those approved by advisory boards. Under a Republican administration, citizens would be guaranteed insurance but not specific approved services.

Economics teaches that there is no such thing as a free lunch. If there are not adequate funds to pay the suppliers of health care their opportunity costs, "guaranteed" services will not be supplied in the quantities demanded. Physicians, nurses, and other health care practitioners will refuse to supply the services that the person is supposed to receive.

Figure 11.7 shows the rising importance of Social Security, *President Roosevelt's **New Deal** was a series of public work, unemployment, and social legislation designed to pull the country out of the Great Depression and to help those harmed by it.* The Social Security Act of 1935 has proven to be the most lasting legacy of the New Deal. Prior to it, individuals were responsible for their own retirement, and they had extended families to fall back on in case of hardship. The Social Security Amendments of 1954 launched a disability insurance program that provided the public with additional coverage against economic insecurity. In 1956, the Social Security Act was amended to provide benefits to disabled workers aged 50 to 65 and to disabled adult children. The most significant change involved the passage of Medicare, which extended health coverage to Social Security beneficiaries aged 65 or older (and eventually to those receiving disability benefits as well). Nearly 20 million beneficiaries enrolled in Medicare in the first three years of the program.

The Social Security Act gave retirees retirement income as designated by the Social Security Administration to be paid for from payroll taxes of those working. At the time the program was introduced, there were four to five active workers for each retiree. Although payroll taxes were supposedly placed in a trust fund, in

FIGURE 11.7   Private versus Public Health and Retirement

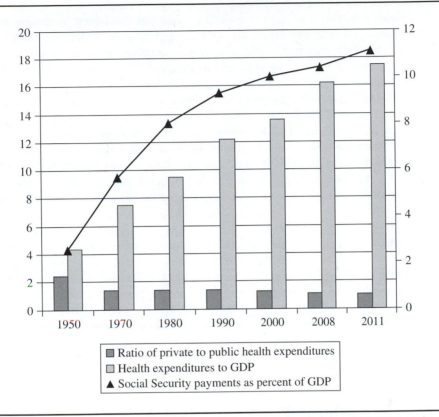

Source: Statistical Abstract, https://www.cms.gov/NationalHealthExpendData/downloads/NHEProjections 2009to2019.pdf.

actual practice payments to retirees have been made out of general revenues. With the aging of the population, the ratio of retirees to active workers has fallen. Depending on assumptions, at some point in the future payroll taxes will not cover retirement obligations, and the Social Security retirement program will have to dip into general tax revenue.

Both Medicare and Social Security have enormous unfunded liabilities. An *unfunded liability* is the shortfall in funds that have been accumulated to meet the future obligations of an entitlement program. In effect, the unfunded liability of Medicare would be the amount of money that would have to be accumulated in a designated account to meet future obligations at under current rules.

Recent calculations of the Social Security Administration show unfunded liabilities of $17.5 trillion, a figure well above annual GDP.[35] Medicare trustees report that the program has an unfunded liability of nearly $38 trillion, more than double U.S. GDP.[36] The combined unfunded liabilities of Social Security and

Medicare are therefore in the neighborhood of $55 trillion, more than three times the annual income of the U.S. economy.

Unfunded liabilities of such magnitudes mean that the current programs are unsustainable. There is no way to set taxes so high that these deficits could be covered. Therefore, our two major entitlement programs must be restructured with less generous benefits or gradual privatization. However, Social Security (and to a lesser degree Medicaid) is called the "third rail" of American politics. Any politician or party that proposes real solutions can be demagogued by their political opponents. This does not mean that entitlement reform is impossible. In the run up to his reelection, Bill Clinton announced famously that "Welfare as we know it should end." Indeed, Clinton worked with a Republican Congress to limit the benefits of welfare mothers. His Personal Responsibility, Work Opportunity and Medicaid Restructuring Act of 1996 brought about a drastic reduction in the number of young mothers on welfare and a dramatic increase in their employment.

It remains to be seen whether the U.S. political system can resolve the impending catastrophe of the unfunded liabilities of Social Security and Medicare. One option would be to dramatically increase tax revenues by a broad-based tax on consumption, such as the value added taxes of Europe. The other approach would be to substantially reduce the benefits of Social Security and Medicare to levels that are affordable at current rates of taxation. If the tax-increase approach is followed, the United States would, in effect, join the European welfare state model. It remains to be seen whether U.S. voters are prepared to accept this option.

The U.S. Federal Tax Code, Social Engineering, and the Percentage Paying Income Taxes

Unlike many governments of Europe and Asia, the U.S. government does not have a national economic plan or a formal industrial policy. This does not mean that the federal government does not attempt to direct economic outcomes. The major instrument of this direction is the federal tax code.

The complete text of the United States Internal Revenue Code, Title 26 of the U.S. Code, is 44,000 pages. Its 5.5 million words and 721 different forms is a patchwork maze of complexity that no single expert can understand. Its main provisions explain the personal income tax and the corporate income tax. The U.S. tax code is administered by the Internal Revenue Service. We have no comparative data, but we suspect that the U.S. tax code is the most complicated among the major industrialized countries.

Changes in the tax code originate in the House of Representatives. Its almost 50,000 words reveal thousands or hundreds of thousands of subsidies, tax preferences, and tax loopholes. Many of these tax preferences favor specific individuals or companies and are influenced by lobbying efforts. There are approximately 40,000 registered lobbyists at the federal and state level. In 2009, Washington lobbyists spent more than $3.5 billion.

Some parts of the tax code aim at specific social-engineering goals. Families with children pay lower taxes to encourage family formation. Homeowners pay less because they can deduct mortgage interest. This provision encourages home ownership. A number of tax breaks encourage energy saving, such as lower taxes for installing insulation or using green energy.

Although one might disagree with social-engineering aspects of the tax code, they at least make some sense. The hundreds of thousands of specific preferences and breaks, however, are simply the result of lobbying, influence buying, and campaign contributions. The complexity of the tax code is a boon for those who write it. It gives Congress enormous leverage, which it can use to gain contributions and other favors.

Although there have been calls for over a century to simplify the tax code, this outcome is unlikely because those who write the tax code benefit from its complexity. Economists favor a flat tax that charges a low single rate for all taxpayers while removing all tax preferences (which has been adopted by many other countries), but it has little chance in the United States.

A complex tax code like that of the United States promotes monopoly rent seeking. **Monopoly rent seeking** *is the expenditure of resources to gain preferences and advantages from the state.* Economists like Gordon Tullock and Anne Krueger have long pointed out that monopoly rent seeking creates huge deadweight losses for society.[37] The losses to society from these preferences far outweigh the gains of those receiving them.

The U.S. Constitution gives citizens the right "to petition government." Lobbyists are, after all, petitioning government and have the right to do so. The First Amendment ensures freedom of speech, which includes "political speech" by the Chamber of Commerce, the Service Employee International Union, and the like. Hence, lobbying will always be with us as long as the government has favors to hand out that individuals, unions, and corporations want. Lobbying cannot be restricted by laws because ways are found around the law. It seems the only way to reduce lobbying is to reduce the power and discretion of the state.

James Madison worried about an overbearing majority as he drafted the Constitution. He worried particularly about a majority teaming up against the "rich." Indeed, slogans like "tax the rich" are appealing the world over. In the United States, about 47 percent will pay no federal income taxes at all for 2009. Either their incomes were too low, or they qualified for enough credits, deductions, and exemptions to eliminate their liability.

Final Comments

The Anglo-Saxon model was developed in England in the eighteenth century. Under it, England became the world's largest and most affluent nation, despite its island status. The tradition of the Anglo-Saxon model was passed on to the United States, which expanded that tradition in its Constitution. The United States appears to follow the Anglo-Saxon model most closely in its capital and labor markets. The rise in regulation of business since the 1930s has made the U.S. economy a highly regulated economy with a regulatory burden of at least $4,000 per capita, despite a significant deregulation of traditionally regulated industries beginning in the late 1970s.

The economic successes of the United States after 1982 have encouraged other countries to adopt some features of the Anglo-Saxon model, such as deregulation and privatization. The "liberalization" of capital and labor markets has proved more difficult in other countries, such as those in Europe, where liberalization efforts encounter significant barriers. Some countries, such as Ireland in the 1990s and, to a lesser extent, the Netherlands, have deliberately adopted some features of the Anglo-Saxon model. In both cases, the move to the Anglo-Saxon model has improved their economic performance.

Summary

- The U.S. Constitution specifies three branches of government—executive, legislative, and judicial—each of which represents a substantial check over the other branches.
- The original intent of the U.S. Constitution was to limit the power and scope of the federal government.
- The private sector (business sector) accounts for approximately 75 percent of economic activity, the government sector for roughly 25 percent.
- There are three primary forms of business organizations: sole proprietorships, partnerships, and corporations.
- Corporate governance is concerned with the issue of for whose interest a corporation is operated.
- U.S. corporations are run for the benefit of shareholders, or owners, as measured by increases in market capitalization.
- The market for corporate control is a market wherein rival management teams have the opportunity to buy control of the corporation from its owners.
- The capital market is the market for long-term financial assets such as stocks and bonds.
- Regulation of private business evolved for the purpose of protecting the public interest, as evidenced by almost thirty different regulatory bodies.
- In 2002, the cost of business regulation was approximately $1 trillion, or about 9 percent of GDP.
- Deregulation, on balance, has reduced real prices and increased services.
- The United States has become an entitlement state that has unfunded liabilities that exceed our ability to pay in the future.
- The U.S. tax code is incredibly complex and encourages monopoly rent seeking.

Key Terms

Board of directors—Elected by the stockholders, makes its major decisions, and appoints management to run the corporation.

Broad and liquid stock market—A large number of shareholders, none of whom hold significant shares, and shareholders can sell their shares readily without affecting the share price.

Capital market—Market in which businesses raise investment finance through the issue of stocks and bonds and bank borrowing.

Corporate governance—Determines in whose interests a corporation, in which owners are not managers, will be run.

Corporate raiders—Mobilize substantial funds to mount hostile takeovers against underperforming corporations.

Corporation—Company owned by its stockholders, who have limited liability, and can act as a legal person.

Counterfactual information—What would have happened in the absence of a particular event.

Deregulation—The reduction of government regulation and the return of decision making back to the private business.

Economic regulation—Government involvement in markets, such as setting prices, restricting corporate decision making, and controlling competition.

Economically rational regulation—Regulation that yields benefits in excess of its costs.

Eminent domain—The right of the state to take property under certain conditions in the public interest (such as buying land for the construction of railways or making way for an interstate highway).

Entitlement program—Recipients are entitled to receive payments once they qualify under the rules of the program.

Fair Labor Standards Act of 1938—Established standards for minimum wages, overtime pay, record keeping, and child labor.

Fiduciary fiduciary responsibility—A relationship in which one person has a responsibility to care for the assets or rights of other persons.

Flexible labor markets—Give employers freedom to hire and fire employees and change conditions of work and pay with few restrictions.

Full disclosure—The principle that the corporations listing stock must make available to potential buyers all relevant information, good and bad, about the company.

Golden parachute—Provides for a limited number of top executives to receive generous severance bonuses if their company is taken over.

Hire and fire labor market—Market in which is one in which workers and employees can be fired or laid off with few limits placed on it by the state.

Hostile merger or acquisition—Targeted company actively opposes the takeover.

Inflexible labor markets—Require employers to follow strict rules and procedures in hiring and firing employees.

Labor or trade union—An organization of employees and workers of a company, occupation, or branch that comes together for the purpose of affecting conditions of work and pay.

Market for corporate control—A rival management team has the opportunity to buy control of the corporation from its share owners.

Market power—Business can affect the price at which it buys or sells.

Mergers and acquisitions—The buying, selling, and merger of one company with another.

Monopoly rent seeking—The expenditure of resources to gain preferences and advantages from the state.

National Labor Relations Act of 1935 (NLRA, also called the Wagner Act)—The union "bill of rights."

New Deal—A series of public work, unemployment, and social legislation designed to pull the country out of the Great Depression and to help those harmed by it.

Partnership—Company owned by two or more partners, who make all the business decisions and share in the profits and losses.

Primary market—Market in which, the corporation, sells (issues) new shares of stocks or bonds to buyers. Such sales of new shares are called **initial public offerings** (IPOs).

Private sector—The business sector in which private ownership prevails and government regulation or intervention is limited.

Shareholder value—The value of the corporation in stock markets as measured by its market capitalization.

Social regulation—The regulation of health, safety, and environment.

Sole proprietorship—Company owned by one individual, who makes all the business decisions and absorbs the profits (or losses) that the business earns.

Stakeholders—Participate in the operation of the corporation as managers, employees, workers, suppliers, or buyers, but not as owners.

Stock option—Grants executives the right to buy a designated number of shares of the company at a specified price (often the stock price on the day the stock options were granted).

Transfer payments—Payments by the state out of revenues from taxpayers to recipients who have not provided a service in return.

U.S. exceptionalism—The notion that the United States is a unique social, economic, and political experiment made possible by a unique confluence of events in the late eighteenth century.

Underwriter—Organize the initial sale of shares, sometimes buying stakes in the company themselves.

Unfunded liability—The shortfall in funds that have been accumulated to meet the future obligations of an entitlement program.

Venture capital fund—Provides start start-up capital to new firms and takes a stake in them in return.

Venture capital—Financing through purchases of shares or loans to start up businesses.

Notes

1. James Madison, *Federalist 51*, "The Structure of the Government Must Furnish the Proper Checks and Balances Between Different Departments," http://federalistpapers.com.
2. James Madison, *Federalist 10*, "The Same Subject Continued (The Union as a Safeguard Against Domestic Faction and Insurrection)."
3. Madison, *Federalist 51*.
4. Douglass North, "Structure and Performance: The Task of Economic History," *Journal of Economic Literature* 41 (September 1978), 968.
5. Harry Scheiber, "Original Intent, History, and Doctrine: The Constitution and Economic Liberty," *American Economic Review* 78, no. 2 (May 1988), 140.
6. http://www.law.emory.edu/FEDERAL/usconst/amend.html.
7. Richard Posner, *Economic Analysis of Law*, 6th ed. (New York: Aspen, 2003) and *Law, Pragmatism, and Democracy* (Cambridge, Mass.: Harvard University Press, 2003).
8. Zechariah Chafee, Jr., "Do Judges Make or Discover Law?" *Proceedings of the American Philosophical Society* 91, no. 5 (3 December 1947), 405–420.
9. W. M. Landes and R. Posner, *The Economic Structure of Tort Law* (Cambridge, Mass.: Harvard University Press, 1987).
10. Francisco Cabrillo, "Law and Economic Development: Common Law Versus Civil Law, 2007," http://www.isnie.org/assets/files/papers2007/cabrillo.pdf.
11. Milton Friedman, "Monopoly and Social Responsibility of Business and Labor," in Edwin Mansfield, ed., *Monopoly Power and Economic Performance*, 3rd ed. (New York: Norton, 1974), pp. 57–68.
12. Frederic Scherer, *Industrial Structure and Economic Performance*, 2nd ed. (Boston: Houghton Mifflin, 1980), p. 519.
13. Clifford Winston, "Economic Deregulation: Days of Reckoning for Microeconomists," *Journal of Economic Literature* 31, no. 3 (September 1993), 1263–1289.
14. Friedman, "Monopoly and Social Responsibility of Business and Labor," pp. 57–68.
15. William G. Shepherd, "Causes of Increased Competition in the U.S. Economy, 1939–1980," *Review of Economics and Statistics*, November 1982, 613–626.
16. See also Frederic Scherer, *Industrial Market Structure*, pp. 68–70; James V. Koch, *Industrial Organization and Prices*, 2nd ed. (Englewood Cliffs, N.J.: Prentice-Hall, 1980), p. 181; and Morris Adelman, "Changes in Industrial Concentration," in Mansfield, *Monopoly Power and Economic Performance*, pp. 83–88.
17. Christopher Caldwell, "Europe's Social Market Economy," *Policy Review* 109 (October–November 2002), 38.
18. Adolf Berle and Gardiner Means, *The Modern Corporation and Private Property* (New York: Macmillan, 1932).
19. Henry Manne, "Mergers and the Market for Corporate Control," *Journal of Political Economy* 73 (1965), 110–120; Philippe Aghion, Oliver Hart, and J. Moore, "The Economics of Bankruptcy Reform," *Journal of Law, Economics and Organizations* 8 (1992), 523–546.
20. "Corporate Governance: Enhancing the Return on Capital Through Increased Corporate Responsibility," http://www.corpgov.net.
21. See, for example, Andrei Shleifer and Lawrence Summers, "Hostile Takeovers as Breaches of Trust," FMG Discussion Papers, June 1987, http://netec.mcc.ac.uk/BibEc/data/Papers/fmgfmgdpsdp0008.html.
22. Caldwell, "Europe's 'Social Market,'" p. 38.

23. Bernard Siegan, *Economic Liberties and the Constitution* (Chicago: University of Chicago Press, 1980), pp. 65, 99, 111–113.
24. North, "On Economic History," p. 969.
25. Scheiber, "Original Intent," p. 142.
26. *The Federal Register, Main Page,* http://www.gpoaccess.gov/fr/.
27. About.com, "Federal Regulations," http://usgovinfo.about.com/od/uscongress/a/fedregulations_2.htm.
28. Federal Reserve Bank of Dallas, *America's Economic Regulation Burden,* Fall 1996, pp. 1–6.
29. Thomas Hopkins, "Profiles of Regulatory Costs," SBA Contract SBAHQ-95-M-0298, Final Report, 1995. The figures have been updated to 2010 by the authors.
30. http://www.epa.gov/airmarkets/trading/2011/11summary.html.
31. Frederic Scherer, *Industrial Structure and Economic Performance,* chap. 18; Paul MacAvoy, "The Rationale for Regulation of Field Prices of Natural Gas," in MacAvoy, *The Crisis of the Regulatory Commissions,* pp. 152–168; Robert E. Litan and William D. Nordhaus, *Reforming Federal Regulation* (New Haven: Yale University Press, 1983); and Lawrence J. White, *Reforming Regulation* (Englewood Cliffs, N.J.: Prentice-Hall, 1981).
32. Elizabeth E. Bailey, "Price and Productivity Change Following Deregulation: The U.S. Experience," *Economic Journal* 96 (March 1986), 1–17. See also C. Winston, "Conceptual Developments in the Economics of Transportation," *Journal of Economic Literature* 23 (1985), 57–94; T. Keeler, *Railroads, Freight, and Public Policy* (Washington, D.C.: Brookings Institution, 1983); A. F. Friedlander and R. H. Spady, *Freight Transport Regulation* (Cambridge, Mass.: MIT Press, 1981); Clifford Winston, "Economic Deregulation: Days of Reckoning for Microeconomists," *Journal of Economic Literature* 31, no. 3 (September 1993), 1263–1289.
33. Robert Bradley Jr., "The Origins of Political Electricity: Market Failure or Political Opportunism?," *Energy Law Journal* 17 no. 59 (1996), 59–102.
34. Our discussion is based on William Bowen and Orley Ashenfelter, eds., *Labor and the National Economy,* rev. ed. (New York: Norton, 1975); H. Gregg Lewis, *Unions and Relative Wages in the United States* (Chicago: University of Chicago Press, 1960); Stanley Masters, *Black–White Income Differentials* (New York: Academic, 1975); Cynthia Lloyd, ed., *Sex, Discrimination and the Division of Labor* (New York: Columbia University Press, 1975); Michael Boskin, "Unions and Relative Real Wages," *American Economic Review* 62 (June 1972), 466–472; George Johnson, "Economic Analysis of Trade Unionism," *American Economic Review, Papers and Proceedings* 65 (May 1975), 23–28; Albert Rees, *The Economics of Trade Unions* (Chicago: University of Chicago Press, 1963); C. J. Paisley, "Labor Union Effects on Wage Gains: A Survey of Recent Literature," *Journal of Economic Literature* 18 (March 1980), 1–31; Richard Freeman and James Medoff, "The Two Faces of Unionism," *Public Interest* 57 (Fall 1979), 73–80; Ronald G. Ehrenberg and Robert S. Smith, *Modern Labor Economics,* 3rd ed. (Glenview, Ill.: Scott, Foresman, 1988); "Rising Wage Inequality in the United States: Causes and Consequences," *American Economic Review: Papers and Proceedings* 84, no. 2 (May 1994), 10–33; "Lessons from Empirical Labor Economics: 1972–1992," *American Economic Review: Papers and Proceedings* 83, no. 2 (May 1993), 104–121.
35. Bruce Barlett, "The 81% Tax Increase," *Forbes,* http://www.forbes.com/2009/05/14/taxes-social-security-opinions-columnists-medicare.html

36. "How Washington Rations: ObamaCare Omen; A Case Study in 'Cost Control,'" *Wall Street Journal*, http://online.wsj.com/article/SB124268737705832167.html.

37. Anne Krueger, "The Political Economy of the Rent-Seeking Society," *American Economic Review* 64 (June 1974), 291–303; Gordon Tullock, "The Welfare Cost of Tariffs, Monopolies, and Theft," *Western Economic Journal* 5 (June 1967), 224–232

Recommended Readings

General Sources

F. M. Bator, "The Simple Analytics of Welfare Maximization," *American Economic Review* 47 (March 1957), 22–59.

———, "The Anatomy of Market Failure," *Quarterly Journal of Economics* 72 (August 1958), 351–379.

H. G. Lewis, *Unionism and Relative Wages in the United States* (Chicago: University of Chicago Press, 1963).

Paul MacAvoy, ed., *The Crisis of Regulatory Commissions* (New York: Norton, 1970).

Product Markets

William J. Baumol, John C. Panzar, and Robert D. Willig, *Contestable Markets and the Theory of Industry Structure* (New York: Harcourt, 1982).

Oliver Williamson, *The Economic Institutions of Capitalism* (New York: Free Press, 1985).

Labor Markets

Ronald Ehrenberg and Robert Smith, *Modern Labor Economics*, 3rd ed. (Glenview, Ill.: Scott Foresman, 1988).

Richard B. Freeman, "Unionism Comes to the Public Sector," *Journal of Economic Literature* 24, no. 1 (March 1986), 41–86.

"Lessons from Empirical Labor Economics: 1972–1992," *American Economic Review: Papers and Proceedings* 83, no. 2 (May 1993), 104–121.

James B. Rebitzer, "Radical Political Economy and the Economics of Labor Markets," *Journal of Economic Literature* 31, no. 3 (September 1993), 1394–1434.

Government and the Economy

Andrew B. Abel and Ben S. Bernanke, *Macroeconomics* (New York: Addison-Wesley, 1992).

Douglas H. Blair and Robert A. Pollack, "Rational Collective Choice," *Scientific American* 249, no. 2 (August 1983), 88–95.

John B. Donahue, *The Privatization Decision* (New York: Basic Books, 1989).

Federal Reserve Bank of Dallas, *America's Economic Regulation Burden*, Fall 1996.

Frank Levy and Richard J. Murname, "U.S. Earning Levels and Earnings Inequality: A Review of Recent Trends and Proposed Explanations" *Journal of Economic Literature* 30, no. 3 (September 1992), 1333–1381.

N. Gregory Mankiw, "Symposium on Keynesian Economics Today," *Journal of Economic Literature* 7, no. 1 (Winter 1993), 3–82.

Robert Moffitt, "Incentive Effects of the U.S. Welfare System: A Review," *Journal of Economic Literature* 30, no. 1 (March 1992), 1–61.

Janet Rotherberg Pack, "Privatization of Public Sector Services in Theory and Practice," *Journal of Policy Analysis and Management* 6(1987), 523–540.

Joseph Pechman, *Who Paid the Taxes, 1966–85?* (Washington, D.C.: Brookings Institution, 1985).

Harvey S. Rosen, *Public Finance*, 3rd ed. (Homewood, Ill.: Irwin, 1992).

F. M. Scherer and David Ross, *Industrial Market Structure and Economic Performance*, 3rd ed. (Boston: Houghton Mifflin, 1990).

Eugene Singer, *Antitrust Economics* (Englewood Cliffs, N.J.: Prentice-Hall, 1968).

James Schmitz, "The Role Played by Public Enterprises: How Much Does It Differ Across Countries?" Federal Reserve Bank of Minneapolis, *Quarterly Review* (Spring 1996), 2–15.

Don E. Waldman, ed., *The Economics of Antitrust* (Boston: Little, Brown, 1986).

Leonard Weiss and Michael Klass, eds., *Regulatory Reform: What Actually Happened* (Boston: Little, Brown, 1986).

Clifford Winston, "Economic Deregulation: Days of Reckoning for Microeconomists," *Journal of Economic Literature* 31, no. 3 (September 1993), 1263–1289.

Richard L. Worsnop, "Privatization," *Congressional Quarterly Researcher* (November 13, 1992), 979–999.

CHAPTER
12

The European Model

Chapter 9 introduced the Anglo-Saxon, European, and the Asian models of capitalism. It described some of the basic characteristics of the European model, such as its use of civil law, the greater concentration of corporate control, reliance on bank financing, the greater role of government, inflexible labor markets, and higher degrees of regulation. The previous two chapters examined the Anglo-Saxon model. We now turn to Europe.

Europe consists of a large number of countries (there are twenty-seven members of the European Union). The countries that created the European model are the first industrializers on the European continent: Germany, Netherlands, Belgium, the Scandinavian countries, and France. Italy joined this group somewhat later, and Spain followed later than that. As participants in the original Industrial Revolution, they counted among the highest-income countries by the second half of the nineteenth century.

The core European countries are surrounded by southern (Greece, Portugal, Spain, and former Yugoslavia), eastern (Poland, the Czech and Slovak Republics, Hungary, and the Baltic states), and northern (Finland and Baltic) peripheries.

Among these early industrializers, we focus principally on Germany, the largest and most successful European economy. Virtually all of the lessons we learn from Germany apply generally to the rest of "old" Europe. We did the same for the Anglo-Saxon model by concentrating on England during the Industrial Revolution and the United States.

Although the older affluent nations of continental Europe vary considerably in history, ethnicity, customs, and traditions, we lump them together for two reasons: First, they share of the core characteristics of the European model despite national variation. Second, "Europe," as represented by the European Union, has become one common market of twenty-seven countries that accounts for almost 500 million people. If Europe proceeds on its path of Europeanization, its institutions will converge, and we will truly be able to speak of a united European model.

The European Union (EU) now constitutes a market larger than the United States because of the accession of new members. *The EU accession states are those that became members of the EU in recent years.* They include countries to the south, such as Portugal, Greece, and Cyprus; countries to the east, such as the Baltic states, Poland, Hungary, and the Czech Republic; and countries to the north, such as Iceland.

A number of the accession states do not share the classic characteristics of the European model, particularly those that were part of the Soviet Empire or of the former Yugoslavia. Presumably membership in the EU will homogenize this diverse mix of countries. We do not know whether this homogenization will make the EU countries generally more like the early European industrializers or like the later accession countries, such as Poland, Lithuania, and Slovenia. Only time will give us an answer.

The European Union

Starting more than sixty years ago with the "one Europe" concept of French statesman Jean Monnet, Europe has gradually developed into a single market that functions in some respects like the fifty states of the United States. Europe stands now at a crossroad: It must decide whether to create a stronger political union directed increasingly by European agencies and a multinational parliament or to retreat back to the earlier status quo of independent but interdependent states.

The European Union was established via a series of treaties, starting in the 1950s. These treaties cumulatively set its rules of the game. *The **European Union** (EU) currently consists of twenty-seven member countries and a number of candidate countries that form a common market with common rules.*

The Treaty of Paris, signed in 1951, established the European Coal and Steel Community. The Treaty of Rome, signed in 1957, established the European Economic Community, otherwise known as the European Common Market. *The **European Common Market** was the precursor of the European Union. It created a common market of member countries by eliminating import duties and quotas.* The European Common Market transformed itself into the European Union through a series of treaties that not only increased economic integration but also increased the number of member countries.

The landmark Maastricht Treaty, signed in February 1992, dictated that the EU should have a common currency and one central bank. *The **Maastricht Treaty** outlined the introduction of a common currency, the euro, for those countries that chose to join the euro zone. The euro's monetary policy would be decided by a **European Central Bank**.*

The Treaty of Amsterdam, signed in October 1997, abolished border patrols and passport requirements among the member states by 2004. The agreements on the free movement of people within the EU were concluded in the Luxembourg city of Schengen. Indeed, citizens of EU countries, with some restrictions on work visas for new members, can now move freely among the EU member countries without visas. Free mobility has continued despite the admission of relatively poor countries, which more affluent countries feared would flood them with low-wage immigrants. The first test came with the "southern expansion" of the EU to Greece and Portugal; later tests came with the admission of Poland, Hungary, and the Czech and Slovak Republics.

The **Nice Summit** of December 2000 spelled out procedures for expansion of membership rights to other countries and for voting rights. Since 2000, twelve EU accession states joined the European Union, and there is a list of candidate and associated countries that one day may join.

Unlike the United States, the European Union lacks a constitution, despite efforts to create one. Instead, it functions on the basis of treaties negotiated over its sixty-year existence. In October 2004, the then twenty-five member states and three candidate countries agreed to draft a constitution to be approved by all member countries. After French and Dutch voters rejected the draft constitution, a reform treaty, the Treaty of Lisbon, was signed in December 2007 in place of a constitution. It codified the previous treaties that had earlier governed the EU into a set of more consistent rules and regulations.

The lack of an overarching constitution has not stymied extraordinary steps toward full economic integration. The most dramatic event was the introduction of a single currency, the euro, managed by the European Central Bank.

On January 1, 1999, the European Central Bank was established, and a common currency, the euro, was adopted for all bank transactions. On January 1, 2002, the euro became the sole currency for the EU. Three countries—England, Sweden, and Denmark—opted out of the common currency. Accession states have to fulfill a number of requirements before admission to the euro zone.

A number of candidate countries remain outside of the euro zone. When they qualify, they must decide whether to adopt the euro in place of their national currency or remain outside the euro zone.[1] Before the euro crisis of 2011 (discussed later), accession countries eagerly joined the euro zone. With the growing problems of the euro, new qualifiers may now decide to remain outside of the zone and continue their own national currency.

A single European central bank means that the individual countries no longer make monetary policy. Instead, interest rates and the money supply are set for the EU zone by the European Central Bank located in Frankfurt. *The **European Central Bank** shares many features with the Federal Reserve Bank of the United States. Its board consists of representatives from the national banks of the various EU members, just as the Federal Reserve Board is comprised of representatives from the district banks. Each member has one vote, unlike other EU bodies that weight votes according to population.* The larger member countries, such as Germany, now propose to change the one-nation-one-vote rule to favor the larger countries.

To prevent radical differences in fiscal policy, the EU countries adopted a stability pact. According to the ***EU stability pact**, no member country could run a public deficit of more than 3 percent of GDP.* If a country failed to meet this condition, it would be subject to fines and other sanctions. The failure of member states to meet the terms of the stability pact, including early on its largest and most prosperous member, Germany, was a major cause of the euro crisis in Europe that struck in 2011.

European Union Governance

*The **European Union (EU)** is governed by a multinational form of government, consisting of a Council of the European Union, an elected European Parliament, a European Commission, a European Central Bank, a European Court of Justice, and a European Council of Auditors.* These organizations reside in Brussels, Strasbourg, Frankfurt, and Luxembourg. The European Commission has more than 33,000 employees. Its approximately $160 billion budget is financed from levies at a uniform rate of the GDPs of member countries and from value-added taxes, customs, and agricultural duties. Many Europeans complain that the EU has become a large and intrusive bureaucracy that clashes too often with national governments.

Exhibit 12.1 shows the governance structure of the European Union.

The EU is a monumental ongoing experiment. Many of its provisions remain to be finalized. Precedents are being set. Voting rules must be established; provisions for enlargement must be approved; and the rights and powers of the elected legislative branch, the European Parliament, must be weighed against those of the European Commission, which is staffed by technocrats. The European Commission is pledged to consider the common interest of the EU, whereas the members of the European Parliament and European Council are supposed to represent the interests of their respective nations. The EU must therefore resolve principal–agent problems between those representing the interests of the EU at large and those representing the interests of member states. The danger of relying entirely on technocrats is that they use rigid bureaucratic rules and are not answerable to voters.

European Union Member Countries

The EU currently consists of twenty-seven countries (see Figure 12.1), seventeen of which are members of the euro zone. The EU's population is 500 million, which exceeds that of the United States (at 312 million) by almost 200 million people. The 2011 combined GDP of the twenty-seven EU member states was around $16 trillion, about the same as the United States. With a larger population and an equivalent GDP, the per capita GDP of the EU is some 65 percent of United States.

The main story of Figure 12.1 is the enormous diversity of the EU member and candidate states. In terms of population, they range from large, such as Germany, the United Kingdom, France, and candidate member Turkey, to tiny, such as Luxembourg and miniscule candidate-member Iceland. Germany's GDP is the world's fourth largest, while Slovenia and Estonia's GDPs are each less than $30 billion. Some EU members have been rich for a long time (the Scandinavian countries, France, and Germany); others are middle-income countries, like Poland and Estonia. Despite its rapid growth, Turkey is still a relatively poor country. It could be the poorest country ever admitted to the EU depending on timing.

The EU's diversity in terms of size, wealth, output, culture, and history suggests a complex cauldron from which to mold an eventual United States of Europe. There is much more diversity among the twenty-seven EU member states than among the fifty U.S. states or, for that matter, the original thirteen American colonies.

Exhibit 12.1   Governance of the European Union

European Commission—Made up of twenty-six commissioners, headed by a president. Commissioners are appointed by their national governments for five-year terms. The commissioners owe their loyalty to the EU, not to their countries. The commission proposes legislation, is responsible for administration, and ensures that provisions of the treaties and the decisions of the institutions are properly implemented. It has investigative powers and can take legal action against entities that violate EU rules. It manages the budget and represents the EU in international trade negotiations.

Council of the European Union—Made up of twenty-seven ministers, one from each member state. The council tries to strike a balance between national and EU interests. It enacts EU laws and can accept or reject legal suggestions made by the European Commission. Unlike the commission, the ministers can defend their national interests. Voting is weighted by country size according to qualified voting rules. The presidency rotates among member states every six months. The council is supported by the European Civil Service, which prepares meetings, drafts legislation, and assists the president.

European Parliament—Made up of 736 members elected to five-year terms by the 500 million citizens of the twenty-seven countries that make up the EU. The parliament's president is elected for a term of two and a half years. Parliament cannot enact laws but can veto legislation in certain policy areas, amend or reject the EU budget, dismiss the entire European Commission through a two-thirds vote, and supervise the EU's new employment policy. The parliament deals with a common foreign policy, globalization, human rights, and fundamental human rights of the European Union.

Court of Justice—Made up of one judge from each member state, appointed for renewable terms of six years. The court is assisted by eight advocate generals. It ensures that the treaties are interpreted and applied correctly by other EU institutions and by the member states. The court has final decision-making powers. Its judgments are binding on EU institutions, member countries, national courts, companies, and private citizens, and they supersede those of national courts.

Court of Auditors—Made up of one member from each country appointed by the Council of the European Union for renewable six-year terms. The court has extensive powers to examine the legality and regularity of receipts and expenditures and the sound financial management of the EU budget.

Member States—Twenty-seven countries are members of the European Union. Four are candidate members (Croatia, Macedonia, Iceland, and Turkey). Five others are potential candidate members.

Source: Based on data pulled from http://europea.eu

FIGURE 12.1A   European Union States, Population (selected members and candidates)

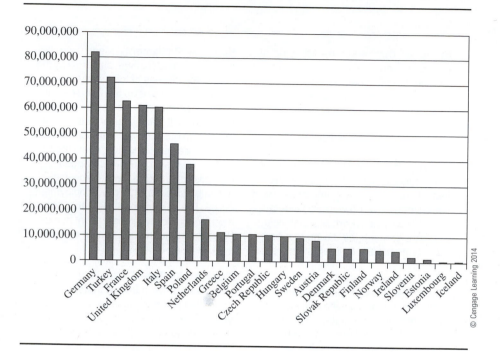

FIGURE 12.1B   European Union Countries GDP (selected members and candidates)

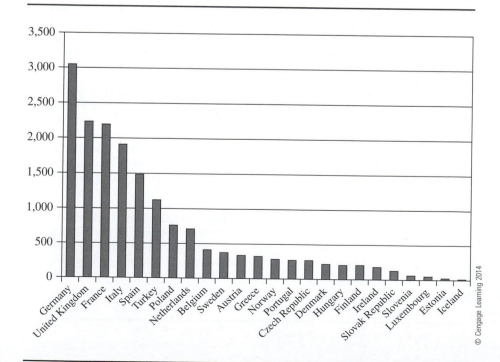

FIGURE 12.1C   European Union Countries, Per Capita GDP (selected members and candidates)

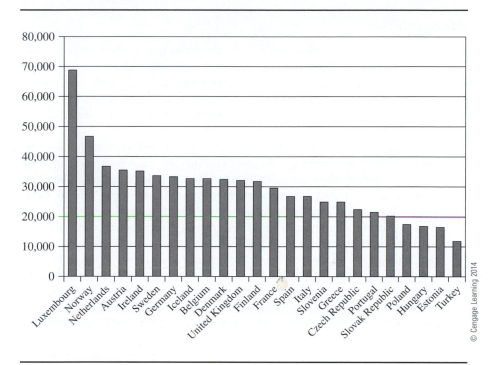

© Cengage Learning 2014

There are now two faces of Europe: There are the European states, with their histories, traditions, and economic and political institutions, and there are the politicians, bureaucrats, and technocrats of the European Union, who approach Europe as a single economic entity. Many would like it to become a single political entity, but Europe must decide which vision of Europe will prevail in the twenty-first century. We shall return to this issue in the concluding chapter.

Intellectual Foundations of the European Model

The ideological and intellectual origins of the Anglo-Saxon model trace back to Adam Smith. The political origins of the Anglo-Saxon model date to the rise of an elected parliament in England and to classical liberal Colonial American political thinkers, such as Thomas Jefferson and James Madison, who argued for limited government and secure property rights.

The European model has quite different ideological origins. Its basic proposition is that a relatively strong state is necessary to promote the general welfare. Individual economic freedoms, property rights, and private contracts may have to be abridged in the public interest. In this sense, the European model borrows more from Thomas Hobbes than from John Locke.

Mercantilism

A pervasive interventionist state was actually the status quo on the European continent on the eve of the Industrial Revolution. State intervention was particularly prominent in France and England in the seventeenth and eighteenth centuries. In fact, Adam Smith wrote his *The Wealth of Nations* as an attack on the mercantilist status quo. Mercantilists argue in favor of a strong state that intervenes directly in economic affairs.

Mercantilism advocates a strong state to regulate and control the domestic and international transactions of a national economy in order to promote its political and economic strength vis-à-vis its neighbors. Unlike economic liberalism, mercantilism has no intellectual founders. Mercantilism was not a "scholar's doctrine but a folk doctrine," and "no scholar of even third rank made a contribution to it."[2] As a folk doctrine, mercantilism offered interest groups benefits, and the state used mercantilism to raise revenue. Only the general welfare suffered.

Mercantilism reached its peak in France under Jean-Baptiste Colbert, France's minister of finance from 1665 to 1683. During that time, mercantilism was "a common approach to the European problem,"[3] which encompassed not only France and England but also Germany and Scandinavia. As a "system of state making," it extended regulation over business and commerce, organized guilds, and managed international trade by issuing charters to select companies. Under mercantilism, the state collected its revenues by selling licenses, charters, and other monopoly rights to special-interest groups.

Mercantilists believed that only a strong state could keep the economy from ruin. If individuals were given economic freedom, the country would quickly lose its wealth and power to rivals.[4]

The English Industrial Revolution was superimposed on a weakening mercantilist infrastructure. Mercantilist institutions remained stronger on the European continent. The Thirteen American Colonies did not import mercantilism from Europe. Instead, they suffered under mercantilist trade laws, such as the Navigation Acts. As the young United States expanded westward, a frontier society emerged with little state presence. But in continental Europe, the traditions of artisan guilds, state control of trade, and government regulation of business continued and influenced the European model.

Most people think almost automatically in mercantilist terms. We are conditioned to think that exports are good and imports are bad, and we think our government should protect us from foreign producers who do not play fair. It is as if mercantilist thought is embedded deeply in our genes.

Marx and Revisionism

Karl Marx's call to revolution in his *Communist Manifesto* raised fears among the leaders of bourgeois Europe of a violent socialist revolution.[5] Some concluded that European capitalism must be reformed before the workers took matters into their own hands. To head off this disaster, the European nations created what would become the European welfare state. *The **European welfare state** replaces families, private savings, and charity with state programs for economic security and welfare.*

Indeed, Marx's predictions appeared to be coming true. In 1871, something resembling a socialist revolution struck France; a coalition of Marxists and anarchists actually ruled Paris for two months. French authorities made short work of this "Paris Commune" as they cracked down on French socialists. The fear of a workers' revolution prompted European politicians elsewhere to be more open to reforms for the working class.

The followers of Marx had to decide whether to work outside the political system for socialist revolution or for reform from within. In Russia, Vladimir Lenin's Marxists rejected reform in favor of revolution. In Europe, they chose reform over revolution. They entered the democratic political process and have been there ever since.

After Marx's death in 1883, the Marxists split between Lenin's Bolshevik revolutionary party and the European revisionists. The Bolsheviks grabbed power in Russia in October 1917 and then attempted to export communism to the rest of the world through the Communist International. In contrast, *Marxist revisionists concluded that the goals of socialism—workers' rights, a fair distribution of income, and state control of the marketplace—could be achieved through the democratic political process.* They worked for reform legislation as members of organized worker parties.

Revisionists in Germany, France, and England worked within the political system to improve the plight of the working class. They ultimately transformed into political parties, such as the Social Democratic Party of Germany, the Socialist Party of France, and the Labor Party in England, which have subsequently alternated in power with Christian democratic or Tory parties to the present day.

Ferdinand Lassalle formed the first worker party in Germany, which became one of the strongest organized labor parties in Europe. Other prominent Marxist revisionists, such as Eduard Bernstein and Karl Liebknecht, were among the early leaders of the German Social Democratic Party. These German Social Democrats worked in the oppressive political climate of Otto von Bismarck's Germany. Bernstein was exiled from Germany and Liebknecht was imprisoned. Liebknecht's colleague in the Spartakusbund, Rosa Luxemburg, was murdered.

It was primarily Bernstein who provided the intellectual foundations of German social democracy. ***Eduard Bernstein** (1850–1932) broke with his Marxist colleagues by arguing against socialist revolution and in favor of reforms for the workers as promoted by political parties that represent the working class.*

Bernstein was born in Germany, where he served as a Social Democratic member of the Reichstag. He also was the editor of the party newspaper. Bernstein lived in exile in Switzerland and London after he was banned from Germany in 1878. In London, he became a colleague of Marx's financial patron and co-author, Friedrich Engels. He parted company with Engels in 1899 with the publication of his most significant work entitled *The Preconditions of Socialism*.[6]

In *Preconditions of Socialism*, Bernstein argued that, with the deep changes in industrial society, the party should devote itself to social reform, not to revolution. Bernstein believed that his goals of equality, commonality, and self-determination could not be achieved in the short run. He advised the Social Democrats that they must work patiently for their goals within the political process.

Bernstein's call to social reform unleashed a revisionist debate within the German social democratic movement, in which his former party colleagues, such as Rosa Luxemburg, Karl Kautsky, and Wilhelm Liebknecht, accused him of forsaking the basic teachings of Marx. *The **revisionist debate** argued whether social democrats should abandon Marx's goal of a socialist revolution and work for change within the existing political system.*

Social democracy evolved into organized political parties. The precursor of the German Social Democratic Party was founded in 1869 and quickly formed alliances with the trade unions, as did socialists in Austria and France. In 1905, the two main French socialist parties merged to win significant numbers of seats in the French parliament. In England, trade unions formed the Labor Party at the turn of the century. By 1910, the British Labor Party was winning significant numbers of seats in Parliament. It had to wait until 1924 for the first labor party government under Ramsay MacDonald.

In Germany, the Social Democratic Party was already winning five million votes in national elections in the 1880s. By the 1890s, it received more votes than any other party, despite persecution by the state. It had its own clubs, newspapers, and women's associations.

Under pressure from the growing popularity of the Social Democrats, German Chancellor Otto von Bismarck introduced social welfare legislation in Germany between 1883 and 1888, despite violent political opposition within his own party. Bismarck felt state pension, unemployment, accident, and health insurance programs were necessary to stave off Marx's socialist revolution. As Bismarck wrote, "My idea was to win over the working class, or maybe I should say to bribe them, for them to see the state as a social institution that exists because of them and for their benefit."[7] Bismarck's introduction of state pensions and other welfare legislation for the working class lay the foundations of the European welfare state.

Contemporary Social Democracy: The Third Way

Bernstein's vision of reform socialism provided the theoretical foundations for workers' parties on the European continent and in England. As time passed, "socialist" parties lost more and more of their Marxist class-struggle foundations as voters turned away from radical politics. Although a number of major parties continue to call themselves "socialist" today, the distinction between the socialist/social democrats and other parties has become blurred.

Clear distinctions between the French Gaullist and socialist parties were still apparent in 1981 when François Mitterrand was elected president of France. His electoral program entitled "110 Propositions for France" called for the expansion of public sector jobs, public works programs, the nationalization of nine industrial groups, reduction of the work week to thirty-five hours, extended unemployment benefits, price controls, minimum wages, a reduction in the value-added tax, a tax on wealth, liberalization of immigration, and an increase in inheritance taxes on the wealthy.

Mitterrand's socialist program called for income and wealth redistribution, expansion of the welfare state, and nationalization of large companies in industry and finance. Mitterrand delivered many of his election promises. The work week was lowered to thirty-five hours, and minimum wage and solidarity wealth taxes were passed. Mitterrand nationalized electricity, mining and metallurgical, chemical and pharmaceutical, and telecommunications companies and large banks. Mitterrand's nationalizations entrenched France's state sector as the largest in Europe. Before Mitterrand, the state already owned major banks, such as Crédit Lyonnais and BNP, Air France, the postal services, and even the automobile manufacturer, Renault.

Jacques Chirac, who succeeded Mitterrand, reversed a number of Mitterrand's nationalizations amid the privatization wave that swept the United Kingdom and the European continent. Many of Mitterrand's social welfare reforms, such as the thirty-five-hour work week, remained in effect.[8]

Mitterrand's socialist government was an exception for its time. Conservative Margaret Thatcher in England (1979–1990) and Helmut Kohl in Germany (1982–1998) each served as heads of state for more than a decade. The Social Democrats in Germany and Labor Party in the United Kingdom decided they could only return to power by offering the electorate a "Third Way" that combined social democratic values of fairness, social justice, liberty, and equality of opportunity with pro-growth policies, such as lower corporate tax rates.[9] In other words, Tony Blair and Gerhard Schroeder favored programs that would get them elected rather than holding out for socialist ideological purity. Blair served as Britain's prime minister from 1997 to 2007. Schroeder served as German Chancellor from 1998 to 2005. In Germany, Schroeder's Third Way led to a split in the social democrat ranks. Those upset with the Third Way formed their own party called The Left.

Social Market Economy

After World War II, a new school of German economic thought—the social market economy—exercised a substantial impact on the European model. Its intellectual heritage can be traced to the Freiburg school of neo-liberalism, headed by Walter Eucken and Alfred Müller-Armack.[10] *The Social Market Economy teaches that the state should ensure the workability of the competitive market system but that the market should allocate resources. The state should be prepared to intervene, however, to achieve necessary social goals.* Intervention should be compatible with the underlying market order; therefore, policies that disrupt the working of the market, such as direct orders and price freezes, should be avoided.

The social market economy dates to the early postwar years of Allied occupation. The Allied occupation continued wartime controls, enforced payment of reparations, and sought to destroy German military potential. Ludwig Erhard, the minister of economics during this period, strongly favored decontrol, deregulation, and the turning of economic decisions over to the impersonal hands of the market.[11] The opposition Social Democrats, remembering the chaos of the inflationary 1920s and the Great Depression of the 1930s, favored a form of central planning. The U.S. occupation commander, Lucius Clay, appeared to agree that strict economic controls should continue.

Over Allied objections, Erhard pushed through the Currency Reform and Price Reform of June 1948. Germany divided into East and West Germany. In May 1949, the German parliament approved the Basic Law of the Federal Republic (the German constitution), which enshrined the sanctity of private property and the principles of the social market economy. The Basic Law set the goals of price stability, a stable currency, full employment, balance-of-payments equilibrium, and stable economic growth. Three social goals, closely associated with the social market economy—social equity, social security, and social progress—were also included. These social goals provided much of the basis for later state intervention in economic affairs in the German Federal Republic.[12]

The balancing of private and public interest, characteristic of the social market economy, can be seen in Article 14 of the German constitution, which guarantees private property rights but also requires that property serves "the public good":

(1) Property and the right of inheritance shall be guaranteed. Their content and limits shall be defined by the laws.
(2) Property entails obligations. Its use shall also serve the public good.
(3) Expropriation shall only be permissible for the public good. It may only be ordered by or pursuant to a law that determines the nature and extent of compensation. Such compensation shall be determined by establishing an equitable balance between the public interest and the interests of those affected.[13]

In current dialogue, German politicians from the major parties all support the concept of a social market economy. By this, they mean a continuation of the welfare state (perhaps not quite so comprehensive for some) combined with the use of market resource allocation.

Legal Foundations: Civil Law

Chapter 9 pointed out that those countries that follow the Anglo-Saxon model use common law. The European economies use civil law, and the Asian countries use mixed legal systems. By language, common law countries largely are English speaking or were ruled by England as a colonial power.

German civil law derives from the Napoleonic Code and from its medieval legal traditions. Germany, as in other European countries, was a Catholic nation until Martin Luther's (1483–1546) reformation. The Roman Catholic Church maintained a system of ecclesiastical courts, whose rules and regulations influenced legal practices. Mercantilism also had its labor and commercial codes, which prevailed in cities and towns. The organizations of merchants, seafarers, craftspeople, and traders followed local custom and practice, which influenced commercial law as it was codified.

German civil law provides citizens with an accessible written collection of laws to govern their behavior as persons, workers, borrowers, lenders, lessors and lessees, and businesspeople. The law is enforced by judges. Only rarely are juries used.

The German civil code is published in the *Buergerlches Gesetzbuch* (BGB), or the *Citizen's Law Book*. German law was first codified in Bavaria, Prussia, and Austria. The unified German Reich created a commission to draft a uniform civil code in the 1870s. Their code was approved in 1896 and went into effect in 1900. The BGB was revised with the passage of new legislation and was amended substantively in 1945 when the Federal Republic of Germany was established. When Germany reunited in 1990, the BGB was applied to the new German states that had been part of East Germany. Germany's well-organized legal system later served as the model for Japan and South Korea, and Taiwan during its early years of modernization.

In German civil courts, the judge is responsible for court proceedings. Civil processes are conducted largely in writing. Lawyers must submit to the court questions for witnesses, which the judge asks only if he or she considers them appropriate. Cross examination is rare, and the lawyers' role is to make sure that the summary of the testimony is complete and correct.

In common law proceedings, opposing lawyers and the judge and jury argue cases based on legal precedent. In a civil law system, lawyers and judges consider themselves legal scientists. They are taught to use rigorous deductive logic to fathom the principles of law as a set of ultimate truths.[14] There is no pretense to legal science in common law countries. The law is discovered primarily through precedent.

The German BGB consists of 2,385 sections that spell out family law and matters of business law such as contracts, leases, debts, and business organization. Each section states general principles of law and, where relevant, the source of the legislation. There are no case studies or precedents cited, only general principles.

Section 258 on the "Right of Removal" is illustrative. It reads: "Anyone entitled to remove an installation from a thing that he must return to another person must in the event of removal restore the thing to its previous condition at his own expense."[15] In this section, the guiding legal principle is that anyone removing an object from someone else's property must restore the property to its previous condition. There are no examples or precedents given. This is all the judge has to go on, although one can imagine many areas of potential conflict, such as the definition of the original condition.

Chapter 11 summarized the arguments of legal theorists, such as Richard Posner and F. A. Hayek, as to why common law, as opposed to German and European civil law, yields more efficient economic outcomes. These theorists maintained that the use of precedent provides a more stable rule of law, that the economic system will reject inefficient legal rules, and that state-made laws can be arbitrary and hence unpredictable. The abuse of civil law, such as in modern Russia or Kazakhstan, shows how an arbitrary state can have a written civil law and yet lack a rule of law.

The differences between civil-law and common-law states were most prominent in the distant past when kings or dictators, rather than elected legislatures, made civil law. Economic historians have argued that the superior performance of England in the nineteenth century was due, in part, to the rising role of parliament and the tradition of common law in England.[16]

Globalization requires greater legal conformity. Multinational corporations cannot operate effectively if they face contradictory legal systems in different countries. Moreover, countries that do not have a rule of law will lose out in the competition for investment and resources. Major countries that have weak rules of law, such as Russia and China, are paying or will pay a steep price in international business.

It is difficult to measure the "rule of law" because it its multidimensional. The World Bank, however, publishes measures of the rule of law for different countries, and they are shown in Figure 12.2.[17] As measured by the World Bank, there do not appear to be major differences in the "quality" of the legal system between the affluent civil law and common law countries, with the exceptions of Italy and Greece, whose rule of law appears to be deteriorating.

FIGURE 12.2   Rankings of Common Law and Civil Law Countries by World Bank Rule of Law Index

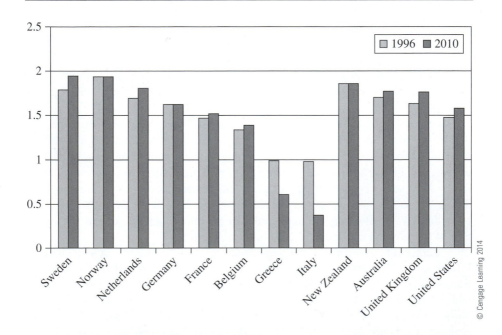

© Cengage Learning 2014

Features of the European Model

We discussed the Anglo-Saxon model in terms of the functioning of its product market, capital market, and labor market and how provision was made for income and job security. We used the United States as the prime example of the Anglo-Saxon model. We use Germany in the same way to describe the European model of corporate governance and capital allocation. We use a more general approach to discuss Europe's labor markets, and we use Sweden to illustrate an extreme case of the state's provision of income security.

Corporate Governance

The previous chapter discussed different models of **corporate governance** in terms of the friction between **stakeholders**, such as workers, suppliers, and buyers, and **shareholders**, the owners of the company. Corporate governance can also refer to frictions between major shareholders, who own enough shares to influence management, and minority shareholders, who do not.

In the Anglo-Saxon model, the primary aim of corporate management is to maximize shareholder value, even if that means sacrificing the interests of stakeholders. In the European model, managerial capitalism replaces shareholder capitalism. With globalization, the starker differences between the Anglo-Saxon and European models are tending to disappear.

Managerial Capitalism

Managerial capitalism is a system of corporate governance that places the interests of stakeholders above those or equal to the shareholders, or owners. Whereas shareholder capitalism requires managers to focus on profitability, managerial capitalism includes other objectives, such as stable employment for managers and employees or maintaining established relationships with banks, suppliers, and major customers, who may also be shareholders or even board members.

Managerial capitalism is presumed to have advantages: Companies should expect more loyalty from their employees, who have a long-term stake in the company. Stakeholder companies can therefore invest more in employee training and education, knowing that trained employees will not leave to join other firms.[11] Managerial capitalism provides more stable employment. Downturns in business will be absorbed by lower profits, not by layoffs. Stakeholder companies create a more nearly equal distribution of income within the company because payments are less tied to profits. Stakeholder corporations may take a longer view of technological improvements than shareholder corporations, which may be more interested in short-term profits.[12]

All listed German companies have a supervisory board that supervises the management board, which is responsible for company operations. Members of the management board cannot serve on the advisory board. Like the board of directors of the U.S. company, the supervisory board appoints the management board and sets the pay of the company's top executives.

Up until the mid-1990s, the German Stock Corporation Act specified that remuneration of management officers should be tied to the annual profit of the company.[18] Unlike U.S. corporations, there were no stock options or other bonus-type payments that were linked to the stock price. Moreover, managerial bonuses were modest compared to those in the United States. Studies show that German executives are paid less than half what American executives in similar companies are paid. There have also been unsuccessful efforts on the part of government to cap executive pay, and supervisory boards have been rebuked for too generous compensation packages for management executives.[19]

Shareholdings   Whereas shareholder corporations in the United States tend to be broadly owned by a large number of investors, stakeholder corporations in Europe tend to be held by a smaller number of investors, many of whom hold significant stakes.

Germany, Inc., *refers to Germany's extensive cross-ownership among corporations and directors serving on the boards of companies in which they own significant shares.* Figure 12.3 illustrates Germany, Inc., by showing the complex pattern of interrelated board directorships. It is not important to know the names of all the corporations in the networks in Figure 12.3, but, as an example, the figure shows the complex maze of directorships emanating from Germany's largest bank (Deutsche Bank, or Deba in the diagram) and its largest insurance company (Allianz, or Alli in the diagram).

FIGURE 12.3   Interrelated Board Directorships in Germany, Inc.

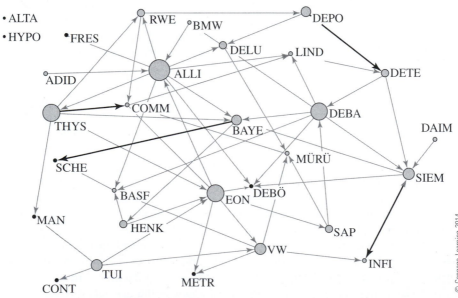

In U.S. corporations, officers of one corporation sitting on the boards of related corporations would not be permitted due to potential conflicts of interest. U.S. board members have a fiduciary responsibility to the company. If they are officers of other companies with whom the company does business, there could be questions regarding in whose interests they were acting. In Germany and other European economies, such potential conflicts of interest are less likely to raise red flags.

Table 12.1 shows the extensive pattern of cross holdings of private and public banks, insurance companies, and industrial companies, who are shareholders of other large companies. **Cross holding** *refers to the ownership of significant blocks of shares by one company in other companies.* For example, Germany's largest insurance company, Allianz, owns 5 percent shares of thirteen of Germany's largest companies,

TABLE 12.1   Cross Holdings and Block Holders of Largest German Companies, 1998

Main targets controlled (voting blocks in large firms sorted by decreasing market value)	Block holders	Voting blocks as % of the market value of all 430 listed corporations
Deutsche Telekom	None, government	4.82
Münchner Rück, VEBA, Dresdner Bank, BASF, Bayr. Hypo, RWE, BDF Beiersdorf, Bayer, Deutsche Bank, Linde, Schering, BHF-Bank, Lahmeyer, Rheinelektra, AMB	Münchner Rück 26%, Bayer. Vereinsbank 10%, Deutsche Bank 10%, Dresdner Bank 10%, Bayer. Hypobank 5%	4.47
Daimler Benz, Allianz, Münchner Rück, Frankfurter Hypo, Südzucker, Linde, Bayerische Vereinsbank, Metallgesellschaft, Heidelberger Zement, Karstadt, Ph. Holzmann, AMB	Allianz 5%	3.09
Allianz, Bayerische Hypo, Victoria, AMB, Hermes Kreditversicherung	Allianz 25%, Bayer. Vereinsbank 10%, Deutsche Bank 10%, Dresdner Bank 10%, DIA VV 6%	2.15
Allianz, Münchner Rück, Deutsche Hypo, OLB, Heidelberger Zement, AMB, Hamburghyp, Bilfinger & Berger, Metallgesellschaft	Allianz 22%, Nona VV 10%, Vermo VV 11%	1.91
Allianz, Münchner Rück, Vereinsund Westbank, BHB, Nürnberger Hypo, Süddeutsche Bodencreditbank	Viag 7%, Bayernwerk 7%, Deutsche Bank 5%	1.45
Sum of all 430 listed corporations		17.89

Source: Ekkehart Boehmer, "Who Controls Germany?" Working Paper No. 71, Humboldt University, October 15, 1998. Reprinted with permission.

including stakes in Daimler, Linde, and Karstadt. Taken together, these large block holders owned almost 20 percent of German companies listed on stock markets as of 1998. Note that these figures relate to the peak of Germany, Inc. Since then, the concentration of block ownership has likely declined, but we lack recent studies to know the extent of the decline.

With a few large shareholders, smaller shareholders have little chance to influence policy, and the rights of minority shareholders may not be of prime concern to the management.

Investors will be reluctant to buy shares of companies if their interests are not protected. In shareholder corporations, the board of directors has a fiduciary responsibility to protect the interests of all shareholders, not just the interests of majority shareholders.

Given the strong protection of property rights under common law, minority shareholders can sue the management or the board of directors for violation of their rights. Countries with a weak rule of law (for example, Russia and China) can abuse minority shareholders without repercussions. They can issue additional shares to majority shareholders, to management, or to related parties, thereby diluting the ownership interests of minority shareholders. With broad public ownership, disgruntled shareholders can also punish corporations for poor performance by selling their shares and pushing down the share price. A low share price makes raising capital more expensive.

Insider Trading

Insiders are board members or managers of the company who have more information about the corporation's performance than do public shareholders. Insiders, who know that the corporation's profits will collapse in the coming quarter, may benefit from this insider information by selling their shares while the price is still high. Outsiders, lacking this information, do not know to sell their shares and will incur losses.

In Anglo-Saxon countries, stock exchanges and securities commissions have stricter laws against **insider trading** than do those in European countries. In the United States, managers and directors are subject to "blackout periods" prior to the public disclosure of information—periods during which they cannot sell or buy shares. Also, insider stock transactions must be reported to the Securities and Exchange Commission for publication. Insider trading does occur, but if it is discovered, it is punishable by civil and even criminal penalties. Martha Stewart, one of the most popular American entertainment figures, was jailed for insider trading.

In the European model, there are fewer restrictions on insider trading. Germany was very slow in implementing rules against insider trading. Prior to 1994, efforts to pass meaningful prohibitions on insider trading were rebuffed through lobbyists' efforts. The Securities Trading Act of 1994 first prohibited trading on private information, defined as a fact that is not publicly known and that, if known, would affect the stock price significantly. Corporate insiders were made subject to this restriction. Apart from this, however, their trading activity was not restricted, and there was no requirement to report such trades. As amended in July 2002, corporate insiders are still allowed to trade freely, as long as they do not trade on private information. There is no blackout period that would ban corporate insiders from trading prior to earnings announcements. Insiders and their spouses and children must now report trades. Securities obtained as a part of the remuneration do not have to be reported, and no report is required if the transaction does not exceed €25,000.[20]

The German insider-trading law has been applied rarely, and offenders have been punished with mild penalties only, unlike the United States or the United Kingdom.[21] Table 12.2 shows that Germany ranks in the middle of European

TABLE 12.2   Ownership, Insider-Trading Laws, and Legal System

	Control Owner	Widely Held	Severity of ITL
Common Law			
Australia	0.19	0.44	4
Canada	0.35	0.31	5
Hong Kong	0.91	0.05	3
Ireland	0.21	0.26	4
Israel	0.95	0.05	3
New Zealand	0.71	0.05	4
Singapore	0.65	0.13	4
United Kingdom	0.02	0.69	3
United States	0.04	0.74	5
Civil Law			
Austria	0.91	0.05	2
Belgium	0.95	0.00	3
Denmark	0.80	0.00	3
Finland	0.64	0.09	3
France	0.36	0.29	4
Germany	0.57	0.13	3
Greece	1.00	0.00	2
Italy	0.86	0.05	3
Japan	0.29	0.36	2
South Korea	0.36	0.29	5
Mexico	1.00	0.00	1
Netherlands	0.50	0.23	3
Norway	0.76	0.05	1
Portugal	0.90	0.00	4
Spain	0.71	0.05	4
Switzerland	0.77	0.10	3
Common Law Avg.	0.301	0.439	4
Civil Law Avg.	0.674	0.133	2.93

Note: ITL stands for Insider-Trading Law; 5 is most strict.

Source: Laura Benny, "Do Shareholders Value Insider Trading Laws? International Evidence," Journal of Law, Economics and Policy, Vol. 4, No. 2, 267, 2008. Reprinted with permission of the journal.

countries in terms of severity of insider-trading laws. European insider-trading laws are relatively toothless compared to those of the United States.

Table 12.2 ranks countries by their ownership structure based on samples of corporations from various countries that use either civil or common law. The "Control Owner" column shows the percentage of firms that are owned by a single controlling interest. The "Widely Held" column shows the percentage of corporations that have broad stock ownership. The "Severity of ITL" column ranks countries according to the severity of their insider-trading laws, where 5 (for example, the United States) denotes the strictest laws and 1 (for example, Mexico) denotes the most lax laws. The table shows that there is more "control ownership" in Europe but relatively little in the United States and the United Kingdom. Conversely, there is little broad ownership of stock in Europe and much broad ownership in the United States and the United Kingdom. Insider-trading laws are stricter in countries that have common law.

Empirical studies show that companies operating with strict insider-trading rules have higher stock market valuations. Investors discount corporations in which there is uninhibited insider trading.[22] Thus U.S. corporations tend to have higher market valuations than their European counterparts, and some think Europe's weak insider trading laws are partially responsible.

Transparency

In order for shareholders to be informed about their ownership interests, corporations must supply transparent information about the company's operations. *Corporate transparency means that companies supply the public with regular, accurate, and readily accessible information concerning their operations and prospects.*

U.S. publicly traded companies must supply transparent accounting and other relevant event information to the public as a requirement of the Securities and Exchange Commission and the stock exchange on which they are listed. European stock exchanges have less strict and comprehensive reporting requirements. Transparency is viewed as less vital in a stakeholder company that is run primarily for the benefit of insiders. Accordingly, stakeholder corporations use less uniform accounting standards and reveal less about company operations.

These accounting differences become apparent when a European corporation wishes to be listed on an American stock exchange, such as the New York Stock Exchange. To be listed according to U.S. standards, the European company must reveal more information about itself than is customary in its home country.

Table 12.3 compares French accounting standards with International Accounting Standards (IAS) used by U.S. companies. Note that French accounting standards do not require the disclosure of transactions with related parties, diluted earnings per share, or changes in equity of the corporation. Such disclosures are considered essential in U.S. stock exchanges. The collapse of Enron Corporation in 2002 was associated with the nondisclosure of transactions with related parties or of changes in equity. Enron officers were sentenced to jail terms for these offenses.

TABLE 12.3   French Accounting Standards

French requirements are based on the Commercial Code, company law and decrees, and rules established by the Committee of Accounting Regulation (including the General Accounting Plan) and interpretations of the Urgent Issues Committee that apply to consolidated financial statements.

French accounting may differ from that required by International Accounting Standards (IAS) because of the absence of specific French rules on recognition and measurement in the following areas:

- Impairment of assets including impairment tests for goodwill and intangibles
- Accounting for employee benefit obligations, because it is not mandatory to recognize a liability for postemployment benefits
- The discounting of provisions
- The calculation of basic and diluted earnings per share

There are no specific rules requiring disclosures of:

- A primary statement of changes in equity
- Transactions with related parties (except for limited requirements)
- Discontinuing operations
- Segment liabilities
- The FIFO or current cost of inventory when LIFO is used
- The fair values of investment properties

Source: GAAP 2000: A Survey of National Accounting Rulesin 53 Countries, page 43. Copyright © 2000 PricewaterhouseCoopers LLP. Reprinted with permission.

Hostile Takeovers and the Market for Corporate Control

A shareholder corporation has shares that are publicly traded. Large blocs may be owned by institutional investors, such as pension funds or mutual funds, who may sell the stock if its performance falters. Large owners of European corporations tend to be stakeholders, who are less inclined to sell the stock if profits decline. They hold shares for reasons other than profits.

Our discussion of corporate governance in the Anglo-Saxon model focused on corporate takeovers, including **hostile takeovers**, as a disciplining device for management. If the current management team is not maximizing shareholder value, the **market for corporate control** will install a new and (it is hoped) more profit-oriented management. That management team may reduce the work force, change suppliers, or work with different banks, thus instituting a wholesale change in stakeholders. Profits count for more than a contented workforce or stable supply chains.

A stakeholder society should weaken the market for corporate control. With cross-ownership of corporations—a supplier may own shares in the company, as does the company's largest bank—there will be a limited market for corporate control. As stakeholders in the company, they are likely to resist hostile takeovers, and they can prevent takeovers by amassing their ownership shares against the corporate raider.

When management changes do occur through mergers and acquisitions, they tend to be friendly takeovers favored by the current management team. *A **merger** or **acquisition** occurs when one corporation buys another either by purchase or through the exchange of stock, corporate debt, or borrowed money.*

Figure 12.4 shows the number of announced mergers and acquisitions from 1995 to 2010. The merger and acquisition movement, especially hostile takeovers, was initiated in the United States in the 1980s at a time when there were few mergers and acquisitions in Europe and elsewhere. Figure 12.4 illustrates the cyclical nature of mergers and acquisitions. There are fewer of them during recessions.

As European integration proceeded, merger and acquisition activity accelerated. Whereas earlier European mergers tended to be few relative to the United States, the European market after 1999 increasingly saw mega deals such as Vodafone acquiring Mannesmann, Daimler acquiring Chrysler, Bayer acquiring Schering, and Allianz acquiring Dresdner Bank.

There were only fourteen hostile takeovers in the European merger and acquisition market in 1996 and five in 1998. Suddenly in 1999 there were 369

FIGURE 12.4   Number of Mergers and Acquisitions (1000)

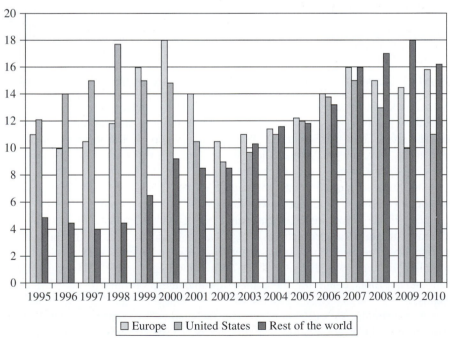

Source: Institute of Mergers, Acquisitions and Alliances, http://www.imaa-institute.org/statistics-mergers-acquisitions.html#MergersAcquisitions_Europe.

hostile bids.[23] Experts say that European companies began to copy the U.S. market for corporate control of the 1980s because they concluded that they can grow faster through acquisitions. Also, they began experiencing competition from international corporate raiders. If they did not act decisively, others would gobble up the companies they wanted to acquire. Moreover, with the growing internationalization of security markets, stocks of European companies became more widely held. As we noted, hostile takeovers require broad and liquid securities markets.[24]

The emergence of a market for corporate control is yet another example of how one economic system learns and adopts practices from others.

Co-determination

The European model is characterized by co-determination (*Mitbestimmung* in German). *Co-determination places worker representatives on the boards of directors of corporations and requires worker participation in decision making at the shop floor level.* Co-determination is widely used in France, Germany, and Italy, but we shall focus on German co-determination as the pioneer.

Co-determination is an integral feature of the German social market economy. Its objective is industrial democracy. *Industrial democracy requires management to consider workers' interests to achieve a consensus.* Co-determination is supposed to create a consensus between workers and management to replace the traditional friction between union and employer and between the worker and owner.

Co-determination was initially applied only to selected industries, but it now covers nearly all sectors since German law was revised in 1976.[16] Firms with 2,000 or more employees fall under the co-determination legislation. A separate co-determination law still applies to the coal, iron, and steel industries.

According to the 1976 law, shareholders and workers have equal numbers of representatives on the company's supervisory board. If the board consists of twelve members, six represent the shareholders and six represent the employees. Of the latter, two must be representatives of the labor union, and at least one must be a "leading employee" (such as a shop foreman). The co-determination law requires that in the absence of a majority, the chairperson is elected by the representatives of the shareholders. The co-determination law avoids stalemates by giving the chairperson the deciding vote. In almost all cases, co-determination laws require the supervisory board members be elected separately by the owners and the employees of the company.

Although labor and stockholders appear to have parity on the board of directors, the shareholders actually have the advantage because of the way the chairperson is selected and "leading employees" often side with the stockholders.[25]

The 1976 co-determination regulations are still being tested in the German courts. Because co-determination rules call for a nearly equal voice for labor, they call into question the protection of private property guaranteed in the German constitution. Another objection to co-determination is that it puts labor representatives on both sides of the collective-bargaining table and thus gives labor an unfair advantage. In past steel industry negotiations, however, labor representatives on the supervisory boards sided with management against the steel workers' demand for a thirty-five-hour work week. It is not obvious, therefore, how labor representatives will behave when they in effect become part of management.

With the expansion of the European Union to low-wage member countries, worker representatives on boards must also take into count the threat of moving the entire operation to another country if labor costs become too high.

Indeed, the record shows that wage increases have been more moderate in Germany than in the rest of Europe. German unions, unlike their counterparts to the south, appear to be sensitive to competitive forces and the need to promote high labor productivity.

The Enterprise Constitution Law (*Betriebsverfassungsgesetz*, or BVG) of 1972 also gives labor a voice in shop-floor decisions. The BVG requires the election of a Works Council in enterprises that employ five or more workers. Leading employees are not eligible. The Works Council has co-determination responsibilities for wages, length of the working day, firings, and layoffs at the shop floor. The influence of the Works Council is strongest in personnel areas where grievances and terminations must be reviewed by the Work Council.

According to the enterprise law, in cases of dismissals:

> (1) The works council shall be consulted before every dismissal. The employer shall indicate to the works council the reasons for dismissal. Any notice of dismissal that is given without consulting the works council shall be null and void. (2) If the works council has objections to a routine dismissal, it shall notify the employer in writing within a week, giving its reasons. If it does not report its objections within the said time limit, it shall be deemed to have given its consent to the dismissal. If the works council has objections against an exceptional dismissal, it shall notify the employer in writing immediately and at any rate not later than within three days, giving its reasons. (3) The works council may oppose a routine dismissal ...[26]

The Works Council law makes it cumbersome for a company to fire or lay off workers and is a source of the labor-market inflexibility, which characterizes the European labor market in general. Inflexible labor markets mean that employers cannot adjust staffing during downturns or make other adjustments to competitive changes. On the positive side, worker protection may raise worker loyalty and enthusiasm and reduce turnover. Worker protection is an integral feature of European industrial democracy, as it is called.

The European Works Council Directive, adopted in September 1994, enacted "consult and inform" requirements obligating employers in the European Union to consult with employees about decisions that could directly or indirectly affect their jobs and to keep them informed about the financial health of the business.

These directives apply to all companies with at least 1,000 employees, and with at least 150 employees in each of at least two member states. By September 1999, more than 2,000 companies had negotiated works council agreements.

When Renault of France closed its two-year-old Belgian plant, which employed more than 3,000 workers, Renault's European Works Council sued Renault for failure to fulfill its information and consultation obligations under the directive. In both France and Belgium, the courts decided against Renault, requiring it to pay heavy fines and provide for a costly layoff plan. The Belgium plant closure became a European Works Council issue because Renault wanted to transfer its production to low-cost Portugal, a move that social policy advocates referred to as "social dumping."[27] Unions have subsequently sought sanctions that would punish a company for taking actions similar to those of Renault and have asked that the threshold of employees for the establishment of a works council be reduced from 1,000 to 500. Given that many European and U.S. companies operate in a large number of countries, works council advocates propose to apply the works council provision on a worldwide scale.

The Works Council Directive was amended in 2009 to ensure European-wide coverage because "Procedures for informing and consulting employees as embodied in legislation or practice in the Member States are often not geared to the transnational structure of the entity which takes the decisions affecting those employees. This may lead to the unequal treatment of employees affected by decisions within one and the same undertaking or group of undertakings."[28]

Co-determination is one of the most distinctive features of the European model because it formally gives non-owners of companies (employees) some of the same rights as owners. Some co-determination principles have been enshrined in EU legislation under its work council provisions as discussed later. EU attempts to pass a single law of co-determination and worker rights have so far failed because of the great diversity of labor-market practices among EU member states.

Mittelstand (Small and Medium-Sized Businesses)

Small and medium-sized businesses play major roles in the American and European economies. In both Germany and the United States, 80 percent of employment is in firms that employ fewer than 500 workers.[29] In both countries, 45 percent of employment is by family-owned small to medium-sized enterprises.[30] The German figures are somewhat lower than the EU averages. In Italy and France, shares of small and medium-sized companies are slightly higher.[31]

Remarkable features of German small and medium-sized enterprises are their concentration in manufacturing and their export orientation. German family owned companies are noted for their precision engineering, quality, and service, and they compete effectively for business in affluent countries like the United States and France and in developing economies like China and India. They compensate for higher wages by offering higher quality and better service. Mittelstand companies have consistently outperformed large corporations with higher profits and higher rates of growth.[32]

The previous chapter showed that in the United States, small businesses provide a hothouse setting for business development. Microsoft, Apple, Google, and Facebook started out as microcompanies with virtually no capital, employees, or office space. They started as visions of their founders. The vast majority of new businesses remained small or disappeared. A few grew into the giant innovative companies that we recognize today.

Germany and Europe have few success stories of "garage companies" developing into leading corporations. Whereas in the United States twelve of the top fifty corporations did not exist in 1950, all of the top fifty European corporations were already major companies.[33] Of the top twenty German companies (or their legal successors), all were established companies before the start of World War II.

There is no single answer to the failure of Germany and Europe as a whole to grow new giant companies. One explanation may be that European family companies wish to remain in the family in Europe, whereas in the United States families wish to cash out their holdings by initial public offerings. Another explanation could be the stricter regulation that larger European companies face. Full co-determination rules apply to them as they cross the 2,000-employee threshold. The lesser-developed venture capital market in Europe than in the United States and Canada offers a third explanation.

Early-stage venture capital is less available in Germany and Europe than it is in North America and Israel. European companies rely on bank financing rather than on the more risky venture capital market for financing. Small companies everywhere find it difficult to convince professional loan officers to take risks with depositor money. Small companies cannot develop into large companies without start-up capital.

Joseph Schumpeter offered creative destruction to explain the natural dynamism of market economies. New companies take advantage of new technologies and changes in consumer tastes to challenge established companies in the market place.

In countries like Germany, the new products offered by new technologies (such as personal computers and Internet services) tend to be produced by established companies as they adapt their product lines. In the United States, entirely new companies like Hewlett-Packard, Microsoft, or Intel establish themselves in the marketplace as new technologies emerge. In Germany, new products are produced by old companies.

A good example would be Siemens Corporation. Founded in 1848, Siemens began as a small company building telegraph systems, electrical engines, and electric trains. In the 1950s, it turned to consumer durables and mainframe computers. Now, Siemens produces medical equipment, nuclear power plants, high-speed trains, wind power equipment, consultancy, along with a myriad of other products.

The failure of new giant concerns to emerge in Germany to replace aging giants appears to be attributable to Germany's capital market and its corporate governance. This system does not promote venture capital well, and cross holdings of stock retard capital from being shifted from declining to rising industries. Rather, when a new type of industry develops, such as personal computers or VCR recorders, old established German companies must change their profile to produce these new goods (for example, Siemens producing PCs and BASF producing VCR tapes), rather than new companies emerging. Schumpeter's "creative destruction" therefore plays a less prominent role in Europe than in the United States.

Capital Markets

In the Anglo-Saxon model, corporations raise capital by issuing stocks and bonds in private capital or equity markets (see Figures 9.2 and 9.3). A prospectus is prepared, the stock or bond issue is registered with the exchanges and with securities regulators, and an initial public offering (IPO) takes place in which, theoretically at least, any and all buyers can participate. In the European model, capital is more likely to be provided by banks.

German and European Banks

In the European model, the initial capital of the company (beyond that provided by the founders) is usually supplied by a bank. Instead of private venture capitalists evaluating projects and providing the initial financing, a bank's loan department makes the determination on start-up capital.

The company's funding bank then normally becomes the company's "house bank" and may eventually arrange to issue shares and sell company debt to raise new capital. The house bank often continues to occupy a seat on the board of directors and, through its retained ownership shares, holds significant interests in the company. These significant interests owned by the house bank and other stakeholder companies prevent hostile takeovers of the company.[34]

Historically, European banks have exercised broader functions than U.S. commercial banks, which until recently could not engage in stock brokerage, insurance, and investment-banking activities. European banks are ***universal banks***, *which perform not only traditional banking but also risk-sharing, stock sales, and merchant-banking functions.*

The large German universal banks (Deutsche Bank, Dresdner Bank, and Commerzbank) are among the largest companies in Germany. They are not the only ones. The postal savings bank, with 27,000 employees, attracts the checking and savings accounts of one in three Germans. It has some 24 million savings accounts.

State Public Banks (*Landesbanken*) from nine German states complement privately owned banks. ***State Public Banks*** *are owned in large part by the German* state governments (such as Bavaria, Berlin, Westphalia) and by local savings banks. They were founded to promote the regional economy. The State Public Banks are linked to a vast system of savings banks (*Sparkassen*), in which German citizens deposit their savings.

The State Public Banks account for 44 percent of loans and for 40 percent of private savings deposits. Of the different types of banks in Germany, State Public Banks have the lowest profit rate.[35]

The German State Public Banks provide a telling lesson for those who blame greedy bankers for recent financial market failures and call for public ownership of banks. The German State Public Banks were established not to make the maximum profit, but rather to promote the regional economy with strategic loans. In earlier times, they could attract funds at a low cost because the financial community considered that the state governments would inject new capital when needed. With tightening public budgets, the German states are no longer prepared to provide new capital at will. The *Landesbanken*, it turns out, also invested heavily in toxic sovereign debt and in unwise investments in the regional economy. Recent stress tests of a bank's ability to withstand an economic downturn showed that *Landesbanken* were particularly vulnerable. Several states have had to inject large sums of taxpayer funds into their *Landesbanken* to keep them solvent.

The shareholders of the third largest *Landesbank*, Westphalia Landesbank, facing an EU ultimatum, has agreed to make it a strictly regional bank serving local needs. As the state economics minister declared, North Rhein Westphalia will no longer have a State Public Bank.[36]

Figure 12.5 reveals the clear distinction between the financing of enterprises in the United States and in Europe. Since the mid-1990s, the equity market capitalization of U.S. companies has been in excess of GDP (except for the substantial stock market decline in the early 2000s). At its peak in the late 1990s, U.S. market capitalization was almost twice GDP. Europe's equity market capitalizations, measured either by EU members or by members of the euro zone, have remained well below GDP with the brief exception of the late 1990s.

Whereas these figures also reflect the stock market's higher evaluation of U.S. companies than of European companies, they show the greater reliance of U.S. corporations on the sale of new stock shares. However, bank assets (primarily loans to businesses, mortgages, and consumer credit) are almost twice GDP in Germany but are just equal to GDP in the United States. Whereas bank loans to businesses in Europe equal over 40 percent of Europe's GDP, they constitute only 7 percent of GDP in the United States.[37]

Advantages and Disadvantages of Bank Financing

Bank financing is presumed to offer some advantages. Banks examine business risks carefully because if they back poorly run companies, their loans will not be repaid. Banks also diversify their risks; therefore, a downturn of one sector will not snowball into downturns elsewhere. Banks monitor any business to which they have lent money to prevent gross mismanagement.

FIGURE **12.5**   Domestic Equity Market Capitalization as a Percent of GDP
(Europe, United States, and Japan)

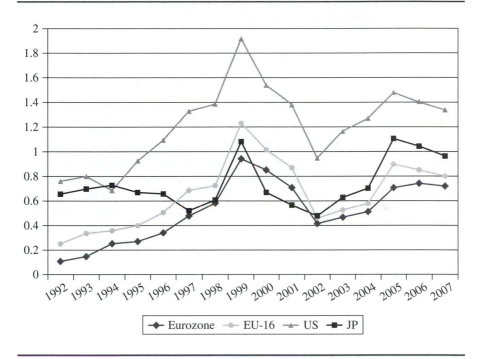

Source: European Capital Markets Institute (2011) Statistical Package, available at www.erurocapital
markets.org

Insofar as the stocks of the universal banks themselves are traded in major stock exchanges, they are ultimately subject to the discipline of the stock market. If these banks make bad loans, their share prices will fall.

The venture capital statistics suggest that the U.S. "market-based" system does a better job of raising venture capital; this may be explained by banks' bureaucratic decision making, which is not well suited to new ventures and new ideas. The corporate governance of European companies also explains the more limited use of stock markets to raise capital. With the lesser protection of property rights by civil law, and the lesser interest in minority shareholder rights, smaller investors may be wise not to purchase stock in European companies.[38]

The Labor Market

The European labor market is more regulated than the United States. Regulation of work conditions began in the second half of the nineteenth century with the introduction of work councils on the shop floors of German businesses. Germany's social market economy, based on a social consensus between management and workers, also allows for regulation of conditions of work through co-determination. Countries such as Germany, France, Italy, and Spain have among the most highly regulated labor markets in the world.

Europe as a Highly Regulated Labor Market

Germany is representative of the extensive regulation and employment protection of the European labor market. In Germany, unemployed workers qualify for unemployment insurance for thirty-two months and are not required to take jobs that necessitate their moving or that offer lower wages than they had earned previously.[39] In Germany, the period of notice varies for the employer depending on the term of employment. The legal notice period for employees is four weeks and must be served so that it ends on the fifteenth day or the last day of any subsequent calendar month. The legal notice period for the employer increases with the length of the employee's service up to a maximum of seven months after twenty years of service. Longer or shorter notice periods are frequently provided in collective bargaining agreements. After six months of employment in an establishment that regularly employs more than ten people, an employment relationship can only be terminated for a limited range of reasons related to the employee, related to the employee's conduct, or due to urgent operational requirements of the employer.[40]

German companies must inform the State Employment Office of the grounds for the termination, the criterion used, and the time period in which the termination will occur. Those to be terminated must be identified by age, gender, and other characteristics. The employer must simultaneously inform the employee's work council and must supply to the Employment Office the work council's position with respect to the planned layoff. The works council has the right to inform the Employment Office independently of its opinions. Workers have the right to appeal in a complicated and time-consuming process. The Employment Office must approve the termination. If the termination does not take place within ninety days, the application process must start from the beginning.

The steps required for a termination of employment can be even more complex in other European countries. Greece has among the most restrictive termination practices in the world.

EU policy generally seeks to create a level playing field in labor markets. Insofar as the European Union consists of high-wage and lower-wage countries, there has been concern that one country could attract employers away from other countries through less restrictive labor practices.

The Treaty of Amsterdam of 1997 called for the creation of a coordinated strategy for employment and for promoting a skilled, trained, and adaptable workforce and labor markets. To implement this objective, the EU put in place social policy directives, regulating such issues as equal pay, minimum annual paid holidays, hours of work, portability of pensions, health and safety standards, maternity and paternity leave, and gender equality.

Exhibit 12.2 offers excerpts from EU labor-market regulations of work time, paid vacations, and work conditions. Member countries can offer even more generous provisions, such as the thirty-five-hour work week in France, the two years of maternity leave available in Germany, and the provision to Swedish parents of 480 days off for each child at 80 percent of pay.

Although the European Union lacks a uniform code of Works Councils and employment protection rules, it does have uniform regulations on conditions of work, some of which are shown in Exhibit 12.2.

EXHIBIT 12.2   EU Labor Regulations (excerpts)

RECOMMENDATION OF 22 July 1975 on the principle of the 40-hour week and the principle of four weeks' annual paid holiday

1. The principle of the *40-hour week* whereby the length of the normal working week (i.e. the period to which provisions for overtime do not apply), as laid down by national legislation, collective agreements or by any other means, must not exceed 40 hours, shall be applied throughout the Community in all sectors by 31 December 1978 at the latest and as far as possible before that date.

2. The application of the principle set out in point 1 *may not entail a reduction in earnings;*

3. The principle of *four weeks annual paid holiday* whereby the minimum standard for annual paid holiday for all persons who have satisfied all the requirements entitling them to full holiday rights must, depending on the Member States' choice, be either four weeks or correspond to the exemption of a number of working days equal to four times that agreed per week, shall be applied throughout the Community in all sectors by 31 December 1978 at the latest and as far as possible before that date.

Council Directive 93/104/EC of *23 November 1993* concerning certain aspects of the organization of working time:

Article 1

1. This Directive lays down minimum *safety and health requirements* for the organization of working time.

2. This Directive applies to:
   (a) *minimum periods of daily rest, weekly rest and annual leave, to breaks and maximum weekly working time*; and
   (b) certain aspects of *night work, shift work and patterns of work.*

3. This Directive shall apply to all sectors of activity, both public and private, within the meaning of Article 2 of Directive 89/391/EEC, without prejudice to Article 17 of this Directive, with the exception of air, rail, road, sea, inland waterway and lake transport, sea fishing, other work at sea and the activities of doctors in training.

(continued)

Exhibit 12.2   EU Labor Regulations (excerpts) (cont.)

Article 3

Daily rest
Member States shall take the measures necessary to ensure that every worker is
entitled to a minimum daily rest period of 11 consecutive hours per 24-hour period.

Article 4

Breaks
Member States shall take the measures necessary to ensure that, where the
working day is longer than six hours, every worker is entitled to a rest break,
the details of which, including duration and the terms on which it is granted,
shall be laid down in collective agreements or agreements between the two
sides of industry or, failing that, by national legislation.

Article 6

Maximum weekly working time
Member States shall take the measures necessary to ensure that, in keeping
with the need to protect the safety and health of workers:

1. The period of weekly working time is limited by means of laws, regulations or
   administrative provisions or by collective agreements or agreements between
   the two sides of industry;

2. The average working time for each seven-day period, including overtime, does
   not exceed 48 hours.

Article 7

Annual leave
1. Member States shall take the measures necessary to ensure that every worker
   is entitled to paid annual leave of at least four weeks in accordance with the
   conditions for entitlement to, and granting of, such leave laid down by national
   legislation and/or practice.

Pattern of work

Member States shall take the measures necessary to ensure that an employer
who intends to organize work according to a certain pattern takes account of
the general principle of adapting work to the worker, with a view, in particular,
to alleviating monotonous work and work at a predetermined work-rate,
depending on the type of activity, and of safety and health requirements,
especially as regards breaks during working time.

Source: Only European Union legislation printed in the paper edition of the Official Journal of the
European Union is deemed authentic. http://eur-lex.europa.eu, © European Union, 1998–2012.

Figure 12.6 provides measures of the degree of employment protection in an
array of countries. These OECD employment protection indicators are compiled
from twenty-one items, including procedural inconveniences that employers face
when starting the dismissal process, notice periods and severance pay, and the

FIGURE 12.6   OECD Indexes of Labor-Market Protection, 2008

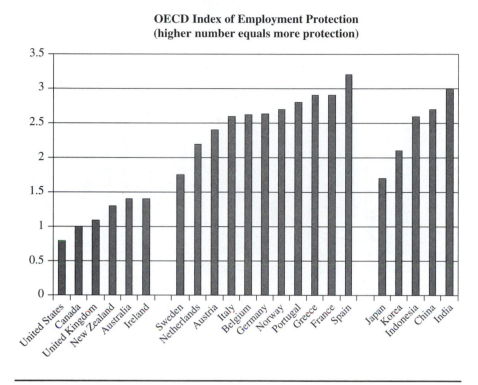

**OECD Index of Employment Protection
(higher number equals more protection)**

Source: Data from OECD, "OECD Indicators of Employment Protection," http://www.oecd.org

difficulty of dismissal and the fines if a dismissal is found to be unfair. The OECD index also measures the additional costs when an employer dismisses a large number of workers at one time. It also includes regulation of fixed-term and temporary work contracts and requirements for temporary workers to receive the same pay and/or conditions as equivalent workers.

Figure 12.6 shows a distinctive pattern of lesser employment protection for the Anglo-Saxon countries (North America, Australia, and New Zealand) and higher levels of employment protection for Europe (with South Europe and France among the highest). The few Asian countries for which the OECD has measures show an intermediate range of employment protection, although we do not know how strictly the laws are enforced in these countries.

Figure 12.7 shows the number of hours worked per year per employed person in Anglo-Saxon, European, and Asian countries. The general trend has been toward fewer hours in Europe compared with the United States and other Anglo-Saxon countries. In 1980, workers in the United States, Germany, and France worked about the same number of hours per year on average (1700–1800). By 2001, U.S. workers still averaged about 1,800 hours per year,

FIGURE 12.7   Hours Worked Per Year, OECD Data, 2010

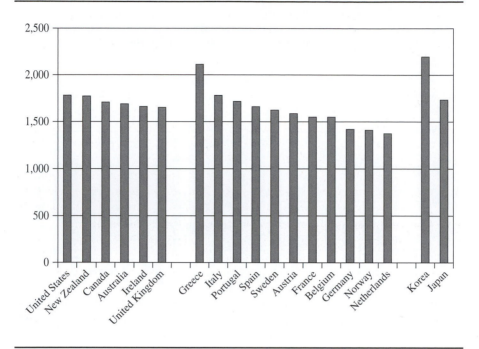

Source: Based on OECD, "Average Annual Hours Actually Worked per Worker," http://stats.oecd.org

but French workers fell to slightly over 1,500, and German workers to well under 1,500 hours per year. German workers averaged about 80 percent of the hours of U.S. workers per year.[41]

Clearly, country regulations of hours worked play a major role in explaining the generally lower hours of work in Europe (with the surprising exceptions of southern European countries). Differences in taxation rates appear to explain little of the variation. Differences in culture also cannot account for lower hours of work in Europe insofar as Europeans worked as many hours as Americans up through 1980.

Labor-union advocates of shorter working hours hoped that with fewer hours worked there would be more jobs. These policies did not increase employment. European unemployment rates have been higher than the United States despite shorter working hours. Instead of jobs, they "may have had a more society-wide influence on leisure patterns."[42] Shorter hours of work have meant lower output and not surprisingly higher unemployment rates. If workers work fewer hours and labor market rules require no reduction in pay, the cost of labor to the employer rises and there is more unemployment.

Costs of Labor-Market Regulations   Labor market regulations cost output and jobs, but they have other costs as well. EU member countries must implement EU's labor regulations, including those that have less regulated labor markets, such as the United Kingdom and Ireland. The UK government estimated the compliance costs of EU labor regulations over $10 billion per year between 2000 and 2003. Since the EU's "Working Time Directives" were implemented in 1999, the number of British workers taking complaints to employment tribunals rose from under 50,000 to more than 100,000 per year.[43]

The cost of labor-market regulations include not only compliance costs but more importantly the extra expense of fewer hours worked per week, generous paid vacations, maternity leaves, and liberal unemployment benefits.

In Germany, the Federal Commission for Labor (BAA) handles payments to unemployed, underemployed, or workers undergoing retraining as well as enforcing employment protection statutes. In 2010, the BAA made payments to labor under employment protection statutes equal to 2 percent of GDP.[44]

European employment protection laws have unanticipated consequences: Employers have become more reluctant to hire full-time workers. They rely instead on temporary workers to whom the labor laws do not apply or apply less strictly. To circumvent the laws, they hire truck drivers or construction workers as "independent contractors."

Throughout Europe, employment protection laws have resulted in a ***two-tier labor market*** *of full-time employees enjoying full protection and part time workers and independent contractors who are not protected.* Full-time employees and their labor representatives must worry that employers will increasingly switch to non-covered workers. Young people entering labor markets also find it increasingly difficult to obtain full-time jobs. Youth unemployment and youths stuck in temporary jobs are further consequences of European labor protection rules.

One consequence of the high cost and rigidity of Europe's labor market has been persistently high unemployment, even during periods of economic expansion.[45]

While the U.S. unemployment rate settled in the 5–7 percent range, European unemployment rates settled, with few exceptions, in the 8–11 percent range. Nevertheless, the political opposition to change in Europe's labor laws is overwhelming and is spearheaded by Europe's unions. In Italy, Spain, and France, even relatively modest proposals to relax rigid labor laws are met with warning strikes and even general strikes. These three countries lead Europe in days lost to strikes for the period 1994–1999, Spain having lost 250 days per year per 1,000 workers; Italy, 100 days; and France, 90 days.[46] In the United States, the comparable figure was about 10 days. In Germany, where there is a close alliance between the SPD party and the labor unions, the government has been warned that any amendments to labor laws will be met by major strike actions.

Tax Wedges and Labor Allocation

Figures 12.8 and 12.9 show that employment protection, health care, social insurance, and state pensions are paid for in the European model primarily by taxes on labor. In the Anglo-Saxon model, Social Security taxes paid by the employee and employer account for smaller percentages of gross wages than in Europe. In Europe, Social Security contributions alone can account for 40 percent or more of gross wages, whereas in the United States they account for less than 13 percent. In Asia, Social Security contributions account for much less.

Social Security and other taxes on labor introduce tax wedges in the labor market. *The **tax wedge** is the difference between the wage received by the worker and the wage paid by the employer.* Taxes on labor transfer revenues and wages from workers and employers to the state, and the state uses these funds to pay benefits and other forms of social transfers to workers.

In addition to taxes, employers must pay nontax compulsory payments that add to the cost of labor. *These **nontax compulsory payments** include pension contributions, unemployment insurance, and health benefits.*

It is compulsory for employers in most affluent countries to pay fringe benefits, such as health insurance, for full-time employees. The majority of European Union countries make obligatory payments for their employees that do not qualify as taxes. Also employees in eight EU countries must pay additional contributions—mainly social insurance contributions—that are not considered as taxes. These nontax compulsory payments either increase the employer's labor costs or reduce the employee's net take-home pay in a similar way to taxes.[47]

In the United States, such nontax payments are called fringe benefits, and employers use them, usually on a voluntary basis, to make their jobs more attractive. Private workers may also accept lower wages and salaries in return for more generous fringe benefits as a form of nontaxable income.

Figure 12.8 shows how taxes on labor, such as Social Security, and nontax compulsory payments raise the cost of labor and reduce the amount of employment (and increase unemployment).

Figure 12.8   The Effect of Tax Wedges on Wages and Employment

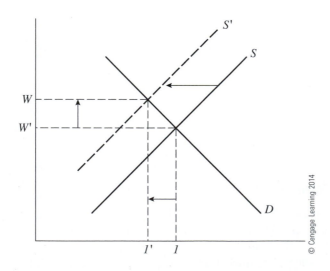

© Cengage Learning 2014

Explanation: The tax on labor causes less labor to be supplied as before. Workers base their supply on the net wage after the tax. The reduction in supply raises the wage and reduces employment. Both employer and employee share the incidence of the tax.

Figure 12.9 shows tax and nontax compulsory payments as a percent of gross wages in a number of countries. In most countries, nontax compulsory payments are only slightly lower than tax payments. Figure 12.9 shows much higher payments on labor in Europe than in the United States or other Anglo-Saxon countries. Japanese and Korean payments are similar to those in the Anglo-Saxon countries.

The high European taxes on labor make workers and employees more expensive. The higher labor costs discourage employment and divert hiring to contract workers, part timers, or illegal workers on whom Social Security taxes need not be paid.

EU member countries such as Germany, France, and Austria have income and Social Security taxes that account for almost half of labor costs. The highest rates are in Belgium, where taxes account for 55 percent of gross labor costs and nontax compulsory payments account for another 54 percent. This means that for every euro of wages Belgian employers pay their workers, they must pay more than a euro in taxes and nontax compulsory payments. In the United States, the same taxes account for about 30 percent of labor costs.

The highly taxed European labor market has therefore created the paradox of a relatively wealthy group of nations, whose per capita income is 60 percent that the

FIGURE 12.9   Tax Wedges: Compulsory Tax and Nontax Compulsory Payments as a Percent of Gross Wages

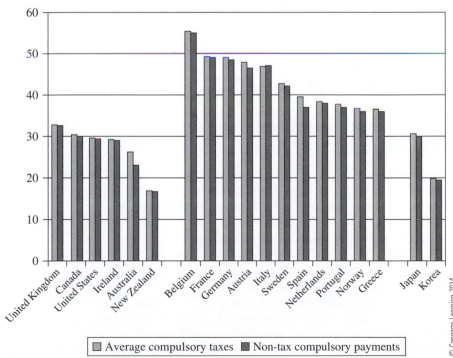

© Cengage Learning 2014

United States, with labor costs equal to or greater than U.S. labor costs. Not only do European workers cost as much as or more than U.S. workers but also they work only 80 percent of the hours of American workers. Hence, unless European workers are at least 20 percent more productive, they will be more expensive than U.S. workers. The highly regulated and taxed European labor market has made its own labor less competitive with other parts of the world.

The natural reaction of employers, is to transfer jobs abroad, perhaps first to the lower-wage countries of the EU ("social dumping") and then to lower-wage countries in Eastern Europe or Asia.

The monetary costs of labor do not include the costs of labor inflexibility to the employer. If labor were a variable cost, the employer could more readily deal with its high cost. During bad times, the employer could cut back on employment through layoffs. In the case of the EU, this option is not as readily available. The employer is saddled with high-priced labor that cannot be shed during economic downturns.

Different EU member countries deal with the problem of high-priced and inflexible labor differently. Throughout Europe, employers deal with rigid labor laws by hiring temporary and part-time workers. From 2005 to 2010, nearly 40 percent of Europe's labor force was in temporary jobs, while in North America the comparable figure was 17 percent.[48] Germany uses "short labor" (Kurzarbeit) to ameliorate business downturns. Instead of laying workers off, employees are put on reduced hours and the firm's payroll is reduced. Workers on short time are compensated out of social benefit funds of the state.[49]

European countries have addressed problems of generous social benefits and labor market rigidities with different degrees of success. But Europe has had a higher rate of unemployment than the United States for more than two decades and a much higher duration of unemployment. Between 2005 and 2011, the average duration of unemployment was ten months in Europe and four months in the United States.[50]

Public Enterprise: Nationalization and Privatization

The Anglo-Saxon model calls for a limited role of government and for protection of private property. Public enterprise should play only a minor part. Figure 9.1 showed the greater amount of state ownership of enterprises in Europe than in the Anglo-Saxon countries.

Indeed, publicly owned enterprises account for between 1 and 2 percent of U.S. GDP. The European model, on the other hand, has welcomed a larger economic role for the state. Therefore, we would expect a greater share of public ownership. Figure 12.10 confirms that there is more extensive public ownership in Europe, including Great Britain, than in the United States.

In the postwar period, Europe has had a relatively even balance between social democratic (trade union) and conservative political parties. The major French political figures of the postwar period were Charles de Gaulle (conservative) and François Mitterrand (socialist). The dominant German political figures were Konrad Adenauer, Ludwig Erhard, Helmut Kohl, and Angela Merkel (conservatives) and Willy Brandt, Helmut Schmidt, and Gerhard Schroeder (social democrats).

In the United Kingdom, there was a succession of relatively weak Labor prime ministers with the exception of the long-serving Tony Blair, and one strong Conservative prime minister, Margaret Thatcher.

This pattern continued through the 1990s and the early 2000s, the political pendulum swinging back and forth between social democrats and conservatives. In the early years of the new century, differences between political parties have become less striking as both major parties seek to position themselves in the middle. Cases in point are Tony Blair in England and Gerhard Schroeder in Germany, who offered voters a "middle way."

In the early postwar years, the choice of party affected the extent of public enterprise. Social democratic and trade union governments favored nationalization, and conservative governments opposed it. Nationalizations were followed by privatizations of major industries in metallurgy, transportation, and banking as political regimes changed. France, at the start of the lengthy Mitterrand tenure in the early 1980s, already had extensive state ownership in industry, transportation, and banking.

Beginning in late 1981 and early 1982, Mitterrand announced a policy of nationalization, especially in the large industrial trusts and banking sectors where state involvement was already substantial. The public sector share rose from 0 to 71 percent in iron ore, from 1 to 79 percent in iron and steel, from 16 to 66 percent in other metals, from 16 to 52 percent in basic chemicals, and from 0 to 75 percent in synthetic fibers.[51] After the return of the Gaullists to power in the mid-1980s, there was a reversal in the trend toward nationalization and growth of the public sector, but state ownership remained substantial relative to other countries.

Public enterprise was highly visible in the British economy throughout the postwar era, but its overall contribution was not a large share of GDP. Although the share of public corporations in capital formation grew, the contribution of public enterprises to output remained moderate. In 1950, public enterprise accounted for just over 8 percent of GDP; the equivalent figure for 1967 was some 7 percent.[52]

It is difficult to quantify the effects of British public enterprise on overall economic performance. What counts is not only the relative size of the public sector but also how well or poorly it was operated. Many public enterprises (such as coal and steel) were nationalized not because of ideology but to prevent bankruptcy. Others were large, visible companies, such as British Airways, that were run by coalitions of unions and management. Others, like British Gas, were operated according to political rather than economic rules.

The role of public enterprise in postwar Germany was also substantial. Not only did state enterprises dominate transportation and communication and the construction of apartment dwellings but there was significant state participation in mining and metallurgy as well.[53] In some cases, government participation was indirect (as in the case of the Krupp industries); in others, it was carried out through holding companies.

Prior to the 1980s, the German experience with nationalization was the reverse of the British experience. In Germany, the emphasis was on denationalization (*Privatisierung*). The Federal Treasury Ministry was established in 1957 to supervise denationalization. Two methods of denationalization were used: (1) the sale of public enterprises to private persons or private groups and (2) social

FIGURE **12.10**   Extent of State Ownership of Industry, 1980

	Telecommunications	Electricity	Gas	Oil Production	Coal	Railways	Airlines	Automobile Production	Steel	Shipbuilding
United States	○	◔	○	○	○	◔	○	○	○	○
Germany	●	◕	◑	◔	◑	●	●	◔	○	◔
France	●	●	●	na	●	●	◕	◑	◕	○
United Kingdom	●	●	●	◔	●	●	◕	◑	◕	●

Private Sector: ○ More than 75 percent

Public Sector: ● More than 75 percent; ◕ 75 percent; ◑ 50 percent; ◔ 25 percent;
na = not available

Source: J. Vickers and V. Wright, *The Politics of Privatization in Western Europe* (London: Frank Cass, 1989), p. 11. Reprinted by permission of the author.

denationalization, achieved by selling a new type of equity, the so-called popular share, to low-income citizens on a preferential basis.

Volkswagen was privatized in 1960 with the sale of 60 percent of its stock to the public. The remaining 40 percent was divided evenly between the German federal government and the government of Lower Saxony. Between 1986 and 1988, the German government sold off its shares in the energy giant VIAG to the public. Union-owned and -organized enterprises also continued and represented a mix of public and private enterprise. The union-owned *Gruppe Neue Heimat* was once the largest European housing construction firm, the union-cooperative *Bank für Gemeinwirtschaft* was the fourth-largest German interregional bank, and the cooperative *Coop-Unternehmen* was the second-largest retail distributor in the 1970s.

When Germany was reunited in 1989, the German government inherited East German state enterprises and state farms. The sale of these public enterprises was handled by a special privatization bureau, which faced the massive task of privatizing thousands of enterprises, most of which were unprofitable. Instead of contributing to the German state budget, the disposition of East German enterprises proved to be a huge strain on public finances.

In the 1990s and early 2000s, discussion of nationalization was replaced by discussion of ***privatization***—*the conversion of enterprises owned by the state into enterprises at least partially owned by private owners*. Wide-scale privatization was begun in England under Thatcher, who argued that private ownership would convert the massive, bureaucratic, and unprofitable public enterprises of Britain into profitable, well-managed companies.

British Telecom was Britain's first privatization in a series of large former state-owned companies—such as British Airport Authority, British Gas, British Airways, Rolls-Royce, British Steel, British Coal, Northern Ireland Electricity, British Rail, the UK nuclear power industry, and even the London Underground. Privatization proceeds covered between 8 and 15 percent of the deficit in the period 1994–1997. The British government sought, through a so-called Private Finance Initiative program, to increase private-sector participation in the provision of both capital assets and services in areas that had previously been restricted to the public sector.[54]

Little empirical evidence has been available for assessing the impact of privatization. A study of a large number of newly privatized firms (including the British case) revealed significant benefits, including performance improvements and sustained employment.[55] For example, British Airways, one of the more poorly performing international air carriers, became more innovative and profitable after its privatization, although it remains subject to the ups and downs of international aviation.

In France, the first period of privatization, from 1986 to 1988, yielded 70 billion French francs to the budget. From 1988 to 1990, official policy aimed at maintaining the status quo ("neither privatization nor nationalization"). Partial privatizations began again in 1991. A law of July 19, 1993, earmarked twenty-one crucial companies in banking and industry for privatization. By 1995, total privatization sales had yielded 185 billion French francs (roughly $37 billion). The sales of this period included the large companies Rhône-Poulenc, Banque Nationale de Paris, Elf Aquitaine, and Union des Assurances de Paris. The total yield of 185 billion French francs covered some 10 percent of total budget expenditures in 1995.[56]

Privatization does not automatically mean that the privatized company will behave as an ordinary private corporation. Nicolas Spulber summarized the situation as follows:

> The role of the government after privatization is also not as simple and transparent as one might assume. Of course, *in principle* privatization aims to free enterprises from government's ownership and control in order to increase their efficiency. Indeed, in some cases, the government does remove itself up to a point from the operation of the privatized firms. But more often than not, the government decides to *continue to play* a role—for instance, that of a critical shareholder—while in other cases, it vests new and extensive controlling powers over the privatized enterprises in the hands of regulatory authorities. Furthermore, shares are not always placed competitively through the financial markets.[57]

In many privatization cases, the government reserved "golden shares" for itself or selected a "hard core" (*noyaux durs*) of strategic investors, with restrictions placed on their disposal over a number of years.

Again, privatization, just like its opposite, nationalization, allows the state bureaucracies and the party in power to transfer wealth and award patronage to their supporters. It also allows for political rather than economic decision-making. An example was the politically motivated firing of the chairman of Deutsche Telekom in the summer of 2002 to clear the decks for Schroeder's reelection campaign. In many cases, reliable political friends have been placed at the head of privatized public enterprises. In other cases, change-resistant employees of public enterprises were encouraged by free or preferential shares to acquire stock as they privatized.

Unions

Although union membership in the United States has fallen below 12 percent, the rapid growth of membership in public sector unions has countered this trend. Of the 14.7 million U.S. labor union members, now a majority are public sector employees. The average union member is no longer the assembly-line worker, but a schoolteacher or government employee. Giant unions such as the American Federation of Government Employees and the American Federation of State and Municipal Employees now represent the majority of American union members.

Union membership in Europe is much higher as a percent of the labor force. Eight EU member states have more than half of the employed belonging to a trade union. Three of the EU's four largest countries—Italy at 30, the UK at 29, and Germany at 27—have unionization rates that are low by historical standards but more than double that of the United States. But, like the United States, the trend is downward. With the exception of Scandinavia and Belgium, labor union membership is declining or at best stable throughout Europe.

European unions can be highly centralized or decentralized by occupation or branch. In Austria, Ireland, and the United Kingdom, a single trade union center represents virtually all union members. In Germany, the German Federation of Trade Unions (Deutscher Gewerkschaftsbund) dominates trade union membership. Civil servants have a separate union. In the Nordic countries of Denmark, Finland, Norway, and Sweden, trade unions essentially divide according to branch and occupation.[58]

Public Employment

There is a big difference between public enterprise and public employment. There are usually few public enterprises, but there can be a lot of public employment, such is in schools, health care, and public services. Whereas the share of public enterprise has been falling, the share of public employment has been rising.

Figure 12.11 provides comparative data on the percent of public workers in the labor force. The rise in the share of unionized public workers helped prevent the decline in union membership in the United States. Higher rates of public employment help explain the higher rates of unionization in Europe.

Figure 12.11 reveals generally higher rates of public sector employment on the European continent, although Germany, Austria, and Spain have about equivalent rates to the United States and other Anglo-Saxon countries. However, none of the Anglo-Saxon countries have public sector employment shares close to Scandinavia, France, Netherlands, or Greece. Public employment shares are uniformly lower in Asia, all well below 10 percent.

FIGURE **12.11**   Public Sector Employment as a Percent of Total Employment
OECD and ILO (2005, 2008)

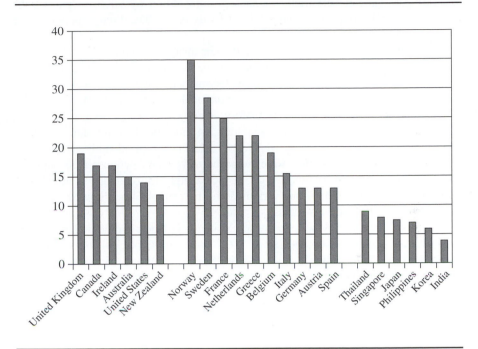

Source: OECD, "Public Employment and Management Working Party," January 28, 2008, http://www.
oecd.org/officialdocuments/displaydocumentpdf?cote=GOV/PGC/PEM(2008)1&doclanguage=en and ILO,
http://laborsta.ilo.org/STP/guest

Deregulation

The deregulation that began in the United States in the late 1970s and early 1980s
was at least partially credited with the rejuvenation of the U.S. economy after 1982.
Thatcher's deregulation of the British economy in the 1980s also appeared to
strengthen the British economy. In light of these successes, deregulation became
an official policy of the European Union.

The European Union's major deregulation initiatives have been in energy and
civil aviation. EU energy policy has aimed for a unified European energy policy
and the opening of national energy markets.

A European-wide energy policy traces its roots to the European Coal and Steel
Community in 1951 and the European Atomic Community in 1957. The 1986 Single European Act gave the European Commission a legal framework and political
mandate to liberalize electricity and gas by introducing free market principles in
place of public controls and exceptions of competition rules.

Deregulation appeared as a necessary component of European industrial
strategy toward previously regulated markets such as transportation, utilities, and

banking, which had been characterized by state ownership in the 1980s. At the EU summit in Barcelona in March 2002, the European Commission proposed opening the European gas and electricity markets to competition by 2005, as part of the drive to make Europe more competitive and dynamic. The French public-sector workers opposed.

Clearly a unified energy policy required doing away with national regulatory agencies, but the individual countries were loathe to part with their own regulatory bodies. Scandinavian countries, Britain, Austria, and Germany largely liberalized their own gas and electricity markets while preserving their national regulatory agencies.[59]

Europe still lacks a single regulatory agency for energy, but independent national regulators have acquired wide-ranging powers. Transmission grids are operated by independent firms, which are independent of incumbent operators. Starting in 2007, all consumers were supposed to be free to choose their supplier. Wholesale energy markets function on an increasingly Europe-wide scale through the progressive integration of the various domestic markets. They now serve as the trading platform for utilities across the entire EU.

European consumers were promised that deregulation would reduce energy prices through competition, but since 2004 prices have been rising due to the increase in oil and natural gas prices. In the face of mounting criticism, the European Commission launched a 2005 inquiry into whether markets were functioning properly. Germany and France, it was discovered, still rely on their own giant energy concerns, such as E.On and EDF. Several governments mandated measures to limit increases in retail energy prices by setting regulated prices below market prices. In short, national specifics continue to dominate in electricity and gas markets. A single European energy market remains to be built.[60]

Another complication in creating a unified European energy market is national differences in atomic energy policy. Whereas France continues to rely heavily on nuclear power generation, Germany and other countries, lead by strong anti-nuclear activists, have decided to shut down all their nuclear power plants.

In telecommunications and aviation, deregulation has been more successful. In telecommunications, consumers have seen expanding service and lower prices. Shoppers in Germany, France, and the Netherlands are barraged by offers of cheap telecommunications services, in place of the stodgy single providers (such as Germany's Telekom) who used to hold national monopolies.

Europe's Open-Skies Treaty of 1992 opened the way for deregulation of passenger air travel, and since 2000, virtually any carrier has been free to compete in any EU market. National carriers, such as BA, Lufthansa, Air France, and KLM, have continued to dominate domestic markets, and higher fuel prices and increased competition have led to acquisitions and mergers. Lufthansa has acquired Swiss Air and Air France has acquired KLM. They continue to have separate operations.

National airlines have been reluctant to challenge the airlines of other countries by setting up competitive operations in other countries. British Air's German affiliate, Deutsche BA, went out of business. The real competition has come not from national carriers but, rather, from low-cost private carriers such as Ryanair, Air Berlin, and EasyJet, which are offering lower fares from smaller airports and are not tied to one country.

The Limits of Income Security

The share of public employment is only one indicator of the role of the state. Figure 9.5 showed that the European countries have higher percentages of taxation and government spending than in the Anglo-Saxon or Asian worlds. These higher rates of government spending and taxation allow for a larger welfare state and a more interventionist role for the state.

Societies wish for prosperity, good jobs, and economic security. Yet market economies are subject to all kinds of shocks. They are subject to business cycles that destroy confidence in markets. You could be employed in an industry where demand is declining or in an industry that is being outmoded by a new technology. As a consequence, you could lose your job and suffer a loss of income. People yearn for economic security, yet even a well-functioning market economy generates insecurities for workers, employees, and employers.

All countries make some kind of provision for economic security, be it through family networks, private charities, or the state. In the European model, economic security is provided by the state, with greater generosity than in the Anglo-Saxon model with its historical emphasis on individual reliance.

Given the economic adage that "there is no such thing as a free lunch," state-delivered economic security has its costs. Traditional societies have relied more on private savings and extended households to insure against risks within the family. They use their own resources and initiatives to deal with poverty and old age.

Private charitable transfers do not appear to be sufficient providers of welfare assistance because of the free rider problem. *Free riding* *exists because potential donors understand that their contributions alone will make little difference, and they rely on others to solve the poverty problem.* Hence, free riding makes a case for state intervention, but state redistribution is not costless.

Arthur Okun used the analogy of a leaky bucket to characterize such a transfer.[61] According to *Okun's leaky bucket*, *as income is being transferred from one person to another, some of the income leaks from the leaky bucket, leaving less income for all.* The reason for the leak is that those losing income in the transfer have less of an incentive to earn income, and the size of the income pie shrinks accordingly.

Paying for the Welfare State

Figure 9.5 showed that the European countries spend between 40 and 55 percent of GDP on government activities. The Anglo-Saxon countries spend from 34 to 43 percent, and the Asian countries spend between 13 and 37 percent of their GDPs. These spending figures speak to quite different conceptions of the role of government in society.

The European welfare state had its origins in Bismarck's Germany. Bismarck introduced public pensions and social insurance, he argued, to stave off a socialist revolution. Since then, citizens of Europe have come to rely more and more on receiving pensions, health care, and social insurance from the state rather than from private savings or private charity.

Figure 12.12 shows government spending on social welfare as a percent of GDP. It reveals that the welfare state is most advanced in northern and Central

FIGURE **12.12**   Government Social Welfare Spending as a Percent of GDP (2005)

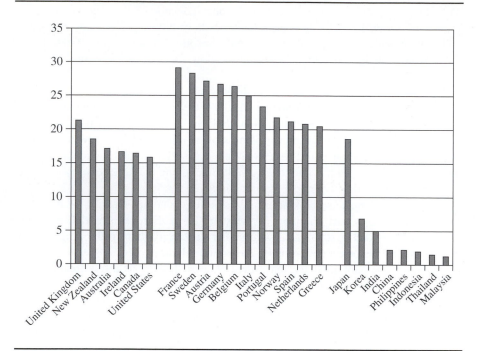

Sources: OECD database, http://www.oecd-ilibrary.org/social-issues-migration-health/how-expensive-is-the-welfare-state_220615515052 and Statistical Database System, https://sdbs.adb.org/sdbs/index.jsp.

Europe, less prominent in the North America and Oceana, and virtually absent in Asia, with the exception of Japan. The share of the welfare state of economic activity has been increasing inexorably over time. Between 1980 and 2005, average European social spending rose by 6 percentage points of GDP. Six percentage points of EU GDP equals slightly less than $1 trillion.

In 2006, the countries of the euro zone spent some $8,200 on social welfare for every man, woman, and child. In the United States, despite its higher per capita income, government spent a lower $6,600 for every man, woman, and child. These figures do not include public spending on education, which would about equal social welfare spending in most countries.

If we add private expenditures on health, pensions, and other social welfare items to government spending, we get roughly equal rates of welfare spending between Europe and the Anglo-Saxon world. In France, private expenditures add on another 4 percentage points of GDP. In the United States, they add on another 11 percentage points of GDP.[62]

The data show that the Anglo-Saxon countries use a combination of private and state provision of public welfare. Europe relies almost exclusively on the state to provide for the social welfare.

Figure 12.13 shows how the elderly in the United States, Europe, and Asia pay quite differently for their consumption. In the United States, those 65 and over combine labor income and private savings to pay for the bulk of their consumption. They continue to transfer income to the younger generation. Public transfers (mainly Social Security) pay for about a third of their consumption. Europe has quite a different pattern: The bulk of the consumption of people 65 years and older is paid for by transfers from the state.

In Sweden and Austria, virtually all consumption by the elderly comes from state welfare programs. Working after retirement is rare, so labor income is not a strong source of consumption. In Asia, the affluent countries, like Japan, Korea, and Taiwan, combine private saving, work after retirement, and public transfers to pay for their consumption, and they receive private transfers from their children. In poorer Asian countries, the elderly receive virtually no public transfers. Instead, they rely on their own savings and work after retirement to pay for their consumption.

FIGURE 12.13   Elderly Population, 65 plus, Sources of Consumption (percent)

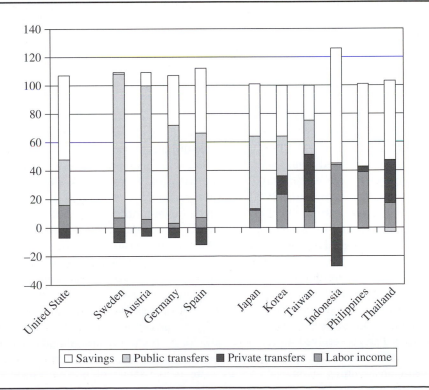

Source: Based on Ronald Lee and Andrew Mason, *Population, Aging and the Generational Economy: A Global Perspective* (New York: Edward Elgar, 2011).

Sweden as a Case Study

Sweden is a cautionary case study for the rest of Europe with respect to the limits of the welfare state. Sweden conducted the most ambitious experiment in transferring income and benefits from one group to another in the 1960s and 1970s.[63] At the start of this experiment, Sweden, as a consequence of its extremely rapid growth over the previous half-century, was the world's fourth most affluent nation. By the time Sweden backed away from its "Swedish model," it was the world's sixteenth most affluent country. Prior to its experimentation in the 1960s and 1970s, Sweden did not stand out relative to its European neighbors in terms of government activity, taxation, or economic policy.

The "Swedish model" aimed at providing economic security, including full employment, and egalitarianism, which included both reducing income differences and eliminating poverty. The institutions created to carry out the Swedish model were a large public sector funded by high tax rates; strong stabilization policies, including active labor-market intervention and centralized wage bargaining; highly centralized decision-making by a small group of individuals; and concentrated holdings of assets by a few financial institutions. These institutions were put in place at different times. Wage bargaining was already centralized by the 1950s, but the decision to squeeze out wage differentials was the result of the "solidarity wage policy" of the late 1960s. Tight regulation of the labor market was not introduced until the 1970s. Tax rates were raised gradually, culminating in the 1971 tax reform that left workers with a marginal take-home pay rate of less than 30 percent and executives with a marginal take-home pay rate of some 10–15 percent. Hence, if workers earned an extra 1,000 kroner, they could keep 300 at the 30 percent rate. If executives earned an additional 1,000 kroner, they could keep between 100 and 150!

Like the German "social market economy," the Swedish model was consensus-oriented, dating back to an agreement between the Swedish trade unions and Swedish employers in 1938 designed to settle disputes peacefully. Union ambitions to gain power reached their peak in the 1970s, when they proposed the creation of a tax-financed wage earners fund to buy Swedish corporate stock and basically make labor the owners of the Swedish private economy. The unions also succeeded in putting in place provisions that would hold down profits and hold down wages in high-productivity firms relative to those in lower-productivity firms.

Sweden's famed cradle-to-grave welfare system matured in the 1960s and 1970s and was based on universal coverage. *Universal coverage means that anyone could qualify for benefits regardless of work situation or other criteria.* Under this system, people without work or not working for reasons such as maternity or sick leave would automatically have 90 percent of their income replaced by state programs. Retirees would automatically have 65 percent of their previous income replaced. Parents received a year of income for each child if they stayed home to care for the infant. Obviously, such benefits were costly, and total public-sector expenditures starting in the late 1970s were in the range of 60–70 percent of GDP, compared to 45–50 percent for the other European countries.

Perhaps the most remarkable feature of the Swedish model was the shift from private-sector employment to living from the state budget. In 1960, 40 percent of individuals were "market-financed" (living from jobs provided by the private sector). In 1995, almost twice as many individuals lived from tax-financed activities (working for a state company or state administration, sick leaves, maternity leaves, pensions, early retirement, etc.). According to the 1995 figures, 2.2 million Swedes lived from market-financed activities and 4.1 million lived from tax-financed activities.

As a consequence of these programs, the Swedish distribution of income became markedly more even. The Swedish Gini coefficient changed from a fairly normal .28 in the mid-1960s to an exceedingly low .20 in the early 1980s. (The higher the Gini coefficient, the more unequal the distribution of income.)

This narrowing of income equalities was entirely due to government income redistribution. The distribution of factor income (before taxes and benefits) had a Gini of .33 whereas the distribution of disposable income (after taxes and benefits) was .20. Unions, in wage bargaining, went from the slogan of "equal pay for equal work" to "equal pay for all work." Under the policy of restricting profits, and as a general consequence of the Swedish model with its state distribution of capital, profit rates fell from between 6 and 10 percent in the 1950s to 2–5 percent in the 1970s and 1980s. With such low profit rates, there was little incentive to invest.

Swedish growth of per capita income began to lag relative to the rest of Europe starting in the 1970s. Whereas Europe's GDP per capita in the late 1990s was nearly double that of 1970, Swedish GDP per capita was only 40 percent higher, and Swedish real wages did not rise at all during this entire period.

The Swedish welfare system provides an extreme microcosm of welfare programs in other parts of Europe. In Germany, France, Italy, and other EU countries, transfers for pensions, unemployment, maternity leaves, and other benefits are paid out of general revenues on a pay-as-you-go basis. Although individuals are free to save on their own for retirement or health emergencies, the generosity of the pay-as-you-go system is such that there is relatively little incentive to save.

The Looming Demographic Bomb

We see major differences between the Anglo-Saxon, European, and Asian models with respect to transfers of the state to the elderly and poor. In the European model, social welfare is primarily assured by the state. In the Anglo-Saxon model, it is provided primarily by the state but with a healthy dose of private spending. In Asia, it is provided by the households themselves with little or no assistance from the state.

Both Europe and the United States are bumping up against limits to the welfare state. With aging populations (population is aging much more rapidly in Europe than elsewhere), the burden of the welfare state on state budgets is intensifying. As the share of older citizens in the population rises and the share of working age population shrinks, the taxes collected on labor fall as a share of GDP and there is insufficient revenue to meet obligations to the retired.

Europe is in a particular bind because the benefits expected by its elderly population are already substantial, only there are now more elderly people. Tax rates on labor income are already high and cannot be pushed higher without irreversible effects on incentives. Why would any working-age person work hard if, say, 70 percent of wages is taken by the state?

In the United States, where people invest in tax-deferred 401K and IRA accounts, massive private savings accumulate to be invested in the private sector. In Europe, with the exceptions of the Netherlands and Switzerland, private pension funds are largely lacking. Instead, Europeans save largely to buy a home, and they plan to retire on a generous state pension. Just as the United States is considering the politically explosive issue of the partial conversion of its pay-as-you-go Social Security system into a private-pension-fund approach, Europe must eventually consider whether it can continue to pay for its generous welfare-state programs.

There is no easy way out of Europe's impending crisis of its welfare state. Tax rates are already high and cannot be raised further. Citizens expect generous benefits from the state. We do not know how this looming crisis will be handled.

The Euro Crisis, 2011

The notion of a single currency for multiple countries was first advanced by Nobel laureate Robert Mundell in 1961.[64] Mundell, in his theoretical work on optimal currency zones, noted that the zone must have free labor mobility across countries, lack cultural barriers to movement such as different languages, have free capital mobility, and have price and wage flexibility. At a more practical level, the drafters of the euro understood that the single currency could be threatened by differences in fiscal policy. If selected countries ran large public deficits while others were fiscally disciplined, the creditworthiness of the entire euro zone could be questioned. These fears were shown to be justified in 2011.

In 2011, a euro crisis broke out, caused in large part by what were perceived as unsustainable deficit spending in Ireland, Greece, Portugal, and Spain. These countries had been running large deficits, well above the stabilization pact's 3 percent of GDP. As members of the euro zone, their governments had been able to borrow at low rates of interest under the assumption that other euro countries would bail them out, if it went that far. As bond markets became wary of these bonds, the borrowing costs of these spendthrift countries rose to such a degree that they could not service their outstanding debt and required bailouts. As members of the Euro zone, they could not devalue their currencies; so the only way out was domestic austerity and severe recession.

The still-solvent euro zone countries were faced with a dilemma: If they did not come to the rescue, they themselves could be threatened with contagion—namely, with substantial increases in their own borrowing costs. Yet, even those with resources available, were loathe to bail out the debtor countries for fear that they would never get their public finances in order and the problem would continue.

As we write these pages, the outcome of the Euro crisis remains unclear.

Summary

- Europe consists of a large number of countries (there are twenty-seven members of the European Union). The countries that most closely represent the European model are the first industrializers on the European continent: Germany,

Netherlands, Belgium, the Scandinavian countries, and France. Italy joined this group somewhat later, and Spain joined later than that.

- Europe, as represented by the European Union, has become one common market of twenty-seven countries that accounts for almost 500 million people. If Europe proceeds on its path of Europeanization, its institutions will converge, and we will truly be able to speak of a united European model.
- The European Union was created by a series of treaties that provided for a common market, free labor mobility, a common currency (the euro), and a European Central Bank. It still lacks a constitution. It is governed by a complex set of commissions and institutions.
- The intellectual foundations of the European model include mercantilism, social democracy, and reform Marxism. Contemporary social democrats have sought to remove the radical elements of Marxism.
- The Social Market Economy teaches that the state should ensure the workability of the competitive market system but that the market should allocate resources. The state should be prepared to intervene, however, to achieve necessary social goals.
- The European model uses civil law, which originated in Rome, France, and church and guild law of the Middle Ages.
- Managerial capitalism is a system of corporate governance that places the interests of stakeholders above those or equal to the shareholders, or owners. Managerial capitalism strives for objectives other than maximum profits, such as providing a stable employment for managers and employees or maintaining established relationships with banks, suppliers, and major customers.
- Germany, Inc., refers to Germany's extensive cross-ownership among corporations and directors serving on the boards of companies in which they own significant shares.
- The European model provides less protection for minority shareholders. European countries provide less transparency for their owners.
- European firms tend to be closely held rather than widely publicly traded, and there is a less active market for corporate control (fewer hostile takeovers). Companies are financed primarily through banks as opposed to stock markets.
- The European capital market depends more on bank than equity financing. The venture capital market is weak.
- The European model uses co-determination in enterprises, which gives employees a greater say in management, such as seats on corporate boards.
- The European labor market is characterized by rigidities caused by numerous rules and regulations that reduce labor mobility and lower hours of work, and thereby raise the costs of labor to employers.
- The European model is characterized by a greater amount of public enterprise, although in recent years European countries have begun to initiate privatization and deregulation.
- State provision of social welfare is more pervasive in Europe than in the Anglo-Saxon world. It is even less pervasive in Asia.
- With an aging population and dependence on the state for health and retirement, Europe is approaching the limits of the welfare state.

Key Terms

co-determination—Worker representatives serve on the boards of directors of corporations and workers participate in decision making at the shop floor level.

corporate transparency—Companies supply the public with regular, accurate, and readily accessible information concerning their operations and prospects.

cross holding—Ownership of significant blocks of shares by one company in other companies.

EU accession countries—Those countries that became members of the EU in recent years.

EU stability pact—The agreement that no member country could run a public deficit of more than 3 percent of GDP.

European Central Bank—Shares many features with the Federal Reserve Bank of the United States. Its board consists of representatives from the national banks of the various EU members, just as the Federal Reserve Board is comprised of representatives from the district banks. Each member has one vote, unlike other EU bodies that weight votes according to population.

European Common Market—A precursor of the European Union. It created a common market of member countries by eliminating import duties and quotas.

European Union (EU)—Consists of 27 member countries and a number of candidate countries that form a common market with common rules. It is governed by a multinational form of government, consisting of a Council of the European Union, an elected European Parliament, a European Commission, a European Central Bank, a European Court of Justice, and a European Council of Auditors.

European welfare state—Replaces families, private savings, and charity with state programs for economic security and welfare.

free riding—Potential donors hold down their contributions and rely on others to solve the poverty problem.

German civil law—An accessible written collection of laws to govern behavior as persons, workers, borrowers, lenders, lessors and lessees, and businesspeople.

Germany, Inc—Germany's extensive cross-ownership among corporations and directors serving on the boards of companies in which they own significant shares.

industrial democracy—Requires management to consider workers' interests to achieve a consensus.

insiders—Board members or managers of the company who have more information about the corporation's performance than do public shareholders.

Maastricht Treaty—A treaty that outlined the introduction of a common currency, the euro, for those countries that chose to join the euro zone.

managerial capitalism—A system of corporate governance that places the interests of stakeholders above those or equal to the shareholders, or owners.

Marxist revisionists—Concluded that the goals of socialism—workers' rights, a fair distribution of income, and state control of the marketplace—could be achieved through the democratic political process. They worked for reform legislation as members of organized worker parties.

mercantilism—Advocates a strong state to regulate and control the domestic and international transactions of a national economy in order to promote its political and economic strength vis-à-vis its neighbors.

merger or **acquisition**—One corporation buys another either by purchase or through the exchange of stock, corporate debt, or borrowed money.

Mitterrand's socialist program—Income and wealth redistribution, expansion of the welfare state, and nationalization of large companies in industry and finance.

nontax compulsory payments—Pension contributions, unemployment insurance, and health benefits.

privatization—The conversion of enterprises owned by the state into enterprises at least partially owned by private owners.

revisionist debate—Argued whether social democrats should abandon Marx's goal of a socialist revolution and work for change within the existing political system.

Social Market Economy—The state should ensure the workability of the competitive market system but the market should allocate resources. The state should be prepared to intervene, however, to achieve necessary social goals.

State Public Banks—Owned in large part by the German state governments (such as Bavaria, Berlin, Westphalia) and by local savings banks. They were founded to promote the regional economy.

tax wedge—The difference between the wage received by the worker and the wage paid by the employer.

two-tier labor market—Full-time employees enjoy full protection, but part-time workers and independent contractors are not protected by labor protection laws.

universal banks—Perform not only traditional banking but also risk-sharing, stock sales, and merchant-banking functions.

Notes

1. For a description of the European Union, see Jay Levin, *A Guide to the Euro* (Boston: Houghton Mifflin, 2002). For the official European Union website, see http://europa.eu. Also see Simon Hix, *The Political System of the European Union* (London: Palgrave Macmillan, 2005).
2. Jacob Viner, "The Economist in History," *American Economic Review* 3, no. 2 (1963), 1–22.
3. Herbert Heaton, "Heckscher on Mercantilism," *Journal of Political Economy* 45 (June 1937), 371.
4. James Buchanan, "Notes on the Liberal Constitution," *Cato Journal* 14, no. 1 (1994), 1–9.
5. Viner, "The Economist in History," p. 20.
6. Eduard Bernstein, *Evolutionary Socialism: A Criticism and Affirmation* (New York: Schocken Books, 1961).
7. Otto von Bismarck, Gesammelte Werke (Friedrichsruher Ausgabe) 1924/1935, Band 9, S.195/196.
8. Howard Machin and Vincent Wright, eds., *Economic Policy and Policy-Making Under the Mitterrand Presidency 1981–1984* (New York: St. Martin's Press, 1985).
9. Tony Blair and Gerhard Schroeder, Europe: The Third Way, http://www.labour.org.uk.

10. H. Jorg Thieme, *Soziale Marktwirtschaft: Konzeption und wirtschaftspolitsche Gestalt-Martwirtschaft: Verschahte Zukunft* (Stuttgart: Seewald, 1973), pp. 40–45.

11. L. Erhard and A. Müller-Armack, *Soziale Markwirtschaft* (Frankfurt am Main: Ullstein, 1972).

12. Gernot Gutman et al., *Die Wirtschaftsverfassung der Bundesrepublik Deutschland* (Stuttgart: Fischer, 1979), chap. 8.

13. Basic Law for the Federal Republic of Germany (English translation of Grundgesetz der BRD, 1949), http://www.iuscomp.org/gla/statutes/GG.htm#14.

14. James G. Apple and Robert Deyling, "A Primer on the Civil-Law System," published by the Federal Judicial Center at the request of the International Judicial Relations Committee of the Judicial Conference of the United States, http://www.fjc.gov/public/pdf.nsf/lookup/CivilLaw.pdf/$file/CivilLaw.pdf.

15. German Civil Code, http://www.gesetze-im-internet.de/englisch_bgb/englisch_bgb.html#p1969.

16. Edward Glaeser and Andrei Shleifer, "Legal Origins," NBER Working Paper 8272, May 2011.

17. World Bank, "Worldwide Governance Indicators," http://info.worldbank.org/governance/wgi/mc_countries.asp.

18. Jeremy Edwards, Wolfgang Eggert, and Alfons Weichenriederrticle, "Measurement of Firm Ownership and its Effects on Managerial Pay," *Economics of Governance* 10 (January 2009), 1–26.

19. "European Executives Make Half Pay," Money Central MSN 2006, http://articles.moneycentral.msn.com/Investing/CompanyFocus/EuropeanCEOsMakeHalfThePay.aspx.

20. A. Betzer and E. Theissenm, "Insider Trading and Corporate Governance: The Case of Germany," CFR-Working Paper No. 07-07, University of Cologne Center for Financial Research, 2007.

21. James Whitman, *Harsh Justice: Criminal Punishment and the Widening Divide between America* (New York: Oxford University Press, 2003), 81–85.

22. Laura Benny, "Do Shareholders Value Insider Trading Laws? International Evidence," Discussion Paper No. 345, 12/2001, Harvard John M. Olin Discussion Papers Series, http://www.law.harvard.edu/programs/olin_center.

23. Marc Goergen and Luc Renneboog, "Value Creation in Large European Mergers and Acquisitions," *Advances in Mergers and Acquisitions* 2 (2003), 92–146.

24. "Trends in European Mergers and Acquisitions," *Leaders Magazine* 29, no. 4 (2006), cited in http://www.skadden.com/content/attorneyFiles/attorneyFiles1029_0.pdf.

25. Bundesministeriumder Justiz in Zusammenarbeit mit der juris GmbH, http://www.juris.de. Gesetz über die Mitbestimmung der Arbeitnehmer (Mitbestimmungsgesetz—MitbestG), date Ausfertigungsdatum: 04.05.1976.

26. Works Constitution Act as promulgated by the Act of September 25, 2001 ("Bundesgesetzblatt", Part I, p. 2518), amended by the Act of December 10, 2001 ("Bundesgesetzblatt", Part I, p. 3443). Official English translation.

27. "The Renault Case and the Future of Social Europe," http://www.eurofound.europa.eu/eiro/1997/03/feature/eu9703108f.htm.

28. Europa, "Summaries of EU Legislation," http://europa.eu/legislation_summaries/employment_and_social_policy/social_dialogue/em0019_en.htm.

29. U.S. Census Bureau, http://www.census.gov/compendia/statab/2012/tables/12s0759.pdf and IFM Institut Bonn, http://www.ifm-bonn.org/index.php?id=108.

30. American Fact Finder, http://factfinder.census.gov/servlet/IBQTable?_bm=y&-geo_id=D&-ds_name=SB0700CSCB06&-_lang=en; Family Firm Institute, http://www.ffi.org/default.asp?id=398.

31. "SBA Fact Sheet: Germany," http://ec.europa.eu/enterprise/policies/sme/files/craft/sme_perf_review/doc_08/spr08_fact_sheet_de_en.pdf.

32. "Germany's Mittelstand: Beating China: German Family Firms are Outdoing Their Chinese Rivals. Can They Keep it Up?" *The Economist*, July 30, 2011.

33. CNN Money, "Fortune 500 Companies," http://money.cnn.com/magazines/fortune/global500/2010/europe/.

34. Ronald Dore, William Lazonik, and William O' Sullivan, "Varieties of Capitalism in the Twentieth Century," *Oxford Review of Economic Policy* 15, 4 (Winter 1999), 102–120.

35. Rudoph Zipf, "Die Zukunft der Landesbanken in Deutschland," *Karlsruhe*, November 2010, http://www.bankendialog-karlsruhe.de/fileadmin/badi/dl/2010/Vortrag-Zipf.pdf.

36. "Problemfall Landesbanken: Nur im Westen was Neues," *Der Spiegel*, 15.04.2011, http://www.spiegel.de/wirtschaft/unternehmen/0,1518,757257,00.html.

37. European Central Bank, "Euro Area Statistics," *Monthly Bulletin* (December 2005), Table 2.4, http://www.ecb.int/pub/pdf/mobu/mb200512en.pdf.

38. Mechthild Schrooten, "*Finanzmaerkte und Gesamtwitschaftliche Dynamik: USA und Europa,*" in *Lars Roller and Christian Wey, eds., Die Soziale Marktwirtschaft in der Neuen Weltwirtschaft, Jahrbuch 2001* (Berlin: WZB, 2001), p. 393–401.

39. "Germany to Tackle Its Labor Taboos," *Wall Street Journal*, August 8, 2002.

40. Global Human Resources Lawyers, "National Employment Laws Across Europe at a Glance," February 2007, http://www.iuslaboris.com/Files/Archives/national-employment-laws-across-europe.pdf.

41. "Short Work Hours Undercut Europe in Economic Drive," *Wall Street Journal*, August 8, 2002.

42. Alberto Alesina, Edward Galeser, and Bruce Sacredote, "Work and Leisure in the U.S. and Europe: Why So Different?" NBER Working Paper No. 11278, April 2005.

43. *Wall Street Journal Europe*, "Focus on Labor," June 21–23, 2002.

44. Statistisches Jauhbuch der BRD, 2011, Table 8.9.2, http://www.destatis.de/jetspeed/portal/cms/Sites/destatis/SharedContent/Oeffentlich/B3/Publikation/Jahrbuch/Sozialleistungen, property=file.pdf.

45. "The Effects of Employment Protection in Europe and the U.S.," *Opuscle*, CREI, 2007.

46. "Caution Could Bog Down Broader Labor Reforms," *Wall Street Journal Europe*, June 21–23, 2002.

47. Bert Brys and Alastair Thomas, "Non-tax Compulsory Payments as an Additional Burden on Labour Income," OECD, http://www.oecd.org/dataoecd/18/17/45120766.pdf.

48. OECD database, "Incidence of Permanent Employment," http://stats.oecd.org/Index.aspx?DatasetCode=TEMP_I.

49. Paul Gregory, "Why Germany's Unemployment Rate is Lower," Advancing a Free Society, Hoover Institution, October, 7, 2010, http://www.advancingafreesociety.org/2010/10/07/why-germanys-unemployment-rate-is-lower/.

50. OECD database, "Incidence of Permanent Employment," http://stats.oecd.org/Index.aspx?DatasetCode=TEMP_I.

51. Bela Balassa, *The First Year of Socialist Government in France* (Washington, D.C.: American Enterprise Institute, 1982), pp. 2–5.

52. For a survey of nationalization in the United Kingdom, see Richard Pryke, "Public Enterprise in Great Britain," in Morris Bornstein, ed., *Comparative Economic Systems: Models and Cases*, 3rd ed. (Homewood, Ill.: Irwin, 1974), pp. 77–92. See also R. Kelf-Cohen, *Twenty Years of Nationalisation* (London: Macmillan, 1969); R. Kelf-Cohen, *British Nationalisation, 1945–1973* (New York: St. Martin's, 1973); and Leonard Tivey, ed., *The Nationalized Industries Since 1960: A Book of Readings* (Toronto:

University of Toronto Press, 1973). For a discussion of issues in the 1970s, see T.G. Weyman-Jones, "The Nationalised Industries: Changing Attitudes and Changing Roles," in W. P. J. Maunder, ed., *The British Economy in the 1970s* (London: Heineman Educational Books, 1980), chap. 8.

53. J. H. Kaiser, "Public Enterprise in Germany," in W. G. Friedman and J. F. Garner, eds., *Government Enterprise: A Comparative Study* (New York: Columbia University Press, 1970).

54. Nicolas Spulber, *Redefining the State: Privatization and Welfare Reform in the East and West* (Cambridge: Cambridge University Press, 1997).

55. William L. Megginson, Robert C. Nash, and Mathias van Randenburgh, "The Financial and Operating Performance of Newly Privatized Firms: An International Empirical Analysis," *Journal of Finance* 44 (June 1994), 403–452.

56. Measures of government involvement are from Frank Gould, "The Development of Public Expenditures in Western, Industrialised Countries: A Comparative Analysis," *Public Finance* 38 (January 1983), 42–43.

57. Nicholas Spulber, *Redefining the State: Privatization and Welfare Reform in Industrial and Transitional Economies* (Cambridge: Cambridge University Press, 1997), p. 59.

58. Eiroline, European Industrial Relations Observatory On-Line, "Trade Union Membership 2003–2008," http://www.eurofound.europa.eu/eiro/studies/tn0904019s/tn0904019s.htm.

59. "French Giving In?" *International Herald Tribune*, March 16–17, 2002.

60. Thomas Veyrenc, "Shake-Ups and Continuity in European Energy Policy," *Paris Tech Review*, http://www.paristechreview.com/2011/09/21/european-energy-policy/.

61. Arthur Okun, *Equality and Efficiency: The Big Tradeoff* (Washington, D.C.: Brookings Institution, 1975).

62. OECD Database, http://www.oecd.org/document/9/0,3746,en_2649_34637_38141385_1_1_1_1,00.html.

63. Assar Lindbeck, "The Swedish Experiment," *Journal of Economic Literature* 35, no. 3 (September 1997), 1273–1319.

64. R. A. Mundell, "A Theory of Optimum Currency Areas," *American Economic Review* 51, no. 4 (1961), 657–665.

Recommended Readings

European Union

Clive Archer and Fiona Butler, *The European Union: Structure and Process*, 2nd ed. (New York: St. Martin's, 1996).

Charles Bean, "Economic and Monetary Union in Europe," *Journal of Economic Perspectives* 6, no. 4 (Fall 1992), 31–52.

Elizabeth Bomberg and Alexander Stubb, *The European Union : How Does it Work?* (New York: Oxford University Press, 2003).

Laura Cruz and Joel Mokyr, editors, *The Birth of Modern Europe: Culture and Economy, 1400-1800: Essays in Honor of Jan de Vries* (Leiden: Brill, 2010).

European Commission, *The Social Situation in the European Union 2009* (Luxembourg: Office of Official Publications, 2010).

Simon Hix, *What's Wrong with the European Union and How to Fix It* (London: Polity Press, 2008).

Robert Leonardi, *Convergence, Cohesion and Integration in the European Union* (New York: St. Martin's, 1994).

S. Stavridis and Elias Mossialos, Roger Morgan, and Howard Machin, *New Challenges to European Union* (Brookfield, Vt.: Ashgate, 1997).

Bart Van Art and Nicholas Crafts, eds., *Quantitative Aspects of Post-War European Economic Growth* (New York: Cambridge University Press, 1996).

Intellectual Origins

James Apple and Robert Deyling, "A Primer on the Civil-Law System," published by the Federal Judicial Center at the request of the International Judicial Relations Committee of the Judicial Conference of the United States.

Eduard Bernstein, *Evolutionary Socialism: A criticism and Affirmation* (New York: Schocken Books, 1961).

Tony Blair and Gerhard Schroeder, *Europe: The Third Way*, http://www.labour.org.uk.

Edward Glaeser and Andrei Shleifer, "Legal Origins," NBER Working Paper 8272, May 2011.

Howard Machin and Vincent Wright (eds.), *Economic Policy and Policy-Making Under the Mitterrand Presidency 1981–1984* (New York: St. Martin's Press, 1985).

Corporate Governance

Laura Benny, "Do Shareholders Value Insider Trading Laws? International Evidence," Discussion Paper No. 345, 12/2001, Harvard John M. Olin Discussion Papers Series, *http://www.law.harvard.edu/programs/olin_center*.

A. Betzer and E. Theissenm, "Insider Trading and Corporate Governance: the Case of Germany," CFR-Working Paper NO. 07-07, University of Cologne Center for Financial Research, 2007.

Marc Goergen and Luc Renneboog, "Value Creation in Large European Mergers and Acquisitions," *Advances in Mergers and Acquisitions* 2 (2003), 92–146.

European Labor Markets

Alberto Alesina, Edward Glaeser, and Bruce Sacredote, "Work and Leisure in the U.S. and Europe: Why So Different?" NBER Working Paper No. 11278, April 2005.

Werner Eichhorst and Paul Marx, *Reforming German Labor Market Institutions: A Dual Path to Flexibility* (Bonn: IZA, 2009).

Stephen Nickell, "Unemployment and Labor Market Rigidities: Europe versus North America," *Journal of Economic Perspectives* 11, no. 3 (Summer 1997), 55–74.

Opuscle, "The Effects of Employment Protection in Europe and the U.S.," Opuscle, CREI, 2007.

Horst Siebert, "Labor Market Rigidities," *Journal of Economic Perspectives* 11, no. 3 (Summer 1997), 37–54.

Works Constitution Act as promulgated by the Act of September 25, 2001 ("Bundesgesetzblatt", Part I, p. 2518), amended by the Act of December 10, 2001.

Germany

Hans-Joachim Braun, *The German Economy in the Twentieth Century* (London: Routledge: 2003).

Jack Knott, *Managing the German Economy* (Lexington, Mass.: Heath, 1981).

Martin Schnitzer, *East and West Germany: A Comparative Economic Analysis* (New York: Praeger, 1990).

———, *Income Distribution: A Comparative Study of the United States, Sweden, West Germany, East Germany, the United Kingdom, and Japan* (New York: Praeger, 1974).

Wolfgang Streek, *Re-forming Capitalism: Institutional Change in the German Political Economy* (Oxford: Oxford University Press, 2009).

Regulation, Deregulation, and Nationalization

Bela Balassa, *The First Year of Socialist Government in France* (Washington, D.C.: American Enterprise Institute, 1982), pp. 2–5.

J. H. Kaiser, "Public Enterprise in Germany," in W. G. Friedman and J. F. Garner, *Government Enterprise: A Comparative Study* (New York: Columbia University Press, 1970).

R. Kelf-Cohen, *British Nationalization, 1945–1973* (New York: St. Martin's, 1973).

Leonard Tivey, ed., *The Nationalized Industries Since 1960: A Book of Readings* (Toronto: University of Toronto Press, 1973).

T. J. Weyman-Jones, "The Nationalized Industries: Changing Attitudes and Changing Roles," in W. P. J. Maunder, ed., *The British Economy in the 1970s* (London: Heineman Educational Books, 1980), chap. 8.

The Welfare State and Sweden

Barry Bosworth and Alice M. Rivlin, eds., *The Swedish Economy* (Washington, D.C.: Brookings Institution, 1987).

Timothy Canova, "The Swedish Model Betrayed," *Challenge* 37 (May–June, 1994), 36–40.

Richard Freeman, Birgitta Swedenborg, and Robert Topel (eds.), *Reforming the Welfare State: The Swedish Model in Transition* (Chicago: University of Chicago Press, 1997).

Peter Lawrence and Tony Spybey, *Management and Society in Sweden* (London: Routledge and Kegan Paul, 1986).

Assar Lindbeck et al., *Turning Sweden Around* (Cambridge, Mass.: MIT Press, 1994).

Assar Lindbeck, "The Swedish Experiment," *Journal of Economic Literature* 35, no. 3 (September 1997), 1273–1319.

Erik Lundberg, "The Rise and Fall of the Swedish Model," *Journal of Economic Literature* 23 (March 1985), 1–36.

Michael Maccoby, ed., *Sweden at the Edge* (Philadelphia: University of Pennsylvania Press, 1991).

Per-Martin Meyerson, *The Welfare State in Crisis—The Case of Sweden* (Stockholm: Federation of Swedish Industries, 1982).

Henry Milner, *Sweden: Social Democracy in Action* (New York: Oxford University Press, 1989).

Arthur Okun, *Equality and Efficiency: The Big Tradeoff* (Washington, D.C.: Brookings Institution, 1975).

Bengt Ryden and Villy Bergstrom, eds., *Sweden: Choices for Economic and Social Policy in the 1980s* (London: Allen and Unwin, 1982).

Nicholas Spulber, *Redefining the State: Privatization and Welfare Reform in Industrial and Transitional Economies* (Cambridge: Cambridge University Press, 1997).

The Swedish Economy Autumn 1993 (Stockholm: National Institute of Economic Research, 1993).

The Asian Model

The Asian model applies to those countries located in South and East Asia, far removed from the industrialized core of Europe and North America. A Eurasian country with some similarities in its pattern of economic development was the Soviet Union—the pioneer of the socialist planned economy model of development. This model is discussed in Chapter 14.

Japan is the notable pioneer of the **Asian model**, followed, in the second half of the twentieth century, by the Four Tigers of Southeast Asia: Taiwan, South Korea, Singapore, and Hong Kong. Another country with Asian development features is China, which has experienced rapid growth in the last three decades. China began its development as a planned socialist economy and now aims to develop as a *market-socialist economy*. China will be discussed in Chapter 15.

The world's second most populous nation, India, has been growing rapidly for more than two decades. India's population will soon exceed China's. Not only has India's growth been rapid but it also is the world's largest democracy. Therefore, it serves as a counterweight to those who argue that democracy is incompatible with rapid growth in poor countries.

The Asian model applies to Asian countries that began their development from a low initial level of per capita income in a largely rural economy. Their main task was not the more efficient utilization of resources and technological progress, as in the affluent West, but the creation of capital and the drawing of labor out of agriculture, where workers were underemployed or redundant, into industry. In order for this transfer to take place, capital formation in industry was necessary, and this requires savings, from the predominant rural sector or from such sources as foreign capital.

Economists and politicians have argued that with Asia's initial low per capita incomes, the state must play a larger role in creating growth and development. A strong state hand is needed to raise the formation of capital, to allocate that capital, and to draw labor from agriculture to industry. Indeed, most of the Asian economies that have grown rapidly have had strong and in many cases impressive rulers, at least early in their development. Even after the transformation into democracies, the state has continued to pursue industrial policy.

Japan and some of the Southeast Asian countries have used state industrial policy to direct investment resources to defined targets. Japan was the pioneer of Asian industrial policy, using land taxes, land purchases from the warrior (Samurai) class, and other devices to shift savings from industry to agriculture. It used a close alliance between the state and big business to carry out its industrial policy.

The focus on capital formation and investment is not unique to Asia. The *Stalinist model*, used extreme state power to force high rates of capital formation and the rapid transfer of workers from agriculture to industry. We shall study the Stalinist model in the next chapter.

Asia is home to the world's two most populous countries. China and India together account for some 40 percent of the world's population. Clearly, what happens in these two countries will determine the shape of the twenty-first century. India, a perennial laggard in economic growth, has shown dramatic signs of life over the past two decades. It is now held back most by corruption. China has grown under the tutelage and control of the Chinese Communist Party, which shows no signs of relinquishing control. If both India and China continue their economic progress, the face of the twenty-first century will be much brighter.

This chapter treats Asia as a single model even though there are substantial differences among countries. Those economies that come closest to the Anglo-Saxon model, Hong Kong and Singapore, are affluent city-states, quite different in many respects from the populous, middle-income countries of South Korea and Taiwan. The poorer, developing-market countries of Thailand, the Philippines, Indonesia, and Malaysia differ as much from these middle-income countries as they do from the gigantic and very poor India.

We devote considerable attention to Japan as the pioneer of the Asian model and its longest practitioner. The fact that Japan has scarcely grown for two decades is scrutinized carefully to determine whether those following it on the path to the Asian model will experience a similar slowdown. *The **unifying features of the Asian model** are the high rates of savings and investment and the distinctive organization of capital markets and corporate governance.*

Ideological and Theoretical Foundations

The ideological, legal, and theoretical lineages of the Anglo-Saxon and European models were described in previous chapters. The foundations of both models could be traced to economic and constitutional philosophies.

The roots of the Asian model are quite different. The Asian model originated in Japan, which, until the late 1860s, was isolated from Western thought. The Asian model spread to the Korean peninsula with its annexation by Japan in 1910. Japan, in its efforts to make Korea a permanent Japanese territory, introduced its style of business, finance, and industrial organization there and assumed ownership of many Korean businesses. When Korea was freed from Japanese occupation in 1945, it was left with a strong imprint of the Japanese system.[1] The Japanese model spread throughout Southeast Asia in the 1960s and 1970s as Japan, by then the world's second-largest economy and by far the dominant Asian economy, exerted influence through its economic miracle and its investments in the region. *Japan's economic miracle refers to its exceptional growth in the first three decades after World War II.*

Modern Japanese History

Modern Japanese history began with two major events. The first was the forced opening of Japan by Admiral Matthew Perry on his second voyage to Japan with eight military ships in February 1854. In the sixteenth century, Japan's rulers had discontinued relations with the West because of its perceived corruptive influences. The imposition of "unequal treaties" on Japan by the more powerful American military came as a profound shock to a nation that believed in its cultural superiority to all things foreign. The humiliation of the forced opening taught Japan that it must modernize to protect itself from foreign enemies—an insight institutionalized in an 1868 imperial memo stating that Japan must stop looking at the world "as a frog from the bottom of a well" and be willing to learn from foreigners and adopt their best points.[2] In the decades that followed, Japanese were sent to the West to learn from universities, industrialists, philosophers, and statesmen. Japan had decided it needed to catch up quickly.

The second major event was the *Meiji Restoration in 1868, which replaced the military regime with a new government of progressive officials determined to embark on modernization.* The Meiji leaders had no blueprint, other than the general acceptance of an "emperor system" that nominally gave the emperor absolute power to be exercised by appointed officials rather than feudal lords. By 1900, Japan's top officials were largely appointed through competitive exams.

Initially, the Meiji rulers lacked a strong centralized government because land, the basic source of revenue, was disbursed among feudal lords. Gradually, however, the central government extended control over feudal land in return for fixed payments to the former owners. Eventually, the central government engineered a massive buyout of feudal lands, and this enabled the state to impose a land tax, which served as its main source of revenue. Deprived of land, talented samurai entered government or business positions. The central government, patterning itself after Western-style governments, became increasingly efficient.

The period's most famous document issued in the emperor's name, the Charter Oath of 1868, stated that all matters would be decided ultimately by the emperor—but on the basis of broad consultation, taking into account the interests of all Japanese. Japan's constitution was prepared after numerous study expeditions to the West. Although there were calls for a democratically elected legislature, the Constitution of 1889 assigned most power to the emperor and his advisors rather than to such an elected body.

Religious Origins

Japan, China, Korea, and other East Asian countries were strongly influenced by Confucianism, the religion of the educated classes in ancient Japan and China. *Confucianism emphasizes the qualities of loyalty, nationalism, social solidarity, collectivism, benevolence, faith, and bravery.* Koreans and Chinese placed emphasis on the last three, whereas the Japanese emphasized loyalty and bravery—a "loyalty centered Confucianism."[3] In Japan, this emphasis led to an amalgamation of civil religion, work ethic, and business ideology. The relationship between religion and law was formalized in imperial edicts, such as the 1872 "Great Teaching" that included injunctions to respect the gods, revere the emperor, love one's country, and obey the rules of moral behavior. The "Great Teaching" constituted a code of civic duty for all Japanese. It institutionalized the emperor as a figurehead who was to preside over Japan's transformation and give legitimacy to those who developed his policies.

Confucianism teaches the notion of a virtuous government, and in China, Japan, and Korea, a positive role of government was taken for granted. *The **virtuous government** as taught by Confucianism suggested a significant and positive role for government in the economy.* Therefore, the public was prepared to accept government administrative guidance in Japan and government instructions in Korea in their early years of industrialization.

Moreover, there was greater acceptance of powerful leadership, such as the authoritarian presidencies of Park Chung Hee in postwar Korea and Chiang Kai-Shek and Chiang Ching-Koo in Taiwan (martial rule was not relaxed until 1988), the symbolic authority of the monarchy in Thailand, the strong rule of Lee Kuan Lew in Singapore, and the intrusive role of the state sultans of Malaysia.

If Japan's political governance was influenced by foreign ideas at all, it was by German notions of the late nineteenth century—the idea of the "right of the state," which gave the state priority over individuals.

The ideas of Japan's rulers were far removed from the teachings of Adam Smith and of classical liberal thinking. It is no surprise, then, that Japan's economy was organized on the principle of a strong state to which the individual was subordinated. In general, whereas common law aims for citizen empowerment, the legal systems of Asia favor state empowerment.[4]

Relative Backwardness and Japan

The economic historian, Alexander Gerschenkron, formulated his theory of relative backwardness to explain how a poor country, such as Japan at the end of the nineteenth century, could rather quickly overcome its relative economic backwardness.[5] *The **theory of relative backwardness** teaches that backward countries grossly underutilizing resources take steps to accelerate economic growth to catch up to more advanced rivals.*

In Japan's case, the necessary shock was delivered when Admiral Perry's forced opening of Japan demonstrated that it could not compete militarily with the West. This experience forced Japan to confront the gap between its actual and its potential economic achievements and to find innovative ways of overcoming its backwardness.

Gerschenkron's theory of substitutions *said that backward countries could find innovative substitutions for missing preconditions.* Lacking bureaucrats, Japan created a professional bureaucracy in short order by adopting Western methods and sending young people abroad. Lacking domestic industrial technology, Japan borrowed technology from other countries. Lacking an entrepreneurial class, it turned to the young samurais who had lost their land. The state substituted industrial policy for market decision making. To economize on entrepreneurial resources, Japan fostered large integrated concerns and syndicates. In short, it made up for missing preconditions with innovative substitutions.

Many of these substitutions were passed on to Korea, which was left, after Japan's brutal occupation, with Japan's educational system; modernized industry, agriculture, and mining; a centralized administrative structure; and the beginnings of the integrated concerns that dominated the Korean economy in the postwar years.[6]

Gerschenkron's empirical prediction was that relatively backward countries would grow more rapidly than the industrialized countries once they decided on a policy of industrialization. Indeed, Japan began its modern era in the late 1880s with a GDP per capita of around $1,000. In the first year of the new millennium, Japan's per capita GDP, despite a decade of slow growth, was $35,000—more than 10 percent above the EU average.[7] Japan's dramatic rise in relative living standards was achieved via higher rates of economic growth. Whereas the major industrial countries grew between 2 and 3 percent per year over the long run, Japan's growth tended to be well above that of other countries and accelerated from the prewar period through the 1970s. And whereas capital grew at the same rate as output in the industrialized countries, there were significant periods in which capital growth exceeded output growth in Japan (see Figure 13.1).

Japan's "economic miracle" dates to the period 1953–1971, when growth averaged 14 percent and capital grew at 9 percent. Growth rates declined thereafter, reaching less than 2 percent for the period 1990–2011.

FIGURE 13.1   Real GDP and Aggregate Gross Capital Stock in Japan (average annual growth rates)

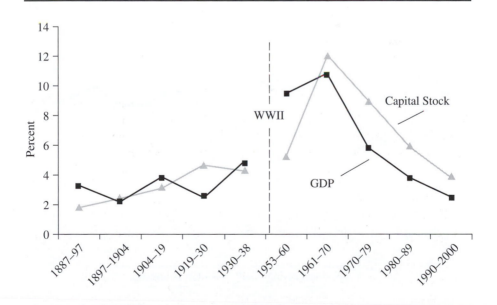

Sources: K. Ohkawa and M. Shinohara, eds., *Patterns of Japanese Economic Development: A Quantitative Appraisal* (New Haven: Yale University Press, 1979); Edward F. Denison and William K. Chung, eds., *How Japan's Economy Grew So Fast* (Washington D.C.: Brookings Institution, 1976); Penn World Table 5.6, Global Development Finance & World Development Indicators, OECD.

Japan's growth was fostered by high rates of investment and national savings. Throughout the postwar period, Japan continued to have exceptionally high national savings rates and investment rates. Figure 13.2 shows that the Japanese economy maintained high investment rates through significant domestic savings. Excess savings were then exported, as national savings exceeded gross domestic investment, especially in 1965–1973 and 1983–1989. One would expect countries with high savings rates to invest more abroad as they mature and domestic rates of return decline. Japanese savings flooded into Southeast Asia, spurring economic development. With this capital went Japanese business methods and technology.

The economic explanations for Japan's rapid economic growth were a technology gap, a high rate of capital formation, and the availability of labor. After being a closed economy for centuries, Japan had a technology gap and could absorb Western technology through imports of capital, a high propensity to save, and the state's promotion of capital formation.[8] The excess of agricultural labor facilitated the shift from agriculture to industry at a rate dictated by the needs of the advanced sector, and wage increases lagged behind advances in productivity.[9]

Japanese growth was export-driven. In the early years of industrialization, exports were primarily traditional industries such as textiles. As modern technology was assimilated, exports shifted toward the high-technology products that Japan, owing to its productive but relatively inexpensive labor, could produce with

FIGURE 13.2   National Savings and Gross Investment Rates in Japan, 1887–2000

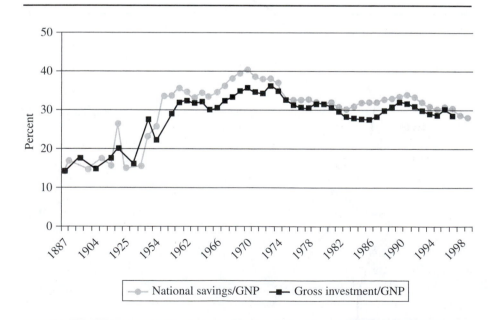

Sources: K. Ohkawa and M. Shinohara, eds., *Patterns of Japanese Economic Development: A Quantitative Appraisal* (New Haven: Yale University Press, 1979); Global Development Finance & World Development Indicators; IMF's International Financial Statistics; Asian Development Bank, Statistical Database, https://sdbs.adb.org/sdbs/index.jsp.

comparative advantage. The state used industrial policy to direct industry to more complex export products, such as electronics, machinery, and automobiles.

Noneconomic factors affected the pattern of growth as well. First, the state gave direction to economic growth through the early use of Industrial Policy. Government offices (*genkyoku*) supervised individual industries, and ministries supervised sectors of the economy. The government was directly involved in the encouragement of industrial projects through low-interest loans from the Development Bank of Japan.[10] Second, workers received "permanent employment" from their companies, and this instilled in them a sense of loyalty to the company and a submissive attitude.[11] Prior to World War II, the government suppressed trade unions. Since their recognition in the postwar period, Japanese trade unions have had a voice in wages, supplemental benefits, and working conditions, but they remain company unions. Giant conglomerates, such as Sony, have their own unions, whose job is to instill loyalty and raise productivity.[12]

Growth in the Rest of Asia: The Four Tigers

The rest of Asia had to wait until the postwar period for its Gerschenkronian burst of economic growth. Perhaps these countries had to wait for Britain's dismantling of its colonial empire after World War II. The **Four Tigers**—Hong Kong, Singapore, South Korea, and Taiwan—are so named because of their exceptionally rapid growth, which started in the early 1970s (see Figure 13.3) and continued high, despite interruption by the Asian crisis of 1997 (discussed in a later chapter).

Note that the rapid growth of the Four Tigers proved contagious, spreading to other parts of Asia, such as Indonesia, Thailand, the Philippines, and Malaysia. In the 1980s, the growth laggard, India, began to grow as well and was one of the world's most rapidly growing economies in the 1990s. Despite their rapid growth, these countries remain poor and must continue their high growth to become middle-income countries.

Figure 13.4 shows that two Asian countries, Hong Kong (which is now a part of China) and Singapore, have reached the level of affluence of Western industrialized countries and Japan. South Korea and Taiwan have become middle-income countries. The other rapidly growing Asian countries remain poor but will approach middle-income status if their growth continues.

The Four Tigers achieved remarkable rapid growth with little if any increases in inequality, as will be shown later. They generated exceptionally high rates of savings; most of these savings were invested at home, but significant amounts were also invested in nearby developing Asian economies. They also invested heavily in human capital through health and education spending. Four Asian countries (Singapore, Taiwan, Japan, and South Korea) are in the top five in science scores for their students.[13] Throughout the last half century, the burden of taxes remained generally low by international standards.

The growth of the Four Tigers was driven by export-led industrialization. Exports have been largely manufactures, but in recent years a somewhat more diversified export pattern has emerged (for example, financial services in the case of Hong Kong and Singapore).

The Four Tigers have different political systems. South Korea and Taiwan began with military dictatorships, which repressed opposition parties, sometimes quite brutally, but kept economic development as a primary goal. After the end of

FIGURE 13.3   Growth of the Four Tigers and Other Asian Countries, 1970 to Present

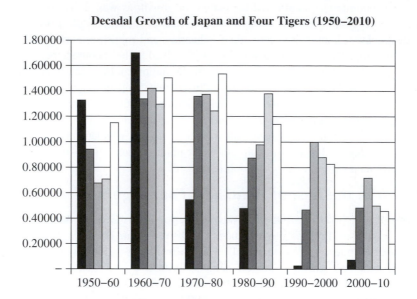

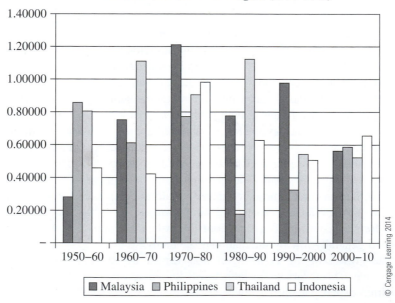

FIGURE **13.4** GDP per Capita, 2011

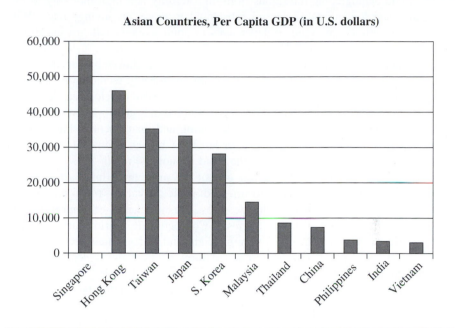

Asian Countries, Per Capita GDP (in U.S. dollars)

Source: Asian Development Bank, http://www.adb.org.

their military dictatorships, South Korea and Taiwan became raucous democracies, characterized by bitter rivalries and even fist fights on the floor of parliament. Assertive trade unions also formed. Singapore has operated under a "benevolent" one-party rule that applies strict rules of behavior on its citizens and suppresses labor unions. Hong Kong inherited a strong democratic tradition from British colonial rule and an honest bureaucracy. It remains to be seen whether these traditions will continue. Hong Kong formally became part of China in December 2010, when the United Kingdom's ninety-nine-year lease expired.

State policy has consistently supported *export promotion* over *import substitution. **Export promotion** consists of state policies to promote exports. Such policies range from subsidies of export industries to free-trade practices for the economy as a whole. **Import substitution** consists of policies that protect domestic industries from foreign competition via tariffs or other barriers.*

The World Bank has classified Hong Kong, Singapore, and South Korea as the world's most outward-oriented economies among the developing countries during the periods 1963–1973 and 1973–1985 and India as among the most inward-oriented during that same period.[14] It was India increasing export orientation after 1990 that is largely credited with its growth. More general statistical studies confirm that the relationship between export orientation and economic growth is positive.[15] There is simply no historical example of successful import-substitution countries.

A number of factors explain the rapid growth of the Four Tigers:

1. The rapid demographic transitions from high fertility and high mortality to low fertility and low mortality caused substantial increases in savings rates. With declining fertility, the ratio of dependents to adult workers fell, freeing discretionary income for savings.[16]
2. Governments in the region promoted a stable investment climate by adopting stable macroeconomic policies and providing stability, reasonably secure property rights, and tranquil industrial relations. Some governments created development banks that took a longer-run view of investment and monitored industrial borrowers.
3. The governments promoted universal education and investment in human capital, such as in public health. The high levels of human capital at the start of growth contributed substantially to the rapid economic growth.[17]
4. Openness to international trade was one of the most important factors in the region's rapid growth. Outward-oriented policies varied from the use of incentives to undervalued exchange rates, the avoidance of import restrictions, and trade liberalization policies.[18] Competing in world markets forced domestic producers to become more efficient and to learn new technologies.
5. Some East Asian governments promoted foreign direct investment to supplement domestic savings and attract new technologies. Policies toward foreign direct investment varied widely: Japan and Korea were initially hostile, whereas Hong Kong and Singapore promoted foreign investment. Foreign direct investment has been significant in parts of East Asia, but only in Singapore was direct foreign investment more than 10 percent of capital formation.

The most controversial issue is the extent to which the Asian miracle was made possible by market-oriented policies versus state-interventionist policies. These matters will be discussed later in this chapter.

The Asian growth figures raise a number of questions: First, what caused growth to be so rapid starting in Japan around the turn of the twentieth century? Second, why did Japanese growth decline over the past decade? Is this a temporary or a permanent setback for Japan, and will other Asian countries eventually experience declining growth as well? Third, what caused the acceleration of growth in other parts of Asia, extending even to India? Did these countries simply follow the Japanese path, or did they create their own models? The ultimate issue is the viability and performance of the Asian model. We have less information on this issue because we have only one long-run experience combined with the shorter-run experiences of a relatively small number of countries. But the Four Tigers have been growing for nearly half a century. There must be systematic long-term factors that explain this growth.

Comparisons with Europe

Table 13.1 compares key benchmarks of the major Asian economies with Europe as of the late 1980s. At that time, Japan, Hong Kong, and Singapore were at comparable levels of per capita income. Taiwan and South Korea were still relatively poor, but they had high rates of investment in both physical and human capital. Japan had already created a society that was 100 percent literate (as is the case in Western Europe) and it had an investment in health (as shown by a people-to-doctor ratio)

Table 13.1   Asian versus European Models, Late 1980s

	Europe	Japan	Hong Kong	Singapore	Korea	Taiwan
Per capita GDP, 93 $	17,089	20,523	16,601	13,021	6,548	7,249
GDI/GDP	20%	33%	27%	35%	35%	27%
Gross saving	20%	34%	35%	43%	37%	32%
Literacy	100	100	88	91	96	92
People/doctor	611	609	933	753	1078	9811
Government revenue/GDP	40%	29%	14%	21%	19%	14%

Sources: Roy Ruffin, "The Role of Foreign Investment in the Economic Growth of the Asian and Pacific Region," *Asian Development Review* 11, no. 1 (1993), 3–5; Cormac O'Grada and Kevin O'Rourke, "Irish Economic Growth, 1945–88," in Nicholas Crafts and Gianni Toniolo, eds., *Economic Growth in Europe Since 1945* (Cambridge: Cambridge University Press), 1996, p. 405; *The World Factbook 1988*, country statistics.

comparable to that of Western Europe. Japan's commitment to investment in physical capital is shown by its much higher rates of national savings and its high rates of domestic investment. The high rate of national savings appears to be a constant of Japanese life. It enabled Japan, particularly in the 1970s and 1980s, to invest its savings surpluses in other countries, such as the Four Tigers of Southeast Asia.

Net foreign investment occurs when a country's national savings rate exceeds its domestic investment rate. Table 13.1 shows Japan's national savings rate (in the mid-1990s) to equal 34 percent, exceeding its domestic investment rate of 33 percent by 1 percent, which constitutes Japan's net foreign investment. Table 13.1 shows that high rates of investment in human and physical capital are common to the Asian model. The Four Tigers all have exceptionally high national savings rates, in excess of their already high domestic investment rates, indicating that they, like Japan, are making net investments in other countries, primarily other Asian countries. They also have high rates of literacy, and they make substantial investments in health, as is indicated by their people-to-doctor ratios.

Table 13.1 reveals yet another common feature: a relatively low tax burden. Whereas Europe's average tax burden was 40 percent of GDP, the Asian countries range from a high of 29 percent for Japan to a low of 14 percent for Hong Kong. The major Asian countries have been able to generate human and physical capital with relatively light burdens of taxation.

Institutions of the Asian Model

In the previous three chapters, we examined the institutional features of the Anglo-Saxon and European models in terms of capital markets, corporate governance, labor markets, privatization, regulation versus deregulation, and provision of income security. We also examined the role of industrial policy, which was largely lacking in the Anglo-Saxon model but present in the European model, particularly in the French case. The same type of analysis can be performed on those countries that adhere to the Asian model.

Corporate Governance

The modern Asian model of corporate governance developed in Japan in the early postwar period. It shares Europe's emphasis on stakeholder over shareholder interests, but its focus is on the overall growth of the conglomerate organization.[19]

Asian corporate governance dates back to the family-owned international trading houses of the prewar period, called the zaibatsu. *The zaibatsu were vertical or horizontal conglomerates that dominated Japanese industry and commerce before World War II.* They were broken up by the occupation forces as the backbone of the Japanese war machine.

Before World War II, Japanese industry was dominated by giant holding-company *zaibatsu*, which formed a complex maze of interlocking directorships, banking relationships, and family ties.[20] By the end of the war, this concentration of ownership had reached the point where fewer than 4,000 zaibatsu-connected families owned almost 50 percent of all the outstanding industry and commerce. The occupation forces sought to eliminate zaibatsu dominance by outlawing holding companies, breaking up monopolies, and making mutual shareholdings among zaibatsu firms illegal.

New industrial groupings called *kieretsu* replaced the old zaibatsu organizations. Kieretsu can be either vertically or horizontally integrated: either a large firm in charge of smaller firms ("children") or a horizontal association of interest groups. These new groups are less powerful than the old zaibatsu, and, at times, a firm within a grouping places its own interests above those of the group.

The zaibatsu were resurrected as keiretsu in postwar Japan. *The keiretsu are horizontal or vertical conglomerates with large banks at their center.* Although often comprised of separate companies or divisions, the keiretsu seek to maximize the growth of the conglomerate as a whole. Historically, the keiretsu have not been in the business of maximizing profits.

The Japanese keiretsu oversaw the Japanese growth boom from 1950 to 1980. Japanese keiretsu are organized around major banks such as Fuji, Mitsubishi, or Dai-Ichi Banks. Mitsui bank, for example, has interests in Mitsui Real Estate, Mitsukoshi, Mitsui Mutual Life, Mitsui Marine & Fire, Nippon Flour Mills, Mitsui Sugar, Suntory, Fuji Photo Film, Mitsui Toatsu Chemicals, Mitsui Petrochemical Industries, Toagosei Chemical Industries, Denki Kagaku Kogyo, Daicel Chemical Industries, Mitsui Pharmaceuticals, Mitsui Toatsu Fertilizers, Mitsui Toatsu Dyes, Toray, Mitsui Bussan, General Sekiyu, Kyokuto Petroleum Industries, Sony Corporation, Yaussa Corporation, Ibiden Company, Toshiba, Japan Steel Works, Sony Computer Entertainment, Sony Pictures, and other Sony subsidiaries.

The Japanese keiretsu were emulated in Southeast Asia and in the Mini Dragon states of Asia and in India, the home of the famous Tata Group. In Korea, they are called *chaebols*. In other Asian countries they are called *gruppo* or by some other local name.

Table 13.2 shows Korea's Daewoo Group's divisions and interrelated ownership structure. One division, Daewoo Electronics, owns 23 percent of Daewoo Motors, and Daewoo Motors owns 45 percent of Daewoo Finance. The family of the founder (the Kim family) owns some 15 percent of the various Daewoo divisions.

TABLE 13.2   Daewoo Group Intraconglomerate Ownership (1997, unit%)

Investor / Investee	Daewoo Corp.	Daewoo Electron.	Daewoo Heavy	Daewoo Telecom	Orion Electric	Daewoo Motor	Daewoo Precisions	Daewoo Auto Sales	Daewoo Develop.	Daewoo Shipbldg.	Daewoo Elect. Comp.	Daewoo Securities	Treas. shares	ESOP	Kim Family	Total
Daewoo Heavy	29.1	5.3		1.1	1.1		2.30	0.04	0.8					0.18	6.87	46.79
Daewoo Corp.		0.4		1.8				0.4					4.34	1.10		8.04
Daewoo Motor	37.0	23.0		8.5												68.50
Daewoo Securit	3.1	6.9		0.2		0.1							2.85	0.13	1.39	14.67
Daewoo Electr					2.0						0.41		1.73	0.47		4.61
Daewoo Tele.		5.7										0.01		2.08		7.79
Orion Electrio								0.4				0.01	2.81	0.53	1.00	4.75
Keang Nam En	4.7	4.7	2.3	2.3			1.55		1.7	3.6		1.1	1.15	2.66		25.76
Daewoo Indust	7.6		6.1	11.1		24.7										49.50
Daewoo Auto Sales						19.1							0.84			19.94
Daewoo Proc.					4.1							0.9		3.34	11.75	20.09
Daewoo Fin.			30.0			45.0		25.0								100
Daewoo Deve.	39.0															39.00
Daewoo Elect. Com	8.5		19.2										0.51	0.08		28.29
Average													1.02	0.76	1.50	31.27 (27.99)*

Source: Joongi Kim, "Anatomy of an Asian Conglomerate: The Rise and Fall of Daewoo and the Formation of Modern Corporate Governance, Graduate School of International Studies," Yonsei University, Seoul Korean, June 2005, Table 1, page 7. Reprinted with permission.

The Japanese keiretsu and Korean chaebols use contracting based on trust, reciprocal shareholdings and trade agreements among the stakeholders, managerial incentives to maximize overall growth, and selective coordination by the associated bank and the state.

The state does not intervene directly in the operation of the keiretsu/chaebol. Rather, the state provides guaranteed lines of credit to the main bank, which then supplies credit to the industrial groups. The keiretsu/chaebols build networks with key stakeholders by negotiating low prices in return for guaranteed purchases and they built up employee loyalty with implicit promises of lifetime employment.

Insofar as the Japanese government and the keiretsu themselves are oriented toward the external market, their decision making has been based on price signals and the state intervened little in their operations. Corporate governance and control have been top down based on vertical and horizontal guarantees and stakeholder interests.

Family Ownership

The Asian corporate governance model differs from the Anglo-Saxon and European models most distinctly in its patterns of ownership and corporate governance. Figure 9.1 showed the greater prevalence of family ownership in Asia than in Europe or the United States. There is considerable family ownership of medium-sized businesses in Europe. In Asia, families own the largest businesses.

A strong Confucian family ideology is reflected in East Asian corporate institutions, where the company is the "head of the family" and the workers are the "children." Instead of management and ownership being separate, the owners tend to be powerful families whose members also serve as part of the management team. Moreover, these families or groups of related individuals own not one company but groups of companies in a complex pattern of cross-ownership.

In Europe, cross-ownership by banks, suppliers, and customers is common. It is common in Asia as well, but instead of institutions owning parts of other institutions, it is one family that owns a number of companies in a kind of overlapping directorate.

Table 13.3 shows that ownership concentrated in the hands of single individuals or families is characteristic of most Asian countries except Japan. Notably,

TABLE 13.3   Ownership Concentration of the Ten Largest Firms (in %)

Asia		Latin America	
India	38	Argentina	50
Indonesia	53	Brazil	31
Korea	23	Chile	41
Malaysia	46	Colombia	63
Philippines	56	Mexico	64
Thailand	44		

Source: Rafael LaPorta et al., "Corporate Ownership Around the World," NBER Working Paper Series, No. 6625, June 1998.

individual and family ownership is also characteristic of Latin America, which shares this feature with the Asian model.[21]

Individual or family ownership applies to both large and small companies, whereas in the United States and Europe, family ownership is common only in small or medium-sized businesses. In the Philippines and Indonesia, one-sixth of all market capitalization can be traced to a single family (the Ayalas in the Philippines and the Suhartos in Indonesia). Even in Hong Kong, the territory that most resembles the Anglo-Saxon model (such as in its use of common law), more than 50 percent of listed companies have a single shareholder or a family that holds the majority of shares. These major families have cross-holdings in other companies. Unlike in Europe, where banks hold significant shares, Hong Kong banks hold insignificant shares and are not part of the corporate governance team.

In Korean *chaebols* (such as Daiwoo, Hyundai, and Samsung), the largest single shareholder owns a relatively small share, such as 10 percent. However, closely affiliated firms own enough of the company—say, an additional 30 percent—to give the largest single shareholder effective control of the conglomerate. Although ownership does not equate directly with control, in most cases the owners either directly manage the company or are represented by a senior executive who manages the company in the interest of the family.

Table 13.4 shows the patterns of ownership in various East Asian countries. It shows that in countries other than Japan, publicly traded companies are owned primarily by family or individual owners. In Singapore, Malaysia, and Thailand, there is significant state ownership as well. Only in Japan are there widely held corporations. Unlike the Anglo-Saxon model, where institutional investors own substantial shares of stock, institutional investors (except for some foreign institutional investors) are not prominent in Asia, and they rarely participate in management.

TABLE 13.4   Control of Publicly Traded Companies in East Asia (weighted by market capitalization)

Country	Number of Corporations	Widely Held	Family	State	Widely Held Financial	Widely Held Corporation
Hong Kong	330	7.0	71.5	4.8	5.9	10.8
Indonesia	178	6.6	67.3	15.2	2.5	8.4
Japan	1240	85.5	4.1	7.3	1.5	1.6
Korea	345	51.1	24.6	19.9	0.2	4.3
Malaysia	238	16.2	42.6	34.8	1.1	5.3
Philippines	120	28.5	46.4	3.2	8.4	13.7
Singapore	221	7.6	44.8	40.1	2.7	4.8
Taiwan	141	28.0	45.5	3.3	5.4	17.8
Thailand	167	8.2	51.9	24.1	6.3	9.5

Source: Stijn Claessens, Simon Djankov, and Larry Lang, "Who Controls East Asian Corporations?" World Bank, December 1998. Reprinted with permission.

Rule of Law, Contracting, and the Market for Corporate Control

Both the Anglo-Saxon and the European models rely on a "rule of law" when they enter into contracts, although the rule of law may be less crucial in the European model, where cross-holdings and bank ownership are prevalent. In Asian countries, which, with the exceptions of Hong Kong and India, use civil law, the "rule of law" appears to be less important in regulating the dealings among companies.

Two generic types of contracting regimes can be identified: ***Relational contracting*** *is based not on a formal rule of law but on personal relationships and trust.* ***Market-based contracting*** *is an impersonal form of contracting based on formal contracts backed by a rule of law.*

Market-based contracting is the primary form of contracting used in the United States, whereas relational contracting is the primary form of contracting used in Asia. Relational contracting is used in countries that have a relatively weak rule of law; prominent examples are modern Russia and China.

Asian firms usually deal with other firms on the basis of personal agreements, informal enforcement mechanisms, customs, or existing trust relationships and rely less on formal contracts and their enforcement by the courts. The courts themselves may be inefficient or even corrupt. As an example, a court-appointed supervisor declared a perfectly solvent Canadian company operating in Indonesia bankrupt after receiving bribes. This and other cases prompted the World Bank's chief representative to Indonesia to declare, "The pattern of outcomes from the courts is very hard to understand except in terms of corruption and probably incompetence."[22]

With their family based ownership system, Asian companies appear to have resolved the key principal–agent problem between owners and manager: Asian family ownership diminishes the principal–agent problem because owners are managers. Principal–agent conflicts do arise, however, between the principal owner and minority shareholders and among the various companies owned by the same family. In cases where relational contracting is used and there is extensive cross-ownership, the rights of minority shareholders tend to be abused.

In Thailand and Korea, shareholder meetings make decisions without a quorum of shareholders. The rights of minority shareholders can be diluted by decisions of the major shareholder to issue new shares to insiders. In Japan, the Asian country with the broadest public ownership of corporations, minority shareholders, and even foreign shareholders with significant minority interests are unable to influence management decisions. T. Boone Pickens, the noted corporate raider, failed in his attempt to gain a directors' position in Koito Manufacturing Company, one of Toyota Motor's major parts suppliers, even though he was the largest single shareholder. A young, American-trained corporate investor, known for challenging Japan's stodgy boards of directors, was arrested as an example for others.

Disputes involving the Japanese company Tokyo Style provide a microcosm of the problems of minority shareholders. In the spring of 2002, a Japanese sort of corporate raider organized minority shareholders (foreign owners held about 30 percent of shares) to force Tokyo Style to pay out some of its huge cash holdings as dividends or, at least, to buy back its own shares to raise the stock price. Minority shareholders attempted to place this proposal on the agenda of a shareholder meeting, an action practically unheard of in Japan. The minority-shareholder proposals were rebuffed by the long-time president of Tokyo Style (he had worked for the company since the age of 18), who marshaled the support of cross-shareholders like Fuji Bank. Fuji Bank was quoted as saying that it would risk ruining its relationships with other customers if it failed to side with management.[23]

Cross-shareholding creates a further risk of expropriation of minority shareholders. The family owner of a number of companies can divert assets from one company to another. In Korea, for example, it is common for companies owned by one family to make uneconomical loans to other family-controlled firms. Shareholders of the lending firm are partially expropriated of their assets via such transfers. Such diversions of assets cannot take place without the collusion of employees and managers, whose careers are controlled by the family owner.

Practices referred to as tunneling and propping benefit insiders at the expense of smaller shareholders are common in Asia.[24] *Tunneling is the awarding of contract to firms, individuals, or interests that are insiders to the conglomerate. Propping refers to the financial and other support given by the more profitable units of the conglomerate to support sister units*. In Korea, a government watchdog agency, for example, fined Hyundai Motors for giving a multibillion-dollar contract to a firm owned by Hyundai's chairman's son.

The price–earnings ratio is the price of a share of stock divided by its earnings (profits) per share. The PE ratio is a measure of optimism concerning the future. A high PE ratio tells us that investors expect profits to rise rapidly in the future. A low PE ratio suggests a slow rise in profits or even stagnation of profits.

The Asian economies have grown more rapidly than the West over the past two decades. More rapid growth brings with it the expectation of the growth of profits. Hence, we would expect to see higher PE ratios in Asian stock markets. This is not the case. The PE ratios of the rapidly growing Asian countries generally fall below those of the United States and the United Kingdom, even during periods, such as 2012, when stock markets were depressed. The 2012 Dow Jones Industrial PE ratio (forward-looking) is 14 and the London Stock Exchange FTSE index is also 14, whereas the PE ratios of Asia range from 13 to 9 despite their higher growth rates.

South Korea ranks at the bottom in terms of PE ratios. Experts say that the prime cause of the discount is poor corporate governance at the family-run chaebol conglomerates that dominate the economy. Schemes to pass control of companies to sons, to avoid taxes, and to use company assets for the benefit of family members place Korea third from bottom in Asia on governance, ahead of only Indonesia and the Philippines.[25]

Given the web of cross-ownership in Asian countries, hostile takeovers are practically impossible. Throughout Asia, there is no active market for corporate control. Poorly run companies protect themselves from takeovers by outsiders. Owners can count on related parties to repel any such attempts. Cross-holdings make bankruptcy a less effective instrument for weeding out poorly managed companies. If the insolvent company is part of a family-owned conglomerate, other companies will bail out the faltering company with loans or asset transfers.

The most fundamental risk is not to minority shareholders but to the company itself. By relying on relational rather than market-based contracting, the company fails to use price signals in its decision making. For example, in an Anglo-Saxon company, transactions would occur "at arm's-length" and would be subjected to rate-of-return calculations by third parties such as investment bankers. Poor investments would be ruled out, as would irrational asset transfers among companies.[26] When relational contracting is used, such "market" controls are largely absent. Business errors, large and small, are the result. Exhibit 13.1 summarizes the features of corporate governance in Asia.

Transparency and Accounting

Publicly traded Asian countries are not required to be as transparent as companies that operate in the Anglo-Saxon legal and accounting environment. Public investors will be reluctant to become shareholders of companies that do not supply adequate accounting information.

Exhibit 13.2 contrasts the disclosure requirements of publicly traded Japanese companies with the disclosures required by the International Accounting System (IAS). The list of deviations is long, and the most significant omission is any requirement to reveal transactions with related parties. Furthermore, Japanese companies can value their assets at their acquisition costs, which means that losses due to declining asset values are not disclosed to shareholders. In Japanese firms there are few outside directors. Virtually all directors are involved in management; therefore, accounting statements cannot be vetted by outside, impartial directors.[27]

The Capital Market

The corporate governance of Asian companies has a profound effect on the functioning of its capital markets. Figure 9.1 showed that widely held publicly traded companies are rare in Asia, with the exception of Japan. Most companies are owned by families with extensive cross-holdings.

Given the widespread use of relational contracting, the lack of protection of minority shareholders, and the limited amount of accounting disclosure, there are only limited purchases of stock by minority buyers. Capital must come from the owners; it will not come from small investors as it does in Anglo-Saxon equity markets. Those with funds to invest, either parties in the country itself or foreigners, would therefore invest in bank deposits or in government debt. Foreign investment would be through the purchase not of shares but of short-term debt. (Share owners know that they have little legal protection, so they invest in the least-risky funds—namely, short-term debt.)

The reliance on debt creates considerable volatility in Asian capital markets because short-term capital, unlike equity capital, can flee a country on a moment's notice if there are signs of weakness of the economy. If there are no restrictions on currency outflows, domestic savers prefer to invest in safe-haven countries, such as the United States, where their holdings are protected by a strong rule of law.

The overall result is that Asian countries finance themselves by borrowing, not by selling new shares of stock. This means that Asian companies are highly leveraged. **Highly leveraged companies** *have heavy debt burdens relative to equity, which must be serviced by regular interest and principal payments.*

EXHIBIT 13.1   Corporate Governance in East Asia and Other Emerging Economies

Variables	Description/Effect	Korea	Indonesia	Malaysia	Philippines	Thailand	Mexico	India
Right to call emergency shareholder meeting	Facilitates shareholders' control	Yes	Yes	Yes	Yes	Yes	Yes	Yes
Right to make proposals at shareholder meeting	Facilitates shareholders' control; increased opportunity to prevent biased decisions by insiders	Yes	Yes	Yes		Yes	NA	NA
Mandatory shareholder approval of interested transactions	Protects against abuse and squandering of company assets by insiders	Yes	Yes	Yes	Yes	Yes	NA	NA
Preemptive rights on new stock issues	Protects against dilution of minority shareholders; prevents insiders from altering ownership structure	Yes	Yes		Yes	Yes	NA	NA
Proxy voting	Facilitates shareholders' control	Yes	No	Yes	Yes	Yes	No	Yes
Penalties for insider trading	Protects against use of undisclosed information at the expense of current and potential shareholders	Yes	Yes	Yes	Yes	Yes		
Provisions on takeover legislation	Protects against violation of minority shareholders' rights	Yes		Yes	Yes	Yes		
Mandatory disclosure of nonfinancial information	Both financial and nonfinancial information data are important in assessment of a company's prospects.	Yes	Yes	Yes		Yes		
Mandatory disclosure of connected interests	Protects against abuse by insiders	Yes			Yes	Yes		
Mandatory shareholder approval of major transactions	Protects against abuse by insiders. Protection can be enhanced through supra-majority voting.	Yes	Yes	Yes	Yes	Yes	Yes	
One share–one vote	A basic right. Some shareholders may waive their voting rights for other benefits such as higher dividends.	Yes	No	Yes	No	No	Yes	No
Allows proxy by mail	Facilitates shareholders' control	Yes	No	No	No	No	No	No

Note: Blank denotes no regulation.

Source: Based on Stijn Claessens, Simon Djankov, and Larry Lang, *East Asian Corporates: Growth, Financing and Risks over the Last Decade* (World Bank, 1998).

Eᴀᴀɪʙɪᴛ **13.2**   Japanese Accounting Standards

Japanese requirements are based on the Commercial Code, the standards of the Business Accounting Deliberation Council, and statements of the Japanese Institute of Certified Public Accountants. Because March year-ends are the most common in Japan, this analysis is prepared on the basis of Japanese standards in force for accounting periods ending on March 31, 2002.

Japanese accounting may differ from that required by IAS because of the absence of specific Japanese rules on recognition and measurement in the following areas:

• The classification of business combinations as acquisitions or unitings of interest	IAS 22.8
• The setting up of provisions in the context of business combinations accounted for as acquisitions	IAS 22.31
• Impairment of assets	IAS 36
• The discounting of provisions	IAS 37.45
• The recognition of lease incentives	SIC 15
• Accounting for employee benefits other than severance indemnities	IAS 19

There are no specific rules requiring disclosures of:

• A primary statement of changes in equity	IAS 1.7
• The FIFO or current cost of inventories valued on the LIFO basis	IAS 2.36
• The fair values of investment properties	IAS 40.69
• Discontinuing operations	IAS 35
• Segment reporting of liabilities	IAS 14.56

There are inconsistencies between Japanese and IAS rules that could lead to differences for many enterprises in certain areas. Under Japanese rules:

• It is acceptable that overseas subsidiaries apply different accounting policies if they are appropriate under the requirements of the country of those subsidiaries.	IAS 27.21
• Under a temporary regulation, land can be revalued, but the revaluation does not need to be kept up to date.	IAS 16.29
• Preoperating costs can be capitalized.	IAS 38.57
• Leases, except those that transfer ownership to the lessee, can be treated as operating leases.	IAS 17.12/28
• Inventories can generally be valued at cost rather than at the lower of cost and net realizable value.	IAS 2.6
• Inventory cost can include overheads in addition to costs related to production.	IAS 2.6
• The completed contract method can be used for the recognition of revenues on construction contracts.	IAS 11.22
• Some trading liabilities are measured at fair value, but the category is not clearly defined.	IAS 39.93
• Provisions can be made on the basis of decisions by directors before an obligation arises.	IAS 37.14

Exhibit 13.2   Japanese Accounting Standards (cont.)

• Proposed dividends can be accrued in consolidated financial statements.	IAS 10.11
• The discount rate for employee benefit obligations can be adjusted to take account of fluctuations within the previous five years.	IAS 19.78
• The discount rate for employee benefit obligations can be adjusted to take account of fluctuations within the previous five years.	IAS 19.78
• Any past service cost of employee benefits is spread over the average service lives of active employees, even if the cost is vested.	IAS 19.96
• The portion of a convertible debenture that is in substance equity is not normally accounted for as such.	IAS 32.23
• Extraordinary items are defined more widely.	IAS 8.6/12
• Segment reporting does not use the primary/secondary basis.	IAS 14.26
In certain enterprises, these other issues could lead to differences from IAS:	
• It is possible, although unusual, for dissimilar subsidiaries to be excluded from consolidation if the consolidation of such subsidiaries would mislead stakeholders.	IAS 27.14
• There are no requirements concerning the translation of the financial statements of hyperinflationary subsidiaries.	IAS 21.36

Source: GAAP 2000: A Survey of National Accounting Rules in 53 Countries, pages 69–70, Copyright © 2000 PricewaterhouseCoopers LLP. Reprinted with permission.

The danger of high leverage is that if revenues fall as a consequence of declining demand, the company will not be able to pay its interest obligations and may become insolvent. In Korea, the weak financial structure of the corporate sector made it vulnerable to mass bankruptcies. Korea's debt-to-equity ratio (the ratio of debt to the underlying value of the company) for the thirty largest chaebols in 1995 was almost 350. These firms had borrowed an average of more than three times the company's net worth. Not all Asian countries have such high debt-to-equity ratios. In the same period, Taiwan's was only one-sixth of Korea's.[28]

Households in Asian countries have exceedingly high rates of savings. Thus, there should be a ready supply of capital for Asian businesses from domestic savings. Given the reluctance of households to invest in stocks as minority shareholders, their savings flow primarily into banks, if not abroad. For many years, most Japanese household savings automatically flowed into the state postal bank. In the European model, banks act as the primary financial intermediaries; therefore, the Asian flow of household savings into banks is similar to the European practice.

Figure 13.5 shows that Japanese households hold their financial assets in cash, deposits, and insurance funds, whereas U.S. households invest in stocks and bonds. The fact that Japanese households hold their substantial savings in banks and

FIGURE 13.5   Japan and U.S. Financial Assets of Households 2003

Japan: Household Financial Assets 2003 (percent)

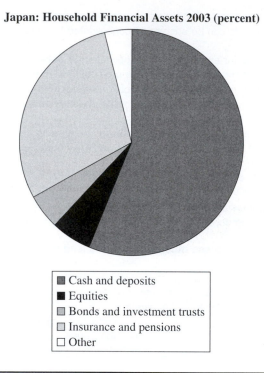

■ Cash and deposits
■ Equities
▨ Bonds and investment trusts
▢ Insurance and pensions
□ Other

insurance funds (as opposed to stock investments) gives banks and insurance companies huge funds to finance industrial investment. In 2009, financial institutions owned 32 percent of Japanese equities, while businesses owned 22 percent; individuals, 20 percent; and foreigners, 24 percent.[29]

To a greater degree than in Europe, Asian banks base their lending on political and industrial policy. For many years, Japan's powerful planning ministry (MITI, renamed METI) directed banks to lend to industries and companies singled out for development.

In Korea, banks were basically owned by the state until their privatization in 1982. Despite financial liberalization and deregulation, strong intervention continued as the government appointed CEOs of banks, and Korean banks continued to function like state-owned institutions.

In the Philippines, banks are owned by families, and there are weak laws to prevent them from serving as a "cash vault" of business groups.[30] In Taiwan, banks were tightly controlled by the government until the early 1990s. After 1992, the banking industry was deregulated, and the government placed restrictions on lending to affiliated groups.

Irrespective of their ownership, most Asian banks are not subject to strong supervision. In Japan, a large number of banks were technically insolvent in the early 2000s as a consequence of bad loans, many backed by real estate, the value

FIGURE **13.5**   Japan and U.S. Financial Assets of Households 2003 (cont.)

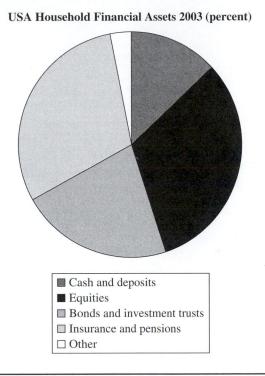

USA Household Financial Assets 2003 (percent)

- ▨ Cash and deposits
- ■ Equities
- ▧ Bonds and investment trusts
- ▣ Insurance and pensions
- ☐ Other

Source: Bank of Japan data.

of which had collapsed. Japan's banking regulatory agency, the Financial Services Agency, continues to support generous deposit insurance that prevents insolvent banks from being restructured and placed on a solid financial footing.

Throughout Asia, banks and other financial institutions are poorly regulated, and large financial institutions count on being bailed out by the government if they are threatened by insolvency. The promise of bailouts encourages bad and risky lending, thereby exacerbating the problems of the banking system. In Japan, the moral hazard problem can be traced to the government's practice of insuring virtually all accounts. Depositors see no risk in depositing their funds in poorly run banks, which are thus not punished for bad lending practices by bankruptcy.[31] A nation's capital market must be judged not only by how much investment finance it raises but also by how it distributes these funds among competing claimants.

Figure 13.6 provides striking evidence on rates of return on capital investments in manufacturing industries in Japan and the United States.[34] For the entire period 1986–2003, the rate of return to U.S. capital investment was markedly higher than in Japan. Rates of return in Japan seemed to be on a declining trend, while they fell in the United States during recessions and recovered thereafter. Differences were huge in the late 1990s, when returns approached zero in Japan and exceeded

FIGURE 13.6   Return on Equity (ROE) in Manufacturing, Japan and the United States

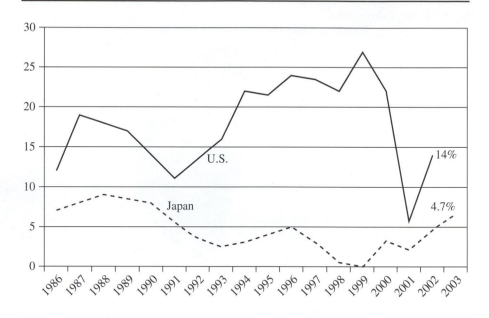

Source: Martin Schulz, "Changing the Rules of the Game: The Reform of (Corporate) Governance in Japan," Mar-04, FRI Research Report No.192, March 2004, p. 12.

20 percent in the United States. Although some blame the increased competition from China and rising wages for low Japanese manufacturing returns, the low Japanese returns suggest poor investment decision making in the capital market.[32]

Labor Markets

The Anglo-Saxon "hire and fire" labor market is flexible and moves labor resources from one activity to another quickly. The European model replaces the Anglo-Saxon model with a highly regulated labor market that makes firing difficult and imposes rules on employment practices.

There are economic theories that claim that more inflexible labor markets may actually be more efficient. Workers who have implicit contracts that promise them long tenure are more loyal to the firm and are willing to get training specific to the firm. Workers who are paid a "fair" wage exert more effort on behalf of the firm, and the fair wage may be above the current market wage. Such views are, however, in the minority. Any system that freezes labor to jobs will eventually result in inefficient allocations of labor.

The Asian labor market has some features of both the Anglo-Saxon and the European labor markets, with the added twist of paternalism toward workers that may be traced back to Confucian philosophy. Labor markets in Asia are the consequence of various forces: Most Asian countries were, at some point in time, under colonial rule or external occupation. These external powers "transplanted" some or all of the labor market regulations into the Asian countries over which they had dominance. These external rules had to contend with local cultural, social, and political morays, resulting in a gap between formal law and practice.[33]

Asian countries, with the exception of ineligible Taiwan, are members of the International Labor Organization (ILO), and ILO membership imposes certain regulatory obligations on all its members. With different backgrounds and histories, there is considerable diversity in Asian labor-market regulation, both in law and in practice.

Labor Market Protection   Unlike in Europe, and with the clear exception of South Korea, unions and employment protection have been weak in Asia. In Japan, labor unions tend to be enterprise unions (such as the Sony union) and do not represent economy-wide branches or crafts. A number of authoritarian governments banned labor unions in the early postwar period, and unions were banned in Japan prior to World War II. In most Asian countries, workers are less protected from "hire and fire" provisions, but they may receive the protection afforded by paternalistic attitudes toward the workforce—workers are regarded as part of an extended family.

Figure 13.7 provides measures of labor market protection in Asia, Europe, and Anglo-Saxon countries. It shows workers in the Anglo-Saxon economies with the

FIGURE 13.7   OECD Index of Labor Market Protection: Asian, European, and Anglo-Saxon Countries

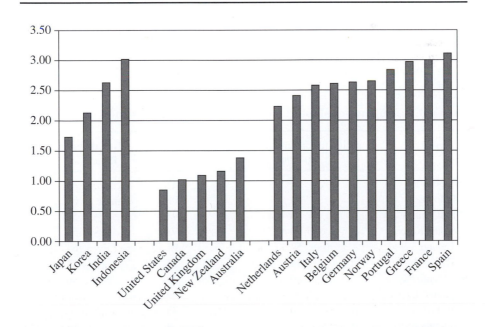

Source: Based on data from OECD statistics.

least amount of protection in the form of dismissal protection, rules against temporary employment, and group dismissals. The European economies clearly have the most labor-market protection. We have few observations of protection of Asian labor markets. The more advanced Asian economies (Korea and Japan) are located between Anglo-Saxon and European levels, but the less advanced (India and Indonesia) have labor-market protections equivalent to Europe.

We do not know the extent to which labor legislation rules are actually observed in the various Asian countries. There are substantial differences between rules and practice, especially in lower-income Asian countries, such as India or Indonesia.

Table 13.5 provides more detailed data on employment protection within East Asia broken down by type of political system. It shows that Asian democracies offer more employment protection than semidemocracies in terms of rigidity of employment, weeks required to execute a firing, and de jure employment protection. Singapore, which is classified as a semidemocracy, has the least amount of protection in its labor markets, whereas Thailand has the most flexible of the democratic labor markets. The number of Asian countries for which we have measures, however, is too small to draw firm conclusions.

Table 13.6 provides richer data on unionization and the prevalence of collective bargaining in Asia versus Europe and Anglo-Saxon countries. With the exception of Taiwan, Asian countries have rates of unionization generally similar to the Anglo-Saxon countries, but well below the unionization rates of Europe. There are even more substantial differences in the prevalence of collective bargaining. Relatively few labor contracts are covered by collective bargaining in Asia, whereas most labor contracts are covered by collective bargaining in Europe. The Anglo-Saxon countries have lesser coverage by collective bargaining than in Europe but more coverage than in Asia.

The lack of collective bargaining means that workers bargain individually with employers. Without collective bargaining and its threat of strikes, we suspect that Asian workers have less bargaining power than in Europe and in the Anglo-Saxon world.

TABLE 13.5 Employment Protection by Type of Political System East Asia

	Rigidity of Employment (0–100)	Cost of Firing (in weeks)	De Jure Employment Protection (0–100)
Democracies	37	87	55
Indonesia	44	108	60
Philippines	35	91	55
South Korea	34	91	54
Taiwan	53	91	64
Thailand	18	54	42
Semidemocracies	20	39	36
Cambodia	49	39	55
Malaysia	10	75	40
Singapore	0	4	13

Source: Terry Caraway, "Labor Rights in East Asia: Progress or Regress?" *Journal of East Asian Studies* Volume 9, Issue 2 (2009), 153–186.

TABLE 13.6   Unions and Collective Bargaining: Asia and Other Countries

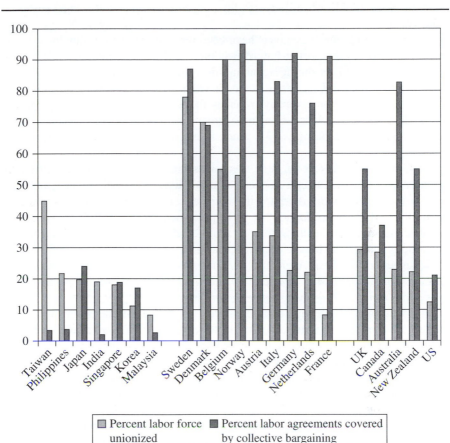

Percent labor force unionized

Percent labor agreements covered by collective bargaining

Source: Based on Sarosh Kuruvilla et al., "Trade Union Growth and Decline in Asia," Cornell University ILR School, 9-1-2002 DigitalCommons@ILS.cornell.edu/ See also Terry Caraway, "Labor Rights in East Asia: Progress or Regress?" *Journal of East Asian Studies* 9 (2009), 153–186.

Affluent Singapore's labor laws feature Asia's most unregulated labor markets. Singapore's "liberal" Employment Act simply limits the work week to forty-four hours and specifies one and one-half times regular pay for overtime. New employees are allowed one week of annual leave and one additional day for each year of service, up to a maximum of fourteen days per year. Employees can be dismissed on one day's notice if they have been employed for less than twenty-six weeks and on four weeks' notice if they have been employed for five years or more.[34]

Paternalism, Lifetime Jobs, and the Share Economy   The stereotype of the postwar Japanese labor market is that of an implicit lifetime labor contract between those working for a large company and the company itself. *An **implicit lifetime labor contract** is an unwritten understanding that employees will keep their* *jobs over the entire course of their working years.* Thus a college graduate hired by Sony or Mitsubishi expects lifetime employment at the company as a "salaryman."

Lifetime employment contracts have been regarded both as a plus for the system (increased loyalty, better-trained workers) and as a minus (companies are unable to shed workers during economic downturns). Indeed, tenure at Japanese firms is longer than in U.S. firms. In the United States, the average male employee spends 7.5 years in one company, whereas the average Japanese male employee spends 12.9 years. The longest Japanese tenures are in large companies. The average tenure in manufacturing is 13.1 years; in electricity, gas, and water, it is 17.3 years.[35]

Established employees of large companies are, in effect, guaranteed lifetime employment. They are taught to think of the company as their family, and they believe that if they work hard for the company, the company will take care of them. John M. Montias found that this "permanent employment" constraint on Japanese management is likely to alter resource-allocation patterns.[36] Indeed, the Japanese economy has been characterized as a share economy, based on a framework suggested by Martin Weitzman.[37] A ***share economy*** *is one in which employees share the risks of the company by having bonuses, based on profits, as a substantial component of their compensation.*

Japanese workers receive bonuses twice a year. The summer bonus is usually the larger of the two. It is not uncommon for Japanese workers to receive $4,000 to $8,000 (or more) for their summer bonuses, which they use to pay for expensive vacations or other purchases. Insofar as bonuses are based on company performance, they tend to lessen the shocks of business downturns. Labor costs fall automatically during downturns and rise pro-cyclically with recovery. Prominent economists who have studied the Japanese bonus system conclude it increases the macroeconomic stability of the economy.[38] Other economists conclude that the bonus system is limited to a minority of Japanese workers and hence has less of an impact on the economy as one might expect.[39] In the Japanese case, the difference between appearance and substance may be considerable.[40]

First, only a minority—20 to 30 percent—of the Japanese labor force are covered by guaranteed employment. The share of workers in industrial core jobs is declining. But the probability of job separations has remained stable for those who are already in the system.[41] Among core employees of Japanese firms, lifetime employment has not changed much over time. The ten-year job retention rate was around 80 percent for the bubble period of 1977–1987. The situation changed little for the post-bubble period of 1987–1997. Approximately four in five core employees of Japanese firms in 1987 survived the turbulent years of the Japanese economy and retained the same job ten years later.

As in Europe, the Japanese (and Korean) labor markets have divided into a two-tier system. In the top-tier positions are the full-time employees of large corporations who enjoy protected job status. In the bottom tier are mainly younger workers who work part-time jobs or lack permanent status, who move from job to job. In Japan, younger employees (ages 20–24 and 25–29) and middle-age employees with short tenure (ages 30–34, 35–39, and 40–44 with 0–4 years of tenure) saw their job retention rates falling noticeably.[42] More than 30 percent of the Japanese labor force in 1992 had part-time jobs.[43] In both Japan and South Korea, derivations of the German word for work (*Arbeit*; Japanese, *Arubaito*) are used to describe low-level temporary jobs occupied largely by young people. With the exception of large corporations, Japanese and Korean firms lay off employees readily. Large firms retire employees early.

Prior to World War II, Japanese companies, large and small, did not hesitate to fire or lay off employees. If lifetime employment had deep-rooted cultural causes, they would have been in effect in this earlier period as well. According to current Japanese labor law, employees cannot be fired unless the company is prepared to argue that it will otherwise fail. Small firms are willing to make such assertions, but large firms are not.[44]

The greater flexibility of the Japanese labor market than its share economy stereotype suggests is supported by its lower unemployment rates, even during periods of economic downturn. Japan's unemployment rate stood at 4.6 percent in December 2011. From 1953 until 2010, it averaged 2.6 percent. These are unemployment figures that would be the envy of the rest of the world.

In the rigid European labor market, unemployment rates are high during normal periods but worsen during economic downturns. Those outside the European job-tenure system simply cannot find work. In Japan, there is apparently enough flexibility, through part-time work and contracting to smaller firms, for the labor market to respond to economic downturns.

Income Distribution

As we have seen, East Asia recorded remarkable economic growth from 1965 to the present. One of the often-overlooked aspects of this growth is that the East Asian economies have combined high growth with relatively low and declining inequality of income.

Figure 13.8 is a scatter diagram for forty economies, showing the relationship between economic growth and income inequality as measured by the ratio of the income share of the richest 20 percent to that of the poorest 20 percent of the population. As the figure shows, there are seven high-growth–low-income-equality countries, and all seven are in East Asia. The East Asian economies began their era of rapid growth with relatively even distributions of income, and most of them have ended with a more nearly equal distribution than when they started.[45] As the author of a substantial survey of the East Asian growth experience comments, "East Asian economies have relatively equal income distributions, and growth in the region is especially noteworthy in that it has not been at the expense of equity."[46]

How was it that East Asia was able to combine growth and equity? One factor has been that the governments of the region adopted policies to ensure that all groups benefited from economic growth. These programs included universal education and public-housing programs, land reform, and control of fertilizer and agricultural prices to raise rural incomes. History also contributed to the more nearly equal distribution of income: Japan's defeat in World War II, the destruction during the

FIGURE 13.8   Income Inequality and Growth of GDP, 1965–1989

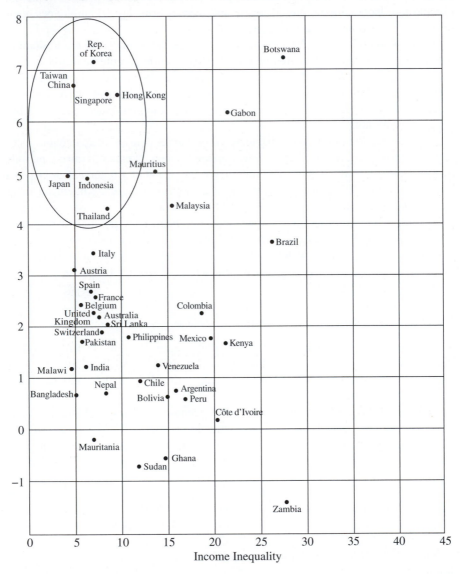

GDP growth per capita (percent)

Note: Income inequality is measured by the ratio of the income share of the richest 20 percent to the income share of the poorest 20 percent of the population.

Source: World Bank data.

Korean War, and the defeat of the Chinese nationalist forces made possible rural land reform and eliminated the property assets of the elite.[47] East Asia's relatively equitable distributions of income may contribute to their more rapid growth. Less inequality usually means greater political stability. It also means a more equitable distribution of education. A high degree of income inequality may promote labor unrest and political conflict, both of which inflict greater risks on the economy and raise the cost of capital.[48] The most likely cause of low income inequality is the more even distribution of human capital (education and health) in Asia.

Industrial Policy

Japan was the pioneer of the Asian brand of industrial policy. The government has played an important role in the Japanese economy since the early years of industrialization.[49] The Japanese ministerial structure has a substantial impact on the economy, not only through direct participation in key aspects of economic life but also through its indirect influence. The Ministry of Finance, along with the Bank of Japan, has been responsible for the traditional functions of monetary control. In the outside world, however, it has been the Ministry of International Trade and Industry (MITI, recently renamed METI) that receives the most attention.[50]

Japan's Ministry of International Trade and Industry (MITI, renamed METI) was responsible for Japan's industrial policy. The close relationships among manufacturing, banks, and government meant that banks could allocate capital on the basis of an implicit industrial policy. Prior to 1998, this meant that Japanese enterprises were virtually guaranteed cheap capital through the banking system.

MITI is responsible for international trade, domestic production, and domestic industrial structure. MITI is the purveyor of an "industrial policy" geared to promoting rapid economic growth. MITI is responsible for guiding and influencing economic decisions by promoting key sectors of the economy and endeavoring to phase out low-productivity sectors. MITI uses public funds for research and development and provides assistance for organizational change, such as mergers.

Traditional measures of government involvement do not capture the essence of the Japanese system. In the absence of a major formal role for government and planning, the government is nevertheless able to influence both short- and long-term decision making. Rather than formal and powerful involvement in a few traditional and noticeable areas, the government exerts its influence through a myriad of arrangements that guide economic growth. Enthusiasts of an industrial policy cite the Japanese experience.

The 1960s saw a worldwide admiration and fascination for Japan's industrial policy, which seemed skilled at picking winners—such as automobiles, trucks, and electronics—that captured world market share. In a time of general economic turmoil, the Japanese were perceived to have found the keys to sustained economic growth.[51] The 1970s, however, were not a tranquil decade for the Japanese economy. In the early 1970s, Japan sustained two major shocks. The first was the end of a long-fixed exchange rate between the American dollar and the Japanese yen and the move toward a flexible exchange rate. The second event was the energy crisis of 1973. The average annual rate of growth of real GDP declined from above 10 percent in the late 1960s to generally lower rates in the mid-1970s. The average annual rate of inflation reached almost 25 percent in 1974. Other performance indicators showed similar trends. Output per labor-hour in manufacturing declined, and manufacturing unit costs increased dramatically. The late 1970s brought on a second, less severe energy crisis and (possibly more important) a sharply increasing positive balance on the current account. Once again, the problem of balancing Japanese–American trade became a major issue.

Japan's dramatic decline in economic performance in the 1990s dimmed the luster of the Japanese model. The reliance on large industrial conglomerates has been seen to inhibit competition and to retard the growth of smaller and more innovative businesses. The intimate relationship between banks and large industrial concerns has caused banks (often prompted by government) to make large, unprofitable loans. The cozy relationship between government and business has created a vast system of corruption, where more than half of Japan's business enterprises have admitted to breaking the law in order to conduct their routine business operations. The close link between government and business has spawned campaign-funding abuses more severe than those encountered in the United States. The lifetime employment offered by Japan's large industrial concerns has prevented them from downsizing to become more efficient in the world marketplace.

Japan's famous industrial policy—the attempt on the part of the state bureaucracy to pick upcoming industrial winners—has also been questioned. An example is the Japanese government's ill-fated decision to promote high-definition television too early. Japan still lags well behind the United States in technological innovation, a gap that many attribute to the Japanese economic system.

The declining reputation of Japanese industrial policy did not prevent its spread into other parts of Asia and throughout the world. The industrial policies of the Four Tigers had one consistent theme—the promotion of exports. In this regard, South Korea is fairly typical.[52] Korean industrial policy aimed at promoting exports and fostering infant industries that had the potential to export. This policy was executed through a virtual free-trade regime for export activity (capital and intermediate goods could be imported without tariffs) and the allocation of credits through government control of banks. The government set quarterly export targets and gave large-scale establishments temporary monopolies and preferential access to credits, rewarding them according to the proportion of output that they succeeded in exporting.

Malaysia under Prime Minister Mahathir Mohamad in the 1980s and early 1990s embarked on an ambitious industrial policy program that called for manufacturing high-tech commercial aircraft. China has conducted industrial policy throughout its reform period as the central government controls and promotes industrial and commercial "national champions."

Promotion of exports has been an extremely important aspect of Asian industrial policy. Asian firms that tied their fate to the export market and to competition according to world market prices had to learn how to compete and how to introduce the technology that would allow them to do so. Countries that used industrial policy to protect their domestic industries effectively cut themselves off from these competitive signals and languished.

We cannot decisively judge the extent to which industrial policy helps (or as some claim hurts) Asian economic growth. Asia has grown for a number of reasons. Critics of industrial policy, however, have a strong case when they doubt that government bureaucrats can pick winners better than the private sector.

Provision of Income Security

One of the prime features of the European model is its generous provision of income security for practically everyone. Sweden served as the extreme example of the European welfare state, but other Western European countries did not lag far behind in terms of benefits. Providing for the public welfare is focused principally on the health and pensions of the aged, although the provision of health care by the state has become an increasingly important factor in Europe and in the United States.

The demand for old-age security depends in part on the age structure of the population. Figure 13.9 shows that all the Asian countries except Japan have a young population. Less than 5 percent of their populations are 65 and older. In Japan, Europe, and the United States, the proportion of older people is much greater.

Partially as a consequence of the different age structure of the population, the Asian countries have a much smaller welfare state. And despite having an age structure that is quite similar to that of Europe, Japan has social security contributions that (as a percent of wage income) are about half of Europe's.

FIGURE **13.9**   The Welfare State: The Asian Model in Perspective

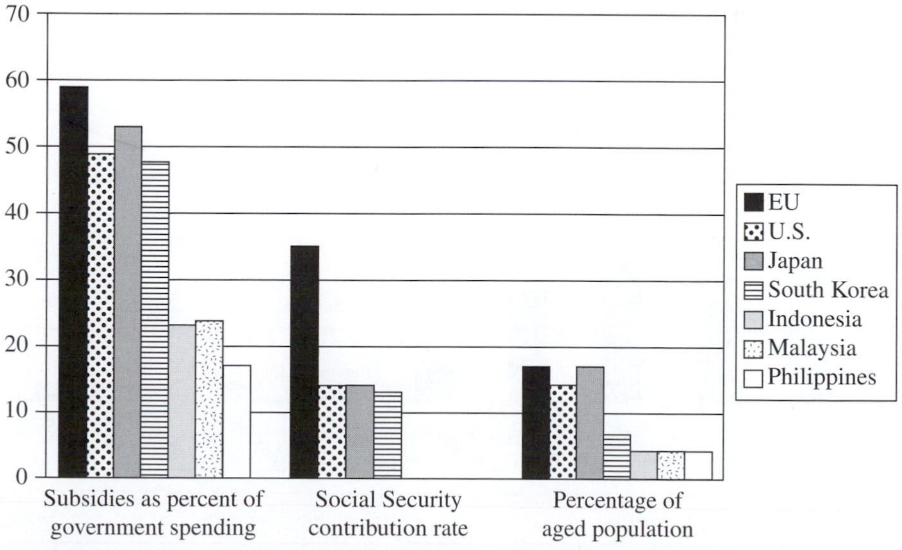

Legend: ■ EU, ▨ U.S., ▦ Japan, ▤ South Korea, ▥ Indonesia, ▨ Malaysia, ☐ Philippines

Categories: Subsidies as percent of government spending; Social Security contribution rate; Percentage of aged population

Sources: World Bank, "Role of Government in the Economy," in *World Development Report; Statistical Abstract of the United States,* International Statistics.

Figure 13.10 shows the huge differences in social security and welfare expenditures as a percent of GDP in Asia versus the United States and Europe. Whereas a high-income European country like France devotes 30 percent of its GDP to social security and welfare and the United State 20 percent, the Asian countries, with the exception of Japan, devote minor shares of GDP to the uses.

Japan did not have a public pension system until 1961, after three-quarters of a century of industrialization. It also did not have public health insurance until 1961, and the system in effect discriminates sharply between employees and those out of the labor force or self-employed. From a European perspective, "Japanese welfare services remain underdeveloped.... Japanese social protection services are still limited compared to other developed countries. But their potential volume is already similar to continental European countries."[53]

The affluent Singapore is an exception to the rule of limited social security protection, but it has relied on a private-market solution.[54] All Singapore employees are required to contribute to a Central Provident Fund for retirement. The contributed funds are invested in Singapore government securities or approved listed stocks. Employees may use these funds to purchase property and also to pay educational expenses. In effect, the contributed funds belong to the contributor and are

FIGURE 13.10   Social Security and Welfare Payments as a Percent of GDP

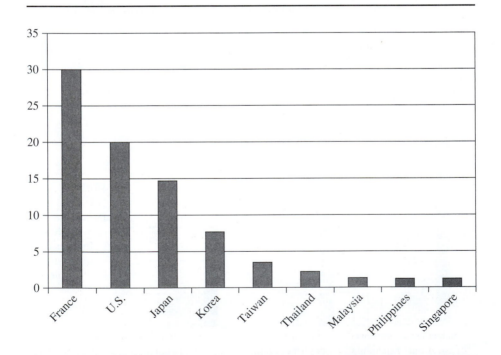

Sources: OECD database, http://www.oecd.org/document/9/0,3746,en_2649_34637_38141385_1_1_1_1,00. html; Asian Development Bank database, https://sdbs.adb.org/sdbs/index.jsp.

intended to be used for retirement and for major investments. A Medisave account is part of the Provident Fund. Each contributor has a medical fund to be used as a standby for exceptional medical expenses. At age 55, the contributor can withdraw his or her fund after setting aside a minimum amount in a retirement account. Thus Singapore has a "privatized" social security system, the cost of which is a 25 percent contribution by the employee and a 15 percent contribution by the employer.

The lesser role of the welfare state in the Asian model can also be attributed to cultural factors and tradition. Confucianism and other Asian religions emphasize the role of the family and the obligation of younger generations to take care of family elders in their retirement years. These cultural norms have been gradually breaking down as Asian countries industrialize and urbanize, but they remain strong.

Because of the relative lack of public pension protection, private households must provide for their own old age, either by relying on their children for assistance or by saving for their own retirement. The high rates of savings that characterize the Asian model are often ascribed to the absence of such a pay-as-you-go retirement system as prevails in Europe and the United States.

Summary

- The Asian model was developed in Japan and China in isolation from Western influence. It is based on history and religion, largely Confucianism, which teaches a positive role for virtuous government. Asian economic development is described by the relative backwardness model of Alexander Gerschenkron.
- The Asian model is characterized by rapid growth fostered by high rates of capital formation. Japan experienced rapid and accelerating growth through the 1970s, and the Four Asian Tigers began to grow rapidly in the 1960s and 1970s.
- The Asian model is characterized by corporations closely held by wealthy families or small groups of individuals, by relational rather than market-based contracting, and by the relatively small role of widely held, publicly traded corporations.
- Asian corporations tend to obtain their financing from banks that are closely related to the enterprises themselves. Asian banks tend to be loosely regulated.
- The Asian labor market combines the limited regulation of the Anglo-Saxon model with paternalistic practices that protect employment during downturns. Paternalism appears to characterize large firms more than small firms, which have considerable flexibility in hiring and firing.
- The Asian model has combined high growth with a relatively even distribution of income.
- Many Asian economies have used heavy-handed industrial policy combined with consistent promotion of export.
- The Asian model has largely rejected the European model of state provision of income and healthy security. The Asian countries' public spending on health is relatively low.

Key Terms

Confucianism—Emphasizes the qualities of loyalty, nationalism, social solidarity, collectivism, benevolence, faith, and bravery.

export promotion—State policies to promote exports. Such policies range from subsidies of export industries to free-trade practices for the economy as a whole.

Gerschenkron's theory of substitutions—Backward countries could find innovative substitutions for missing preconditions.

highly leveraged companies—Heavy debt burdens relative to equity, which must be serviced by regular interest and principal payments.

implicit lifetime labor contract—An unwritten understanding that employees will keep their jobs over the entire course of their working years.

import substitution—Policies that protect domestic industries from foreign competition via tariffs or other barriers.

Japan's economic miracle—Exceptional growth in the first three decades after World War II.

Japan's Ministry of International Trade and Industry (MITI, renamed METI)—Responsible for Japan's industrial policy.

keiretsu—Horizontal or vertical conglomerates with large banks at their center.

market-based contracting—An impersonal form of contracting based on formal contracts backed by a rule of law.

Meiji Restoration in 1868—Replaced the military regime with a new government of progressive officials determined to embark on modernization.

net foreign investment—When a country's national savings rate exceeds its domestic investment rate.

propping—Financial and other support given by the more profitable units of the conglomerate to support sister units.

relational contracting—Based not on a formal rule of law but on personal relationships and trust.

share economy—Employees share the risks of the company by having bonuses, based on profits, as a substantial component of their compensation.

theory of relative backwardness—Backward countries grossly underutilizing resources take steps to accelerate economic growth to catch up to more advanced rivals.

tunneling—Awarding of contract to firms, individuals, or interests that are insiders to the conglomerate.

unifying features of the Asian model—The high rates of savings and investment and the distinctive organization of capital markets and corporate governance.

virtuous government—As taught by Confucianism suggested a significant and positive role for government in the economy.

zaibatsu—Vertical or horizontal conglomerates that dominated Japanese industry and commerce before World War II.

Notes

1. Lee-Jay Cho and Yoon Hyung Kim, "Political and Economic Antecedents," in Lee-Jay Cho and Yoon Hyung Kim, eds., *Economic Development in the Republic of Korea: A Policy Perspective* (Honolulu: East–West Center, 1991), pp. 3–9.

2. This historical section is largely based on W. G. Beasley, *The Rise of Modern Japan* (New York: St. Martin's, 1995), chaps. 1–6, p. 55.

3. Lee-Kay Cho, "Culture, Institutions, and Economic Development in East Asia," in Lee-Jay Cho and Yoon-Hyung Kim, *Korea's Political Economy* (Boulder, Colo.: Westview, 1991), pp. 5–19.

4. Sean Cooney at al, *Law and labour market regulation in East Asia* (London: Rutledge, 2002), p. 14.

5. Alexander Gerschenkron, *Economic Backwardness in Historical Perspective* (Cambridge, Mass.: Harvard University Press, 1965).

6. Cho and Kim, "Political and Economic Antecedents," pp. 6–7.

7. Angus Maddison, *The World Economy: A Millennial Perspective* (Paris: OECD, 2001); and http://www.OECD.org.

8. For a survey of Japanese economic growth, see Kazushi Ohkawa and Henry Rosovsky, *Japanese Economic Growth* (Stanford, Calif.: Stanford University Press, 1973), chap. 2.

9. Various aspects of the Japanese labor market are discussed in G. C. Allen, *The Japanese Economy* (London: Weidenfeld and Nicolson, 1981), chap. 9; Taira, *Economic Development*.

10. For a survey of organizational features of the Japanese economic system, see Kanji Haitani, *The Japanese Economic System* (Lexington, Mass.: Heath, 1976).

11. Ohkawa and Rosovsky, *Japanese Economic Growth*, chap. 5.

12. In addition to Taira, *Economic Development*, see Robert E. Cole, *Japanese Blue-Collar: The Changing Tradition* (Berkeley: University of California Press, 1971); for a summary, see Robert E. Cole, "Industrial Relations in Japan," in Morris Bornstein, ed., *Comparative Economic Systems, Models and Cases*, 3rd ed. (Homewood, Ill.: Irwin, 1974), pp. 93–116.

13. RealOnlineDegrees.com, "Education Rankings by Country," http://www.realonlinedegrees.com/education-rankings-by-country/.

14. World Bank, *World Development Report 1987* (Oxford: Oxford University Press, 1987).

15. Sebastian Edwards, "Openness, Trade Liberalization and Growth in Developing Countries," *Journal of Economic Literature* 31 (September 1993), 1387.

16. Ronald Lee, Andrew Mason, and Timothy Miller, "Saving, Wealth, and the Demographic Transition in East Asia," Conference on Population and the East Asian Miracle, Program on Population, East-West Center, Honolulu, Hawaii, January 7–10, 1997; Jeffrey Williamson and Mathew Higgins, "The Accumulation and Demography Connection in East Asia," Andrew Mason, ed., *Population and the East Asian Miracle* (East-West Center Working Papers, Population Series, No. 88-24, August 1997).

17. Geoffrey Carliner, "Comment on Anne Krueger, 'East Asian Experience and Endogenous Growth Theory,'" in Taakatoshi Ito and Anne Krueger, eds., *Growth Theories in Light of the East Asian Experience* (Chicago: University of Chicago Press, 1995), pp. 30–33; and Joseph Stiglitz and Marilow Uy, "Financial Markets, Public Policy, and the East Asian Miracle," *World Bank Research Observer* 1, no. 2 (August 1996), 249–276.

18. Robert Barro and Xavier Sala-l-Martin, *Economic Growth* (New York: McGraw-Hill, 1995).

19. Carl Kester, *Japanese Takeovers: The Global Contest for Corporate Control* (Boston, 1991); Martin Schulz, "The Reform of (Corporate) Governance in Japan," in *Japan: How to Overcome the Difficult Decade*, Vierteljahrshefte zur Witschaftsforschung, Heft 4, no. 70; Martin Schulz, "Changing the Rules of the Game: The Reform of (Corporate) Governance in Japan," Mar-04, FRI Research Report No.192, March 2004.

20. Kozo Yamamura, "Entrepreneurship, Ownership and Management in Japan," in M. M. Postan et al., *Cambridge Economic History of Europe*, Vol. 7, Part 2 (Cambridge: Cambridge University Press, 1978), pp. 215–264. See also Eleanor M. Hadley, *Antitrust in Japan* (Princeton, N.J.: Princeton University Press, 1970); Richard E. Caves and Masu Uekusa, *Industrial Organizations in Japan* (Washington, D.C.: Brookings Institution, 1976); and Kanji Haitani, *The Japanese Economic System* (Lexington, Mass.: Heath, 1976).

21. Il Chong Nam, Yeongjae Kang, and Joon-Kyong Kim, "Comparative Corporate Governance Trends in Asia," *Korea Development Institute*, December 1999.

22. "World Banker Assails Indonesia's Corruption," *New York Times*, August 28, 2002.

23. "Proxy Fight to Redress Tokyo Style," *Wall Street Journal*, May 13, 2002.

24. "The Korea Discount: Corporate Governance Explains Korea's Law Stock Market Ratings," *The Economist*, February 11, 2012.

25. "The Korea Discount."

26. Schulz, *The Reform of (Corporate) Governance*, p. 528.

27. Schulz, *The Reform of (Corporate) Governance*, p. 528–537.

28. Joon-Kyung Kim and Chung H. Lee, "Insolvency in the Corporate Sector and Financial Crisis in Korea," *Journal of the Asian Pacific Economy* 7, no. 2 (2002).

29. Tokyo Stock Exchange Factbook 2010, http://www.tse.or.jp/english/market/data/factbook/b7gje60000003o32-att/fact_book_2010.pdf.

30. Nam, Kang, and Kim, "Comparative Corporate Governance Trends in Asia."

31. "Rough Start for Regulator in Japan," *New York Times*, World Business, August 23, 2002.

32. Kim and Lee, "Insolvency in the Corporate Sector and Financial Crisis in Korea."

33. Sean Cooney et al., *Law and Labour Market Regulation in East Asia* (London: Rutledge, 2002).

34. Geoffrey Murray and Audrey Perera, *Singapore: The Global City State* (New York: St. Martin's, 1996), pp. 231–233.

35. These figures are cites in Y. Miwa and J. M. Ramsauer, "The Myth of the Main Bank, Japan, and Comparative Corporate Governance," Harvard Law School, Discussion Paper 333, September 2001.

36. John M. Montias, *The Structure of Economic Systems* (New Haven: Yale University Press, 1976), Part 5.

37. Martin Weitzman, *The Share Economy* (Cambridge, Mass.: Harvard University Press, 1984).

38. Richard Freeman and Martin Weitzman, "Bonuses and Employment in Japan," NBER Working Paper No. 187, Issued in February 1989.

39. Merton J. Peck, "Is Japan Really a Share Economy?" *Journal of Comparative Economics* 10 (1986), 427–432.

40. Gregory B. Christiansen and Jan S. Hagendorn, "Japanese Productivity: Adapting to Changing Comparative Advantage in the Face of Lifetime Employment Commitments," *Quarterly Review of Business and Economics* 23 (Summer 1983), 23–39. For a discussion of the labor–management issue in a growth context, see Harry Oshima, "Reinterpreting Japan's Postwar Growth," *Economic Development and Cultural Change* 31 (October 1982), 1–43.

41. Hiroshi Ono, "Lifetime Employment in Japan: Concepts and Measurements," Stockholm School of Economics, October 2005, http://www.japanfocus.org/data/Ono.pdf.

42. Takao Kato, "The End of Lifetime Employment in Japan: Evidence from National Surveys and Field Research," *Journal of the Japanese and International Economies* 15 (2001), 489–514.

43. Susan Houseman and Machiko Osawa, "Part Time and Temporary Employment in Japan," *Monthly Labor Review* (October 1995), 12.

44. Christiansen and Hagendorn, "Japanese Productivity," p. 30.

45. World Bank, *The East Asian Miracle: Economic Growth and Public Policy* (Oxford: Oxford University Press, 1993), Fig. 1.3, p. 31; Fig. 3, p. 4.

46. John Bauer, "Economic Growth and Policy in East Asia," Conference on Population and the Asian Economic Miracle, Program on Population, East-West Center, Honolulu, Hawaii, January 7–10, 1997.

47. D. H. Perkins, "There Are at Least Three Models of East Asian Development," *World Development* 4 (April 1994), 655–662.

48. For a discussion of income distribution and growth, see Vito Tanzi and Ke-young Chu, eds., *Income Distribution and High-Quality Growth* (Cambridge Mass.: MIT Press, 1998).

49. Assessing the role of government in the importance of the "public" sector in the Japanese economy is difficult for definitional reasons. For a discussion, see Chalmers Johnson, *Japan's Public Policy Companies* (Washington, D.C.: American Enterprise Institute, 1978).

50. Much has been written about MITI. For basics, see Haitani, *The Japanese Economic System*. For more detail, see Chalmers Johnson, *MITI and the Japanese Miracle* (Stanford, Calif.: Stanford University Press, 1982); and Christiansen and Hagendorn, "Japanese Productivity."

51. For a more skeptical view of MITI in the 1970s, see Kozo Yamamura, "Success That Soured: Administrative Guidance and Cartels in Japan," in Kozo Yamamura, ed., *Policy and Trade Issues of the Japanese Economy* (Seattle: University of Washington Press, 1982), pp. 77–112. On the role of the state in supporting key sectors, see also Gary R. Saxonhouse, "What Is All This About 'Industrial Targeting' in Japan?" *World Economy* 6 (September 1983), 253–273.

52. Larry Westphal, "Industrial Policy in an Export-Propelled Economy: Lesson from the South Korean Experience," *Journal of Economic Perspectives* 4 (Summer 1990), pp. 41–60.

53. Tetsuo Fukawa, "Japanese Welfare State Reforms in the 1990s and Beyond: How Japan Is Similar to and Different from Germany," in *Japan: How to Overcome the Difficult Decade*, p. 572.

54. Geoffrey Murray and Audrey Perera, *Singapore: The Global City State* (New York: St. Martin's, 1996), pp. 231–233.

Recommended Readings

Japan

J. G. Abegglen, *The Japanese Factory* (Glencoe, Ill.: Free Press, 1958).

G. C. Allen, *The Japanese Economy* (London: Weidenfeld and Nicolson, 1981).

W. G. Beasley, *The Rise of Modern Japan*, 2nd ed. (New York: St. Martin's, 1995).

Thomas F. Cargill, Michael M. Hurchison, and Takatoshi Ito, *The Political Economy of Japanese Monetary Policy* (Cambridge, Mass.: MIT Press, 1997).

Edward F. Denison and William K. Chung, *How Japan's Economy Grew So Fast: The Sources of Postwar Expansion* (Washington, D.C.: Brookings Institution, 1976).

Ronald Dore, *Flexible Rigidities* (London: Athlone Press, 1986).

Kanji Haitani, *The Japanese Economic System* (Lexington, Mass.: Heath, 1976).

Christopher Hause, *The Origins of Japanese Trade Supremacy: Development and Technology in Asia from 1540 to the Pacific War* (Chicago: University of Chicago Press, 1996).

Ronald I. McKinnon and Kenichi Ohno, *Dollar and Yen: Resolving Economic Conflict Between the United States and Japan* (Cambridge, Mass.: MIT Press, 1997).

Toru Iwami, *Japan in the International Financial System* (New York: St. Martin's, 1996).

Japanese Economic Research Center, *Economic Growth: The Japanese Experience Since the Meiji Era*, Vols. I and II (Tokyo: Japanese Economic Research Center, 1973).

Chalmers Johnson, *Japan's Public Policy Companies* (Washington, D.C.: American Enterprise Institute, 1978).

———, *MITI and the Japanese Miracle* (Stanford, Calif.: Stanford University Press, 1982).

Lawrence Klein and Kazushi Ohkawa, eds., *Economic Growth: The Japanese Experience Since the Meiji Era* (Homewood, Ill.: Irwin, 1968).

Edward J. Lincoln, *Japan: Facing Economic Maturity* (Washington, D.C.: Brookings Institution, 1988).

William Lockwood, ed., *The State and Economic Enterprise in Japan* (Princeton, N.J.: Princeton University Press, 1965).

Angus Maddison, *Economic Growth in Japan and the USSR* (London: Allen and Unwin, 1969).

Ryoshim Minami, Kwan S. Kim, Fumio Makino, and Joung-Hae Seo, *Acquisition, Adaptation and the Development of Technologies* (New York: St. Martin's, 1994).

Ryoshin Minami, *The Economic Development of Japan* (London: Macmillan, 1986).

Carl Mosk, *Competition and Cooperation in Japanese Labor Markets* (New York: St. Martin's, 1994).

Takafusa Nakamura, *The Postwar Japanese Economy* (Tokyo: University of Tokyo Press, 1981).

Meiko Nishimizu and Charles R. Hulten, "The Sources of Japanese Economic Growth, 1955–71," *Review of Economics and Statistics* 60 (August 1978), 351–361.

Kazushi Ohkawa and Henry Rosovsky, *Japanese Economic Growth* (Stanford, Calif.: Stanford University Press, 1973).

Kazushi Ohkawa and Hirohisa Kohama, *Lectures on Developing Economies: Japan's Experience and Its Relevance* (Tokyo: University of Tokyo Press, 1989).

Hugh Patrick and Henry Rosovsky, eds., *Asia's New Giant: How the Japanese Economy Works* (Washington, D.C.: Brookings Institution, 1976).

M. M. Postan et al., eds., *Cambridge Economic History of Europe*, Vol. VII, Part 2 (Cambridge: Cambridge University Press, 1978), chaps. 3–5 on Japan.

Kazuo Sato, *The Transformation of the Japanese Economy* (Armonk, N.Y.: Sharpe, 1996).

———, *The Japanese Economy and Business* (Armonk, N.Y.: Sharpe, 1996).

Ryuzo Sato, "U.S.–Japan Relations Under the Clinton and Hosokawa Administrations," *Japan and the World Economy* 6, no. 1 (1994), 89–103.

Yoshio Suzuki, *Money, Finance, and Macroeconomic Performance in Japan* (New Haven: Yale University Press, 1986).

Ozawa Terutomo, *Multinationalism Japanese Style* (Princeton, N.J.: Princeton University Press, 1979).

Yosho Tsurumi, *The Japanese Are Coming: A Multinational Interaction of Firms and Politics* (Cambridge, Mass.: Ballinger, 1976).

Kozo Yamamura, ed., *Policy and Trade Issues of the Japanese Economy* (Seattle: University of Washington Press, 1982).

M. Y. Yoshino, *Japan's Multinational Enterprises* (Cambridge, Mass.: Harvard University Press, 1976).

South Korea, Singapore, Taiwan, Hong Kong

Edward K. Y. Chen, *Hyper-Growth in Asian Economies* (London and Basingstoke, England: Macmillan, 1979).

Shirley W. Y. Kao, Gustav Ranis, and John C. H. Fei, *The Taiwan Success Story: Rapid Growth with Improved Distribution in the Republic of China, 1952–1979* (Boulder, Colo.: Westview, 1981).

Paul Krugman, "The Myth of Asia's Miracle," *Foreign Affairs* 73 (November–December 1994), 62–78.

Paul Kuzner, "Indicative Planning in Korea," *Journal of Comparative Economics* 14 (December 1990), 657–676.

Eddy Lee, ed., *Export-Led Industrialization and Development* (Geneva: ILO, 1981).

Roy A. Matthews, *Canada and the Little Dragons* (Montreal: Institute for Research on Public Policy, 1983).

Miron Mushkat, *The Economic Future of Hong Kong* (Boulder, Colo., and London, England: Hong Kong University Press, 1990).

George Rosen, *Economic Development in Asia* (Brookfield, Vt.: Ashgate, 1996).

J. L. Saking, "Indicative Planning in Korea: Discussion," *Journal of Comparative Economics,* 14, no. 1 (December, 1990), 677–680.

Robert A. Scalapino, Seizaburo Sato, and Jusuf Wanandi, eds., *Asian Economic Development—Present and Future* (Berkeley: University of California Press, 1985).

Miyohei Shinohara and Fu-chen Lo, *Global Adjustment and the Future of the Asian-Pacific Economy* (Tokyo and Kuala Lumpur: Institute of Developing Economies and Asian and Pacific Development Centre, 1989).

A. H. Somjee and Geeta Somjee, *Development Success in Asia Pacific* (New York: St. Martin's, 1995).

Julian Weiss, *The Asian Century* (New York: Facts on File, 1989).

Jon Woronoff, *Asia's "Miracle" Economies* (Armonk, N.Y.: Sharpe, 1986).

World Bank, *The East Asian Miracle: Economic Growth and Public Policy* (Washington, D.C.: World Bank, 1993).

India

A. N. Agrawal, *Indian Economy*, 2nd ed. (New Delhi: Vikas, 1976).

Kaushik Basu, *Agarian Questions* (New Delhi: Oxford University Press, 1998).

Jagdish Bhagwati and Sukhamoy Chakravaty, "Contributions to Indian Economic Analysis: A Survey," *American Economic Review* 59 (September 1969), 4–29.

William A. Byrd, "Planning in India: Lessons from Four Decades of Development Experience," *Journal of Comparative Economics* 14 (December 1990), 713–736.

Pramit Chaudhuri, ed., *Aspects of Indian Economic Development* (London: Allen and Unwin, 1971).

Francine R. Frankel, *India's Green Revolution* (Princeton, N.J.: Princeton University Press, 1971).

———, *India's Political Economy, 1947–1977* (Princeton, N.J.: Princeton University Press, 1978).

Ira N. Gang, "Small Firm 'Presence' in Indian Manufacturing" *World Development* 20 (1992), 1377–89.

Raj Krishna and G. S. Raychaudhuri, "Trends in Rural Savings and Capital Formation in India, 1950–1951 to 1973–1974," *Economic Development and Cultural Change* 30 (January 1982), 271–298.

William A. Long and K. K. Seo, *Management in Japan and India* (New York: Praeger, 1977).

Angus Maddison, *Class Structure and Economic Growth: India and Pakistan Since the Moghuls* (New York: Norton, 1971).

Wilfred Malenbaum, "Modern Economic Growth in India and China: The Comparison Revisited, 1950–1980," *Economic Development and Cultural Change* 31 (October 1982), 45–84.

Rakesh Mohan and Vandana Aggarwal, "Commands and Controls: Planning for Indian Industrial Development, 1951–1990," *Journal of Comparative Economics* 14 (December 1990), 681–712.

Dilip Mookhergee, *Indian Industry: Policies and Performance* (New Delhi: Oxford University Press, 1997).

Arvind Panagariya, "Indicative Planning in India: Discussion," *Journal of Comparative Economics* 14 (December 1990), 736–742.

Prabhat Patnaik, *Macroeconomics* (New Delhi: Oxford University Press, 1997), pp. 12–36.

C. H. Shah and C. N. Vakil, eds., *Agricultural Development of India: Policy and Problems* (New Delhi: Orient Longman, 1979).

Subramanian Swamy, "Economic Growth in China and India, 1952–1970: A Comparative Appraisal," *Economic Development and Cultural Change* 21 (July 1973), 1–84.

CHAPTER
14

The Soviet Command Economy

Although the institutions of the Soviet economy varied over its sixty-year existence, Communist Party control, state ownership, national economic planning, and the collectivization of agriculture remained constants of the system. The Soviet experience therefore represents the prime attempt to create a socialist society and to forge rapid economic development through planning and minimal use of markets.

The economic reforms that received a great deal of attention from mid-1950 onward did little to change the fundamentals of the system. From 1929 through 1987, when Mikhail Gorbachev introduced his perestroika reforms, we have a long period in which to examine the Soviet economic system.

Since the demise of communism in the late 1980s and early 1990s, we have engaged in endless debate as to the causes of its collapse. Did the administrative-command system fail because of weak economic performance? Was the system unable to keep up with its primary competitor, the United States? And what lessons should we learn? Was the Soviet system not viable, or was it viable but run by the wrong people? We will probably never have conclusive answers to these questions.

Intellectual Origins

The Soviet administrative-command system drew its intellectual origins from Karl Marx and other revolutionary socialist thinkers. In his 1848 *Communist Manifesto*, Marx called on the workers of the world to unite and throw off their capitalist chains. Many Russians heeded his call. Other revolutionary writers, such as anarchist Mikhail Bakunin, called for the overthrow of the czarist regime. Followers of Marx formed the underground Social Democratic Labor Party of Russia to organize a socialist revolution. V. I. Lenin broke off his Bolshevik Party from the Menshevik faction of the Social Democratic Labor Party in 1903, but the two factions continued to meet jointly in illicit party congresses. At the time of the October 1917 revolution, there was an array of socialist parties supporting the revolution, the best organized of which was Lenin's Bolsheviks.

The October Revolution of 1917 did away with czarist rule and brought to power a group of dedicated Marxist revolutionaries under the leadership of Lenin.[1] The Bolsheviks, in fact, were astonished at their good fortune. They had expected a much longer wait until they could seize power.

Lenin's Bolsheviks immediately began what they called a Red Terror to liquidate opposition parties, including former allies, supporters of the old regime, and clergy. The October Revolution victory was tested by a bloody civil war that the Red Army won primarily due to the disorganization of opposition forces.

Lenin's communists inherited the fifth largest economy in Europe, about equal in size to the Austro-Hungarian Empire, but it was among the poorest nations of Europe. The economy had grown rapidly after the construction of the railroads and the linking of Russian agriculture to the outside world in the 1880s. The Russian Empire, which included the breadbasket of Europe—Ukraine—became the world's second largest exporter of grain behind the United States. It attracted considerable foreign investment to finance its industry, energy, and other natural resources. In the 1890s, Russia was the Klondike for adventurous entrepreneurs. Lenin's default on Russia's foreign debt was the largest in history at the time.

Lenin died in January 1924 after a series of debilitating strokes. His death prompted a bloody power struggle that ended with the triumph of I. V. Stalin, who put in place one of the most brutal dictatorships of history. After Stalin's death in March 1953, the Soviet Union was run by collective rule. The top party official continued to bear Stalin's title of General Secretary of the Communist Party.

As the Soviet system expanded into China and Eastern Europe after the war, the Stalin precedent continued. The nation's leader was the top official of the country's Communist Party. Each new communist country adopted the Soviet system as its own. To explain the workings of the USSR, Soviets sent advisors to each Soviet satellite, which then copied the Soviet system right down to its repressive secret police. In the early part of the postwar era, the Soviet system had considerable appeal for poor countries: It appeared to promise a quick path out of poverty based on state control.

ABC of Communism and Socialism in One Country

The Bolsheviks came to power with little guidance from the spiritual father of communism. Marx wrote about the inevitable demise of capitalism but had precious little to say about how the first communist state would be run. It was left to Lenin, Stalin, and Stalin's successors to decide how this was to be done.

Two young Bolshevik leaders published a textbook in 1920 explaining how a Soviet planned economy was to work. In their 1920 *ABC of Communism*, *Nikolai Bukharin and Evgeny Preobrazhensky described an economy in which the workers collectively own the means of production, goods are kept in public warehouses, and people take what they* need.[2] Although the *ABC of Communism* was the most widely read of the early writings of Bolshevism, it remained the vision of its young and idealistic authors (both of whom were to be executed under Stalin's terror).

The Bolsheviks also had to address the fact that Marx's writings called for a global socialist revolution. Yet they found themselves in charge of only one country with little immediate prospect for socialist revolutions elsewhere. They had to ask whether they could be content with building "socialism in one country" or to devote their efforts to world revolution. *Socialism in one country refers to the argument about whether the Bolsheviks should set as their goal the building of socialism in the USSR or promote a world socialist revolution.*

Among the Bolsheviks, I. V. Stalin (supported by Bukharin) argued that the socialist revolutions of Europe had failed, and it was the responsibility of the USSR to build a strong socialist society in Russia. Leon Trotsky, the founder of the Red Army and among the most charismatic of Bolshevik leaders, argued that socialism in one country violated the basic tenets of Marx. The Russian Bolsheviks should focus on world revolution, without which Soviet communism could not survive. It was Stalin who won this argument when the Russian Communist Party adopted the policy of socialism in one country in 1925.

The Experiments of the 1920s

The future course of the Soviet Union was dictated more by events on the ground than by philosophical differences among Bolshevik leaders. Two economic experiments were conducted in the decade following the revolution of 1917: War Communism (1917–1921) and the New Economic Policy (NEP, 1921–1928).[3] Both responded to the needs to consolidate power and to marshal economic resources in a time of crisis.

War communism involved the nationalization of most of the economy, the attempt to eliminate market relationships in industry and trade, and the forced requisitioning of agricultural products from the peasants. Some suggested that Lenin was attempting to bypass socialism and move directly to a communist system with War Communism. Others argued, including Trotsky, these were the measures of a "besieged fortress." Whatever the intent, the economic consequences were disastrous. By the end of the civil war, the economy was in ruin. By 1920, the index of industrial production (1913 = 100) had fallen to 20, the index of agricultural production to 64, and the index of transportation to 22.[4]

To promote economic recovery, Lenin introduced the New Economic Policy in March 1921 over the objections of party true believers. *The New Economic Policy (NEP) returned smaller enterprises to private ownership, legalized private trade, and introduced a tax on agriculture to replace grain requisitions.* By 1927, the Soviet economy had recovered from the losses of civil war and war communism and was at, and in some cases above, the prewar level. In effect, NEP was a form of market socialism, with its combination of state ownership of industry and market allocation.

The period from 1917 to 1928 provided lessons that permeated Soviet thinking. First, if the market were to be eliminated, some mechanism for coordination had to take its place. During War Communism, Lenin nationalized industries and eliminated the market, but he did not replace the market with a plan or some other substitute mechanism. Second, partly as a result of inept state policies, the peasants came to be viewed as having a dangerous influence on the pace of industrialization.[5] Stalin hated them because he felt they resisted Soviet power in the countryside. After all, the economy was largely agricultural, so resources would have to come primarily from the rural sector. Third, attempts to introduce payment in kind or to downgrade the importance of money during War Communism made it obvious that incentives were crucial to motivate labor.

The Industrialization Debate

In addition to the experience of War Communism and NEP, the 1920s witnessed remarkably open discussions within the upper reaches of the party over the proper course of industrialization and planning.[6] The debate on industrialization focused on modes of industrialization and, in particular, on differing roles for the agricultural and industrial sectors. All participants agreed that industrialization was essential and that the peasants would play a key role.

With the opening of the Russian archives in the 1990s, we now have an even closer view of the debate within the upper ranks of the party. We have the actual transcripts of the debates over industrial and agricultural policy within the Party's Central Committee and its Politburo.[7] These debates show the growing tension between Stalin and his party opponents, who wished to continue the NEP economy.

Stalin favored a more radical approach, which had to wait for his consolidation of power. Bukharin argued in favor of continuing the NEP economy with its private trade, peasant agriculture, and absence of coercion of the peasantry, whereas Stalin argued in favor of state control of agriculture, a great leap forward for industrialization, and eventually for the end of private peasant agriculture.

Stalin's Great Break

At the end of the 1920s, Stalin, ensconced as the unquestioned dictator of the USSR, was ready for his Great Break. *Stalin's Great Break refers to the policies he put in place starting in 1929 to establish the administrative command economic and political system.* First, he put in place a system of central planning based on compulsory state and party directives. He put an abrupt end to the system of market allocation in retail and agricultural trade that Lenin had installed in March 1921. Planning was carried out by a ministerial system in which national state planners prepared plans for ministries, while ministries drew up the plans for enterprises subordinated to them. Limited first to two ministries, the number of ministries grew as planning became more comprehensive.

Second, Stalin ordered the collectivization of agriculture. Lenin brought the Bolsheviks to power on the slogan of land to the peasants. Stalin distrusted the peasantry, especially the more prosperous ones. Moreover, he chafed that Soviet power was virtually absent from the Russian village. Stalin forced peasants to enter collective farms. *Collective farms (called **kolkhozy**) were compulsory collectives of peasant households that delivered their products to the state at prices dictated by the state.* The countryside burst into open rebellion as peasants were forced to give up their livestock and possessions. The peasant rebellion has been called a second Russian revolution, but Stalin suppressed it with brutal force. The more prosperous peasants were deported, imprisoned, or killed. By the mid-1930s, more than 90 percent of Soviet peasant households were living in collective farms.[8]

Third, Stalin perfected a totalitarian system of political governance that enshrined the Communist Party and its leaders or leader in the "leading role." The Communist Party's economic commands were communicated throughout the system by the "general line" of the party.[9] Under Stalin (and later under China's Mao Zedong and North Korea's Kims), a "cult of the personality" elevated the party's leader to god-like status.[10]

Fourth, Stalin continued Lenin's use of an extraordinarily powerful secret police (called at various times, the Cheka, OGPU, NKVD, and finally KGB), which served as the party's "unsheathed sword" to track down and punish political and economic enemies. Throughout the Soviet era, the secret police was directly subordinated to the top leaders or the leadership collective.[11]

The economic system that Stalin put in place in the early 1930s was radically different from any prior system. It was the greatest socioeconomic experiment of the twentieth century, and it failed. Communism's collapse caused Francis Fukuyama (see Chapter 1) to conclude that history had ended with the triumph of capitalism over socialism.

The Institutions of the Soviet Economy

Economic systems are characterized by basic attributes, such as decision-making levels, market and plan mechanisms of information, property rights, incentive systems, and system of political governance. As we examine the Soviet command economy and its organizational arrangements, we must ask three questions: How did the system operate in reality as opposed to its official description by Soviet authorities? How did this system differ from the ideal of planned socialism? How well did it perform relative to alternative economic systems?

The Soviet economic system was organized in a vertical hierarchical fashion as described in Chapter 2. It constituted the world's first attempt to plan and manage an entire economy, a kind of "USSR incorporated." The Soviet political system of party and state institutions shared authority and responsibility, although the primacy of the party was never in question. There were several decision-making layers, including the state and party structure at the top, the ministries and regional authorities and sometimes trust organizations in the middle, and the basic production units (enterprises and farms) at the lower level.

The Decision-Making Hierarchy

The conceptual framework of planning did not change after its introduction in the early 1930s. Throughout its entire existence, the Communist Party played, what was termed, the leading role. ***The leading role of the party*** *refers to its recognized status as the primary decision-making body of the Soviet Union.* At the time of the

October Revolution, there were only 200,000 members. In the mid-1990s, it had almost 20 million members, about 10 percent of the adult population. It was this organization that ran the USSR, and its members constituted its elite.

The Communist Party   Figure 14.1 shows that the Soviet Union was formally directed by the Communist Party of the Soviet Union. At its apex stood the Central Committee, which met periodically in Plenums to decide major issues. Between the plenums, a Politburo made the decisions. In most case, the Politburo made the decisions; the Central Committee met to rubber stamp the Politburo's decisions. Only during periods of major change (such as the dismissal of Nikita Khrushchev in 1964 or the choice of a new party leader) did the Central Committee play more than a nominal role.

In theory, the ultimate power rested with party congresses in which the party elite assembled to vote on the party leadership and other matters. Party congresses were held at infrequent intervals, but some became historic events. Khrushchev

FIGURE 14.1   The Organization of the Soviet Economy: The Command Model

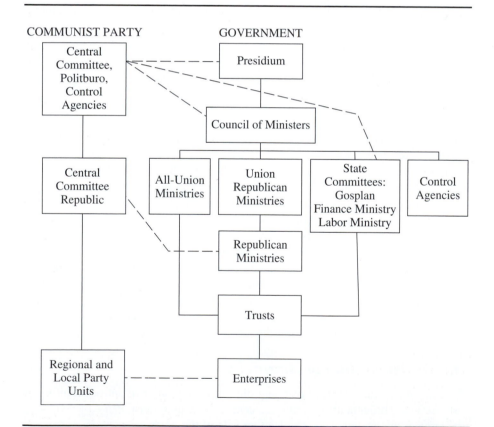

Source: From GREGORY, Comparing Economic Systems in the Twenty-First Century, 7E. © 2004 Cengage Learning.

used the Twentieth Party Congress of 1956 to denounce Stalin and inadvertently set in motion the Hungarian revolution.

The Communist Party was itself highly centralized with all of its branches and regional and local entities reporting directly to Moscow. The Communist Party maintained branches at virtually all levels of the economy and society. It operated through a complex centralized structure beginning at the national level, with its Politburo of top leaders and Central Committee of national and regional leaders, and terminating with individual party cells in each industrial enterprise, farm, and organization. Each organization had its own party organization. Each enterprise had a primary party organization. *The **primary party organization** represented the interests of the party at the local enterprise level.* In large enterprises, the head of the party organization was considered as the second boss alongside the enterprise manager.[12]

The party maintained republican and metropolitan divisions, each headed by a central committee, such as the Central Committee of Ukraine or of Uzbekistan. The top regional party heads served in the Central Committee and Politburo, depending on their importance.

The parallel organization of the party to the economy was put in place so that the party could monitor and inspire the organizations to which it was attached. The party organization's job was to ensure that their units were fulfilling the plan and acting in the interests of the party as the purported representative of workers and peasants.

Figure 14.1 showed that both the party and the state had their own control commissions to ferret out and punish illegal managerial behavior. The party control commission, for example, had the right to punish any and all party members (except those in the top leadership).

One of the most potent powers of the party was its power to appoint through the nomenklatura system. *The **nomenklatura** was a list of responsible positions that were to be filled by the personnel department of the party.* The most important positions were filled by the personnel division of the party Central Committee. Other key jobs were filled by the personnel departments of the Council of Ministers or ministries. *Because of this appointment procedure, the political, economic, and military elite were referred to as the **nomenklatura**.*

The State   The Soviet system differentiated between the party and the state. The party gave the direction and the state executed the party directives. *The **Soviet state**, with the **Council of Ministers** at its apex, was responsible for executing the directives of the Communist Party.* In the early years of Soviet power, in fact, the government was called the Central Executive Committee. Its head was the nominal head of state, although everyone knew the real position of power was the General Secretary of the party.

At the Council of Ministers level, the state and party overlapped. Members of the Politburo and Central Committee occupied the most important posts in government, such as the heads of ministries and state committees. Relatively few top party officials had open portfolios that allowed them to look after general issues as opposed to more narrow departmental or territorial interests.[13] The Council of

Ministers directed the industrial and agricultural ministries, the general branches of government. They were advised by various state committees, the most important being the State Planning Commission and the State Committee on Prices.

The economy was divided into industrial ministries, which received plans from the Council of Ministers as devised by the State Planning Commission, or Gosplan, as it was known. ***Gosplan** is the Russian name for the State Planning Commission.* The ministries themselves were divided into main administrations, which prepared plans for and supervised the enterprises that fell under their purview.

The Communist Party formulated the general outline of resource allocation. Gosplan then converted those directives into operative plans, with the aid of ministries and, to a degree, the individual enterprises.[14] It was the responsibility of the individual enterprises to carry out the plan directives. Information flowed from top to bottom and vice versa. Transactions among enterprises were coordinated by a plan, and money and markets were supposed to play only a limited role.

The most important branches of industry were governed by all-Union ministries. Union republican ministries dispersed a measure of decision-making authority at the level of the fifteen republics. The ministries were the organizational superiors of the industrial and agricultural enterprises. Organizational reforms experimented with combining enterprises into trusts to serve as an intermediary between the enterprise and the ministry.

The state organization, like the party, also had republican and territorial divisions that duplicated the national structure at the territorial level. In cases where production tended to be localized by region, such as in the oil and timber industry, republican ministries managed the affairs of enterprises. In a number of cases, enterprises were dual subordinated, subject to orders from the national and republican governments.

Motivation, Managers, and Principal–Agent Problems

The Soviet command system was divided between those who gave orders and those responsible for fulfilling them. In the Soviet terminology, those who gave the orders were termed (loosely translated) "administrators" and those responsible for fulfilling them were called "economic managers." *In the Soviet system, **administrators** issued the orders and intervened when they felt it was necessary. The **economic managers** were responsible for fulfilling these orders and were rewarded or penalized based on the level of fulfillment.*

It is an interesting question why the Soviet system did not also make those who drew up the plans responsible for their fulfillment. The likely answer is that the top leadership needed some agents who were likely to tell them the truth without bias. The State Planning Commission has been singled out as a "truth-telling organization" on the grounds that the top leadership needed at least one organization that was not held responsible for final results and could therefore be relied on to tell the truth.[15]

The divergence in roles and responsibilities between administrators and economic managers created a fundamental tension. Administrators felt free to order economic managers to fulfill herculean tasks but bore no responsibility for setting unrealistic targets. Economic managers, facing punishment for plan failure, resented the unrealistic and trivial orders of administrators. In order to survive in this environment, economic managers had to systematically provide false information on capacity and material requirements.

The clash between administrators and economic managers continued throughout the entire Soviet period. Administrators knew they could not trust economic managers, and economic managers resented the intrusions and interventions from uninformed administrators, which they called petty tutelage.[16] ***Petty tutelage*** *refers to the constant interventions in the affairs of enterprises by superiors.*

Responsibility for final results defined the difference between producers and planners. Producers complained that superiors gave orders but bore no responsibility. The minister of heavy industry, in an outburst in a Politburo meeting of August 1931, protested: "You want to play the role of bureaucrat, but when my factories fall apart, it is I who must answer not those of you who engage in such 'serious discussions' here."[17] The deputy chairman of a military industrial plant echoed these sentiments some fifty years later: "They [the defense branch department of the Central Committee] would inquire why the plan isn't being fulfilled, they acted like they were another Council of Ministers. But they had more authority and none of the responsibilities."[18]

Who were the administrators and who were the economic managers? The administrators were those members of the state and party elite not held responsible for concrete results. They were the experts in state committees such as the State Planning Commission, the State Pricing Commission, or the State Supply Committee; they were experts who drew up plans, set norms, and determined prices. They gave orders or assisted those giving orders. The economic managers were industrial ministry officials, industry administration heads, and, above all, enterprise managers.

The economic managers faced a success indicator problem. They were confronted with all kinds of orders from above, not all of which were consistent. *The* ***success indicator problem*** *refers to the managers' need to select which orders they were to fulfill among the multitude of orders they received.* Managers received rewards or were punished based on plan performance. But the plan itself consisted of an array of output, financial, labor staffing, technological, and quality targets.[19] Gross value of output served as the most important target throughout the Soviet period. ***Gross value of output*** *is the planned output of the ministry or enterprise expressed either in physical units or in value terms.* The manager's performance was usually judged on the basis of fulfillment of production targets and one or two other supplemental targets. The tension was that the planners could specify a number of objectives but the manager decided which of them was most important. This "freedom to choose" made the manager a key cog in the Soviet system rather than simply an automaton that followed orders from above.

Managers could ignore items that made a small contribution, relative to their use of scarce resources, to gross value and would overproduce items that made a large contribution. The mix or assortment of goods within the plan could also be ignored. A classic cartoon from a Soviet satirical magazine showed an enterprise's monthly output of ten tons of steel nails being fulfilled by a truck hauling away ten 1-ton nails.

Gross output came increasingly to be stated in value terms, as output mixes became more complicated. Instead of ten tons, the production target would be ten million rubles. Given that producers operated in a seller's market, they were often in a position to negotiate prices—known or unknown to their superiors. Managers could therefore trade off less output for higher prices.

Figure 14.2 shows that the enterprise is expected to produce $Q*$ and to sell it at the state price of $P*$. If it does so, the enterprise fulfills the plan as desired by the state. It has produced the right amount of output, which it sells at the right price. The manager, however, can fulfill the gross output plan in rubles by selling a smaller quantity at a higher price. The curved line shows all the possible price–quantity combinations that fulfill the ruble value plan.

Such managerial opportunistic behavior could be rewarding to the manager and the enterprise. The bonus system typically paid little or nothing until the output plan was 100 percent fulfilled. Then rewards were paid for production over this level, resulting in an average managerial bonus of 25 or 35 percent of base salary.[20] Top managers received bonuses in excess of 50 percent. Managerial behavior was clearly affected by the reward system.[21] There were other rewards, such as housing, vacations, automobiles, and promotions. On the negative side, managers who did not perform were dismissed or even imprisoned or executed—sanctions that were widely used in the early days of Soviet planning.[22]

Generally taut targets and uncertain supply (especially for "limited" goods) were combined with substantial rewards for fulfillment of planned output targets. The result was informal and dysfunctional managerial behavior—a problem not anticipated by the socialist theorists, who assumed that managers would obey all rules handed down by superior authorities.

FIGURE 14.2   Enterprise Tradeoffs between Price and Quantity

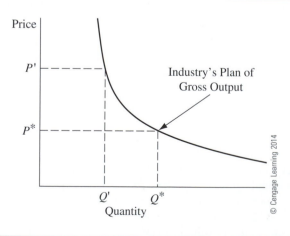

The combination of different objectives and different access to information created a classic principal–agent conflict between enterprise managers and their superiors. The manager was required by law to fulfill the plan, primarily to produce the output targets and the assortment, and would suffer presumably dire consequences in the event of failure. But only the manager knew the true productive capacity of the enterprise and its true needs for materials. The manager's superiors in the ministry or in Gosplan could only guess at capacity or material requirements.

This information asymmetry enabled the manager to engage in opportunistic behavior relative to principals in the hierarchy who wanted maximum production with the minimum expenditure of society's resources. The manager's opportunism extended into the following areas: First, managers, during the plan formulation stage, attempted to secure "easy" targets—that is, targets that were well below the actual capacity of the enterprise. An easy target meant low outputs and ample inputs and investment.

Second, managers emphasized what was important in terms of their rewards and neglected other areas. Thus cost-saving targets, along with assortment targets, were sacrificed for the sake of meeting the gross output targets. Neglect of assortment explained the shortage of spare parts, whose manufacture disrupted production lines and did not contribute sufficiently to rewards.

Third, managers sought "safety" in various other practices. They could stockpile materials that were in short supply; they could avoid innovation; and they could establish informal or "family" connections to ensure a supply of crucial inputs. Managers were able to focus on production at the expense of other targets—most notably, the efficiency with which output was produced—because they understood that their production was so valuable to their principals that they would not be allowed to fail.

The emphasis on fulfilling output plans meant that Soviet enterprises operated on the basis of a soft budget constraint. *The **soft budget constraint** meant that enterprises that failed to cover their costs received automatic subsidies from their ministry, which redistributed profits from profitable to unprofitable enterprises, or from the state budget.* With a soft budget constraint, enterprises were free to overuse resources and to avoid cost-saving innovations. It also meant that profitability was not an important indicator of managerial success. Therefore, later efforts to introduce profits as a criterion for success were doomed as long as the soft budget constraint was retained.

We can view the reform process as a game of catch-up between administrators and economic managers. As managers "cheated" by substituting higher prices for less output, their superiors placed stricter controls on prices. With stricter controls on prices, managers cheated by reducing product quality or ignoring the assortment. When superiors placed more emphasis on marketing assortments that no one wanted, enterprise managers used new tricks. This never-ending game began in the first years of the administrative command system and continued until its final days.

Planning in Theory and Practice

Ludwig von Mises and Friedrich Hayek (Chapter 4) argued that a single planning organization cannot plan all economic activity from the center. The economy consists of hundreds of thousands of enterprises that produce millions of products. Everyone realized that planning in such detail was an impossible task.

The founders of the Soviet system resolved this "complexity problem" by planning only a limited number of activities, presumably the most important. Gosplan planned only a limited number of products and planned the work of ministries, not the work of enterprises. In only very rare cases were actual enterprises planned from the center, such as defense plants or huge enterprises that affected the national interest. Other activities were planned wholly by the ministries or by regional or local bodies.

Figure 14.3 shows the usual planning sequence: from the State Planning Commission to the ministry, to the main administration, and finally to the enterprises.

The ministries produced the real operational plans of the economy, whereas Gosplan concentrated on more general directives. Gosplan prepared short-term (one-year and quarterly), longer-term (five- or seven-year), and even twenty-year "perspective" plans. The five-year plans were not broken down into annual operational segments. The annual and quarterly plans were the economy's operational plans, if there were any. Ministries and main administrations even issued decadal (ten-year) plans. The essence of the plan was the material balance system, which we examined in Chapter 6.

FIGURE 14.3   The Sequence of Planning

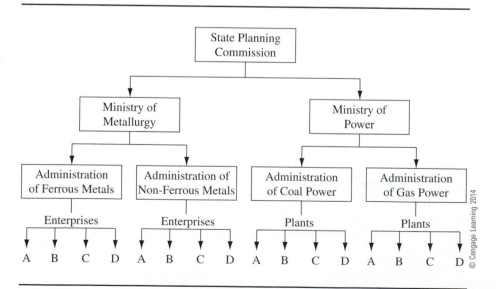

Output and Supply Plans

As the material balance system suggests, the "plan" must actually consist of two plans. *The **output plan** tells the producers what to produce and in what assortments.* But the planners were not indifferent to who received the output. Deliveries had to be made in accordance with the material balance. Hence, the second component of the plan was the supply plan. *The **supply plan** told producers to whom to deliver their outputs.*

Planners therefore had to engage in both the planning of outputs and the planning of their deliveries. In the early years, Gosplan handled both tasks. After the war, the State Supply Committee (Gossnab) became a separate entity for the planning of deliveries. It worked out a more detailed set of delivery balances than Gosplan's output plans.

In theory, the plan was formulated in the following manner. General directives were provided by the CPSU and converted into control figures by Gosplan. ***Control figures** were the preliminary output targets of the national economic plan.* The control figures, or tentative production targets, were transmitted through the ministries and main administrations down to the level of individual enterprises, with comment and informational input being sought from each level in the hierarchy. The control figures then moved back up through the hierarchy and at the Gosplan level were "balanced"; that is, for major items in the plan, supply and demand had to balance.

Once balance was achieved, the plan was disaggregated and the targets were once again disseminated down through the ministries to the individual enterprises. The final result, the techpromfinplans (technical–industrial–financial plans), were legally binding and contained detailed directives for enterprise operations during the forthcoming year.[23] *The **techpromfinplan** (technical–industrial–financial plan) was the enterprises plan, including output, assortment, labor staffing, and financial plans.* As the saying went, "the plan is the law." All economic managers were obligated to fulfill the plan.

The formulation of this plan was time-consuming and complex, and clearly could not approach the theoretical ideals outlined in Chapter 6. Intense bargaining, haggling, interplay among the various units, and delays were integral parts of planning. Frequently the new plan was late in arriving, so the enterprise continued to operate under the old plan or on the basis of informal agreements. This planning system worked in large part because it had built-in simplifications.

Planning from the Achieved Level

The planning process did not start from scratch each year. The plan for year *t* was, in effect, little more than a revision and update of the plan for year *t* − 1. This practice of planning from the achieved level simplified the planning process. ***Planning from the achieved level** refers to the practice of planning based on last year's targets plus marginal changes.*

Planning from the achieved level simplified planning, but it created rigidities. Gosplan planned only major commodities such as steel and machinery, which were called funded commodities or limited commodities. ***Funded commodities** were those whose "limits" were assigned to enterprises by the planning system.*

Their number varied over time from a few hundred to a few thousand. *The recipients of funded commodities were called **fund holders**.*

Other commodities were planned at progressively lower levels, depending on their importance. This simplified the planning process but left much to be done at the lower levels, in the various republics and ministries.

In constructing balances, planners faced a dilemma. They wanted the balance to be achieved at the most challenging level. On the other hand, they knew that the more taut the plan—that is, the closer the targets were to maximum capacity—the more likely it was that errors and supply imbalances would occur. Planners had to compile a plan that was demanding yet in balance.

Planners did not employ sophisticated planning techniques to "balance" supplies and demands. In fact, ad hoc tallies of sources and material requirements were compiled, and past experience was the principal guide. Accordingly, planners were usually satisfied if they were able to come up with a consistent plan; they did not have the luxury of seeking out the optimal plan from among all possible consistent plans.

Soviet planning was supposed to be "scientific planning"—a procedure that produced the best economic results possible for the country using scientific methods. The reality of Soviet planning was far different from the image Soviet planners tried to project.

Planning or Resource Management

Eugene Zaleski, in his classic study of Soviet planning from 1933 to 1952, found that the deviations of actual performance from planned performance were so great that he doubted that this was a planned economy at all.[24] Rather, he suggested that resources were actually allocated by resource managers in the party and state apparatus after the plan had been completed. Zaleski's ***resource managers*** *were the actors, not the plan itself, that made the actual resource allocation decisions for the economy in the course of plan implementation.*

The plan, Zaleski found, was simply a vision of the future, designed to show the population that better times are ahead. No manager, however, is prepared to limit the demand for resources, and the plan declares that production will be abundant. Hence the material balance will be grossly unbalanced by excess demands. As enterprises and ministries clamor for resources, state and party officials decide who gets what. They, not the plan, allocate resources.

No less an authority than Stalin himself confirmed that resources were allocated by resource managers and not by the plan:

> For us, for Bolsheviks, the five year plan is not something that is a law that is forever given. For us the five year plan, like any plan, is only a plan approved *as a first approximation* which must be made more precise, to change and improve on the basis of experience, on the basis of executing the plan.... Only bureaucrats can think that planning work ends with the creation of the plan. The creation of the plan is only the beginning. The real direction of the plan develops only after the putting together of the plan.[25]

Studies of actual Soviet planning based on the open Soviet state and party archives show planning to be a chaotic process that produced virtually no "final" plans.[26] All plans were preliminary and subject to change at any time by virtually any resource manager in the state or party. Although the enterprise plan was supposed to contain numerous plan targets, the operational plans usually gave only output and assortment targets. Labor, costs, productivity, new technologies, and new products were reconstructed retrospectively at the end of the planning period. Ministries and enterprises, when ordered by resource managers to amend the plan, could not appeal to earlier agreements because they were all preliminary.

Enterprises and ministries therefore developed a number of devices to protect themselves from arbitrary resources managers: They either failed to provide planners with information or provided them with false information. They prepared two plans, one for internal use, the other for external consumption, and they formed networks of informal resource allocation with others at the same level in the hierarchy.[27]

The archives reveal a high-level of "unplanned" exchanges among ministries—a system in which disputes were largely adjudicated informally rather than through appeal to the center. Even products that were subject to the strictest level of planning and control, such as vehicles, were subject to informal allocation.[28]

The Soviet system of resource allocation was therefore incredibly complex and multifaceted. Some products were "planned," others were "resource-managed," still others were allocated by the participants themselves via horizontal unplanned exchanges. In effect, these unplanned exchanges formed a quasi-market in which state enterprises or even ministries engaged in unsanctioned and perhaps illegal exchanges. Clearly, central authorities were aware; they had control commissions that investigated wrongdoing by party members.[29] Their toleration of unplanned exchanges suggests that these were probably essential to keeping production moving.

Ruble Control

In theory at least, output and supply planning was carried out in physical units. But these physical units inevitably were expressed in money terms. Enterprises had to pay their suppliers in money terms. Workers had to be paid their wages in cash. Trading enterprises needed credit. All real transactions had to be expressed in money terms. That financial flows mirror real flows suggested a powerful control mechanism, especially given that all financial transactions were handled by one monopoly bank, called the State Bank, or Gosbank (in Russian). ***The State Bank, Gosbank** in Russian, was the monopoly bank that handled all enterprise transactions throughout the economy.*

Gosbank was a huge institution. It had tens of thousands of branch banks located in every city, town, and village. At a later date, its savings arm, Sberbank, separated from Gosbank and became the prime repository for household savings (and still exists to the present day). There were other specialized banks, such as for foreign trade or housing construction, but it was Gosbank that handled all transaction among enterprises.[30] Each enterprise was required to hold all its accounts with the state bank, where all transactions were recorded. Not only were the firm's labor requirements specified in the plan but also the fund that was used to pay for the labor was held and monitored by the state bank.

Ruble control is the monitoring of plan fulfillment by monitoring the financial transactions among enterprises. Let us consider how ruble control was supposed to work: If an enterprise is ordered to produce 10 tons of steel and sell it to a buyer at 20 rubles per ton, the seller should receive 200 rubles in its bank account, as the buyer's account is debited 200 rubles. Planners therefore can follow the financial flows to see what is happening to physical flows. If Gosbank does not see the 200 ruble transaction, this means the physical plan is not being fulfilled.

In theory, this ruble control should work well. All enterprises must maintain their bank accounts in the state bank, which can serve as a huge financial monitoring center. In practice, however, ruble control did not offer such a panacea.

Plan targets were usually stated in aggregated terms, such as tons of steel or meters of textiles. Financial flows, on the other hand, were for actual transactions conducted at lower levels. The plan might call for the production of 10 tons of steel, but the delivery plan would break deliveries into different types of steel, and then the main administration plan would break deliveries into finer and finer units. The actual financial transactions would be almost impossible to trace back to the 10-ton output plan.

For ruble control to work, physical plans must be as detailed as financial plans, which was impossible. Moreover, just as enterprises could receive "unofficial" supplies by trading with other enterprises, they could evade ruble control by granting each other unofficial credits or by paying cash. The use of cash transactions to circumvent the plan was widespread. Throughout its history, Gosbank had to fight back against informal credit among enterprises. Cash transactions formed the foundation of the Soviet "second economy," to be discussed in a later section.

Prices and Money

The founders of the administrative-command economy hoped money and prices would play only a small role in the economy. Bukharin and Preobrazhensky in their *ABC of Communism* wrote that goods and services should be directly distributed to consumers by a rationing system and money would disappear.

Even the most idealistic early communists realized that prices would continue to exist. They were needed as accounting units to add things together, unlike market economies where relative prices tell us what is cheap or expensive. But if resources are allocated by an administrative plan, prices should not play an allocative role nor should they be indicators of relative scarcity.

Wholesale Prices and the Labor Theory of Value

Soviet prices were primarily set by administrative authorities.[31] In the case of collective farm markets, and with services provided by moonlighting workers, prices were formed by supply and demand, but market prices were the rare exception.

Wholesale prices were set by the State Pricing Commission (Goskomtsen), which decreed that prices should be based on costs, not on demand. Two goods produced at the same cost should have the same price irrespective of demand. Therefore the State Pricing Commission had to conduct extensive and repeated censuses of enterprises to check their costs.

In fact, wholesale prices were changed very infrequently, such as every decade. When wholesale prices were changed, they were rolled out as a price reform. Soviet pricing authorities could not keep prices in line with costs. As years passed with no change in prices, more and more enterprises operated at a loss. Pricing authorities sought, through periodic price "reforms," to raise prices enough to make the average branch enterprise profitable. Wholesale prices established in 1955 remained in effect until 1966. The 1966–1967 price reform remained in effect until the general price reform of 1982. Prices had limited use because they were unrelated to relative scarcities.

The State Pricing Commission set wholesale prices according to a simple formula familiar to utility regulators in capitalist countries: ***Industrial prices*** *were set to equal the average cost of the industrial branch plus a profit markup.* Pricing officials used average branch costs because they found that different enterprises produced at different costs. They therefore had to average the costs to get the official price. In calculating costs, they followed Marx's labor theory of value by excluding rental and interest charges. ***Marx's labor theory of value*** *stated that value is determined by labor alone and therefore excludes interest and rent from allowable costs.*

There was, for the most part, no rental price for agricultural land. Planners determined land utilization within the framework of the plan, taking into account technical and local conditions. There were no rental costs for underground resources, whose recovery costs depended on the location and richness of reserves.

The exclusion of interest and rent rendered enterprise profits an unreliable indicator of managerial performance. Consider the example in Exhibit 14.1 of a coal-mining ministry that has two mines, A and B. A produces at a low cost; B produces at a high cost. According to the average branch formula, the price of coal is set at the average cost for the branch, which means an automatic loss for the high-cost

EXHIBIT 14.1   Average Branch Cost Pricing Results in Redistribution of Profits

	Cost per ton	Profit per ton	Profit Redistribution
Coal mine A	100 rubles	+120 rubles	Ministry redistributes
Coal mine B	300 rubles	−80 rubles	part of A's profits to
Average for the branch	200 rubles	+40	B to cover its
Price = Average branch cost plus 10% profit	220 rubles		losses

producer and an automatic profit for the low-cost producer. To balance the ministry books, the ministry redistributes profits from A to cover B's losses.

This example shows why profits are not meaningful in a world of average branch cost pricing. The minister will not know whether A's costs are low due to advantages, such as more capital or richer ore deposits that are not reflected in the price, or due to better management.

Average branch cost pricing means that profits cannot be used to gauge managerial performance. The various reform proposals presented in the early 1960s that proposed to elevate profits to a key indicator of managerial success failed to recognize that profits cannot be used for this purpose.

Retail Prices and Turnover Taxes

When a product left the wholesale level to be sold at the retail level, the pricing mechanism did take demand factors into account. If consumer goods are priced only according to costs, there will be either shortages or surpluses.

Figure 14.4 shows that the supply of consumer goods was determined largely by the planners, although producers, if they had a choice in output mix, choose products with higher relative prices. Thus the supply curve (*S*) has a steep positive slope. The consumer demand curve (*D*) is a function of relative prices, incomes, and tastes and could not be controlled by the planners. Planners sought to achieve a balance of supply and demand by setting the retail price at or near a market-clearing level, such as *P'*, by adding a turnover tax.

The turnover tax was a differentiated tax on consumer good that depended on consumer demand for the product and is the difference between the wholesale and

FIGURE 14.4   Soviet Turnover Tax

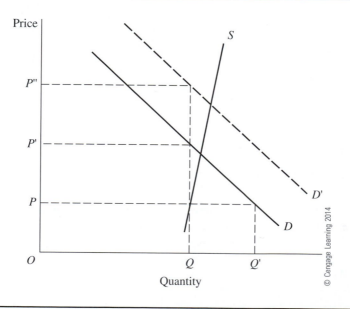

© Cengage Learning 2014

retail price. If the retail price were set at the wholesale price (*P* in Figure 14.4), there would be an excess demand of *Q'Q*, for *OQ* would be produced and *OQ'* demanded. Some form of rationing would be required in this case. Pricing authorities, however, could impose a turnover tax to balance supply and demand. They could set the retail price at *OP'* and a near-equilibrium would prevail. Raising the retail price *did not* raise the quantity supplied above *OQ* because the enterprise continued to receive the wholesale price *OP* for the product.

Unlike Western sales taxes, the turnover tax, in this case *PP'*, differed widely from one product to another, and it was included in the price rather than being added on at the time of sale. Its share of retail prices declined over time, as planners increased supplies of consumer products and raised the wholesale prices of farm products.

Although prices approached equilibrium at the retail level, the result was different from a market economy. What in the Soviet case was a tax would in the capitalist system be something resembling a profit, signaling existing producers to expand supply and new producers to enter the market. There was no such signal in the Soviet case because the producer was unaware of and largely uninterested in retail prices. The link between consumer demand and the producer was broken. Suppose that demand increases from *D* to *D'*. As the producer continues to receive the wholesale price *OP*, the quantity produced remains at *OQ*. But at the old retail price *OP'*, there is now an excess of quantity demanded over quantity supplied. The state reacts by raising the turnover tax by *P'P"*. Note that higher demand does not result in more output, only in a higher price.

Financial Planning and Money

Value categories, such as prices, costs, and profits, always existed in the Soviet system, but they were supposed to play only a limited role in allocating resources. In a centralized economy where few decisions are made at local levels, households still made decisions about working and what they would buy. How could planners ensure that there would be a macroeconomic balance of consumer goods when households determined what they would buy? A ***macroeconomic balance*** *would occur when the supply of consumer goods at established prices equaled desired consumer spending.*

The balancing of aggregate consumer demand and supply can be illustrated in the following formulas:

$$D = WL - R \qquad\qquad (14.1)$$

$$S = P_1 Q_1 \qquad\qquad (14.2)$$

where

D = aggregate demand
S = aggregate supply
W = the average annual wage
L = the number of worker-years of labor used in the economy

R = the amount of income not spent on consumer goods (equal to the sum of direct taxes and savings)

Q_1 = the real quantity of consumer goods produced

P_1 = the price level of consumer goods

Note the unusual interpretation this balance attaches to savings, which are included in the term R. Savings are the result of not having enough goods to buy.

Savings were regarded as evidence of repressed inflation, assuming that people save because there is nothing to buy at prevailing prices. Soviet authorities feared a savings overhang. *A **savings overhang** referred to the accumulation of forced savings that resulted from having nothing to buy.* It was feared that the savings overhang could destabilize consumer markets. The literature on this subject therefore debated whether Soviet household savings behaved similarly to the West, where people save for retirement, human investment, and contingencies, or was simply the result of nothing to buy.[32]

The financial-balance problem of the early Soviet period was quite obvious. As the Soviet economy grew rapidly in the early plan years, it paid labor increasingly high wages to motivate higher participation and greater effort, but the state wanted that labor to produce producer goods, not consumer goods (Q_1). Thus the state permitted wages (W) to rise to encourage labor inputs (L) to rise. In so doing, planners were hoping that labor force decisions would be based on nominal and not real wages—in other words, that Soviet workers would be subject to money illusion. ***Money illusion** occurs when economic agents base their decisions on nominal prices and wages rather than on relative prices and real wages.*

In the absence of sharp increases in Q_1, however, alternative steps were required to achieve a balance between S and D—notably to let P_1 rise along with R (the latter through forced bond purchases). However, prices were not allowed to rise fast enough to absorb the full increase in demand; an imbalance between aggregate supply and demand was allowed to develop. This phenomenon, known as repressed inflation, was used widely throughout the entire Soviet era.[33] After World War II, the quantity of consumer goods increased, although simultaneous increases in purchasing power made it difficult to determine to what degree excess demand was reduced.

The consumer-goods-balance formula shows the importance of money. Virtually all consumer purchasing power originated from wage earnings, which were paid by enterprises in cash. Enterprises typically preferred more labor rather than less. The more labor they had, the easier it would be to meet production targets, even if some of this labor might be redundant. They were persistently requesting more labor from planners and more cash to pay labor from Gosbank.

Although the enterprise had a soft budget constraint for the purchase of materials, it appeared to have a hard budget constraint on cash to pay labor.[34] In fact, the highest political authorities in the land had to approve the emission of new currency, and ministers of finance could be fired if the money supply expanded too rapidly.[35]

The consumer-goods-balance equation shows why enterprise cash for wages was a hard budget constraint. Basically, the demand for consumer goods roughly equaled the amount of cash paid as wages throughout the economy. If financial authorities had treated wages like materials and allowed enterprises virtually unlimited access to cash, the inflationary consequences would have been substantial. As it was, the problem of too much purchasing power plagued the Soviet economy in its final years.

Labor Markets and Jobs Rights

The Soviet labor market came close to functioning as a real market.[36] Wage differentials were the primary mechanism to allocate labor. The demand for labor was primarily plan-determined. Once output targets were established, labor requirements were determined by applying technical coefficients of labor required per unit of output under existing technology. On the supply side, households were substantially free to make their own occupational choices. The state set wage differentials—for example, by occupation and by region—in an attempt to induce appropriate supplies to meet planned demands.[37]

Wage-setting was straightforward. For an industrial branch, a base rate determined the relative wage level for that branch. A branch schedule of skill grades established the pattern of wage differentials within the branch. Therefore the level and differential could be adjusted by manipulating either the base or the schedule. Trade unions and workers played virtually no role in setting wages; wages were set by administrative authorities. Unlike other areas, planners were willing to use these differentials to manipulate labor supply. There was a substantial degree of market influence on the structure of Soviet wages.

In addition to wage differentials, nonmarket devices were used to manipulate labor supply. Higher- and technical-education institutions expanded in direct relation to the desired composition of the labor force, as directed by state control.[38] Nonmonetary rewards, adulation in the press, social benefits, and other moral incentives were also used to control the supply of labor. Soviet citizens, moreover, were limited in their locational choice by an internal passport system that required residency permits for various cities. Organized recruitment was used in early years but declined after World War II, except for the seasonal needs of agricultural production.

Soviet labor policies, including the forced-labor campaigns of the 1930s, ensured a high rate of labor force participation to promote rapid economic development. The participation rate (the civilian labor force as a proportion of the able-bodied population) generally exceeded 90 percent. Structural problems grew more serious as the system matured and became a major test of the ability of central planning to allocate labor. The rapid rate of urbanization left shortages in some areas, surpluses in others. Labor imbalances especially characterized the regional distribution of labor. Soviet authorities were consistently unable to meet the labor needs of Siberia and the far north.[39] In addition, the restrictive role of Soviet trade unions and the policy of "full employment" resulted in overemployment—artificially high levels of staffing at the enterprise level. It was quite difficult to lay off workers even if they were redundant.

Earlier chapters contrasted the Anglo-Saxon hire-and-fire labor market with the protected labor markets of Europe. The Soviet economy had its own version of labor market protection, which David Granick termed a job rights economy.[40] A *job rights economy is one in which workers are guaranteed a job by the state.*

The notion of a job rights economy arose in the early years of Soviet power. The new Bolshevik leaders pointed to the high unemployment rates of capitalism versus the guaranteed jobs of the world's first socialist economy. Job rights worked both ways, however. Labor laws required able-bodied citizens to work, or else be subject to penalties as parasites. There was also a problem with enterprises bidding against each other for scarce labor, which led to what the authorities regarded as excessive labor turnover. The fear of excessive turnover caused authorities to introduce penalties for unauthorized job changes.

By the postwar period, the jobs rights economy was entrenched. Workers knew they had guaranteed jobs. Employers were willing to keep marginal workers because they might need them in times of taut plans.

A job rights economy carries with it certain costs. If employees know they cannot be fired, they will shirk at work and labor productivity will suffer. The job rights economy produced a classic implicit agreement between labor and management summarized in the expression: "We pretend to work and you pretend to pay us."

Although there was experimentation with programs to encourage the firing of unproductive workers, the problems of guaranteed-employment policies were not solved and remained a grave difficulty for the transition.

Capital Allocation

Capital is not a value-creating input according to Marx's labor theory of value. Hence it should not generate an interest charge. Nevertheless, capital has an implicit value because less is available than is demanded, and some means must be devised for its allocation. Furthermore, if a "price" of capital is allowed, presumably all capital is owned by the state, and the "income" from capital accrues to the state, not to individuals.

Soviet investment was controlled by planning authorities and the ministries. In drawing up the output plan, planners used technical coefficients to determine and authorize the investment necessary to produce the planned increases in output. Some funds were available from internal enterprise sources, but even those funds remained under state control.

The aggregate supply of investment funds was largely under the control of planners. It is not surprising, therefore, that the ratio of saving to GDP was higher than under industrialized capitalism.[41]

In a capitalist economy, saving is largely determined by individuals and businesses as they choose between consumption in the present and greater consumption in the future. In the Soviet context, the state controlled savings (primarily by the state and by enterprises). In a capitalist economy, savings arise as undistributed profits in enterprises and as income that is not consumed in households. Both *types* of savings existed in the Soviet case, but because wages and prices were set by the state, the state itself could determine savings rates. The control of savings and investment was a powerful mechanism to promote more rapid capital accumulation than would be tolerated in an economy directed by consumer sovereignty.

Starting in the late 1960s, Soviet enterprises paid an interest charge for the use of capital. This charge was typically low and was designed to cover the administrative costs of making the capital funds available to the enterprise. The introduction of interest charges was less significant than it might appear. Interest charges were simply added as a cost of production, but, as noted earlier, production costs did not determine the use of outputs or inputs.

At the micro level, authorities devised rules for choosing among investment projects. Suppose there was a directive to raise the capacity to generate the volume of electric power. Will the new capacity be hydroelectric, nuclear, coal-fueled, or what? How can one compare the capital-intensive variant that has low operating costs with the variant that requires less capital initially but has high annual operating costs? Although Stalin rejected quasi-market techniques for making this sort of decision in the 1930s in favor of planners' wisdom, those methods surfaced again in the late 1950s and were used widely until the end of the Soviet Union.

Planners accepted the principle that the selection among competing projects should be based on cost-minimizing procedures. A general formula, called the coefficient of relative effectiveness, was used to compare projects, where *the **coefficient of relative effectiveness** was an interest rate disguised using another technical term.*

$$C_i + E_n K_i = \text{minimum} \tag{14.3}$$

where

$$C_i = \text{current expenditures of the } i\text{th investment project}$$
$$K_i = \text{the capital cost of the } i\text{th investment project}$$
$$E_n = \text{the normative coefficient}$$

This formula was used to weigh the tradeoff between higher capital outlays (K_i) and lower operating costs (C_i). The principle was that the project variant should be selected that yields the minimal full cost, where an imputed capital charge is included in cost. The capital cost was calculated by applying a "normative coefficient" (E_n) to the projected capital outlay.

To illustrate, assume that a choice must be made between two projects, the first having an annual operating cost (C) of 10 million rubles and a capital cost (K) of 30 million rubles, the second having a C of 7 million rubles and a K of 50 million rubles. Applying a normative coefficient of 10 percent yields a full cost of 13 million rubles for the first project and 12 million rubles for the second. The second project should be chosen because it is the minimal-cost variant. However, suppose a normative coefficient of 20 percent is applied. In this case, the full cost of the first variant is 16 and that of the second variant is 17. In this case—and all that has changed is the normative coefficient—the first variant should be chosen.

The principle that capital should be allocated on the basis of rate-of-return calculations should not obscure the fact that the basic allocation of capital still proceeded through an administrative investment plan, which itself was a derivative of the output plan. The rate-of-return calculations were used only to select among projects that followed planners' preferences in the first place. Thus they were used to decide what type of plant should be used to generate electricity, not whether the investment should be in the generation of electricity or in steel production. In fact, the standardized coefficient introduced in 1969 was watered down thereafter by numerous exceptions for particular branches of heavy industry and for various regions.

Market Forces: The Second Economy

In some areas of the Soviet economy—for example, labor allocation—planners used markets to influence outcomes. Wage differentials were used to influence the distribution of labor by region, by season, and by profession; retail prices were used to allocate consumer goods. The fact that wages and retail prices were set by planners does not rule out market forces. In such instances, planners were actually using the market as a tool.

Unlike labor and retail prices, the second economy fell outside the range of state control. The second economy has been analyzed extensively by Gregory Grossman, Dimitri Simes, Vladimir Treml, Michael V. Alexeev, Aron Katsenelinboigen, and others.[42] It consisted of a number of market activities of varying importance and degrees of legality, all facilitating "unplanned" exchange among consumers and producers. According to Grossman, *the second-economy encompasses activities that meet at least one of the following two criteria: (1) the activity is engaged in for private gain; (2) the person engaging in the activity knowingly contravenes existing law.*

Examples of second-economy activities abound. Indeed, since the demise of the Soviet Union, a good deal more has been learned about the second economy. A physician would treat private patients for higher fees. A salesperson would set aside quality merchandise for customers who offered large tips. The manager of a textile firm would reserve goods for sale in unofficial supply channels. A collective farmer would divert collective farm land and supplies to his private plot. Black marketeers in port cities would deal in contraband merchandise. Owners of private cars transported second-economy merchandise. In some cases, official and second-economy transactions were intertwined. Managers would divert some production into second-economy transactions to raise cash to purchase, unofficially, supplies needed to meet the plan. The official activities of an enterprise would serve as a front for a prospering second-economy undertaking.

It is difficult to estimate accurately the magnitude of second-economy activity. In a survey of Soviet émigrés conducted by Gur Ofer and Aron Vinokur, earnings derived during the early 1970s from activity other than that at the main place of employment were found to account for approximately 10 percent of earnings.[43] A study of Soviet alcohol production and consumption, conducted by Treml in the mid-1980s, found that between 20 and 25 percent of transactions were illegal. Although the second economy was important in the overall command economy, there were substantial variations from one sector to another. It was not surprising for secondary activities to arise in a setting of increasing incomes and devotion of limited resources to the service sector.

The second economy had its advantages and disadvantages as far as the planners were concerned. It helped to preserve incentives because higher wages and bonus payments could be spent in the second economy. Moreover, the second economy reduced inflationary pressures on the official economy. On the negative side, the second economy diverted effort from planned tasks and loosened planners' control. Soviet authorities long tolerated the second economy. Reforms of the late 1980s moved to legalize a number of second-economy activities that did not involve the use of hired labor.

Yet another area of market influence was the private sector of Soviet agriculture. Under certain restrictions, the farm family could use a plot of land, hold animals, and raise crops. The resulting products were sold in the kolkhoz market—a practice the authorities tolerated—at prices established by supply and demand. Such sales accounted for a substantial portion of the farm family's income. It was not by accident that the private plots produced farm products that were poorly suited to planning, such as fruits, vegetables, and dairy products—all of which required much personal care and motivation.

International Trade

Foreign trade played a substantive but less important role in the Soviet development experience than in that of other industrialized economies.[44] The policies and the systemic arrangements of foreign trade in the command model differed widely from those in market economies.

Throughout the Soviet period, foreign trade was planned and executed by the foreign trade monopoly. *The **Soviet foreign-trade monopoly** handled all international transaction between Soviet and foreign enterprises.* Decision making—what will be traded, with whom, and on what terms—was centralized in three major institutions: the Ministry of Foreign Trade (MFT), the *Vneshtorgbank* or Bank for Foreign Trade (BFT), and the various foreign-trade organizations (FTOs).

The formal organization of Soviet foreign trade is represented in Figure 14.5. The MFT, like other Soviet ministries, was a centralized body concerned with issues of foreign-trade planning—the development of import/export plans, material supply plans, and balance-of-payments plans—all of which were an integral part of the Soviet material balance planning system.

Individual Soviet enterprises did not deal with the external world until the reforms of Gorbachev in 1987. Rather, for both imports and exports, enterprises dealt with the FTOs in domestic currency at domestic prices, and the FTOs dealt with the external world via financial arrangements handled by the MFT and the BFT. The domestic users or producers of goods entering the foreign market were isolated from foreign markets by this foreign-trade monopoly. Soviet foreign trade operated according to the rule, "Export what is available to be exported to pay for necessary imports, and limit the overall volume of trade to control the influence of market forces on the Soviet economy."

FIGURE 14.5   The Organization of Soviet Foreign Trade: The Command Model

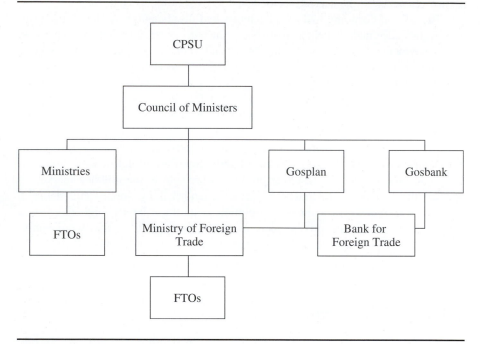

Source: From GREGORY, Comparing Economic Systems in the Twenty-First Century, 7E. © 2004 Cengage Learning.

Most Soviet trade, even with other socialist countries, was bilateral—that is, directly negotiated for each trade deal with each trading partner. Bilateral trade meant that Soviet exports and imports were handled largely on a barter basis. The difficulties of operating according to offsetting barter deals hampered Soviet trade volume through the years. In part, bilateral trading arrangements arose from and contributed to the nonconvertibility of the Soviet ruble, which was not used as a medium of exchange in world markets.

Soviet trading arrangements were not conducive to an expanding and competitive position in world markets, but Western economists generally argued that the Soviet Union followed a policy of deliberate trade aversion.[45] ***Trade aversion** is the deliberate underutilization of trade potential.*

Dating from the late 1920s and early 1930s, Soviet trade ratios (that is, the ratio of imports and exports to GDP) generally declined. For many years, the Soviet trade ratio remained low by world standards. This pattern partially resulted from the Soviet Union's adverse position in world markets at that time, or it may have been in part a deliberate policy response. In any event, for the trade that was conducted, a very successful effort was made to redirect Soviet imports away from consumer goods and toward producer goods, an outcome that contributed to the development effort.

Despite changes in attitudes toward international markets near the end of the Soviet period, the Soviet economy remained isolated from world product and capital markets. Whereas other countries became increasingly a part of globalized markets, the Soviet economy remained isolated.

When the Soviet system collapsed, the foreign-trade monopoly collapsed along with it. As enterprises and individuals gained the right to hold foreign currency and engage in foreign transactions, mass confusion resulted. Few knew the intricacies of international trade and credits. Western sellers did not understand that the state did not stand behind the foreign debts of state enterprises. There was confusion about who would take responsibility for the foreign debts of the USSR.

In this environment of confusion, former foreign trade officials had a comparative advantage over others. Many of today's Russian oligarchs cut their teeth in the foreign-trade monopoly.

Economic Performance

The Soviet administrative-command economy collapsed in the late 1980s and early 1990s as the former republics of the USSR and Eastern European satellites began their different roads to transition. China introduced significant reforms to its command system starting in the late 1970s. By the time of the collapse of communism, its economy bore little resemblance to the administrative-command system other than preserving the leading role of the Chinese Communist Party.

Scholars and officials debated for more than a half century whether the Soviet administrative-command economy would outperform capitalism in its various manifestations. We now have a definitive answer: No. But this answer was not evident until near the end, and the failure of the intelligence community to see the collapse coming was a matter of great embarrassment.

The various performance indicators of the administrative-command economy explained why we failed to see its collapse coming. According to conventional indicators, the system performed reasonably well in its early years. But, as time passed, its performance was worsening. Most experts thought, however, that the communist system would continue to "muddle along." The system itself seemed stable and capable of surviving at lower levels of economic performance. Confusing the matter more was the fact that the West went through trying times itself. In the 1970s, growth was depressed by the energy crisis. In the late 1970s and early 1980s, the West grappled with stagflation. Pain seemed to be shared all around, but the Western economies showed resilience. The communist economic system did not.

If we take away one lesson from the collapse of the administrative-command system, it is that what appear to be stable working arrangements can be actually quite fragile and require only a small push to send them over the edge.

Although we know the ultimate answer, it is nonetheless instructive to reexamine the performance of the administrative-command economy to see the strengths that kept it going and the weaknesses that contributed to its collapse.

Economic Growth

The huge research effort that went into studying the growth of communist countries during the Cold War was explained by military considerations and by the competition between the two economic systems on the world stage. When Western economists began recalculating the growth of the Soviet economy, they had to make a fundamental decision. In the Soviet case, the mix of goods produced was set by planners' preferences, not by consumer demand. ***Planners' preferences*** *refer to the setting of economic priorities by political authorities not by households acting as consumers.*

Planners' preferences meant that a Soviet-type economy produces a quite different mix of goods from a market economy. Some of them might appear quite useless to us, such as funds spent on "Red education circles" or "unfinished construction." We knew that such goods and services would not be demanded in a market economy. If the Soviet economy ever reverted to a market economy, their value would be zero. However, we were not in a position to impose our own value judgments. Soviet leaders had concluded that these goods were worth their resource costs. Hence the scholars doing the first independent reconstructions of Soviet economic growth—most notably Abram Bergson—decided to value all goods and services at the cost of producing them in their calculations.[46]

After the collapse of the Soviet economy, its successor economies summarily ceased the production of about a third or more of the products that they had earlier produced. These products were simply not wanted by a market economy.

We cannot summarize the mammoth literature on the performance of the Soviet administrative-command economy in a few pages. At best, we can hope to learn something from some group averages, noting that we could draw different conclusions from studies of country pairs, such as the United States versus the Soviet Union.

Figure 14.6 provides the average growth rates for the seven communist economies as contrasted with a larger number of capitalist countries. These averages conceal variability within the two groups, but we must content ourselves with such a global overview.

Figure 14.6 summarizes the growth rates of real GDP for the postwar period from 1950 to the collapse that was underway in 1990 and adversely affected the command economy results. The figure also shows average growth rates for middle-income market countries—a valid contrast in that the seven command economies were themselves middle-income countries.

Figure 14.6 illustrates why the verdict was out until fairly late in the game. Until the mid-1970s, the planned socialist and capitalist countries grew at about the same rate, one higher than the other depending on time period and circumstances. The planned socialist group, for example, outgrew the West during the West's troubles with the first energy crisis and during the beginning phases of stagflation. However, after 1975, it became clear that the socialist countries were experiencing declining growth. They were in what Gorbachev described as a period of stagnation. ***The period of stagnation*** *referred to the declining growth of the Soviet economic starting in the early 1970s.*

Economic growth in the West fluctuated according to the business cycle and external events, but it did not exhibit a pronounced secular trend toward decline. In the 1990s, the West entered a period of protracted growth called the Great Moderation, but that is not part of this story.

Throughout the postwar era, middle-income capitalist countries like Spain, Greece, South Korea, and Taiwan grew more rapidly than their mature

FIGURE 14.6   Growth Rates of Real GDP, Socialist Countries, Capitalist Countries and Middle-Income Capitalist Countries

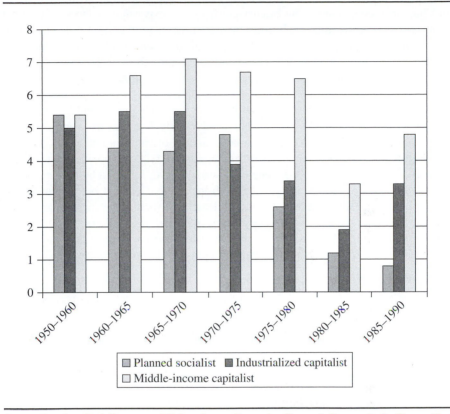

Source: Based on Paul Gregory and Robert Stuart, *Comparing Economic Systems in the Twenty-First Century* (Boston: Houghton Mifflin, 2004), pp. 348–349. The middle-income growth rates are from the conference board's statistical database, http://www.conference-board.org/data/economydatabase/

counterparts. Throughout much of the 1950–1990 period, their per capita income levels were in the same range as the planned socialist countries. Comparing growth rates of middle-income countries with different economic systems makes sense.

The middle-income country comparisons show striking differences: Whereas the middle-income capitalist economies grew rapidly, their socialist counterparts did not. The middle-income capitalist countries did not follow a secularly declining trend in growth rates.

The pattern of decline of planned socialist growth rates goes a long way toward explaining the decision to transition from planned socialism to market resource allocation. The growth explosion that began in China after its reform gave added impetus for change. The Soviet Union under Gorbachev felt that it could derive as many benefits from reform as China. Gorbachev was sorely disappointed in this regard.

Dynamic Efficiency and Productivity Growth

We can look behind these growth rates to examine the sources of growth. As noted in Chapter 3, economies grow extensively from the expansion of labor and capital inputs, or they grow intensively from increased factor productivity. *The **growth of factor productivity** measures the rate of growth of output per unit of capital and labor input.*[47] Although the link is imperfect, the growth of factor productivity is thought to capture the effects of technological advances on economic performance.

Figure 14.7 supplies information on the dynamic efficiency of the planned socialist and the industrialized capitalist countries. It records real GDP growth and factor productivity growth for two periods: 1950–1960 and 1960–1985. It uses the average rates of growth of each group, which conceals a large amount of variation within the group.

Figure 14.7 shows, as in the growth comparisons, relatively rapid growth of factor productivity for the socialist group in the early period, followed by a steep decline after 1960. Factor productivity growth fell from above 3 percent per annum to less than 1 percent between the two periods. At least, on average, the socialist group did achieve intensive growth in the early years, but that was followed by extensive growth after 1960. The socialist countries had reached the point where they could grow only by increasing labor and capital inputs, which is an "expensive" way to

FIGURE 14.7   Growth Rates of Real GDP and Total Factor Productivity, Socialist Countries and Capitalist Countries, 1950–1985

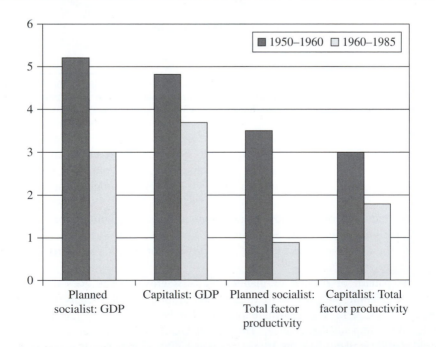

Source: Based on Paul Gregory and Robert Stuart, *Comparing Economic Systems in the Twenty-First Century* (Boston: Houghton Mifflin, 2004), pp. 356–357.

grow. Their populations were no longer growing, and there was no will to defer consumption to build up the capital stock.

If we compare factor productivity growth with GDP growth, we see that after 1960, increase in output per unit of inputs explained about half of the growth of capitalist economic growth and less than a third of socialist growth.

Intensification of growth proved to be a Holy Grail that the planned socialist economies could never find. Without intensification, they were doomed to limp along at modest rates of growth at best, while their Western competitors, particularly the middle-income countries, outpaced and overtook them.

Static Efficiency

Dynamic efficiency measures an economy's rate of increase in efficiency. *Static efficiency takes a snapshot of an economy's efficiency at one point in time.*

To measure a country's static efficiency, we must know its productive potential, as defined by its total resources. We measure static efficiency by how closely

FIGURE 14.8   Why It Is Difficult to Evaluate Static Efficiency: Different Country Production Possibilities

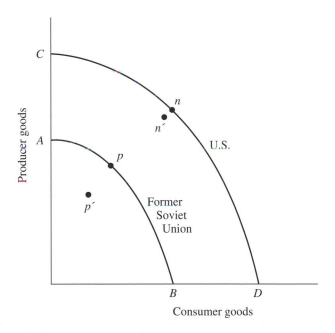

Explanation: CD represents the production possibilities frontier (PPF) of, say, the United States. AB is the PPF of, say, the former Soviet Union. The U.S. PPF is to the northeast of the Soviet PPF because of greater resources and better technology. The relevant measure of static efficiency is how closely each economy comes to operating on its PPF. If, for example, the United States operates very close to *n* at *n'* and the Soviet Union operates at *p'*, which is very far from *p*, then the United States is more efficient. In real-world measurement, all we observe is *p'* and *n'*. We have no way of knowing what *p* and *n* are.

Source: From GREGORY, Comparing Economic Systems in the Twenty-First Century, 7E. © 2004 Cengage Learning.

the economy comes to meeting that potential. Figure 14.8 explains this. To show that the Soviet Union, for example, obtained half as much output as the United States from a given amount of conventional labor and capital inputs would not unambiguously prove the greater static efficiency of the American economy. The measurement of conventional inputs may fail to capture the full range of resources (in both qualitative and quantitative terms) at the disposal of each economy.

Abram Bergson has made a careful study of comparative productivity under capitalism and socialism that sheds light on static efficiency.[48] Bergson's data for 1975 are reproduced in Table 14.1. They give per capita outputs and labor (adjusted for quality differences), capital, and land inputs of various capitalist and socialist countries (where the socialist group includes Yugoslavia) as a percentage of the U.S. per capita figures. Table 14.1 shows, for example, that Italy had a per capita output 61 percent, a per capita employment 75 percent, and a per capita capital stock 62 percent of the United States. The Soviet Union had a similar per capita output (60 percent) of the United States, but it had higher per capita employment (104 percent) and per capita capital stock (73 percent) than Italy.

The issue is whether the socialist countries systematically obtained less output from their available inputs than the capitalist countries. The data for Italy and the Soviet Union show that Italy obtained more output from its available inputs. Italy and the Soviet Union had the same per capita output when compared with the United States, yet the Soviet Union used more labor and capital per capita to produce that output.

Bergson demonstrated that there was a systematic tendency for the output per worker (labor productivity) in socialist economies to fall short of output per worker in capitalist countries, when other inputs are held constant. According to Bergson's

TABLE **14.1**   Per Capita Output, Employment, Capital, and Land, 1975
(United States = 100)

Country	Output per Capita	Employment per Capita Adjusted for Labor Quality	Reproducible Capital per Capita	Farm Land per Capita
United States	100.0	100.0	100.0	100.0
West Germany	90.0	84.0	107.3	14.8
France	92.2	88.3	83.0	40.1
Italy	61.3	75.2	61.6	24.9
United Kingdom	67.2	89.6	77.2	14.5
Japan	82.8	129.0	95.2	5.4
Spain	64.6	95.4	47.7	67.0
Soviet Union	60.0	104.1	73.2	103.5
Hungary	61.1	115.6	70.9	59.8
Poland	54.8	122.7	51.6	50.4
Yugoslavia	41.5	98.8	35.9	45.6

Source: Abram Bergson, "Comparative Productivity: The USSR, Eastern Europe, and the West," *American Economic Review* 77 (June 1987), 347. Used by permission.

calculations, output per worker in the socialist group fell 25 percent to 34 percent short of output per worker in the capitalist group *ceteris paribus.*

Bergson's findings suggest that socialist economies have relatively lower productivity, *ceteris paribus*, than industrialized capitalist countries.[49] The planned socialist economy is dead, so we cannot repeat these experiments using larger samples. However, this and other studies lead to the general presumption that efficiency was lower in the planned socialist systems than in market capitalist systems.

Declining Performance

A number of explanations have been advanced for the slowdown of the planned socialist economies. Some explanations are technical; others are associated with political-economy failings.

On the technical side, scholars have argued that diminishing returns and/or declining marginal product of capital occurred in a setting where capital was substituted for labor inputs that were no longer growing.[50] Others argued that planning and management had simply become more complex as the economy matured. Mature economies have to make more complex choices than the simpler economies of the 1930s or early 1950s, when priorities were more obvious. The growing complexity of the planned socialist systems also contributed to the lagging performance. The growing complexity was made even denser in an environment of persistent excess demand, along with shortages and bottlenecks in the material supply system.[51] Moreover, lack of innovative activity became understandable in a system where few if any rewards were reaped for either product or process innovation.[52] Others claim that the evolutionary approach to change may have conferred a growth advantage for the early years, but it became a disadvantage in later years.[53] As time passed, enterprises and interest groups learned how to collude and manipulate information, which limited the effectiveness of the central planners and their control over the economy.

Income Distribution

Another measure of performance is the distribution of income among households. What constitutes a good income distribution must be subjective, but most would agree that a distribution in which the top 1 percent of the population receives 95 percent of all income is "unfair" and that a completely even distribution is "unfair."

Marx himself rejected an equal distribution of income during the transition from socialism to communism, arguing instead for a distribution that reflected the individual's contribution to the well-being of society. He understood that differential rewards would have to be offered for effort until a new sort of communist human being was created.

What differences would one expect in the distribution of income under capitalism and socialism? In capitalist societies, inequality derives from the unequal distribution of property ownership (land and capital resources) and of human capital. Both forms of capital yield income—the first in the form of property income from rent, interest, dividends, and capital gains, the second from wages and salaries.[54]

Under both planned and market socialism, property other than consumer durables and housing is owned by the state, and the return from this state-owned property is at the state's disposal. Under capitalism, the bulk of property is owned privately, and property income accrues to private individuals.

The distribution of human capital depends on schooling and on-the-job training. Free or subsidized public schooling is available in both types of societies, although there is a greater tendency for the state to pay for higher education in socialist societies. Nevertheless, the differences between the two systems would not be expected to be great. If anything, the distribution of labor incomes could be more equal under socialism because of the more equal distribution of education and training, the absence of real labor unions, and the greater doctrinal commitment to equality.[55]

The major distinction is the absence of private ownership of income-earning property under socialism. Unless offset by higher earnings differentials, the distribution of income should be more equal under socialism. The distribution of income after taxes and benefits depends on the extent to which the state engages in income redistribution.

Frederic Pryor made an extensive econometric study of the distribution of labor income among workers for the late 1950s and early 1960s. He found that the distribution of labor income was more nearly equal under socialism, once per capita income and the size of the country were held constant. He also found that labor incomes were less equal in the Soviet Union than in the other socialist countries; therefore, studies that generalize from the Soviet experience are likely to give a false impression.[56]

Subsequent data on the distribution of earnings for full-time wage and salary earners confirm most of Pryor's findings for the 1950s and early 1960s. Earnings were more nearly equally distributed in Eastern Europe and the Soviet Union than in the United States in the 1970s. For the USSR, this was a relatively new phenomenon because as late as 1957 Soviet earnings were less nearly equal than those in the United States.

Data calculated by P. J. D. Wiles on the distribution of per capita income, after income taxes, for a limited number of planned socialist and capitalist countries generally exclude top income–earning families (party leaders, government officials, artists, and authors) and include only families of workers and employees.[57] Many second-economy activities considered legal in capitalist societies (the provision of private repair and medical services, for example) are also not recorded. Also, resources (even excluding free educational and medical benefits) provided in socialist societies on an extra market basis—shopping privileges, official cars, vacations—and are not included. We could point out similar flaws in the capitalist distributions, but we think that the results will capture the main differences in income distribution between socialist and capitalist systems.

Wiles' data show that income was distributed more unequally in those capitalist countries in which the state played a relatively minor redistributive role (the United States, Italy, and Canada). Yet even where the state played a major redistributive role (the United Kingdom and Sweden), the distribution of income appeared to be slightly more unequal than in the planned socialist countries

(Hungary, Czechoslovakia, and Bulgaria). The Soviet Union in 1966 appears to have had a less egalitarian distribution of income than its East European counterparts. The USSR distribution was scarcely distinguishable from the British and Swedish distributions (it may even have been more unequal). The Soviet income distribution was more nearly equal than that in Australia, Canada, and the United States but not much different from that in Norway and the United Kingdom.

The **Gini coefficient** is a convenient summary measure of income inequality. The higher the Gini coefficient, the more unequal the distribution of income. A Gini coefficient of zero denotes perfect equality; a Gini coefficient of 1 denotes perfect inequality. Gini coefficients for the distribution of income after taxes and benefits for Great Britain and Sweden for the early 1970s are both approximately 0.25. The Czech, Hungarian, and Polish Gini coefficients for the same period are 0.21, 0.24, and 0.24, respectively—that is, very close to the British and Swedish coefficients. The Canadian and U.S. Gini coefficients, on the other hand, are 0.34 and 0.35, respectively, well above the socialist coefficients.[58]

In general, we conclude that the differences in distribution of income between the planned socialist economies and the capitalist welfare states were relatively minor. This is a surprising conclusion. One would have expected the absence of private ownership of property to make more of a difference. Nevertheless, differences are apparent when one contrasts the socialist distributions with those of the capitalist nations in which the state does not play a major redistributive role. In this instance, the expected contrast emerges, although we must reiterate the difficulty of interpreting the socialist distributions because of the omitted income categories.

As the former planned socialist economies began their transitions, income inequality soared. In a market context, the notion of income inequality was rejected rather emphatically.

Summary

- State ownership, national economic planning, and the collectivization of agriculture characterized the Bolshevik Revolution.
- The administrative-command economy was the resource-allocation model used in the former Soviet Union for more than sixty years.
- The Soviet system was a relatively centralized economic system. The broad objectives of the Communist Party were implemented through Gosplan (the state planning agency), the ministries, and individual firms and agricultural units.
- The essence of Soviet planning was the material balance system, in which balances were developed to equate the demand and supply of key industrial commodities, labor inputs, and the like. This system emphasized consistency, not optimality, and there was only minimal reliance on money and prices for the allocation of resources.
- Soviet enterprises were responsible for fulfilling plan targets, and managers were motivated within an incentive framework.
- Prices were cost-based, and the demand side had little or no influence. Capital was allocated primarily by administrative decree.

- Market-type influence existed in the allocation of labor. Market mechanisms played an important role in the private sector of Soviet agriculture.
- Collective farms, state farms, and the private sector traditionally dominated Soviet agriculture. In later years, agro-industrial integration became an important mechanism for combining farm activity with industrial processing.
- Soviet foreign trade was a state monopoly. Soviet domestic enterprises were largely isolated from world markets through the intermediary function of the foreign-trade organizations and the nonconvertible ruble.

Key Terms

ABC **of Communism**—Nikolai Bukharin and Evgeny Preobrazhensk's book, describing an economy in which the workers collectively own the means of production, goods are kept in public warehouses, and people take what they need

Administrators—issued the orders and intervened when they felt necessary.

Average branch cost pricing—profits cannot be used to gauge managerial performance.

Coefficient of relative effectiveness—an interest rate disguised using another technical term.

Collective farms (*kolkhozy*)—compulsory collectives of peasant households that delivered their products to the state at prices dictated by the state.

Control figures—preliminary output targets of the national economic plan.

Economic managers—responsible for fulfilling these orders and rewarded or penalized based upon on the level of fulfillment.

Foreign foreign-trade monopoly—handled all international transaction between Soviet and foreign enterprises.

Fund holders—recipients of funded commodities.

Funded commodities—those whose "limits" were assigned to enterprises by the planning system.

Gosplan—the Russian name for the State Planning Commission.

Gross value of output—the planned output of the ministry or enterprise expressed either in physical units or in value terms.

Growth of factor productivity—measures the rate of growth of output per unit of capital and labor input

Industrial prices—set to equal the average cost of the industrial branch plus a profit markup.

Job rights economy—workers are guaranteed a job by the state.

Labor theory of value (Marx)—value is determined by labor alone and therefore excludes interest and rent from allowable costs.

Leading role of the party—the recognized status of the communist party as the primary decision decision-making body of the Soviet Union.

Macroeconomic balance—supply of consumer goods at established prices equaled desired consumer spending.

Money illusion—economic agents base their decisions on nominal prices and wages rather than on relative prices and real wages.

New Economic Policy (NEP)—returned smaller enterprises to private ownership, legalized private trade, and introduced a tax on agriculture to replace grain requisitions.

Nomenklatura—a list of responsible positions that were to be filled by the personnel department of the party.

Output plan—tells the producers what to produce and in what assortments.

Period of stagnation—the declining growth of the Soviet economic starting in the early 1970s.

Petty tutelage—the constant interventions in the affairs of enterprises by superiors.

Planners' preferences—the setting of economic priorities by political authorities not by households acting as consumers.

Planning from the achieved level—the practice of planning based on last year's targets plus marginal changes.

Primary party organization—supposedly represented the interests of the party at the local enterprise level.

Resource managers—the actors, not the plan itself, that made the actual resource allocation decisions for the economy in the course of plan implementation.

Ruble control—the monitoring of plan fulfillment by monitoring the financial transactions among enterprises.

Savings overhang—the accumulation of forced savings that resulted formfrom having nothing to buy.

Second-economy—activities that meet at least one of the following two criteria: (1) the activity is engaged in for private gain; (2) the person engaging in the activity knowingly contravenes existing law.

Socialism in one country—the argument about whether the Bolsheviks should set as their goal the building of socialism in the USSR or promote a world socialist revolution.

Soft budget constraint—enterprises that fail to cover their costs received automatic subsidies from the ministry, which redistributed profits from profitable to unprofitable enterprises, or from the state budget.

Stalin's Great Break—the policies Stalin put in place starting in 1929 to establish the administrative command economic and political system.

State Bank (Gosbank)—the monopoly bank that handled all enterprise transactions throughout the economy.

Static efficiency—takes a snapshot of an economy's efficiency at one point in time.

Success indicator problem—managers' need to select which orders to fulfill among the multitude of orders they received.

Supply plan—tells producers to whom to deliver their outputs.

Techpromfinplan (technical–industrial–financial plan)—the enterprises plan, including output, assortment, labor staffing, and financial plans.

Trade aversion—the deliberate underutilization of trade potential.

Turnover tax—a differentiated tax on consumer good that depended on consumer demand for the product and is the difference between the wholesale and retail price.

War communism—the nationalization of most of the economy, the attempt to eliminate market relationships in industry and trade, and the forced requisitioning of agricultural products from the peasants

Notes

1. Paul R. Gregory and Robert C. Stuart, *Soviet and Post-Soviet Economic Structure and Performance*, 6th ed. (Reading, Mass.: Addison Wesley Longman, 1997); Alec Nove, *The Soviet Economic System*, 3rd ed. (New York: Unwin Hyman, 1986); and Michael Ellman, *Socialist Planning* (New York: Cambridge University Press, 1989). For useful background papers, see U.S. Congress, Joint Economic Committee, *Soviet Economy in the 1980s: Problems and Prospects*, Parts 1 and 2 (Washington, D.C.: U.S. Government Printing Office, 1982). For a briefer treatment of the Soviet economy, see Franklyn D. Holzman, *The Soviet Economy: Past, Present, and Future* (New York: Foreign Policy Association, 1982); and James R. Millar, *The ABC's of Soviet Socialism* (Urbana: University of Illinois Press, 1981).
2. Nikolai Bukharin and Evgeny Preobrazhensky, *The ABC of Communism: A Popular Explanation of the Program of the Communist Party of Russia* (Ann Arbor: University of Michigan Press, 1966). A translation of the 1920 Russian edition.
3. Alec Nove, *An Economic History of the U.S.S.R.*, rev. ed. (London: Penguin Books, 1982); Eugene Zaleski, *Planning for Economic Growth in the Soviet Union, 1928–1932* (Chapel Hill: University of North Carolina Press, 1971); Maurice Dobb, *Soviet Economic Development Since 1917*, 5th ed. (London: Routledge and Kegan Paul, 1960); E. H. Carr and R. W. Davies, *Foundations of a Planned Economy, 1926–1929*, Vol. I, Part 2 (New York: Macmillan, 1969); Roger Munting, *The Economic Development of the USSR* (London: Croom Helm, 1982); R. W. Davies, *The Socialist Offensive, the Collectivization of Soviet Agriculture 1929–30* (London: Macmillan, 1980); and Thomas F. Remington, "Varga and the Foundation of Soviet Planning," *Soviet Studies* 34 (October 1982), 585–600.
4. Gregory and Stuart, *Soviet and Post-Soviet Economic Structure and Performance*, p. 58.
5. Jerzy F. Karcz, "From Stalin to Brezhnev: Soviet Agricultural Policy in Historical Perspective," in James R. Millar, ed., *The Soviet Rural Community* (Urbana: University of Illinois Press, 1971), pp. 36–70; and Davies, *The Socialist Offensive*.
6. Alexander Erlich, *The Soviet Industrialization Debate, 1924–1928* (Cambridge, Mass.: Harvard University Press, 1960). For a translation of original contributions to the debate, see Nicolas Spulber, *Foundations of Soviet Strategy for Economic Growth* (Bloomington: Indiana University Press, 1964).
7. Paul Gregory, *Politics, Murder and Love in Stalin's Kremlin: The Story of Nikolai Bukharin and Anna Larina* (Stanford: Hoover Press, 2010). The actual debate transcripts have not been translated and must be read in Russian.
8. M. Lewin, *Russian Peasants and Soviet Power* (London: Allen and Unwin, 1968) and R. W. Davies, *The Socialist Offensive, the Collectivization of Soviet Agriculture 1929–30* (London: Macmillan, 1980).
9. Paul Gregory, *The Political Economy of Stalinism* (New York: Cambridge University Press, 2003), chap. 1.
10. Jan Plamper, *The Stalin Cult: A Study in the Alchemy of Power* (New Haven: Yale University Press, 2012).

11. Paul Gregory, *Terror by Quota: State Security from Lenin to Stalin* (New Haven: Yale University Press, 2008).

12. Leonard Shapiro, *The Communist Party of the Soviet Union* (New York: Random House, 1971); and Jerry F. Hough and Merle Fainsod, *How the Soviet Union Is Governed* (Cambridge, Mass.: Harvard University Press, 1979). For a statistical survey of party membership, see T. H. Rigby, *Communist Party Membership in the U.S.S.R., 1917–1967* (Princeton, N.J.: Princeton University Press, 1968). For further evidence, see T. H. Rigby, "Soviet Communist Party Membership Under Brezhnev," *Soviet Studies* 28 (July 1976), 317–337; and Jan Adams, *Citizen Inspectors in the Soviet Union: The People's Control Committee* (New York: Praeger, 1977). For evidence on how the party financed itself, see Eugenia Belova and Valery Lazarev, *Funding Loyalty: The Economics of the Communist Party* (New Haven: The Yale-Hoover Series on Stalin, Stalinism, and the Cold War, 2012).

13. Hough and Fainsod, *How the Soviet Union Is Governed*; and T. H. Rigby, *Political Elites in the USSR* (Brookfield, Vt.: Edward Elgar, 1990).

14. For a remarkable inside look at how Stalin directed the economy through his deputies, see R.W. Davies et al., *The Stalin-Kaganovich Correspondence, 1931–1936* (New Haven: Yale University Press, 2003).

15. Paul Gregory and Mark Harrison, "Allocation under Dictatorship: Research in Stalin's Archives," *Journal of Economic Literature* XLIII (September 2005), 725–729.

16. Paul Gregory, *The Political Economy of Stalinism* (New York: Cambridge, 2004), chap. 4.

17. O. V. Khlevnyuk, R. Davies, L.P. Kosheleva, E.A. Ris, L.A. Rogovaia, *Stalin i Kaganovich. Perepiski. 1931–1936 gg.* (Moscow: Rosspen, 2001), p. 55.

18. Michael Ellman and Vladimir Kontorovich, *The Destruction of the Soviet Economic System: An Insiders' History* (Armonk, N.Y.: M.E. Sharpe, 1998), p. 46.

19. Joseph Berliner, *Factory and Manager in the USSR* (Cambridge, Mass.: Harvard University Press, 1957); David Granick, *The Red Executive* (New York: Doubleday, 1960); David Granick, *Managerial Comparisons of Four Developed Countries: France, Britain, United States and Russia* (Cambridge, Mass.: MIT Press, 1972); William J. Conyngham, *The Modernization of Soviet Industrial Management* (New York: Cambridge University Press, 1982); and Jan Adams, "The Present Soviet Incentive System," *Soviet Studies* 32 (July 1980), 360.

20. Gregory and Stuart, *Soviet and Post-Soviet Economic Structure and Performance*, pp. 215–216.

21. David Conn, special ed., *The Theory of Incentives*, published as *Journal of Comparative Economics* 3, no. 3 (September 1979); and J. Michael Martin, "Economic Reform and Maximizing Behavior of the Soviet Firm," in Judith Thornton, ed., *Economic Analysis of the Soviet-Type System* (New York: Cambridge University Press, 1976).

22. Paul Gregory, *Terror by Quota: State Security from Lenin to Stalin* (New Haven: Yale University Press, 2008).

23. J. M. Montias, "Planning with Material Balances in Soviet-Type Economies," *American Economic Review* 49 (December 1959), 963–985.

24. Eugene Zaleski, *Planning for Economic Growth in the Soviet Union, 1928–1932* (Chapel Hill: University of North Carolina Press, 1971).

25. I. V. Stalin, *Voprosy Leninizma*, 10th ed. (Moscow, 1937), p. 413.

26. Paul Gregory, *The Political Economy of Stalinism*, chap. 8.

27. Eugenia Belova and Paul Gregory, "Dictators, Loyal and Opportunistic Agents: The Soviet Archives on Creating the Soviet Economic System," *Public Choice* 113 (2002), 265–286.

28. Valery Lazarev and Paul Gregory, "The Wheels of a Command Economy," *Economic History Review* 55, no. 2 (July 2002), 324–328.

29. Eugenia Belova, "Economic Crime and Punishment," in Paul Gregory (ed.), *Behind the Façade of Stalin's Command Economy* (Stanford, Calif.: Hoover Institution Press, 2001).

30. Paul Gekker, "The Banking System of the USSR," *Journal of the Institute of Bankers* 84 (June 1963), 189–197; and Christine Netishen Wollan, "The Financial Policy of the Soviet State Bank, 1932–1970" (Ph.D. dissertation, University of Illinois, Urbana, 1972).

31. Gregory and Stuart, *Soviet and Post-Soviet Economic Structure and Performance*, chap. 8; Morris Bornstein, "Soviet Price Policy in the 1970s," in U.S. Congress, Joint Economic Committee, *Soviet Economy in a New Perspective* (Washington, D.C.: Government Printing Office, 1976), pp. 17–66; Morris Bornstein, "The Administration of the Soviet Price System," *Soviet Studies* 30 (October 1978), 466–490; and Morris Bornstein, "Soviet Price Policies," *Soviet Economy* 3, no. 2 (1987), 96–134.

32. Gur Ofer and Joyce Pickersgill, "Soviet Household Saving: A Cross-Section Study of Soviet Emigrant Families," *Quarterly Journal of Economics* 95 (August 1980), 121–144; and Joyce Pickersgill, "Soviet Household Saving Behavior," *Review of Economics and Statistics* 58 (May 1976), 139–147; D. W. Bronson and Barbara S. Severin, "Recent Trends in Consumption and Disposable Money Income in the USSR," U.S. Congress, Joint Economic Committee, *New Directions in the Soviet Economy*, Part II-B (Washington, D.C.: Government Printing Office, 1966); and Igor Birman, *Secret Income and the Soviet State Budget* (Boston: Kluwer, 1981).

33. Studies of repressed inflation in the former Soviet Union include D. H. Howard, "The Disequilibrium Model in a Controlled Economy: An Empirical Test of the Barro-Grossman Model," *American Economic Review* 66 (December 1976), 871–879; Richard Portes, "The Control of Inflation: Lessons from East European Experience," *Economics* 44 (May 1977), 109–130; Richard Portes and David Winter, "A Planners' Supply Function for Consumption Goods in Centrally Planned Economies," *Journal of Comparative Economics* 1 (December 1977), 351–365.

34. David Granick, *Job Rights in the Soviet Union: Their Consequences* (Cambridge: Cambridge University Press, 1987).

35. Gregory, *The Political Economy of Stalinism*, chap. 9.

36. Leonard J. Kirsch, *Soviet Wages: Changes in Structure and Administration Since 1956* (Cambridge, Mass.: MIT Press, 1972); B. Arnot, *Controlling Soviet Labour* (London: Macmillan, 1988); D. Granick, *Job Rights in the Soviet Union: Their Consequences* (New York: Cambridge University Press, 1987); and Silvana Malle, *Employment Planning in the Soviet Union* (Basingstoke, England: Macmillan, 1990).

37. Abram Bergson, *The Economics of Soviet Planning* (New Haven: Yale University Press, 1964), chap. 6.

38. Murray Feshbach and Stephen Rapawy, "Soviet Population and Manpower Trends and Policies," in Joint Economic Committee, *Soviet Economy in a New Perspective*, 113–154. For the specific case of agriculture, see Karl-Eugen Wadekin, "Manpower in Soviet Agriculture—Some Post-Khrushchev Developments and Problems," *Soviet Studies* 20 (January 1969), 281–305.

39. Murray Feshbach, "Population and Labor Force," in Abram Bergson and Herbert S. Levine, eds., *The Soviet Economy: Towards the Year 2000* (Winchester, Mass.: Allen and Unwin, 1983), pp. 79–111; Jan Adams, ed., *Employment Policies in the Soviet Union and Eastern Europe*, 2nd ed. (New York: St. Martin's, 1987); and P. R. Gregory and I. L. Collier, "Unemployment in the Soviet Union: Evidence from the Soviet Interview Project," *American Economic Review* 78 (September 1988), 613–632.

40. Granick, *Job Rights in the Soviet Union*; and Malle, *Employment Planning in the Soviet Union*.

41. Alan Abouchar, "The New Soviet Standard Methodology for Investment Allocation," *Soviet Studies* 24 (January 1973), 402–410; P. Gregory, B. Fielitz, and T. Curtis, "The New Soviet Investment Rules: A Guide to Rational Investment Planning?" *Southern Economic Journal* 41 (January 1974), 500–504; Frank A. Durgin, "The Soviet 1969 Standard Methodology for Investment Allocation versus 'Universally Correct' Methods," *ACES Bulletin* 19 (Summer 1977), 29–53; Frank A. Durgin, Jr., "The Third Soviet Standard Methodology for Determining the Effectiveness of Capital Investment (SM-80, Provisional)," *ACES Bulletin* 24 (Fall 1982), 45–61; and Janice Giffen, "The Allocation of Investment in the Soviet Union: Criteria for the Efficiency of Investment," *Soviet Studies* 33 (October 1981), 593–609. For a useful summary, see David Dyker, *The Process of Investment in the Soviet Union* (New York: Cambridge University Press, 1981).

42. Gregory Grossman, "The 'Second Economy' of the USSR," *Problems of Communism* 26 (September–October 1977), 25–40; Aron Katsenelinboigen, "Coloured Markets in the Soviet Union," *Soviet Studies* 29 (January 1977), 62–85; Dimitri Simes, "The Soviet Parallel Market," *Survey* 21 (Summer 1975), 42–52; and *Studies on the Soviet Second Economy* (Durham, N.C.: Berkeley–Duke Occasional Papers on the Second Economy in the USSR, December 1987); Vladimir Treml, "Alcohol in the USSR: A Fiscal Dilemma," *Soviet Studies* 41 (October 1973), 161–177; Dennis O'Hearn, "The Consumer Second Economy: Size and Effects," *Soviet Studies* 32 (April 1980), 221; and Vladimir G. Treml, *Purchase of Food from Private Sources in Soviet Urban Areas* (Durham, N.C.: Berkeley–Duke Occasional Papers on the Second Economy in the USSR, September 1985).

43. Treml, "Alcohol in the USSR"; O'Hearn, "The Consumer Second Economy"; and Treml, *Purchase of Food from Private Sources in Soviet Urban Areas.*

44. Gregory and Stuart, *Soviet and Post-Soviet Economic Structure and Performance,* chap. 9.

45. Steven Rosefielde, "Comparative Advantage and the Evolving Pattern of Soviet International Commodity Specialization, 1950–1973," in Steven Rosefielde, ed., *Economic Welfare and the Economics of Soviet Socialism* (New York: Cambridge University Press, 1981), pp. 185–220.

46. Abram Bergson, *The Real National Income of Soviet Russian Since 1928* (Cambridge, Mass.: Harvard University Press, 1961).

47. To calculate the rate of growth of output per units of capital and labor inputs, we must first calculate the growth rates of labor and capital combined ($\hat{L} + \hat{K}$), or total factor input. This is typically done by taking a weighted average of the growth rates of labor and capital, where the weights represent each factor's share of national income. Therefore total factor productivity is defined as $\hat{Q} - (\hat{L} + \hat{K})$. The ^ denote annual rates of growth of Q (real GDP), L (labor input), and K (capital input), where

$$\hat{K} + \hat{L} = \hat{K}W_K + \hat{L}W_L$$

where

$$W_K = \text{capital's share of income}$$
$$W_L = \text{labor's share of income}$$

48. Abram Bergson, "Comparative Productivity: The USSR, Eastern Europe, and the West," *American Economic Review* 77 (June 1987), 342–357. For Bergson's earlier work on this subject, see his discussion of relative Soviet output per unit in Abram Bergson, *The Economics of Soviet Planning* (New Haven: Yale University Press, 1964), chap. 14. Also see Bergson, *Production and the Social System: The USSR and the West* (Cambridge, Mass.: Harvard University Press, 1978).

49. See also Frederic L. Pryor, *Property and Industrial Organization in Communist and Capitalist Nations* (Bloomington: Indiana University Press, 1973), p. 80.

50. For a summary of views, see "The Soviet Growth Slowdown: Three Views," *American Economic Review: Papers and Proceedings* 76 (May 1986), 170–185.

51. Abhijii V. Banerjee and Michael Spagat, "Productivity Paralysis and the Complexity Problem: Why Do Centrally Planned Economies Become Prematurely Gray?" *Journal of Comparative Economics* 15 (December 1991), 646–660.

52. Joseph S. Berliner, *The Innovation Decision in Soviet Industry* (Cambridge, Mass.: MIT Press, 1976).

53. Peter Murrell and Mancur Olson, "The Devolution of Centrally Planned Economies," *Journal of Comparative Economics* 15 (June 1991), 239–265.

54. P. J. D. Wiles, *Economic Institutions Compared* (New York: Halsted Press, 1977), chap. 16; Martin Schnitzer, *Income Distribution: A Comparative Study of the United States, Sweden, West Germany, East Germany, the United Kingdom, and Japan* (New York: Praeger, 1974); Abram Bergson, "Income Inequality Under Soviet Socialism," *Journal of Economic Literature* 22 (September 1984); C. Morrison, "Income Distribution in East European and Western Countries," *Journal of Comparative Economics* 8 (1984), 121–138; and Anthony B. Atkinson and John Micklewright, *Economic Transformation in Eastern Europe and the Distribution of Income* (Cambridge: Cambridge University Press, 1992).

55. P. J. D. Wiles, *Economic Institutions Compared* (New York: Halsted Press, 1977), p. 443; Pryor, *Property and Industrial Organization in Communist and Capitalist Nations*, pp. 74–75.

56. Pryor, *Property and Industrial Organization in Communist and Capitalist Nations*, pp. 74–89.

57. Wiles, *Economic Institutions Compared*, p. 443. For other studies, see Janet Chapman, "Earnings Distribution in the USSR, 1968–1976," *Soviet Studies* 35 (July 1983), 410–413; See also Alastair McAuley, "The Distribution of Earnings and Income in the Soviet Union," *Soviet Studies* 29 (April 1977), 214–237.

58. Atkinson and Micklewright, *Economic Transformation in Eastern Europe and the Distribution of Income*.

Recommended Readings

General Works

Robert W. Campbell, *The Soviet-Type Economies: Performance and Evolution*, 3rd ed. (Boston: Houghton Mifflin, 1981).

R. W. Davies, ed., *The Soviet Union* (Winchester, Mass.: Unwin Hyman, 1989).

David A. Dyker, *The Future of the Soviet Planning System* (Armonk, N.Y.: M. E. Sharpe, 1985).

Paul R. Gregory and Robert C. Stuart, *Soviet and Post-Soviet Economic Structure and Performance*, 5th ed. (New York: HarperCollins, 1994).

Franklyn D. Holzman, *The Soviet Economy: Past, Present, and Future* (New York: Foreign Policy Association, 1982).

Tania Konn, ed., *Soviet Studies Guide* (London: Bowker–Saur, 1992).

James R. Millar, *The ABC's of Soviet Socialism* (Urbana: University of Illinois Press, 1981).

Alec Nove, *The Soviet Economic System*, 2nd ed. (London: Unwin Hyman, 1981).

United States Congress, Joint Economic Committee, *Gorbachev's Economic Plans*, Vols. I and II (Washington, D.C.: U.S. Government Printing Office, 1987).

Soviet Economic History

E. H. Carr and R. W. Davies, *Foundations of a Planned Economy, 1926–1929*, Vol. 1, Parts 1 and 2 (New York: Macmillan, 1969).

R. W. Davies, *The Industrialization of Soviet Russia*, Vols. I and II (Cambridge, Mass.: Harvard University Press, 1980).

R. W. Davies, Mark Harrison, and S. G. Wheatcroft, eds., *The Economic Transformation of the Soviet Union 1913–1945* (Cambridge: Cambridge University Press, 1994).

Maurice Dobb, *Soviet Economic Development Since 1917*, 5th ed. (London: Routledge and Kegan Paul, 1960).

Alexander Erlich, *The Soviet Industrialization Debate, 1924–1928* (Cambridge, Mass.: Harvard University Press, 1969).

Paul R. Gregory, *Russian National Income, 1885–1913* (New York: Cambridge University Press, 1983).

Gregory Guroff and Fred V. Carstensen, *Entrepreneurship in Imperial Russia and the Soviet Union* (Princeton, N.J.: Princeton University Press, 1983).

Moshe Lewin, *Political Undercurrents in Soviet Economic Debates: From Bukharin to the Modern Reformers* (Princeton, N.J.: Princeton University Press, 1974).

Roger Munting, *The Economic Development of the USSR* (London: Croom Helm, 1982).

Alec Nove, *An Economic History of the U.S.S.R.*, rev. ed. (London: Penguin Books, 1982).

Nicolas Spulber, *Soviet Strategy for Economic Growth* (Bloomington: Indiana University Press, 1964).

The Communist Party and the Manager

Donald D. Barry and Carol Barner-Barry, *Contemporary Soviet Politics: An Introduction*, 2nd ed. (Englewood Cliffs, N.J.: Prentice-Hall, 1982).

William J. Conyngham, *The Modernization of Soviet Industrial Management* (New York: Cambridge University Press, 1982).

Andrew Freiis, *The Soviet Industrial Enterprise* (New York: St. Martin's Press, 1974).

David Granick, *Managerial Comparisons of Four Developed Countries: France, Britain, United States, and Russia* (Cambridge, Mass.: MIT Press, 1972).

Leslie Holmes, *The Policy Process in Communist States* (Beverly Hills: Sage Publications, 1981).

Jerry F. Hough and Merle Fainsod, *How the Soviet Union Is Governed* (Cambridge, Mass.: Harvard University Press, 1979).

David Lane, *Politics and Society in the USSR*, 2nd ed. (London: Martin Robertson, 1978).

Nathan Leites, *Soviet Style in Management* (New York: Crane Russak, 1985).

Leonard Shapiro, *The Government and Politics of the Soviet Union*, 6th ed. (Essex, England: Hutchinson Publishing Group, 1978).

Selected Aspects of the Soviet Economy

R. Amann and J. M. Cooper, eds., *Industrial Innovation in the Soviet Union* (New Haven: Yale University Press, 1982).

Joseph S. Berliner, *The Innovation Decision in Soviet Industry* (Cambridge: MIT Press, 1976).

Morris Bornstein, ed., *The Soviet Economy: Continuity and Change* (Boulder, Colo.: Westview, 1981).

Robert W. Campbell, *Soviet Energy Technologies* (Bloomington: Indiana University Press, 1980).

David A. Dyker, *The Process of Investment in the Soviet Union* (Cambridge: Cambridge University Press, 1983).

Franklyn D. Holzman, *International Trade Under Communism* (New York: Basic Books, 1976).

Alastair McAuley, *Women's Work and Wages in the Soviet Union* (London: Unwin Hyman, 1981).

Mervyn Matthews, *Education in the Soviet Union* (London: Allen and Unwin, 1982).

————, *Poverty in the Soviet Union* (New York: Cambridge University Press, 1987).

James R. Millar, *Politics, Work, and Daily Life in the USSR* (New York: Cambridge University Press, 1987).

Henry W. Morton and Robert C. Stuart, eds., *The Contemporary Soviet City* (Armonk, N.Y.: M. E. Sharpe, 1984).

Robert C. Stuart, ed., *The Soviet Rural Economy* (Totowa, N.J.: Roman and Allenheld, 1983).

Murray Yanowitch, *Social and Economic Inequality in the Soviet Union* (London: Martin Robertson, 1977).

Eugene Zaleski, *Planning Reforms in the Soviet Union, 1962–1966* (Chapel Hill: University of North Carolina Press, 1967).

Planning

Alan Abouchar, ed., *The Socialist Price Mechanism* (Durham, N.C.: Duke University Press, 1977).

Edward Ames, *Soviet Economic Processes* (Homewood, Ill.: Irwin, 1965).

Abram Bergson and Herbert S. Levine, eds., *The Soviet Economy: Towards the Year 2000* (London: Allen and Unwin, 1983).

Martin Cave, Alastair McAuley, and Judith Thornton, eds., *New Trends in Soviet Economics* (Armonk, N.Y.: M. E. Sharpe, 1982).

Michael Ellman, *Soviet Planning Today: Proposals for an Optimally Functioning Economic System* (Cambridge: Cambridge University Press, 1971).

David Granick, *Job Rights in the Soviet Union: Their Consequences* (New York: Cambridge University Press, 1987).

Kenneth R. Gray, ed., *Soviet Agriculture* (Ames: Iowa State University Press, 1990).

Donald W. Green and Christopher I. Higgins, *SOVMOD I: A Macroeconometric Model of the Soviet Economy* (New York: Academic, 1977).

Paul R. Gregory, *The Soviet Economic Bureaucracy* (Cambridge: Cambridge University Press, 1990).

John Hardt et al., *Mathematics and Computers in Soviet Planning* (New Haven: Yale University Press, 1977).

Peter Murrell, *The Nature of Socialist Economies: Lessons from Eastern European Foreign Trade* (Princeton, N.J.: Princeton University Press, 1990).

Steven Rosefielde, ed., *Economic Welfare and the Economics of Soviet Socialism* (New York: Cambridge University Press, 1981).

Robert C. Stuart, ed., *The Soviet Rural Economy* (Totowa, N.J.: Roman and Allenheld, 1983).

Judith Thornton, ed., *Economic Analysis of the Soviet-Type System* (New York: Cambridge University Press, 1976).

Alfred Zauberman, *Mathematical Theory in Soviet Planning* (Oxford: Oxford University Press, 1976).

CHAPTER

15

China: Party Dictatorship, Markets, and Socialism

Unlike the other models of economic systems—market capitalism and planned socialism, both of which can be illustrated with real-world examples—market socialism (Chapter 7) lacks a clear-cut real-world manifestation. This chapter asks whether China fits the bill.

Recall that market socialism combines market resource allocation with state ownership. In market-socialist models, state ownership need not be pervasive. There may be private ownership of smaller businesses, but the state should own the most significant "means of production" in the form of state ownership or ownership by workers or farmers. The market could allocate consumer goods and labor, but there might be extensive state intervention in the case of producer goods and labor. Under market socialism, enterprises might be managed by state-appointed managers answerable to the state, or, in the cooperative model, by managers appointed by worker-owners.

With the exception of the Soviet administrative-command economy, we have not covered economies with significant shares of state ownership. State ownership accounts for a minimal share of the economy in the United States. It is more significant in Europe but still a minor share. In China, at least until the early 1990s, state-owned enterprises accounted for more than half of GDP. *State-owned enterprises (SOEs) are owned by the state under the jurisdiction of a government entity and run by a state-appointed manager.*

If we search for real-world models of market socialism, we could cite the Yugoslav economy before the disintegration of what was once Yugoslavia. The Yugoslavs abandoned the Soviet-planned economy in the aftermath of World War II as they, under the leadership of Josip Broz Tito, avoided being swallowed up in the Soviet bloc. Having rejected the Soviet model, the Yugoslavs settled on worker ownership and management, a relatively open economy, and extensive use of market allocation tempered by strong state intervention. Interest in the Yugoslav form of market socialism lessened with the collapse of Yugoslavia as a nation-state.

China has retained a one-party dictatorship, and its leaders wish to retain some socialist roots. One way to classify an economic and political system is to look at how China wishes to classify itself. To get an answer, we should look to the Chinese Constitution.

The Constitution: Is China a Socialist State or Something Else?

The 1954 Constitution of the People's Republic of China assigns the Communist Party to lead the "continuous revolution under the dictatorship of the proletariat … to achieve great victories both in socialist revolution and socialist construction…. by practicing economic planning on the basis of socialist public ownership."[1] Thus, in its early years, China described itself as a nation on the road to building a planned socialist state directed by its Communist Party.

With the passage of time, the goal of building planned socialism receded into the background. According to the 1982 Constitution and subsequent amendments, China now aims for "socialist modernization." Instead of "continuous revolution," the Communist Party advances society "along the road of Chinese-style socialism … persists in reform, improves socialist institutions, develops a socialist market economy, advances socialist democracy, improves the socialist legal system and turns China into a powerful and prosperous socialist country." With such tasks, national planning is no longer necessary because the state has put into practice a socialist market economy."[2] China is pictured as evolving into a more complex social, economic, and political order that offers blends of capitalism and socialism.

Early drafts of the Constitution designated the state sector *under ownership by the whole people, as the leading force in the economy*. The individual economy, operating within the limits prescribed by law, served as a complement to the socialist sector. Later revisions elevated individual, private, and other non-public economies that exist within the limits prescribed by law to be "major components of the socialist market economy." Unlike the Soviet economy where most private activity was "informal," the Chinese Constitution has recognized private economic activity as a legal and "major component" of its socialist economy.

Constitutional revisions also strengthened private property rights from "The State protects the lawful rights and interests of individual and private economies, and guides, supervises and administers individual and private economies" to "Citizens' lawful private property is inviolable" and "The State, in accordance with law, protects the rights of citizens to private property and to its inheritance." Constitutional revisions even added a quasi-due process clause: "The State may, in the public interest and in accordance with law, expropriate or requisition private property for its use and shall make compensation for the private property expropriated or requisitioned."[3]

A Law on Property passed the national congress after a number of unsuccessful attempts in March 2007. It formally allows private property along with state and collective property. The state continues to own all land but individuals can possess a land-use right, such as a long-term lease.[4]

The People's Republic of China clearly began as an administrative-command system like its mentor, the Soviet Union. That goal morphed into a ***Chinese-style socialism*** *in which the state and private economies coexist, national planning is absent, and private property rights are supposed to be protected.* Although it remains difficult to categorize the current Chinese economic system, it is a market-socialist economy in that it combines significant state ownership and control with private economic activity but under the supervision of a monopoly communist party.

The Chinese Reforms

Changes in the Chinese Constitution followed the changes in the economic system brought about by Chinese economic reform. China began its economic reform in the late 1970s. Before that, the Chinese economy strongly resembled the Soviet administrative-command economy (almost complete state ownership, collectivized agriculture, an industry managed by directive plans, with priorities set by the Communist Party). The reforms begun by Mao's successor, Deng Xiaoping, permitted a form of private ownership in agriculture, trade, and small-scale industry; opened the economy to world markets with a vengeance; and created financial markets and institutions, albeit primitive in their early phases.

Throughout the reform process, China retained two features of the administrative-command model: significant state ownership of heavy industry and other "commanding heights" and the continued political dictatorship of the Chinese Communist Party. The brutal crackdown on dissidents in June 1989 in Tiananmen Square in Beijing told the world the party did not intend to give up its power. Since that landmark event, there has been no serious challenge to the party's monopoly of political power.

The Chinese Puzzle

We are attracted to the study of China for a number of reasons other than its size, its participation in the Asian economic miracle, and its growing super power status. One of these reasons is that China hosts the testing ground for twenty-first-century state capitalism combined with one-party rule. Whereas state capitalism was discredited in France in the 1960s and in Japan in the 1980s, it has appeared in new form as "the emerging world's new model."[5] With China's clout and communist rule, it has become the ultimate test case of a state-directed market economy.

We wish to know whether China can break the ***middle-income trap***, *which refers to the inability of fast-growing poor countries to raise per capita income from middle-income to affluent status.* Over the past century, only Japan and the Four Southeast Asian Tigers have accomplished this feat. China currently ranks ninetieth for per capita income at roughly $8,500 per capita, wedged between the Maldives and Ecuador. Meanwhile, its Chinese counterpart—Taiwan—has a per capita income of $38,000.[6]

Whether China can break the middle-income trap depends on whether China can solve the China Puzzle. The **China Puzzle** *is how a country such as China, with its poor protection of private property, weak corporate governance, lack of democratic accountability, and absence of a rule of law, can grow rapidly over more than three decades.*[7] Can it extend this growth long enough to break the middle-income trap?

The Setting

China's 1.3 billion inhabitants make it the world's most populous country. China has a land area of just over 3.6 million square miles, nearly the size of Canada, making it one of the most densely populated countries of the globe. China is a relatively resource-rich country. Although coal is a major source of energy, only recently has China undertaken to utilize its oil reserves. Sharp variations in climate and fertility, along with large areas of rough terrain, mean that large amounts of capital are needed to exploit its mineral and land resources. Although China has vast natural resources, it must import huge amounts of minerals and raw materials to support its rapid growth. For this reason, China has become a major buyer of raw materials in Africa and Latin America to the extent that China's thirst for raw materials tends to drive up their prices worldwide.

China is the world's oldest existing civilization, a source of great pride to the Chinese people. Although there are numerous ethnic minorities in China (primarily in the western part of the country), the dominant group is the Han nationality. Hans populate China's political class, even in provinces where they are distinct minorities. The Chinese language comprises many varying dialects; the Mandarin dialect is dominant. The rich heritage of the Chinese people is an important if immeasurable influence on their attitudes toward and participation in the modernization process.

China remains today a poor country despite more than three decades of rapid growth. China's 2011 per capita income of about $8,400 was above its immediate neighbors India and Pakistan ($3,700 and $2,800, respectively), but it ranks well below that of Taiwan at $38,000 and South Korea at $32,000.

Another unique feature of China is the notion of a Greater China. **Greater China** *refers to the presence of vast numbers of Chinese both inside and outside of China proper.* Geographically, Greater China encompasses mainland China plus Taiwan, Hong Kong, and Macao, the last Portuguese colony. Hong Kong is now under the rule of mainland China but retains a great deal of it autonomy. In addition to its geographic boundaries, Greater China includes the diaspora of more than 50 million ethnic Chinese located mainly in Southeast Asia.

Prosperous Taiwan maintains its independence in the face of mainland Chinese threats of eventual reunification. Greater China has played an underrated role in Chinese economic development. Greater Chinese have brought foreign direct investment and entrepreneurial expertise to China. With ancestral ties to China, they have been better at understanding local business practices and using the relational contracting that characterizes business relations throughout Asia. Currently, a large number of private Chinese enterprises are owned and operated by Hong Kong and Taiwanese partners.

China's History of Revolution and Upheaval

China's prereform history is one of violence and upheaval, much like that of the Soviet Union with its bloody civil war, disastrous collectivization and famine, and blood-curdling power struggles.

The Chinese Empire evolved over a 2,000-year period. Starting with the Qin dynasty in 225 BC, the emperor appointed regional officials. Because of poor transportation and vast territories, regional officials exercised a great deal of autonomy, as they do today.

The Chinese Empire split apart as colonial powers divided China into concessions and warlords assumed control of remote provinces. The modern Chinese state, the Republic of China, was founded in 1912 under its first president, Sun Yat-sen. After Sun's death in 1925, China was divided between the communists, eventually led by Mao Zedong, and the nationalists under General Chiang Kai-shek. The Japanese invasion in August of 1937 caused the warring factions to unite to fight the invaders, with the nationalists doing the lion's share of fighting. As the war ended, the communists and nationalists engaged in a bitter civil war from which the communists under Mao Zedong emerged victorious and Chiang retreated with his forces to Taiwan.

The People's Republic of China was founded in October 1949 with the victory of the Red Army over the nationalist forces. Mao Zedong was the unquestioned leader. He, like Josef Stalin and Kim Jong Il and Kim Il Sung in North Korea, built a personality cult *that portrayed him as the supreme and infallible leader*. Mao's personality cult gave him supreme power and the ability to order extreme and costly economic and social experiments in the name of a purer form of communist ideology. Campaigns such as the Great Leap Forward and the Cultural Revolution set back economic progress, often for a decade or more, and resulted in the loss of millions of lives.

The Early Years and the Soviet Model

China was much more backward in 1949, when it adopted the Soviet economic model, than Russia was in 1917. Chinese leaders faced several key problems in adapting the Soviet model to Chinese circumstances. In developing such a planned socialist economy, modifications of the Soviet model had to be made to account for the very large Chinese population, its relative poverty, and its primarily rural character.

China in 1949 was a classic poor country with low per capita income, significant population pressure on arable land and other resources, and an absence of institutions appropriate for economic development. China, with a land mass about half that of the Soviet Union, and with a population roughly three and one-half times that of the Soviet Union, began its implementation of the Soviet model as Stalin dispatched advisors to instruct his fellow Chinese communists how to plan an economy and how to control the population through party cadres and secret police.

The result was sporadic economic growth and development interrupted when ideological and political factors gained supremacy over economic factors. Many of the policies and institutions developed in China were similar to those used in the Soviet Union. There were, however, important differences, especially the impact of ideology.

Between 1949 and 1952, two goals were pursued in China. First, land was redistributed to individual households in preparation for an eventual collectivization. Collectivization was to be pursued without undue haste. Land reform was a bloody affair. Estimates of the number of executions of land owners and political oppositionists range from two to five million in the first three years of power.[8] Second, nationalization and consolidation of industry took place in preparation for national economic planning. Financial reform, educational reform, and other changes were undertaken to prepare for the beginning of the first five-year plan in 1953. In this respect, China's first steps were much like those of the Soviet Union in the 1920s, as it prepared for its five-year-plan era.[9]

China's approach to agriculture differed from the Soviet's in the early 1930s. The Chinese leadership initially wished to avoid Soviet mistakes, but both countries used land reform and similar experimental forms of organization to eliminate class differences, distribute machinery through centralized facilities, and apply pressure to hold down rural food consumption. China, however, avoided substantial destruction of cattle, facilities, and equipment when it began the first step of collectivization in the 1950s.[10]

The early 1950s also saw the nationalization of industry and the development of a system of national economic planning. There was a gradual transition from private to socialist industry—certainly more gradual than in the Soviet Union after 1928. The shift was intended to be slow, but toward the latter part of the first five-year plan it became rapid. The pattern of change was from private ownership to what the Chinese called elementary state capitalism, then to advanced state capitalism, and finally to socialist industry.

By 1955, 68 percent of the gross value of output was produced by state industry and only 16 percent by joint state–private enterprises. Eventually, even handicraft production was brought under state control like under Soviet war communism dating from 1918 to 1920. The socialist transformation of both agriculture and industry accelerated in 1955–1956 as ideology and political considerations dominated economic considerations.

Chinese planning, put in place in the early 1950s, was initially similar to the Soviet model.[11] The basic unit of production activity was the enterprise. As in the Soviet Union, a dual party–state administrative structure drew up and implemented (and often interrupted) five-year plans for both agriculture and industry. Chinese plans were formulated by a State Planning Commission, which, like Gosplan in the Soviet Union, operated through an industrial ministry system communicating with regional and enterprise officials. Once approved by the State Council, that plan became law for enterprises. Chinese planning produced problems similar to those in the Soviet case: imbalance and shortages, poor quality, late plans, and deviation of results from targets. Chinese thinking on reform began to surface in the mid-1950s, but it was overshadowed by the political and ideological upheavals of the late 1950s.

The first ten years of the Chinese industrialization show the influence of the Soviet model. "In general, it can be said that during 1953–1957, the Chinese followed the broad outlines of the Stalinist strategy of selective growth under conditions of austerity with three important qualifications."[12] Unlike the Soviet case, where state resources were directed through state farms and Machine Tractor Stations, agriculture was largely self-financed in the early years, a consequence of the much lower economic development of China in 1949 than of the Soviet Union in 1928.

The Chinese relied heavily on the state enterprise as a revenue source for state investment funds. Revenue from state enterprises accounted for roughly 35 percent of total budgetary revenue in 1953 and for 46 percent by 1957. In comparison, the most important source of budgetary revenue in the early years of Soviet industriali-zation was the turnover tax. The decision not to rely on taxes on peasants reflected the realities of subsistence agriculture.

During the 1950s, the Chinese generally followed the Soviet "industry first" strategy. Between 1953 and 1957, heavy industry absorbed an average of 85 percent of industrial investment. Only 8 percent of state investment was devoted to agricul-ture, whereas aggregate investment accounted for 20 to 25 percent of GDP.[13] These investment figures suggest a relatively high rate of accumulation for a poor country, with emphasis on industry in general and heavy industry in particular.

China's economic growth during the 1950s was generally strong, but uneven. There was an impressive 50 percent increase in GDP per capita between 1950 and 1958, with faster growth of industrial production and more modest increase in agriculture. After 1958, China's growth was determined and retarded by cataclys-mic political and ideological upheavals: the Great Leap Forward followed by the Cultural Revolution.

The First Upheaval: The Great Leap Forward

Chinese economic development from the late 1950s through the late 1970s was characterized by massive political upheavals that tended to reverse earlier economic progress. Massive ideological disruptions appealed to the aging group of commu-nist revolutionaries led by Mao, who worried about the decline of revolutionary fervor and the bureaucratization of economic and political life.

After the brief liberal Hundred Flowers Campaign (1956–1957), during which open discussion and criticism of the system were encouraged, Mao launched the Great Leap Forward in 1958.[14]

Mao had already broken with the Soviet Union at this time. He was infuriated that Soviet party leader Nikita Khrushchev had denounced Stalin in 1956, a move that prompted the Hungarian revolution and cast doubt on communism. Mao also felt that the USSR had abandoned the goal of world socialist revolution. He decided that China had to follow its own revolutionary path. China should take advantage of its vast population and agricultural resources to shift production from the cities to the countryside.

*The **Great Leap Forward** was a massive resurgence of radical ideology, which replaced rationality.* Campaigns were instigated with revolutionary fervor to emphasize a new role for the peasantry, especially through small-scale industry in the countryside and the introduction of communes. Development of water resources was also stressed. A brutal campaign against the educated elite was mounted. The movement of industry from the city to the countryside violated economic principles of mass production and economies of scale as foundries were set up in villages, fed largely by scavenged scrap metals.

Villagers were forced to enter massive people's communes encompassing thousands of households. *The rural people's commune was the Chinese version of the Soviet collective farm, although on a scale of thousands of families rather than hundreds.* Farm households were required to contribute even their household appliances to the commune. Families had to eat in massive dining halls. The family unit was broken up. The commune became the unit of local government.

The people's communes combined a number of collectives (advanced cooperatives) to produce agricultural and handicraft products and to serve as local units of government. The original communes (roughly 26,000 in number and averaging about 4,600 households each) faced obvious difficulties. They were too large to coordinate, and individual incentives were lacking.

Mao attempted to use the people's communes to follow Stalin's model of extracting a surplus from agriculture. The people's communes were supposed to deliver planned quantities of agricultural products to state agencies despite low state prices. Presumably this was to give the state a surplus to finance further economic development.

The exacting of farm products from the countryside combined with poor harvests created massive starvation, even in those provinces that were exporting grain "surpluses." Chinese authorities initially concealed the true toll of the Great Leap Forward, but later studies show the loss of life from famine to be between 40 and 60 million—the largest famine in world history.[15] Unlike Soviet famines from which cities were largely spared, the Chinese Great Leap famine affected almost every family in China. Although the Great Leap Forward was mainly abandoned by 1960, the commune system remained with some modifications until it fell apart during the reform period.[16]

The Great Leap's effect on economic performance was disastrous. Per capita GDP fell by 20 percent between 1958 and 1962. The 1958 living standard was not reached again until 1965.[17] Factor productivity declined at 1 percent per year between 1957 and 1965.[18]

The Great Leap Forward was also accompanied by a wave of decentralization from the Soviet top-down model. During the Great Leap Forward, central ministries handed over control of state-owned enterprises to regional governments. At that time, most state revenues came from profit taxes on state enterprises. Regional government tax revenues increased from 20 percent in 1958 to 79 percent of the total in 1961, signifying a huge shift in resources from the center to the regions. Supervision of SOEs was delegated from the ministries to the regions, and central planning was largely replaced by the organization of production at regional and local levels.[19]

Many decisions were shifted to the local level. Local industrial establishments were set up to serve local (especially rural) needs. The decentralizations of the Great Leap Forward laid some of the foundations for later regionalization and centralization of Chinese governance.

1960–1978: Development and Cultural Revolution

Like the 1950s, the 1960s were divided into two very different periods: moderation in the early 1960s and upheaval in the late 1960s. The early 1960s was a period of relative calm in which Chinese leaders looked toward balance in economic development, modernization of agriculture, and recovery from the Great Leap Forward. In industry, the 1960s was a period of reform—a movement away from the overwhelming importance of gross output (the major success indicator of the 1950s) toward quality in production and the elimination of major deficiencies in the planning system. Mao's own political influence diminished as a consequence of the disaster of the Great Leap. He would regain the upper hand, however, within a few years to impose yet another disaster on China.

During the early 1960s, new emphasis was placed on mechanization and reorganization of agriculture. Because communes were too large, the intermediate (brigade) and lower-level (team) units assumed new importance. Emphasis on nonmaterial rewards, a hallmark of the earlier commune system, was changed in favor of material incentives and the reintroduction of private plots. Although the number of communes was reduced during the 1960s, their role in the social, cultural, and political affairs of the countryside remained intact through the 1970s.

If the early 1960s was a period of reform and change, the opposite could be said of the Cultural Revolution of 1966–1969. Mao's **Cultural Revolution** *sought to restore socialist zeal and discipline by liquidating capitalist and traditional elements from Chinese society.*

The Cultural Revolution signaled Mao's return to absolute power after the disaster of the Great Leap Forward. He charged that capitalist elements were trying to restore capitalism and must be crushed. Mao called on the youth to eradicate traditional and capitalist elements. Schools and universities were shuttered, and mobs sent the intellectual and political elite into exile in the countryside or in jails. Mobs of young people waved small red books containing quotations from Mao as they terrorized the party and technical elites.

The Cultural Revolution had a dramatic effect on China's educated classes. Scholars and officials were ignominiously shipped to hard industrial labor or labor in the countryside by radical bands of youths motivated by Mao's revolutionary ideas. China's entire educational establishment ceased to function in the backlash against education and Western teaching.

Like the Great Leap Forward, the Cultural Revolution had a devastating effect on economic performance. Disruption was so great that meaningful estimates of GDP during the Cultural Revolution are not available, but GDP per capita failed to increase between 1965 and 1970—a loss of output equal to or more severe than that of the Great Leap.[20]

As the Cultural Revolution immersed the economic and political system into chaos, there was a further loss of central power. Between 1966 and 1975, regional revenue rose from 65 to 88 percent of the total. As a result, China had literally hundreds of self-contained and self-sufficient regional economies. Most of the 2,000 counties had SOEs producing machinery, steel, fertilizers, and cement. More than twenty provinces had SOEs that produced cars and tractors. The number of centrally planned targets had been reduced to fewer than 800, and there were fewer than thirty ministries.[21]

In effect, the Great Leap Forward and the Cultural Revolution destroyed the Chinese centralized planning and control system "in sharp contrast to all other formally centralized economies in which specialization and monopoly are hallmarks." [22] The ensuing destruction of communist institutions and society led to disillusion with communist ideology, weakened resistance to reforms, and paved the way for post-Mao reforms.

The early 1970s was a period of recovery from the Cultural Revolution. The return to normalcy was interrupted, however, by events of the early and mid-1970s. Head of state, Zhou Enlai, a supposed advocate of a moderate path of industrialization, died in early 1976. The following September, Mao Zedong, the father of the revolution and an advocate of continuing the revolutionary mentality, died. Shortly thereafter, in October 1976, the Gang of Four, representing the revolutionary left and espousing a continuation of the Stalinist mode of industrialization, were arrested amid great ideological fervor.[23]

These events paved the way for what would be fundamental changes in the Chinese economic system under the leadership of Deng Xiaoping. Deng had been a right-hand man of Mao during the Great Leap Forward, but he fell from favor and was a victim of the Cultural Revolution. Both experiences made him amenable to reform.

China's Modernization Reform: Deng Xiaoping and His Successors

Both China and the Soviet Union sought to make the administrative-command system work—the Soviet Union from 1928 to 1985, China from 1950 to 1978. Both, disillusioned by the weaknesses of the administrative-command system, turned to reformers to modify their systems. The Soviet Union turned to a young and vigorous general secretary of the Communist Party, Mikhail Gorbachev, who opted to alter the Soviet political, social, and economic system, with the result that the Soviet Union and its centralized party dictatorship ceased to exist. China turned to Deng Xiaoping, an elderly veteran of the Chinese civil war, a trusted Mao deputy, and a victim of the Cultural Revolution, to reform the Chinese system.

The path chosen by Deng roughly a decade before Gorbachev yielded quite different results: Deng ultimately opted to avoid the political democratization and openness that Gorbachev later introduced into the Soviet system. He chose instead to preserve the dictatorship of the Chinese Communist Party and not to tolerate dissent, but rather to unleash the productive and entrepreneurial talents of the Chinese people while retaining significant control and ownership of the "commanding heights" of the Chinese economy.

Deng's moves can be likened to V. I. Lenin's decision in 1921 to return the Soviet economy to a mixed economic system that encouraged private initiative and openness to the outside world, while the state retained control of the "commanding heights." During the Gorbachev era, agrarian reform was of limited importance. In China, agrarian reform would be the initial catalyst of change.[24]

Although the Deng reforms, which began to be introduced in 1978, were intended to be a process Deng later described as "fording the river by feeling for the stones," in reality the reforms moved quickly, particularly in the countryside.

The fruits of Chinese reforms have been immense. China has grown rapidly for more than three decades and promises to become a world superpower. In seeking to explain China's success (and its durability), scholars have latched on to a number of explanations. Which explanation proves correct may tell us about the durability of China's success.

In effect, the reforms that began in 1978 and 1979 created a new Chinese economic system, which we shall describe in the rest of the chapter.

The Chinese Economic System

The China Puzzle asks what has made China "work" in the absence of what are considered "good institutions." We now examine those "questionable" economic institutions that make China one of the world's most intriguing economic systems. We begin with the question of how China is governed and how this form of governance overcame resistance to reform and the opening to world markets. We then look at China's industrial structure, namely, its mix of SOEs and private enterprise, both domestic and foreign. After that, we examine China's capital and labor markets and its provision of income security.

A Regionally Decentralized Authoritarian Regime

Some see the answer to China's reform success in the unique decentralized nature of the Chinese economic and political system as it emerged from the cataclysms of the 1950s and 1960s. Others see it as the result of spontaneous risk taking and initiative at the individual level taking place contrary to government wishes. Other explanations include the opening of a very poor economy to trade with abundant reserves of labor that could be drawn from the countryside to the city. According to this explanation, growth will eventually dry up as reserves are exhausted. It is only a matter of time, but if that time is long, considerable progress can be made.

The Great Leap Forward and the Cultural Revolution both served to weaken or destroy the centralized top-down state administrative structure that had earlier planned and managed the economy. In both cases, planning and administration were switched from party headquarters and central ministries in Beijing to regional party and state bodies.

By the time of Mao's death in 1976, China had achieved what Chenggang Xu characterizes as a regionally decentralized authoritarian regime, called RDA for short. *A **regionally decentralized authoritarian regime (RDA)** is characterized as a combination of political centralization and economic regional decentralization.*[25]

RDA combines political centralization of the communist party with substantial autonomy of regional and other sub-national governments. The highly centralized political and personnel governance structure appoints and promotes regional government officials. The power to appoint, demote, and promote gives national figures considerable leverage over sub-national officials. Note that regional officials are not elected by or held accountable by the constituents. Instead, their loyalty is to the national party.

Meanwhile, the governance of the economy is delegated to sub-national governments in provinces, municipalities, and counties. These, due to the destruction of central planning and central ministerial control, are relatively self-contained and self-sufficient. They have the responsibility for managing the regional economy, initiating and coordinating reforms, providing public services, and making and enforcing laws within their jurisdictions.

In the RDA regime, sub-national governments have influence or even direct control rights over a substantial amount of resources, such as land, firms, financial resources, energy, raw materials, and others. Nearly 70 percent of total public expenditure in China takes place at the sub-national level (i.e., provincial, prefecture, county, and township), of which more than 55 percent takes place at sub-provincial levels. In terms of population size, provinces, regions, and large municipalities equal medium-sized countries elsewhere. Sub-national governments, under the supervision of the central government, can initiate, negotiate, implement, divert, and resist reforms, policies, rules, and laws.

The Regional Governance Structure of the Chinese Economy   Figure 15.1 illustrates RDA in practice. It shows a central government that oversees a population of 1.3 billion, employs 2.75 million, and manages slightly more than two thousands SOEs. Below the central government are twenty-two provinces, five autonomous regions, and four provincial level municipalities, whose average populations are between 18 and 46 million, and which manage almost 270,000 SOEs, collectives, joint companies, and foreign companies. Below these provinces and regions are 333 municipality-level units, averaging slightly fewer than four million residents.

Central Government   The central government depicted in Figure 15.1 is an interlocking directorate of party and state officials. Like in the Soviet Union, the party's highest body is nominally the National Congress of the Communist Party, which meets at least once every five years to ratify policies proposed by the Central Committee, headed by its General Secretary. The Central Committee meets periodically in plenums, but party business is conducted by the Politburo and its smaller standing committee.

The Politburo is the most powerful political force and is comprised of key regional party leaders and those with national responsibilities. *The **Politburo** is headed by the **General Secretary of the Party**—the most important position in China*. Currently, the General Secretary is Hu Jintao, who also carries the title of President. He will be replaced by his designated successor, Xi Jinping, the current vice president of China.

As in the Soviet Union, the Central Committee's cadres department handles high-level appointments. *The **cadres department** appoints officials to elite positions in the party and state. The party uses promotions and other rewards to incentivize regional officials.*

The Central Committee's inspection commission roots out corruption and punishes misdeeds of party officials. It is the party's disciplinary arm.

FIGURE 15.1   Regional Governance Structure of the Chinese Economy

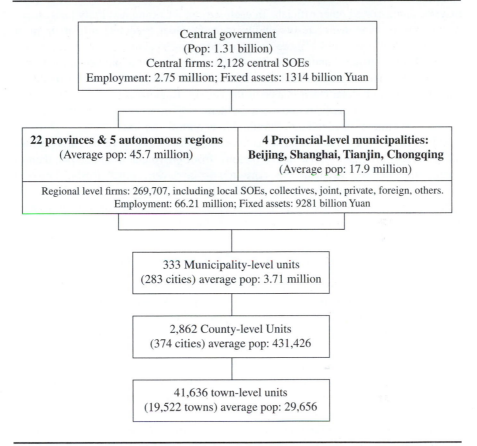

Source: Chenggang Xu, "The Fundamental Institutions of China's Reforms and Development," *Journal of Economic Literature* 49, no. 4 (2011), 1084.

The basic policy directives of the Communist Party are carried out by an executive State Council. *The* **State Council** *is the executive branch of the central government.* It is headed by a premier, which is the equivalent to prime minister in parliamentary governments. This position is currently occupied by Wen Jiabao. He is scheduled to be replaced by his top lieutenant, Li Keqiang.

In a precedent set by Mao's immediate successor Deng Xiaoping, the top leaders of China are term limited. The new General Secretary is chosen as a main agenda item of the National Party Congress. For example, Hu Jin Tao's and Wen Jiabao's successors were chosen in the Eighteenth Party Congress of March 2012.

Unlike other communist states where top officials serve in office until their deaths, China's top officials are retired according to an orderly procedure. The orderly retirement of China's top officials was a major political innovation introduced by Deg Xiaoping and may explain a portion of China's success. New leaders should bring new ideas.

Regional (Sub-national) Government: Leaders and Competition   The provinces, autonomous regions, and provincial-level municipalities are headed by governors, mayors, and assorted other officials. In each region, a Communist Party boss shares power and to some degree responsibility with the chief executive officer. In most cases, the local party boss is more powerful than his executive counterpart.

Both the top party and state official of the region are appointed through the cadres department of the Central Committee. Their career trajectories depend on the economic and social performance of the region. Regions compete among themselves with respect to growth rates, employment, reform successes, the attraction of foreign investment, or success in introducing economic reform.

This nested network of appointments extends the central government's personnel control to officials of all levels of regions, from provincial to municipal, then to county until the bottom of the hierarchy, township government.[26] Reshuffling and rotation of regional leaders has kept central control over sub-national officials intact. From 1978 to 2005, 80 percent of provincial governors have been rotated by the central government.[27]

M-Form Versus U-Form Organizations

The Soviet administrative-command system was organized as a vertical hierarchy based on industrial branches. A central planning commission planned the activities of sectoral ministries, which managed the affairs of subordinated enterprises. In this U-Form organization, a metallurgy department in the state planning commission developed plans for the metals ministry, which developed plans for metal-producing enterprises. Metals producers in different parts of the country were managed by the same planners and ministers in Moscow.

In the Chinese M-Form organization, the central government has central functional agencies subordinated to it that cover administration, finance, and general economic issues, but the major economic control functions are exercised at the territorial level. *An **M-Form organization** organizes and manages economic tasks on a regional rather than a sectoral basis.* (See accompanying figure) Each province exercises functional controls and produces outputs. The bulk of output is

FIGURE **15.2**   The M-Form Organization Structure: Stylized Version

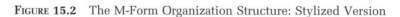
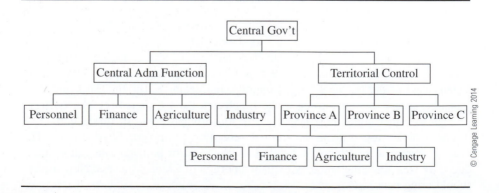

produced under territorial controls in the territories.[28] In fact, the M-Form organization was briefly tried by Khrushchev in 1964, only to be rejected by his successors as too radical a reform.

Regional Competition and Experimentation   With an M-Form organization, production is carried out by relatively independent sub-national organizations that are each large enough to marshal resources to produce large scales of output. They are relatively independent in the sense that central authorities use a hands-off approach to monitoring and control.

The more "successful" sub-national state and party bosses are promoted to higher positions, leaving less successful regional colleagues behind. Sub-national leaders whose regions produce high growth rates, create new types of non-state firms, achieve high rates of employment, or attract foreign direct investment can look forward to Central Committee appointments or even a place in the Politburo.

Sub-national regions therefore serve as testing grounds for reform initiatives, which sub-national leaders can select better than the central government because of their knowledge of local conditions. Regional reform experiments cause fewer disruptions, if the reform fails. Once a regional reform has proven successful, the central government can try to achieve a consensus in its favor by using its national influence.[29]

Soviet reforms were consistently sabotaged by the bureaucracy. The Chinese RDA model seeks to promote enthusiasm for reform and sweep away bureaucratic resistance. It offers sufficient rewards to encourage risk taking by regional officials.

Tournament Models of Promotion   Our chapter on the Soviet administrative-command economy emphasized the success indicator problem that "resource managers" faced. Managers, confronted with diverse performance indicators, had to choose which targets to fulfill and which to ignore. Given that their superiors in the ministries had incomplete information about local operations, they underreported capacity, overstated material requirements, and cheated on quality and prices. Their goal was said to be a "comfortable life," not mercuric rise through the bureaucratic ranks.

Although the Soviet system attempted to organize "socialist competition" among firms, Soviet managers did not have the discretionary resources to compete with their counterparts, and attempts at socialist competition came to naught. Soviet managers were far from self-sufficient. Experiments could not be restricted to a regional level because the region depended on other regions for supplies, while the experiment applied only to one region. Some likened Soviet experimental reform attempts to telling one city district to drive on the left side of the road, while all others remained on the right.

The M-Form Chinese economic model does allow regions to compete against each other. They are sufficiently large and self-sufficient. They are not hampered by the petty tutelage of Beijing bureaucrats. If a regional official is promoted as a result of successful reform, his successors would have to make it work, not the official. In sum, in the Chinese M-Form organization, sub-national economies can engage in independent experiments and complete against each other.

Sub-national regional competition makes sense only if the sub-national leaders are properly motivated. The center, in setting rules for regional competition, must offer sufficient rewards for good performance to compensate for higher risks. In setting rewards, the center had to decide whether sub-national regions should be rewarded for achieving, say, a high target rate of growth, or whether they would be rewarded for outperforming other regions.

Chinese central authorities chose to use tournament competition that rewards *relative performance*. **Tournament competition** *is present when the players in the competition are judged by their relative performance (relative to other players)*. In a golf tournament, for example, prize money is not awarded to all players who beat a par score. The awards go to the players who score better than their opponents.

The economic theory of tournament competition suggests that this reward system works better than other incentive arrangements when the tasks of agents are similar and they are similarly affected by random events.[30] In the golf analogy, tournaments work if the players play under the same rules and if random effects (such as weather conditions) apply to all. For regional competition to work, the regions must face similar tasks. If one is told to innovate, the other to experiment, and the third to produce high growth, they cannot compete because they are pursuing different goals.

Studies of Chinese sub-national regions suggest they are basically similar. They produce a wide assortment of products and have their own resource bases. If they produce specialized products (as did Soviet ministries) or if their regional circumstances were quite different, performance differences could be the result of factors specific to the region or to bad managerial performance. Suppose a governor performs poorly and tries to blame the outcome on bad luck in his region. This excuse is unconvincing if similar regions are prospering under similar conditions.

Political resistance to reform is weakened when a new reform is tried on a regional basis. Reformist national leaders reduce their own risks because the regional leader is responsible for the reform's success or failure. Regional reforms also allows for "learning by doing." Top leaders, including those who pioneered market reform in China, knew little about how to transform China into a market economy. Regional experiments allowed them to "ford the river by feeling for the stones," as Deng Xiaoping advised. Local experimentation also renders reform progress more stable because reforms create interest groups not only among central leaders but also among sub-national officials, who benefit from the success of their own reforms.

Empirical studies of career paths of Chinese officials conclude that the center does indeed judge sub-national leaders on their tournament performance. Studies show that regions that grow fast relative to others gain more representation on the Central Committee.[31] The promotions of top provincial leaders depend on their performances relative to the national average or relative to their immediate predecessors.[32] Other studies find that regional officials' promotions depend on the performance of their jurisdiction relative to the national average, everything else being equal.[33]

Compared to Soviet reforms, Chinese reforms have been remarkably consistent. They have continued through a number of changes in leadership. There remains the question of the limits of reform. The general tenor of reforms has been to increase the role of market allocation, to reduce the role of ideology, and to allow private economic activity to prosper. The relative share of the state sector has declined and could decline even more.

As the leaders of the party assembled for the National Party Congress in March 2012, a faction of the party, represented by a powerful party boss from Chongqing, appealed for a revival of the "collectivist spirit of Chairman Mao." He was replaced as party chief in a rare public rebuke, suggesting that reformists still have the upper hand.[34] One of the biggest ideological issues is whether the state will retain ownership of China's largest companies. State ownership, it will be recalled, is part of China's claim to being a socialist state.

Agricultural Reform

The land reforms and de-collectivization of the late 1970s early 1980s illustrate how major breakthroughs can occur without the apparent support of the central leadership. If necessary, the central leadership can even appear openly to oppose the reform.

Spontaneous De-collectivization Prior to 1978, the commune was the unit of organization in agriculture. Agricultural production was in the hands of production teams, which comprised a number of households within a village. Production teams combined to form brigades, brigades to form a commune. Above the commune, the county government was responsible for directing agricultural activity. It implemented the national economic plan administered by the Ministry of Agriculture and Forestry.[35] The commune had a reward system based on points for daily work done. The value of the points hinged on communal income, which was not known until the end of the period.

On a November night in 1978, eighteen Chinese peasants from Xiaogang village in Anhui province secretly divided communal land to be farmed by individual families, who would keep what was left over after meeting state quotas. Such a division was illegal and highly dangerous, but the peasants felt the risks were worth it. The peasants took action one month before the agenda of the 1978 party conference. Deng Xiaoping and his supporters, contrary to popular legend, did not agree on a reform program at the Third Plenum of the Eighth Party Congress in 1978, which installed him in power. A Chinese reform official by the name of Bao Tong later admitted as much: "In fact, reform wasn't discussed. Reform wasn't listed on the agenda, nor was it mentioned in the work reports."[36] Deng Xiaoping's famous description of Chinese reform as "fording the river by feeling for the stones" is not incorrect, but it was the Chinese people who placed the stones under his feet. Throughout the early stages of the reform process, the Chinese Communist Party simply reacted to (and wisely did not oppose) bottom-up reform initiatives that emanated largely from the rural population. Thus, without fanfare, began the economic reform of agriculture as spontaneous land division spread to other villages.

Why were the peasants of Xiaogang village willing to take the risk of breaking the law? They had vivid memories of the catastrophes of the Mao years. They had witnessed the chaos of the Great Leap Forward and had seen their parents and children die from starvation during the 1958–1961 famine. They learned they had to take care of themselves.

Starting with the peasants of Anhui province, China's farmers de-collectivized agriculture spontaneously from below. They created their own contract responsibility system.[37] *The **contract responsibility system** is an agreement of a group of peasant households to collectively deliver quotas to the state while keeping the rest for their consumption or sale.*

The contract responsibility system spread from village to village and from province to province without endorsement or encouragement from regional authorities. It spread almost as a plague. To quote one farmer: "When one family's chicken catches the pest, the whole village catches it. When one village has it, the whole county will be infected."[38]

Figure 15.3 shows the success of the agricultural reform. As agricultural production soared, Deng Xiaoping and his party realized they could not resist and could take advantage of something that was working. By 1982, more than 90 percent of rural dwellers were engaged in the household production system. Even after Deng Xiaoping officially supported grassroots rural reform, he did not give farmers long-term commitments. Farmers were allowed one- to three-year contracts in 1982. It was only in 2003 that the state gave long-term leases in its Rural Land Contracting Law.

Governors Zhao Ziyang of Sichuan and Wan Li of Anhui were the beneficiaries of the success of the land reform program. Although they did not initiate the

FIGURE 15.3   The Growth of Agriculture in the Early Years of Chinese Reform

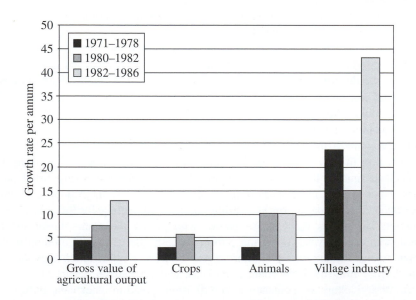

Source: State Statistical Bureau, cited in Dwight Perkins, "Reforming China's Economic System," *Journal of Economic Literature* 36, 2 (June 1988), 612.

grassroots change, they recognized its success. They were promoted to national level posts. Zhao and Wan became the premier and executive deputy premier of the state council, respectively, responsible for national reform.[39]

Creating the Private Sector

The spontaneous developments in agriculture meant new supplies of food products that needed to make their way to a market that still had to be created. At the time Deng Xiaoping came to power, domestic trade was dominated by state trading networks. Consumers received coupons for different types of goods and stood in long lines for each rationed product. In Wuhan, Hubei Province, there were more than eighty types of ration coupons for items like soap, cooking oil, meat, eggs, fish, tofu, grain, watches, bikes, furniture, and matches.[40]

China's first entrepreneurs got their start by marketing farm products in the cities. Farm products had to be moved over long distances in violation of laws and without contracts that could be enforced in courts. In effect, Chinese farmer-trader-entrepreneurs had to create completely new institutions for transporting and selling agricultural products. Once in place, they could be used for other goods and services.

China's pioneering entrepreneurs had to find ways to overcome socialist institutional barriers and create markets. The Chinese entrepreneur had to juggle profits and security. For most, a mistake meant confiscation, a jail sentence, or worse.[41] In the early 1960s, such traders were labeled as "bad elements." Some lost their jobs or were sent to labor camps while others were put on neighborhood watch lists. Even in the late 1970s and early 1980s, the sight of police officers chasing and confiscating a rural peddler's goods was common.

The entrepreneur, operating in the grey area of legality, had no access to state capital. The state banks refused to serve any private businesses until June 1988 and even then did so with tight restrictions. Bank lending even today remains reserved for state companies.

Throughout the early 1980s, farmers in north Jiangsu packed their bikes with chickens, ducks, and other fowl; crossed the Yangzi River; and shipped their products by rail to urban centers in the Yangzi basin. "A million roosters cross the mighty Yangzi" was the expression of the day.[42] By 1983, the majority of consumers in major cities purchased their products in free markets rather than in government stores. Within one year (1979 to 1980), most state vegetable markets, except the highly subsidized Beijing and Shanghai markets, were out of business.

Other new private markets, such as hotels and service facilities, followed. Private traders had to develop a network of hotels because they could not stay in state-run hotels. After their release from the communes in the early 1980s, rural entrepreneurs left their villages to establish restaurants, laundries, and other small manufacturing businesses in major cities. Friends and relatives followed. Like entrepreneurs elsewhere, Chinese private entrepreneurs set up their businesses through the three Fs: friends, family, and fools.

Chinese rural dwellers used "township enterprises" or "township and village enterprises" (TVEs) to circumvent state or collective ownership requirements. *Township and village enterprises (TVEs) were enterprises that were at least nominally owned by the township or village. They provided official cover for what were often purely private owners.* Private ownership was not recognized until 2003. In the meantime, TVEs provided a suitable collective form of ownership to disguise private economic activity.

Remarkable stories of hardy entrepreneurs abound: A rural minority woman from Hunan began her business by buying shoes in cities and selling them in her hometown, Baojing. She returned from her sales trips with herbs, mushrooms, and other goods and resold them in local markets. After a decade of hard work, she settled down and collected rent every month from the six houses she had built over the years. The richest Chinese citizen in the 2007 was the daughter of a poor farmer from Guangdong, whose family became wealthy by building affordable townhouses and holiday homes for China's growing middle class.[43]

Corruption served as an unexpected asset for the new private businesses. Entrepreneurs had to "wear a red hat" (register a family business as a part of a formal legal organization), set up their business as a sham collective enterprise, or find "big shots" or "mothers-in-law" as patrons to give them protection. Without such cover, they could not issue receipts, keep books, pay taxes, write contracts, or open bank accounts.

Private business spread to the cities, and then started to return to the countryside as rural-based industry. Many large private manufacturing firms developed in predominantly agricultural provinces (Zhejiang, Shandong, Guangdong, Hunan, and Sichuan). China's largest agribusiness was founded by brothers who left the city to found their company in a rural part of Sichuan province. Rural entrepreneurs built the largest refrigerator maker and air conditioning companies.

In 1978, state enterprises generated about 80 percent of China's GDP; the rural commune produced the other 20 percent.[44] There were no private businesses. By 1997, there were 961,000 private enterprises and 28,500,000 small family private firms. By 2002, the share of GDP produced by truly private companies comprised more than half.[45] By 2004, there were more than 3 million private companies employing more than 47 million workers.[46]

Before 1980, entrepreneurial activity in China was illegal. Today, there are over 40 million entrepreneurs, whose businesses employ over 200 million and generate two-thirds of industrial output. Private entrepreneurs are even encouraged to become members of the party, although old-line party members have resisted their entry.

Opening the Chinese Economy

The Chinese reform leadership relied on experiments—some unsanctioned, such as the spontaneous land reform—to feel their way down the path of reform. As part of Asia, however, one thing was clear: Developing Asian countries grew rapidly after they opened themselves to trade with the rest of the world. They used their low-wage labor force to compete in world markets. Competing for international market share imposed discipline. Companies that do not produce high-quality products efficiently and with modern technology simply cannot sell. Countries that do not offer reasonable protection to investors cannot attract foreign capital.

The opening of China's economy was probably the most significant step in the Chinese reform process. The opening of China's economy began in 1977 and 1978.

Within three years, the volume of international trade tripled. In 2009, China overtook Germany to become the world's largest exporter. Less widely known is the fact that China will become the world's largest importer by 2014.[47]

"Greater China" played a significant role in opening the Chinese economy. Greater Chinese numbered in the millions in Hong Kong, Taiwan, Macao, Southeast Asia, and North America. Especially those in Hong Kong and Taiwan still had roots on the mainland. They understood China's potential as a low-wage country with abundant human resources strategically situated in the heart of booming Southeast Asia. Greater Chinese intermediaries could explain to investors how and with whom to do business and which government officials were reliable.

China's first lesson in global exchange was from nearby Hong Kong. Before communist rule, the inhabitants of the capital of Guangdong adjacent to Hong Kong were considered city slickers, whereas Hong Kong was full of country bumpkins. As Hong Kong surged, several million Guangdongese fled to Hong Kong's economic miracle. Friends and families lined up in long queues in Guangzhou to receive hand-me-downs from Hong Kong. Young urban women wanted to marry only men with overseas family relations.[48]

In focusing on the outside world, Chinese reformers knew that they had to take advantage of nearby Hong Kong, Taiwan, and East Asia. However, capital would not be forthcoming from them unless the Chinese could offer reasonable safety for foreign investment.

Given that Chinese legal protection of property rights was weak and that Chinese courts could not be counted on to enforce the property rights of foreigners, Chinese reformers set up various "free enterprise or trade zones," most located initially in close proximity to Hong Kong. They exempted them from Chinese taxation and regulatory arrangements and liberalized joint-venture laws to encourage export-oriented joint ventures in these zones.

The Chinese government first set up special economic zones in Shenzhen near Hong Kong; Zhuhai near Macao; Shantou, the hometown of Hong Kong refugees; and Xiemen, near Taiwan to promote trade. *Special economic zones were areas freed of trade restrictions and barriers that were allowed to operate under foreign legal regimes.*

At first, the Chinese borrowed their new rules and regulations directly from Hong Kong. Guangdong entrepreneurs copied the Hong Kong model of "Front Shop, Back Factory," while others set up joint factories together with Hong Kong small business owners. Hong Kong, with the largest container port in Asia, provided both hard and soft infrastructure for China through which Chinese goods first reached global markets.

Taiwanese investors began to flood into China in the early 1990s, circumventing a ban on business with China by going through Hong Kong. They used China for manufacturing bases to contend with increasing world competition. By 2004, Taiwanese investment comprised close to three percent of China's GDP.

In 2001, the Chinese state took a giant step forward by becoming a member of the World Trade Organization (WTO). *WTO membership obligated China to comply with WTO rules and regulations concerning international copyright laws, trademarks, visas, business licenses, and protection of domestic industries.*[49] The obligation to comply with

WTO rules represented a serious test for China's economic practices. The WTO does not allow governments to subsidize their domestic industries. Under WTO rules, foreign banks must be allowed to compete against Chinese banks. WTO membership can force China to reform corporate ownership and governance. To date, China has avoided implementing many of its obligations under the WTO.

China passed joint-venture laws to encourage foreign companies to set up shop in China with Chinese partners. Remarkably, China became the world's top recipient of foreign direct investment among the developing economies. *Foreign direct investment (FDI) is investment by foreign investors in the form of acquiring substantial shares in domestic companies or entering into partnerships with domestic companies through joint ventures.* FDI contrasts with *portfolio investment, whereby foreign investors simply purchase shares or debt of domestic companies.*

The result was a massive influx of Western capital. Starting initially with modest amounts, FDI in China exceeded a cumulated total of $40 billion by 1996. Almost 60 percent of this FDI came from "Greater China" sources, particularly Hong Kong, Macao, and Taiwan.

A major payoff from this foreign investment was the acquisition of modern technology and marketing savvy that permitted China to increase its exports. In 1985, Chinese companies with foreign investors exported goods worth less than $1 billion per annum and accounted for about 1 percent of Chinese exports. By 1995, they accounted for almost $50 billion in exports and for 32 percent of Chinese total exports.

Table 15.1 shows China's astonishing success in attracting FDI, which reached a peak of 40 percent of world FDI in the mid-1990s. China began its reform era with less than $2 billion of FDI annually and entered the twenty-first century with over $40 billion annual FDI. China financed some 40 percent of its gross capital formation in the decade of the 1990s with FDI; the remaining 60 percent was financed through domestic savings.[50]

TABLE 15.1   China's Share in FDI Inflow in the World and as a Share of Developing Countries, 1982–2010

	Year			
	1982–1987 (annual average)	1990	2000	2010
China (billion $US)	1.4	3.5	41	106
All Countries (billion $US)	67.2	159.1	1271	1244
China's Share in World FDI	2	2.2	3.2	8.5
All Developing Countries (billion $US)	14.7	34.7	240	574
China's Share in Developing Countries FDI	9.5	10.1	17.1	18.5

Sources: Data for 1982–1987 annual averages are cited from the United Nations, *World Investment Report 1994*, Annex table 1. Data for 1990, 1994, and 2000 are from the United Nations, *World Investment Report 2001*. The 1982–1987 averages are cited from Chen Chunlai, *Foreign Direct Investment in China*, Chinese Economy Research Unit (Adelaide, Australia: University of Adelaide, April 1996). The 2010 data are from UNCTAD, Global Investment Trends, 2011, http://www.unctad-docs.org/files/UNCTAD-WIR2011-Chapter-I-en.pdf.

FIGURE 15.4 Distribution of FDI in China by Source Country, 1996

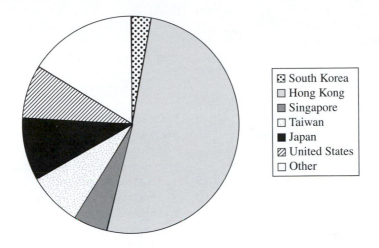

Legend:
- South Korea
- Hong Kong
- Singapore
- Taiwan
- Japan
- United States
- Other

Source: From GREGORY, Comparing Economic Systems in the Twenty-First Century, 7E. © 2004 Cengage Learning.

Figure 15.4 shows that most FDI to China came from Asia, the largest donor being Hong Kong (perhaps playing the role of intermediary for overseas Chinese in various countries). Less than one-quarter of FDI in the mid-1990s came from countries outside of Asia, although this proportion has increased since then.

Some 400 of the 500 world's largest companies have invested in over 2,000 projects in China. They include the world's leading computer, electronics, telecommunications equipment, pharmaceutical, and petrochemical companies. Transnational corporations such as Microsoft, Motorola, GM, GE, Samsung, Intel, Nokia, and Siemens, to name just a few, have established R&D ventures in China. Microsoft, for example, has invested $80 million in a Chinese research institute and intends to make additional investments to create a Microsoft Asian Technology Center. The effect of FDI can be seen in China's increasing ability to export high-technology products. In 2000, China exported $37 billion worth of high-technology products, 81 percent of which were produced by foreign affiliates in China.[51]

When transnational companies make foreign direct investments in China, they must usually partner with a Chinese joint-venture partner or affiliate. Hence, they must deal, through their local partner, with the peculiarities and problems of Chinese corporate governance. The assets that foreigners acquire through their direct investments must be managed within China according to Chinese business practices and are subject to the interventions and frequent irrationalities of the Chinese economic system.

Table 15.2 shows the enormous size and scope of China's foreign trade as of 2010. China is the world's largest merchandise exporter, accounting for 10 percent of the world total, 94 percent of which is manufactures. Its main markets are the European Union and the United States. It exported $1.6 trillion worth of merchandise and ran a merchandise surplus of almost $200 billion in 2010.

TABLE 15.2   Indicators of Chinese Foreign Trade

	Value		
	2010		
Merchandise *exports*, f.o.b. (million US$)	1 577 824		
Merchandise *imports*, c.i.f. (million US$)	1 395 099		

	2010		2010
Share in world total exports	10.36	**Share in world total imports**	9.06
Breakdown in economy's total exports		**Breakdown in economy's total imports**	
By main commodity group (ITS)		By main commodity group (ITS)	
Agricultural products	3.3	Agricultural products	7.8
Fuels and mining products	3.0	Fuels and mining products	26.7
Manufactures	93.6	Manufactures	64.1
By main destination		By main origin	
1. European Union (27)	19.7	1. Japan	12.6
2. United States	18.0	2. European Union (27)	12.0
3. Hong Kong, China	13.8	3. Korea, Republic of	9.9
4. Japan	7.7	4. Taipei, Chinese	8.3
5. Korea, Republic of	4.4	5. China	7.6

Source: World Trade Organization 2011, http://stat.wto.org/CountryProfile/WSDBCountryPFView.aspx?Language=E&Country=CN.

Figure 15.5 shows China's trade proportion as of 2006 (on the eve of the world economic downturn). It shows that China's exports plus imports constituted more than 70 percent of GDP, which is a high ratio for a country as large as China (see, for example, India's and the United States' smaller trade proportions).

China has changed the face of world trade. Its exports have held down consumer prices in its export destinations. U.S. consumers shop at Walmart and Target for goods produced in China that earlier would have cost double or more. China's huge manufacturing centers offer Microsoft, Apple, and Adidas factory facilities and a trained labor force that can produce huge scale of output quickly. In its thirst for raw materials throughout the world, China has bid up the prices of crude oil and minerals.

China's phenomenal entry into the world economy has increased the interrelatedness of the world economy. The West now depends on Chinese growth as an engine for recovery from economic downturns. China faces shrinking export markets during economic recessions elsewhere in the world.

The Chinese trade model has also created China's future competitors. Countries like Malaysia, Indonesia, Vietnam, and Thailand also offer low-wage labor that competes with China for foreign investment and manufacturing facilities. As China's wages rise, export business will increasingly shift to other parts of Asia.

FIGURE 15.5   China's Trade Proportion (exports plus imports as a percent of GDP) versus Other Countries, 2006

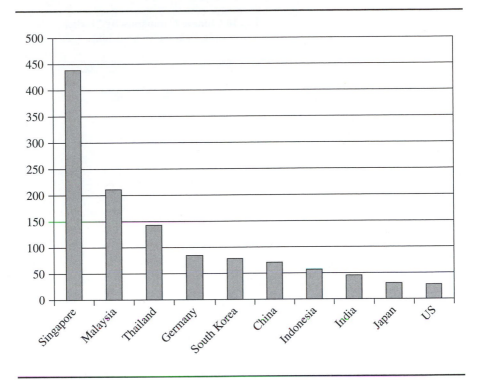

Source: Asian Development Bank, *http://www.adb.org.*

SOEs and Private Enterprise

China began its reforms in the late 1970s with virtually complete state or collective ownership of industry, agriculture, transportation, and commerce.[52] Reforms began with changes in ownership relationships in agriculture and in small-scale trade, manufacturing, and services and then spread to larger-scale economic activities.

Although the share of the private sector has been growing over time, Chinese leaders have maintained that their national champions must remain under state ownership and control. *National champions are companies deemed of such national importance that they must be owned and managed by the state.* The Chinese state continues to be protective of its SOEs.

Chinese SOEs are state sole-funded corporations and enterprises with the state as the biggest shareholder. According to the latest census, they number more than 150,000 (some 3 percent of the total number of enterprises), and they account for a substantial portion of total enterprises assets.[53] SOEs account for more than 90 percent of the market value of listed Chinese companies. If indirectly controlled entities, urban collectives, and public TVEs are included, the share of GDP owned and controlled by the state is approximately 50 percent.[54] Figure 15.6 shows the market capitalization of China's top ten companies—all SOEs.

FIGURE 15.6   Top 10 Chinese Companies by Market Capitalization (in US $ bil.)

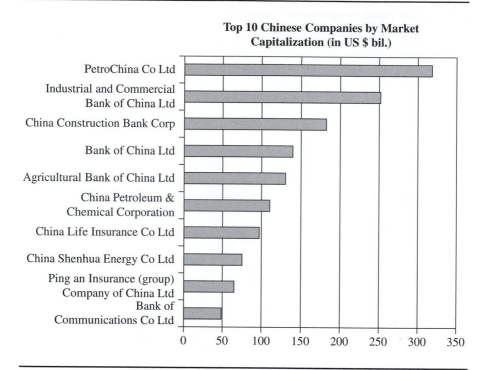

Top 10 Chinese Companies by Market Capitalization (in US $ bil.)

Source: Financial Times. Thanks to David Hunkar for finding. Reprinted with permission of Seeking Alpha.

Figure 15.7 shows that the relative importance of SOEs has been declining. The steeper decline in shares of the number of enterprises than in shares of industrial assets (which remains around 50 percent) suggests that SOEs are growing increasingly large relative to private enterprises.

Power and Influence of SOEs   The Chinese have stubbornly resisted turning the "commanding heights" of the economy over to private hands. State ownership is the hallmark of market socialism. If China were indeed to privatize its SOEs, it would lose its claim of being a market-socialist economy. For hard-liners in the party, this would be a serious blow.

The first two decades of economic reform incrementally reduced the scope of planning, increased managerial authority, and relied more on market forces. The late 1990s saw a clearly enunciated SOE policy of "retain large SOEs and release small ones." Smaller state-owned companies could go to private owners, but the state should continue to own the largest.

Current Chinese policy is captured by the phrase, "the state advances, the private sector retreats." Or, as the Chinese prime minister stated in a March 2010 address, "The socialist system's advantages enable us to make decisions efficiently,

FIGURE 15.7   Shares of Chinese SOEs: Number of Enterprises and Shares of
Assets

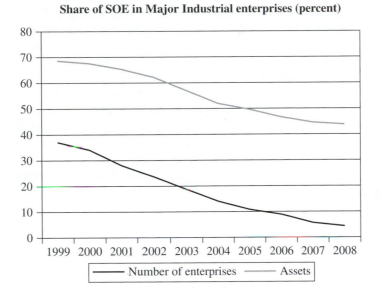

Share of SOE in Major Industrial enterprises (percent)

Source: Gao Xu, "State Owned Enterprises in China: How Big Are They?" January 19, 2010; CEIC.
Reprinted with permission.

organize effectively and concentrate resources to accomplish large undertakings."
One Chinese official described the "state advance, private sector retreats" more
frankly as "leaving the private sector drinking the soup while the state enterprises
are eating the meat."[55]

As the Chinese reforms proceeded, state ownership was "corporatized" from
direct state management to state "shareholding" by a state asset-management commission, outside directors, and supervisory committees. Corporatization *means the
state remains the owner of the majority of shares but management is supposedly
independent*. The hope was that corporatized SOEs would operate like corporations
in industrialized market economies.

De-politicization of SOEs has proven difficult for Chinese officials to accept.
Their control of large companies has been a source of political power, patronage,
and corruption, and their ideology is biased to favor state ownership. Chinese leaders, pursuing "socialism with Chinese characteristics," believe that companies
important to economic and national security should remain "national champions."
Under national champions, they include not only strategic industries but also technological firms that foster indigenous innovation.[56] SOEs continue to enjoy privileges, such as preferred access to bank credit at below market rates, favorable tax
treatment, and favored access to state procurement markets.

In many cases, state companies use their advantages to drive out private competitors, as the following account explains:

> Six years ago, the central government invited private investors to enter the civil aviation business. By 2006, eight private carriers had sprung up to challenge the three state-controlled majors, Air China, China Southern and China Eastern. The state airlines immediately began a price war. The state-owned monopoly that provided jet fuel refused to service private carriers on the same generous terms given the big three. China's only computerized reservation system—currently one-third owned by the three state airlines—refused to book flights for private competitors. And when mismanagement and the 2008 economic crisis drove the three majors into financial straits, the central government bought stock to bail them out.[57]

The government also uses SOEs to facilitate structural change in the Chinese economy, to acquire technology from foreign firms, and to secure raw material from beyond China's borders. The state used SOEs and state-owned banks to carry out a stimulus policy in 2008 during the world economic downturn.

Chinese leaders keep SOE executives under control through appointments and promotions managed by the Central Committee cadres department. SOE executives, who wish to advance or keep their jobs, must follow the government's policy guidance. If maximizing shareholder value conflicts with state goals, SOE managers are likely to pursue the goals of the state.

Soft Budgets, Banks, and Profits   Under the old Soviet-style system, SOEs could count on state bailouts; that is, they faced a soft budget constraint. Insolvent SOEs were kept afloat by cash infusions and rollovers of nonperforming debt. This practice continued throughout the reform era.

It was thought that bankruptcy of large SOEs could harm the regional or national economy; therefore, banks continued to lend to troubled companies. At times, Chinese banks were left holding large quantities of non-performing loans and had to be bailed out themselves. In 2001, for example, between 40 and 45 percent of outstanding loans equaling between 45 and 55 percent of GDP were non-performing.[58] Since 2004, the volume of non-performing loans has fallen with the improved financial performance of SOEs.[59] Chinese practice did not allow the market to winnow out the low performers and replace them with the high performers. To a great extent, the cost of keeping insolvent SOEs afloat has been shifted to private enterprise and taxpayers.[60]

Figure 15.8 shows the rates of return on equity of the ten largest Chinese SOEs. It shows that SOEs that enjoy monopolies (such as energy, utilities, and telecoms) or benefit from government procurements (Baoshan Iron and Steel) enjoy healthy profits. SOEs engaged in banking and life insurances (as lenders to SOEs) earn miniscule profits. These meager rates of return are largely the result of "political lending."

Chinese banks make only 4 percent of their loans to private businesses. In years of high inflation, banks lend at negative real rates of interest. Meanwhile, private businesses must borrow in unofficial credit markets at high rates of interest, such as the "Wenzhou rate" of 18 percent or more, or they must finance business

FIGURE 15.8   Rates of Return of Equity, China's Ten Largest Companies (2010)

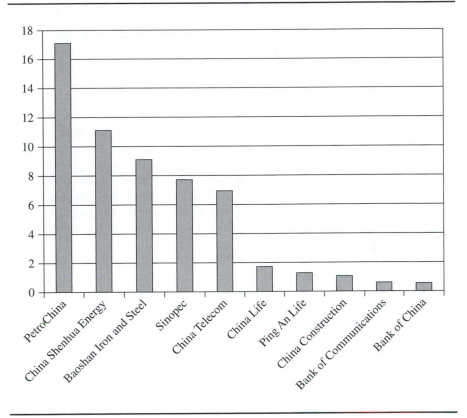

Source: Based on data from Yahoo Finance, http://finance.yahoo.com

expansion out of enterprise savings. Private credit markets often violate Chinese laws. Private businesses do not know if and when their private lending and borrowing will land them in jail or worse. For example, one prominent female lender faced the death penalty for illegal lending.[61]

Despite their disadvantages, private companies are more than twice as productive as wholly owned SOEs. Indeed, productivity increases as the form of ownership moves from direct state to private ownership. Private companies, whether foreign-owned, domestic-owned, or joint ventures, have consistently outgrown SOEs, and an OECD study finds that total factor productivity of privately controlled enterprises is approximately twice that of SOEs. Nevertheless, SOEs continue to receive almost all of the official bank credits.[62]

Corporate Governance, Corruption, and Property Rights

As we noted in Chapter 2, ownership entails formal ownership, control rights, and the right to receive the income and other benefits the property generates. China's formal property rights are remarkably weak, even after the passage of property laws in 2003. In agriculture and small-scale enterprises, formal private ownership is disguised by long-term "leases" or by "township" or "cooperative" ownership. There exist few formal-ownership registers, which establish clear-cut documentation of property ownership. Property rights instead are guaranteed by an implicit contract with state and party authorities, who tacitly agree to the exercise of these property rights.

China's "property rights limbo" is nowhere more evident than in the corporatized SOEs. The state is the formal owner, and the management is supposed to operate the company according to market criteria. One expert on China, however, concludes that "shareholding enterprises, despite receiving a great deal of attention, have not been able to deliver markedly better results than the Soviet-style SOEs they replaced.... . property rights relations remain relatively confused."[63]

Although management is theoretically guided and supervised by shareholders, the monitoring capacity of corporate shareholders is not yet established. Some enterprise managers have complete authority; others are directed by state and political leaders. Corporate directors are ill-informed about the enterprises on whose boards they serve. Corporate directorates are often simply renamed government offices.

In the Anglo-Saxon and European models, the "rule of law" that assures contract fulfillment requires clearly defined property rights and an accepted enforcement mechanism, such as courts. If a contract is violated, the injured party must have the expectation of getting back damages. This threat (plus other factors, such as harm to reputation and image) induces parties to honor contracts in countries with mature institutions.

In the Chinese case, the transnational corporation operating in China would not expect local courts to protect its property rights; rather, it would use government or party officials—be they local, regional, or national—to act as guarantors of contracts. Hence Chinese contracts are primarily regulated by *relational contracting*, as in other parts of Asia.

Despite its shortcomings, Chinese relational contracting appears, to date, to have provided sufficient protection to allow the influx of billions of dollars of investment every year. How it has been able to work in this fashion is one of the many missing pieces of the China Puzzle mentioned at the beginning of this chapter.

With insecure property rights and relational contracting, obtaining licenses, permits, bank loans, protection from competition, and other advantages depend on whom you know, on who is willing to help and who can harm your business. These uncertainties create huge opportunities for corruption. It might be necessary to bribe an official to get an operating license or export permission. Bank officials might require a side payment before releasing a loan.

Insofar as the ultimate source of power is the party, those with party status and rank are in a position to offer favors in return for under-the-table rewards. Often influential party members themselves are constrained by party ethics from profiting on their position. Their children and relatives are not.

China was ranked in seventy-fifth place on Transparency International's 2011 corruption index (located between Tunisia and Romania). China's corruption ranking has in fact fallen relative to other countries. China tied with Saudi Arabia and Syria for seventy-first place in 2008.[64]

China has as many billionaires as the United States (Russia is in third place). China's superrich tend to be princelings. ***Princelings*** *refer to the offspring of the older generation of party leaders who have profited from their family connections.*

Foreign companies normally partner with SOEs in order to have a state entity on their side to handle the bureaucracy, but Western and Chinese partners approach problem solving differently. When Yahoo! teamed with a Chinese partner, it discovered that a major company asset had been transferred to the Chinese owner without Yahoo!'s knowledge. The Chinese owner justified the action on the grounds that the transfer was necessary to preserve the company's operating licenses.[65] After a face-saving compromise, Yahoo! quietly withdrew from the Chinese market. Yahoo!'s CEO was subsequently replaced.

The fact that the Chinese Communist Party has a procedure for orderly transition of power has helped China attract foreign investment. If a transnational company is contemplating a billion-dollar investment that will pay off only over decades, it must be confident of the continuity of leadership over this period of time. Moreover, if aging leaders refuse to retire (perhaps they fear retribution for earlier decisions), a new generation of leaders with new ideas cannot advance. How the Chinese Communist Party itself adapts to change and handles the myriad of principal–agent problems within its hierarchy will determine how long it can serve as an anchor for the relational contracts on which the Chinese economy is based.

It must be recognized as well that there is no such thing as "the party." The national party has one set of goals; regional party officials must look after the interests of their regions; municipal party leaders are interested in the success of their city. Regional, municipal, and local party leaders represent narrow vested interests that pursue narrow goals. For example, the national interest may require the closing of a large, inefficient plant, but the city party leadership must lobby against its closing to prevent the loss of local employment.

For international investors, agreements with municipal mayors or provincial governors could be overridden by national figures. To succeed, they must transverse the complicated maze of intraparty relationships that are too complicated even for the Chinese to understand.

Capital Markets, Minority Shareholders, and Banks

State ownership of the majority of shares of corporatized companies discourages share purchases by minority shareholders, who rightly fear the enterprise will be run for political rather than economic gain.

Although minority shareholders should, in principle, avoid minority shareholdings in Chinese corporations, the lure of the China market has allowed Chinese companies to issue IPOs in Chinese, Hong Kong, and even Western stock exchanges, such as in Canada.

In 2010, China was the world's top IPO market, selling $131 billion worth of new shares on various exchanges, more than double the depressed IPO business in the United States.[66] But even this substantial figure accounted for just 5 percent of Chinese gross capital formation in 2010.

Stock Exchanges versus Bank Lending   Buying Chinese stocks holds a number of pitfalls for foreign investors. The "A Share" market consists of companies whose shares are denominated in local currency and are off limits to non-Chinese investors. "B share stocks" are denominated in dollars and can be bought by foreigners, but the rights are usually restricted. Quite often, foreign buyers must pay higher prices for the same stock. Foreigners can also buy on Western exchanges in the form of American Depository receipts or reverse mergers in Canadian or other stock markets, but listing requirement for Chinese stock are highly deficient and their disclosure rules are among the most lax in the world. There are currently some seventy Chinese companies listed in the United States, and the list continues to grow.[67]

Scandals are diminishing the allure of Chinese stocks. Major shareholders of the Canadian-Chinese company Sino-Forest Corporation learned that their Chinese partners could not deliver proof of rights to its timber reserves. A Chinese coal company sold stock on one of Canada's stock exchange after listing as assets mines that had been transferred to a state company.[68] The value of Chinese companies delisting from U.S. exchanges in 2011 exceeded the amount Chinese companies raised via initial public offerings.[69]

There can be no real market for corporate control in China. The state's majority ownership means that it can block unwelcome takeover bids. Foreign owners who have large blocs of shares have no way of changing management or influencing agenda items. In short, Chinese officialdom remains hostile to the development of a healthy private financial and industrial sector. Laws and the tax system favor state-owned enterprises over private corporations, and few tax incentives are offered for private companies.[70]

China has been able to attract huge amounts of FDI—a more important source of investment finance—but Chinese SOEs finance their investment primarily through bank lending. The greater reliance on bank lending is seen in the comparison of market capitalization of Chinese listed companies with bank lending to companies as a percent of GDP.

According to World Bank figures, the market capitalization of listed companies was 81 percent of GDP in 2010, up from 62 percent in 2008 but down from 100 percent during the run up of the Chinese stock market in 2009.[71] In contrast, domestic credit provided by banking sector to companies was 146 percent of GDP in 2010 and 145 percent in 2009.[72]

Political Capital Markets   The investment decisions of private companies in China are based on rate-of-return considerations. The private owners have their own capital at risk, and they should seek to invest capital in the highest and best use. Private Chinese companies affiliated with Western partners would also make investment decisions based on commercial principles.

In the state-owned sector, investment decision making still suffers from political intervention. Because the approval process takes into account the impact of investment on regional economic development, large investment projects are decided by the clout of their high-level political supporters, not by market research or rate-of-return analysis. One expert on China draws the following conclusions about investment choice in China: "Despite the impact of two decades of reform, the fundamental nature of investment processes in China has not changed substantially from the pre-reform circumstances."[73]

Insofar as the bulk of investment capital for SOEs comes from banks, it is worthwhile to consider whether the banks themselves operate on commercial or other principles. Chinese banks are state owned and they have faced relatively little foreign competition despite the WTO requirement that foreign banks and investment firms be given access to China's financial markets.

Under China's old Soviet-style banking system, there was no distinction between the central bank and commercial banks. The monopoly banking system allocated credit according to credit plans tied to the economic plan. The reform created a two-tiered banking system of a central bank and commercial banks, and commercial banking remained concentrated in the hands of a few large state banks.

Throughout the reform period, banks remained the property of the state, and they disbursed loans according to the directives of government and party officials, giving preferential treatment to state enterprises. Private-sector companies had to finance their own activities through their retained earnings and were starved of banking services. Banks not owned by the state are taxed heavily and in a discriminatory fashion. Interest rates are regulated on both the loan and deposit sides, although private banks operating underground can charge what the market will bear.[74]

The Big Four commercial banks—Bank of China, Industrial and Commercial Bank of China, Agricultural Bank of China, and China Construction Bank—control about two-thirds of the banking system. Each of these giant banks employs hundreds of thousands of people at thousands of branches. Even when top management has tried to institute reforms, it is hard to get such massive bureaucratic organizations to change their way of doing business. Despite some attempts to make banks lend to private business, this has not happened.

China's accession to the WTO was supposed to shake up Chinese banking. Under WTO provisions, domestic banks must compete with foreign banks. Under promises that Beijing made when China joined the WTO, by the end of 2006 foreign banks were supposed to have the same rights as domestic banks. The year 2006 has long passed, and foreign banks scarcely have a presence in the difficult Chinese financial market. Chinese banking officials' worries that transnational banks would come to dominate the Chinese banking market have not materialized. Although foreign banks continue to consider Chinese financial services as a lucrative investment opportunity, their share of China's financial market remains below 2 percent.[75]

Private enterprises, largely cut out of the bank lending market, turn to China's informal lending system comprised of small lenders, loan sharks, and wealthy individuals. There are no official figures on the size of this market (because much of it is illegal), but informal estimates place its annual lending at 10 percent of GDP. Given its size and importance, the national party congress of March 2012 mulled ways to legalize parts of the informal lending market. Specifically, the China Banking Regulatory Commission has launched trial reforms of informal lending in the Chinese city of Wenzhou, a city known for its informal lending markets.[76]

National Savings and Financial Intermediation   Faced with little competition, Chinese banks attract the bulk of savings that does not go into informal lending markets. As Figure 15.9 shows, China's national savings rate is the highest in the world and has been rising steadily.

Undergirding China's exceptionally high national saving rate is the high rate of household savings. Chinese families save more for a number of reasons: The state welfare system applies only to state employees and offers meager retirement income. Chinese families must save to finance expensive educations for their children or to buy a home or apartment in the absence of borrowing opportunities. Chinese families also remember the upheavals of the Great Leap Forward and the Cultural Revolution and understand the meaning of uncertainty.

Knowing the risks of Chinese stocks and the lack of competition from foreign banks, Chinese households can hoard cash, deposit in banks, or lend money directly without financial intermediation. The fact that informal lending may account for between $316 billion and $632 billion, a bit less than 10 percent of the country's GDP, suggests that many households and businesses avoid the financial intermediation of banks by direct borrowing and lending.[77] Private businesses also generate savings by retaining profits and by hiding profits to reduce their tax liabilities.[78]

FIGURE 15.9   National Savings Rates, China and Other Asian Countries, 1982–2007

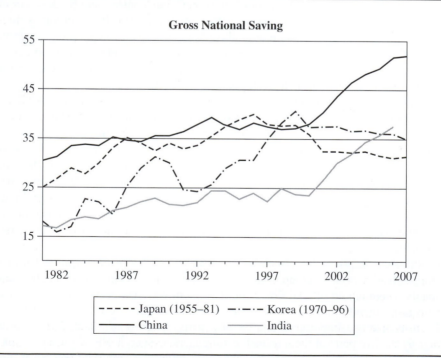

Gross National Saving

1982   1987   1992   1997   2002   2007

----- Japan (1955–81) —·—·— Korea (1970–96)
——— China   ——— India

Source: Guonan Ma and Wang Yi, "China's High Saving Rate: Myth and Reality, June 2010," Bank for International Settlements, BIS Working Paper 3123.

Chinese Financial Markets and Efficiency   Capital will not be allocated efficiently if it does not go to the highest and best use. If the bulk of investment capital goes to projects that yield a 5 percent rate of return while projects that yield 20 percent go unfunded, we can say the capital market is inefficient. ***Capital market inefficiency*** *occurs when investment finance does not go to uses that yield the highest rates of return (adjusted for risk).*

Most Chinese capital is allocated by banks that do not necessarily use economic criteria in making loans. Only 4 percent of bank loans go to private business, and it is private businesses that earn the highest profit rates. State enterprises are estimated to earn a 4 percent return on capital versus a minimum of 14 percent for registered private companies.[79] Insofar as private companies borrow at the Wehzhou rate of 18 percent and above, this means they must earn profit rates above that if they are to survive and prosper.[80] If state enterprises indeed average profit rates of 4 percent, their real profit rate is negative whenever inflation exceeds 4 percent. As *The Economist* writes, "China is often held up as an object lesson in state-directed capitalism. Yet its economic dynamism owes much to those outside the government's embrace."[81]

The remarkable feature of China is that its private sector has been able to advance and outgrow the privileged state sector, especially given its disadvantages in credit markets. An authority on Chinese financial markets writes that political authorities are reluctant to turn control over this "bountiful source of political resources" to the market. He writes: "Although the Chinese leadership willingly liberalized other sectors of the economy, the enormous pool of savings in the banking sector made it an indispensible policy and political instrument."[82]

Labor Markets

Under China's former Soviet-style system, people either worked for state enterprises or in collective farms. Large SOEs were often the major employer in the city or region, providing for the social, health, educational, and cultural needs not only of employees but also of the community. Labor unions, if they existed at all, ensured that workers fulfilled the plan. Under the old system, the plan was supposed to ensure that every able-bodied person had a job. Enterprises operated under soft budget constraints. With little interest in profits, enterprises kept too many employees on the payroll. Even redundant employees could be useful at times to fulfill a difficult plan.

This labor market was not suited to new market conditions. As private enterprises gained ascendancy in agriculture and small and medium-scale establishments, they limited their hiring to employees who could add to profits. Competition required labor costs be held down in export industries. The last haven for redundant workers was the SOE, which still received subsidies and credits to keep it in business.

In the reform era, China had to create a private labor force that worked primarily for private enterprises according to commercial principles. It had to create a labor market that transferred workers from low productivity to high productivity jobs in geographically distant areas. The whole working-age population had to be reshuffled.

Migrant Workers: Hukou   China's rapid growth began along its Eastern coast and then gradually spread inland. In 1978, at the start of the reform, China's population lived inland and was locked into collective farms and communes from which they could not legally exit. Then and today, Chinese citizens are subject to a household registration system, which regulates where they are allowed to live. ***Hukou** is a residence registration system that registers households by place of urban or rural location.* The household registration system was set up in 1958 to provide data for government welfare and resource distribution, migration control, and criminal surveillance.

Only those with residence permits are legally entitled to live permanently in the designated city. To change urban locations, they have to receive a new residence permit. Those residing in a city without a residence permit are not entitled to housing and other social benefits, such as education and medical care. Residents are not allowed to work or live outside the administrative boundaries of their household registration without approval of the authorities. Once they leave their place of registration, they leave behind all of their rights and benefits. For the purpose of surveillance, temporary residents are required to register with the police of their place of residence and their temporary residence.

For all appearances, the hukou system seemed incompatible with the movement from underemployment in rural areas to manufacturing jobs on the eastern coast. But Chinese industrial growth has been fueled since its beginnings by vast flows of migrant workers from the countryside to the cities under the auspices of the hukou system. Migrant workers travel to cities and construction sites where they receive no benefits and are not entitled to regular housing. They live in employer-provided dorms. They periodically return to their places of residence and move from one location to another according to job availability.

Over the last three decades, the number of cities increased more than three times from 191 in 1978 to 661 in 2005. The proportion of urban population increased from 18 percent in 1978 to its present 50 percent. As urbanization expanded, so did the gap between urban and rural incomes. In 1978, urban incomes were 2.6 times those of rural incomes, but by 2005, that gap had widened to 3.22 times, and in 2006 to 3.3 times. The discrepancy between rural and urban incomes spurred rural workers to move to the cities in search of better pay.

The six provinces of Henan, Anhui, Hunan, Jiangxi, Sichuan, and Hubei contribute just less than 60 percent of migrant workers nationally; the six municipalities and provinces of Beijing, Shanghai, Zhejiang, Jiangsu, Guangdong, and Fujian have absorbed almost 70 percent of cross-province migrant workers. In Beijing in 2011, about 40 percent of the total population was migrant workers; in Shenzhen, 12 million of the total 14 million people were migrants.

In 1989, there were already about 30 million migrant workers in China. In 1993, the number increased to 62 million and by the end of 2006 to 131.8 million. By the end of 2010, there were an estimated quarter of a billion rural migrant workers in China, accounting for about one third of the rural workforce. The migration of workers made possible huge changes in the composition of output. At the start of the reform, some one third of output originated in agriculture. Currently it is close to 10 percent.[83]

According to a 2006 national survey on migrant workers, 64 percent were males, and half of migrant workers were aged between 16 and 30. Only 10 percent of migrant workers had education beyond middle school. The proportion of migrant workers in manufacturing industries and in construction reached as high as 68 percent and 80 percent respectively.[84]

Layoffs in the State Sector   As employment opportunities for migrant workers and private-sector employees expanded, they shrank in SOEs. In 1995, the central government decided to leave or sell medium to small-scale SOEs. By 1998, one quarter of China's 87,000 industrial SOEs had been restructured and another quarter were scheduled for restructuring. In most cases, restructuring meant shedding excess workers. From 1998 to 2004, six in ten SOE workers were laid off, and the proportion of SOE employees in the labor force dropped from 16 percent in 1994 to 8 percent in 2005. Some 21 million workers were laid off from SOEs between1994 and 2005 alone. It was up to the private sector to take up this slack.

Local governments used a number of methods to encourage employee retention and rehiring. SOE buyers were required to sign contracts for the redeployment of employees. The government also offered discounts in return for a commitment to find employment for workers. In some extreme cases, they even offered the free transfer of ownership rights and tax holidays.

Despite these efforts, redeployment of labor through official channels worked in only three in ten cases. Laid-off SOE workers received redundancy packages of three years' salary, but most of it went for contributions to their own pension and insurance schemes. In enterprises with limited resources, poor, or corrupt management, it was not unusual for laid-off workers to get no compensation.[85]

National and regional government efforts to help laid-off workers were tied to concern about labor unrest. Chinese workers do not have the right to form independent unions. They lack the right of free assembly. They work under difficult and dangerous conditions. For a state fearful of civic unrest, the specter of unemployed urban masses raised a red flag. Chinese authorities sought to head off social problems with new labor laws.

Two labor contract laws of 2008 guaranteed contracts for full-time employees and provided for lawsuits and arbitration. Employees immediately began to take advantage of these laws. In 2008 alone, there were 700,000 labor disputes under arbitration for cases of unpaid wages, unlawful overtime, and cheating on minimum wages, among other things. Honda workers, for example, demanded the creation of an independent union along with wage increases. One of the most common complaints was not paying overtime pay when the work week exceeded forty hours.[86]

China faces pressure on another front. Its WTO membership requires it to observe certain international working conditions standards. The two it openly violates are the right to form independent labor unions and prohibition on prison labor. Audits show that Chinese companies routinely violate WTO labor codes against unpaid overtime, substandard working conditions, and labor-related accidents. The March 2012 audit of Apple's manufacturing of iPads and iPhones operations through a Chinese employer, Foxconn Technology Group, resulted in higher pay and improved working conditions. Due to its high-profile nature, the Apple case may raise wages generally in Chinese manufacturing operations.[87]

China is locked in a competitive struggle with lower-wage Asian economies in Indonesia, Vietnam, Thailand, and elsewhere. Higher wages and improved working conditions come at a cost: China's low-wage advantage may be lost as jobs and contracts shift to other parts of Asia.

Economic Security

The Chinese Constitution of 1982 (Articles 44 and 45) provides that retirees shall enjoy the benefits of social security and that the state shall establish a system of social insurance, social assistance, and medical care. Under current provisions, state enterprises are supposed to pay a social security tax equal to 20 percent of their payroll, plus another 8 percent for health and unemployment insurance. The state finances only the administration of the system; it makes no other contribution. As in Europe and the United States, the Chinese state social security system is a pay-as-you-go system. Financially weak state-owned enterprises often fail to pay in. The state system covers employees in urban state enterprises and excludes those out of the labor force, migrant workers, and those living in the countryside.

In all, the state system covers less than 20 percent of the population. Privatized social security accounts are meant to cover the remainder. The state system currently replaces only 20 percent of pre-retirement income for those covered.[88] Although retirement ages of state employees remain the same, there is now the question of how pensions will be funded, particularly if large state-owned enterprises fail. Those falling outside the state system must see to their own retirement.

The weakness of the official social security system explains, to some degree, the high rate of household savings in China. Cultural factors explain the rest—self-reliance and family support are strong values.

Income Distribution

Like other Soviet-type systems, China began its reform era with a relatively even distribution of income. All property was owned by the state; able-bodied persons worked either in collective or state farms or in state enterprises earning wages set by the state. Entrepreneurial incomes were illegal. Workers, with a guarantee of lifetime employment and an obligatory retirement age of 60 (men) and 55 (women), received state pensions upon retirement.

China's market reforms changed the distribution of income dramatically. China now boasts a hundred or so billionaires. There are almost eight million private enterprises. Wealthy Chinese business owners buy expensive real estate in China and in luxury home markets abroad. Meanwhile, the average Chinese worker or farmer earns a modest income.

Figure 15.10 shows that China's income distribution is now similar to that of other relatively poor Asian countries and is about the same as the United States. The dramatic rise in inequality is exactly what would be expected from the move to private enterprise, the increase in entrepreneurship, and the stagnation of the large SOEs.

FIGURE 15.10   Inequality of Income Distribution as Measured by the Gini
Coefficient: China and Other Countries (latest estimates)

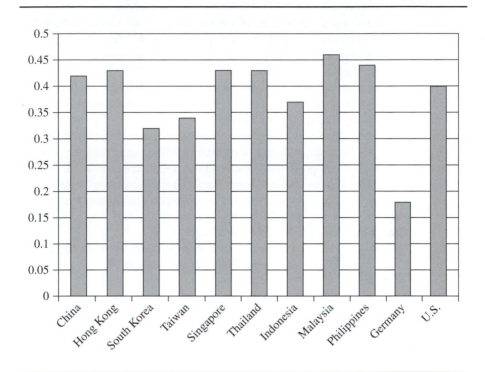

Source: Asian Development Bank, Poverty Database, http://www.abd.org.

It is important to recognize that three decades of rapid growth have reduced in
a dramatic fashion the percentage of population living in poverty. Using Chinese
standards of poverty, China's poverty rate fell from three quarters of the population
in 1995 to its current rate of some 30 percent.[89]

Those who focus on the increase in inequality must also recognize the remarkable increase in the living standards at the bottom of the income distribution. It
would be virtually impossible to have three decades of rapid growth without the
rising tide lifting all boats.

Summary

- China retained a one-party dictatorship and some socialist roots to create Chinese-
  style socialism with a large state sector and a leading role of the Communist Party.
- The China Puzzle is how a country like China with its poor protection of private
  property, weak corporate governance, lack of democratic accountability, and
  absence of a rule of law can grow rapidly over more than three decades.
- The People's Republic of China was founded in October 1949 with the victory
  of the Red Army under Mao Zedong, the unquestioned leader. It adopted the
  Soviet model.

- China's development was set back by the Great Leap Forward, which established communes in agriculture, and by the Cultural Revolution. Reform had to wait until Mao died in 1976.
- China is governed by a regional decentralized authoritarian regime, which has used regional competition to grow and to experiment with reforms.
- China uses an M-Form organization to organize and manage economic tasks on a regional rather than a sectoral basis.
- Economic reform began in agriculture on a spontaneous basis when peasants created the contract responsibility system. Reform spread from agriculture into services, trade, and then to manufacturing.
- The reforms begun by Deng Xiaoping opened the Chinese economy to world trade and FDI and created new forms of ownership while maintaining the political monopoly of the Communist Party. These reforms created rapid economic growth.
- The Chinese leadership has opted to keep control of the largest state enterprises, which receive special advantages in financing, protection, and other benefits.
- The fastest growing segment of the Chinese economy has been the private sector, but state policy favors the state sector.
- State banks dominate the capital market even though China has been the largest recipient of foreign direct investment. Political intervention has contributed to the vast corruption of Chinese officials.
- China's labor market consists of state employees who receive benefits and pensions and who have urban residential permits. It also consists of a vast migrant labor force; migrants travel from job to job with few protections. China's growth has markedly reduced poverty in China, but it has led to an increase in income inequality.

Key Terms

cadres department—Appoints officials to elite positions in the party and state. The party uses promotions and other rewards to incentivize regional officials.

capital market inefficiency—Investment finance does not go to uses that yield the highest rates of return (adjusted for risk).

China Puzzle—How China with its poor protection of private property, weak corporate governance, lack of democratic accountability, and absence of a rule of law can grow rapidly over more than three decade.

Chinese SOEs—State sole-funded corporations and enterprises with the state as the biggest share holder.

Chinese-style socialism—The state and private economies coexist, national planning is absent, and private property rights are supposed to be protected.

contract responsibility system—An agreement of a group of peasant households to collectively deliver quotas to the state while keeping the rest for their consumption or sale.

Cultural Revolution—Sought to restore socialist zeal and discipline by liquidating capitalist and traditional elements from Chinese society.

foreign direct investment (FDI)—Investment by foreign investors in the form of acquiring substantial shares in domestic companies or entering into partnerships with domestic companies through joint ventures.

Great Leap Forward—Massive resurgence of radical ideology, which replaced rationality.

Greater China—Vast numbers of Chinese both inside and outside of China proper.

hukou—Residence registration system, which registers households by place of urban or rural location.

M-Form organization—Organizes and manages economic tasks on a regional rather than a sectoral basis.

middle-income trap—The inability of fast-growing poor countries to raise per capita income from middle-income to affluent status.

national champions—Companies deemed of such national importance that they must be owned and managed by the state.

Politburo—Headed by the **General Secretary of the Party**—the most important position in China.

portfolio investment—Foreign investors simply purchase shares or debt of domestic companies.

Princelings—The offspring of the older generation of party leaders who have profited from their family connections.

regionally decentralized authoritarian regime (RDA)—Combination of political centralization and economic regional decentralization.

rural people's commune—Chinese version of the Soviet collective farm, although on a scale of thousands of families rather than hundreds.

special economic zones—Areas freed of trade restrictions and barriers that were allowed to operate under foreign legal regimes.

State Council—The executive branch of the central government.

state-owned enterprises (SOEs)—Owned by the state under the jurisdiction of a government entity and run by a state-appointed manager.

tournament competition—Players in the competition are judged by their relative performance (relative to other players).

township and village enterprises (TVEs)—Enterprises that are at least nominally owned by the township or village. They provided official cover for what were often purely private owners.

WTO membership—Obligated China to comply with WTO rules and regulations concerning international copyright laws, trademarks, visas, business licenses, and protection of domestic industries.

Notes

1. Constitution of the People's Republic of China, 1954, preamble, http://e-chaupak.net/database/chicon/1954/1954bilingual.htm#a.
2. Constitution of the People's Republic of China (December 1982), http://www.purdue.edu/crcs/itemResources/PRCDoc/pdf/Constitution.pdf.
3. Constitution of the People's Republic of China (December 1982) (With amendments), http://english.people.com.cn/constitution/constitution.html.
4. BBC, "China Passes New Law on Property," March 16, 2007.
5. "The Rise of State Capitalism," *The Economist*, January 21–27, 2012.
6. World Economic Outlook Database, September 2011.
7. Chenggang Xu, "The Fundamental Institutions of China's Reforms and Development," *Journal of Economic Literature* 49, no. 4 (2011), 1080.

8. Maurice Meisner, *Mao's China and After: A History of the People's Republic, Third Edition* (New York: Free Press, 1999); Lee Feigon, *Mao: A Reinterpretation* (Chicago: Ivan R. Dee, 2002).

9. Arthur G. Ashbrook, Jr., "China: Economic Modernization and Long-Term Performance," in U.S. Congress, Joint Economic Committee, *China Under the Four Modernizations*, Part 2, Section 5 (Washington, D.C.: U.S. Government Printing Office, 1982), pp. 151–368.

10. Jan S. Prybyla, *The Political Economy of Communist China* (Scranton, Pa.: International Textbook, 1970), chap. 5.

11. Thomas G. Rawski, "China's Industrial System," in U.S. Congress, Joint Economic Committee, *China: A Reassessment of the Economy* (Washington, D.C.: U.S. Government Printing Office, 1975), pp. 175–198; Robert F. Dernberger, "The Chinese Search for the Path of Self-Sustained Growth in the 1980s: An Assessment," in Joint Economic Committee, *China Under the Four Modernizations*, Part 1, pp. 19–76.

12. Prybyla, *The Political Economy of Communist China*, pp. 144–145.

13. Prybyla, *The Political Economy of Communist China*, pp. 135 ff.

14. Roderick MacFarquhar, *The Hundred Flowers Campaign and the Chinese Intellectuals* (New York: Praeger, 1960).

15. Roderick MacFarquhar, *The Origins of the Cultural Revolution, volume 3: The Coming Cataclysm, 1961–1966* (New York: Columbia University Press, 1997).

16. Kenneth R. Walker, "Organization of Agricultural Production," in Alexander Eckstein, Walter Galenson, and Ta-Chung Liu, eds., *Economic Trends in Communist China* (Chicago: Aldine, 1968), pp. 440–452; Kenneth R. Walker, *Planning in Chinese Agriculture: Socialization and the Private Sector, 1956–1962* (Chicago: Aldine, 1965); Frederick W. Crook, "The Commune System in the People's Republic of China, 1963–74," in Joint Economic Committee, *China: A Reassessment of the Economy*, pp. 366–410; Frederic M. Surls and Francis C. Tuan, "China's Agriculture in the Eighties," in Joint Economic Committee, *China Under the Four Modernizations*, Part 1, pp. 419–448.

17. The Conference Board, "The Conference Board Total Economy Database," http://www.conference-board.org/data/economydatabase/.

18. Dwight Perkins and Thomas Rawski, "Forecasting China's Economic Growth to 2025," in Loren Brandt and Thomas Rawski eds., *China's Great Economic Transformation* (New York: Cambridge University Press, 2008), pp. 829–886.

19. Chenggang Xu, "The Fundamental Institutions of China's Reforms and Development," 1084–1085.

20. Subramanian Swamy, "Economic Growth in China and India 1952–1970: A Comparative Appraisal," *Economic Development and Cultural Change* 21 (July 1973), 62.

21. Cited in Xu, "The Fundamental Institutions of China's Reforms and Development, 1085–1087.

22. Xu, "The Fundamental Institutions of China's Reforms and Development, 1086.

23. Robert F. Dernberger and David Fasenfest, "China's Post-Mao Economic Future," in U.S. Congress, Joint Economic Committee, *Chinese Economy Post-Mao* (Washington, D.C.: U.S. Government Printing Office, 1978), pp. 3–47.

24. Paul Gregory and Kate Zhou, "Why China Won and Russia Lost." *Policy Review*, December 2009.

25. Xu, "The Fundamental Institutions of China's Reforms and Development, 1078–1079.

26. John P. Burns, "Strengthening Central CCP Control of Leadership Selection: The 1990 Nomenklatura," *The China Quarterly* 138 (1994), 458–491.

27. Xianxiang Xu, Wang Xianbin and Shu Yuan, "Local Officials and Economic Growth," *Economic Research (Jingji Yanjiu)*, September 2007.

28. Eric Maskin, Yingyi Qian, and Chenggang Xu, "Incentives, Information, and Organizational Form," *Review of Economic Studies* 67, no. 2 (April 2000), 359–378.
29. Barry Naughton and Dali L. Yang (eds.), *Holding China Together: Diversity and National Integration in the Post-Deng Era* (New York: Cambridge University Press, 2004).
30. Edward Lazear and S. Rosen, "Rank-Ordered Tournaments as Optimal Labor Contracts," *Journal of Political Economy* 89 (1981), S.841–S.864.
31. Maskin et al., "Incentives, Information, and Organizational Form."
32. Ye Chen, Hongbin Li, and Lian Zhou, "Relative Performance Evaluation and the Turnover of Provincial Leaders in China," *Economics Letters* 88 (2005), 421–425.
33. Hongbin Li and Lian Zhou, "Political Turnover and Economic Performance: The Incentive Role of Personnel Control in China," *Journal of Public Economics* (2005).
34. "Chinese Party Chief Falls After Rebuke: Bo Xilai Is Removed From Post; Premier's Open Criticism Illustrates Divide Among Communist Elite," *Wall Street Journal*, March 15, 2012.
35. Henry J. Groen and James A. Kilpatrick, "China's Agricultural Production," in Joint Economic Committee, *Chinese Economy Post-Mao*, Vol. 1, pp. 607–652.
36. Bao Tong, "A Pivotal Moment For China," broadcast on RFA's Mandarin service. Director: Jennifer Chou. Translated by Luisetta Mudie. Edited by Sarah Jackson-Han. December 12, 2008. http://newsblaze.com/story/20090106100021zzzz.nb/topstory.html.
37. Kuan-I Chen, "China's Changing Agricultural System," *Current History* 82 (September 1983), 259–263, 277–278; Kuan-I Chen, "China's Food Policy and Population," *Current History* 82 (September 1983), 257–260, 274–276; Yak-Yeow Kueh, "China's New Agricultural-Policy Program: Major Economic Consequences, 1979–1983," *Journal of Comparative Economics* 8 (December 1984), 353–375; Nicholas R. Lardy, *Agriculture in China's Modern Economic Development* (Cambridge: Cambridge University Press, 1983); Dwight Perkins and Shahid Yusuf, *Rural Development in China* (Baltimore: Johns Hopkins University Press, 1984); Kenneth R. Walker, "Chinese Agriculture During the Period of Readjustment, 1978–83," *China Quarterly* 100 (December 1984), 783–812; Kenneth R. Walker, *Food Grain Procurement and Consumption in China* (Cambridge: Cambridge University Press, 1984); Peter Nolan and Dong Fureng, eds., *Market Forces in China* (London: Zed Books, 1990); and Anthony Y. C. Koo, "The Contract Responsibility System: Transition from a Planned to a Market Economy," *Economic Development and Cultural Change* 38 (July 1990), 797–820.
38. This section is based on Paul Gregory and Kate Zhou, "How China Won and Russia Lost," *Policy Review* 158 (December 2009); Kate Zhou, *How the Farmers Changed China: Power of the People* (Boulder, Colo.: Westview Press, 1996).
39. Xu "The Fundamental Institutions of China's Reforms and Development."
40. Gregory and Zhou, "How China Won and Russia Lost."
41. Keming Yang, "Double Entrepreneurship in China's Economic Reform: An Analytical Framework," *Journal of Political and Military Sociology* (Summer 2002); Douglas North, *Institutions, Institutional Change, and Economic Performance* (Cambridge: Cambridge University Press, 1990).
42. Kate Zhou, *How The Farmers Changed China: Power of the People* (Boulder, CO: Westview Press, 1996).
43. Robin Kwong, "China's Billionaires Begin to Add Up," *Financial Times*, October 22, 2007, http://us.ft.com/ftgateway/superpage.ft?news_id=fto102220071307209730.
44. Guojia Tongjiju, *Zhongguo tongji nianjian 1987 (Statistical Yearbook of China)* (Beijing: Zhongguo tongji chubanshe, 1988).

45. "People's Republic of China: The Development of Private Enterprise," http://www2. adb.org/documents/studies/PRC_Private_Enterprise_Development/default.asp.

46. "Private Enterprises Expanding Quickly," *People's Daily Online*, February 4, 2005, http://www.chinadaily.com.cn/english/doc/2005-02/04/content_414858.htm.

47. Helen Wang, "China to Become the World's Largest Importer by 2014," http://www. forbes.com/sites/helenwang/2012/01/11/china-to-become-the-worlds-largest-importer-by-2014/.

48. Gregory and Zhou, "How China Won and Russia Lost."

49. Nicolas Lardy, "China Enters the World Trade Organization," in *Integrating China into the Global Economy* (Washington, D.C.: Brookings Institution, 2002), p. 2.

50. United Nations, *World Investment Report 2001*, p. 27, Figure 1.

51. World Investment Report 2001, p. 26.

52. Thomas G. Rawski, "Is China's State Enterprise Problem Still Important?" prepared for a Workshop on "China's SOE Reform and Privatization," University of Tokyo, June 25, 2000.

53. Geo Xu, "State-Owned Enterprises in China: How Big are They?" July 19, 2010, http:// blogs.worldbank.org/eastasiapacific/state-owned-enterprises-in-china-how-big-are-they.

54. Andrew Szamosszegi and Cole Kyle, "An Analysis of State-Owned Enterprises and State Capitalism in China," U.S.-China Economic and Security Review Commission, October 26, 2011. http://www.uscc.gov/researchpapers/2011/10_26_11_CapitalTrade SOEStudy.pdf

55. Patrick Chonanec, "China State Enterprises Advance, Private Sector Retreats," Forbes.com, August 31, 2010, http://www.forbes.com/sites/china/2010/08/31/guo-jin-min-tui/.

56. Andrew Szamosszegi and Cole Kyle, "An Analysis of State-Owned Enterprises and State Capitalism in China."

57. Michael Wines, "China Fortifies State Businesses to Fuel Growth," *New York Times*, August 29, 2010.

58. Victor Shih, *Factions and Finance in China* (New York: Cambridge University Press, 2008), 27–28.

59. Xiao Geng, "Non-Performing Debts in Chinese Enterprises: Patterns, Causes, and Implications for Banking Reform," *Asian Economic Papers* 4, no. 3 (Cambridge, MA: MIT Press, 2006), 61–113.

60. Edward Steinfield, "Challenges Facing China's Reform," presented at Summer Conference of American Enterprises Institute, May 3, 2001, http://www.aie.org.

61. "When Fund Raising is a Crime," *Economist* (April 16, 2011), 69; "Entrepreneurship in China: Let a Million Flowers Bloom," *Economist*, March 10, 2011.

62. Andrew Szamosszegi and Cole Kyle, "An Analysis of State-Owned Enterprises and State Capitalism in China," 123.

63. Thomas Rawski, "What's Happening to China's GDP Statistics?" China Economic Review (Symposium on Chinese Statistics), Vol. 12, 4, December 2001).

64. Transparency International Corruptions Perception Index 2011, http://cpi.transparency. org/cpi2011/results/.

65. "Alibaba and the Chinese Thieves (Yahoo in China): Serious Questions About China's Growth Prospects," http://paulgregorysblog.blogspot.com/2011/05/alibaba-and-chinese-thieves-yahoo-in.html.

66. Ernst & Young, "Global IPO Trends," http://www.ey.com/Publication/vwLUAssets/ Global-IPO-trends_2011/$FILE/Global%20IPO%20trends%202011.pdf.

67. John Christy, "Investing in China—Types of Chinese Stocks," http://internationalinvest. about.com/od/globalmarkets101/tp/ChineseStocks.htm.

68. Paul Gregory, "Chinese Stock Alarm? Sino-Forest May Be the Best of the Bunch," http://paulgregorysblog.blogspot.com/2011/11/chinese-stock-alarm-sino-forest-may-be.html.

69. "Investors Steer Clear of Chinese IPOs in US," *Financial Times.com*, January 3, 2012, http://www.ft.com.

70. John Langlois, "Challenges Facing China's Reform," presented at Summer Conference of American Enterprises Institute, May 3, 2001, http://www.aei.org.

71. Trading Economics, "Market Capitalization of Listed Companies (% of GDP) in China," http://www.tradingeconomics.com/china/market-capitalization-of-listed-companies-percent-of-gdp-wb-data.html.

72. Trading Economics, "Domestic Credit Provided by Banking Sector (% of GDP) in China," http://www.tradingeconomics.com/china/domestic-credit-provided-by-banking-sector-percent-of-gdp-wb-data.html.

73. Rawski, "Is China's State Enterprise Problem Still Important?" Prepared for a Workshop on "China's SOE Reform and Privatization," University of Tokyo, June 25, 2000. http://www.pitt.edu/~tgrawski/papers2000/SKETCH.HTM

74. Yasheng Huang, "Challenges Facing China's Reform," presented at Summer Conference of American Enterprises Institute, May 3, 2001, http://www.aei.org.

75. PWC, "Foreign Banks in China," June 2011, http://pwccn.com/webmedia/doc/634442705425169010_fs_foreign_banks_china_jun2011.pdf.

76. Dinny McMahon, "China Mulls Legalizing Informal Lending," *Wall Street Journal*, March 14, 2012, http://online.wsj.com/article/SB10001424052702303863404577281030976537026.html.

77. McMahon, "China Mulls Legalizing Informal Lending."

78. Qiao Liu and Geng Xiao, "Look Who Are Disguising Profits: An Application to Chinese Industrial Firms," Hong Kong University, May 2004, http://www.sef.hku.hk/~qliu/wp/profit.pdf.

79. "Entrepreneurship in China: Let a Million Flowers Bloom," *The Economist*, March 10, 2011.

80. Qiao Liu and Alan Siu, "Institutions, Financial Development, and Corporate Investment: Evidence from an Implied Return on Capital in China," Hong Kong Institute of Economics and Business Strategy, December 2006.

81. "Entrepreneurship in China," *The Economist*.

82. Shih, *Factions and Finance*, 191.

83. CLB Research Reports No.5, "Speaking Out: The Workers' Movement in China (2005–2006)," December 2007, http://www.clb.org.hk; State Council (2006). (Research report on Chinese migrant workers). Shiyan Chubanshe.

84. "Migrant Workers in China," *China Labor Bulletin*, June 6, 2008, http://www.clb.org.hk/en/node/100259.

85. "Reform of State-Owned Enterprises," *China Labor Bulletin*, December 19, 2007, http://www.clb.org.hk/en/node/100153.

86. "As China Aids Labor, Unrest Is Still Rising," *New York Times*, June 20, 2010.

87. "Audit Finds Apple's Chinese Factories in Violation of Employment Laws," *The Guardian*, March 30, 2012, http://www.guardian.co.uk/technology/video/2012/mar/30/apple-foxconn-employment-audit-china-video.

88. Yang Yansui, "The Analysis of the Structure of the Social Security System in China," CCER-NBER Annual Meeting, Analysis and Structure of the Social Security System in China, March 2002, http://www.ccer.edu.cn/en/.

89. Based on data from the Asian Development Bank, http://www.adb.org.

Recommended Readings

General Works

Richard Baum, ed., *China's Four Modernizations: The New Technological Revolution* (Boulder, Colo.: Westview Press, 1980).

Chu-yuan Cheng, *China's Economic Development: Growth and Structural Change* (Boulder, Colo.: Westview Press, 1982).

Gregory Chow, *The Chinese Economy* (New York: Harper & Row, 1984).

Robert Dernberger, ed., *China's Development Experience in Comparative Perspective* (Cambridge, Mass.: Harvard University Press, 1980).

Audrey Donnithorne, *China's Economic System* (New York: Praeger, 1967).

Alexander Eckstein, *China's Economic Development: The Interplay of Scarcity and Ideology* (Ann Arbor: University of Michigan Press, 1975).

———, *China's Economic Revolution* (New York: Cambridge University Press, 1977).

Alexander Eckstein, Walter Galenson, and Ta-Chung Liu, eds., *Economic Trends in Communist China* (Chicago: Aldine, 1968).

Christopher Howe, *China's Economy: A Basic Guide* (New York: Basic Books, 1978).

Gary Jefferson and Wenyi Yu, "The Impact of Reform on Socialist Enterprises in Transition: Structure, Conduct, and Performance in Chinese Industry," *Journal of Comparative Economics* 15 (January 1991), 45–54.

Nicholas Lardy, *Economic Growth and Distribution in China* (New York: Cambridge University Press, 1979).

Zhiling Lin and Thomas Robinson, eds., *The Chinese and Their Future: Beijing, Taipei, and Hong Kong* (Washington, D.C.: American Enterprise Institute, 1994).

Thomas Lyons, *Economic Integration and Planning in Maoist China* (New York: Columbia University Press, 1987).

Jan Prybyla, *The Chinese Economy: Problems and Policies*, 2nd ed. (Columbia: University of South Carolina Press, 1981).

U.S. Congress, Joint Economic Committee, *An Economic Profile of Mainland China*, Vols. 1 and 2 (Washington, D.C.: U.S. Government Printing Office, 1967).

———, *China: A Reassessment of the Economy* (Washington, D.C.: U.S. Government Printing Office, 1975).

———, *China's Economic Dilemmas in the 1990s: The Problems of Reforms, Modernization, and Interdependence*, Vols. 1 and 2 (Washington, D.C.: U.S. Government Printing Office, 1991).

———, *Chinese Economy Post-Mao* (Washington, D.C.: U.S. Government Printing Office, 1978).

———, *China Under the Four Modernizations* (Washington, D.C.: U.S. Government Printing Office, 1982).

The Rural Economy and Rural Reform

William A. Byrd and Lin Qingsong, eds., *China's Rural Industry* (New York: Oxford University Press, 1991).

Kang Chao, *Man and Land in Chinese History: An Economic Analysis* (Stanford, Calif.: Stanford University Press, 1987).

Kuan-I Chen, "China's Food Policy and Population," *Current History* 86 (September 1987), 257–260, 274–276.

Christopher Findlay, Andrew Watson, and Harry X. Wu, eds., *Rural Enterprises in China* (New York: St. Martin's, 1994).

Paul Gregory and Kate Zhou, "How China Won and Russia Lost," *Policy Review* 158 (December 2009).

Anthony Y. C. Koo, "The Contract Responsibility System: Transition from a Planned to a Market Economy," *Economic Development and Cultural Change* 38 (July 1990), 797–820.

Yak-Yeow Kueh, "China's New Agricultural-Policy Program: Major Economic Consequences, 1979–1983," *Journal of Comparative Economics* 8 (December 1984), 353–375.

Nicholas R. Lardy, *Agriculture in China's Modern Economic Development* (Cambridge: Cambridge University Press, 1983).

Justin Yitu Lin, "Rural Reforms and Agricultural Growth in China," *American Economic Review* 82 (March 1992), 34–51.

Victor Nee and Frank W. Young, "Peasant Entrepreneurs in China's 'Second Economy': An Institutional Analysis," *Economic Development and Cultural Change* 37 (January 1991), 293–310.

Ole Odgaard, *Private Enterprises in Rural China* (Brookfield, Vt.: Ashgate, 1992).

Dwight Perkins, *Agricultural Development in China, 1368–1968* (Chicago: University of Chicago Press, 1969).

————, ed., *Rural Small-Scale Industry in the People's Republic of China* (Berkeley: University of California Press, 1977).

Shugiei Wao, *Agricultural Reform and Grain Production in China* (New York: St. Martin's Press, 1994).

Kate Zhou, *How the Farmers Changed China: Power of the People* (Boulder, CO: Westview Press, 1996).

Industrial and Political Organization

William Byrd, ed., *Chinese Industrial Firms Under Reform* (Oxford: Oxford University Press, 1992).

David Granick, *Chinese State Enterprises: A Regional Property Rights Analysis* (Chicago: University of Chicago Press, 1990).

Deborah A. Kaple, *Dream of a Red Factory* (New York: Oxford University Press, 1994).

Edward Lazear and S. Rosen, "Rank-Ordered Tournaments as Optimal Labor Contracts," *Journal of Political Economy* 89 (1981), S.841–S.864.

Hongbin Li and Lian Zhou, "Political Turnover and Economic Performance: The Incentive Role of Personnel Control in China," *Journal of Public Economics* (2005).

Jun Ma, *Intergovernmental Relations and Economic Management in China* (New York: St. Martin's, 1997).

Eric Maskin, Yingyi Qian, and Chenggang Xu, "Incentives, Information, and Organizational Form." *Review of Economic Studies* 67, no. 2 (April 2000), 359–378.

Jan Prybla, *The Political Economy of Communist China* (Scranton, Pa.: International Textbook, 1970).

Carl Riskin, *China's Political Economy* (New York: Oxford University Press, 1987).

Kai Yuen Tsui, "China's Regional Inequality, 1952–1985," *Journal of Comparative Economics* 15 (March 1991), 1–21.

Christine P. Wong, "The Economics of Shortages and Problems of Reform in Chinese Industry," *Journal of Comparative Economics* 10 (December 1986), 363–387.

Xianxiang Xu, Wang Xianbin, and Shu Yuan, "Local Officials and Economic Growth," *Economic Research (Jingji Yanjiu)*, September 2007, 30–41.

Susumi Yabuki, *China's New Political Economy: The Giant Awakes* (Boulder, Colo.: Westview, 1995).

Chen Ye, Hongbin Li, and Lian Zhou, "Relative Performance Evaluation and the Turnover of Provincial Leaders in China," *Economics Letters* 88 (2005), 421–425.

Economic Reform

Kang Chen, Gary H. Jefferson, and Inderjit Singh, "Lessons from China's Economic Reform," *Journal of Comparative Economics* 16 (1992), 201–225.

Richard Conroy, *Technological Change in China* (Paris: OECD, 1992).

Directorate of Intelligence, *China's Economy in 1992 and 1993: Grappling with the Risks of Rapid Economic Growth* (Washington, D.C.: Central Intelligence Agency, 1993).

———, *China's Economy in 1994 and 1995: Overheating Pressures Recede, Tough Choices Remain* (Washington, D.C.: Central Intelligence Agency, 1995).

———, *China's Economy in 1995–97* (Washington, D.C.: Central Intelligence Agency, 1997).

———, *The Chinese Economy in 1991 and 1992: Pressure to Revisit Reform Mounts* (Washington, D.C.: Central Intelligence Agency, 1992).

Qimiao Fan and Peter Nolan, *China's Economic Reforms* (New York: St. Martin's, 1994).

Joseph Fewsmith, *Dilemmas of Reform in China* (Armonk, N.Y.: M.E. Sharpe, 1994).

Keith Griffin and Zhao Renwei, *China's Economy in 1983 and 1984: The Search for a Soft Landing* (Washington D.C.: Central Intelligence Agency, 1994).

———, eds., *The Distribution of Income in China* (New York: St. Martin's, 1993).

Gary Jefferson and Thomas G. Rawski, "Enterprise Reform in Chinese Industry," *Journal of Economic Perspectives* 8 (Spring 1994), 47–70.

Gary Jefferson, Thomas G. Rawski, and Yuxin Zheng, "Growth, Efficiency, and Convergence in China's State and Collective Industry," *Economic Development and Cultural Change* 40 (1992a), 239–266.

Hsueh Jien-tsung, Sung Yun-wing, and Yu Jingyuan, *Studies on Economic Reform and Development in the People's Republic of China* (New York: St. Martin's, 1993).

Deepak Lal, "The Failure of the Three Envelopes: The Analytics and Political Economy of the Reform of Chinese State-Owned Enterprises" *European Economic Review* 34 (September 1990), 1213–1231.

Barry Naughton, *Growing Out of the Plan: Chinese Economic Reform, 1978–1993* (New York: Cambridge University Press, 1993).

Dwight Perkins and Thomas Rawski, "Forecasting China's Economic Growth to 2025," in Loren Brandt and Thomas Rawski eds., *China's Great Economic Transformation* (New York: Cambridge University Press, 2008), pp. 829–886.

Dwight H. Perkins, "Completing China's Move to a Market Economy," *Journal of Economic Perspectives* 8 (Spring 1994), 23–46.

Elizabeth J. Perry and Christine Wong, *The Political Economy of Reform in Post-Mao China* (Cambridge, Mass.: Harvard University Press, 1987).

Jan S. Prybyla, "Mainland China's Economic System: A Study in Contradictions," *Issues & Studies* 30, no. 8 (August 1994), 1–30.

Susan L. Shirk, *The Political Logic of Economic Reform in China* (Berkeley: University of California Press, 1993).

Clement Tisdell, *Economic Development in the Context of China* (New York: St. Martin's, 1993).

George Totten and Zhou Shulian, eds., *China's Economic Reform* (Boulder, Colo.: Westview, 1992).

Lim Wei and Arnold Chao, eds., *China's Economic Reforms* (Philadelphia: University of Pennsylvania Press, 1983).

Gordon White, "The Politics of Economic Reform in Chinese Industry: The Introduction of the Labour Contract System," *China Quarterly* 11 (September 1987), 365–389.

Chenggang Xu, "The Fundamental Institutions of China's Reforms and Development," *Journal of Economic Literature* 49, no. 4 (2011), 1080.

Susumi Yusuf, "China's Macroeconomic Performance and Management During Transition," *Journal of Economic Perspectives* 8 (Spring 1994), 71–92.

China and the Global Economy

Nicholas R. Lardy, *China in the World Economy* (Washington, D.C.: Institute for International Economics, 1984).

Justin Yitu Lin, Fang Cai, and Zhou Li, *The China Miracle* (Hong Kong: Chinese University Press, 1996).

Ike Mathur and Chen Jui-Sheng, *Strategies for Joint Ventures in the People's Republic of China* (New York: Praeger, 1987).

Finance

Xiao Geng, "Non-Performing Debts in Chinese Enterprises: Patterns, Causes, and Implications for Banking Reform," *Asian Economic Papers* 4, no. 3 (2006), 61–113.

Victor Shih, *Factions and Finance in China* (New York: Cambridge University Press, 2008), 27–28.

Party and Politics

Constitution of the People's Republic of China (December 1982), http://www.purdue.edu/crcs/itemResources/PRCDoc/pdf/Constitution.pdf.

"The Rise of State Capitalism," *The Economist*, January 21–27, 2012.

Chenggang Xu, "The Fundamental Institutions of China's Reforms and Development," *Journal of Economic Literature* 49, no. 4 (2011), 1080.

Dwight Perkins and Thomas Rawski, "Forecasting China's Economic Growth to 2025," in Loren Brandt and Thomas Rawski eds., *China's Great Economic Transformation* (New York: Cambridge University Press, 2008), pp. 829–886.

Xianxiang Xu, Wang Xianbin and Shu Yuan, "Local Officials and Economic Growth," *Economic Research (Jingji Yanjiu)*, September 2007.

Eric Maskin, Yingyi Qian, and Chenggang Xu, "Incentives, Information, and Organizational Form," *Review of Economic Studies* 67, no. 2 (April 2000), 359–378.

Edward Lazear and S. Rosen, "Rank-Ordered Tournaments as Optimal Labor Contracts," *Journal of Political Economy* 89 (1981), S.841–S.864.

Ye Chen, Hongbin Li, and Lian Zhou, "Relative Performance Evaluation and the Turnover of Provincial Leaders in China," *Economics Letters* 88 (2005), 421–425.

Hongbin Li and Lian Zhou, "Political Turnover and Economic Performance: The Incentive Role of Personnel Control in China," *Journal of Public Economics* (2005).

Andrew Szamosszegi and Cole Kyle, "An Analysis of State-Owned Enterprises and State Capitalism in China," U.S.-China Economic and Security Review Commission, October 26, 2011. http://www.uscc.gov/researchpapers/2011/10_26_11_CapitalTradeSOEStudy.pdf

PART

IV

Systemic Change in a Global Perspective: Transition

An Introduction to Transition

Concepts and Context

The concepts of economic reform and transition have been discussed from the broad perspective of socioeconomic change. We resume our examination of transition to explore the dramatic events of the post-command era of the 1990s and thereafter. **Transition** is *the process of change from one economic system to another.*[1]

Why are the transition economies of special interest to us, justifying the attention we pay to them? First, there is no recent example of systemic change more expansive and pervasive than the contemporary shift of the socialist command systems to market arrangements. Second, there are a significant number of systems that have undergone transition, systems that differ from one another in measurable ways. These differences facilitate research on regularities that can be extended to other and future cases. Third, transition generated a new interest and fundamental reassessment of the role of institutions in explaining performance across economic systems. Fourth, in many cases, a major result of transition has been the establishment of databases heretofore unknown in the field of comparative economic systems. These databases allow us to apply econometric analysis to a number of hypotheses generated by institutional economics, and in particular, attempt to measure the impact of institutions on economic outcomes. These results apply not only for the analysis of transition economies but also for understanding institutional change in both emerging and developed market economic systems. Fifth, although many in the early years of transition thought that the transition process would be relatively rapid, in reality transition has been a lengthy and complex process taking place in highly varied settings with differing outcomes. Finally, the results of our analysis of transition economies can also be useful for the analysis of other economies.

As we examine the transition economies, we discuss countries like China and Vietnam as systems that have undergone significant change. We do not classify them as transition economies, however, because both countries remain under the political governance of a single Communist Party. Both political change and democratization have been pivotal parts of the transition experience. In some cases, former leaders of the Communist Party have become new leaders no longer identifying themselves as communists.

However, key components of transition—for example, privatization and the development of markets (liberalization)—have been major policy imperatives in China and Vietnam as well as many other countries, especially the newly emerging market economies. Their combination of monopoly communist rule with other aspects of transition has been discussed earlier and will be important as we examine economic growth in differing economic systems.

Discussion of an eventual transition took place in the West and in the future transition countries starting in the 1960s. It intensified as the performance of the command economies of the Soviet Union and Eastern Europe showed significant decline that appeared irreversible. But few anticipated the sudden collapse of the command economies following the failure of Mikhail Gorbachev's perestroika reforms that were introduced to improve the command system in the USSR during the late 1980s. Because the collapse was rapid, there were no clear theoretical or practical models from which the course of transition could be charted. In a sense, the early transition era was a case of "learning by doing" replacing economic reform with systemic change. It was therefore unclear whether the same transition model would fit all sizes and shapes of the transitions to come let alone the exact nature of lessons learned for systemic change in nontransition economies.

The Background of Transition Economies: Meaning and Impact

Differences in background affect economic outcomes irrespective of the economic system. The transition economies had different histories, geography, and culture and operated under the planned socialist model for differing periods of time. In Table 16.1, we present a set of basic indicators to illustrate the magnitude of basic country differences.

Judging the size of transition economies from the perspective of origin, land area, population, or incomes, we can see that the transition economies differed markedly at the dawn of the transition era. Countries such as Kazakhstan and Russia are both large in terms of land area and population. At the same time, there are many very small transition economies, for example the Baltic states (Latvia, Lithuania, and Estonia). The political changes created by the collapse of the USSR and later Yugoslavia created fundamental changes in the size and nature of decision-making units.

The Soviet Union was an immense entity, composed of fifteen union republics that functioned under the command economic system introduced in 1928. In Eastern Europe, the command economic system dated from the end of World War II. Yugoslavia was first a command economy but then switched to a form of market socialism under worker management, a set of arrangements very different from the command economies. In the Soviet Union, the command economy functioned for sixty years; in Eastern Europe, it functioned for roughly forty years. The extent and impact of economic reform from within also differed widely in these economies.

TABLE 16.1   Transition Economies: Basic Indicators

Country	Pre Transition Economic System	Origin	Land Area Square Kilometer	Population Millions July 2001 Estimate	Per Capita GDP (US$), Mid-2001 Est. (ppp)[a]	Per Capita GDP, 1999 (1989 = 100)
Albania	Command	USSR	27,398	3.5	3,000	95
Armenia	Command	USSR	28,400	3.3	3,000	42
Azerbaijan	Command	USSR	86,100	7.8	3,000	47
Belarus	Command	USSR	207,000	10.4	7,500	80
Bosnia/Herzegovina	Mkt-soc	YUGOSLAVIA	51,129	3.9	1,700	n.a.
Bulgaria	Command	INDEPENDENT	110,550	7.7	6,200	67
Croatia	Mkt-soc	YUGOSLAVIA	56,414	4.3	5,800	78
Czech Republic	Command	CZECH REP[b]	77,276	10.3	12,900	95
Estonia	Command	USSR	43,211	1.4	10,000	77
FYR Macedonia	Mkt-soc	YUGOSLAVIA	24,856	2.0	4,400	74
Georgia	Command	USSR	69,700	5.0	4,600	34
Hungary	Command	INDEPENDENT	92,340	10.1	11,200	99
Kazakhstan	Command	USSR	2,669,30	10.7	5,000	63
Kyrgyzstan	Command	USSR	191,300	4.8	2,700	63
Latvia	Command	USSR	64,589	2.4	7,200	60
Lithuania	Command	USSR	65,200	3.6	7,300	62
Moldova	Command	USSR	33,371	4.4	2,500	31
Mongolia	Command	INDEPENDENT	1,565,00	2.2[c]	n.a.	na
Montenegro	Mkt-soc	YUGOSLAVIA	13,812	n.a.	1,780	na
Poland	Command	INDEPENDENT	304,465	38.6	8,500	122
Romania	Command	INDEPENDENT	230,340	22.4	5,900	76
Russia	Command	USSR	16,995,8	145.5	7,700	57
Slovakia	Command	USSR	48,800	5.4	10,200	100
Slovenia	Mkt-soc	YUGOSLAVIA	20,253	1.9	12,000	109
Tajikistan	Command	USSR	142,700	6.6	1,140	44
Turkmenistan	Command	USSR	488,100	4.6	4,300	64
Ukraine	Command	USSR	603,700	48.8	3,850	36
Uzbekistan	Command	USSR	425,400	25.2	2,400	94

[a]purchasing power estimate

[b]Czechoslovakia

[c]estimate

Source: Central Intelligence Agency, *The World Factbook 2001* (Washington, D.C.: CIA, 2001); European Bank for Reconstruction and Development, *Transition Report 2000* (London: EBRD, 2000). Output for Mongolia is mid-2000; Mkt-soc refers to market socialist economic systems.

During the 1980s, there was significant economic reform in Hungary and Poland but minimal reform in the Soviet Union.[2] In no case was reform significant enough to change the economic system, but it affected the starting points of transition.

The collapse of the command order in the Soviet Union presented problems very different from those in a single political and geographic entity such as Hungary. The Soviet republics had existed as countries for a long period of time. There was no question of creating entirely new political entities.

However, as the former Soviet republics became independent countries, new questions arose: How would the infrastructure be divided, and how would formerly national issues (such as the USSR's debt) be handled?

By any of the very basic indicators chosen in Table 16.1, the countries that have emerged from the former Soviet Union, and indeed the entire set of transition economies, are fundamentally very different from each other. There are major differences in the transition economies when we examine levels of output and output change in the early years. Hungary and the Czech Republic are both relatively high income countries, and yet in almost all of the transition economies output levels were lower a decade after transition began. This result would eventually change, as we will see when we examine the empirical evidence on transition in the next chapter.

Figure 16.1 provides us with a spatial and regional perspective on the transition economies. A similar perspective emerges in Figure 16.2 and illustrates how geographically close to the European Union (EU) many of the transition economies are located.

Most of the transition economies remained as identifiable entities before and during transition, although there were important and interesting exceptions. Czechoslovakia split into the Czech Republic and Slovakia (1993), and the German Democratic Republic (GDR) became unified with the Federal Republic of Germany (FRG) to form a single country and economy.[3] Isolating the elements of transition

FIGURE 16.1   The Independent Republics of the Former Soviet Union

Source: Directorate of Intelligence, Central Intelligence Agency, *Handbook of International Economic Statistics* (Washington, D.C.: U.S. Government Printing Office, 1996), p. 57.

FIGURE 16.2   Europe

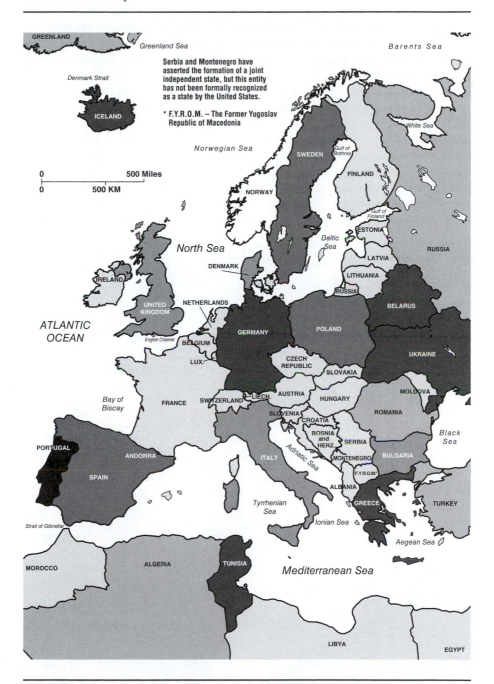

in the German case is especially interesting yet difficult because the entire process has taken place under a single political entity in a unique cultural, historical, and geographic setting. Yugoslavia's experience has been complicated by internal conflict.[4] However, the republics of the former Yugoslavia finally became independent entities by 2006. The geographic and spatial setting of these new countries is illustrated in Figure 16.3.

Country size and location are significant in many ways beyond geography. Some countries, especially the smaller East European countries, were relatively **open economies** even during the command era, whereas others experienced only very limited trading engagement with the external world.[5] This differing trade experience not only had an impact on resource allocation during the command era

FIGURE 16.3   The Former Yugoslavia

Source: Central Intelligence Agency, Washington, D.C., 1996.

but also left some of the new countries with limited trading experience to exploit as they entered a global environment during transition. Arguably, the republics of the Soviet Union were "closed" to a much greater degree than Hungary and Poland. This fact affects far more than the simple mechanics of exporting and importing, influencing areas such as specialization patterns (industrial structure) and the potential impact (or lack of impact) of foreign technology as a major example. Geography also matters in another important respect: the proximity of the countries of Eastern and Central Europe to the European Economic Community and the impact of globalization.

In the transition economies, the **resource bases** differ greatly, a fact that influenced industrial structure and trade patterns during the command era. These differences have largely persisted during the transition era in critical areas such as energy supplies. Anyone who has followed the economics and politics of oil in contemporary Russia can appreciate the importance of these differences. Economists have a special interest in the performance of these "resource-rich" countries whatever the nature of their economic system.

Effects of the Rapidity of Transition

The fact that the transition era emerged quickly presented a variety of special difficulties that have had a significant impact during the early years of transition. First, transition has always been much more than an economic phenomenon. It is also fundamentally a political and a social phenomenon with far-reaching implications for populations long isolated from Western democratic ideas and institutions. The extent and impact of this isolation varied a great deal from country to country. Clearly, Albania and Belarus were far more isolated over a longer period of time than Hungary and Poland. There are countries like Belarus that today remain substantially unchanged from earlier times.

Second, social policies—or, more narrowly, economic incentives—were fundamentally different in the command economies. Great reliance was placed on the socialization of incentives, and this became an important issue as social policies began to change dramatically during transition. The new incentive structure would be a major determinant of population support for the new political regime and its transition policies. One could argue that in the command economies, the attempted socialization of incentives failed. However, citizens became accustomed to "full employment," access to education, and the provision of old-age pensions on reasonable terms, even if consumer goods were not always available in retail stores and living levels were arguably low. Changes, and especially sudden changes, in the safety net during the transition of the 1990s have been of major importance in all the transition economies during an era when the social contract has been fundamentally redefined. During the early years of transition, there was a continuing fear that that the process of transition could be **reversed**, an issue long forgotten in the twenty-first century but very important during the early 1990s.

Third, it is perhaps ironic that many countries, suddenly faced with the need for institutional change, would look to the discipline of economics for guidance. We have emphasized that neoclassical economics had not, until recently, embraced institutional change as a fundamental component of its paradigm. Simple models of systemic change were simply not available to guide policy makers in the emerging market economies, although economists have argued that system differences were important as a force influencing outcomes.[6]

Fourth, we must not overlook the impact of European, Asian, and other cultural and historical forces on the outcomes of transition. The former command economies have pursued the development of market capitalism, although the forms of capitalism may themselves differ considerably from those we are familiar with in the industrialized world. Transition economies may well be identified as mixed economic systems to a greater degree than the traditional industrialized (market) economies. In the transition context, it is important to identify a mixed system as mixed in at least two important dimensions: (1) There may well be a tendency to combine systemic elements from the command era—specifically, instruments of state control and/or intervention—with traditional market mechanisms; (2) It is likely that there will be important policy differences (for example, greater concern for the safety net in transition economies) to soften the outcomes more typical of market economies. Indeed, it is the sustained differences in institutional arrangements in market economics that is at the core of the newly emerging vision of comparative economic systems.

The decade of the 1990s was dominated by interest in and observation of these emerging systems, the different paths they have chosen, and the varied outcomes they have achieved. The lessons learned from these transition economies have been important for the other emerging market economies. However, judging the success of the transition economies themselves and assessing the relevance of their experiences to other countries is a complex undertaking. Even after more than two decades of transition experience, there are some countries (such as Ukraine and Belarus) where the impact of transition has been constrained. And there are other countries (such as Hungary and the Czech Republic) where some would argue that models of transition no longer apply to these small, open, market economies.

Finally, the mechanics of the transition process that is the early stages of transition and the development, harmonization, and implementation of the transition components in a sequential fashion brought to the forefront problems of **timing**. To understand these issues, we turn to a brief examination of important themes from the early transition experiences.

Approaches to Transition: A Retrospective of Basic Themes

For convenience, we frame transition in a series of stages as presented in Table 16.2.

As the old order collapsed, the search for a new path began. In cases like Russia, hindsight tells us that conceptions of a quick and relatively smooth transition path (the "500-day plans") were naïve, perhaps in the extreme. Indeed, as the old arrangements and institutions collapsed, so did output. This in turn placed a

TABLE 16.2   Transition: The Major Early Phases

The Collapse (1989–1991)	Stabilization: Considering policy alternatives and limiting output collapse
The Early (initial) Transition Era (1992–1995)	Legislation: Developing and implementing a new policy framework
The Secondary Transition Era (1992 onward)	Facing the initial complications of implementation and potential crises
The End of Transition	Entering a long-run "normal" growth path

Source: Compiled by the authors.

significant emphasis on the need for **stabilization**, or *the development of institutions and polices to limit the decrease of output in the transition economies.*

Second, during the early transition era, emphasis was placed on the political sphere, and especially the development of legislation that would, it was hoped, guide the admittedly complex process of transition. Much of the old order remained as the new order was emerging, and yet the legislative process was complex because new legislation seldom remained in place for very long. Turbulent conditions existed, with outcomes difficult to assess as statistical indicators changed on a regular basis.

Toward the end of the 1990s, the notion that transition might be reversed became less and less likely, although economic crises were difficult (for example Russia in 1998) and few were discussing the end of transition and the return to a "normal" growth path. Much of the contemporary literature on transition focuses on long-term economic growth, although once again world events after 2008 have led many to ask how transition economies will respond to new difficulties. We turn to a discussion of economic growth in the next chapter.

Modeling Transition: The Early Dichotomy

During the transition era, two major approaches to the transition process emerged. The first approach, often characterized as a "big push," was based on the notion that transition policies, specifically the replacement of socialist policies and command planning arrangements by markets, could be implemented as quickly as possible. The second approach, termed "gradualist" or "evolutionary," was based on the idea that markets are best developed through an iterative path-dependent and properly sequenced approach, a model that we have already discussed in earlier chapters of this book. Both of these approaches were products of the early transition era cast against the "Washington Consensus," which was a set of views about transition emerging in the West as international organizations became involved in the transition debate.

As transition began in the late 1980s and early 1990s, attention quickly turned to the collapse of the command systems, the gradual emergence of new arrangements, and, perhaps most important, changes in output. We turn our attention to these issues.

Differences in Output Performance: The Initial Collapse

The index of output for transition economies given in Table 16.1 and the graphical presentation in Figure 16.4 demonstrate the existence of major differences in output performance among the transition economies presented during the initial transition era of the 1990s. Thus in 1999, the per capita output of Moldova (as an example) was 31 percent of its level in 1989. This is a significant collapse and was experienced in many but not all transition economies. Exceptions were countries such as Poland and Slovenia, and in countries such as Estonia and Romania the collapse existed but was less severe. This pattern of change is of significant interest to policy makers in contemporary economies where important systemic changes are contemplated.

This evidence on the output patterns of transition economies presents us with one of the most frequently discussed stylized pictures of transition: the "**J curve**,"

FIGURE 16.4   GDP: Percentage Change (year to year in constant prices) Selected
Transition Economies, 1990–2002[a]

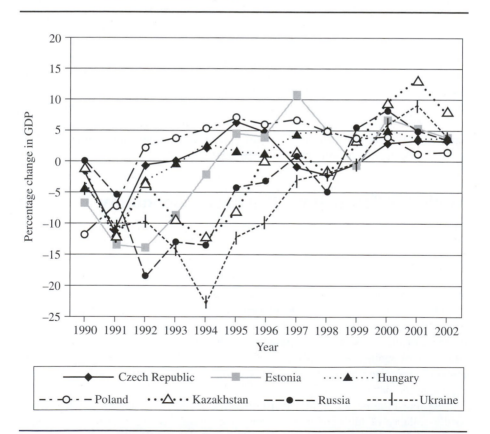

[a]Data for 2001 are preliminary; data for 2002 are projections.

Source: Data are from EBRD, *Transition Report Update* (London: EBRD, May 2002), Annex 1.1.

or *the pattern of severe collapse and subsequent recovery observed in virtually all transition economies.*[7] What accounts for the striking pattern we observe and for the important differences in output growth from one country to another?

Can We Account for the Early Collapse?

We now turn to a discussion of the causes of the "J curve," or the collapse followed by recovery.[7] It is important to emphasize that the complete characterization of the "J curve" as a cycle is difficult. Moreover, variations in the pattern are important. For example, there are cases of a steep decline and a speedy recovery, and there are other cases of a shallow decline and a very slow recovery. Interest has focused on the depth and length of the decline. Why did output collapse in so many transition economies, and what caused that collapse to be severe in some cases?

At first glance, this question might seem simplistic. After all, if an economy "collapses," would it not be reasonable for output to collapse? In the transition economies during the very early stages of transition (unlike market economies in recession), there was no "failure" of monetary and fiscal policies because these institutions and arrangements did not exist. Moreover, unlike a case of war, all of the production capacity remained fully in existence. What, then, explains the collapse? In fact, there are a variety of explanations, all of which help us to understand the transition process.

First, there is the possibility that at least part of the collapse is explained by differences in accounting methods, notably the calculation of net material product (NMP) used during the command era and that of gross domestic product (GDP) used during the transition era. Consider, for example, the issue of the service sector. It was widely argued during the command era that the accounting methods used to determine NMP underestimated the growth and size of the service sector. Thus, as the output of an economy measured in NMP standards is recomputed in GDP standards, the result could be an increase in output even though output calibrated in physical terms has not changed.

Consider a different example: agriculture. It has been observed that during the transition era, agricultural output has, on balance, declined less than industrial output. Therefore, an economy with a larger share of agricultural output would decline less in the aggregate, even though it might be (in fact, typically would be) at a lower level of economic development. One suspects that in the agricultural economy, daily decisions and actions are guided much more by tradition than is the case in an industrial economy, where, during the early years of transition, the guidance rules have essentially disappeared. One could also argue that in-kind exchanges in the rural economy would be less likely to be disrupted than those taking place under plan directives (and perhaps using "family connections") in the industrial economy.

Second, it is interesting to note that issues related to the shadow economy, or second economy, could affect our assessment of transition. Is it likely that the shadow economy will be measured differently as the command system collapses and markets emerge? The empirical evidence on this issue is intriguing. The magnitude of the shadow economy in Eastern Europe during the transition era of the

1990s has been relatively small, whereas its magnitude in the states of the former Soviet Union has been relatively large. In the Russian case, the magnitude of the shadow economy increased significantly in the latter half of the 1990s, a puzzling outcome because it is in this period that one would expect market arrangements to have emerged making the shadow economy less meaningful except during periods of rapid inflation. The issue of the shadow economy thus complicates the task of measuring transition performance, and yet it is less clear that transition differences have been systematically affected by levels and changes in the levels of shadow economies.

Third, an approach to understanding the magnitude of the collapse is more directly related to the nature of the command economy. This approach focuses on the fact that during the command era, enterprises were governed by directives from planners. What happened when these directives ceased as the command economy collapsed? One could argue that the answer depended on the nature of the relations between a firm and its suppliers and the firm and its customers. Without directives, "market" arrangements, such as prices and information, would become increasingly important, and yet in many early transition settings, these signals were weak. Under these circumstances, it is not surprising that it grew difficult to sustain supplies and, on the demand side, to maintain customers. These issues were especially important in the post-Soviet setting, when former republics of a single country became independent nations.

Fourth, it has been popular to blame the policy makers and claim that output fell because policy makers "got it wrong." Although it is difficult to isolate policy issues, the emergence of the "Washington Consensus" has remained controversial in the policy arena. There are probably as many variants of this criticism as there are countries, but the focal point is frequently the problem of the speed and sequencing of transition components. For example, it is argued that privatization cannot be implemented before **corporatization**; banks cannot be privatized before the development of bank supervision and bank insurance arrangements; and the pressure to sustain real interest rates should not result in a severe credit crunch. The criticisms of policy tend to be country-specific, but they are still important to our understanding of transition.

Finally, a major (and original) approach to understanding the collapse of transition economies has focused on the supply and demand components of output. For example, we have already noted that in the transition economies, output of agricultural sectors has generally shown less cyclical fluctuation. Therefore, an economy with a larger agricultural sector is likely to show a lesser decline than an economy with a smaller agricultural sector. There are other examples. In most transition economies, there has been a sharp decline in investment. This decline is understandable, given the fundamental change in investment arrangements. This initial decline in investment was also accompanied by changes in the other components of aggregate demand.

Obviously, any judgment about transition tends to focus on output—specifically, the magnitude of the collapse and its pattern and duration thereafter. Even with this seemingly simple indicator, there are disagreements about measurement and interpretation, and yet striking differences emerge.

The collapse of the Polish economy was by any measure modest and the recovery rapid. By contrast, the collapse of the Russian economy was deep and the recovery very slow; after the collapse in 1989, positive economic growth appeared for the first time in the late 1990s! Consequently both the nature and the pattern of economic growth are major indicators for judging transition, although in many cases there are serious problems of data availability, accuracy, and interpretation.[8] In the important case of Russia, the presence of a large virtual (shadow) economy, especially in the late 1990s, makes traditional measurement approaches inadequate.[9]

Output is of course a function of many underlying forces, so naturally all of these forces are of interest. Privatization and liberalization are critical first steps, but subsequent restructuring is essential and is a major indicator of continuing systemic change. The development of international trade is important, but the contribution of trade to economic growth and to the enhanced well-being of the population is also of fundamental importance. Therefore, both the nature of economic growth and the forces that contribute to this growth are crucial to a successful transition. Characterizing systemic change and the components of systemic change is a major challenge as we seek to understand the transition experience. We need to examine more than changes in output.

As much as economists favor examination of institutional, policy, and other underpinnings of the growth experience, we cannot assess transition without considering the populace's quality of life. The socialist era may have had a leveling effect on living standards, imposing a more even income distribution than tends to occur under alternative systemic and policy arrangements. But the era of markets has been very different: Some economies have prospered, some have held their own, and some have found their standard of living significantly lowered. Increasing inequality was to be expected. At the same time, human adjustment to these new conditions is a major story of the transition experience. The human side of transition is especially important in the European setting, where there is less tolerance for inequality than in the United States. Fortunately, we have a considerable body of literature on labor force issues to be examined later in this book.

Should we emphasize the starting points, or **initial conditions**, that prevailed at the beginning of transition some twenty years ago? Or is the major emphasis to be placed on other factors, such as the natural environment, the extent of political modernization, and the emerging policy framework? Although these questions will interest scholars and policy makers long into the twenty-first century, a decade of practical experience can certainly provide us with important perspectives. If transition is successful, clearly the impact of initial conditions will decline, and, as some say, transition will be over.

Transition in a Global Setting

We have noted that the emergence of transition in the late 1980s was a relatively sudden event. Its impact, however, is far more than local (domestic) in character—a fact that dominates the contemporary discussion of transition economies. There are a variety of reasons for this global emphasis.

First, when transition began, it did so in economies that had been largely isolated from the globalization process. Although we have noted that this isolation was of greater consequence for some countries (such as the Soviet Union) than for others (such as Poland and Hungary), the structural impact of years of isolation from both the negative and the positive effects of world market forces left many countries with archaic resource allocation arrangements and resulting **structural distortions** (for example, the serious heavy industry emphasis) in resource allocation. The normal market influences of specialization and trade, for example, were sharply modified in countries such as the Soviet Union. Furthermore, the Soviet Union was almost totally isolated from the impact of world financial markets and world financial forces. Some of the distortions that grew out of the isolation of the command economies were quite basic (distorted commodity trade patterns), and some were more complex (the lack of impact of foreign technology). The emergence of markets and market forces in the transition economies brought necessary—but sudden and sometimes brutal—changes as noncompetitive industries collapsed while new, formerly nonexistent industries emerged. Another important example is the command economies' well-known bias in favor of industry and heavy industry, which resulted in sectoral allocation patterns very different from what one might expect under market arrangements. Of course, structural changes have occurred in many countries (consider the production of steel in the United States after World War II), but in market economies, these changes occurred relatively slowly. Large segments of the command economies were isolated from world competitive forces, and inefficient domestic economic activity was sustained by large state subsidies funded by the extraction of surplus value from the population. These arrangements changed suddenly during transition as state subsidies came to an end. The associated social disruption (for example, significant unemployment in declining sectors) was important.

Second, the transition economies have had to adapt to an external (global) environment that itself has been undergoing rapid change. Perhaps the most dramatic example of such change is the development of the **European Union**. The emergence of the EU has been controversial in the West, but even more so in the East, where EU rules of entry prescribe the implementing of difficult but critical policy, structural, and other changes. More than twenty years from the beginning of transition, the importance of EU arrangements have taken center stage, especially during the past decade.

Third, the global setting has prompted some to ask about the end of transition. For example, one could argue that the Czech economy is a small open economy at a medium level of economic development pursuing stable and sustained economic growth. Why not simply characterize the Czech economy in this way rather than thinking about it in terms of the framework of transition? Our choice in this matter will dictate what tools are appropriate for analyzing the Czech economy. If we abandon the characterization of the Czech economy as a transition economy, then we imply that we understand the objectives of transition and that these objectives have been achieved. Moreover, we imply that the impact of the command era has been erased or, at a minimum, has no impact on contemporary economic events. In other words, the Czech economy would be characterized as returning to its long-term "normal" growth path having eliminated the structural distortion of the command era. These important and controversial issues will be discussed further in subsequent chapters of this book.[10]

Assessing Transition: Contemporary Perspectives

How might we characterize the end of transition? The end of transition is much more than growth outcomes. There are a variety of indicators, none of which is completely satisfactory and most of which are difficult to measure precisely. It is, however, critical that we be able to characterize both the successes and the failures of the transition experience. The output data presented in Table 16.1 and Figure 16.4 gives us only a modest start in our assessment of transition outcomes. But, we need to focus on varying frames of reference that can be used to characterize transition and to assess outcomes.

During the early years of the transition era, there has been a tendency to look at organizational indicators of transition (for example, the importance of private ownership) and to argue that when this indicator reaches a level comparable to that in other economies at similar levels of economic development, this element of transition has been completed. That level would be reached when private property had replaced state property, and markets had been put in place. One could make a similar argument for policy measures—for example, using the development of monetary and fiscal institutions and associated macroeconomic policies to gauge the extent to which institutions and policies of the command era have in fact been replaced by market-based institutions and policies. It is for this reason that liberalization has been a major theme of the literature on transition. **Liberalization** is *the reduction of state controls and the introduction of markets.* There have been a variety of attempts to develop indexes measuring the degree to which markets and market policies have emerged in the transition economies. In a sense, such a perspective looks at transition in terms of organizational arrangements (inputs) rather than outputs. We are fortunate to have a series of indices (for example, those provided by the EBRD) that assist us in assessing these changes.

One could argue that from a longer-term perspective, transition is really over when the economy in question has returned to a long-term market trajectory of economic growth. Such an outcome might be measured in terms of such long-term structural characteristics as sectoral output shares, trade shares, and aggregate growth patterns. This was, after all, a popular framework in which to view the command economies as suffering from distortion in their earlier outcomes. Indeed, we often characterized the command economies as being distorted, a concept that implied nonmarket outcomes (an example is the well-known industry bias in these economies). From this point of view, the changing institutional arrangements and policies are secondary characteristics that we examine to determine the outcome of the allocation process and to observe when such outcomes revert to "normal," or noncommand, patterns. The empirical literature on transition has yet to fully characterize transition from this perspective. Moreover, this type of assessment brings the field of transition economics very close to the field of development economics. Indeed, for some transition economies that had only limited success in the 1990s, one could argue that the tools of economic development may be more relevant than the tools of transition. That is, the tools of transition are inappropriate for those economies that have not experienced any measurable amount of economic growth and development.

Finally, much of the transition literature focuses on quite traditional indicators of success. We have already emphasized the importance of output patterns in the transition economies. Equally important are indicators such as employment, medical care, pension benefits, and elimination of poverty.

A Systems Perspective

Those who observe transition economies in the context of comparative economic systems tend to take a long-term view of the transition process. From a systems perspective, it can be argued that differences in outcomes are to be expected when institutional arrangements and policy imperatives differ even moderately. It might also be argued, especially in cases such as Russia, that the long-term impact of socialist policies in the command setting is very difficult to erase. The analyst of differing economic systems would maintain, therefore, that even when we do not impose the traditional simplistic characterization of systems inherent in the "isms" framework, economic systems remain very different from one country to another. Indeed the concept of a mixed system may receive much more attention in the transition economies than has been typical in market economies, a central theme in the new comparative economic systems. The economic systems of Great Britain and the United States are very different, as are the economic outcomes in these countries. These differences will remain important as the discipline of economics becomes better able to provide useful theoretical and analytical tools with which to understand them. The disappearance of simplistic categories of economic systems is a positive but complex outgrowth of the transition era. However, system differences persist, as do other fundamental differences such as natural setting and resource endowment. In the end, and with only limited exceptions, most transition economies are in fact mixed systems and differ significantly from one another. They will, however, be analyzed not in terms of simple categorizations (the "isms"), but rather in terms of their architecture and internal working arrangements using agency theory, information economics, and so on.

The impact of the global era is important in yet another dimension: Transition has not taken place in isolation from more general changes occurring in various nontransition countries, such as the emergence of the European Union. Consider, for example, the role of the state and public sector in the economy. This issue can be approached in ideological terms, but it can also be cast within the framework of public-choice theory in market-capitalist economies. In the past, these two approaches have been quite distinct.

Whereas explicit policies of **privatization** have been pursued in transition economies to replace command instruments with market mechanisms of resource allocation, Western market economies have placed major emphasis on privatization with the immediate objective of increasing economic efficiency. Thus replacing public enterprise with private enterprise has been a major policy imperative in both East and West, but in very different settings and with somewhat different objectives and results. Indeed, as we will observe, the decline of the state sector in economies East and West, developed and developing, is a contemporary phenomenon of great importance, with implications far beyond the singular case of privatization in the transition setting. The contribution that examining this process will make to our knowledge of differing economic systems promises to be immense.

Finally, the social impact of transition is a complex issue of great importance to our assessment of transition outcomes. Although social policies differed considerably from one command economy to another, on balance all pursued a social contract very different from that pursued under contemporary capitalism.[11] It is understandable that the former command economies saw the need for efficiency, but it is also necessary to emphasize the long-run importance of equity issues. The latter will be critical to defining the successes or failures of the transition economies.

The Framework of Transition: Theory and Evidence

In the remaining chapters of this book, we examine the transition era of the 1990s and thereafter. Our approach relies heavily on the experiences of individual countries for the light they shed on similarities and differences between various transition scenarios and on the components of the transition process. Framing the experience of transition is not a straightforward task. Much of the literature generated during the early years of transition is cast in terms of the big push and the evolutionary approaches. Most analysts now treat these early transition models as simplistic and prefer to address the underlying and basic issues of speed, sequencing, and complementarities when formalizing the transition experience. The modeling of transition approaches is not ideal, but there is much agreement on the typical components of the transition experience. It is these components that form the framework of the remainder of this book.

Traditionally, the literature on transition has been usefully characterized in **four** major dimensions. First, there is a large literature on *the process of privatization and the development of factor and product markets.* During the early years of transition, this literature focused on the mechanisms for privatization and typically assessed the immediate results by examining the sectoral shares of output and employment derived from private economic activity. During the latter years of the 1990s and into the new century, the literature has focused mainly on **restructuring**, or the *changing the nature of corporate governance to achieve efficiency objectives.*

The second major component of the transition literature has been the *development of the macroeconomy,* both institutions and policies. Immediately after the collapse, the focus was on stabilization, but the more recent focus has been on "normalization" of the macroeconomy, specifically the budgetary process and the banking system, including the development of financial markets for the purpose of financial intermediation. These issues are especially important during transition because financial institutions had limited influence on resource allocation in the command economies. The challenge here is to develop new institutions and a new stock of human capital to guide them.

Third, although integration of the command economies into the global economy is fundamentally intertwined with development of the macroeconomy, it is useful to examine foreign trade as a major and identifiable policy issue for transition economies. Beyond the development of new market-oriented institutional arrangements for both physical and financial flows, a major issue has been the introduction of a convertible currency and the implementation of an exchange rate regime capable of sustaining a reasonable foreign and domestic balance.

Fourth, the literature on transition economies has placed a great deal of emphasis on safety-net issues, both in and of themselves and as part of a more general assessment of the successes and failures of transition. Interest in safety-net issues derives in part from our appreciation of the major social impact of transition, an issue we have emphasized in this chapter. But we must also remember that, because in the former command economies the safety net was largely socialized in the hands of the state, maintaining that safety net is challenging as the functions of the state diminish in the transition era.

The unifying theme for the systemic change that the transition economies are experiencing is liberalization, the replacement of command mechanisms with market mechanisms and market policies.

In the end, assessing the evidence on transition is difficult. Some twenty-eight countries have been engaged in the transition process, and we have had more than two decades to observe transition and to collect empirical evidence on it. How will the successes and the failures of transition be judged? Once again, the choice depends on the interests of the observer. We turn to an examination of the empirical evidence.

Summary

- Transition is the replacement of one economic system by another economic system.
- There are many transition economies, most having originated from the collapse of the former Soviet Union, the collapse of economic systems in Eastern Europe, or the collapse of the market-socialist experience of the former Yugoslavia.
- Beyond those countries that we generally and typically classify as transition economies, important aspects of transition (for example, privatization) have been fundamental components of change in other emerging market economies, such as Vietnam and China.

- As the command economies collapsed quickly in the late 1980s, models of system change were not readily available. This led to considerable experimentation and controversy, much of the latter arising from Western advice on how markets should emerge in the new transition economies.
- The transition economies, with their varying backgrounds and very different initial conditions, have pursued the introduction of markets to varying degrees, through varying approaches, and with very different results. Nearly all transition economies, however, experienced an initial decline in output and then a subsequent recovery (the "J curve") although the patterns of change in output varied from case to case throughout the transition era of the 1990s. There are a variety of explanations for this, including the end of the guidance system, changes in trade patterns, sectoral shifts, and institutional collapse.
- Transition emerged in countries that had been largely isolated from the global economic community during the command era. This fact has been of great importance as the transition economies have developed and implemented new institutions and policies to facilitate their participation in the growing global economy.
- From a systems perspective, analysis of the transition era has moved us away from the era of "isms" toward an era in which organizational (institutional) arrangements and policy variants are the central components of new economic systems that are emerging in settings where very different command arrangements recently dominated. The economic analysis of these emerging arrangements is based on contemporary microeconomic theory—for example, agency theory and information economics.
- We have emphasized the fact that our discussion will focus on the beginnings of transition—that is, the setting inherited from the command era, measurement issues, and assessing transition alternatives. Finally, we examine the content of transition by isolating its main components: privatization, restructuring and liberalization, development of the macroeconomy, introduction of new trade regimes, and, finally, the building of a new safety net.

Key Terms

command economy—An economic system where resources allocation is directed by a central planning agency, the function of which is to give directives to enterprises.

economic reform—Changes in arrangements within an economic system; often applied to attempts to change command economies and to improve their performance.

economic system—The organizational arrangements, institutions, and policies responsible for resource allocation in a given geographic (country) setting.

emerging market economies—Economies typically at a lower level of economic development pursuing economic growth through market institutions.

European Union—An economic and political association of twenty-seven European nations designed to create a single market.

initial conditions—Characteristics of economies observed at the beginning of transition; for example, the heavy industry bias typical of the command economies.

"J curve"—A characterization of the pattern of output change observed in a number of transition economies; sever collapse followed by subsequent recovery.

liberalization—The reduction of state controls over economic activity typical of the early stages of transition.

market economy—An economic system where resource allocation is directed through market arrangements and the forces of supply and demand.

open economies—Economies engaged in international trade—the development of exports and imports and the expansion of direct foreign investment.

privatization—The movement away from state ownership of economic activity and toward private ownership.

resource base—Typically a reference to natural resources (minerals, timber, agricultural land, favorable climate for agricultural production, etc.).

restructuring—The change of corporate governance arrangements in enterprises as private economic activity replaces state economic activity.

stabilization—The development of institutions and policies designed to limit the decrease of output exhibited during the early phases of transition.

structural distortions—Usually deviations from market patterns regarding sectoral shares; for example, the importance of heavy industry, the service sector, etc.

transition—The replacement of one economic system by another.

Notes

1. The major examples of transition are the former command economies from the Soviet Union and the separate economies of Central and Eastern Europe; we include the market socialist economies that emerged from the former Yugoslavia.

2. We have emphasized that although there was much discussion of **economic reform** in the Soviet Union, there is general agreement that it had little impact on the economic system or performance outcomes. At the same time, the long-term pursuit of economic reform in countries such as Hungary (the New Economic Management, or NEM) probably achieved results especially important for the post-command privatization and restructuring.

3. The German case is of special interest to observers of transition. During the command era in the German Democratic Republic (GDR), many of the nonsystem factors such as cultural and historical factors were basically the same in the GDR and the Federal Republic of Germany (FRG). Unlike Czechoslovakia where there was a split, in Germany there was unification, a setting very different from most other transition economies.

4. Prior to the death of Josip Broz Tito and the eventual disintegration of Yugoslavia as a single political entity, there was considerable interest in Yugoslavia as an example of market socialism and workers management, an economic system discussed in earlier chapters.

5. Recall that in the Soviet Union the conduct of foreign trade was centralized in the Ministry of Foreign Trade and Foreign Trade Organizations (FTOs). Arguably, the impact of foreign trade on an individual republic was quite limited.

6. It is useful to note that in recent years the fields of comparative economic systems and economic development have become much more closely identified with each other. Many of the critical elements of transition, for example privatization and restructuring, have been of great importance in a wide variety of both developed and less developed economic systems.

7. The "J curve" has been of considerable interest since output fell in most but not all transition economies during the early years of the transition process. In the next chapter, we discuss the empirical literature on economic growth in transition economies and provide extensive references to the literature that focuses on the collapse.

8. The issue of data availability is fundamental to our examination of transition economies. During the early years of transition, these economies generally converted to standard world accounting systems. However, one could argue that data for the early years of transition are less reliable, and comparisons with subsequent years very difficult.

9. This issue is discussed in Dominik H. Enste, "Shadow Economies: Sizes, Causes, and Consequences," *Journal of Economic Literature* 38, no. 1 (March 2000), 77–114.

10. We have emphasized rates of economic growth in transition economies. A different and complex issue is the determination of levels of output in command economies at the end of the command era, such that reasonable comparisons can be made with levels of output in subsequent years. Output levels are especially important as we attempt to compare living levels across transition (and other) economies.

11. This theme is emphasized in Janos Kornai and Karen Eggleston, *Welfare, Choice, and Solidarity in Transition: Reforming the Health Sector in Eastern Europe* (Cambridge: Cambridge University Press, 2001).

Recommended Readings

General and Russia

Daron Acemoglu, Simon Johnson, and James Robinson, "Institutions as the Fundamental Cause of Long Run Growth," *NBER Working Paper* 10481, May 2004.

Anders Aslund, *How Capitalism Was Built: The Transformation of Central and Eastern Europe, Russia, and Central Asia* (New York: Cambridge University Press, 2007).

Erik Berglof and Gerard Roland (eds), *The Economics of Transition: The Fifth Nobel Symposium in Economics* (New York: Palgrave Macmillan, 2006).

Erik Berglof, Andrei Kunov, Julia Shvets, and Ksenia Yudaeva, *The New Political Economy of Russia* (Cambridge Mass.: The MIT Press, 2003).

Oliver Blanchard, *The Economics of Post-Communist Transition* (New York: Oxford University Press, 1997).

Oliver Blanchard, Kenneth A Froot, and Jeffrey D. Sachs, *The Transition in Eastern Europe*, 2 vols (Chicago: University of Chicago Press, 1994).

Horst Brezinski and Michael Fritsch, eds., *The Emergence and Evolution of Markets* (Lyme, Conn.: Elgar), 1997.

Christopher Clague and Gordon C. Rausser, eds., *The Emergence of Market Economies in Eastern Europe* (Cambridge, Mass.: Blackwell, 1992).

David A. Dyker, *Catching Up or Falling Behind: Post Communist Transformation in Historical Perspective* (Imperial College Press, 2004).

Maurice Ernst, Michael Alexeev, and Paul Marer, *Transforming the Core: Restructuring Industrial Enterprises in Russia and Central Europe* (Boulder, Colo.: Westview Press, 1996).

Saul Estrin, Grzegorz W. Kolodko, and Ilica Uvalic, *Transition and Beyond* (New York: Palgrave, 2000).

European Bank for Reconstruction and Development, *Transition Report 2000: Employment, Skills and Transition* (London: EBRD, 2000).

——, *Transition Report 2002* (London: EBRD, 2002).

——, *Transition Report 2009* (London: EBRD, 2009).

Elisabetta Falcetti, Martin Raiser, and Peter Sanfey, "Defying the Odds: Initial Conditions, Reforms and Growth in the First Decade of Transition," *EDRD Working Paper*, July 2000.

Elisabetta Falcetti, Tatiana Lysenko, and Peter Sanfey, "Reforms and Growth in Transition: Re-Examining The Evidence," *Journal of Comparative Economics* 34, no. 3 (September 2006), 421–45.

Harvey Feigenbaum, Jeffrey Henig, and Chris Hamnett, *Shrinking the State* (New York: Cambridge University Press, 1998).

Hubert Gabrisch and Jens Holscher, *Transformation to a Market Economy* (New York: Palgrave Macmillan, 2005).

Yegor Gaidar, *The Economics of Russian Transition* (Cambridge, Mass: The MIT Press, 2003).

Brigitte Granville and Peter Oppenheimer, *Russian Economy in the 1990's* (New York: Oxford University Press, 2001).

Philip Hanson and Michael Bradshaw, eds., *Regional Economic Change in Russia* (Northampton, Mass.: Edward Elgar, 2000).

Oleh Havrylyshyn, *Divergent Paths in Post-Communist Transformation: Capitalism for All or Capitalism for the Few?* (New York: Palgrave Macmillan, 2006).

Ian Jeffries, *Socialist Economies and the Transition to the Market: A Guide* (New York: Routledge, 1993).

David Kennett and Marc Lieberman, *The Road to Capitalism* (New York: Dryden, 1992).

Michael Keren and Gur Ofer, eds., *Trials of Transition: Economic Reform in the Former Communist Bloc* (Boulder, Colo.: Westview Press, 1992).

Lawrence K. Klein and Marshall Pomer, eds., *The New Russia: Transition Gone Awry* (Stanford: Stanford University Press, 2001).

János Kornai, *Struggle and Hope* (New York: Edward Elgar, 1999).

——, *Reforming the State* (New York: Cambridge University Press, 2001).

János Kornai and Susan Rose-Ackerman, eds., *Building a Trustworthy State in Post-Socialist Transition* (New York: Palgrave Macmillan, 2004).

János Kornai, Bo Rothstein, and Susan Rose-Ackerman, eds., *Creating Social Trust in Post-Socialist Transition* (New York: Palgrave Macmillan, 2004).

David Lane, ed., *The Transformation of State Socialism: System Change, State Socialism, or Something Else?* (New York: Palgrave Macmillan, 2007).

Marie Lavigne, *The Economics of Transition* (New York: Palgrave Macmillan 1999).

Jim Leitzel, *Russian Economic Reform* (New York: Routledge, 1995).

Roger Manser, *Failed Transitions* (New York: The New York Press, 1993).

Eric S. Maskin and Andras Simonovits, eds., *Planning. Shortage, and Transformation: Essays in Honor of Janos Kornai* (Cambridge, Mass.: The MIT Press, 2000).

Martha de Melo, Cevdet Denizer, and Alan Gelb, "Patterns of Transition from Plan to Market," *World Bank Economic Review* 10, no. 3 (September 1996), 397–424.

Tomasz Mickiewicz Masrek, *Economic Transition in Central Europe and the Commonwealth of Independent States* (New York: Palgrave Macmillan, 2006).

Peter Murrell, ed., "Symposium on Economic Transition in the Soviet Union and Eastern Europe," *The Journal of Economic Perspectives* 5, no. 4 (Fall 1991).

Zbigniew Nahorski, Jan Owsinski, and Tomasz Szapiro, *The Transition to Market Economies* (New York: Palgrave Macmillan, 2000).

OECD, *Russian Federation* (Paris: OECD), 2000.

———, *Russian Federation* (Paris: OECD), 2010.

Lucanj T. Orlowski, ed., *Transition and Growth in Post-Communist Countries* (Northampton, Mass.: Edward Elgar, 2001).

Richard Pomfret, *Creating a Market Economy* (New York: Edward Elgar, 2002).

J. L. Porket, *Modern Economic Systems and Their Transformation* (New York: St. Martin's, 1998).

Sheila M. Puffer, Daniel J. McCarthy, and Alexander I. Naumov, eds., *The Russian Capitalist Experiment* (Northampton, Mass.: Edward Elgar, 2000).

Gerard Roland, *Transition and Economics: Politics, Markets, and Firms* (Cambridge, Mass.: MIT Press, 2000).

Andrei Schleifer and Daniel Triesman, *Without a Map* (Cambridge, Mass.: MIT Press, 2000).

Paul Seabright, ed., *The Vanishing Rouble: Barter Networks and Non-Monetary Transactions in Post-Soviet Societies* (Cambridge: Cambridge University Press, 2000).

Nicolas Spulber, *Redefining the State* (Cambridge: Cambridge University Press, 1997).

———, *Russia's Economic Transitions: From Late Tsarism to the New Millennium* (New York: Cambridge University Press, 2006).

David Stark, *Postsocialist Pathways: Transforming Politics and Property in East Central Europe* (New York: Cambridge University Press, 1998).

Kitty Stewart, *Fiscal Federalism in Russia* (Northampton, Mass.: Edward Elgar, 2000).

"Symposium of Economic Transition in the Soviet Union and Eastern Europe," *Journal of Economic Perspectives* 5, no. 4 (Fall 1991), 3–217.

Joseph E. Stiglitz, *Whither Socialism?* (Cambridge, Mass.: MIT Press, 1994).

Pier-Angelo Toninelli, ed., *The Rise and Fall of State-Owned Enterprises in The Western World* (New York: Cambridge University Press, 2000).

World Bank, *From Plan to Market: World Development Report 1996* (Washington, D.C.: World Bank, 1996).

OECD, *Russian Federation* (Paris: OECD, 2000).

Salvatore Zecchini, ed., *Lessons from the Economic Transition* (Boston: Kluwer, 1997).

The Baltic Countries

Juris Dreifrelds, *Latvia in Transition* (New York: Cambridge University Press, 1996).

Helena Hannula, Slavo Radosevic, and Nick von Tunzelmann, eds., *Estonia: The New EU Economy: Building a Baltic Miracle* (New York: Ashgate, 2006).

Central Asia

Anders Aslund, *How Capitalism Was Built: The Transformation of Central and Eastern Europe and Central Asia* (New York: Cambridge University Press, 2007).

Mehrdad Haghayeghi, *The Economies of the Central Asian Republics* (New York: Palgrave Macmillan, 2002).

Yelena Kalyuzhnova, "The First Decade of Transition in Central Asia: An Introduction to the Symposium," *Comparative Economic Studies* 45, no. 4 (December 2003).

Hungary

OECD, *Hungary* (Paris: OECD, 2010).

Xavier Richet, *The Hungarian Model: Markets and Planning in a Socialist Economy* (New York: Cambridge University Press, 1989).

Anna Seleny, *The Political Economy of State-Society Relations in Hungary and Poland: From Communism to the European Union* (New York: Cambridge University Press, 2006).

Poland

John E. Jackson, Jacek Klich, and Krystyna Poznanska, *The Political Economy of Poland's Transition: New Firms and Reform Governments* (New York: Cambridge University Press, 2005).

David Lipton and Jeffrey Sachs, "Creating a Market Economy in Eastern Europe: The Case of Poland," *Brookings Papers on Economic Activity* 1 (1990).

OECD, *Poland* (Paris: OECD, 2010).

Germany

Jens Holscher, ed., *Germany's Economic Performance: From Unification to Euroization* (New York: Palgrave Macmillan, 2006).

CHAPTER

17

Transition Economies: Output Patterns and Measurement Issues

In Chapter 16, we presented a broad survey of contemporary transition economies and identified twenty-eight economies that would be the focus of attention in this book. Here, we will find it useful to examine the transition economies in selected subgroups—for example, those emerging from the former Soviet Union, Central and Eastern Europe (CEE), and Central Asia. By almost any standard, the transition economies differ significantly from one another, both at the dawn of transition and at the present time, almost twenty-five years after the initial collapse of the command economies. Moreover, these differences (be they geographic, economic, or social) have affected the degree to which transition has succeeded in different settings well beyond the initial decade of the 1990s and the first decade of the twenty-first century.

As we attempt to measure the success of transition, the variables that are important are usually not readily captured. We need to define what success in transition means, and then attempt to model those forces that seem to influence success. In this chapter, our focus is relatively narrow, namely economic growth. For our broader discussion of transition outcomes in subsequent chapters, we will focus on a variety of generally identifiable characteristics of success—for example, privatization and the development of markets, the emergence of macroeconomic institutions and policies, the expansion of foreign trade and economic relations, and finally, the development of labor markets and the safety net.

Explaining Patterns of Growth in Output Transition Economies

Initial Conditions and Distortion

In Chapter 16, we examined the early collapse of output evident in many transition economies, but we did not consider the empirical evidence (see Figure 16.4).[1] Now we turn to an examination of the forces more broadly responsible for changes in output in the transition setting. The reader may wonder why we are addressing these issues before we discuss the transition process, given that outcome is in effect a summary of transition results. Understanding transition performance patterns from the outset will help us ask the right questions as we study the components of transition—and will help us appreciate the difficulties of assessing the transition process, and especially the nature of systemic change in the long run.

Modeling the patterns of performance during the transition era has proved to be a complex but essential task. Most observers would argue that there are at least **three** main explanatory forces. The first is **initial conditions**, which are the *conditions prevailing at the onset of transition (the level of economic development, the nature of institutions, the availability of natural resources, the openness of the economy etc.).* The second are **policy measures**—*a factor that can be changed without changing the underlying economic system*—chosen during transition (for example with regard to privatization and the development of financial institutions). The third are a variety of **environmental factors**—*country size, geographic features, resource endowments, and so on*; it is necessary to consider differences among countries by examining performance in groups of countries, such as the former USSR and Eastern Europe. Much of the literature on transition, especially the literature related to performance, focuses on the transition process in these selected groups of transition economies: those performing well in Eastern Europe and those performing less well among the Commonwealth of Independent States (CIS) countries. In part, this is a statistical issue, but we will watch it carefully as we attempt to characterize transition patterns and to understand why there are important differences among transition economies.

One significant factor is different **initial conditions**—that is, differences in resource allocation at the outset of transition. These differences are often characterized as representing **distortion**, simply because in many cases, allocation patterns differed from those typically found in market economies.[2] What do we mean by differences in allocation patterns, and why do we care whether these historical differences existed?

Some of the ways in which command and market economies differ in resource allocation are given in Table 17.1. This table reflects structural differences in the pre-transition era—specifically, differences in the sectoral outcomes of resource allocation under the command systems. In other words, if we examine the sources of output (for example, industry versus agriculture) and the uses of output (for example, consumption versus investment), it is evident that the outcomes in the former command economies did not reflect market forces. As we have discussed earlier, the command systems used both systemic features (state ownership and control) and policy imperatives (an industry-first policy) to ensure that there would be an emphasis on industry, and on heavy industry in particular. Specifically, if we measure the importance of industry (for example, the share of industrial output in total output) and control for the level of economic development of the countries in question, we find that the command economies tended to exhibit systematically larger shares of industrial output than market economies at similar levels of economic development.[3] There are many such examples of what might be broadly termed **structural distortion**, which is *a type of distortion usually related to sectoral shares in the economy*.

TABLE 17.1   Structural Differences Between Command and Market Economies[a]

Target Variable	Command Economies	Market Economies
GDP: *sources*		
Industry	+	normal
Agriculture	−	normal
Services	−	normal
GDP: *uses*		
Consumption	−	normal
Investment	+	normal
Government	+	normal

[a]In this table, we provide a stylized comparison of selected target variables for command and market economies. A plus (+) indicates an above-normal share; a minus (−) indicates a below-normal share. A "normal" share is the share that would occur if a large sample of market economic systems were compared, controlling for the level of economic development measured in terms of per capita GDP. Thus a plus for industry in a command setting indicates an industry share larger than would typically be found in market economies, controlling for the level of GDP per capita. Likewise, a minus for the service share in command systems indicates a service share smaller than would typically be found in a sample of market economies, controlling for the level of GDP per capita. Thus market resource-allocation patterns are assumed to be "normal" as a reference point from which to understand deviations in command systems.

Source: Compiled by the authors.

Our characterization of systemic distortion in Table 17.1 is simplistic but reflects our earlier discussion of command systems and would generally be supported by statistical analysis. Moreover, deviations from market patterns of resource allocation in command systems emerge on many levels, not just in terms of the sources and uses of output. For example, socialist regional policies could and did dictate the nature of resource allocation on a regional basis. Thus, in the case of the former Soviet Union, a region such as Siberia received much more attention than would, for example, northern Canada within the Canadian political and economic systems. Many of the urban centers that emerged during the Soviet era were planned "socialist" cities in terms of their location, their size, and many of their characteristics, such as transportation and housing. One does not have to make a judgment about the merits of these differences in allocation; the point is that market arrangements and policies will not typically sustain socialist patterns. For example, whatever the merits of the Soviet development of Siberia, it is very unlikely that this level of development would be sustained under market arrangements.

Another important example is foreign trade. In the command systems, currencies were not convertible, and trade was conducted by the state. Although the state must respect world market forces, state preferences could and did prevail with regard not only to the overall volume of trade but also to many of the important details, such as the commodity composition and geographic distribution of trade (both imports and exports). The latter, for example, was strongly influenced by the socialist trade block The Council for Mutual Economic Assistance (CMEA), which collapsed prior to the onset of transition. The socialist trading mechanisms and policies created a pattern of trade sharply different from patterns that occur under market arrangements. As we will see when we examine trade patterns before and after the collapse of the command economies, major shifts in trade patterns occurred.

Indeed, the impact of the command era was significant in many dimensions. Consider, for example, the case of bias in favor of industry. Not only was there an industry bias in the general sense outlined above, but the structure of industry also differed from the industrial structures found in a market setting. For example, it is well known that Soviet industrial enterprises were, for a variety of reasons, large, capital-intensive, and integrated. Both horizontal and vertical integration were favored to resolve the irregularities of the material supply system. In a market economy, the "make or buy" decision is made on different (cost/benefit) grounds. Thus, policies and allocational decisions in the command economies created organizational arrangements different from those found in market economies. The introduction of markets is bound to change these organizational arrangements. We will examine this critical element of corporate governance when we discuss privatization.

There were also important differences in the rules guiding enterprises. For example, in Soviet enterprises, workers could not generally be dismissed. This fact, combined with state budgeting of enterprises, created artificial levels of employment—a condition inconsistent with market arrangements. Thus, as privatization occurs and the role of the state is reduced, we would expect significant changes in decision making arrangements within the enterprise, and thus, changes in the use of labor and other inputs.

Why do these initial conditions, which differ widely from market patterns, matter? They matter because as markets are introduced, one can expect allocation patterns under different systemic arrangements and different policies to revert to more "normal" patterns—that is, patterns that resemble long-term market outcomes. Thus, one can argue that the more serious the distortions, the greater the distance that an economy must travel to reach market dimensions, and thus, the more difficult the transition process will be. In part, the magnitude of these distortions reflects the length of time that socialist arrangements prevailed, although other factors are also important. For example, one might expect, even under socialist arrangements, that a resource-constrained economy such as Hungary would be more open to foreign trade than a large, resource-rich country such as the former Soviet Union. Thus, at the beginning of the transition era, we might expect foreign trade to have had a greater impact on resource allocation in Hungary than in the former Soviet Union.

Can the effect of initial conditions—and thus distortions—be measured? The answer is yes, but the task of defining, measuring, and accounting for the impact of these distortions is difficult. In Figure 17.1, we provide a simple scatter diagram and a trend line to demonstrate the relationship between initial conditions and the growth of output as captured by European Bank for Reconstruction and Development (EBRD) indexes.[4] Larger positive numbers indicate better initial conditions; larger negative numbers indicate inferior initial conditions. Although there is considerable variation around the trend line, there is a positive relationship between growth and initial conditions as characterized by these indexes. Indeed, the trend line that we have drawn illustrates the basic nature of this relationship, even though there are interesting outliers.

FIGURE 17.1   Economic Growth and Initial Conditions

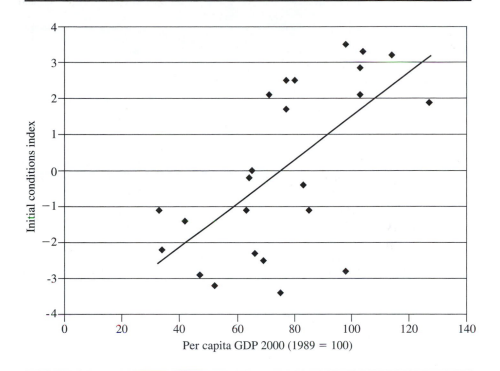

Source: Based on EBRD, *Transition Report 2001: Energy in Transition* (Paris: EBRD, 2001), pp. 19 and 59.

Assessing Transition Patterns

To understand how we might assess the patterns of performance exhibited by different transition economies, we begin with a simple illustrative approach, working with some of the variables (forces) discussed above. Let's assume that the performance of transition economies is determined by just one variable and that this variable can be measured: the extent to which **liberalization** (the movement toward markets) has taken place. This view, although simplistic, has been popular in the literature, especially among those who favor significant reliance on markets. We formalize this idea in the following simple functional relationship (omitting the error term):

$$\text{Gr}_i = f(\text{Lib}_i) \tag{17.1}$$

where

> Gr_i = an index of growth, 1989–1999 with 1989 = 100
> Lib_i = an index of liberalization

Rather than estimating this simple relationship, in Figure 17.2, we provide a scatter diagram relating liberalization and economic growth based on EBRD indicators.[5] The trend line indicates that there is a positive relationship between

FIGURE 17.2   Economic Growth and Liberalization

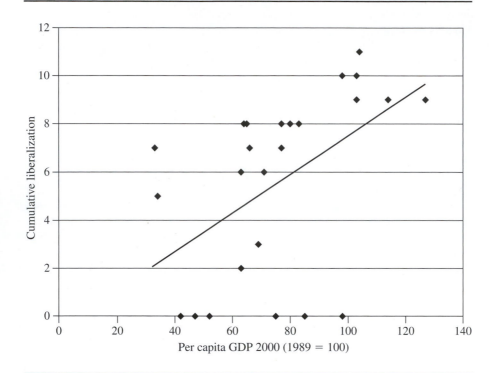

Source: EBRD, *Transition Report 2001: Energy in Transition* (Paris: EBRD, 2001), pp. 19 and 59.

increases in per capita GDP and liberalization as assessed by the EBRD index. This index characterizes greater liberalization with a positive number, less liberalization with a negative number. It is evident from Figure 17.2 that there is considerable variation around the trend line. However, as a group, the countries of the former Soviet Union have done less well than the countries of Eastern Europe. However, there is much more that we can do in the measurement of these patterns of transition performance.[6]

We turn to a more complex model of the transition process. We examine the impact of initial conditions, policies (for example, liberalization), and environmental factors on growth. We specify the following basic relationship:

$$Gr_i = (IC_i, Lib_i, Env_i) \tag{17.2}$$

where

$$
\begin{aligned}
Gr_i &= \text{an index of growth, 1989–1999 with 1989} = 100 \\
Ic_i &= \text{an index measuring initial conditions} \\
Lib_i &= \text{an index of liberalization} \\
Env_i &= \text{a measure of environmental factors}
\end{aligned}
$$

We now have a relationship that cannot be readily examined in graphical terms, and we have some variables rather more complicated than those in equation 17.1.

However, as we shall see, this model provides us a mechanism to observe the important yet complicated issues involved in understanding the growth patterns. Obviously, this model could be more carefully specified and estimated using basic econometric techniques. We do not take this step (although we do examine the available empirical evidence on these issues) the importance of understanding the variables used in this type of model and the difficulties encountered in determining actual empirical results.

Typically, in equation 17.2, we might measure growth and our policy variable (liberalization) in the same manner as in equation 17.1. The variable capturing initial conditions might well be an index—for example, one of the sort provided by EBRD. Finally, as an environmental variable, we use per capita GDP of the transition economies. This variable requires additional explanation.

Many have argued that, apart from the issue of distortions left behind from the command era, transition experiences are likely to differ depending on the level of economic development of the transition economy.[7] As noted in Table 16.1, the transition economies that we examine began the process from very different levels of economic development. One could argue that a country with a per capita GDP of US$1,000 is very different from a transition economy with a GDP of US$10,000. Indeed, the former might be characterized as an economy in need of a policy framework for economic development, not transition. Having said this, however, per capita income is difficult to interpret because it presumably captures a variety of past and present economic and noneconomic forces.

In a model such as this, it is important to provide some theoretical underpinning for our expected results. We would expect that better initial conditions (less distortion) would make the transition process easier, and thus, there would be a positive relationship between these two variables. Note that in equation 17.2, our measure of initial conditions indicates better conditions with a higher index number, and hence an expected positive relationship in this example (see Figure 17.1).

We would expect that economic growth would be better with more aggressive liberalization (the argument made in equation 17.1 and illustrated in Figure 17.2). Hence, again, we would expect a positive relationship between these two variables. Finally, the potential impact of our environmental variable—per capita output—is less clear. We have already noted that this sort of variable captures a variety of influences. It is, in a sense, an overall measure of the achieved level of economic development, including the development of institutions. At the same time, our argument that economies at higher levels of economic development should be better able to handle transition implies the existence of a positive relationship.

We turn to a brief discussion of statistical issues, after which we examine the available empirical evidence on growth patterns.

Problems of Specification and Estimation[8]

The most serious problem is that of **specification**, which is *the form taken by a model that relates a result to a series of explanatory variables*. How were the included variables chosen, and why do we believe that equation 17.2 as we have specified it actually captures the forces that we believe are important? For example, an important omission is that of country differences, which are only partially captured by a variable such as per capita GDP. What might be helpful in this case would be to use a fixed-effects model—that is, a model that captures country differences directly. In this case, we might well isolate the countries of the former Soviet Union and those of Eastern Europe, arguing that in transition these two groups of countries are structurally different. These differences could be examined statistically.

A second major problem with this model is endogeneity. Simply put, this model assumes that the variables on the right-hand side are **exogenous**—that is, determined outside the model. By contrast, the variable on the left-hand side—in our case, a measure of economic growth—is an **endogenous variable**, which is *a variable on the left-hand side of the equation that is to be explained by estimating this model*. This is an important and a strong assumption in this model. Thus, in equation 17.2, we make the (probably incorrect) assumption that liberalization is an **exogenous variable** unrelated to our measure of economic growth. Moreover, we assume that the independent variables on the right-hand side are themselves not related to each other—a different issue, but an important assumption here. Why do these assumptions matter in our case? If a variable such as liberalization is not exogenous but rather is endogenous, then there is the possibility of simultaneity between liberalization and the growth of output, and that would require a different specification from the one proposed here.

Third, we need to address the issue of **time lags**—*in a formal model, a difference in time between changes in the explanatory variables and the dependent variable*. Equation 17.2 assumes that there are no time lags. If liberalization affects growth, the impact is presumed to be simultaneous. Clearly, this assumption may be inappropriate, but introducing lags would complicate our analysis. Again, if time lags are thought to be important, then a different specification would be suggested.

A final problem with this type of model is selecting the dependent variable (in our case, the rate of growth over the transition era). If one wishes to assess the results of transition, a variety of possible variables come to mind. Is the rate of inflation, or perhaps the rate of unemployment, an important outcome of transition? The question to be considered is whether the rate of inflation (for example) is a variable that explains the rate of growth, or whether, instead, the rate of economic growth explains (in part) the rate of inflation? These issues are important to our modeling effort, especially when the variables themselves are often difficult to characterize with precision.

During and after the 1990s, the empirical literature examining the results of transition has wrestled with the complications we have noted. We turn to an examination of the literature.

The Empirical Evidence: Collapse and Economic Growth

In Table 16.1 and Figure 17.1, we presented empirical evidence on economic growth in transition economies both for the initial decade of change (the 1990s) and also for the subsequent decade at the beginning of the twenty-first century.

What does the empirical evidence—and the statistical analysis of this evidence—tell us about economic growth in the transition economies?

Early studies on economic growth in transition economies usually examined both the observed early collapse and the emerging patterns of longer-term growth. Although specific explanations of the "J curve" vary, in fact, there is a degree of uniformity among explanations. For example, Brada and King argue that declines in output were the result of "exogenous shocks to the balance of trade, to investment and to autonomous consumption." Repkine and Walsh argue that "the U shaped experience of industrial sectors is an outcome driven by an inter-sector change, induced by investment demand shocks, in the market orientation of production away from products traditionally sold into the CMEA market and towards products traditionally sold into the EU market." Kornai adds emphasis to the decline or coordinating mechanisms, the end of a sellers' market, and the hardening of financial discipline in a setting where financial discipline was traditionally weak. Kornai emphasizes the transformation of the real structure of the economy and, as other studies have done, emphasizes the potential negative impact of inflation. A broader survey of the measurement issues is found in de Melo and Gelb and also Stuart and Panayotopoulos.[9]

In the early analysis, Krueger and Ciolko focus on policy measures arguing that measures such as a liberalization index may be endogenous to measures of performance (such as output decline), the result being an overstatement of the impact of policies on performance.[10] An analysis by Levine and Renelt argues that while the share of investment in GDP and the share of trade in GDP were important to performance, the results of growth analysis are sensitive to the sorts of specification and estimation issues that we have discussed earlier. Specifically, it is argued that results are fragile to small changes in the underlying information set. An analysis by Barro examines a larger sample of countries for a longer period of time and finds that economic growth is inversely related to the share of government consumption in GDP but unrelated to the share of public investment. Perhaps not surprising, Barro also finds that growth is "positively related to measures of political stability and inversely related to a proxy for market distortions."[11]

Subsequent studies have built on earlier studies with considerable refinement as more data are available over longer periods of time. Campos argues that the underlying assumptions in the modeling of transition are important. He argues that earlier specifications perform poorly and that "almost a decade after the transition began, the former centrally planned economies are still structurally different from market economies at similar levels of per capita income." This type of evidence suggests that growth convergence has not been achieved during the initial decade of transition.[12]

Subsequent studies have tended to emphasize convergence patterns. Falcetti, Lysenko, and Sanfrey suggest that reforms have a positive impact on growth in the transition economies but with feedback, and argue further that the impact of initial conditions decline over time. However, growth in one period serves as a spur to growth in a subsequent period and stimulates a continuation of economic reform. A similar conclusion, emphasizing the importance of macroeconomic fundamentals for convergence in the CEE economies is emphasized by Kocenda.

However, Kutan and Yigit examine the issue of convergence and find less convergence than that found by Kocenda.[13]

A number of studies have emphasized the importance of macroeconomic issues and especially the development of financial markets. Moers emphasizes the importance of Foreign Direct Investment (FDI) and macrostabilization during the early years of transition. Havrylyshyn also emphasizes the role of stabilization and structural reforms, as does Denizer. Bayesian analysis done by Lyroudi, Papanastasiou, and Vamvakidis sees a lesser impact for FDI on performance.[14]

A strong endorsement for the need to control inflation is provided in the empirical literature. Nath, examining the CEE and Baltic countries, stresses the need for inflation control and also macroeconomic stabilization. The issue of inflation is also addressed by Fischer, Sahai, and Vegh.[15]

Using dynamic panel data, Estrin, Urga, Lazarova and Vegh argue that privatization has influenced economic growth, but perhaps indirectly via capital markets. They also find that trade and FDI are probably collinear in these studies because FDI is unimportant when a trade variable is included in the specification. However, Godoy and Stiglitz argue that the speed of privatization has a negative impact on growth with the development of legal institutions being more important. However, Staehr argues that reform policies and especially policy changes influence economic growth. Institutional issues and especially property rights in an analysis of the Russian regions can be found in Sonin.[16]

Data on Transition: What's in the Numbers?

In our discussion thus far, we have assumed that we can look at the data and provide a reasonable assessment of transition issues, especially performance, from simple indicators such as changes in output over time. Although the conclusions we present from the available empirical evidence are probably reasonable, there is more to the story.

Any observer of the command economies knows that measurement problems are serious. Indeed, our earlier discussions of these economies, and of their collapse, focused on critical measurement issues. Basic data series such as those pertaining to national income were fundamentally different from those generated and used in Western market economies. Obviously, these issues have not disappeared, but transition economies have largely shifted to widely accepted national accounting procedures, and, depending on the issues being investigated, we can now have greater confidence in the comparability of data for transition and Western market economies. This confidence does not extend uniformly to all issues, however.

Consider the critical matter of measuring changes from the command era through the transition era, whether we focus on structural issues (for example, how important was heavy industry in the command economies?) or general performance (what was the level of output in Russia in 2000 compared to 1988?). Obviously, to investigate these sorts of issues, one needs output for both the pretransition and the transition eras measured in a comparable manner—in terms of basic definitions, price weights, or the like. These types of estimates are tenuous, and the observer should expect the evidence to vary as a consequence of different, although quite reasonable, assumptions about such things as price weights.

A second issue has been the important changes that have occurred in basic statistical indicators. Consider, for example, the issue of inflation. Any long-time observer of the transition experience is aware that the nature of inflation was very different in the early years of transition, when formerly fixed prices were released, than during the middle and latter years of the decade. These issues present a challenge to the observer of transition who wants to characterize inflation from the late 1980s through the present.

A third problem with transition data is the important qualitative differences among data series—an issue that of course also matters in market economies. For example, measures of unemployment or poverty are likely to be much less reliable than measures of electricity output. One must be concerned about definitional issues, how data are collected, and, if data are aggregated, how this aggregation is accomplished.

A fourth problem with data from transition economies is the issue of "nonstandard" components and influences. For example, a number of transition economies have informal or underground economies that are significant but very difficult to measure. We know that the informal economy is important—indeed, in some cases and some times it is critical—yet its impact on "traditional" economic variables can be difficult to capture. A recent study suggests that "substantive results from many studies examining the consequences of the radical transition from planned to market economies must be viewed with considerable skepticism."[17]

In sum, those who study transition economies can access vast amounts of empirical evidence that was not generally available for these economies during the command era. At the same time, the special circumstances of the transition era suggest the need for caution when accessing and interpreting transition data.

Economic Growth and the Output Levels in Transition

We have now examined some of the empirical evidence relating to transition economies choosing to look first at the distortions of the early transition era (the 1990s) and thereafter the perhaps more "normal" early years of the first decade of the twenty-first century. Although the diversity of this empirical evidence makes a summary difficult, some observations are useful.

First, although we should be careful "selecting" periods in which we examine transition performance, the modeling effort is complicated by the fact that the patterns of output change clearly differ between the early years of transition and the more recent years.

Second, it is evident that country responses to the transition process have been quite different from one country to another. In this sense, country effects are important in a modeling effort.

Third, it is necessary to emphasize that almost all of the caveats that we discussed when examining approaches to modeling are in fact relevant. We need to bear this fact in mind as we examine the empirical literature.

Fourth, although generalizations can be made, it is clear that "the devil is in the details." Analysts have quite different results looking at similar issues but with different data sets, specifications, and modeling techniques.

Fifth, it is evident that many of the forces that we would expect to be positive with regard to the growth experience are in fact positive. For example, institutional development (a legal framework), privatization, liberalization, and the development of markets and policy development all seem to influence growth in a positive fashion, whereas not unexpectedly factors such as inflation are generally negative influences. At the same time, there are at least two caveats: The precise channels through which growth is influenced can be difficult to observe and country effects can account for significant differences in the magnitude of causal influence.

Having examined the growth patterns of transition economies for the first twenty years of the transition process, what can be said about the **level** of output in these economies as we enter a third decade? In Table 17.2, we present indices of the level of output for the period 1989 through 2008.

Our earlier discussion suggested that the first decade saw significant declines in output in a number of transition economies. Specifically, from the evidence on per capita GDP from 1989 through 1999 (Table 17.1), of the twenty-eight economies listed, twenty-two showed declines, not including three for which data were not available.

For the overall transition era through 2008, and using the indicator of real GDP, we provide evidence on twenty-nine transition economies, of which only seven showed decreases over the twenty-year period. Of twenty-five countries for which we have comparable data for the first decade of transition, eighteen showed declines in output. For the first decade of transition, output in all transition economies decreased by 24 percent, whereas for the second decade (with a slightly larger sample of transition economies), output increased by 40 percent, a significant overall improvement.

One could argue that overall, transition economies that performed less well in the early years of transition have continued to fare poorly, whereas other have done well (with considerable variation among countries) and an overall growth rate of roughly 2 percent per year.

The Transition Experience in the Twenty-First Century

Thus far, we have examined some of the underpinnings of the early growth experience of transition economies. What does the evidence say about longer-term outcomes?

First, if we characterize a successful transition as one where underlying organizational arrangements and allocational patterns have changed producing sustained economic growth, then clearly there are marked differences among the transition economies. In general, the transition economies emerging from the former Soviet Union have done least well, whereas those in CEE have done the best. There are important differences among subgroups, although on balance, liberalization has produced economic improvement.

Second, the transition economies that have done the best are those that have been able to institute organizational change and develop a new market

TABLE **17.2**   The Level of Output in Transition Economies

Country	Real GDP 2001 (1989 = 100)	Real GDP 2008 (1989 = 100)
Croatia	85	111
Czech Republic	106	142
Estonia	90	147
Hungary	112	136
Latvia	75	118
Lithuania	72	120
Poland	129	178
Slovak Republic	110	164
Slovenia	121	156
Albania	116	163
Bosnia and Herzegovina	na	84
Bulgaria	80	114
FYR Macedonia	77	102
Montenegro	na	92
Romania	84	128
Serbia	na	72
Armenia	74	153
Azerbaijan	62	177
Belarus	91	161
Georgia	37	61
Moldova	37	55
Ukraine	46	70
Russia	64	108
Kazakhstan	84	141
Kyrgyz Republic	71	102
Mongolia	na	167
Tajikistan	56	61
Turkmenistan	96	226
Uzbekistan	105	163
All transition countries	**76**	**140**

Source: EBRD, *Transition Report 2009* (EBRD: 2009), Table A.1.1.1; EBRD *Transition Report 2002* (EBRD: 2002). Annex 3.1.

infrastructure and appropriate supporting mechanisms in the regulatory sector (limitation of policy constraints), the banking sector, and legal arrangements.

Third, our earlier examination of growth in the transition economies focused on the first decade, an era of striking change and collapse, but with recovery as the first decade of transition came to an end. What has happened to the transition economies in the twenty-first century, and where do they stand today?

We begin with an examination of output levels and rates of change, using the United States as a useful comparator. In Table 17.3, several issues emerge. Although these comparisons need to be interpreted with caution due to well-known measurement issues, as a reasonable estimate, they tell us that there are significant differences

TABLE **17.3**   Transition Economies: Per Capita GDP (U.S. dollars) estimates 2010

Country	PCGDP (USD)	Gini Coefficient	Country	PCGDP (USD)	Gini Coefficient
USA	47,200	40.8	Romania	11,600	31.0
Slovenia	28,200	28.4	Azerbaijan	10,900	36.5
Czech Republic	26,600	25.4	Serbia	10,900	
Slovakia	22,000	25.8	Macedonia	9,700	
Estonia	19,100	35.8	Albania	8,000	28.2
Poland	18,800	34.5	Ukraine	6,700	28.1
Hungary	18,800	26.9	Kosovo	6,600	
Croatia	17,400	29.0	Armenia	5,700	33.8
Lithuania	16,000	36.0	Georgia	4,900	40.4
Russia	15,900	39.9	Mongolia	3,600	30.3
Latvia	14,700	37.7	Uzbekistan	3,100	26.8
Belarus	13,600	29.7	Moldova	2,500	33.2
Bulgaria	13,500	29.2	Kyrgyzstan	2,200	30.3
Kazakhstan	12,700	33.9	Tajikistan	2,000	32.6

Note: The United States is included for comparative purposes.

Source: Central Intelligence Agency, *The World Factbook, 2011* (Washington D.C.: CIA, 2011).

between the higher-income and the lower-income transition economies, differences that seem to be sustained over time. If one examines the higher-income economies as compared to the lower-income economies, there is at least a tenfold difference in per capita output (income). Moreover, it is worth noting that all of the transition economies have levels of income inequality less than that of the United States. On average, income levels are less than half that of the United States, perhaps to be considered a significant achievement, although the devil is to some degree hidden in the details. The higher-income transition economies are mostly those that were not a part of the former Soviet Union, whereas the lower-income transition economies are mostly those that were part of the former Soviet Union.

Although measures of output and inequality of its distribution are basic for cross-country comparisons, it is also useful to examine what are perhaps more subjective indicators, broadly those related to quality of life issues.

In Table 17.4, we examine three major indicators of country achievement, specifically levels of corruption, an index of freedom, and the United Nations Human Development Index (HDI). Again, we use the United States as a comparator.

Perhaps as we look ahead, the most important indicator of success for the transition economies is economic growth. Although estimates of future economic growth are always precarious, it is important to have some sense of what might be expected. In Table 17.5, we assemble estimates presented by the Office of the Chief Economist of the EBRD.[18] As we consider these estimates, it is important to appreciate the fact that there are now many organizations preparing such estimates, a summary of which can be found in the EBRD Transition Reports. What can we learn from these estimates?

TABLE 17.4   Transition Economies: Selected Socioeconomic Indicators

Country	Corruption Index	Freedom Index	HDI 2010	Country	Corruption Index	Freedom index	HDI 2010
USA	7.1	77.8	.908	Azerbaijan	2.4	59.7	.699
Slovenia	5.9	64.6	.864	Serbia	3.2	58.0	.764
Czech Republic	4.4	70.4	.863	Montenegro	4.0	62.5	.771
Slovakia	4.1	69.5	.832	Macedonia	3.9	66.0	.726
Estonia	6.4	75.2	.832	Albania	3.1	64.0	.737
Poland	5.5	64.2	.811	Turkmenistan	1.6	43.6	.681
Hungary	4.6	66.6	.814	Ukraine	2.3	45.8	.725
Croatia	4.0	61.3	.794	Kosovo	2.9		
Lithuania	4.8	71.3	.805	Armenia	2.6	69.9	.729
Russia	2.4	50.5	.751	Georgia	4.1	70.4	.647
Latvia	4.2	65.8	.802	Mongolia	2.7	59.5	.647
Belarus	2.4	47.9	.751	Uzbekistan	1.6	45.8	.636
Bulgaria	3.3	64.9	.768	Moldova	2.9	55.7	.644
Kazakhstan	2.7	62.1	.740	Kyrgyzstan	2.1	61.1	.615
Romania	3.2	64.7	.779	Tajikistan	2.3	53.5	

Sources and Notes: The transition economies in this table are ordered from highest per capita GDP (U.S. dollars 2010) with the United States included as a comparator. The Corruption Perception Index is for 2011 from Transparency International; the scale ranges from 10 (least corrupt) to 1 (most corrupt).

The Index of Economic Freedom ranks as follows: 100–80 (free); 79.8–70 (mostly free); 69.9–60 (moderately free); 59.9–50 (mostly unfree); 49.9–0 (repressed). The Freedom Index is from the Heritage Foundation in collaboration with the *Wall Street Journal*. For details, see http://www.heritage.org/index/.

The Human Development Index (HDI) is from the United Nations, Human Development Report http://hdr.undp.org/en/statistics/hdi/ and ranges from 0 (lowest level) to 1 (highest level).

TABLE 17.5 Transition Economies: Economic Growth, 2009–2012

Country	2009	2110	2111	2112	Country	2009	2010	2011	2012
Slovenia	-8.1	1.2	2.0	2.0	Romania	-7.1	-1.3	1.8	3.8
Czech Republic	n.a.	n.a.	n.a.	n.a.	Azerbaijan	n.a.	n.a.	n.a.	n.a.
Slovakia	-4.8	4.0	3.7	4.1	Serbia	-3.1	1.8	2.9	4.1
Estonia	-13.9	3.1	6.1	3.8	Macedonia	-0.9	0.7	2.5	3.1
Poland	1.7	3.8	3.8	3.5	Albania	3.9	3.9	3.0	3.3
Hungary	-6.7	1.2	2.7	2.8	Ukraine	-14.8	4.2	4.5	4.5
Croatia	-6.0	-1.3	1.4	2.0	Kosovo	n.a	n.a	n.a	n.a
Lithuania	-14.7	1.3	6.5	3.5	Armenia	-14.2	2.1	4.5	4.0
Russia	-7.8	4.0	4.8	4.7	Georgia	-3.8	6.4	5.4	4.5
Latvia	-18.0	-0.3	2.9	4.0	Mongolia	-1.6	6.1	9.0	12.0
Belarus	0.2	7.6	3.0	3.5	Uzbekistan	8.1	8.5	8.5	9.0
Bulgaria	-5.5	0.2	3.1	3.6	Moldova	-6.0	6.9	5.0	4.5
Kazakh	1.2	7.0	7.0	7.3	Kyrgyzstan	3.0	-1.4	6.3	6.0
					Tajikistan	3.4	6.5	6.7	5.0

Source: EBRD, *Regional Economic Prospects in EBRD Countries of Operations: May 2011* (London: EBRD, Office of the Chief Economist, 2011).

First, although we have already discussed growth in the earlier years, a quick glance at the growth data reveals, even with some important variations, how serious the recent economic decline has been. For the year 2009, for example, fully seventeen of twenty-four transition economies for which we have data had negative rates of economic growth, in some cases of significant magnitude.

Second, and perhaps even more significant, the estimates for 2011 and 2012 suggest a significant and positive reversal of economic fortunes in the transition economies. Although it is true that for some countries growth rates are projected to be modest, it is also necessary to focus on the notable improvement that is expected, for example for the Baltic nations.

Third, in light of these expectations, it remains to be seen to what extent these more positive outcomes will put the transition economies back on a more healthy growth path. To an important degree, world economic conditions will influence this outcome through the mechanisms and channels discussed in earlier chapters.

Summary

- We have focused in this chapter on the changing output patterns in the transition economies, specifically the "J curve," and on the various explanations for the very different patterns observed across the transition economies.
- The measurement of performance frequently identifies those forces thought to affect the growth of output: differences in starting positions (**initial conditions and distortions** inherited from the command era), **policy differences**, and **country effects**.
- It is hard to characterize these variables—initial conditions, policy variables, and country effects—in such a way that a more formal statistical investigation can be conducted. In addition to both theoretical and econometric issues, we have emphasized the difficulties of working with data from the transition era, and especially the issues related to the assessment of transition performance over time.
- We have examined the forces leading to the decline of output in transition economies, emphasizing both supply and demand forces and other factors, such as the collapse of command instructions and the absence or slow emergence of price and other market-type information signals.
- The empirical evidence on economic growth suggests limitations on the achievement of convergence with market economies. However, there is support for the positive influence of variables such as privatization and institutional development, and an indication that forces such as inflation inhibit economic growth. At the same time, many of the difficulties of modeling economic growth are conformed and emphasized by the authors of empirical studies.
- Assessment of transition results is complicated by the presence in many cases of a non-monetary barter economy. Empirical evidence suggests that this presence of a non-monetary economy is greater in the CIS countries, especially Russia, and can be explained by the absence of appropriate market-type organizational arrangements, the limited role of financial markets, and the holdover of patterns of exchange that prevailed during the command era.

Key Terms

distortion—In the transition setting, usually refers to differences in structure and allocation of resources when, for example, command economic systems are compared to market economic systems at similar levels of economic development.

endogenous variable—In an economic model, a variable whose value is explained within the model being studied.

environmental factors—Factors such as resource endowments arguably likely to influence resource allocation in economic systems.

exogenous variable—In an economic model, a variable whose value is explained outside the model being studied.

initial conditions—Conditions existing at the beginning of the transition era, for example, institutional arrangements, industrial structure, and so on.

liberalization—The reduction of state controls and the implementation of decentralized (usually market) forces to influence resource allocation.

policy measures—The framework of political directives designed to influence and direct patterns of resource allocation in an economic system.

specification—The nature of an equation, for example, that has been designed to measure the impact of selected explanatory variables on a dependent variable.

structural distortion—Usually refers to differences in sectoral structures, for example, an emphasis on heavy industry, when former command systems are compared to market economic systems.

time lags—For example, the time that elapses between the development of a policy measure, the implementation of that measure, and changes in real-world outcomes resulting from this policy measure.

Notes

1. The concept of the "J curve" derives from international trade but has been used to characterize the pattern of output decline in transition economies. See Josef Brada and Arthur King, "Is There a 'J' Curve for the Economic Transition from Socialism to Capitalism?" *Economics of Planning* 25, no. 1(1992), 37–42. For a broad perspective, see Vladimir Popov, "Shock Therapy versus Gradualism: The End of the Debate (Explaining the Magnitude of the Transformational Recession)," *Comparative Economic Studies* 42, no. 1 (Spring 2000), 1–57.
   Robert Holzmann, Janos Gacs, and Georg Winckler, eds., *Output Decline in Eastern Europe* (Boston: Kluwer Academic, 1995). For a theoretical discussion, see Gerard Roland, *Transition and Economics: Politics, Markets, Firms* (Boston, Mass.: MIT Press, 2000), Ch. 7. For an interesting comparison, see Jacek Rostowski, "Comparing Two Great Depressions: 1929–33 to 1989–93," in Salvatore Zecchini, ed., *Lessons from the Economic Transition* (Boston: Kluwer Academic, 1997), pp. 225–239.

2. The concept of distortion is often difficult to characterize in a simple fashion. Note that we are not really arguing that there is only one pattern of resource allocation that is "good" but, rather, that under command arrangements, allocation patterns differed sharply from those typically found in market economies. Obviously, this means that as market arrangements replace command arrangements, the allocation of resources will change, and the command economies will in the end come to resemble market

economies more closely. As we will note later, such a characterization might be useful for understanding when the process of transition comes to an end.

3. Sectoral shares are frequently characterized in terms of output, although other measures such as labor inputs can be used. Conceptually, these measures ought to be straightforward, but in reality there are many measurement difficulties associated with the national income accounting procedures used in the command economies.

4. The data are from EBRD, *Transition Report 2001: Energy in Transition* (Paris: EBRD, 2001), pp. 19 and 59. The index of initial conditions is "derived from factor analysis and represents a weighted average of measures of the level of development, trade dependence on CMEA, macroeconomic disequilibria, distance to the EU, natural resource endowments, market memory and state capacity."

5. The data are from EBRD, *Transition Report 2001: Energy in Transition* (Paris: EBRD, 2001), pp. 19 and 59. The index of liberalization is based on the number of years that a country achieved a liberalization score of at least 3 on price liberalization and at least 4 on trade and foreign exchange liberalization, as computed by the EBRD. These scales vary from 0 to 4+ for increasing price and foreign exchange liberalization.

6. For a recent assessment, see Nauro F. Campos and Fabrizio Coricelli, "Growth in Transition: What We Know, What We Don't, and What We Should," *Journal of Economic Literature* 40, no. 3 (September 2002), 793–836.

7. The relationship between the level of development and what we have termed initial conditions is in fact a complex but interesting issue. For example, Uzbekistan was for many years under Soviet (command) governance, and yet we know that at the beginning of transition, there were important differences between Uzbekistan and Russia, not only in the level of output per capita but also in the extent to which distortions could be found in each case. These differences are potentially important to our understanding of transition differences.

8. This section can be skipped without loss of continuity.

9. Josef Brada and Arthur King, "Is There a "J" Curve for the Transition from Socialism to Capitalism? *Economics of Planning* 25, no. 1 (1992), 35–52; Alexandre Repkine and Patrick Paul Walsh, "Evidence of European Trade and Investment U-Shaped Industrial Output in Bulgaria, Hungary, Poland and Romania," *Journal of Comparative Economics* 27, no. 4 (December 1999), 730–752; Martha de Melo and Alan Gelb, "A Comparative Analysis of Twenty-Eight Economies in Europe and Asia," *Post-Soviet Geography and Economics* 37, no. 5 (May 1996), 265–285; Robert C. Stuart and Christina M. Panayotopoulos, "Decline and Recovery in Transition Economies: The Impact of Initial Conditions," *Post-Soviet Geography and Economics* 30, no. 4 (June 1999), 267–280; Janos Kornai, "Transformational Recession: The Main Causes," *Journal of Comparative Economics*, 19, no. 39 (1994).

10. See Gary Krueger and Marek Ciolko, "A Note on Initial Conditions and Liberalization During Transition," *Journal of Comparative Economics* 26 (1998), 718–734.

11. Ross Levine and David Renelt, "A Sensitivity Analysis of Cross Country Growth Regressions," *The American Economic Review* 82, no. 4 (September 1992), 942–963; Robert J. Barro, "Economic Growth in a Cross Section of Countries," *Quarterly Journal of Economics* 106, no. 2 (1991), 447–463.

12. Nauro F. Campos, "Will the Future be Better Tomorrow? The Growth Prospects of Transition Economies Revisited," *Journal of Comparative Economics* 29, no. 4 (December 2001), 663–676; Nauro F. Campos and Frabizio Coricelli, "Growth in Transition: What we Know, What we Don't, and What We Should," *Journal of Economic Literature* 40, no. 3 (December 2002), 793–836.

13. Elizabetta Falcetti, Tatiana Lysenko, and Peter Sanfey, "Reforms and Growth in Transition: Re-examining the Evidence," *Journal of Comparative Economics* 34 (2006), 421–445; Evzen Kocenda, "Macroeconomic Convergence on Transition Countries," *Journal of Comparative Economics* 29 (2001), 1–23; Ali M. Kutan and Taner M. Yigit, "Nominal and Real Stochastic Convergence of Transition Economies," *Journal of Comparative Economics* 32, no. 1 (March 2004), 23–36.

14. Luc Moers, "How Important are Institutions for Growth in Transition Economies?" 16 February 1999; Oleh Havrylyshyn, "Recovery and Growth in Transition Economies: A Decade of Evidence," IMF Staff Papers, fo. 45, Special Issue, 2001; Cevdet Denizer, "Stabilization, Adjustment, and Growth Prospects in Transition Economies," World Bank Research Working Paper No. 1855, November 1997; Katerina Lyroudi, John Papanastasiou, Athanasios Vamvakidis, "Foreign Direct Investment and Economic Growth in Transition Economies," *South Eastern Journal of Economics* 1 (2004), 97–110.

15. Hiranya K. Nath, "Trade, Foreign Direct Investment and Growth: Evidence From Transition Economies," Sam Houston State University, Department of Economics and International Business, Working Paper Series, No. SHSU_ECO_WP05-044; Stanley Fischer, Ratna Sahay, and Carlos A. Vegh, "Stabilization and Growth in Transition Economies: The Early Experience," *Journal of Economic Perspectives* 10, no. 2 (Spring 1996), 45–66.

16. Saul Estrin, Giovanni Urga, Stephana Lazarova, and James W. Maw, "Privatization Methods and Economic Growth in Transition Economies," Cass Business School Research Paper FEEM, Working Paper No. 105.04, July 2004; Sergio Godoy and Joseph E. Stiglitz, "Growth, Initial Conditions, Law and Speed of Privatization in Transition Countries," NBER Working Paper No. 11992, January 2006; Karsten Staehr, "Reforms and Growth in Transition Economies: Complementarity, Sequencing and Speed," Institute for Economics in Transition, Bank of Finland, Discussion Paper 1/2003; Constantin Sonin, "Private Protection of Property Rights, Inequality, and Economic Growth in Transition Economies," Russian-European Center for Economic Policy, New Economic School, Moscow.

17. Edgar L. Feige and Ivica Urban, "Measuring Underground (Unobserved, Non-observed, Unrecorded) Economies on Transition Countries: Can We Trust GDP?" *Journal of Comparative Economics* 36, no. 2 (June 2008), 287–306; See, for example, the discussion in Paul Seabright, ed., *The Vanishing Ruble: Barter Networks and Non-Monetary Transactions in Post-Soviet Societies* (Cambridge: Cambridge University Press, 2000); Wendy Carlin, Steven Fries, Mark Schaffer, and Paul Seabright, "Barter and Non" *Working Paper No. 50*, June 2000; Eric Friedman, Simon Johnson, Daniel Kaufmann, and Pablo Zoido-Lobaton, "Dodging the Grabbing Hand: The Determinants of Unofficial Activity in 69 Countries," *Journal of Public Economics* 76 (2000), 459–493; Friedrich Schneider and Dominik H. Enste, "Shadow Economies: Size, Causes, and Consequences." *Journal of Economic Literature* 38, no. 1 (March 2000), 77–114; "Monetary Transactions in Transition Economies: Evidence from a Cross-Country Survey," *EBRD*.

18. The EBRD provides a useful summary of estimates. For example, in the Transition Report 2009, there is a summary of fourteen different estimates for GDP growth in 2009. See EBRD, Transition Report 23009: "Transition in crisis?" (London: EBRD, 2009).

Recommended Readings

George T. Abed and Hamid R. Davoodi, "Corruption, Structural Reforms, and Economic Performance in the Transition Economies," IMF Working Paper *WP/00/132*, July 2000.

Paschalis A. Arvanitidis, George Petrakos, and Sotiris Pavleas, "On the Dynamics of Growth Performance: An Expert Survey," *Contributions to Political Economy* 29, no. 1 (2010), 59–86.

A. Aslund, P. Boone, and S. Johnson, "How to Stabilize: Lessons from Post-Communist Countries," *Brookings Papers on Economic Activity* 81, no. 1, 217–234.

David Barlow, "Growth in Transition Economies: A Trade Policy Perspective," *Economics of Transition* 14, no. 3 (July 2006), 505–515.

Robert J. Barro, "Economic Growth in a Cross Section of Countries," *Quarterly Journal of Economics* 106, no. 2 (1991), 447–443.

Robert J. Barro and Sala-I-Martin, "Convergence Across States and Regions," *Brookings Papers on Economic Activity*, no. 1 (January–March, 1991), 107–158.

———, "Convergence," *Journal of Political Economy* 100, no. 2 (April 1992), 223–251.

Thorston Beck and Luc Laeven, "Institution Building and Growth in Transition Economies" (Washington, D.C.: World Bank, April 2005).

Oliver Blanchard and Michael Kremer, "Disorganization," *Quarterly Journal of Economics* 112, no. 4 (1997), 1091–1126.

———, Kenneth A. Froot, and Jeffrey D. Sachs, (eds), *The Transition in Eastern Europe*, Vol. 2 (Chicago: University of Chicago Press, 1994).

———, *The Transition in Eastern Europe*, Vol. 1 (Chicago: University of Chicago Press, 1994).

Josef Brada and Arthur King, "Is There a 'J' Curve for the Transition from Socialism to Capitalism?" *Economics of Planning* 25, no. 1 (1992), 37–52.

———, "The Transformation From Communism to Capitalism: How Far, How Fast?" *Post-Soviet Affairs* 9, no. 2 (1993), 87–110.

Nauro F. Campos, "Will the Future be Better Tomorrow? The Growth Prospects of Transition Economies Revisited" *Journal of Comparative Economics* 29, no. 4 (December 2001), 663–676.

——— and Fabrizio Coricelli, "Growth in Transition: What We Know, What We Don't, and What We Should," *Journal of Economic Literature* 40, no. 3 (September 2002), 793–836.

Wendy Carlin, Steven Fries, Mark Schaffer, and Paul Seabright, "Barter and Non-Monetary Transactions in Transition Economies: Evidence from a Cross-Country Survey," EBRD Working Paper *No. 50*, June 2000.

Bernard Chavance, "Formal and Informal Institutional Change: The Experience of Post-Socialist Transformation," *The European Journal of Comparative Economics* 5, no. 1 (June 2008).

Simon Commander and Christian Mumssem, "Understanding Barter in Russia," EBRD Working Paper No. 37, December 1998.

Mark De Broeck and Vincent Koen, "The Great Contractions in Russia, the Baltics and Other Countries of the Former Soviet Union: A View from the Supply Side," IMF Working Paper *QW/00/32*, March 2000.

Martha de Melo and Alan Gelb, "A Comparative Analysis of Twenty-Eight Transition Economies in Europe and Asia," *Post-Soviet Geography and Economics* 37, no. 5 (May 1996), 265–285.

——— and Cevdet Denizer, "From Plan to Market: Patterns of Transition," *World Bank Economic Review* 10, no. 3 (1996), 397–424.

Cevdet Denizer, "Stabilization, Adjustment, and Growth Prospects in Transition Econo-mies," World Bank Research Working Paper *No. 1855*, November 1997.

Axel Dreher, Christos Kotsoglannis, and Steve McCorriston, "Corruption Around the World: Evidence From a Structural Model," *Journal of Comparative Economics* 35, no. 3 (September 2007), 443–466.

EBRD, *Transition Report 2000* (Paris: EBRD, 2000).

———, *Transition Report 2001: Energy in Transition* (Paris: EBRD, 2001).

———, *Transition Report Update* (Paris: EBRD, 2002).

———, *Transition Report 2009: Transition in Crisis?* (Paris: EBRD, 2009).

———, Transition Report 2011: Crisis and Transition: The Peoples Perspective (Paris: EBRD, 2011).

Maurice Ernst, Michael Alexeev, and Paul Marer, *Transforming the Core* (Boulder, Colo.: Westview Press, 1996).

Saul Estrin, Giovanni Urga, and Stepana Lazarova, "Testing for Ongoing Convergence in Transition Economies, 1970–1998," *Journal of Comparative Economies* 29 (2001), 677–691.

———, John Bennett, Giovanni Urga, and James W. Maw, "Privatisation Methods and Economic Growth in Transition Economies," *Cass Business School Research Paper*, FEEM Working Paper No. 105.04, July 2004.

Pauyl Evans and Georgios Karras, "Convergence Revisited," *Journal of Monetary Economics* 37, no. 2 (April 1996), 249–265.

Elisabetta Falcetti, Tatiana Lysenko, and Peter Sanfey, "Reforms and Growth in Transition: Re-Examining the Evidence," *Journal of Comparative Economics* 34 (2006), 421–445.

Edgar L. Feige and Ivica Urban, "Measuring Underground (Unobserved, non-Observed, Unrecorded) Economies in Transition Countries: Can We Trust GDP?" *Journal of Comparative Economics* 36, no. 2 (June 2008), 287–306.

Jan Fidrmuc, "Economic Reform, Democracy and Growth During Post-Communist Transition," *European Journal of Political Economy*.

Stanley Fischer and Ratna Sahay, "The Transition After Ten Years," IMF Working Paper WP/00/30, 2000.

———, and Carlos A. Vegh, "Stabilization and Growth in Transition Economies: The Early Experience," *Journal of Economic Perspective* 10, no. 2 (Spring 1996), 45–66.

John Foster and J. Stanley Metcalfe, *Frontiers of Evolutionary Economics* (Northampton, Mass.: Edward Elgar, 2001).

Eric Friedman, Simon Johnson, Daniel Kaufmann, and Pablo Zoido-Lobaton, "Dodging the Grabbing Hand: The Determinants of Unofficial Activity in 69 Countries," *Journal of Public Economics* 76 (2000), 459–493.

Norbert Funke, "Timing and Sequencing of Reforms: Competing Views and the Role of Credibility," *Kyklos* (1993), 337–362.

Sergio Godoy and Joseph E. Stiglitz, "Growth, Initial Conditions, Law and Speed of Privat-ization in Transition Countries: 11 Years Later," NBER Working Paper No. 11992, January 2006.

Stanislaw Gomulka, "Output: Causes of Decline and Recovery," in Peter Boone, Stanislaw Gomulka, and Richard Layard, eds., *Emerging from Communism: Lessons from Russia, China and Eastern Europe* (Cambridge, Mass.: MIT Press, 1998), 13–41.

Daniel Gros and Marc Suhrcke, "Ten Years After: What Is Special About Transition Countries?" EBRD Working Paper *No. 56*, August 2000.

Paul Hare and Tamas Revesz, "Hungary's Transition to the Market: The Case Against a Big-Bang," *Economic Policy* 14 (1992).

Oleh Havrylyshyn, "Recovery and Growth in Transition: A Decade of Evidence," *IMF Staff Papers* Vol. 45, Special Issue, 2001.

Geoffrey M. Hodgson, *Evolution and Institutions: On Evolutionary Economics and the Evolution of Economics* (Northampton, Mass.: Edward Elgar, 2000).

Herman W. Hoen, "Shock Versus Gradualism in Central Europe Reconsidered," *Comparative Economic Studies* 38, no. 1 (Spring 1996), 1–20.

Robert Holzman, Janos Gacs, and George Winckler, *Output Decline in Eastern Europe* (Dordrecht: Kluwer Academic, 1995).

Grzegora W. Kolodko, "Globalization and Catching-Up: From Recession to Growth in Transition Economies," IMF Working Paper, WP/00/100, June 2000.

Janos Kornai, "Transformational Recession: The Main Causes," *Journal of Comparative Economics* 19, no. 39 (1994).

Gary Krueger and Marek Ciolko, "A Note on Initial Conditions and Liberalization During Transition," *Journal of Comparative Economics* 28, no. 4, (December 1998), 718–734.

Ali M. Kutan and Taner M. Yigit, "Nominal and Real Stochastic Convergence of Transition Economies," *Journal of Comparative Economics* 32, no. 1 (March 2004), 23–36.

Ross Levine and David Renelt, "A Sensitivity Analysis of Cross-Country Growth Regressions," *The American Economic Review* 82, no. 4 (September 1992), 942–963.

Katerina Lyroudi, John Papanastasiou, and Athanasios Vamkadidis, "Foreign Direct Investment and Economic Growth in Transition Economies," *South Eastern Europe Journal of Economics* 1 (2004), 97–110.

Karen Macours and Johan F. M. Swinnen, "Causes of Output Decline in Economic Transition: The Case of Central and Eastern European Agriculture," *Journal of Comparative Economics* 28, no. 1 (March 2000), 172–206.

Pak Hung Mo, "Corruption and Economic Growth," *Journal of Comparative Economics* 29, no. 1 (March 2001), 66–79.

Peter Murrell, "The Transition According to Cambridge, Mass.," *Journal of Economic Literature* 33, no. 1 (March 1995), 164–178.

———, "Can Neoclassical Economics Underpin the Reform of Centrally Planned Economies?" *Journal of Economic Perspectives* 5, no. 4 (Fall 1991), 59–76.

———, Evolution in Economics and in the Economic Reform of Centrally Planned Economies," in Christopher C. Clague and Gordon Rausser, eds., *The Emergence of Market Economies in Eastern Europe* (Cambridge: Blackwell, 1992), 35–53.

———, "What is Shock Therapy? What Did it do in Poland and Russia?" *Post-Soviet Affairs* 9, no. 2 (April–June 1993), 11–40.

———, "Evolutionary and Radical Approaches to Economic Reform," *Economics of Planning* 25, no. 1 (1992), 79–95.

———, and Mancur Olson, "The Devolution of Centrally Planned Economies," *Journal of Comparative Economics* 15 (1991), 239–265.

Hiranya K. Nath, "Trade, Foreign Direct Investment and Growth: Evidence From Transition Economies," Sam Houston State University, Department of Economics and International Business, Working Paper Series, No. SHSU_ECO_WP05-04.

Gur Ofer and Richard Pomfret, eds., *The Economic Prospects of the CIS: Sources of Long Term Growth* (New York: Edward Elgar, 2004).

Vladimir Popov, "Shock Therapy versus Gradualism: The End of the Debate (Explaining the Magnitude of the Transformational Recession)," *Comparative Economic Studies* 42, no. 1 (Spring 2000), 1–57.

Roxana Radulescu and David Barlow, "The Relationship Between Policies and Growth in Transition Economies," *Economics of Transition* 10, no. 3 (November 2002), 719–745.

Alexandre Repkine and Patrick Paul Welsch, "Evidence of European Trade and Investment U-Shaping Industrial Output in Bulgaria, Hungary, Poland, and Romania," *Journal of Comparative Economics* 27, no. 4 (December 1999), 730–752.

Gerard Roland, *Transition and Economics: Politics, Markets, and Firms* (Boston: MIT Press, 2000).

Jeffrey D. Sachs, "The Transition at Mid-Decade," *American Economic Review Papers and Proceedings* 86, no. 2 (May 1996), 128–133.

Paul Seabright, ed., *The Vanishing Ruble: Barter Networks and Non-Monetary Transactions in Post-Soviet Societies* (Cambridge: Cambridge University Press, 2000).

Constantin Sonin, "Private Protection of Property Rights, Inequality, and Economic Growth in Transition Economies," Russian-European Center for Economic Policy, New Economic School, Moscow.

Karsten Staehr, "Reforms and Economic Growth in Transition Economies: Complementarity, Sequencing and Speed," Institute for Economies in Transition, Bank of Finland, Discussion Paper 1/2003.

Joseph E. Stiglitz, *Whither Socialism?* (Cambridge, Mass.: MIT Press, 1991).

———, "More Instruments and Broader Goals: Moving Towards the Post-Washington Consensus" (Helsinki, Finland: 1998 WIDER Annual Lecture, January 7, 1998).

———, *Globalization and Its Discontents* (New York: Norton, 2002).

Pasquale Tridico, "Institutional Change and Governance Indexes in Transition Economies: The Case of Poland," *The European Journal of Institutional Economics* 3, no. 2 (December 2006), 197–238.

Jozef van Brabant, "Lessons From the Wholesale Transformation in the East," *Comparative Economic Studies* 35, no. 4 (1993), 73–102.

Hans van Ees and Harry Garretsen, "The Theoretical Foundations of Reform in Eastern Europe: Big Bang versus Gradualism and the Limitations of Neo-Classical Theory," *Economic Systems* 18, no. 1 (March 1994), 1–13.

Paolo Verme, "Pro-Poor Growth During Exceptional Growth: Evidence from a Transition Economy," *The European Journal of Comparative Economics* 3, no. 1 (2006), 3–14.

World Bank, *From Plan to Market: The World Development Report*, 1996 (Washington, D.C.: The World Bank, 1996).

Introducing Markets: Privatization and the Decline of Government

The most fundamental element in the identification of differing economic systems is property rights. The cornerstone of a market economy is private property, based on clearly identified **property rights** (*claims for the ownership and use of real property*) and a system of markets and exchange resulting in prices that appropriately reflect relative scarcities in both factor and product markets. These prices serve as the most basic mechanism of resource allocation in a market economy. Given the almost complete absence of private property in the command economies, the ill-defined nature of state property rights, and the minimal use of prices (set administratively) for resource allocation, it is not surprising that the initial policy focus of transition was the creation of markets through a process of privatization along with the abandonment of state-set prices.[1]

Beyond these general observations, however, both the theory and the practice of privatization have proved to be complex and controversial, and privatization has become a contemporary policy issue that extends well beyond the transition economies. Indeed, although our focus in this chapter is the nature of privatization in the transition economies, we will see that privatization is a worldwide phenomenon. We begin this chapter with a discussion of the background of privatization. Then we will address theory, policy, real-world applications, and finally results. The outcomes of privatization worldwide are relevant to our analysis, but we will focus mainly on the transition economies.

Privatization in Transition

The Background

The story of privatization is much more significant than one might suspect from the contemporary transition setting. As we have emphasized before, the role of the state in the process of economic development is of great importance. This is especially clear to systems analysts because differing roles of the state imply very different organizational arrangements and hence different economic systems. Traditionally, the role of government in an economy has been a key element in system classification. A socialist economic system would be likely to have a larger role for government (measured in terms of government spending as a portion of total output) than a capitalist system. Also, in any economic system we characterize as a "welfare state," the role of government is in part as a mechanism for both production and redistribution.

Even judged within a narrow framework of privatization, where **state-owned enterprises (SOEs)**—*firms or businesses whose assets are owned by the state*— are replaced by private firms, the contemporary setting of privatization extends far beyond the transition economies. Indeed, the onset of a declining role for SOEs pre-dates the transition era. In both developed and developing market and mixed economies, reducing the role of the state through privatization has been a major policy thrust since the early 1980s. One can argue that this choice fundamentally defines the nature of the **social contract**—*the relationship between the people and the state as defined through institutions, laws, policies, etc.*—and thus will differ according to cultural and historical settings.

In the field of comparative economic systems, the role of government in an economy, measured in various ways, has been studied extensively.[2] However, before the contemporary era of privatization, there had been only modest theorizing about why the importance of government differs significantly from one case (country) to another as well as varying over time. Moreover, there has been considerable controversy over how best to measure the role of government in different economies. Although this issue has already been discussed in Chapters 3 and 4, it is useful to return to the subject as we assess the nature and meaning of privatization in the 1990s.

In Figure 18.1, we present a picture of the role of government in a number of very different economies, characterizing the importance of government in terms of the ratio of government spending to total output—in this case, for the year 1997. Several conclusions can be drawn from this simple comparison. First, even a quick glance suggests that the role of government as measured here is quite different in different economies, varying from a low of 8 percent in Azerbaijan to a high of 30 percent in Croatia. In spite of the fact that conceptual and measurement issues make comparison difficult, these are clearly important differences. Second, some of the evidence in Figure 18.1 seems to conform to our expectations, even though simple explanations for the observed outcomes are not always available. For example, we would probably expect Sweden (often characterized as a welfare state) to have a large government role, whereas the United States, at the other end of the spectrum, should have a much smaller role for government. The data broadly conform to these expectations. But why is the role of government fully ten points greater in Croatia than in the Czech Republic, two countries that were part of a larger single country until 1993? And why is the role of government apparently so small (just over 10 percent) in Russia, when many view the role of the state as traditionally very important there? To some degree, differences may be explained by measurement problems. One could argue that the higher the level of

FIGURE **18.1**   G/GDP for Selected Countries, 1997

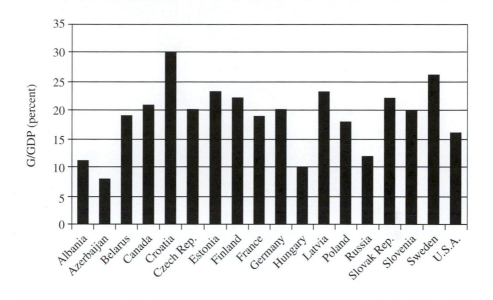

Source: World Bank, *World Development Indicators 1999* (Washington, D.C.: World Bank, 1999), Table 4.9. Reprinted with permission.

development of an economy, the more accurate it is to use government spending as a measure of the government's role in the economy. Thus comparing Canada and the United States in these terms is more meaningful than comparing Croatia and Canada. However, the more fundamental concern is probably how we measure the role of government in a mixed economy and the extent to which government spending actually captures the impact of government. This is a different issue, although an important one in our assessment of transition economies.

Figure 18.2 provides a summary of the role of government from 1950 through 2000 (at five-year intervals) for the United States. The picture that emerges here can be readily explained by reference to historical facts. For example, the growth of the government sector during the era of the "Great Society" (the 1960s) is evident, as is its decline during the era of privatization (the 1980s and thereafter). Even during this relatively short time, the changes in the importance of government in this context are quite significant. These changes can be explained in part by privatization implemented before the beginning of the transition era.

What are the traditional explanations for the varying roles of government in the economic systems of different nations? Traditionally, government involvement has been justified on the grounds of either *equity* (*fairness*) or *efficiency* (*the relationship between inputs and outputs*). From an equity viewpoint, government is involved in redistribution, usually sanctioned by society through a voting process. From an efficiency standpoint, much of the contemporary literature on privatization argues that, other things being equal, production can be conducted more efficiently by private

FIGURE **18.2**   G/GDP for the United States, 1950–2000

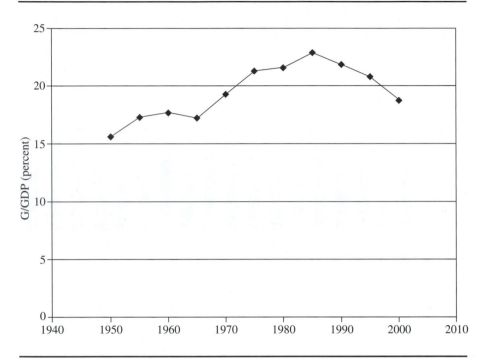

Source: U.S. Census Bureau, *Statistical Abstract of the United States* (Washington, D.C.: U.S. Department of Commerce, various issues).

than by nonprivate enterprise.[3] However, from both equity and efficiency standpoints, the case in support of government activity has been rather broader. For example, there are traditional public good and/or externality arguments justifying a role for government. And there are regulatory arguments, although these can extend to equity issues in different national settings. Thus on one end of the spectrum, our views of government as a regulatory mechanism in a market economy have changed significantly over time, while at the other end of the spectrum, so have our views on government as a component of financing the welfare state.[4] These issues are just as important in the Western European economic systems as they have been (and still are) in the East European transition settings.

Finally, we have argued that before the contemporary era in which privatization has been emphasized, theoretical explanations for the growth of government have generally been sparse. One might expect some degree of cyclical variation, but explanations for long-term change tend to focus on issues such as wars and the idea of displacement, in part fueled by a self-aggrandizing bureaucracy. Therefore it is common to argue that when the role of government increases (for example, as a consequence of war), that role will decline after the war is over, but not to prewar levels.[5]

To put it differently, the sense that a strong role for government in an economy is important has declined sharply, especially in the latter decades of the twentieth century, to be replaced in both East and West by a view that the unfettered market is superior. Thus, beginning in the 1980s and continuing into a new century, privatization has become a front-burner issue, often described in the transition setting as *mass privatization*, or *shifting the ownership of real property from the state to individuals on a wide scale rather than on a selective basis*. As we shall see, privatization in existing market economies, both developed and less developed, is very different from privatization in the transition setting. It is for these reasons that interest in privatization in the postcommand economies is so intense. Moreover, many would argue that the Western degree of reliance on privatization and markets is inappropriate for many transition economies, where a long-term trajectory is much more likely to be based on a mixed system.

The Context

Although state ownership was not, technically, universal in the command economies, nevertheless in most cases there was very limited private property, limited private economic activity, and for the most part an absence of markets. If a state-dominated command economy is to become a market economy dominated by the private marketplace, then state-owned property must be conveyed into an emerging private sector. Such a process implies that it will be possible to identify property rights and, through a process of sale or distribution, to convey these rights to new owners. Unfortunately, these preconditions were seldom met in the transition economies. Property rights were difficult to identify and hence difficult to convey. Without purchasing power and markets through which demand could be exercised, it was not clear how the property rights would be conveyed (in most cases sold) to new owners. The initial absence of financial intermediation meant that investment funds would generally not be available as a mechanism to create investment from savings. Moreover, because state claims to property were largely a result of confiscation during the command era, the issue of **restitution** (*compensation for property seized by the state under Communist governments*) arose during the transition era, especially in those countries where confiscation had been relatively recent (Eastern Europe as opposed to the former USSR).[6] These and related considerations have sharply delineated the process of privatization as it has unfolded in the transition economies and in the Western market economies.

The initial conditions that existed in the planned economies at the onset of transition were also important in other respects for the process of privatization. For example, the absence of a legal framework made it hard to define initial property rights—and thus especially hard to change ownership arrangements so that private property rights could be clearly delineated. Much of the legal infrastructure that we take for granted in a market economy, such as the ability to develop, sign, and enforce **contracts** (*an enforceable agreement between two or more individuals*), was largely absent at the onset of transition. At the very least, significant modification of these arrangements was necessary to suit new and very different circumstances. Moreover, the assets that were to be privatized—especially industrial firms—bore little relation to their brethren in market economies, a matter we emphasized during our discussion of initial conditions in Chapter 16.[7] In many cases, there was a ***soft budget constraint*** (*in command economies, the concept that enterprise budgets can be exceeded without consequences*), staffing levels were inordinately high to sustain a state-supported ***full-employment policy*** (*a government policy whose objective is the ability to sustain jobs for all who want them*), and, most important, ***scale*** (*the size of an enterprise*) issues were often dominant. We have already emphasized the extent to which both vertical and horizontal integration were used to resolve difficulties in the command era—for example, irregular availability of supply (inputs) from sources external to the firm. In many cases, the impact of foreign trade had been minor, and enterprises were overly large, with significant but technologically dated capital structures. In these settings, privatization would prove difficult, and various approaches were used.

Although our emphasis here is privatization in the transition economies, the privatization experience in market economies (both industrialized economies and emerging market economies) offers us a sharp contrast with which to assess the transition experience.

In a market economy, privatization is conceptually feasible, and easier to achieve, under a variety of conditions. First, most privatization in market economies is not mass privatization but rather selective privatization, sometimes related to production but often related to services, regulation, and other government activities. Second, the product or service to be privatized can often be clearly identified. Thus it is not surprising that in the early stages of privatization in market economies, services such as trash collection, janitorial duties, security services, and the like can be readily privatized. In such cases, the product or service is known and most often homogeneous. Third, in the market setting, the legal infrastructure is critical in that a contract can be written, and performance in the fulfillment of the contract can be monitored and ultimately enforced. Note, then, that even in cases where the provision of a service is being privatized, rather than an asset's (such as a firm) being sold, the process is relatively clear. Fourth, markets and financial arrangements exist, so it is possible to make reasonable decisions based on cost/benefit analysis, including some assessment of both private and social costs and benefits.

Finally, it is possible to assess the outcomes of privatization, largely within the framework of efficiency. For example, indicators of firm-level behavior (for example, profitability, dividend payout, and labor productivity) can be measured to examine changes in performance. Thus at the firm level in a market economy, we can examine the results of economic activity before and after privatization to arrive at an assessment of outcomes. In the transition economy where markets are imperfect, obtaining and assessing this type of evidence is difficult. Moreover, we will discover that assessing the results of privatization is not a simple task, especially when we move away from the firm toward a higher level of (societal) aggregation. It is this theme that in the end returns us to the role of the state as a purveyor of regulatory and well-being components in what may become mixed economic systems. These are important issues, especially in different national and historical settings, and they are a fundamental reason why, even among Western market economies, the roles played by the government sector have been and will probably remain very different.

The Transition Setting

The Stages of Privatization

Thus far we have emphasized that the contemporary era of privatization pre-dates, and is much more significant historically than, the privatization taking place under the rubric of transition. At the same time, it is well to note the immense magnitude and difficult circumstances of mass privatization in the transition setting. We will see that although national differences are significant, mass privatization neverthe-less exhibited broad similarities in different settings as the need to proceed rapidly took center stage.

It is useful to characterize mass privatization as taking place in the four stages outlined in Table 18.1. These four stages have generally been developed and imple-mented under some form of **state privatization agency**, which, *in transition econo-mies, is a state agency responsible for organizing and executing privatization.* These agencies were conceptually the holders of state property rights and would, under rules and regulations promulgated by the government, have the responsibility of shifting the economy from a state-property base to a private-property base.[8]

Before we deal with these stages in greater detail, it is important to appreciate the fact that the rules governing these stages were themselves a matter of contro-versy. For example, in the case of Russia, it was the Duma that had to define the role of the state sector in a new, privatized economy. This proved to be—and indeed remains—a difficult task. Nevertheless, some boundaries were established; for example, sustaining natural resources and providing for national defense remained responsibilities of the state sector for a variety of traditional reasons. Issues such as common property and the privatization of sectors other than produc-tion (housing, for example) involved special problems. These sorts of issues tended to make privatization more appealing for small-scale enterprises, such as those in the service sector.

Carrying out the steps identified in Table 18.1 has turned out to be very prob-lematic in some cases, less so in others. Although the identification of properties to privatize is in theory a reasonable task, in many cases the nature of existing SOEs (large or very large scale, vertical integration, capital-intensiveness) made the pro-cess of privatization difficult. **Corporatization**, or *the creation of a corporate type of ownership with shares that can be traded*, implied a means of control, although sale would be difficult without standard mechanisms for the valuation of shares. Indeed, the issue of **valuation** (*assessing and determining the value of an asset*

TABLE **18.1**   Stages of Privatization in the Transition Setting

Develop a legal framework.	Identify properties to privatize.	Create a corporate structure.	Distribute corporate shares.	Restructure enterprises.

Source: Compiled by the authors.

such as an enterprise for sale purposes) assumed great importance during the early years of transition.

For example, if a firm is to be sold in a market economy, there are standard mechanisms for establishing some concept of market value. Where a share structure exists, this is an obvious mechanism for valuation. Moreover, even in the absence of a share structure, accounting approaches or some variant of the ***present value*** (*the value on a given date of a future stream of monies usually discounted*) of expected future profit streams can provide an assessment of value at a particular time. In the transition setting, however, there were no markets, legal and accounting rules were typically weak and inadequate, and as a consequence, ***transparency*** (*the openness of a process such that all aspects of the process can be observed and assessed*) in valuation would be impossible to achieve.

Perhaps the most important constraints on privatization in the transition economies have been the absence of purchasing power, limited foreign interest, and the fact that entrepreneurial spirit had so long been stifled in countries with state-controlled systems. This may be why privatization vouchers were widely used to distribute shares to the population. Vouchers seemed to make sense in the transition setting, although, as we will see, they were subject to significant abuse and limitations.

Before we turn to a discussion of the mechanics of privatization and then attempt to assess the results, it is important to note that restructuring, the final stage of the process outlined in Table 18.1, is in many ways the most critical stage of the privatization process. Restructuring is a key focal point as we examine the results of mass privatization in a new century. Many have argued that, whether privatization is based on equity, efficiency, or more general concepts of a role for the state, the transfer of a state-owned enterprise to private owners is not meaningful unless the new owners change the way the property rights are exercised. That is, the fundamental purpose of privatization is to change the nature of resource allocation. This restructuring implies that decision-making arrangements within the firm will change, and when they do change, the results of the firm's operation will be different. This process has been described as making changes in ***corporate governance***, which is *the manner in which the internal operations of an enterprise are observed and assessed*. Such restructuring has been very difficult.

The Privatization Process

As transition began in the late 1980s and early 1990s, there were no simple road maps for the privatization process. Moreover, important differences in the conditions that prevailed when the transition began were to influence the approach to privatization in various settings. Finally, although economic theory would provide some guidelines, political issues also affected the policy process. Much of the early literature devoted to privatization in the transition economies focused on "strategies" of transition—specifically the speed and sequencing of change, issues that we examined in Chapter 17. From the perspective of privatization, however, the issue was one of guarding against ***reversibility*** (*the possibility, during transition, that the process of moving from plan to market might be reversed or slowed*) by finding the optimal pace at which privatization should take place to ensure completion of the movement toward a market economy. As privatization proceeded, the issue of cost, and especially social cost (growing levels of unemployment, for example), became a crucial theme in policy discussions.

Finally, it is important to understand that the implementation of privatization *by sector* and *by industry* has been uneven. In all cases, certain sectors (such as defense and energy) were to be retained, at least for some time, by the state. In addition, although Western attention had focused on agriculture, especially in the Soviet case, privatization in agriculture has been uneven and for the most part unsuccessful in the Russian case. Privatization *by region* has also been uneven in large countries such as Russia, partly because of differences in the emerging regional administrative structures and also because of regional differences inherited from the past.

The scale of the industrial establishment also turned out to be important in the process of privatization. Understandably, much of the policy focus centered on medium-sized and large industrial establishments. However, for a variety of reasons, privatization has proved to be more difficult when the largest enterprises are the targets—a problem evident in the contemporary evolution of the Chinese economy. At the other end of the spectrum, privatization has proved to be much easier for **de novo privatization**, which is *expansion of the private sector usually by the creation of new (usually small) firms*.

Although the process of privatization has varied from one transition setting to another, two major approaches (or combinations of these approaches) dominated. In **direct sale** (*the transfer of ownership directly from one person to another usually absent intermediate mechanisms, such as an auction*) of enterprises to buyers, sale could take place either through **outsider privatization** (*the sale of an enterprise to persons not connected in any way to the enterprise*) or through **insider privatization**, (*the sale of an enterprise to those who are employed by the enterprise*). The actual method of sale could vary from a direct negotiation between buyer and seller to an auction or other indirect method.

A second major approach to privatization was the use of **vouchers**, which are *documents that represent an ownership claim that can be executed to acquire the shares of an enterprise*. Note that these approaches might overlap in that vouchers could be used by "insiders" to gain control of enterprises in which they were employed.[9] Also, depending on the rules established, an employee of one firm who possessed a voucher could use this mechanism to purchase shares in a different firm. In the Russian case, with financial markets very limited, the intent of the voucher program was to pass equity to workers and others within the firm and to do so reasonably quickly. However, voucher privatization did not raise funds, and this was a major problem in a setting where enterprises needed access to new capital.

The approaches were, however, different. Vouchers were appealing because there was little purchasing power available to buy shares of stock. The population did not have sufficient funds, and hence buyers (except perhaps external buyers) could not be found. At the same time, it was argued that the use of vouchers would not provide working capital for the enterprise, a critical issue given that the state was withdrawing from this function, a hard budget constraint would be imposed, and both events would occur largely in the absence of traditional capital markets. This aspect of privatization has been viewed as especially important because significant capital investment would be necessary for restructuring. Finally, a major focus of early privatization discussions was the issue of restructuring—specifically, what would the different approaches to privatization imply for desired changes in decision making? Would external buyers be more likely to make changes, or would the knowledge of internal buyers be required?

During the early stages of transition, the voucher approach (used, for example, in Russia and the Czech Republic) was proposed as a means to achieve mass privatization very quickly. Note that during the early years, both theoretical and practical arguments were advanced for pursuing privatization at a rapid pace. These arguments were based in part on the simultaneous privatization of SOE components and on the political sense of creating and setting in motion an irreversible process.[10] The threat of reversibility arose from fear that the long-term economic gains to be derived from privatization might well be offset by short-term costs, hence eroding popular support for privatization programs.

In the Russian case (one of the most important), the Russian government distributed to every person, in 1993, a voucher with a face value of 10,000 rubles. These vouchers could then be exchanged for shares of stock at a place of work, exchanged elsewhere through financial intermediaries, or, as a last resort, sold in a secondary (street) market. Direct sale of an enterprise or organization, sometimes through an auction, was one transaction in which these vouchers could be used, along with ruble cash and/or credit, where the latter was available.[11]

The difficulties with the voucher process immediately became evident. Judged in terms of the importance of the private sector (for example, private sector output as a share of total output), the private sector grew rapidly in many transition economies. But such measurements, although clearly necessary, were inadequate as indicators of the effectiveness of changes in the allocation of resources.

In the Russian case, share structures were defined, and yet "insider privatization" emerged, in which small numbers of influential individuals (former managers, party members, and the like) in effect gained control of the enterprises being privatized. The result was a growing concentration of wealth and what became known as *asset stripping, the acquisition of valuable assets during privatization with the intent of financial gain rather than eventual enterprise restructuring.* Asset stripping can be seen as the attack on assets of value and the abandonment of other assets. Ironically, in earlier years it was generally thought that creating owners out of workers would be an effective route to privatization and revisions of corporate governance by those who knew the organization best. Evidence has shown, however, that the emerging internal coalitions did not always have the best interests of the organization at heart, resulting in a negative view of insider privatization.

Privatization: Assessing the Early Results

During the early stages of the transition era (the early 1990s) it was popular to assess privatization by examining the extent to which economic activity had in fact been privatized. For example, in Table 18.2 we present estimates of the percentages of economic activity privatized in various transition economies during the 1990s.

TABLE **18.2**   Private Sector Output as a Share of GDP (Percent)

	1992	1996	2000	2009
Russia	25	60	70	65
Kazakhstan	10	40	60	65
Ukraine	10	50	60	60
Poland	45	60	70	75
Estonia	25	70	75	80
Hungary	40	70	80	80
Czech Republic	30	75	80	n.a.

Source: EBRD *Transition Report: Energy in Transition* (London: EBRD, 2001), country assessments; EBRD *Transition Report 2006: Transition in Crisis?* (London: EBRD, 2009), Country Assessments.

Table 18.2 illustrates several points. First, judging from the evidence for the year 2000, in all of the economies there has been a very significant degree of privatization of output. Second, the starting positions were very different. In some countries, such as Ukraine, there was little private activity in the early 1990s, whereas in other cases, such as Poland, almost half of the output in the early 1990s was derived from the private sector. These two facts suggest that the pace of privatization has differed widely among the transition economies.

A useful way to assess the nature of privatization is the EBRD privatization index. This index, which ranges from 1 (little private ownership) to 4+ (standards typical of advanced industrial economies with at least 75 percent of enterprise assets in private ownership) is summarized in Table 18.3.

The data in Table 18.3 tell a similar story about privatization, with one important exception. In those countries that have pursued privatization less aggressively (such as Ukraine), there is a tendency for the privatization of large-scale enterprises to lag behind. We noted earlier in this chapter that privatizing small-scale enterprises is easier.

TABLE **18.3**   The EBRD Index of Privatization in Selected Transition Economies[a]

	1992	1996	2000	2009
Russia	2.0 (2.0)	4.0 (3.0)	4.0 (3.3)	4.0 (3.0)
Kazakhstan	2.0 (1.0)	3.3 (3.0)	4.0 (3.0)	4.0 (3.0)
Ukraine	1.0 (1.0)	3.0 (2.0)	3.3 (2.7)	4.0 (3.0)
Poland	4.0 (2.0)	4.3 (3.0)	4.3 (3.3)	4.3 (3.3)
Estonia	2.0 (1.0)	4.3 (4.0)	4.3 (4.0)	4.3 (4.0)
Hungary	2.0 (2.0)	4.0 (4.0)	4.3 (4.0)	4.3 (4.0)
Czech Republic	4.0 (2.0)	4.3 (4.0)	4.3 (4.0)	n.a.

[a]The data in parentheses refer to large-scale privatization; the remaining data refer to small-scale privatization.

Source: EBRD, *Transition Report 2001: Energy in Transition* (London: EBRD, 2001), country assessments; EBRD, *Transition Report 2009: Transition in Crisis?* (London: EBRD, 2009), country assessments.

Although this sort of evidence has been important for assessing the pace of transition and understanding sectoral differences, there is more to the story. Much of the contemporary literature on privatization quite correctly focuses on what we broadly term **restructuring**, or *the changing of the manner in which an enterprise is organized and functions internally*. What is restructuring? Why is it important? And why is it so difficult to measure and to assess?

The fundamental objective of creating new property rights is to change the nature of the decision-making arrangements in the newly privatized enterprises and organizations and, by so doing, to change the allocation of resources to improve efficiency. Restructuring is therefore the changing of decision-making arrangements (corporate governance) within an organization, predominantly, although not exclusively, in enterprises in the producing sector of the economy. In the end, restructuring is the critical outcome of the privatization process. Can we judge the success of restructuring?

Although the measures of private-sector shares that we have examined suffer from measurement problems, they are much simpler to gauge than restructuring. The latter would typically be judged by a wide variety of indicators—for example, efficiency indicators (real sales per employee), indicators of the effectiveness of financial markets (percentage of working capital raised in financial markets), and such performance indicators as profitability and dividends per share. An important indicator of restructuring is changes in levels of employment. This variable is often emphasized in the analysis of privatized enterprises on the theory that state firms might be expected to shed excess labor to become more attractive to potential purchasers. Unfortunately, although studies that examine key operating variables both before and after privatization are readily available for an assessment of restructuring in Western market economies, these types of studies are hard to come by for transition economies.

There are a great many studies on privatization and restructuring and, fortunately, some good surveys of these studies.[12] The studies of privatization in Western market economies generally suggest that restructuring does in fact occur, improving indicators of operating and financial performance. Privatized firms generally seem to show better performance than nonprivate firms, although the evidence on employment effects and issues pertaining to equity are less clear. However, studies reveal that more than privatization per se is necessary. Also essential are the emergence of new institutions, the existence of a legal infrastructure, and progress in the hardening of budgets. Most studies of privatization have been less successful in identifying the sources of improvement, but outside ownership and changes in management, along with the sorts of institutional changes noted, are all important in these studies.

Compared to studies done on privatization in Western market economies, studies on privatization and restructuring in the transition economies are generally survey-based and limited in scope.[13] Transition studies have focused on differences in ownership arrangements (for example, insider versus outsider ownership), the role of managers, the issue of soft budgets (an important holdover from the command era), product market competition, and the nature of the legal framework. Broadly speaking, the literature supports the view that enterprise restructuring has been less successful in the CIS countries than in the transition economies of Eastern Europe. Whereas this contrast is evident in many transition indicators, there is less agreement on why the CIS countries have performed less well on restructuring. A common argument is that in these cases, the institutions of the command era had been in place much longer and thus were harder to modify.[14] Again, we see the key influence that initial conditions had on progress in the transition era.

Studies of restructuring in the transition economies generally agree on several basic issues, although there are important differences by sector, region, method of privatization, and the like. First, performance improvements are generally better where there is some measure of outsider privatization—either new domestic owners external to the firm or (preferably) foreign owners. (Of course, it is possible that foreigners are simply more likely to be attracted to involvement in better-performing enterprises.) Second, most studies confirm the importance of management and (especially) managerial turnover—that is, the replacement of command era managers by new managers. Third, the development of hard budgets has been a critical factor, and empirical studies show that it is more likely to be achieved in Eastern European than in the CIS countries. Problems in this area doubtless result from a lengthy command era experience and also, in cases such as Russia, from the emergence of an important shadow economy.[15] Finally, recent studies have emphasized the importance of privatization and restructuring in sectors where competitive product markets exist, representing either domestic or foreign competition. Again, regional experiences differ. There is also growing emphasis on the emergence of new institutions, although the empirical evidence on this issue is recent and much research remains to be done.

Another approach to improving our understanding of mass privatization and restructuring in transition economies is to focus on indexes developed by various international organizations, such as the EBRD. Table 18.4 gives the recent scores of several transition economies on indexes of changes in corporate governance and commercial law.

TABLE 18.4   Changes in Corporate Governance and Commercial Law

Country	Corporate Governance and Restructuring[a]	Overall: Effectiveness and Extensiveness of Commercial Law, 2001[b]
Russia	2+	3+
Kazakhstan	2	4
Ukraine	2	3
Poland	3+	3+
Estonia	3+	4−
Hungary	3+	4

[a]Scale from 1 to 4+, where 1 indicates soft budget constraints and limited changes in corporate governance, and 4+ indicates performance standards of advanced industrial economies.
[b]Scale from 1 to 4+ indicating extensiveness and effectiveness of commercial law—pledge, bankruptcy, and company law.

Source: EBRD, *Transition Report 2001: Energy in Transition* (Paris: EBRD, 2001), Tables 2.2 and 2.1.1.

From the evidence presented in Table 18.4, it is clear that there have been significant improvements in corporate governance and the legal infrastructure surrounding the enterprise.[16] At the same time, there are important variations among the transition economies.

On balance, the evidence suggests that privatization has proceeded quite rapidly in the transition economies, although assessing the progress of restructuring has been difficult, and the experiences of individual transition economies have differed significantly from one another. Moreover, as the research literature is beginning to emphasize, there is more to the story of privatization than reduction of the state sector and gains in industrial efficiency. There is an important relationship between privatization and the emergence of financial markets, an issue of critical importance in all the transition economies—and especially in the CIS states, where financial markets are limited in scope and depth. The development of an appropriate legal infrastructure is also critical and will affect the distribution of ownership that ultimately emerges in the transition economies.[17]

Summary

- Privatization is much more than a process to change property-holding arrangements. Privatization implies fundamental changes in the role of the state in the economy.
- Privatization has occurred worldwide, in both industrialized and emerging market economies, but mass privatization in the transition economies has been the major focus of this chapter.
- Although there have been significant country differences in privatization, the process has generally involved a series of stages: development of a legal framework, identification of properties to be privatized, creation of a joint stock framework, and, finally, sale of the properties.
- The mechanisms for transference of property rights from the state to the private sector have varied from some form of direct sale (including the auction process) to a voucher arrangement used in Russia and the Czech Republic. The latter involves the distribution of vouchers (with a specified face value) that can be used to redeem shares in, for example, an enterprise.
- Early research interest focused on an overall assessment of the growth of the private sector in transition economies, whereas the contemporary literature focuses on restructuring, or changes in corporate governance (that is, changing resource allocation and decision making in the enterprise) with the objective of improving efficiency.
- Privatization has been broadly achievable, although controversial, and the impact and results of privatization have been much more evident in industrialized and emerging market economies than in transition economies.
- There is general agreement that among the transition economies, privatization and restructuring have been less successful in the CIS countries than in Eastern Europe, although the degree of variation from one case to another can be significant.

- The extent of privatization has been significant in many of the transition economies; assessing the extent and meaning of restructuring has been more difficult. In the transition economies, new (outsider) ownership enhances privatization, as does devoting attention to management and to the necessary financial and legal arrangements.
- In recent years, the emphasis has been on the development of competitive product markets and on the emergence of new institutions, such as financial markets capable of providing capital to restructuring enterprises. The development of a commercial legal framework is an important element in the transition settings. There remain, as always, important differences among countries, regions, and industrial sectors.

Key Terms

asset stripping—The acquisition of valuable assets during privatization with the intent of financial gain rather than eventual corporate restructuring.

contracts—An enforceable agreement between two or more individuals.

corporate governance—The manner in which the internal operations of an enterprise or business are organized and operated.

corporatization—The creation of a corporate type of ownership with shares that can be traded.

de novo privatization—Expansion of the private sector by the creation of new and usually small firms.

direct sale—The transfer of ownership from one person or persons to others usually absent intermediate mechanisms, such as an auction.

efficiency—The relationship between inputs and outputs.

equity—Fairness.

full-employment policy—A government policy whose objective is the ability to sustain jobs for all who want them.

insider privatization—The sale of an enterprise to those who are employed by the enterprise.

mass privatization—Shifting the ownership of real property from the state to individuals on a wide scale rather than on a selective basis.

outsider privatization—The sale of an enterprise to persons not connected in any way with the enterprise.

present value—The value on a given date of a future stream of monies usually discounted.

property rights—Claims for the ownership and use of real property.

restitution—In transition economies, the compensation for property seized by the state when Communist governments assumed power.

restructuring—Changing the manner in which an enterprise is organized and functions internally.

reversibility—The possibility, during transition, that the process of moving from plan to market might be slowed or reversed.

scale—The size of an enterprise.

social contract—The relationship between people and government defined through institutions, laws, policies, etc.

soft budget constraint—In command economies, the concept that enterprise budgets can be exceeded without consequences.

state-owned enterprises (SOEs)—Firms or business enterprises owned by the state.

state privatization agency—In transition economies, a state agency responsible for organizing and executing privatization.

transparency—The openness of a process such that all aspects of the process can be observed and assessed.

valuation—Assessing the worth of an enterprise for the purpose of sale.

vouchers—A document that represents an ownership claim that can be exercised to acquire the shares of an enterprise.

Notes

1. In most of the transition economies of Eastern Europe and the former Soviet Union, prices were released from state control during the early 1990s. Although the release of prices was selective, there was in nearly all countries a sharp spike of inflation, as expected.

2. There is a growing literature on the more general issues relating to the role of the state in differing economic systems. For a useful discussion, see Pier Angelo Toninelli, ed., *The Rise and Fall of State-Owned Enterprise in the Western World* (Cambridge: Cambridge University Press, 2000); and Nicolas Spulber, *Redefining the State: Privatization and Welfare Reform in Industrial and Transitional Economies* (Cambridge: Cambridge University Press, 1997). Political issues are addressed in Harvey Feigenbaum, Jeffrey Henig, and Chris Hamnett, *Shrinking the State: The Political Underpinnings of Privatization* (Cambridge: Cambridge University Press, 1997).

3. Although this broad distinction between state and nonstate (private) ownership is reasonable for our examination of mass privatization in the transition economies, classifying differing equity arrangements is a complex and important issue. Moreover, as transition economies tend to converge toward allocational arrangements found in long-standing market economic systems, simplistic classification in terms of state and nonstate property rights will become less meaningful.

4. The changing role of the state in the provision of social services is an important issue in any economy—and especially in the transition economies, where state involvement was formerly dominant. We will discuss this in greater detail in Chapter 21 when we address issues related to the provision of a safety net.

5. A common interpretation of the apparently expanding role of government in Western industrial economies was provided by displacement theory. This view was also expressed in popular writings on Marxism–Leninism in support of the argument that an expanding state sector (fueled by imperialism, military interactions, and the like) was an essential element of capitalist economic development.

6. The statistical importance of restitution (that is, restitution as a percentage of all forms of privatization) has been small in the transition economies (seldom over 10 percent of privatization). However, the issues involved in cases of restitution are interesting and important.

7. There is a tendency (evident in our discussion here) to emphasize initial conditions in transition economies as those "left over" from the command era, generally organizational arrangements, policies, and structural outcomes that will have an impact on transition policies—in this case, privatization. In addition, however, it is important to note that in the Western literature on privatization, a great deal of emphasis is placed on what steps might be taken, prior to privatization, to facilitate the process. These issues are important in transition economies because they affect the policy mix (the nature of privatization arrangements) and thus the patterns of privatization by region, by sector, and over time.

8. Note that it is useful to distinguish two sorts of rules related to privatization. First, transition economies had to decide, through the political process, what state property rights should be transferred to nonstate ownership. In a sense, these emerging rules came to define the public sector (defense, transportation infrastructure, energy, etc.) in these economies. Second, it was necessary to establish a set of rules pertaining to privatization arrangements, such as any limits on the distribution of enterprise shares to various groups, such as insiders, outsiders, and managers. Both concepts obviously had an important impact on the outcomes of privatization in differing transition economies during the 1990s.

9. The Russian case is instructive in this respect. Rules governed the distribution of shares to various groups, but it was easy to bypass the rules.

10. As we have emphasized, a common argument in favor of rapid privatization focused on the possibility that privatization (and transition in general) could be reversible if the process moved slowly and the immediate negative impact (for example, the reduction of output) was significant. A second important argument, however, involves theoretical issues. For example, it has been shown that complementarities are critical in transition in general and privatization in particular. For example, if a firm uses two inputs and the sources of these inputs are private and nonprivate, the progress of privatization may be slowed.

11. Manipulation of ownership arrangements and avoidance of legal requirements have been a problem. In the Russian case, the "loans for shares" scandal provides an important example. In the mid-1990s, Russian banks provided loans to the state in return for shares in large state-owned enterprises. Banks, through auctions of shares and the provision of loans, were able to acquire significant holdings. For a discussion, see Juliet Johnson, *A Fistful of Rubles: The Rise and Fall of the Russian Banking System* (Ithaca and London: Cornell University Press, 2000), pp. 184 ff.

12. The literature on privatization and restructuring is now very large. A major source on the transition economies is Simeon Djankov and Peter Murrell, "Enterprise Restructuring in Transition: A Quantitative Survey," *Journal of Economic Literature* (forthcoming). A major survey of privatization and restructuring in both transition and Western economies is William Megginson and Jeffrey Netter, "From State to Market: A Survey of Empirical Studies on Privatization," *Journal of Economic Literature* 39, no. 2 (2001), 321–389. A useful survey of the Russian case is Carsten Sprenger, "Ownership and Corporate Governance in Russian Industry: A Survey," EBRD, Working Paper No. 70, January 2002. See also Saul Estrin and Mike Wright, eds., "Corporate Governance in the Soviet Union," *Journal of Comparative Economics* 27, no. 3 (September 1999), 395–474.

13. This is not to be critical of these studies, but rather to make the reader aware that hard data on restructuring indicators such as profitability, sales, product development, capital structure, dividend payouts, and the like are much less likely to be available for the transition economies.

14. This is a theme that was emphasized in Chapters 14 through 16. It remains important in our assessment of privatization and restructuring, suggesting that both privatization and restructuring have been significantly more difficult in those transition economies whose history included a longer time span under the influence of command institutions and policies.
15. It is not easy to characterize and measure the shadow economy with precision. However, as we will emphasize , the apparent size and nature of the shadow (informal) economy varies considerably from one transition economy to another. It was especially large in the Russian case during the latter half of the 1990s and thus complicates measurement issues.
16. For a discussion of these indicators, specifically their compilation and meaning, see EBRD, Transition Report 2001: Energy in Transition (Paris: EBRD, 2001), Annex 2.1.
17. As emphasized in earlier chapters, the broad concept of liberalization, although difficult to characterize and to measure with precision, is nevertheless viewed as an important mechanism for success in the transition experience. Just as the length of time under the command experience can be viewed as important in explaining transition outcomes, so too can the extent to which liberalization has taken place during the 1990s. By most indicators, those economies that have experienced greater degrees of liberalization have generally performed better in transition.

Recommended Readings

General Works

Joan W. Allen et al., *The Private Sector in State Service Delivery: Examples of Innovative Practices* (Washington, D.C.: Urban Institute, 1989).

William J. Baumol, "On the Perils of Privatization," *Eastern Economic Journal* 19 (Fall 1993), 419–440.

Matthew Bishop, John Kay, and Colin Mayer, *Privatization and Economic Performance* (New York: Oxford University Press, 1994).

Deiter Bos, *Privatization: A Theoretical Treatment* (Cambridge, Mass.: Blackwell, 1992).

Maxim Boycko, Andrei Shleifer, and Robert W. Vishny, "A Theory of Privatization," *Economic Journal* 106 (March 1996), 309–319.

John B. Donahue, *The Privatization Decision* (New York: Basic Books, 1989).

Ahmed Galal, Leroy Jones, Pankaj Tandon, and Ingo Vogelsgand, *Welfare Consequences of Selling Public Enterprises: An Empirical Analysis* (New York: Oxford University Press, 1994).

Leroy P. Jones, Tankaj Tandon, and Ingo Vogelsgang, *Selling Public Enterprises: A Cost-Benefit Methodology* (Cambridge, Mass.: MIT Press, 1990).

J. A. Kay and D. J. Thompson, "Privatization: A Policy in Search of a Rationale," *Economic Journal* 96 (March 1986), 18–32.

Sunita Kikeri, John Nellis, and Mary Shirley, *Privatization: The Lessons of Experience* (Washington, D.C.: World Bank, 1992).

V. V. Ramanad Lam, ed., *Privatization and Equity* (New York: Routledge, 1995).

William C. Megginson, Robert C. Nash, and Matthias van Radenborgh, "The Financial and Operating Performance of Newly Privatized Firms: An International Empirical Analysis," *Journal of Finance* 49 (June 1994), 403–452.

Philip Morgan, ed., *Privatization and the Welfare State: Implications for Consumers and the Workforce* (Brookfield, Vt.: Dartmouth, 1995).

OECD, *Methods of Privatizing Large Enterprises* (Paris: OECD, 1993).

————, *Valuation and Privatization* (Paris: OECD, 1993).

Janet Rothenberg Pack, "Privatization and Public-Sector Services in Theory and Practice," *Journal of Policy Analysis and Management* 6 (1987), 523–540.

Andrew Pendleton and Jonathan Winterton, eds., *Public Enterprise in Transition* (London and New York: Routledge, 1993).

E. S. Savas, *Privatization: The Key to Better Government* (Chatham, N.J.: Chatham House, 1987).

Horst Seibert, ed., *Privatization: A Symposium in Honor of Herbert Giersch* (Tubingen, Germany: Institut fur Weltwirtschaft an der Universitat Kiel, 1992).

E. E. Suleiman and J. Waterbury, *The Political Economy of Public Sector Reform and Privatization* (Boulder, Colo.: Westview Press, 1990).

John Vickers and George Yarrow, *Privatization: An Economic Analysis* (Cambridge, Mass.: MIT Press, 1988).

Charles Wolf, Jr., *Markets or Governments: Choosing Between Imperfect Alternatives* (Cambridge, Mass.: MIT Press, 1988).

Regional Literature

Joseph R. Blasi, Maya Kroumova, and Douglas Kruse, *Kremlin Capitalism: Privatizing the Russian Economy* (Ithaca: Cornell University Press, 1997).

Dieter Bos, "Privatization in Europe: A Comparison of Approaches," *Oxford Review of Economic Policy* 9, no. 1 (1993), 95–110.

Maxim Boycko, Andrei Shleifer, and Robert Vishny, *Privatizing Russia* (Cambridge, Mass.: MIT Press, 1996).

Trevor Buck, Igor Filatotchev, and Mike Wright, "Employee Buyouts and the Transformation of Russian Industry," *Comparative Economic Studies* 36 (Summer 1994), 1–16.

Wendy Carlin and Colin Mayer, "The Truhandanstalt: Privatization by State and Market," in Oliver Jean Blanchard, Kenneth A. Froot, and Jeffrey D. Sachs, eds., *The Transition in Eastern Europe,* Vol. 2 (Chicago: University of Chicago Press, 1994), pp. 189–207.

Simeon Djankov and Peter Murrell, "Enterprise Restructuring in Transition: A Quantitative Survey," *Journal of Economic Literature,* forthcoming.

Maurice Ernst, Michael Alexeev, and Paul Marer, *Transforming the Core* (Boulder, Colo.: Westview Press, 1993).

Saul Estrin, "Privatization in Central and Eastern Europe: What Lessons Can Be Learnt from Western Experience," *Annals of Public and Cooperative Economy* 62, no. 2 (April–June 1991), 159–182.

Saul Estrin and Xavier Richet, "Industrial Restructuring and Microeconomic Adjustment in Poland: A Cross-Sectional Approach," *Comparative Economic Studies* 35, no. 4 (Winter 1993), 1–19.

Roman Frydman and Andrzej Rapaczynski, *Privatization in Eastern Europe: Is the State Withering Away?* (Budapest: Central European University Press, 1994).

Eva Marikova Leeds, "Voucher Privatization in Czechoslovakia," *Comparative Economic Studies* 35, no. 3 (Fall 1993), 19–38.

Susan J. Linz, "Russian Firms in Transition: Champions, Challengers, and Chaff," *Comparative Economic Studies* 39, no. 2 (Summer 1997), 1036.

Susan J. Linz and Gary Krueger, "Enterprise Restructuring in Russia's Transition Economy: Formal and Informal Mechanisms," *Comparative Economic Studies* 40, no. 2 (Summer 1998), 5–52.

Ivan Major, *Privatization and Economic Performance in Central and Eastern Europe* (Northampton, Mass.: Edward Elgar, 1999).

William L. Megginson and Jeffrey M. Netter, "From State to Market: A Survey of Empirical Studies on Privatization," *Journal of Economic Literature* 39, no. 2 (June 2001), 321–389.

Lynn D. Nelson and Irina Y. Kuzes, "Evaluating the Russian Voucher Privatization Program," *Comparative Economic Studies* 36 (Spring 1994), 55–68.

Marsha Pripstein Posusney and Linda J. Cook, eds., *Privatization and Labor* (Northampton, Mass.: Edward Elgar, 2000).

Clemens Schutte, *Privatization and Corporate Control in the Czech Republic* (Northampton, Mass.: Edward Elgar, 2000).

Marko Simoneti, Saul Estrin, and Andreja Bohm, eds., *The Governance of Privatization Funds* (Northampton, Mass.: Edward Elgar, 1999).

Darrell Slider, "Privatization in Russia's Regions," *Post-Soviet Affairs* 10, no. 4 (October–December 1994), 367–396.

Carsten Sprenger, "Ownership and Corporate Governance in Russian Industry: A Survey," EBRD, Working Paper No. 70, January 2002.

Pier Angelo Toninelli, ed., *The Rise and Fall of State-Owned Enterprise in the Western World* (Cambridge: Cambridge University Press, 2000).

Milica Uvalic and Daniel Vaughan-Whitehead, eds., *Privatization Surprises in Transition Economies* (Lyme, N.H.: Edward Elgar, 1997).

Western and Developing Countries

Paul Cook and Colin Kirkpatrick, eds., *Privatisation in Less Developed Countries* (New York: St. Martin's, 1988).

Harvey Feigenbaum, Jeffrey Henig, and Chris Hamnett, *Shrinking the State: The Political Underpinnings of Privatization* (Cambridge: Cambridge University Press, 1998).

Dominique Hachette and Rolf Luders, *Privatization in Chile* (San Francisco: ICS Press, 1993).

Steve H. Hanke, ed., *Privatization and Development* (San Francisco: Institute for Contemporary Studies, 1987).

Attiat F. Ott and Keith Hartley, eds., *Privatization and Economic Efficiency: A Comparative Analysis of Developed and Developing Countries* (Brookfield, Vt.: Edward Elgar, 1991).

Jonas Prager, "Is Privatization a Panacea for LDC's? Market Failure versus Public-Sector Failure," *Journal of Developing Areas* 26 (April 1992), 301–322.

Jeremy Richardson, ed., *Privatization and Deregulation in Canada and Britain* (Brookfield, Vt.: Aldershot, 1990).

Gabriel Roth, *The Private Provision of Public Services in Developing Countries* (Oxford: Oxford University Press, 1987).

Nicolas Spulber, *Redefining the State: Privatization and Welfare Reform in Industrial and Transitional Economies* (Cambridge: Cambridge University Press, 1997).

Pier Angelo Toninelli, ed., *The Rise and Fall of State-Owned Enterprises in the Western World* (Cambridge: Cambridge University Press, 2000).

CHAPTER

19

The Macroeconomy: Fiscal and Monetary Issues

One of the fascinating aspects of the transition era has been the development of macroeconomic arrangements in settings where such arrangements typically did not exist in a traditional (market) form during the command era. During the era of classical socialism, the role of the state sector was dominant, and state access to resources was achieved directly through state enterprises and other state organizations, obviating the need for an indirect **"Western-style" tax system**, which is the *tax system used in market economies (sales, vat, and so on) as opposed to command economies (turnover tax and the like).*

Banking systems in the command economies were primitive, playing largely a formal role in a system arguably driven by real, rather than monetary, forces. In many instances, the money supply was a state secret, and the role of money was viewed as passive from the perspective of influencing resource allocation. There were no financial markets (and therefore effectively no financial intermediation), state enterprises being funded directly from the state (consolidated) budget. Foreign trade was directly under state control, with both exports and imports controlled by the state. The currency was not convertible, so the balance of payments was not a function of (external) market forces and commodity and financial flows. And at least in theory, external financial forces had very little impact on the domestic monetary arrangements. This is a situation that was destined to change dramatically during transition.

It may be that the foregoing view of the macroeconomy in the command setting is simplistic. Certainly, as the Soviet economy faltered under perestroika in the late 1980s, **monetary overhang**, *excess monetary emissions in an otherwise state-controlled economy*, was viewed as a growing problem. The macro balance, however, was traditionally viewed in terms of a simple balance between aggregate demand and aggregate supply and, within reason, the state could exercise considerable control over both sides of the equation.

It is not surprising, given the almost complete absence of a macroeconomic system, that the initial collapse of the old order and the early years of transition to market arrangements were difficult for the command economies. Moreover, the initial conditions differed significantly from one country to another. A similar set of arguments could be made for the macroeconomy, where the potentially important initial conditions in transition economies included the existence of macroeconomic distortions (for example, the possibility of excess demand in a shortage economy where price controls were pervasive). These are issues that have already been addressed, although the specifics of the macroeconomic environment remain to be investigated.

Creating the Macroeconomy: The Early Years of Transition

The early years of transition unfolded largely in the absence of models or obvious alternatives for the policy makers in charge of the transition processes. As the old order began to collapse, state control of economic activity collapsed with it, and the decentralization of decision making often occurred in an institutional and legal vacuum. In this setting, both the actors and the setting in which these actors would function changed quickly, often with limited policy guidance. During the early years of transition, the emphasis understandably fell on **stabilization**, or the *adoption of policies that would limit the downslide of economic activity*, occurring as the state exited and market arrangements were not yet in place. Even so, the downslide of economic activity was significant—although very different in both pattern and magnitude from one country to another.[1]

In many transition economies, the introduction of familiar institutional underpinnings (financial markets, banking arrangements, and the like) created the appearance of market-type arrangements, but the financial institutions did not always work like their counterparts in established market economies. Financial markets were generally shallow and nontransparent. Moreover, the existence of financial institutions that played only a limited role in the macroeconomy made policy choices especially difficult, understanding both the selection of targets and the impact of those targets.

In a market economy, the debate over the nature and effectiveness of various macro policy instruments continues unabated. However, the policy environment of the semireformed transition economies has been much more complex than that of developed market economies, especially during the early years of the transition process.

Policy formulation and execution has been much more complex in the transition economies for several basic reasons, some of which we have addressed in earlier chapters. First, in semireformed economic systems, an optimal policy mix is not generally obvious. Can a policy on interest rates be implemented in a system that has a limited emerging banking system and limited (if any) financial markets? For example, if enterprises do not and cannot obtain funds from financial intermediaries, of what relevance is a policy designed to change investment patterns through these intermediaries (for example, by the manipulation of interest rates)?

Second, in a market economy, the channels through which policies affect economic outcomes are generally understood. Thus, the impact of policy variants can be predicted, and intelligent policy judgments can be made.[2] For example, it is well known that interest rates have a significant impact on the purchase of durable goods (housing) in market economies. If it is thought desirable to stimulate the sectors that produce and sell these durable goods, then one obvious mechanism to do so is adjustments to interest rates. In the transition economies, especially during the early stages of transition, the policy channels were generally unknown, and thus, the potential impact of policy variants could not be predicted. Credit for the purchasing of consumer durables was generally not available, so varying the charges made for the use of credit would have little, if any, impact on the consumption of durables.

Third, although there is continuing debate about policy objectives even in developed market economies, these issues arguably have been more serious in the transition economies. For example, beyond the basic policy issues raised earlier, the macroeconomic policy framework is especially fragile in the transition setting, where the external economy will have a major impact on the domestic economy, but under emerging and fragile financial arrangements, especially the exchange rate.[3] Specifically, it is possible—indeed likely—that there will be conflicts between internal and external balance. In most transition economies, the conflict between alternative, yet attractive, policy objectives made the policy mix especially difficult to determine.

Fourth, in some transition economies, there is yet another critical dimension: the presence of an important **shadow economy**, *that part of the economy that is outside official channels usually conducted in non-monetary terms, although not necessarily in violation of laws.* In Russia, for example, informal arrangements for resource allocation, dating from the command era, have been sustained. In addition, the shadow economy assumed a variety of new forms in the semireformed Russian economy of the 1990s.[4] Worse, however, is the fact that money surrogates were of major importance by the second half of the 1990s, in some cases replacing traditional mechanisms and channels and thus necessitating very different policy variants. For example, a considerable share of enterprise activity—for example, the payment of taxes to local and higher-level governments—has been conducted in kind. Whatever the reasons for this turn of events, the policy environment in a barter economy is clearly very different from the policy environment in a functioning market economy.

A Macroeconomic Framework

What challenges face the policy makers as they ponder the macroeconomic balance in the transition economies? Perhaps the best way to organize our thinking on these issues is to return to a simple macroeconomic framework (balance) of the sort presented in equation 19.1.

$$I = S + (T - G) + (M - X) \tag{19.1}$$

where

$$I = \text{investment}$$
$$S = \text{private savings}$$
$$T - G = \text{government balance}$$
$$M - X = \text{foreign balance}$$

An understanding of each of the components of this balance will provide us with an overview of the macroeconomic problems of the transition economies.

Investment

Command economies typically devoted a relatively large share of output to investment. Moreover, the state was the dominant mechanism through which accumulation and investment took place, facilitating its concentration in the industrial sector, as opposed to the service and other sectors. As the command economies collapsed, two major changes occurred. First, the state apparatus through which the investment process took place began to crumble, and it was generally not quickly replaced by alternative (market) arrangements. As we have seen, however, there were considerable differences among transition economies as a consequence of initial conditions, level of development, pre-collapse reform in countries such as Hungary and Poland, and so on. Second, in the absence of the organizational arrangements to facilitate it, investment might be expected to fall. There were important differences in the evolution of banking systems, for example. In cases such as Russia, banks did not generally perform the usual functions of banks (attracting deposits and making loans), and this denied the system a major channel through which savings might be converted into investment. Moreover, the emergence of financial markets was slow and uneven, usually resulting in limited and very shallow markets.

The absence of adequate sources of enterprise investment was an important aspect of the initial collapse of output, an issue that we have examined.[5] Equally important as the transition era evolved, limitations on investment had a negative impact on the nature and the pace of enterprise restructuring. It is difficult to assemble accurate data for the early and tumultuous years of transition, but let's examine what evidence is available.

In Figure 19.1, we show the year-to-year percentage change in real gross fixed investment through the mid- and late 1990s for selected transition economies. The patterns here generally conform to the general pattern outlined, although there are important differences among countries and some surprising outcomes, such as the improvement in Russia. On balance, these changes through the 1990s have led to changes in the command era pattern of sustaining a very high investment share relative to the patterns typical in market economies. Figure 19.2 shows investment shares for a sample of transition economies. Both the Czech Republic and Estonia have sustained high investment shares, but the other countries examined here have generally moved toward more modest shares.

During the twenty-first century, investment as a percentage of GDP generally increased, although significant fluctuations and variations across transition countries persisted. Countries like Kazakhstan experienced significant increases, whereas increases in countries such as Russia, the Czech Republic, and Latvia were modest.

Private Savings

The mechanism of accumulation in the command economies was fundamentally different from that found in most market economies. Under a system where control of resources and production is in the hands of the state, and returns to factors (wage payments to labor in the socialist economy) are set by the state, there is no need for

FIGURE 19.1   Percentage Change in Real Gross Fixed Investment: Selected
Transition Economies

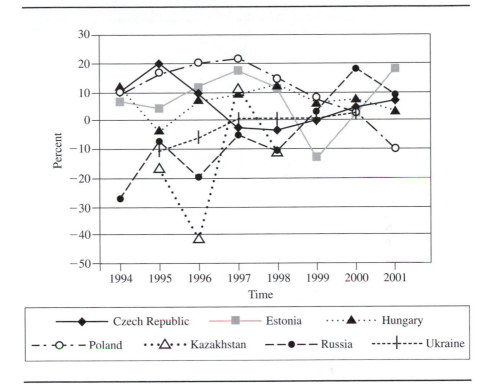

Source: EBRD, *Transition Report Update* (London: EBRD, 2001), country assessments.

indirect systems of taxation for the purpose of accumulation. The state has direct
access to the product generated in the economy and can, within reason, determine
the magnitude of accumulation, assuming that this burden will be tolerated by the
population. No wonder that under these arrangements, accumulation and investment could be high by international standards.

    Command systems did, however, facilitate savings in savings accounts or in
cash hoards where savings banks were not viewed by citizens as trustworthy. It is
perhaps not surprising that as the command system collapsed, patterns of household
savings changed, and not always in fully predictable ways. Although data on
household savings during the early years of transition are often questionable, overall there was a tendency for savings rates to fall, arguably from roughly 30 percent
of household income to some 15 percent or less.[6] Then, somewhat surprisingly,
savings rates increased to some extent (from their lowest levels) during the transition era. The Russian pattern is instructive.[7] There was an initial collapse, but more
important, Russian households moved away from making deposits in Sberbank (the
Russian savings bank) and toward simply holding rubles in cash. Thereafter, there
was a sharp movement out of rubles toward dollars as ruble convertibility was

FIGURE **19.2**   Investment as a Percent of GDP: Selected Transition Economies

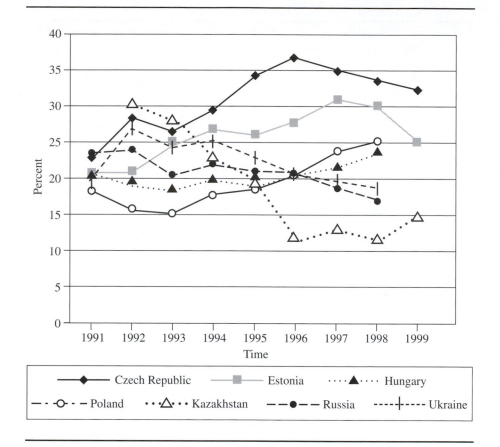

Source: EBRD, *Transition Report 2000* (London: EBRD, 2000), country assessments.

introduced. Although Russians initially defected from Sberbank, commercial banks did not pick up the slack, so household savings were not generally available to investors through financial intermediaries.

The Government Balance

In equation 19.1, $(T - G)$ represents the government balance—that is, the difference between government revenues (T) and government expenditure (G). During the command era, both elements of the government balance were directly under the control of the state. There was therefore no need to incur either a surplus or a deficit, although this issue has been the subject of controversy, especially during the latter years of the command era.

During the early years of transition, as the command arrangements collapsed, two major changes occurred. First, government enterprises, with no plan directives to guide them, reduced output and thus were unable to pay their expenses (such as wages and materials outlays), let alone accumulate a surplus to be used for financing government expenditure. In the absence of a tax system, government revenues inevitably declined, although again with considerable variation from case to case and over time.

Second, although government expenditure could be shrunk, this alternative proved to be very difficult. In most cases, there was a reluctance to close enterprises because unemployment would result. Moreover, there was continuing pressure to sustain major components of government spending—for example, the social safety net, which was viewed as necessary for maintaining popular support for new political regimes and associated transition programs.

The result of the pressures on both T and G was a budget deficit. Figure 19.3 presents the government balance for the transition economies of Central and Eastern Europe, Southeastern Europe, and the Commonwealth of Independent States (CIS). It is evident that during the early years of the transition there were serious imbalances, especially in Southeastern Europe and the CIS.[8] These imbalances were a major element of the **Washington Consensus**. Second, although the budgetary story improved considerably by the mid- and late 1990s, there remain persistent deficits that vary in magnitude among the individual transition economies. It is clear that these deficits occurred because of pressure to sustain

FIGURE **19.3**   Government Balance: Transition Economies

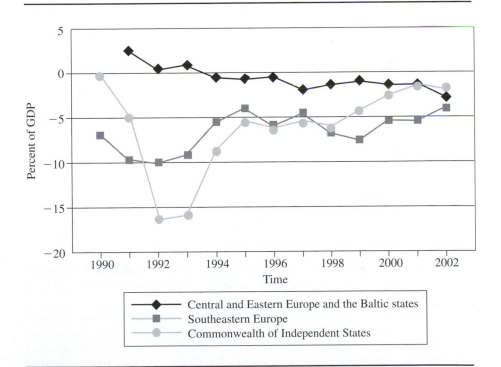

Source: EBRD, *Transition Report 2001* (London: EBRD, 2001), Table A.3.4.

government spending in an environment where old sources of revenue were shrinking and were only slowly being replaced by new sources.

During the past decade, trends in the government balance have been encouraging except for the final few years. In general, balances have remained negative but of declining magnitude until the latter part of the decade. By the end of the decade, balances in the transition economies were almost all negative, and in some cases of significant magnitude. By the end of this past decade, however, the budget problem was pervasive. For example, in 2011, of forty-two economies reported in the *Economist* (of which only five are transition economies), fully thirty-four or 81 percent were experiencing a negative budget balance as a percent of GDP. According to European Bank for Reconstruction and Development (EBRD) estimates for 2011, for twenty-nine transition economies (including Turkey), only five will have a positive fiscal balance. But why should we be concerned with these deficits?

The major problem with the existence of a budget deficit has been the issue of monetizing the deficit, or the impact of financing mechanisms. In the absence of significant financial markets, how could a budget deficit be sustained unless obviously inflationary measures (such as printing money) were used? The issue of the budget deficit took center stage in policy debates for several important reasons. First, during the early years of transition, prices were (more or less) released. This markedly boosted inflation in many transition economies and, of course, the potential for continuing inflation resulting from the macroeconomic imbalance.

Second, domestic financial markets were generally not available as a source of finance. This led to the emergence of various other (often controversial) financial instruments, such as treasury bills in the Russian case. The extent to which domestic borrowing could be contemplated was limited in many of the transition economies. Third, the budget deficit had an immediate and obvious connection to the external economy. This resulted in the emergence of serious policy issues related to the introduction of a convertible currency and the closely related matter of external financial balance. Given the very different transition experiences with the foreign sector, it is not surprising that in many cases the foreign sector did not provide a simple solution to the domestic budget crisis. Finally, because the budget balance was an observable indicator of macrobalance or lack of macrobalance, it became a key and controversial indicator that would be used (for example, by the IMF) to gauge the effectiveness of transition measures and thus eligibility for bank support. These issues, as we have noted earlier, became the focus of the Washington Consensus.

Inflation and Emerging Markets

During the early years of transition, a critical issue was the development of domestic monetary policy and the closely related matter of inflation. Recall that during the command era, prices were set by the state and bore no necessary relation to basic demand and supply conditions. In most of the transition economies, prices were released from state control during the early 1990s. The process was uneven and occurred under political directives that dictated which prices would be released and which would remain subject to state control. Understandably, in a disequilibrium setting, prices generally increased sharply. Figure 19.4 offers an overview of

FIGURE 19.4   Average Annual Inflation in Transition Economies, 1990–2002

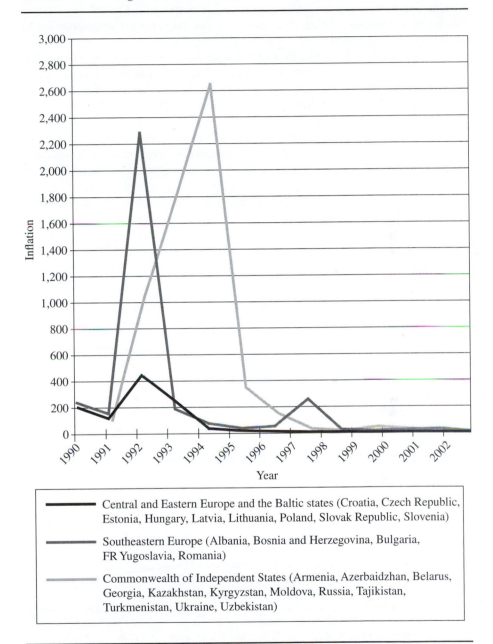

Central and Eastern Europe and the Baltic states (Croatia, Czech Republic, Estonia, Hungary, Latvia, Lithuania, Poland, Slovak Republic, Slovenia)

Southeastern Europe (Albania, Bosnia and Herzegovina, Bulgaria, FR Yugoslavia, Romania)

Commonwealth of Independent States (Armenia, Azerbaidzhan, Belarus, Georgia, Kazakhstan, Kyrgyzstan, Moldova, Russia, Tajikistan, Turkmenistan, Ukraine, Uzbekistan)

Source: Based on EBRD, *Transition Report Update* (London: EBRD, May 2002), Table A-2.

inflation for the period 1990–2002, using the annual mean value of inflation. Two observations are important: The magnitude of inflation in the CIS and Southeastern European states was dramatic as price controls were removed. And the differences in the spike in inflation, especially comparing these cases to the Central and Eastern European states, are striking. The inflation spikes in Central and Eastern Europe were important within these countries but very modest in comparison to the other transition settings.

It is important to appreciate the fact that inflation in the transition economies has been caused by two very different sets of forces. The first set of forces, the release of formerly state-controlled prices, is evident in Figure 19.4: Inflation in the early 1990s exceeded 2,000 percent in Southeastern Europe and the CIS. Figure 19.5 shows that the average annual rate of inflation (using an un-weighted mean value) for the latter part of the decade is on a very different scale. In one sense, the rate of inflation came under control, especially in the latter years of the decade, across most transition economies. What has caused a sustained (if much more modest) rate of inflation in recent years in transition economies?

During the early years of transition, stabilization was a difficult task from both a fiscal and a monetary standpoint. As prices increased, a major effort was made to bring monetary and fiscal variables under control, with the goal of achieving a positive real rate of interest. In Figure 19.6, it is evident that during the initial years of transition in some of the transition economies, the growth of broad money (M2)

FIGURE 19.5   Transition Economies: Average Annual Inflation

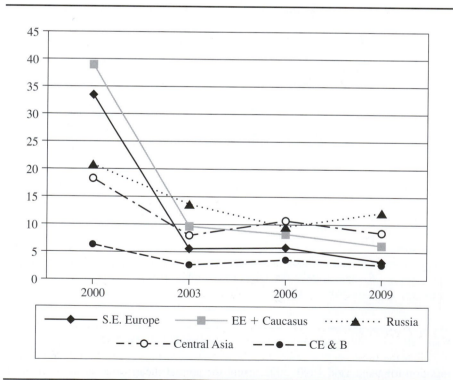

Source: EBRD, *Transition Report Update* (London: EBRD, 2002), Table A.2.; EBRD *Transition Report 2009: Transition in Crisis* (London: EBRD, 2010).

FIGURE 19.6   Broad Money (end-year M2): Percentage Change in Selected
Transition Economies

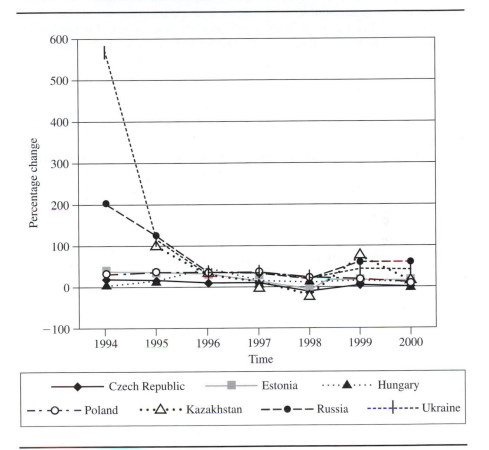

Source: EBRD, *Transition Report 2001* (London: EBRD, 2001), country assessments.

was rapid, although much more modest rates of growth (in money terms) occurred during the latter half of the 1990s. What are the current prospects for inflation?

The EBRD in its projections for 2011 suggested an inflation rate (year-over-year percentage change) of roughly 3.3 percent for Central Europe and the Baltics, 5.5 percent for Southeastern Europe, 9.2 percent for Eastern Europe and the Caucasus, 12 percent for Central Asia, and 9.6 percent for Russia.[9] For most transition economies, these estimates represent an increase (in some cases a significant increase) over the rates of inflation in 2010.[10]

The External Balance

Possibly the most complex aspect of the macroeconomic balance in transition economies during the 1990s was the external balance. Although we devote Chapter 20 to trade and payments, it is important to relate these issues to the domestic macroeconomy and the developments of the early transition years.

As is well known in the economic literature, an imbalance between the export and import of goods and services implies the movement of capital, which, along with investment flows (either through portfolio investment, loans and grants, or direct foreign investment), implies that an external mechanism may be available for assisting with the budget deficit. Specifically, during the early years of transition, the devaluation of transition currencies led to an increase in exports and financial inflows in the form of loans and grants and direct foreign investment. These flows expand the monetary base and can fuel domestic inflation. Thus, although capital inflows are attractive, they expand the domestic money supply and thus must be controlled by some **sterilization** policy—for example, the sale of state securities by the central bank to shrink the money supply. To the extent that these capital inflows are short-term, creating instability, they can be the focus of attacks on the domestic currency. It is these issues that came to the forefront in the Czech financial crisis of 1997 and the Russian financial crisis of August 1998.

The Macroeconomic Agenda and Its Early Evolution

Thus far, we have focused on the basics of the macroeconomic balance and the initial problems unfolding in the transition economies. Their responses to these problems were quite different, as were the outcomes.[11] As we have emphasized, the focus of the early transition years was on stabilization, as the old order collapsed and new institutions were yet to be established. Table 19.1 lists some of the formal stabilization programs enacted in the various transition economies. All included the introduction of banking arrangements and related laws, the introduction of stock exchanges, and a myriad of legal regulations governing financial institutions, markets, pensions, and the like. In most transition economies, there has been continuing modification of these arrangements.

Banking in Transition Economies

One of the most controversial aspects of the transition process has been the emergence of new market-type banking arrangements.[12] Conceptually, the agenda for banking is, at least in hindsight, quite clear. It is necessary to create a central bank, as well as distinct and separate commercial banks, and to establish the liberalization of interest rates and the convertibility of the currency such that the banking system can serve the usual functions that it performs in market economies. It is also necessary to create the appropriate legal structure governing the operation of banks. An assessment of banking arrangements should focus on the extent to which they develop as commercially viable operations by attracting a deposit base and contributing to investment through financial markets. What has been the experience in transition economies?

TABLE **19.1**   The Macroeconomic Agenda: Early Organizational and Policy Changes

---

The Czech Republic   1990, two-tier banking system introduced; 1991, bankruptcy law; 1992, initial bank privatization; 1993, beginning of stock exchange trading; 1993–1998, changes in bankruptcy laws; 2001, completion of bank privatization

Estonia   1991, foreign investment law; 1992, bankruptcy law; 1993, securities laws and new banking regulations; 1995, initial bank privatization; 1996, stock exchange established; 1998, pension reform, and deposit insurance becomes effective

Hungary   1990, securities laws introduced, stock exchange established, and banking laws adopted; 1991–1993, bankruptcy laws introduced; 1994, first state bank privatization; 1995, securities and exchange commission established; 1997, pension laws and banking reform; 2001, new central banking act

Poland   1991, banking laws introduced and stock exchange opens; 1992–1993, changes in banking laws and first bank privatization; 1998, changes in banking and bankruptcy laws; 1999, pension reform

Kazakhstan   1991, securities and stock exchange laws passed; 1993, initial banking laws introduced; 1995, decree on bankruptcy, bank and enterprise restructuring agency developed; 1997, bankruptcy law and pension reform; 1999, first domestic bond issues; 2001, national development bank established

Russia   1990, initial banking laws and central bank initiative; 1993, bankruptcy law established; 1995, federal securities commission established; 1998, new bankruptcy laws; 1999, laws on bank insolvency, restructuring, and foreign investment; 2001, banking laws amended

Ukraine   1991, central bank law, securities and stock exchange law; 1992, stock exchange opens, bankruptcy laws; 1995, securities and exchange commission established; 1998, foreign ownership of banks permitted; 2000, new bankruptcy law and new laws on banking

---

Source: EBRD, *Transition Report 2001* (London: EBRD, 2001), country assessments.

Figure 19.7 offers evidence on the development of banks and non-bank financial institutions, using the index of liberalization of EBRD. These ratings fall on a scale of 1 to 4+, where 1 indicates little progress and 4+ indicates standards of advanced industrial economies. The ratings here suggest a mixed record of early banking reform. Some improvements made during the first half of the 1990s were sustained during the latter half of the decade (in the Czech Republic and Estonia, for example), whereas there were declines in the index for Russia and little change for Ukraine and Kazakhstan. By 2009, eighteen of twenty-nine transition economies had a score of 3 or better with only two countries (Turkmenistan and Uzbekistan) having a score below 2. Figure 19.8 shows that the development of non-bank financial institutions exhibited a similar pattern. By 2009, eleven of the twenty-nine transition economies had a score of 3 or better in this category. If the emergence of the financial infrastructure has been a mixed experience, what can be said about the abilities of these institutions to provide appropriate intermediation in the transition economies?

FIGURE 19.7   EBRD Index of Banking Sector Reform: Selected Transition
Economies

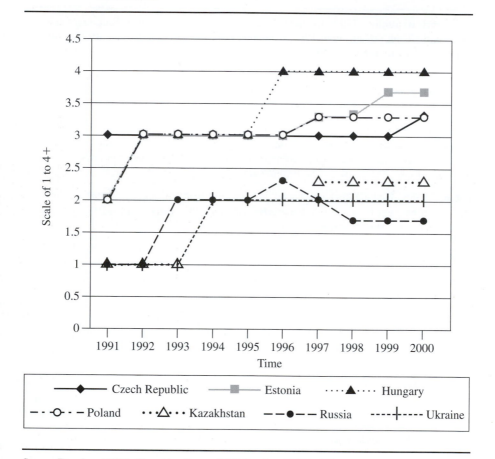

Source: Based on EBRD, *Transition Report 2001* (London: EBRD, 2001), Table 2.2.

Figure 19.9 confirms the importance of "domestic credit to enterprises as a percent of GDP," a ratio discussed earlier in this chapter. With the decline of state budgetary subsidies for enterprises, one would expect other sources to replace the state
role. The Czech Republic is a distinct case among the transition economies examined
in Figure 19.9, but the levels of domestic credit to enterprises have generally been
modest, although gradually increasing, in the latter half of the 1990s. However, there
is another side to the story. To the extent that the banking sector has emerged slowly,
and in many cases has been only a modest source of financing, financial difficulties
might be expected. These difficulties are illustrated by the importance of bad loans as
a share of all loans during the early years of transition (see Figure 19.10). During the
first decade of the twenty-first century, nonperforming loans as a percentage of all
loans generally declined, and, even where they increased, the increases were modest.

The macroeconomic experience of the transition economies has been a challenging
one. Most of these economies began the transition experience with an attempt to

FIGURE 19.8   EBRD Index of Reform of Non-bank Financial Institutions: Selected Transition Economies

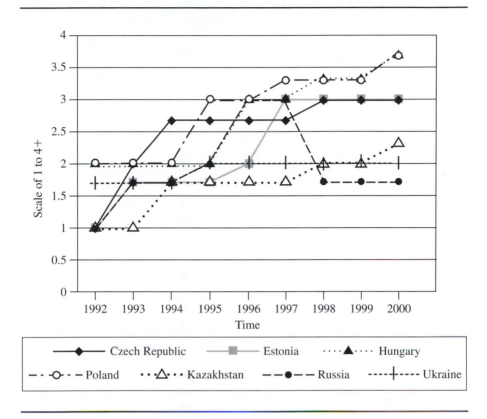

Source: Based on EBRD, *Transition Report 2001* (London: EBRD, 2001), Table 2.2.

stabilize their economies through a combination of emerging fiscal and monetary policies for both domestic and foreign economic activities. As new legislation was drafted to govern the emergence of new institutional arrangements and related policy measures, progress was in many cases modest, and financial markets remained shallow (see Figure 19.11) and nontransparent. The net result, by the late 1990s, was a fragile macroeconomic setting that varied considerably among the transition economies. As we will see, a degree of stability seems to have unraveled somewhat with the European financial crisis in the latter part of the last decade and continuing into 2011–2012.

The Transition Macroeconomy in a Turbulent Era

Our discussion of the macroeconomics of transition has focused on the years and changes toward the end of the twentieth century and the first decade of the twenty-first century. A major theme that dominates our discussion is the turbulence of the

FIGURE 19.9   Domestic Credit to Enterprises as a Percent of GDP: Selected
Transition Economies

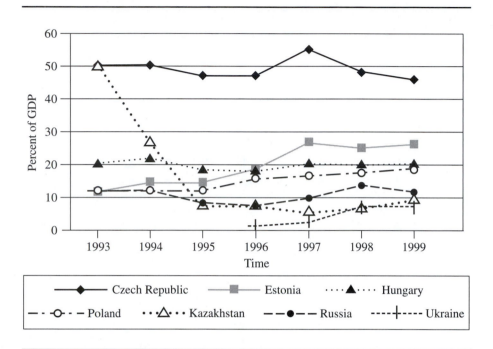

Source: Based on EBRD, *Transition Report 2001* (London: EBRD, 2001), Table 2.2.

early years of transition, which was followed by a measure of calm. However, if there was a measure of normalcy as the twentieth century ended, world economic problems changed events of the transition economies beginning around 2007, when world economic expansion came to an end and debt issues surfaced. Although the events in Russia in the late 1990s brought attention to macroeconomic issues in the transition economies, the early years of the twenty-first century seemed to suggest a measure of stability and sustained economic growth.

By 2005, a considerable measure of economic integration had occurred among the transition economies. By 2004, the Czech Republic, Estonia, Latvia, Lithuania, Poland, Slovenia, and the Slovak Republic had joined the EU. Bulgaria and Romania followed suit in 2007. After a time of increasing integration through 2007, a number of negative indicators began to emerge: increasing unemployment, a negative fiscal balance, reduction of reserves, and a reduction of demand, the latter driven in part by lagging exports and lagging financial inflows.

Rates of economic growth in 2009 were mostly negative (fourth quarter 2009 compared with fourth quarter 2008 as estimated by the EBRD), and in some cases, the negative growth rates were of significant magnitude. By 2010, EBRD estimates suggest a return to positive rates of economic growth, a pattern EBRD forecasted would persist through 2012.[13]

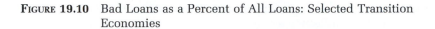

FIGURE 19.10   Bad Loans as a Percent of All Loans: Selected Transition Economies

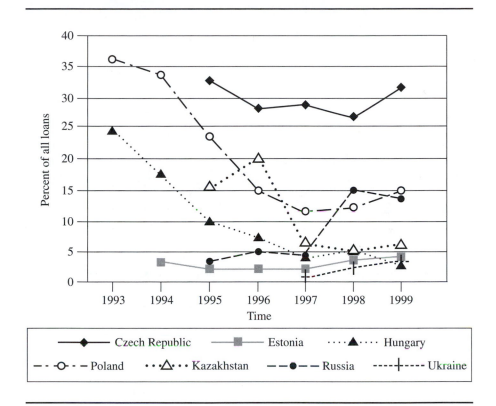

Source: EBRD, *Transition Report 2000* (London: EBRD, 2000), country assessments.

However, the basic issues underlying the world economic crises of 2009–2010 remain at the forefront in the euro zone. There have been a variety of policy responses, and for the most part, economic reforms in the transition economies have been sustained, although the significant differences among the development patterns of the transition economies have also been sustained. Certainly in the immediate future, the maintenance of financial stability in the transition economies will remain a front-burner issue, especially with sustained debt concerns in the EU. We will examine the issues further in the next chapter.

Summary

- Investment initially collapses in the early years of transition; it subsequently recovers, although not generally to levels sustained during the command era.
- Household savings rates (savings as a proportion of household income) declined significantly during the early years of transition, with some recovery in the latter part of the 1990s. The composition of savings changed, and there was a tendency to hold hard currency following the introduction of convertibility.

FIGURE **19.11**   Stock Market Capitalization as a Percent of GDP: Selected
Transition Economies

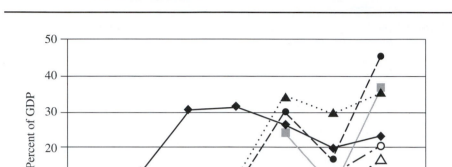

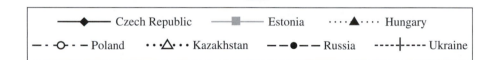

Source: EBRD, *Transition Report 2001* (London: EBRD, 2001), Table 2.2.

- The government balance typically ran a deficit, as government revenues declined but pressure for sustained government spending proved difficult to resist. From initially high levels, the budget deficit has generally become more modest throughout the transition era.
- Inflation has been a major problem in transition economies. As prices were released from state control in the early 1990s, they increased dramatically in many cases. Thereafter, price increases were more modest.
- The macroeconomic agenda has been similar in the various transition economies but has had differing outcomes. Beginning in the early 1990s, the nature of banking arrangements changed significantly, along with the emergence of stock markets, the development of the safety net, and an emergent legal environment. Russia was tested in the late 1990s, and all of the transition economies have been tested during the era of world economic problems in 2007–2011.

Key Terms

monetary overhang—Excess monetary emissions in an otherwise state-controlled economy.

shadow economy—That part of an economy that is outside official channels often conducted in non-monetary terms but not necessarily in violation of laws.

stabilization—The adoption of policies designed to limit the downslide of economic activity as command economies replaced state mechanisms with market mechanisms.

sterilization—Policy designed to prevent the loss of foreign exchange reserves from affecting the domestic money stock.

Washington Consensus—Set of guidelines developed and implemented by the IMF to promote economic growth through macroeconomic stabilization and privatization.

"Western-style" tax system—The tax system used in market economies (sales, VAT, and so on) as opposed to command economies (turnover tax and the like).

Notes

1. A useful discussion of the early years of transition can be found in "Symposium on Economic Transition in the Soviet Union and Eastern Europe," *Journal of Economic Perspectives* 5, no. 4 (Fall 1991), 3–236; Christopher Clague and Gordon C. Rausser, eds., *The Emergence of Market Economies in Eastern Europe* (Cambridge: Blackwell, 1992), Part II.

2. Specifically, policy targets can be known, and the leads and lags associated with policy variants can be known, at least within reasonable ranges.

3. There is considerable controversy surrounding the movement from a nonconvertible to a convertible currency in the transition economies. These issues are discussed in Chapter 9.

4. The magnitude of the shadow economy differs considerably among the transition economies, and arguably it is much smaller in Eastern Europe than in the CIS countries. A case of special interest is Russia, where the shadow economy has been very large. See, for example, OECD, *Russian Federation* (Paris: OECD, 2000); for a more general discussion, see Eric Friedman, Simon Johnson, Daniel Kaufmann, and Pablo Zoido-Lobaton, "Dodging the Grabbing Hand: The Determinants of Unofficial Activity in 69 Countries," *Journal of Public Economics* 76 (2000), 459–493; Simon Commander and Christian Mumssen, "Understanding Barter in Russia," EBRD Working Paper No. 37, December 1998; Wendy Carlin, Steven Fries, Mark Schaffer, and Paul Seabright, "Barter and Non-Monetary Transactions in Transition Economies: Evidence from a Cross-Country Survey," EBRD Working Paper No. 50, June 2000.

5. The theoretical underpinnings of these issues are developed in Gerard Roland, *Transition and Economics* (Cambridge, Mass.: MIT Press, 2000), Ch. 12.

6. For a discussion of savings rates during transition, see Cevdet Denizer and Holger C. Wolf, "The Savings Collapse During the Transition in Eastern Europe," a part of the World Bank project entitled "Saving Across the World," EBRD, *Transition Report 1996* (London: EBRD, 1996). Note also that comparison of savings rates before and during transition is difficult, in part because of conceptual and definitional differences and the controversy surrounding the magnitude of savings during the command era.

7. For a discussion of the Russian case, see Juliet Johnson, *A Fistful of Rubles* (Ithaca: Cornell University Press, 2000); Michael S. Bernstam and Alvin Rabushka, *Fixing Russia's Banks: A Proposal for Growth* (Stanford: Hoover Institution Press, 1998).

8. It is important to note that during the early years of transition, there were a number of estimates of the size of the budget deficits. These estimates differed considerably one from another, thus further fueling the debate over actual magnitude of deficits.

9. See EBRD *Regional Economic Prospects in EBRD Countries of Operations: May 2011* (EBRD: London, May 2011).
10. Ibid.
11. For a useful summary, see Marie Lavigne, *The Economics of Transition*, 2nd. ed. (London: St. Martin's, 1999), Ch. 7.
12. For a discussion, see Steven Fries and Anita Taci, "Banking Reform and Development in Transition Economies," EBRD Working Paper No. 71, June 2002; Charles Enoch, Anne-Marie Gulde, and Daniel Hardy, "Banking Crises and Bank Resolution: Experiences in Some Transition Economies," IMF Working Paper WP/02/56, March 2002.
13. In addition to the EBRD Transition Report, *Recovery and Reform* (London: EBRD, 2010), see EBRD "Regional Economic Prospects in EBRD Countries of Operations: May 2011" (London: EBRD Office of the Chief Economist, 2011), Table 2.

Recommended Readings

P. Aghion, P. Bolton, and S. Fries, "Optimal Design of Bank Bailouts: The Case of Transition Economies," *Journal of Institutional and Theoretical Economics* 155, no. 1 (1999), 51–79.

Lorand Ambrus-Lakatos and Mark E. Schaffer, eds., *Fiscal Policy in Transition* (New York: Institute for East–West Studies, 1997).

————, *Monetary and Exchange Rate Policies, EMU and Central and Eastern Europe* (New York: Institute for East–West Studies, 1999).

Ronald W. Anderson and Chantal Kegels, *Transition Banking* (New York: Oxford University Press, 1998).

Age F. P. Bakker and Bryan Chapple, eds., *Capital Liberalization in Transition Countries: Lessons from the Past and for the Future* (New York: Edward Elgar, 2003).

James R. Barth, Gerard Caprio, and Ross Levine, "Bank Regulations are Changing: For Better or Worse?" *Comparative Economic Studies* 50 (2008), 537–563.

Michael S. Bernstam and Alvin Rabushka, *Fixing Russia's Banks: A Proposal for Growth* (Stanford: The Hoover Institution Press, 1998).

Mario I. Blejer and Marko Skreb, *Financial Sector Transformation: Lessons From Economies in Transition* (New York: Cambridge University Press, 1999).

————, *Macroeconomic Stabilization in Transition Economies* (Cambridge: Cambridge University Press, 2006).

John Bonin and Istvan P. Szekely, eds., *The Development and Reform of Financial Systems in Central and Eastern Europe* (London: Edward Elgar, 1994).

Frank Bonker, *The Political Economy of Fiscal Reform in Eastern Europe* (Northampton, Mass.: Edward Elgar, 2002).

Michael D. Bordo and Forrest Capie, *Monetary Regimes in Transition* (New York: Cambridge University Press, 1993).

Jozef M. Brabant, *Adjustment, Structural Change, and Economic Efficiency: Aspects of Monetary Cooperation in Eastern Europe* (New York: Cambridge University Press, 1987).

G. Caprio and R. Levine, "Reforming Finance in Transitional Socialist Economies," *World Bank Research Observer* 9, no. 1 (1994), 1–24.

Era Dabla-Norris, "The Challenges of Fiscal Decentralization in Transition Countries," *Comparative Economic Studies* 48 (2006), 100–131.

Cevdet Denizer and C. Holgzer, "Household Savings in Transition Economies," National Bureau of Economic Research, Working Paper No. 6457, 1998.

————, Raj M. Desai, and Nikolay Gueorguiev, "Political Competition and Financial Reform in Transition Economies," *Comparative Economic Studies* 48 (2006), 563–582.

EBRD, *Transition Report 2000* (London, EBRD, 2000).

————, *Transition Report 2001* (London: EBRD, 2001).

————, *Transition Report Update* (London: EBRD, 2001).

————, *Transition Report 2010* (London: EBRD, 2010).

————, *Transition Report 2011* (London: EBRD, 2011).

Steven Fries and Anita Taci, "Banking Reform and Development in Transition Economies," The European Bank for Reconstruction and Development, Working Paper No. 71, June 2002.

David M. A. Green and Karl Petrick, eds., *Banking and Financial Stability in Central Europe* (Northampton, Mass.: Edward Elgar, 2002).

Steven H. Hanke, Lars Jonung, and Kurt Schuler, *Russian Currency and Finance: A Currency Board Approach to Reform* (New York: Routledge, 1993).

Hansjorg Herr, ed., *Macroeconomic Problems of Transformation: Stabilization Policies and Economic Restructuring* (Cheltenham, England: Edward Elgar, 1994).

Jens Holscher, ed., *Financial Turbulence and Capital Markets on Transition Countries* (New York: Palgrave Macmillan, 2000).

Yelena Kalyuzhnoa and Michael Taylor, eds., *Transitional Economics: Banking, Finance, Institutions* (New York: Palgrave Macmillan, 2001).

Grzegorz W. Kolodko, *From Shock to Therapy: The Political Economy of Postsocialist Transformation* (Oxford: Oxford University Press, 2000).

David Lane, ed., *Russian Banking: Evolution, Problems and Prospects* (Northampton, Mass.: Edward Elgar, 2002).

Donato Masciandaro, ed., *Financial Intermediation in the New Europe: Banks, Markets and Regulation in EU Accession Countries* (New York: Edward Elgar, 2004).

Ronald I. McKinnon, "Financial Control in the Transition from Classical Socialism to a Market Economy," *Journal of Economic Perspectives* 5, no. 4 (Fall 1991), 107–122.

————, *The Order of Economic Liberalization: Financial Controls in the Transition to a Market Economy* (Baltimore: Johns Hopkins University Press, 1991).

Anna Meyendorff, "Transactional Structures of Bank Privatizations in Central Europe and Russia," *Journal of Comparative Economics* 25 (1997), 5–30.

————, and Anjan Thakor, *Designing Financial Systems in Transition Economies: Strategies for Reform in Central and Eastern Europe* (Ann Arbor, Mich.: Davidson Institute, 2002).

Janet Mitchell, "Managerial Discipline, Productivity and Bankruptcy in Capitalist and Socialist Economies," *Comparative Economic Studies* 32 (Fall 1990), 93–137.

Milan Nikolic, *Monetary Policy in Transition: Inflation Nexus Money Supply in Postcommunist Russia* (New York: Palgrave Macmillan, 2006).

OECD, *Transformation of the Banking System: Portfolio Restructuring, Privatization, and the Payment System* (Paris: OECD, 1993).

Michael Pettis, *The Volatility Machine: Emerging Economies and the Threat of Financial Collapse* (New York: Oxford University Press, 2001).

Stanislav Poloucek, *Reforming the Financial Sector in Central European Countries* (New York: Palgrave Macmillan, 2004).

Carmen M. Reinhart and Kenneth S. Rogoff, *This Time is Different: Eight Centuries of Financial Folly* (Princeton: Princeton University Press, 2009).

Gregg S. Robbins, *Banking in Transition: East Germany After Unification* (New York: Palgrave Macmillan, 2000).

Alex Segura-Ubiergo, Alejandro Simone, Sangeev Gupta, and Qiang Cai, "New Evidence on Fiscal Adjustment and Growth in Transition Economies," *Comparative Economic Studies* 52 (October 2009), 18–37.

Gerard Turley, *Transition, Taxation and the State* (Burlington, Vt.: Ashgate, 2006).

Mariko Watanabe, ed., *Recovering Financial Systems: China and Asian Transition Economies* (New York: Palgrave Macmillan, 2006).

World Bank, *Russia: The Banking System During Transition* (Washington, D.C.: World Bank, 1993).

———, *The World Development Report 1996* (Washington, D.C.: World Bank, 1996).

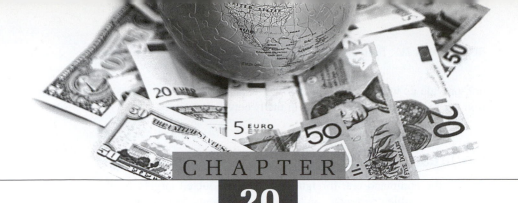

CHAPTER
20

Transition and the Global Economy: International Trade and Finance

Throughout this book, we have emphasized the unique organizational arrangements, policies, and outcomes of the command economic systems. A striking example of these differences can be found in the arena of international trade—both the organizational arrangements and policy imperatives for the trading of goods and services, and the financial arrangements associated with the state trading systems of the command era. Although there were significant differences from country to country at the end of the command era, generally speaking the peculiarities of the command era made the early transition era difficult. In some cases, it made the early transition area very difficult. Two factors combined during the command era to create significant complications that have persisted in many cases during the transition era. The first factor was the absence of a *convertible currency—currency for which there is a market and thus a market-determined rate of exchange available to participants within and beyond the borders of the country.* The second factor was the resulting dominance of *barter (exchange of goods and services between two parties when money is not involved as an intermediary)* arrangements functioning through state trading organizations. As the old order collapsed, it was essential to shrink the role of the state, create new institutions (in both trade and finance), and pursue the establishment of a convertible currency. As we will see, the trading arrangements and exchange rate regimes that were chosen varied considerably from one economy to another and have been subject to considerable change during the transition era. As the new trading arrangements emerged during the early transition years, patterns of trade and the financial outcomes of trade changed fundamentally and, for the most part, quite quickly. These ongoing adjustments and differing outcomes have been the subject of a growing volume of scholarly literature. The difficulties of implementing major changes during the transition era, and also the difficulties of the recent recession era, provide us with a base from which we can assess the prospects for the transition economies in a global setting in the twenty-first century.

Collapse and the Early Years of Transition

During the command era, foreign trade was conducted largely by the state with a nonconvertible currency and no arrangements for multilateral clearing. Although attempts were made to achieve the latter—for example, through the **Council for Mutual Economic Assistance (CMEA)** *trade bloc established by the former command economies in 1949 to promote trade and coordinate planning, which was abolished in 1989*—these attempts largely failed, and integration was not achieved.[1] In addition, given the lack of financial markets in the command economies, there were no mechanisms for the inflow of foreign capital, whether through **portfolio investment** *(investment from one country to another that occurs through the purchase of financial instruments such as stocks as bonds rather than directly as FDI)* or through **foreign direct investment (FDI)** *(investment flows from one country to another that occur directly rather than through instruments such as stocks)*. The impact of these command-era arrangements has been widely debated in the literature, but basic distortions were evident. The complexities of these arrangements tended to limit the volume of foreign trade, and thus to limit the extent of integration. Moreover, both the commodity composition of trade and its geographic distribution differed from what might be expected under market arrangements, although again, there were significant differences from country to country. Finally, the absence of scarcity-based domestic prices and of a meaningful exchange rate made the foreign trade decision itself exceedingly difficult. Consequently, in the measurement of transition performance during the 1990s, foreign-trade distortions have become a critical element of initial conditions, an issue we discussed earlier. Indeed, the extent to which these initial conditions have been modified over time is itself a matter of dispute, as we noted when we discussed the issue of growth convergence in transition economies.

Beyond the obvious distortions and the possibility that the volume of trade was limited, however, the lack of integration meant that the development trajectories of the command economies were not dictated by external market forces to any degree, and critical benefits often derived through the foreign sector (for example, the importation of foreign technology) were largely absent. Therefore, as transition began in the early 1990s, attention focused on the appropriate organizational changes and associated policy measures that would lead to liberalization of foreign trade, or the opening of largely "closed" economies, to pursue integration with Western market economies. As a result, it was expected that during the transition era patterns of foreign trade would undergo significant change, and the financial aspects of trade would take on added importance. The latter would of course be fundamental to the closely related emergence of new domestic macroeconomic arrangements in a transition setting.

It is important to emphasize that there is a close relationship between the foreign sector and the domestic sector and that this relationship is especially fragile in the transition economies. Specifically, financial flows and domestic monetary creation are typically closely related, especially in cases where balance-of-payments flows are of a significant magnitude. This means that domestic monetary and fiscal policies must both be coordinated with the financial arrangements in the foreign-trade sector. What will be the nature of this coordination?

In a market economy, the exchange rate regime is the fundamental link between the domestic economy and the external economy, the goal being "to provide a nominal anchor, to ensure adequate competitiveness, and to insulate the economy from shocks."[2] However, it is important to recognize that because of the isolation of the transition economies from the global economy during the command era, in many cases it was at first difficult, if not impossible, to assess differences in real levels of economic activity between transition economies and their possible market-oriented trading partners in a new era. Thus choosing an exchange rate regime became a very difficult task. In addition to the problems of choosing and implementing a new exchange rate regime, the transition economies were experiencing continuing deflation, which suggested that any regime established during the early years of transition would be subject to continuing, possibly major change. It is for this reason that there was a serious search for a nominal anchor, or a mechanism to understand differing real levels of economic activity among the transition economies vis-à-vis potential trading partners.[3] The nature of price setting in the command economies significantly distorted any comparisons between command and market economies. If a real anchor could be found, the real differences could be understood, facilitating the establishment of an appropriate exchange rate between, for example, a former command economy in transition and a market economy.

As the foreign exchange regimes were established in the transition economies, another important set of issues emerged—specifically, the matter of policy targets and instruments, both in the macroeconomy and in the foreign sector. Although there is a large literature on the relationship among exchange rate regimes, associated policies, and economic performance, there is unfortunately no real consensus on, for example, the nature of the relationship between the exchange rate and the rate of economic growth. Although this fact greatly complicates planning, it is understandable because many forces beyond the exchange rate influence the rate of economic growth. Nevertheless, it is still necessary to decide on appropriate targets—for example, a particular rate of inflation or a balanced budget—and to define the nature of the policy instruments that will be used to achieve these policy targets. This effort is further complicated in the transition economies because the policy channels—that is, the routes through which policy targets can be achieved by the manipulation of policy instruments—are not always known and are always subject to change. Consider the case of the macroeconomy during early transition in Russia and the use of interest rates to influence levels of economic activity. If there is a very limited domestic financial market from which firms may borrow, and if the magnitude of the shadow economy is significant, one can argue that changes in interest rates will have little if any impact on the level of economic activity. Indeed, it may be difficult to know the potential impact of any policy variable, an impossible situation.

If changes in the foreign-trade regimes of the newly emerging transition economies were anticipated, what were these changes, and what factors would influence their nature? First and foremost, as the state exited from the active management of these economies, liberalization would imply the replacement of state trading organizations by private organizations, including banking and financial organizations. But liberalization would imply much more. These economies would move toward the establishment of trading arrangements patterned after those found in market economies. Therefore there would be an effort to reduce restrictions on foreign trade—both quantitative restrictions (such as import and export quotas) and financial restrictions (such as import and export tariffs).

Along with trade liberalization, the major issue that arose in the early days of the transition economies was the establishment of a convertible currency and of an exchange rate regime that could sustain **external balance** *(when the demand and supply of foreign exchange is equalized, the market is in equilibrium)* and **internal balance** *(equilibrium in the internal economy, usually defined as full employment of resources and the absence of inflation)* under very difficult and volatile circumstances. As we can see in Table 20.1, the steps taken in the economies that we examine varied considerably from one economy to another. However, most transition economies pursued the introduction of a convertible currency quickly but sequentially and on a piecemeal basis. The initial step was typically the introduction of **current-account convertibility**, followed later by **capital-account convertibility**. These changes, as we will see, had important implications for the overall macroeconomy and for the continuing effort to sustain economic growth with reasonable levels of unemployment and inflation.

Later in this chapter, we will examine the changes in trading patterns brought about by these new regimes. However, the changes that occurred were obviously a function of the sorts of new trading regimes that were established. Moreover, basic issues such as factor endowments and the legacies of the command era—that is, the initial conditions—were influential. Thus, in general, those economies that were more "open" during the command era (for example, the economies of Eastern Europe) were likely to find the changes more comfortable than those economies that were less "open" (for example, the countries emerging from the former Soviet Union). Indeed, the collapse of the Soviet Union and the emergence of fifteen separate and independent nations, which had been one nation for many years, presented a unique setting.[4] In this setting, political issues and past arrangements were important and would shape the nature of trading systems in the emerging transition economies—a matter that warrants further discussion.

TABLE **20.1**   Early Changing Foreign Trade Regimes: Selected Transition
Economies

The Czech Republic: 1991, fixed exchange rate adopted; 1993, new currency (koruna) adopted; 1995, full convertibility (current account); 1998, exchange rate band widened; 1998, managed float exchange rate adopted.

Estonia: 1990, state trading eliminated; 1992, new currency (kroon) and currency board adopted; 1994, full current-account convertibility introduced and nontariff trade restrictions removed; 1994, WTO membership; 2000, capital account fully liberalized.

Hungary: 1995, WTO membership; 1996, full current-account convertibility; 1997, currency basket changed, import surcharge abolished; 2000, currency basket changed; 2001, full convertibility (forint) with a fixed band and a euro peg.

Poland: 1990, trade controls removed and nontariff restrictions removed, fixed exchange rate introduced; 1991, crawling peg introduced; 1992, EFTA and CETA arrangements; 1995, managed float with a fluctuation band, current account convertible, WTO membership; 1999, new foreign exchange laws; 2000, exchange rate floated.

Kazakhstan: 1993, custom union with Belarus and Russia introduced; foreign exchange surrender abolished; 1996, full current-account convertibility; 1999, reintroduction of some trade restrictions.

Russia: 1992, state trade monopoly abolished, exchange rate unified; 1993, ruble zone collapses; 1995, currency corridor introduced; 1996, trade liberalization and full current-account convertibility introduced; 1999, dual exchange rate regime.

Ukraine: 1993, multiple exchange rates introduced; 1994, exchange rates unified, reduction of exchange rate quotas; 1996, new currency (hryvnia) introduced; 1997, full current-account convertibility; 1998, trade restrictions (autos) introduced, currency band widened; 1999, currency band further widened; 2000, floating exchange rate introduced.

Source: EBRD, *Transition Report 2000* (Paris: EBRD, 2000), country assessments; Padma Desai, *Going Global: Transition from Plan to Market in the World Economy* (Cambridge, Mass.: MIT Press, 1997).

Emerging Trading Arrangements:
Regional and Political Issues

Transition was clearly different in the early 1990s than in the middle and late 1990s. This fact helps us to analyze transition patterns. However, we have also emphasized that spatial and related political issues have been important, hence our emphasis on differentiating between the transition economies that are often described as "winners" and those that are often described as "losers." Although the dichotomy is far too simplistic, we emphasize again that the countries that emerged from the former Soviet Union seemed to have a much more difficult transition path during the 1990s than the countries of Eastern Europe.

These differences are potentially of great importance for other economies that we have not directly classified as transition economies—for example, in Asia.

When the Soviet Union collapsed as a political and economic entity, fifteen separate countries emerged. Often termed the **newly independent states (NIS)**, these were *states (countries) emerging from the former Soviet Union sometimes referred to in Russia as the "near abroad,"* and all of them (along with other command economies) had been members of the CMEA. The CMEA may not have been a particularly effective organization, but when the USSR ceased to exist there was an immediate attempt to develop and sustain a political and economic union, absent the Baltic states of Latvia, Lithuania, and Estonia. This attempt culminated in the **Commonwealth of Independent States (CIS)**, an *organization that comprised the states emerging from the former Soviet Union with the exception of Latvia, Lithuania, and Estonia.* The motivation for such an organization was strong: the republics of the former USSR were integrated to a significant degree, and their dawning independence would result in benefits but also costs. Indeed, costs could be significant, especially during the time before new institutional arrangements and trading patterns could emerge. According to economic theory, integration could take a variety of forms. One form could be a **monetary union**, which is *one of several forms of integration in which member countries agree to use a common currency*, essentially the use of a single currency (in this case, a ruble zone). Another form could be a **customs union**, *a form of integration that eliminates trade barriers among member countries using a single common external tariff on non-member countries.* In a customs union, a group of countries form to lower trade barriers among themselves and establish a common policy regarding barriers between themselves and nonmember countries.[5]

Following the breakup of the Soviet Union in 1991, the CIS was formed. During the initial period of transition, the countries of the CIS continued to use the ruble as a national currency, so foreign trade among the CIS states was conducted in rubles. However, because Russia was the sole producer of rubles, these arrangements immediately created problems, and by the mid-1990s all of the CIS states had introduced their own national currencies. Understandably, patterns of trade among the CIS countries changed, an issue we address later in this chapter. Also, during the first half of the 1990s, there were numerous attempts among the former Soviet republics to integrate in various ways, but the impact of these arrangements was arguably quite limited.[6] The assets of the USSR were largely disbursed according to location, although in the case of military assets (for example, in Ukraine) ultimate ownership was a matter of controversy. Russia officially assumed the foreign debt of the USSR in 1993, an issue that grew in importance throughout the 1990s until a major agreement on debt restructuring was achieved with the London Club in 2000.

The situation in Eastern Europe was quite different from that of the newly independent states. Beginning in 1991, the countries of Central Europe (Poland, Hungary, and at the time Czechoslovakia) edged toward the abolition of trade restrictions and toward the free movement of capital and labor. By 1992, the **Central European Free Trade Area (CEFTA)**—*a free trade area formed in 1992 among Poland, Hungary, and Czechoslovakia*—began to expand. Although trade patterns changed under the emerging arrangements, the impact of CEFTA has generally been viewed as modest, The critical issue through the process of accession to CEFTA is membership in the **European Union (EU)**—*a group of European countries that make up a single economic community.*

What is accession and why is membership in the EU important for the transition economies? **Accession** is the process of becoming a member of the European Union.[7] For both political and economic reasons, joining the EU has been an important goal for the transition economies of Central and Eastern Europe. Membership, however, requires that countries meet a variety of both economic and political criteria that are often difficult to achieve in the transition setting. These criteria involve political democracy and the liberalization of trade, capital flows, and migration.

Between 1991 and 1996, ten countries (see Table 20.2) became candidate members.[8] By 1996, all ten had become members of the **World Trade Organization (WTO)** and the **General Agreement on Tariffs and Trade (GATT)**. The **WTO** is the *successor to GATT, providing a forum for the discussion of world trade issues.* **GATT** was the *predecessor to the WTO, serving as a mechanism to discuss world trade issues.* Membership in both was required for accession to the EU. Toward the end of the decade, discussions about accession were begun with five additional countries (see Table 20.2). This pattern of integration has been much more aggressive than that exhibited by the CIS states. CIS states have been slow to pursue GATT/WTO membership, although they have signed partnership agreements with most other CIS countries.

TABLE 20.2   Transition Economies: Early Membership Commitments

	GATT/WTO Membership	IMF Article VII Status	EU Association Agreement	Entry
Albania	July 2000	—	—	—
Bulgaria[a]	December 1996	September 1998	March 1993	2007
Croatia	July 2000	May 1995	—	—
Czech Republic[a]	January 1995	October 1995	October 1993	2004
FYR Macedonia	—	June 1998	—	—
Hungary[a]	January 1995	January 1996	December 1991	2004
Poland[a]	July 1995	June 1995	December 1991	2004
Romania[a]	January 1995	March 1998	February 1993	2007
Slovak Republic[a]	January 1995	October 1995	October 1993	2004
Slovenia[a]	July 1995	September 1995	June 1996	2004
Estonia[a]	November 1999	August 1994	June 1995	2004
Latvia[a]	February 1999	June 1994	June 1995	2004
Lithuania[a]	—	May 1994	June 1995	2004

[a]EU accession countries.

Source: EBRD, *Transition Report 2000* (London: EBRD, 2000), p. 22, Table 2.3; EBRD, *Transition Report 2001* (London: EBRD, 2001), sec. 2.7

Many of the changing trade patterns and the resulting integration stem from the liberalization of trade or the changing of organizational arrangements and policies. We now turn to a discussion of the changes that have been made. Then we will attempt to assess the impact of these changes.

Transition and Emerging Outcomes in the Foreign Sector

The monetary regimes adopted in the transition economies varied considerably, as did the nature of the policy framework. Therefore, it is possible to generalize about outcomes, but there are also important distinctions from case to case. If a flexible exchange rate is used, then the exchange rate adjusts to bring equilibrium to the balance of payments—that is, the inflows and outflows of capital. In contrast, if a fixed exchange rate is used, then the adjustment takes place though changes in the domestic money supply. The issue of choosing a fixed versus (some form of) flexible exchange rate regime continues to be of interest in the assessment of trade regimes in varying settings. What has happened in the transition economies?

The extent of change in the trade and foreign exchange arrangements of transition economies can be judged to some degree by the evidence presented in Figure 20.1. However, there are other useful indicators. For example, the EBRD compiles a system of transition indicators, including an indicator of the degree of liberalization of the foreign trade and exchange system. These indicators range from 1 (little change) to 4+ (standards of advanced industrial economies, including enforcement of policy on competition). In their *Transition Report 2001*, the EBRD identifies fully thirteen countries (Albania, Bulgaria, Croatia, the Czech Republic, Georgia, Hungary, Latvia, Lithuania, Moldova, Poland, the Slovak Republic, and Slovenia) that achieve a score of 4+.[9] There are four other countries that come close, with a score of 4 (Armenia, Former Yugoslav Republic Macedonia, Kyrgyzstan, and Romania). The lagging countries are Azerbaijan, Belarus, Bosnia and Herzegovina, Federal Republic of Yugoslavia, Kazakhstan, Russia, Tajikistan, Turkmenistan, Ukraine, and Uzbekistan.

The EBRD also provides, for selected transition economies, indicators of competitiveness (for example, changes in industrial productivity and measures of competitiveness based on changes in the real manufacturing wage and changes in unit labor costs measured using the deutsche mark). These indicators show important differences in competitiveness among the selected transition countries.[10] For example, deutsche mark–denominated unit labor costs between 1996 and 2000 increased by 98 percent in Lithuania and increased by only 0.1 percent in Croatia and 6.7 percent in Slovenia.

An important indicator of change in the foreign sector is the real exchange rate. The pattern in the transition economies has generally been a decline (in some cases, a significant decline) in the real exchange rate during the early years of transition, followed by an increase in the real exchange rate during the second half of the 1990s. What explains these changes in real exchange rates? Although a

FIGURE 20.1   Transition Economies: Current-Account Balance, 1994–2009

	1994	1997	2000	2003	2006	2009
CEE + Baltic	−0.8	−6.3	−4.8	−6.1	−8.8	−1.5
S.E. Europe	−3.6	−9.2	−5.6	−8.0	−12.1	−12.9
E.E. + Caucasus	na	na	−4.8	−7.5	−2.5	−7.67
Russia	2.0	0.0	18.0	8.2	9.6	3.1
Central Asia	na	na	1.2	−6.0	6.7	0.3
All Transition	−4.8	−8.7	3.0	−4.9	−4.5	−4.9

Source: EBRD, *Transition Report 2002: Agriculture and Rural Transition* (London: EBRD, May 2002), p. 20, Table A.4; *Transition Report 2009: Transition in Crisis?* (London: EBRD, 2009), Table A.1.1.6.

potentially important issue is the nature of initial conditions and the difficulty of implementing a new exchange rate regime during the early years of transition, a popular explanation is changes in the fundamentals underlying determination of the exchange rate—notably, changes in productivity and the real wage relative to changes experienced by trading partners. This hypothesis has been tested by examining the pattern observed in many of the transition economies.[11] A recent examination of this issue using panel data seems to confirm the view that appreciation in real exchange rate is productivity based.[12]

The balance of payments involves the current account and the capital account. If the sum of current-account and capital-account transactions is zero, then the quantity of foreign exchange being demanded is equal to the quantity of foreign exchange being supplied. An imbalance implies an adjustment process, typically a change in the exchange rate, assuming that a flexible exchange rate regime is in place. What is the evidence pertaining to the balance of payments? Figure 20.1 shows the current-account balance for transition economies from the beginning of the transition era through the beginning of the new century. The pattern of decline and limited recovery during the latter part of the 1990s is striking, as is the fact that the outflows are of significant size compared with GDP. What is the nature of capital flows?

Capital Flows: Aid and Foreign Direct Investment

A major component of the opening up of the transition economies has been the integration of these economies with the global economy, and especially with global financial markets. To the extent that cross-border capital flows are increased, from an allocative standpoint the outcome is likely to be positive. However, increased financial flows present important challenges to domestic policy makers because the domestic (host country) monetary and fiscal regime is no longer fully under domestic control, as we have noted. In the case of Russia in 1998 and the Czech Republic in 1997, for example, the financial crisis therefore led to a search for both signals and cures. Financial (capital) flows typically take the form of aid, portfolio investment, or foreign direct investment.

Aid and foreign direct investment are very different. For the transition economies during the 1990s, aid was provided mainly by two organizations: the **International Monetary Fund (IMF)**, a *world organization helping member nations to manage international financial transactions*; and the **World Bank**, *an international organization founded in 1944 that provides loans to member countries for the purpose of promoting growth and development*. Both organizations have been involved with transition economies, although largely on a country-by-country basis rather than under any general umbrella. The IMF has been largely concerned with domestic stabilization, whereas the World Bank has been more concerned with loans to stimulate long-term economic growth. Both have functioned under guidelines that proved controversial but were important barometers of achievement in the transition economies.

Figure 20.2 offers evidence on total capital flows for all transition economies (including a linear trend line) and for selected transition economies. The size and growth of capital flows to the transition economies are impressive, although there are important differences among the transition economies and significant fluctuations over time.[13] Portfolio investment in transition economies has increased (irregularly) over time, but foreign direct investment deserves special attention as a major component of capital flows (see Table 20.3).

Issues surrounding FDI in the transition economies have been controversial. The size and growth of FDI in Central and Eastern Europe has been significant, whereas the opposite has been true for countries of the CIS. How big are these investment flows, and what accounts for these significant regional differences?[14] Table 20.3 presents a more detailed picture of FDI by country. Note that as a group, the CIS countries have fared poorly in attracting FDI, and for some cases, such as Russia, the importance of FDI is strikingly small and much less understandable than in cases such as Belarus, where there has been only very limited economic change during the 1990s.[15] There are other cases, such as Bulgaria and Armenia, where FDI, judged as a share of GDP, is important, although not comparable to that in the front-running countries such as Hungary and the Czech Republic. What accounts for these differences?

There is a large literature devoted to FDI, and especially to the determinants of FDI. Typically, a host country is attractive if it has a reasonable combination of features, including a low country risk assessment, a functional and effective legal framework, a reasonable resource base (for example, available human capital), and an infrastructure appropriate to the sort of investment being contemplated. At the same time, there are a variety of motives for engaging in investment abroad, much of which in recent years has occurred within the framework of **multinational enterprises**—*firms that function in two or more countries*. As a portion of financial inflows to the transition economies, FDI has been important, although there are sharp differences among countries and also over time. Variations in level of FDI

FIGURE 20.2   Transition Economies: Total Capital Flows, 1992–1999

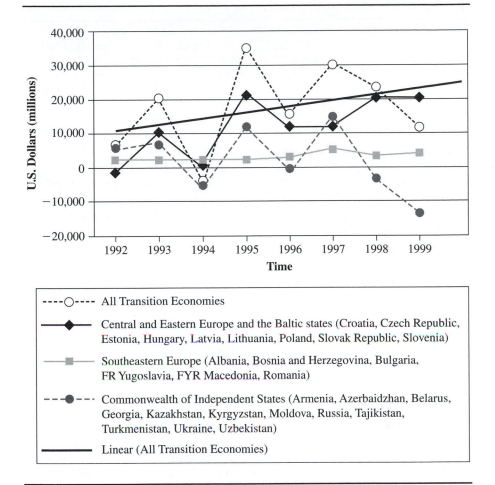

----○---- All Transition Economies

——◆—— Central and Eastern Europe and the Baltic states (Croatia, Czech Republic, Estonia, Hungary, Latvia, Lithuania, Poland, Slovak Republic, Slovenia)

——■—— Southeastern Europe (Albania, Bosnia and Herzegovina, Bulgaria, FR Yugoslavia, FYR Macedonia, Romania)

---●--- Commonwealth of Independent States (Armenia, Azerbaidzhan, Belarus, Georgia, Kazakhstan, Kyrgyzstan, Moldova, Russia, Tajikistan, Turkmenistan, Ukraine, Uzbekistan)

——— Linear (All Transition Economies)

Source: EBRD, *Transition Report 2000* (London: EBRD, 2000). From GREGORY, Comparing Economic Systems in the Twenty-First Century, 7E. © 2004 Cengage Learning.

may result from traditional cyclical factors or from changing patterns of privatization. For example, in the Eastern European economies, substantial portions of FDI inflows during the late 1990s have been from the sale of major enterprises, in effect a one-time source of financial inflows. At the same time, the transition economies' access to Western financial markets has increased, and this access can change the exposure to financial risk through diversification. Finally, capital flows and the FDI component of these flows can be very sensitive to country differences, notably the extent to which there may be natural resources (for example, in the case of Russia) that attract foreign investment.

TABLE 20.3   Foreign Direct Investment in Transition Economies: Selected Indicators

	Cumulative FDI, 1989–2001 (million US$)	Cumulative FDI per Capita, (US$)		FDI as a Percent of GDP	
		1989–2001	2001–2008	2001	2008
Czech Republic	26,493	2,570	7287	8.5	4.2
Estonia	2,358	1,637	6530	6.4	3.7
Hungary	21,869	2,177	5295	4.3	3.0
Poland	34,426	890	2927	3.6	2.7
Bulgaria	815	241	5454	5.3	17.0
Armenia	642	213	1006	4.3	6.5
Belarus	1,315	132	694	0.7	3.6
Russia	9,702	67	304	0.6	1.2
Ukraine	3,866	79	889	1.4	5.4
Central and Eastern Europe	98,297	1,365	n.a.	4.7	n.a.
Southeastern Europe	15,206	296	2669	5.1	9.2
CIS	34,368	196	n.a.	3.3	n.a.

Source: EBRD, *Transition Report Update* (Paris: EBRD, May 2002), Table 2.1; EBRD, *Transition Report 2010: Transition in Crisis?* (London: EBRD, 2010), Table A.1.1.7.

The Integration of Transition Economies

The foreign trade and payments regimes of the transition economies have been a focal point of attention for a variety of reasons. These regimes were difficult to establish in a new setting, requiring important changes and adjustments throughout the 1990s and reacting to changes that have differed considerably among the transition economies. Although it is difficult to make an overall assessment, several observations are appropriate. First, given the very different transition settings and the difficulties of establishing new trade and payments regimes in these settings, there has been impressive forward movement in many countries. Second, the differences in this forward movement are, on balance, what we would expect from our examination of other transition indicators. The changes in the Eastern and Central European transition economies have generally been much more progressive than those in the countries of the former Soviet Union.

Third, patterns of integration have changed fundamentally during the transition era. Generally speaking, trade among the CIS countries declined as trade was reoriented toward the West. The same has been true for the Eastern European transition economies, although there have been important country-to-country differences.[16]

Transition in a Turbulent Era

Perhaps it is fortunate that the transition economies enjoyed a significant period of time for the introduction of and adaptation to new systemic arrangements and policies prior to the recent worldwide financial crisis, dubbed by Carmen Reinhart and Kenneth Rogoff "The Second Great Contraction."[17] For the transition economies, the focus since roughly 2007 has been the troubled Euro environment, its impact on the transition economies, and, perhaps most important, the extent to which the difficulties of recent years may have an impact on the continuation of reform and change in these transition economies.

Earlier, we examined the literature on economic growth in transition economies. We return to the broader issues of economic growth and performance outcomes in Chapter 21. However, the external environment has been and will remain important as we examine recent performance indicators in transition economies. The EBRD identifies three main areas of importance.[18] First, as troubles emerge in the world economies, finance, and specifically the availability of external finance, remains important. Second, trade and remittances (imports and exports, and the remittances of, into transition economies when some of their workers are abroad) will fluctuate as nontransition economies face economic difficulties, especially the impact of debt in countries such as Greece and Italy. Finally, as we have emphasized, differences among the transition economies remain important as each tries to respond to these factors.

Although efforts have been made to avert default (for example, the creation of an EU/IMF fund to assist troubled countries), few expect the Euro area to be trouble free in the immediate future.

Summary

- The arrangements of the command era (state control of foreign trade, a nonconvertible currency, and barter trade) caused significant distortions in both trading arrangements and outcomes, creating major problems for the transition era.
- The major emphasis in the early years of transition has been on a sharply reduced role for the state in the conduct of foreign trade and on the creation of financial arrangements for the conduct of trade, especially the introduction of a convertible currency for both the current account and the capital account.
- The emergence of new trading arrangements opened an ongoing discussion about the appropriate policy targets and instruments for the conduct of foreign trade in a new setting.
- Most transition economies pursued the reduction of state involvement in foreign trade and the introduction of a convertible currency.
- The pursuit of integration and membership in world trading organizations has differed considerably among the transition economies. Generally speaking, the countries of the CIS have moved more slowly than those of Eastern and Central Europe.
- Throughout the transition economies, real exchange rates declined during the early years of transition and thereafter increased. Trade patterns have changed, with a reduction of intra-transition trade and an increase in the degree of integration with Western market economies. Capital flows have increased, significantly in Eastern Europe and more slowly in the CIS states. FDI has been an important component of capital flows, especially in Eastern Europe.

During the latter years of the first decade of the twenty-first century, performance in the transition economies has been highly variable. This variability has been driven in large part by the world debt crisis, the specific issues of importance in the Euro area, and the ability of the transition economies to respond to these forces both in terms of their external impact and the need for changing domestic policies to adapt to a new era.

Key Terms

accession—Process through which states (countries) become members of the European Union.

barter—Exchange of goods and services between two parties when money is not involved as an intermediary.

capital account convertibility—Exists when a currency can be purchased and sold in a market for the purpose of engaging in transactions pertaining to capital assets.

Central European Free Trade Area (CEFTA)—Free trade area (common market) formed in 1992.

Commonwealth of Independent States (CIS)—Organization that comprises those states emerging from the former Soviet Union except the Baltic states of Latvia, Lithuania, and Estonia.

convertible currency—Currency for which there is a market (supply and demand), and thus a market determined rate of exchange, available to participants within and beyond the borders of an economy.

Council for Mutual Economic Assistance (CMEA)—Trade bloc established by the former administrative command economies in 1949 to provide integration of the command economies through coordinated economic planning and trade; abolished in 1989.

current-account convertibility—Exists when a currency can be purchased and sold in a market for the purpose of engaging in transactions pertaining to the current account.

customs union—One of a variety of forms of economic integration that eliminates the trade barriers among member countries and imposes a common external tariff on nonmember countries by Poland, Hungary, and Czechoslovakia.

European Union (EU)—Group of European nations making up a single economic community.

external balance—When the demand side for foreign exchange is equalized with the supply of foreign exchange; in other words, the market for foreign exchange is in equilibrium.

foreign direct investment (FDI)—Investment flows from one country to another that occur directly—for example, through the construction of plant and equipment by a donor country in a host country—rather than through financial instruments such as stocks.

General Agreement on Tariffs and Trade (GATT)—Predecessor to the World Trade Organization (WTO); established as a framework for the discussion of world trade policies and negotiations.

internal balance—Equilibrium of the domestic economy usually characterized by full employment and the absence of inflation.

International Monetary Fund (IMF)—World organization helping member nations manage international financial transactions.

monetary union—One of a variety forms of integration in which member countries agree to use a common currency.

multinational enterprises—Firms that function in two or more countries.

newly independent states (NIS)—States (countries) emerging from the former Soviet Union sometimes known in Russia as the "near abroad."

portfolio investment—Investment flows from one country to another that occur through the purchase of financial instruments such as stocks and bonds rather than as direct investment (FDI).

World Bank—An international organization making loans to member countries for the purpose of promoting economic growth and development. Founded in 1944 and located in Washington, D.C., it works closely with the International Monetary Fund.

World Trade Organization (WTO)—Successor to GATT; provides a forum for the discussion of world trade issues.

Notes

1. The issues pertaining to foreign trade in the command economies are discussed in Paul R. Gregory and Robert C. Stuart, *Russian and Soviet Economic Structure and Performance,* 7th ed. (New York: Addison-Wesley, 2001).

2. Lorand Ambrus-Lakatos and Mark E. Schaffer, eds., *Monetary and Exchange Rate Policies, EMU and Central Eastern Europe* (New York: East–West Institute, 1999), p. 1.

3. For a discussion of these issues and the nature of the dollar wage as a nominal anchor, see Ambrus-Lakatos and Schaffer, chap. 2.

4. For an excellent discussion of the Soviet breakup, see Bert van Selm, *The Economics of the Soviet Breakup* (New York: Routledge, 1997). For a discussion of the impact of the demise of the CMEA, see Dariusz K. Rosati, "The Impact of the Soviet Trade Shock on Central and East European Economies," in Robert Holzmann, Janos Gacs, and Georg Winckler, eds., *Output Decline in Eastern Europe* (Boston: Kluwer Academic, 1995), chap. 6.

5. These issues vis-à-vis the collapse of the Soviet Union are discussed in Bert van Selm. For a background discussion on differing forms of integration, see Beth V. Yarbrough and Robert M. Yarbrough, *The World Economy,* 5th ed. (New York: South Western, 2000), chap. 9.4.

6. See van Selm, *The Economics of the Soviet Breakup.*

7. For a summary of these issues, see Lorand Ambrus-Lakatos and Mark E. Schaffer, eds., *Coming to Terms with Accession* (New York: East–West Institute, 1996).

8. For a summary of trends in the 1990s, see EBRD, *Transition Report 2001* (London: EBRD, 2001), sec. 2.7.

9. See EBRD, *Transition Report 2001* (London: EBRD, 2001), p. 12, Table 2.1. See also Constantine Michalopoulos, "The Integration of Transition Economies into the World Trading System," Paper presented at the Fifth Dubrovnik Conference on Transition Economies, Dubrovnik, Croatia, June 23–25, 1999. For recent scores, see *Transition Report 2011: Crisis and Transition: The Peoples Perspective* (London: EBRD, 2011).
10. See EBRD, *Transition Report 2001* (London: EBRD, 2001), pp. 66–67, Table A.3.8. See also EBRD *Transition Report 2011: Crisis and Transition: The Peoples Perspective* (London: EBRD, 2011).
11. See Laszlo Halpern and Charles Wyplosz, "Equilibrium Exchange Rates in Transition Economies," *IMF Staff Papers* 44 (December 1997), 430–461; Lorand Ambrus-Lakatos and Mark E. Schaffer, eds., *Monetary and Exchange Rate Policies, EMU and Central and Eastern Europe* (New York: East–West Institute, 1999).
12. Mark De Broeck and Torsten Slok, "Interpreting Real Exchange Rate Movements in Transition Countries," IMF Working Paper WP/01/56 (Washington, D.C.: IMF, May 2001).
13. For a discussion of early patterns, see EBRD, *Transition Report Update* (London: EBRD, May 2002), Part 1, chap. 2.
14. See, for example, Pietro Garibaldi, Nada Mora, Ratna Sahay, and Jeromin Zettelmeyer, "What Moves Capital to Transition Economies?" IMF Working Paper WP/02/64 (Washington, D.C.: IMF, April 2002).
15. The Russian case is especially instructive. Although capital flight is difficult to measure accurately, it was arguably a problem in the Russian case during the mid-1990s.
16. For a summary of changing trade patterns, see Michalopoulos, "The Integration of Transition Economies into the World Trading System."
17. Carmen Reinhart and Kenneth S. Rogoff, *This Time is Different: Eight Centuries of Financial Folly* (Princeton N.J.: Princeton University Press, 2009).
18. For a good survey of these issues, see EBRD *Transition Report 2009: Transition in Crisis?* (London: EBRD, 2009), chap. 2. Useful updates can be found in the subsequent EBRD Transition Reports of 2010 and 2011.

Recommended Readings

Lorand Ambrus-Lakatos and Mark E. Schaffer, eds., *Monetary and Exchange Rate Policies, EMU and Central and Eastern Europe* (New York: East–West Institute, 1999).

——, Coming to Terms with Accession (New York: East–West Institute, 1996).

Patrick-Maksimento Artisien and Yuri Adjubei, eds., *Foreign Investment in Russia and Other Successor States* (New York: St. Martin's, 1996).

Erik Berglof, Yevgeniya Korniyenko, Alexander Plekhanov, and Jeromin Zettelmeyer, *Understanding the Crisis in Emerging Europe*, EBRD Working Paper 109, 2009.

Alan A. Bevan and Saul Estrin, *The Determinants of Foreign Direct Investment in Transition Economies*, The William Davidson Institute, Working Paper 342, October 2000.

Richard N. Cooper and Janos Gacs, eds., *Trade Growth in Transition Economies* (Cheltenham, England: Edward Elgar, 1997).

Martin Dangerfield, *Subregional Cooperation in Central and Eastern Europe* (Northampton, Mass.: Edward Elgar, 2001).

Ralph De Haas and Neeltje Van Horen, *Running for the Exit: International Bank Crisis Transmission*, EBRD Working Paper 124, 2011.

Padma Desai, ed., *Going Global* (Cambridge, Mass.: MIT Press, 1997).

David G. Dickinson and Andrew W. Mullineux, eds., *Financial and Monetary Integration in the New Europe* (Northampton, Mass.: Edward Elgar, 2002).

EBRD, *Transition Report 2009: Transition in Crisis?* (London: EBRD, 2010).

———, *Transition Report 2002: Agriculture and Rural Transition* (London: EBRD, 2002).

———, *Transition Report 2011: Crisis and Transition: The Peoples Perspective* (London: EBRD, 2011).

Barry Eichengreen, "Crisis and Growth in the Advanced Economies: What We Know, What We do Not, and What We Can Learn From the 1930s" *Comparative Economic Studies* 53 (2011), 383–406.

Hubert Gabrisch and Klaus Werner, "Advantages and Drawbacks of EU Membership—The Structural Dimension," *Comparative Economic Studies* 40, no. 3 (Fall 1998), 79–103.

Janos Gacs, Robert Holzmann, and Michael L. Wyzan, eds., *The Mixed Blessing of Financial Inflows* (Northampton, Mass.: Edward Elgar, 1999).

Gábor Hunya, ed., *Integration Through Direct Foreign Investment* (Northampton, Mass.: Edward Elgar, 2000).

Hilary Ingham and Mike Ingham, eds., *EU Expansion to the East* (Northampton, Mass.: Edward Elgar 2002).

Marie Lavigne, "Conditions for Accession to the EU," *Comparative Economic Studies* 40, no. 3 (Fall 1998), 38–57.

Enrico Marelli, "Specialisation and Convergence in the European Regions," *The European Journal of Comparative Economics* 4 (2007), 149–78.

John McCormick, *Understanding the European Union: A Concise Introduction* (New York: Palgrave, 2002).

G. Michalopoulos and D. Tarr, eds., *Trade Performance and Policy in the Newly Independent States* (Washington, D.C.: World Bank, 1996).

M. V. Miklalevich, I. V. Sergienko, and L. B. Koshlai, "Simulation of Foreign Trade Activity Under Transition Economy Conditions," *Cybernetics and Systems Analysis* 34, no. 4 (2001).

OECD, *Barriers to Trade with the Economies in Transition* (Paris: OECD, 1994).

———, *Trade Policy and the Transition Process* (Paris: OECD, 1996).

Lucjan J. Orlowski, "Exchange-Rate Policies in Central Europe and Monetary Union," *Comparative Economic Studies* 40, no. 3 (Fall 1998), 58–78.

Eric J. Pentecost and Andre Van Poeck, eds., *European Monetary Integration* (Northampton, Mass.: Edward Elgar 2002).

Carmen M. Reinhart and Kenneth S. Rogoff, *This Time is Different: Eight Centuries of Financial Folly* (Princeton N.J.: Princeton University Press, 2009).

Josef van Brabant, *Centrally Planned Economies and International Economic Organizations* (New York: Cambridge University Press, 1991).

———, *Integrating Europe—The Transition Economies at Stake* (Boston, Mass.: Kluwer Academic, 1996).

———, "On the Relationship Between the East's Transitions and European Integration," *Comparative Economic Studies* 40, no. 3 (Fall 1998), 6–37.

Bert van Selm, *The Economics of the Soviet Breakup* (London: Routledge, 1997).

Christian von Hirschhausen and Jurgen Bitzer, eds., *The Globalization of Industry and Innovation in Eastern Europe* (Northampton, Mass.: Edward Elgar, 2000).

Jan Winiecki, *Transition Economies and Foreign Trade* (New York: Routledge, 2002).

Iliana Zloch-Christy, ed., *Eastern Europe and the World Economy* (Northampton, Mass.: Edward Elgar, 1998).

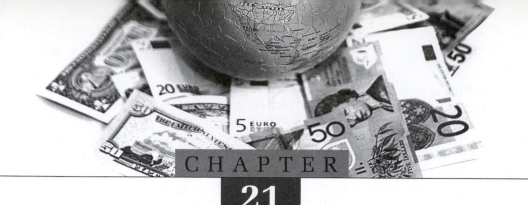

CHAPTER

21

Transition and the Safety Net

One of the most striking features of the command era was the dominant role of the state in the development and implementation of **social policies** (*policies adopted for sustaining the well-being of the population*), termed the provision of a **safety net**, *policies established to sustain a minimum level of living for the population.* Whatever the availability and quality of the various components of the safety net during the command era, most elements—unemployment benefits, medical care, and pensions for the elderly—were provided by the state in most command economies. Moreover, although it was widely argued that differences in achievement should be rewarded, the constraints of ideology often led to "leveling," or the elimination of significant differences in rewards. The incentive effects of social benefits provided by the state have always been a matter of controversy, whether in the command economies or in market economies. Thus, it might be reasonable to characterize command economies as systems in which it was very difficult, even through hard work and education, to extract a significantly larger share of the economic pie. At the same time, those who shared in the economic pie seem to have done so more evenly than in market economies.[1]

As the state structure collapsed in the command economies, inevitably it became difficult to sustain the social services. Non-state variants of social services were slow to emerge, yet many citizens were not able or prepared to make other arrangements. Moreover, in the absence of adequate revenue sources and growing budget deficits, states were ill prepared to sustain the benefit programs of the command era. The inevitable result has been, by almost any measure, a significant decline in well-being for many citizens, although there have been important variations from one country to another, and, within countries, important variations among various geographic regions and subgroups of the population.

Of course, safety-net issues are a component of any overall assessment of performance in the transition economies, but there is more to the story—and hence a separate chapter on these issues. Indeed, although economists usually assess the well-being of human populations through basic indicators such as per capita output and quality-of-life indexes, we know that the issues are complex, especially in countries undergoing rapid systemic change. Ultimately, the well-being of the population must be assessed by examining a broad array of indicators, such as access to education, employment, and (for those who need them) support services.

A major component of transition has inevitably centered on population issues—specifically, the reallocation of labor, the dramatic readjustment of the uses of human capital, and the uses of the significant volume of human capital accumulated during the command era. In this chapter, we explore issues broadly related to population and the labor force, in effect examining the winners and losers in the transition era, the changes in the safety net, and the adjustment patterns that led to new outcomes, such as the impact of widespread privatization.

In recent years, there has been extensive questioning of welfare programs and their impact on performance (often economic growth) in Western market economies.[2] Although the evidence on these issues is mixed, it has been argued that even in countries not normally identified as "welfare states," welfare programs constrain rates of economic growth and thus ultimately inhibit the long-term growth of well-being. We leave these arguments for others, although it is important to note that the development of new, market-based social welfare programs in transition economies occurs from a unique base (programs during the command era) and in a unique time frame, when such programs are under increasing scrutiny in market systems worldwide.

Finally, we would be remiss not to note the critical interaction between social welfare programs and the popular support for new regimes and new market-type policies in the transition economies. Inasmuch as political support is essential, we should not be surprised to discover that transition economies have faced very difficult policy choices. For example, in a setting where labor-market adjustment is essential but where widespread (even short-term) unemployment was historically unacceptable, what is the optimal tradeoff between unemployment and adjustment in the new transition setting, and how will it be sustained? For social policies used to provide an economic floor for the population, what is the tradeoff between the nature and the size of these benefits and any possible negative work incentives? Labor-market adjustments and the costs of these adjustments are key issues because the command economies lacked adjustment mechanisms over long periods of time. We begin with a discussion of labor markets, after which we turn to the matter of compensation for those unable to adjust to new arrangements.

The Labor Force in the Command Era

We have already emphasized several important elements of labor allocation under very different organizational arrangements. First, a major element of the command era was education, especially technical training as opposed to broader liberal arts education. Most transition economies began their passage through the transition era with major stocks of human capital. It is striking to note that compared to economies at similar levels of economic development, the stock of human capital achieved in the command economies was impressive. This human capital would be available in the transition era, and yet issues related to the use of this human capital in very different settings have been of central importance. Could the stock of human capital available from the command era be readily deployed under emerging market arrangements?

Second, most command economies pursued a policy of what has been termed a ***job right constraint***—a *policy in command economies effectively guaranteeing full employment by restricting dismissals and budget funding of unneeded workers*—or full employment.[3] Such policies bore little relation to the Western "full-employment" policies implemented as part of fiscal and monetary policies in a market economy. In the command economies, there was underemployment in a setting where the dismissal of workers, whether productive or not, was generally difficult. However one may assess this type of arrangement, unemployment was not a major issue in the command economies, and making adjustments to the allocation of labor (by field or sector) was difficult. In effect, the unemployment "problem" was incorporated into the enterprise system (in part through a soft budget), at the major cost of unproductive labor and a very ineffective system of labor allocation and reallocation. Be that as it may, many people thought they had jobs, and few were accustomed to the idea of unemployment.

Third, although the command economies did not pursue absolute equality, empirical evidence suggests that income differentials in the command economies were significantly less than would be the case in market economies. Wage differentials were used to reward differential inputs and to motivate effort, but even so the outcome was generally egalitarian compared with market economies. This has been an important legacy of the command era, but its impact during transition has been difficult to assess. Inevitably, the distribution of income changed sharply in many transition economies as market arrangements were introduced during the 1990s.

Labor in the Transition Era

During the transition era, a central issue has been the movement of labor from the former state sector to the newly emerging private sector. A prominent model with which to analyze this process is the Aghion–Blanchard model.[4] This model focuses on (1) the speed with which production (and hence inputs) will be transferred from the state to the emerging private sector and (2) the nature of the mechanisms involved—specifically, changes in the wage level in the declining state sector and in the emerging private sector, and the level of unemployment. The speed and ease with which labor can be released from the state sector and absorbed into the emerging private sector depends in part on wage levels in both sectors. However, these wage levels are increasingly a function of market forces as state wage-setting procedures of an earlier era are dismantled. Unemployment may lead to lower wage levels and thus enhance the demand for labor in the private sector. At the same time, there are significant fiscal and social costs associated with unemployment. Interest in this adjustment process has generated a considerable body of literature on the optimal speed of transition in general and especially in labor markets. How rapidly has labor moved from the public to the private sector? The evidence presented in Table 21.1 suggests considerable variation among the transition

TABLE 21.1 Employment in the Private Sector as a Percentage of Total Employment

	1992	1996	2000	2008
Albania	3.8	78.6	82.2	83.0
Azerbaijan	35.6	48.5	63.7[a]	67.0
Belarus	n.a.	9.3	18.6[a]	n.a.
Bulgaria	18.0	47.0	65.0[a]	74.0
Czech Republic	31.1	58.9	65.0	n.a.
Hungary	n.a.	76.8	81.4[b]	78.1
Poland	54.0	63.0	72.0	74.4
Romania	41.0	52.0	n.a.	69.0

n.a. = not available.
a. 1999.
b. 1998.

Source: EBRD, *Transition Report 2001: Energy in Transition* (London: EBRD, 2001). *EBRD Transition Report 2009: Transition in Crisis?* (London: EBRD, 2009), country assessments.

economies listed. Private-sector employment at the onset of transition differed significantly from one country to another; for example, it was very low in Albania and very high in Poland.[5] These differences are not surprising, given what we know about the initial conditions in these cases. We also note that the growth of private-sector employment has generally been very rapid. Once again, the differences that we observe (for example, the slow emergence of private-sector employment in Belarus) conform closely to our knowledge of the countries (of Belarus as a country) with limited emphasis on transition.

Empirical research on the labor-adjustment process has extended the basic Aghion–Blanchard model. Generally speaking, the reallocation has had results somewhat different from what was commonly anticipated. Unemployment was expected to result from the closure of state enterprises, but it was generally of greater magnitude than expected, and often with important sectoral and regional differences. Unemployment has indeed risen as the result of job quitters' entry into unemployment, closure of both state and private enterprises, and limited exit from unemployment back into employment; on balance, adjusting to unemployment has been less successful than might have been expected. As we will see, there have often been unusual forms of adjustment such as the emergence of family safety nets. Moreover, the evidence suggests that sectoral and regional adjustment (for example, in Russia) has been limited, with important differences by age and sex.[6]

Along with the shift of employment by sector, there have been marked changes in aggregate employment levels and in the extent and nature of unemployment. Employment levels declined significantly in the transition economies during the early 1990s. There were, however, marked differences among the various countries. Throughout the decade of the 1990s, the level of total employment in the Commonwealth of Independent States (CIS) countries declined steadily, from roughly 11.8 million in 1990 to 10.2 million in 1998. At the same time, in Central

TABLE 21.2   Unemployment Levels in Selected Transition Economies

Country	1994	1998	2001	2008	2011
Russia	7.8	11.9	9.0	7.8	6.6
Kazakhstan	8.1	6.6	11.0	6.6	5.4
Ukraine	0.3	3.7	3.7	6.4	7.0
Poland	16.0	10.4	17.3	6.7	12.4
Estonia	7.6	9.9	12.7	5.5	12.1
Hungary	12.4	10.1	8.4	7.8	10.9
Czech Republic	3.2	7.5	8.9	n.a.	8.5

Source: EBRD, *Transition Report Update* (London: EBRD, May 2002), country assessment; EBRD, *Transition Report 2008: Transition in Crisis?* (London: EBRD, 2009), Country assessments; data for 2011 are estimates from CIA, World Factbook, http://www.CIA.gov/library/publications/the-world-factbook.

and Eastern Europe and the Baltic States and in Southeastern Europe, employment levels initially declined. They began to recover in the mid-1990s, but with only limited gains made toward the end of the decade. During these years, the level of unemployment also increased.

In Table 21.2 we present a summary of unemployment levels for a selected group of transition economies.

Unemployment data for transition economies need to be interpreted with caution. First, it is troubling for the observer to note that evidence about unemployment differs considerably from one source to another and has been subject to major revisions over time. Second, although they are not unreasonable, levels of unemployment are generally high in the transition economies. The increases in unemployment through the transition era have been the result of various factors that we have noted, but adjusting to them has been difficult for populations generally not accustomed to unemployment of the sort experienced in market economies. In other words, both the decline in employment levels and the increase in unemployment levels hide patterns of adjustment in the transition economies.

Unfortunately, in spite of significant differences among countries, labor-market adjustments in transition economies have not generally been significant. There has been only limited adjustment by sector and by region. Moreover, the movement out of unemployment has generally been slow, in spite of a major policy effort to create appropriate components of a safety net while encouraging mobility. Understandably, mobility has generally been greater into and also out of the emerging private sector.

Employment, Earnings, and the Safety Net

Adjustment in labor markets of the transition economies has varied significantly from country to country. Typically, and especially in the CIS countries, many who are employed are not employed full-time. One adjustment strategy is holding multiple jobs. A second strategy is sometimes termed a "subsistence" approach, such as informal employment or family activities. According to a recent EBRD report, "family helpers," measured as a percentage of the population over 16, varied from a low of 4 percent in Poland in 1998 to a high of 31.16 percent in Russia in 1998.[7] For the most part, males dominate the "multiple employment" category; females, the "family helper" category.

To the extent that unemployment has been a serious problem that has persisted at relatively high levels, unemployment benefits and the possibility of entry into poverty are important issues in the transition setting. The transition economies have generally developed systems of unemployment compensation. These programs differ from country to country and have typically been more generous in Eastern Europe than in the CIS, although the level of generosity has declined over time. In Poland and Hungary, these programs accounted for 2.4 and 2.0 percent of GDP, respectively, in 1994; in Russia they accounted for just 0.4 percent of GDP. The percentage of registered unemployed who were receiving benefits has been high in some cases (77.1 percent in Russia in 1995) and quite low in other cases (23.6 percent in Slovakia in 1992 and 31.2 percent in Bulgaria in 1995).[8]

The budgetary impact of unemployment benefits has been a matter of concern, although it is arguably not large. However, the empirical evidence seems to suggest that these programs do not have a significant impact. Thus with sustained high unemployment (especially for particular segments of the population, such as women and older men), poverty becomes a greater threat. There is also the likelihood of increasing income inequality, an issue to which we return below.

The concept of poverty always involves cultural, regional, and historical characteristics.[9] Two main issues arise in the process of identifying poverty: definition and measurement. In terms of *definition*, it is necessary to establish a poverty line in terms of an appropriate variable, such as income, health conditions, or the availability of basic consumption items such as housing. What does a society deem to be a reasonable minimum level of income? *Measurement*, in this context, means determining what portion of the population is in poverty and thus falls below the established minimum. Thus it is necessary to analyze income levels—a critical issue in transition economies because the composition of household income (reported and unreported) has changed significantly from earlier socialist patterns during the transition era. The existence and importance of underground (unreported and unmeasured) economic activity is important in this effort. Finally, having identified a poverty line and counted those who are statistically below this line, it is important both to analyze poverty incidence (how widespread and how deep it is) and to understand who is in poverty, identifying causal factors.

How widespread is poverty in the transition economies? Although there are always measurement difficulties, there is considerable agreement on the magnitude and depth of poverty in the transition economies (see Table 21.3).

A number of observations emerge from the data in Table 21.3. First, there are important differences in the incidence of poverty, which is significant in the CIS states (for example, Russia and Ukraine) and much less significant in the Eastern European cases (for example, Hungary and the Czech Republic). Second, understandably, the **poverty deficit**—*the amount of funding that would be necessary to raise all those below an established poverty level up to that level*—also differs considerably among the transition economies. Third, although different approaches to measurement yield broadly comparable results for the incidence of poverty, there

TABLE 21.3   Poverty in Selected Transition Economies, 1993–1995

	Poverty Head Count (HBS)[a]	Poverty Deficit as a Percent of GDP	Poverty Head Count (Macro)[b]	Poverty Deficit as a Percent of GDP[c]
Russia	44	3.3	39	3.7
Kazakhstan	62	8.2	n.a.	n.a.
Ukraine	63	6.9	26	2.3
Poland	14	0.9	10	0.5
Estonia	37	4.2	34	2.9
Hungary	2	0.1	7	0.3
Czech Republic	Less than 1	0.0	n.a.	n.a.

a. Based on income as measured by (HBS) household budget surveys.
b. Based on macroeconomic (income) data.
c. Based on estimates of household expenditures.

Source: Compiled from Branko Milanovic, *Income, Inequality, and Poverty During the Transition from Planned to Market Economy* (Washington, D.C.: World Bank, 1998), Tables 5.2 and 5.3.

are nevertheless cases where measurement issues are important. In the case of Ukraine, the importance of the poverty deficit varies considerably, depending on the manner in which it is measured. It has been argued that poverty is generally a more serious problem in the CIS countries than in the transition economies of Eastern Europe, although even where the incidence of poverty seems high the depth of poverty is generally not great.

Thus far we have focused on the safety-net issues related to labor-market adjustments, earnings, unemployment, and the possibility of poverty. Earnings, however, are a function of a wide variety of factors, such as schooling, work experience, length of employment, and a bevy of important personal characteristics such as age, sex, and health status. All are important for our understanding of transition and especially of the critical bottom line: the overall well-being of the population. In this section, we examine the relationship among basic demographic issues, population well-being, and the health care and other support mechanisms.

Demographic Issues and the Safety Net

Many would argue that basic demographic patterns—including birth rates, death rates, and the rate of growth of the population—are typically stable over the long term, barring a catastrophe such as war. An examination of basic data on life expectancy (and birth rates and death rates) in the transition economies reveals two important patterns. First, in some transition economies (notably the CIS countries), a significant decline and then a modest recovery in life expectancy occurred during the early years of the transition era. The pattern is especially striking when compared to similar data from the pretransition era and to data from other countries. Second, an analysis of these patterns of life expectancy suggests that they have been much more severe in the CIS countries and much less severe or virtually nonexistent in Eastern Europe, although in general the impact on males has been greater than the impact on females. What has accounted for these patterns, and what policy implications emerge?

Studies have shown that the reduction of life expectancy has been primarily a result of rising mortality rates, especially for males. Mortality rates have seemingly risen for identifiable reasons (cancer and cardiovascular disease, for example), but this change is serious and cannot be attributed to possible measurement problems. Specifically, these adverse demographic developments have been in part the result of changing income patterns and an inability to access adequate health care. Consider, for example, the case of Russia.[10]

Figure 21.1 shows crude birth and death rates for Russia from 1990 through 2010. The pattern here is striking and has received a great deal of attention as a "demographic crisis." What is the essence of this crisis, and how is it related to transition and the safety net? An analysis of death rates in the Russian case indicates that especially among males, age-specific death rates from some historically common causes (cancer and cardiovascular disease) increased significantly during the early years of transition. Deaths from these diseases, along with a continuing alcohol problem and increasing crime rates, were associated with the sharp declines in income and the general disruption in the provision of social services that accompanied the end of the command era. The latter issue is not easy to chronicle. However, there is now considerable debate over the demographic issues: Are they directly related to transition, or are they in part related to longer term demographic changes? These rates have remained strikingly similar in the twenty-first century with a crude birth rate of 10 per 1,000 population and a crude death rate of 15 per 1,000 population in 2011.

The data in Table 21.4 indicate significant and sustained expenditure on health and education (as a portion of GDP), but in cases like Russia, there are significant regional differences in the level at which such services are provided, financed, and delivered and in how much disruption of services occurred.

FIGURE 21.1   Russia Birth and Death Rates per 1,000 Population: 1990–2010

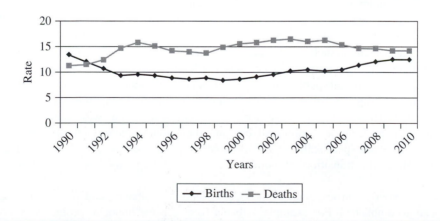

Source: Goskomstat Rossii, *Demograficheskii ezhegodnik Rossii* (Moscow: Goskomstat, 2002), p. 55; http://www.en.wikipedia.org.

TABLE 21.4   Expenditures on Health and Education as a Percentage of
GDP Health Only

	1992	1994	1996	1998	2000	2008
Russia	6.0	7.7	7.4	7.4	5.4	4.8
Kazakhstan	6.1	5.3	7.2	6.2	4.2	3.9
Ukraine	8.6	10.1	8.7	7.9	5.6	6.8
Poland	10.8	10.7	10.8	9.9	5.5	7.6
Estonia	12.1	13.4	12.2	12.0	5.3	6.1
Czech Republic	10.1	11.9	11.7	10.8	n.a.	n.a

n.a. = not available.
Source: EBRD, *Transition Report 2001: Energy in Transition* (London: EBRD, 2001), country assessments; http://www.who.int/whosis/whostat/enwhs2011_part2.xls.

Transition and the Social Sector

Thus far we have observed that changing employment conditions along with declining income and demographic changes have led to the emergence of social problems in the transition economies and that these problems have been more serious in the CIS economies than in the transition economies of Eastern Europe. What has been done to address these difficulties? A number of generalizations can be made.

First, it is well known that the command economies provided significant—if controversial—social programs.[11] During transition, however, the arrangements made in the command era were eroded and often could not serve the needs of a new era. For example, unemployment was theoretically nonexistent during the command era but became an important problem during transition. Second, the modes of adjustment (for example, increasing unemployment, severe inflationary pressures, and increases in retirement prompted by inability to adjust to a new employment setting) created pressure on available benefit programs, financial distress, and inevitably worsening standards of living for many. Third, there have been significant policy differences among the transition economies. In advanced cases such as Poland, the typical pattern is a combination of both state and private funding for pensions, partly on a pay-as-you-go basis. Health insurance (again both public and private) has been introduced, along with financial reform, to bring contributions and tax levels in line with expenditures for fiscal solvency. These countries have achieved a reduction in the widespread benefits carried over from the command era and their replacement with targeted programs directed specifically at the most needy groups of the population. Indeed, throughout the transition economies, the issue of targeting has assumed major importance.

In other countries, such as the Czech Republic, Albania, and Russia, less has been accomplished. For example, Albania faces serious financial problems in sustaining pensions, and in the Czech Republic these problems are related to longer-term demographic changes—specifically, the aging of the population.

As the transition economies move toward market arrangements, the problems they face become increasingly similar to those debated in the developed market economies. Expenditures on both health care and education are major budget items and must be approached in such a way as to ensure fiscal responsibility. Pension arrangements must account for the increasing dependency ratio, and unemployment schemes must strike an appropriate balance between providing essential benefits and sustaining incentives that lead to critical adjustments in labor markets.

Transition, Inequality, and Levels of Well-Being

Throughout this book we have emphasized the importance of the initial conditions, or factors from the past, that influence development during the transition era. In this chapter we have stressed the fact that dramatic changes have occurred in standards of living during transition, partly because of the erosion of social-sector programs. These programs, significant during the command era, have undergone important changes, which have had rather different results in different transition economies. What can we expect in a new century?

Empirical evidence suggests two conclusions regarding inequality.[12] First, the populations of transition economies generally prefer a more egalitarian distribution of income than would be the case in Western economies. Second, these views are not necessarily generated from the sometimes sharp changes in the distribution of income that occurred during transition but, rather, are based on long-standing views about the nature of the social contract. Understanding this evidence is important because during transition there have been significant changes in the distribution of income—changes that are having, and will continue to have, important social and economic consequences.

In nearly all transition economies, inequality (measured by the **Gini coefficient**, which is the *standard measure of income inequality that usually expresses the gap between low income earners—say the bottom 10 percent of income earners—and the top 10 percent of income earners*) increased during the early years of transition (see Table 21.5), in some cases significantly.[13] In part, these changes are the result of changes in the composition of income, but these changes have themselves had a disproportionate impact on certain social groups. Specifically, the burden of inequality has been borne by the elderly, farmers, those not fully employed, and (to some degree) women.

It is important to appreciate that these changes in the Gini coefficient, especially in cases such as Russia, are very large, particularly in a setting accustomed to a more egalitarian distribution of income. This outcome conforms to a popular view in Russia—namely, that the benefits of transition, broadly defined, have been very unevenly distributed. These issues are important for our overall assessment of transition and of the mechanisms and policies that have been used in the various transition economies.

Table 21.5   Inequality in Selected Transition: Economies: Annual
Gini Coefficient

	2011	1987–1988	1993–1995
Russia	39.9	24	48[a]
Kazakhstan	33.9	26	33
Ukraine	28.1	23	47[b]
Poland	34.5	26	28[c]
Estonia	35.8	23	35[a]
Hungary	26.9	21	23
Czech Republic	25.4	19	27[b]

Note: In most cases, income in 1987–1988 is gross income and in 1993–1995 is disposable income.

a. Quarterly.
b. Monthly.
c. Semiannual.

Source: Compiled from Branko Milanovic, *Income, Inequality, and Poverty During the Transition from Planned to Market Economy* (Washington, D.C.: World Bank, 1998), p. 41, Table 4.1. Data for 2011 from http://www.nationmaster.com economic statistics—income inequality—UN Gini index.

Summary

- During the command era, the state provided the safety net. During transition, it has been difficult for the state to sustain the safety net, private-sector alternatives have been slow to emerge, and state budgets have lacked an adequate revenue base. However, safety-net benefits such as reduction of poverty and the provision of pensions, medical care, and unemployment benefits are all important elements for our assessment of transition. They also influence the extent to which there is popular support for transition programs.

- Our analysis of safety-net issues begins with a discussion of the allocation of labor, the end of state employment, and the entry into private-sector employment. To the extent that this process is uneven, the ineffective use of a significant stock of human capital in the transition economies has important implications for economic growth, and the resulting growth of unemployment boosts the demands placed on the safety-net programs.

- We emphasize the fact that although transition economies are struggling with safety-net issues in countries not accustomed to widespread unemployment, the debate over these programs and their potential impact on economic growth is also a major issue in Western industrialized economies.

- Although the labor-allocation adjustment in the transition economies has generally entailed a decline in state-sector employment and an increase in private-sector employment, the process has grown more complicated as the structure of household incomes has changed and aggregate levels of unemployment have risen significantly.

- One major outcome of these difficult labor-market changes has been significant increases in the levels of poverty in transition economies. However, studies suggest that there are significant differences in the incidence of poverty (aggregate levels of poverty and its impact on different population groups by region, age, and gender). As with other indicators of transition, there are important differences between the transition economies of Eastern Europe and the CIS states.

- Considerable attention has been paid to the broad relationships between safety-net issues and the emerging demographic patterns in transition economies. Although the evidence suggests that expenditures on health have largely been sustained (measured as a portion of state spending), difficulties in the delivery of health services have contributed to what in some countries (such as Russia) has been termed a "demographic crisis": increases in death rates and reductions in birth rates. Again, there are significant differences between the patterns observed in the CIS states and those observed in Eastern Europe.
- An important and controversial outcome of the transition era has been changes—sometimes sharp changes—in the extent of income inequality, measured by the Gini coefficient.

Key Terms

social policies—A broad concept referring to policies adopted for preserving the well-being of a society, for example income maintenance programs, unemployment benefits, and the like.

safety net—Policies designed to maintain a minimum standard of living for the population. Examples are unemployment insurance benefits and pensions for the elderly.

job right constraint—A policy, prevalent in command economies, in which full employment would in effect be guaranteed through limitations on the firing of unneeded workers and the provision of funds to finance unneeded workers.

poverty deficit—Amount of funding that would be necessary to raise all those below an established poverty line up to that line.

Gini coefficient—A standard measure of income equality that usually expresses the gap between low income earners (say the bottom 10 percent of income earners) and high income earners (say the top 10 percent of income earners).

Notes

1. Inequality varied regionally in command economies such as the Soviet Union and generally increased during the 1980s, when the Gini coefficient ranged from the mid- to upper twenties. For a discussion of inequality during the command era, see Paul R. Gregory and Robert C. Stuart, *Russian and Soviet Economic Performance and Structure* (New York: Addison Wesley Longman, 2001), Ch. 7.
2. For a useful discussion of these issues, see A. B. Atkinson, *The Economic Consequences of Rolling Back the Welfare State* (Cambridge, Mass.: MIT Press, 1999).
3. The classic work is David Granick, *Job Rights in the Soviet Union: Their Consequences* (New York: Cambridge University Press, 1987).
4. See the discussion in Oliver Blanchard, *The Economics of Post-Communist Transition* (Oxford: Clarendon Press, 1997), Ch. 2; and P. Aghion and O. Blanchard, "On the

Speed of Transition in Central Europe" *National Bureau of Economic Research Macro-economics Annual*, 1994, pp. 283–320.

5. Again, as we have emphasized, some of the command economies (for example, Poland and Hungary) experienced considerable economic reform and change during the latter years of the command era. These experiences are in sharp contrast to cases like the Czech Republic (then Czechoslovakia), where there was little economic reform in the post-1968 period.

6. There is a large literature on employment policies in transition countries. For a survey, see Tito Boeri and Hartmut Lehmann, eds., "Unemployment and Labor Market Policies in Transition Countries," *Journal of Comparative Economics* 27, no. 1 (March 1999), 1–130; for a discussion of the Russian case, see J. David Brown and John S. Earle, "Gross Job Flows in Russian Industry Before and After Reforms: Has Destruction Become More Creative?" IZA, Discussion Paper No. 351, August 2001; for a discussion of the Polish case, see Andrew Newell and Francesco Pastore, "Regional Unemployment and Industrial Restructuring in Poland," IZA, Discussion Paper No. 194, August 2000. See also Hartmut Lehmann and Jonathan Wadsworth, "Tenures That Shook the World: Worker Turnover in Russia, Poland, and Britain," *Journal of Comparative Economics* 28, no. 4 (December 2000), 639–664; Elizabeth Brainerd, "Winners and Losers in Russia's Economic Transition," *American Economic Review* 88, no. 5 (December 1998), 1094–1116; EBRD, *Transition Report 2000* (London: EBRD, 2000), Ch. 5.

7. For a discussion of these issues, see EBRD, *Transition Report 2000,* Ch. 5.

8. These data are from ibid.

9. There is a large literature on poverty in the transition economies. See, for example, Sandra Hutton and Gerry Redmond, eds., *Poverty in Transition Economies* (London: Routledge, 2000); Branko Milanovic, *Income, Inequality, and Poverty During the Transition from Planned to Market Economy* (Washington, D.C.: World Bank, 1998); World Bank, *From Plan to Market: World Development Report 1996* (Washington, D.C.: World Bank, 1996); Janos Kornai and Karen Eggleston, *Welfare, Choice and Solidarity in Transition* (Cambridge: Cambridge University Press, 2001); Ethan B. Kapstein and Michael Mandelbaum, eds., *Sustaining the Transition: The Social Safety Net in Post-communist Europe* (New York: Council on Foreign Relations, 1997).

10. See, for example, the discussion in Julie DaVanzo and David Adamson, "Russia's Demographic 'Crisis': How Real Is It?" Rand Corporation, Center for Russian and European Studies, Labor and Population Program, July 1997; Mark G. Field, "The Health Crisis in the Former Soviet Union: A Report from the 'Post-War' Zone," *Social Science Medicine* 41, no. 11 (1995), 1469–1478; Elizabeth Brainerd, "Death and the Market," Department of Economics, Williams College, typescript. A useful set of articles on population in Russia can be found in *The World Development Report* 26, no. 11 (1998).

11. A useful survey of basic issues is Peter S. Heller and Christian Keller, "Social Sector Reform in Transition Economies," IMF Working Paper WP/01/35.

12. See the discussion in Marc Suhrcke, "Preferences for Inequality: East vs. West," UNI-CEF, Innocenti Working Paper No. 89, October 2001.

13. There is a significant body of literature addressing issues of inequality in transition economies. See, for example, Branko Milanovic, *Income, Inequality, and Poverty During the Transition from Planned to Market Economy* (Washington, D.C.: World Bank, 1998); John Flemming and John Micklewright, "Income Distribution, Economic Systems and Transition," UNICEF, Innocenti Working Paper, No. 70, May 1999.

Recommended Readings

Joachim Ahrens, *Governance and Economic Development* (Northampton, Mass.: Edward Elgar, 2002).

Dirk J. Bezemer, "Poverty in Transition Countries," *Journal of Economics and Business* IX, no. 1 (2006), 11–35.

Jeanine Braithwaite, Christian Grootaert, and Branko Milanovic, *Poverty and Social Assistance in Transition Economies* (New York: Palgrave Macmillan, 2000).

Annette N. Brown, ed., *When is Transition Over?* (Kalamazoo, Mich.: Upjohn Institute, 1999).

Tilman Bruck, Alexander M Danzer, Alexander Muravyev, and Naralia Weibhaar, "Determinants of Poverty During Transition: Household Survey Evidence From Ukraine," DIW Berlin, December 7, 2007.

Michael Cuddy and Ruvin Gekker, eds., *Institutional Change in Transition Economies* (Burlington, Vt.: Ashgate, 2002).

Patricia Dillon and Frank C. Wykoff, *Creating Capitalism* (Northampton, Mass.: Edward Elgar, 2002).

Robert Gilpin, *The Challenge of Global Capitalism* (Princeton, N.J.: Princeton University Press, 2000).

Louis Haddad, *Towards a Well-Functioning Economy* (Northampton, Mass.: Edward Elgar, 2003).

Christian von Hirschhausen, *Modernizing Infrastructure in Transformation Economies* (Northampton, Mass.: Edward Elgar, 2002).

Sandra Hutton and Gerry Redmond, eds., *Poverty in Transition Economies* (New York: Routledge, 2000).

ILO, *Global Employment Trends 2011: The Challenge of a Jobs Recovery* (Geneva: ILO, 2011).

Hay H. Levin, *A Guide to the Euro* (Boston: Houghton Mifflin, 2002).

Tomasz Mickiewicz and Janice Bell, *Unemployment in Transition: Restructuring and Labor Markets in Central Europe* (London: Routledge, 2000).

Vladimir Mikhalev, *Inequality and Social Structure During Transition* (New York: Palgrave Macmillan, 2003).

Richard Pomfret, *Constructing a Market Economy* (Northampton, Mass.: Edward Elgar, 2002).

Linda M. Randall, *Reluctant Capitalists* (New York: Routledge, 2001).

James N. Rosenau, *Distant Proximities: Dynamics beyond Globalization* (Princeton, N.J.: Princeton University Press, 2003).

Peter Saunders and Harry X. Wu, eds., "Measuring Growth, Productivity, Income Distribution and Poverty in Transition Economies: Progress, Challenges and Prospects," *Review of Income and Wealth Series* 55, special issue, July 2009.

Andrei Shleifer and Robert W. Vishny, *The Grabbing Hand* (Cambridge, Mass.: Harvard University Press, 1998).

Horst Seibert, *The World Economy*, 2nd ed. (London and New York: 2002).

Max Spoor, ed., *The Political Economy of Rural Livelihoods in Transition Economies: Land, Peasants and Rural Poverty in Transition* (London: Routledge, 2010).

Gerturde Tumpel-Gugerell and Peter Mooslechner, eds., *Economic Convergence and Divergence in Europe* (Northampton, Mass.: Edward Elgar, 2003).

World Bank, *The World Development Report 2003* (Washington, D.C.: World Bank, 2003).

PART

V

Assessing the World Economies in a New Era: Performance

CHAPTER
22

Prospects for 2050: Economic Institutions and Economic Performance

The study of economic systems is definitely a long-run endeavor. Institutions change slowly and their impact on economic performance can be gleaned only over a long period of time. Yet, the short run attracts most of our attention and diverts us from understanding the role of institutions on economic performance. In writing a book on comparative economic systems, we must keep our eye on long-run trends and not be distracted by current events.

Has Capitalism Failed? Cycles versus Secular Trends

Writing as we are in the second decade of the twenty-first century, we are barraged with screaming headlines of financial crises, high unemployment, budget deficits, impending defaults, and other calamities. This attention on what is occurring right now is understandable. As we write, the world economy is slowly emerging from what has been termed the "second great contraction." Some say this contraction is unique.[1] Others say it is like most other contractions, only somewhat more severe. The second great contraction was less severe than the Great Depression of the 1930s but similar in magnitude to the severe downturns of the late 1970s and early 1980s. We live in the short run, as John Maynard Keynes emphasized, so we naturally focus our attention on today not the future.

Reputable publications and the blogosphere feature forums to discuss the "failure" of capitalism. They herald the arrival of a new and better form of economic organization—perhaps state capitalism, as practiced in China, Brazil, and Russia.[2]

Critics of capitalism use economic downturns, especially severe ones, to prove the failure of market capitalism. The communist and socialist movements in the

United States were strongest during the Great Depression. We even had a socialist as vice president.

In a familiar refrain, critics cite the recession of 2008–2010 as a distinctive failure of the market economy, but business cycles have always been an integral part of the capitalist model. Their persistence shows we have not been able to eradicate them, despite our best efforts. Students of the planned socialist economy were duly surprised to find business cycles under planned socialism.[3] However under planned socialism, the bigger problem was one of secular decline not cycles.

Recessions, financial crises, and bubbles do not prove the failure of capitalism. They are a part of capitalism, and they always will be. The issue instead is whether capitalism's growth during upturns compensates for the loss of output during downturns. It is difficult to take this longer-term view when businesses are failing, unemployment is high, and an election is just around the corner.

This book addresses timeless questions that transcend transitory booms and busts: We want to know which constellation of economic arrangements yield superior economic performance. Answers to this question are vital as a guide to public policy, assuming we could ever convince our politicians to focus on the really important issues.

Economic Systems: Models and Performance

There is no easy answer to the question of ideal institutional arrangements for economic performance. We have enough on our hands just to cluster economic arrangements into something we can call distinctive economic systems. The world's economic systems are no longer demarcated into capitalism and socialism. In those days, when classification was simpler, getting answers was easier: Capitalism did clearly outperform planned socialism, which is a discredited economic system except in a few odd circles. Instead of capitalism versus socialism we have a more nuanced conception of what constitutes an economic system.

Throughout this book, we have focused on four models of economic systems:

1. Anglo-Saxon model
2. Planned socialist model
3. European model
4. Asian model

We have treated China separately as an economic system in the process of defining itself, and one that insists on calling itself market socialism "with a Chinese face." Additionally, the models we have studied are far from comprehensive. In particular, they leave out Latin America, Africa, and large parts of Asia, such as Pakistan and Bangladesh.

The transition model that occupied the last few chapters is not a real model in the sense that it studies economies in the process of converting from one economic system to another. Once the transition is "over," we will cease studying it, other than as an object of historical interest or as a lesson for others, such as North Korea or Cuba.

The measurement of economic performance is also nuanced. Although economic growth remains the most widely used performance indicator, we have to consider alternative measures, such as efficiency and income distribution, and even broader measures, such as "quality of life" or what we broadly call "happiness." Even if we could agree on quantifiable measures of economic systems and economic performance, we would still face complex econometric problems in establishing relationships and causality.

The Chinese proverb says: "May you live in interesting times." We have been eyewitnesses to unprecedented and unexpected change in the second half of the twentieth century and the first decade of the twenty-first. In 1936, Keynes in his *General Theory of Employment, Interest and Money* warned that we are all captives of the philosophies and economic ideas of the past.[4] But over long enough periods of time, we in a better position to understand which ideas of the past were incorrect and which have merit.

The Past Half Century: A Helicopter View

The last sixty years have taught us to expect the unexpected. Few anticipated the collapse of the Soviet Union and its East European empire. The best experts in the field anticipated that Soviet-style communism would muddle along for quite a while. We were caught off guard by the early postwar economic miracle of Japan. We had thought that the Japanese were capable only of producing low-quality knock-offs of American products. Now we consider Japanese manufacturing as high quality but recognize that Japan's better days are a thing of the past.

We were surprised when the Four Southeast Asian Tigers duplicated and improved on the Japanese model. Early postwar prognosticators expected Africa, not Asia, to be the next developing region. They did not foresee the Asian boom and the African bust.

We did not expect that China would emerge from the chaos of the Mao dictatorship to become the world's second largest and most rapidly growing economy—one that promises to become a world superpower as a result of its economic success. Will we be similarly surprised by the hidden weaknesses of the Chinese model that came to light as the Chinese Communist Party prepared for its Eighteenth Party Congress amid rumors of murder, corruption, and power struggles?

The biggest surprise of all has been India, which for the past quarter century has been among the world's fastest growing economies. India has shown that liberalization can yield immediate and long-lasting benefits if the nation's leaders, from all parties, hold firm to the reform approach. If India continues its rapid growth, it belies the myth that democracy cannot produce rapid growth in a poor country. However India, like its neighbor China, must overcome political corruption if it is to continue its progress.

The rise of Asia reversed the centuries-old "Great Divergence" between the West and the East.[5] Asia's two largest countries, India and China, are growing rapidly under quite different political conditions. China retained its one-party dictatorship after the suppression of student demonstrations in the spring of 1989. In contrast, India is the world's largest democracy, albeit a messy one. If India continues its growth, it will refute the claim that poor countries need a strong and benevolent leader to develop. Experience shows that there are many dictators who wish to exercise a strong hand, but few of them are benevolent.

Our forefathers were also caught off guard almost seventy years ago when Germany and Japan rose from the ashes of defeat at the end of World War II to become "economic miracles." Japan's economic miracle lasted through the 1970s before it entered an extended period of malaise. Germany cemented its status as Europe's largest and most solid economy, but the heavy burden of integrating the failed East German economy bore its costs. German growth slowed considerably, but it still remains the anchor of the emerging European Union.

The European Union was the idea of French politicians, who considered economic integration the best protection against resurgence of German militarism and nationalism. Beginning modestly as an iron and coal community, Europe expanded into a common market and then into a full-fledged European Union, with free mobility of labor and capital, no customs barriers, and a single currency and central bank. As the European Union expanded to the south and the east, it absorbed less affluent countries, many with weak economic institutions. This expansion was ad hoc and treaty based. The European Union could not agree on a common constitution.

We were also caught off guard by the EU crisis of 2011 and 2012. EU governments to the south took advantage of their Eurozone membership to borrow freely at low EU-zone interest rates to finance profligate state spending. As they faced insolvency, the solvent EU members to the North had to decide whether to bail them out or impose austerity on them. The Eurozone crisis continues, so we do not know its ultimate resolution. Much depends on the national elections of 2012 and the actions of the European Central Bank.

The affluent world of North America, Europe, and Japan are confronting another issue, which has been long anticipated because it is based on demographic fundamentals. Over the course of the past half century, the affluent world erected generous safety nets for the middle class and the less fortunate. Among the most expensive state programs are old age retirement and medical care. Insofar as these welfare programs are paid for out of tax revenue, primarily taxes on labor, the affluent world has had to confront the issue of affordability. We face aging populations and fewer younger workers to pay the taxes on labor that fund medical care and retirement programs. These programs face billions or trillions of dollars of unfunded liabilities usually hidden from public view. Governments must either find new sources of revenue and risk reductions in economic growth or make their welfare programs less generous, a move that would impose enormous political costs on parties in power.

The affluent countries of the world are currently testing the limits of the welfare state. Some have clearly gone too far, such as Sweden, Netherlands, and to some extent Germany, and have cut back. Others, such as Greece, have gone too far but do not understand how they can reduce the welfare state in feasible economic and political terms. The 2012 U.S. election is being fought over the size of the welfare state. The Republican platform will call for reining in entitlement spending. The Democrat platform will be relatively silent on this issue, meaning tacit support for no cuts and perhaps even further expansion. In Europe, social democratic, socialist, and labor parties fight for the preservation of the existing welfare state against conservative and liberal parties.

Few expected the transition in what was the Soviet Empire to be as difficult as it was. Beginning in the late 1980s, almost a decade after China's reforms began, many experts thought the transition would proceed smoothly as the transition countries moved from planned socialism to capitalism. Even the most successful experienced transition recessions. Poland, Hungary, and the Czech Republic lost 10–15 percent of their output and resumed growth only after three or four years. Others lost almost half of their output and did not resume growth for almost a decade. The upheaval of the transition was immense and reflects itself in non-economic indicators such as heightened mortality and collapsing birth rates.

The success of the transition countries must be measured in both economic and political terms, although the two are related. Here we see a clear divide between the transition countries of Central Europe, southeastern Europe, and the Baltic States that had less distant experiences with democracy and markets than the republics of the former Soviet Union. The former group of countries joined the European Union; they are, by and large, working democracies and can be generally considered economic successes. Russia, Ukraine, Central Asia, and the Caucasus states are totalitarian or, at best, tenuous democracies, and their economic performance has been weak. Many are nominal democracies, but they are governed largely by the elite of Soviet times, they are plagued by massive corruption, and they are run by oligarchies. In Russia, Kazakhstan, and Azerbaijan, the ruling class is kept afloat by oil and natural resource wealth. In natural resource–poor countries, the dictatorship is kept afloat by extreme repression, such as in Belarus.

Other Economic Systems

The scope of this book is broad, but it cannot cover everything. Latin America, the Middle East, and Africa are notably absent, not because these areas are not interesting but because of space limitations. We cannot conclude, however, without a few highlights from these parts of the globe.

Latin America

Latin America has been torn in the postwar period between political and economic extremes. Authoritarian political regimes and populist economic policies have alternated with movements toward political democracy and free-market reform.

Most Latin American countries have had their share of military dictatorships and economic populist leaders, the best known being the Perón dynasty in Argentina, which favored nationalized industries, strict government control, and highly redistributive policies. Inspired by Juan Perón and also communist thinking, Argentina under the Kirchners and Venezuela under Hugo Chávez have pursued populist, anticapitalist, and anti–foreign investment policies that have retarded economic progress. They have expropriated foreign companies, to the delight of the masses. They have rejected market allocation in favor of massive rationing and lines. They have driven out the propertied class. They have taken control of national statistical offices so as to churn out low inflation and high growth figures.

Latin American economists, trained in free-market traditions in the United States, enacted liberalization reforms in a number of Latin American countries, beginning in Chile under the military dictatorship of Augusto Pinochet, who ruled Chile from September 1973 to March 1990. Under this military dictatorship, a team of young economists trained at the University of Chicago opened up the Chilean economy, liberalized prices, eliminated state controls, and privatized state industries. After a rocky start, a Chilean "economic miracle" began in 1975, a period of rapid economic growth that was interrupted by a number of setbacks. The Chilean economy began to grow rapidly, and its investment rate soared. The democratically elected governments that followed the military dictatorship have retained Chile's basic free-market export-oriented policies. Today, despite some setbacks, Chile is one of Latin America's more successful economies.

Largely inspired by Chile's example, a number of Latin American economies embarked on free-market reforms, including Brazil, Columbia, and Peru. The most notable success among this group of countries has been Brazil, whose rapid growth and large population have made it the world's seventh largest economy between Russia and Great Britain. Notably, Brazil's reforms began under a former leftist trade union leader, whose policies have been continued under another leftist leader.

The Latin America reform model of privatization, reduction of trade barriers, and deregulation is still too fragile to classify it as an alternative economic system. Vested interests that control large state enterprises, such as Mexico's, Brazil's, and Argentina's national oil companies, resist change and continue to supply patronage and benefits to political allies and workers. Corruption is rampant, and mafia groups that control illegal drugs constitute a state within a state.

We can hope that Latin America, as a whole, will embrace the liberal model, but the appeal of Marxism and populism remains strong. The reform process in Latin America swings like a pendulum that never seems to rest.

Africa

Africa, struggling under the artificial boundaries left behind by its colonial rulers, has suffered from tribal warfare and incredibly cruel dictators. It has some bright spots, such as South Africa and Botswana, but it also has some of the world's most dysfunctional dictatorships, such as Zimbabwe.

Over the past decade, six of the world's ten fastest-growing countries were African. In eight of the past ten years, Africa has grown faster than East Asia. As we are writing this book, Africa's rate of economic growth is projected to equal that of Asia over the next few years.

A commodities boom is partly responsible. In the first decade of the new century, roughly a quarter of Africa's growth came from higher revenues from natural resources. China's rapid growth has translated into rising demand for Africa's raw materials.[6] Also, Africa is the last remaining continent with substantial population growth. While Europe and Asia shrink in size of population and labor force, demographers project that half of the increase in population over the next forty years will be in Africa.

Africa continues to be a study in contrasts, although the 2012 Index of Economic Freedom showed net gains in economic freedom in twenty-two African countries. Countries like Mauritius, Botswana, Rwanda, and Cape Verde have made substantial positive structural reforms, whereas countries like Eritrea and Zimbabwe continue to record the world's lowest rankings.[7] Africa has also made substantial political gains, although it remains home to some of the world's worst dictators. In 1987, only two African countries achieved the ranking of "free." In 2012, twelve African countries were ranked as "free." In 1987, thirty African countries were ranked as "unfree." In 2012, the number had been reduced to sixteen.[8]

If Africa's gains continue, it might eventually one day reach the promise that was forecast for it as we began the second half of the twentieth century.

The World of Islam and the Islamic Economic Model

Islam is the world's second largest religion after Christianity. In 2009, Islam had 1.6 billion adherents, or almost one quarter of the world's population. A number of countries designate themselves as Islamic states, such as Iran, Pakistan, and Saudi Arabia. In many Muslim countries, sharia, or Islamic law, is either the dominant legal code or it coexists with other forms of law. Muslims are divided into different sects, the two most important being the Shias and Sunnis. *A fatwa in the Islamic faith is a religious opinion concerning Islamic law issued by an Islamic scholar. A mufti is a person who issues a fatwa.* The fatwa can be legally binding or not legally binding depending upon the branch of Islam and the issuer.

None of the economic systems we have discussed so far is strictly tied to religion, although the Asian model was influenced by Confucian thought, and the Anglo-Saxon model was influenced by Protestantism. The term *Islamic economics* derives from the teachings of the Koran and from centuries-old practices, but it was coined by the Pakistan social thinker Sayyid Abdul A'la Maududi in the late 1940s.[9]

Islamic economics was practiced throughout the Muslim world in the Middle Ages, when Islamic merchants were active traders from the Mediterranean to the Baltic Sea, spreading instruments of Islamic finance throughout Europe. Two contemporary nations—Iran and Pakistan—have legislated that their economies be run according to Islamic principles. Their state constitutions require their banking systems to be fully compatible with Islamic law. In Egypt, Indonesia, Malaysia, Sudan, and the Gulf Cooperation Council (GCC) countries, Islamic banking exists alongside conventional banking. There is no single Islamic financial center that is the equivalent of New York or London. The stock markets in Iran and Sudan come closest to operating in compliance with Islamic principles.

The three basic principles of Islamic economics are said to derive directly from the Koran. They are the *prohibition of interest*; the *zakat* system, which transfers income from the wealthy to the poor; and the use of *Islamic moral norms* in business. Islamic economists disagree on other matters, such as private property and the role of state regulation, but there is agreement on these three points, especially on the prohibition of interest.

The prohibition of interest stems from the belief that it is unjust to earn money without risk. Insofar as the lender is presumed not to take risks, it is therefore unjust to accept a reward in the form of a fixed rate of interest. Profit is legitimate only as a reward for risk. Hence the lender should accept some risk either by sharing of profit and loss or by more innovative risk-sharing methods. Interest payments are prohibited even when the lending market is competitive and the interest rate yields the lender a normal rate of return. Profits symbolize successful entrepreneurship and wealth creation; interest is a cost that is accrued irrespective of the business outcome and does not create wealth. Social justice demands that borrowers and lenders share rewards as well as losses in an equitable manner, although it remains unclear how this sharing is to proceed.

More than one hundred financial institutions in over sixty countries practice some form of Islamic finance today. Sharia-compliant banks have assets of approximately half of a trillion dollars. Depositors in Islamic banks are said to earn not interest but "profit shares" that tend to fluctuate. Borrowers do not pay interest, but they are assessed markups and service charges that resemble interest payments. In fact, in Turkey, where Islamic banks coexist with conventional banks, depositors receive the same rates of interest from Islamic and conventional banks.[10] In practice, therefore, Islamic finance has proved flexible and has created financial instruments that allow profitable banking operations without being called interest charges.

There is little uniformity in the religious principles applied in Islamic countries. In the absence of a universally accepted central religious authority, Islamic banks have formed their own religious boards for guidance. Islamic banks have to consult their sharia advisors to seek approval for each new instrument. Differences in interpretation of Islamic principles by different schools of thought mean that identical financial instruments are rejected by one board but accepted by another. Thus the same instrument may not be acceptable in all countries.

The second feature of Islamic economics is the zakat system of redistributing wealth from the rich to the poor. In most cases, the zakat is voluntary, but in six countries (Yemen, Saudi Arabia, Malaysia, Libya, Pakistan, and Sudan), zakat is run by the government. The zakat system accumulates funds from wealthy donors, or taxpayers if the system is obligatory, and distributes these funds to widows and to religious or educational institutions. Zakat obligations can apply both to individuals and to businesses. The empirical evidence suggests that the obligatory zakat system has not put a dent in poverty in those nations with a government-run system. There is also evidence that it leads to corruption, with funds going to connected individuals, even to religious leaders, rather than to the poor.

A third principle of Islamic economics is the substitution of Islamic norms for capitalist norms. Businesspeople are supposed to deal fairly with their business partners in observing Islamic morality. They should charge fair prices, provide accurate information, and not engage in fraud or deceit. The principle of fairness is difficult to apply because people have different notions of fairness. In the Islamic Republic of Iran, morality committees attached to factories and institutions are supposed to enforce Islamic morality, and various religious leaders issue edicts on morality. But in general, each person, group, or country has its own notion of Islamic morality, and there is no central authority to define it.

The growth and development of Islamic economies has probably not been seriously retarded by the prohibition of interest, zakat, or the use of Islamic norms. More problematic is the legal organization of Islamic enterprises. Islamic partnerships, by Islamic law, must be liquidated at the death of one partner. They are therefore set up for small sums with limited time horizons and, as such, cannot be long-lived like Western corporations. Additionally, Islamic inheritance laws require inheritance to be divided among heirs.

Islamic law also does not recognize nonpersons as legal persons. The recognition of the corporation as a legal person allows it to enter into contracts and conduct business as a person could. The notion of limited liability was also not recognized in the early years of Islamic businesses.

Probably the lack of development of the corporate form of governance and ownership hindered the growth of Islamic economies. The first Islamic corporations were not recognized until the 1850s in Turkey. It would be hard to conceive of a strong economic development in the West without the corporation. The late development of the corporation in the Islamic world has therefore been a factor retarding growth.

Until recently, no economy that operates on the principles of Islamic economics experienced rapid growth. Turkey has proven to be the major exception, with its rapid growth over the past decade and its possibly impending membership in the European Union. Indonesia has also experienced economic growth as an economy with a majority Muslim population. All eyes are, however, on Turkey, as a path breaker for the Islamic economic model.

The Performance of Economic Systems: Institutional Quality

There is a direct and indirect approach to determining which type of economic system is in some sense better than others. Recall from Chapter 3 that economic outcomes depend on the economic system (ES), the economic environment (ENV), and economic policies (POL):

$$O = f(\text{ES, ENV, POL}) \tag{22.1}$$

where

$$
\begin{array}{ll}
O & \text{denotes economic outcomes} \\
\text{ES} & \text{denotes the economic system} \\
\text{ENV} & \text{denotes environmental factors} \\
\text{POL} & \text{denotes policies pursued by the economic system}
\end{array}
$$

According to the direct approach, we evaluate economic systems according to the quality of their institutions. The direct approach requires being able to measure economic institutions and agree on what constitute "good" or "bad" institutions.

A "good" institution would be one that leads to better performance. A "bad" institution leads to worse performance.

The indirect approach examines economic outcomes and links them to the economic system. If we observe good economic outcome that tend to be related to a particular system and are not explain by ENV and POL, we conclude that that economic system is better than the others.

We have delineated a number of economic systems—the Anglo-Saxon, European, and Asian models, and also China. If we could rate each of them according to the quality of their institutions, we might have a quick and easy answer to our question: "Which economic system is, in some sense, the 'best'?" Answer: It is the one with the best institutions.

A group of prominent economists proposed an Institutional Possibilities Frontier to depict the effects of economic institutions on economic performance.[11] *The **Institutional Possibilities Frontier (IPF)** measures the social costs (losses) associated with different combinations of economic institutions.* At any point in time, the social losses are constant along a given IPF. Societies, with given institutional possibilities, must select the "optimal" (for them) location on the existing IPF.

Figure 22.1 shows a society that chooses among combinations of markets/free enterprise and plan/state enterprise along a given institutional possibilities frontier. The curve labeled IPF shows its array of choices that yield equal social losses. Presumably that choice would depend on societal preferences as expressed by the people in a democracy or by a ruling elite in a totalitarian regime.

If the society "improves" its economic institutions, the institutional possibilities frontier moves inward from IPF to IPF'. At the new IPF, it can again choose its optimal combination, each choice being at a lower level of social cost.

Similarly, the IPF diagram could illustrate two societies at the same time operating on different IPFs. The society on the higher IPF operates with higher social

FIGURE 22.1   The Institutional Possibilities Frontier

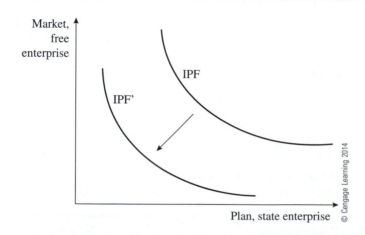

losses than the one on the lower IPF. The improvement of economic institutions is depicted as an inward movement of the frontier.

The IPF offers a conceptual way to evaluate institutions. "Good" institutions lower social costs or losses. "Bad" institutions raise social costs or losses. Given that we now have a number of empirical measures of institutions, we can try to rate economic system by the good or bad institutions that they embody.

Figure 22.2 gives countries grouped by economic system according to the level of economic freedom and corruption—two of the most prominent measures of institutional quality. (In the figure, a higher number represents more economic freedom and more freedom from corruption.) The first group represents the European model; the second, the Anglo-Saxon model; the fourth, the Asian model. China is listed separately. Few would argue that more corruption is a better outcome. Some may argue that more economic freedom is a worse outcome, but they are likely in the minority.

FIGURE 22.2   Economic Systems Rated by Economic Freedom and Freedom from Corruption

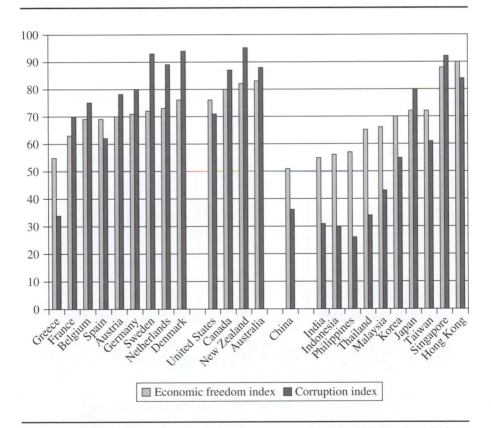

Source: Based on data from Heritage Foundation, Economic Freedom Index 2012, http://www.heritage.org/index/explore.

Figure 22.2 shows that the European and Anglo Saxon models have roughly equal freedom from corruption, but that the Anglo-Saxon model has more economic freedom. China has relatively low economic freedom and limited freedom from corruption, similar to the poorer countries of Asia (such as India, Indonesia, Philippines, and Thailand). Asia has less freedom from corruption than the Anglo-Saxon and European models, with the exception of the two Asian super-affluent city-states of Hong Kong and Singapore that enjoy among the highest levels of economic freedom and freedom from corruption in the world. The rest of Asia, however, has less economic freedom than either the European or Anglo-Saxon models.

Figure 22.3 examines specific institutional practices that affect the social costs of doing business, such as measures of ease of doing business, firing costs, and start-up costs.

Figure 22.3 shows a greater ease of doing business in the Anglo-Saxon model (and in Hong Kong and Singapore). Note that the *higher the number*, the more difficult it is to do business, to fire workers, or to start up a business. Europe has

FIGURE 22.3   Various Institutional Measures of Costs of Doing Business (In each case, the higher the figure, the more difficult it is to do business)

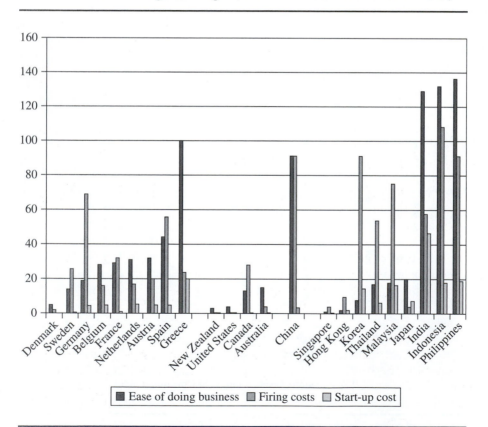

Source: Based on data from World Bank, World Development Report, http://data.worldbank.org/indicator/all.

higher start-up costs, less ease of doing business, and higher firing costs than the Anglo-Saxon countries. China has a very low ease of doing business, high firing costs (we guess for state employees), and low start-up costs.

Figures 22.2 and 22.3 show that the Anglo-Saxon countries are less constrained by rules, bureaucracy, corruption, and other impediments to free enterprises. This fact does not "prove" the superiority of the Anglo-Saxon system. Some could argue that there is too much freedom in the Anglo-Saxon world, or that more regulation of labor markets is required to protect workers. Few, however, could argue that corruption is a positive institutional feature, and in this regard, the Chinese and Asian models perform poorly.

Economic Systems and Economic Performance

The indirect approach to evaluating economic systems is to judge them by the economic performance they generate. These performance indicators are the outcome of the quality of institutions. Remember that economic performance is affected by ENV and POL as well as by ES. The fact that economic performance is determined by a multiplicity of factors greater complicates our analysis. Another complication is that there is no single measure of economic performance. The most commonly used indicator is economic growth, but there are other measures—efficiency, income distribution, or stability—that could be used as well.

Economic Growth

The most common measure of economic performance is economic growth. Economic growth can be measured either as the growth rate of real GDP or of real GDP per capita. The growth rate of real GDP measures the annual increase in total economic output adjusted for inflation. The growth rate of real GDP captures, albeit imperfectly, the growth rate of living standards. The growth rate of real GDP per capita is equal to the growth rate of real GDP minus the growth rate of population. If real GDP growth is 3 percent and population growth 1 percent, real GDP growth per capita is 2 percent.

The choice of GDP or GDP per capita growth is complicated by the fact that population growth can be affected by GDP growth. If young people do not anticipate advances in real GDP growth, they may be reluctant to have children. Stagnant countries do not attract immigrants. Population growth may be endogenous to economic growth.

The choice of GDP or GDP per capita makes a difference in international comparisons. For example, North America, Latin America, and Africa still experience population growth through natural fertility and immigration. Europe and Japan have for all practical purposes ceased replacing their populations. So GDP growth comparisons will favor North America and Africa and disfavor Europe and Japan. The comparisons look more even if we use per capita GDP.

Table 22.1 summarizes growth rates of GDP, population, and GDP per capita for various parts of the globe.

TABLE **22.1**   Growth of Real GDP, Population, and Per Capita GDP, The World

	GDP growth	Population growth	GDP per capita growth
A. Western Europe			
1950–70	5.5	0.9	4.6
1971–90	2.8	2	0.8
1991–2011	1.6	0.3	1.3
B. United Kingdom			
1950–70	2.7	0.5	2.2
1971–90	2.3	0.1	2.2
1991–2011	2.1	0.4	1.7
C. North America plus Oceania			
1950–70	3.9	1.6	2.3
1971–90	2.3	1	1.3
1991–2011	2.6	1	1.6
D. China			
1950–70	4	2	2
1971–90	6.3	1.6	4.7
1991–2011	9.5	0.8	8.7
E. India			
1950–70	3.8	2.1	1.7
1971–90	4.5	2.1	2.4
1991–2011	7	1.7	5.3
F. Japan			
1950–70	9.6	1.1	8.5
1971–90	4.2	0.8	3.4
1991–2011	0.3	0.1	0.2
G. Southeast Asia			
1950–70	5.4	2.4	3
1971–90	3.6	1.2	2.4
1991–2011	3.2	0.1	3.1
H. Latin America			
1950–70	5.8	2.8	3
1971–90	3.6	2.2	1.4
1991–2011	3.2	1.4	1.8
I. Middle East			
1950–70	8.4	2.9	5.5
1971–90	2.8	3.6	−0.8
1991–2011	4.6	2.3	2.3
J. Africa			
1950–70	4.4	2.5	1.9
1971–90	3.1	2.8	0.3
1991–2011	4.2	2.4	1.8

TABLE 22.1   Growth of Real GDP, Population, and Per Capita GDP, The World
             (cont.)

	GDP growth	Population growth	GDP per capita growth
K. Eastern Europe			
1950–70			
1971–90			
1991–2011	1.7	−0.1	1.8
L. Former Soviet Union			
1950–70			
1971–90			
1991–2011	0.09	−0.01	0.1

© Cengage Learning 2014

Table 22.1 divides the world into the economic systems we covered in the book: the European model (Western Europe), the Anglo-Saxon model (North America and Oceana, primarily), the Asian model (Southeast Asia), China, and then the transition countries of Eastern Europe and the former Soviet Union. We include Latin America, Africa, and the Middle East as areas we were not able to cover as identifiable economic systems.

The European model began the postwar period with rapid economic growth, low population growth, and high per capita GDP growth. Experts say that this "golden age" of growth was the result of closing the technology gap with the United States that had opened during the war. After 1991, Europe's growth fell to about 1.5 percent; its population growth had virtually ceased, and its per capita growth was a modest 1.3 percent.

The United Kingdom, which does not fit neatly into the European or Anglo-Saxon model, failed to experience the growth spurt of the continent after the war. (It was said to suffer from the "English disease" at the time.) Its population growth also sank, but from 1991 to 2011 its GDP and GDP per capita growth was generally higher than that on the European continent.

The Anglo-Saxon world, which is dominated by the United States, missed out as the dominant technology leader on the early postwar economic miracle of the European continent, but it maintained its growth of GDP, population, and GDP per capita. Although continental growth gives the appearance of a secular downward trend, there is no discernible trend for the Anglo-Saxon countries.

In China, we see the results of the remarkable growth that followed the Deng reform of the late 1970s accompanied by the demographic effects of the state-imposed one-child policy. China largely avoided the economic downturn of the second half of the first decade of 2000 and recorded exceptionally rapid growth of GDP combined with a decline to a modest rate of population growth. The country is currently experiencing an "easy growth" as the labor force transfers from the countryside; whether Chinese growth will continue unabated after this process is completed is one of the biggest unknowns of current times.

India's reform began in 1990. Before that its population growth ate up much of its GDP growth, but in its reform period it has experienced accelerating GDP growth and declining population growth.

Japan, the pioneer of the Asian model, experienced a remarkable collapse of both GDP growth and population growth after its own economic miracle of the first two postwar decades. It grew at nearly 10 percent per annum in the early period with a population growth of 1.1 percent. After 1991, it scarcely grew in terms of GDP, population, or real GDP. Japan's sluggish growth and low fertility rate may alarm other high-income Asian partners such as Taiwan and South Korea. All three share high rates of saving and export orientation. Will South Korea and Taiwan share Japan's fate? We do not know. What we do know is that Japan has reached a high level of affluence. South Korea and Taiwan count today among the world's affluent economies.

Southeast Asia captures the rapid growth of the Asian model. It began the postwar era with rapid growth of GDP and population. After 1991, its GDP growth was lower but its population growth declined to a near standstill; therefore, its per capita growth remained largely unchanged at a rapid 3 percent.

In the Middle East and Africa, population growth has remained stubbornly high. These regions must yet go through the demographic transition. They still follow the model of extensive growth based on growth of population and labor. Latin America has begun the demographic transition, and it has maintained GDP at a rapid enough pace to achieve positive per capita growth. All three regions combine successful and unsuccessful economies, so the average figures have less significance than in other regions.

Finally, we have the transition economies of Eastern Europe and the former Soviet Union. Both regions experienced declining populations, but in Eastern Europe GDP growth has occurred, assuring a reasonable growth rate of per capita GDP. In the former Soviet Union—Russia, Ukraine, Central Asia, and the Caucasus—GDP growth basically ground to a halt between 1990 and 2011. It was hoped that the transition economies, after they restructured their institutions, could experience rapid enough growth to compensate for some of the losses of the Soviet and early transition periods. So far, there has been no exceptional payoff in terms of a sustained growth spurt for the former Soviet states.

Comparisons of growth rates reveal dramatic differences between Europe and the rapidly growing Asian countries. They show the malaise of Europe and the greater resiliency of the Anglo-Saxon model in terms of GDP growth and continued population growth. The transition economies neatly divide into the transition failures of the former Soviet Union and the transition successes of Eastern Europe, now largely members of the European Union. Yet, the successful transitioners do not appear to have experienced a big payoff in terms of Asian-like growth upon completion of their transitions. The transition economies of Central Europe, however, are now outgrowing Western Europe. They are also bringing new life and new institutions to the European Union, which should prove of benefit to the European continent.

In virtually all regions, population growth rates have declined, except in Africa and the Middle East. The demographic transition appears inevitable, but it must wait its turn to happen. As per capita income grows, Africa and the Middle East will eventually experience declining birth rates as have the other regions of the world. In Botswana, one of the fastest growing African nations, the total fertility rate dropped from 3.8 to 2.5 between 2000 and 2011.[12] As African growth occurs, other countries will follow the Botswana example.

Missing from Table 22.1 is data on long-term growth rates for countries that reached high levels of affluence early. Growth rates of affluent countries during their own peak periods of growth were comparable in many cases to the Asian growth rates of today. For example, the U.S. economy grew at 4.1 percent per year between 1850 and 1900 and there were subperiods of even more rapid growth.[13] Sweden grew at an annual rate of almost 5 percent between 1921 and 1939 (even counting the Great Depression).[14]

Natural Experiments with Economic Growth

Sorting out the impact of the economic system on economic outcomes is a difficult business. The figures on economic growth in Table 22.1 do not provide conclusive evidence of which system works better. If we look at long-run evidence, the nature of the economic system can change over a century or so. The European model really evolved in the 1970s, and the Anglo-Saxon model may have peaked in the years before the Great Depression. Economic systems may grow the fastest in their early stages, particularly when they start from a low base.

History does, however, provide a few natural experiments in which the differences in the economic system are great and other factors appear to be reasonably the same. The most prominent example is the experiment with planned socialism that began in the Soviet Union in the late 1920s and spread to Eastern Europe and Asia after World War II.

The Great Soviet experiment gave us two striking natural experiments of formerly united countries split off into communist and capitalist systems: East and West Germany and North and South Korea. In both cases, the regions of the formerly unified countries had roughly equal per capita output and resources and a common history and culture. Differences in economic performance should therefore be attributed to the different economic systems under which the divided countries operated.

In both cases, the capitalist twin outperformed the socialist twin by a wide margin. The living standards of the German "Wessis" exceeded those of the "Ossis" by a huge margin. Eastern factories and businesses could not find buyers because of their inefficiencies, and the best products from the East (such as the famed Trabbi car) disappeared from the economy.

North and South Korea remain divided, and the performance differences are even more striking (see Figure 22.4). Both Koreas started with roughly equal per capita income in 1950. In 1998, North Korean GDP per capita was, at best, equal to what it had been in 1950, whereas South Korea had become an affluent industrial power—part of the Four Southeast Asian Tigers success story. Today, South Koreans own their own homes and cars, travel internationally, and are

FIGURE 22.4   Per Capita Income, North and South Korea

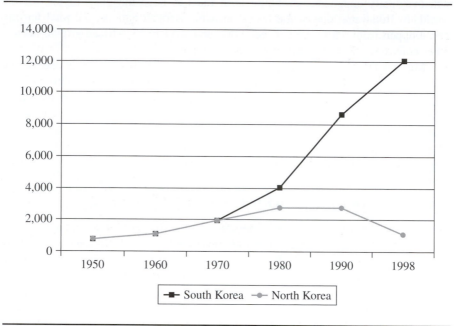

Source: Daron Acemoglu, Simon Johnson, and James Robinson, "Institutions as the Fundamental Cause of Long-Run Growth," Figure 3, page 97, http://www.growthcommission.org/storage/cgdev/ documents/LeadershipandGovernance/Paper%20Acemoglu_Robinson.pdf.

more likely to suffer from being overweight than starvation. North Koreans eke out a subsistence living and are subject to periodic famines, which would claim hundreds of thousands of lives were it not for outside assistance. Even more important, South Koreans have a vibrant democracy, whereas their North Korean cousins live under a brutal dictatorship that maintains a vast Gulag to imprison those out of favor.

Divided Germany and divided Korea provide us with the most conclusive evidence of the failure of the planned socialist system. We could use other natural experiments such as Cuba versus the rest of Latin America. We also present evidence (in a later section) on the relatively poor productivity performance of the Soviet-type economies.

This evidence of the poor performance of planned socialism comes as no surprise. We know that this type of economic system has been abandoned, and no one appears to be arguing for its revival.

Efficiency, Invention, and Institutions

Economies grow *extensively* through the expansion of labor and capital inputs. They grow *intensively* through technological progress that is through improvements in technology, science, and business organization. The Institutional Possibilities

Frontier makes the point that efficiency can also increase through improvement in economic institutions.

The Production Possibilities Frontier (PPF) of Figure 22.5 illustrates these relationships. Consider an economy operating at a low level of output—on the PPF labeled A. It experiences an increase in labor and capital inputs and shifts its frontier outward to PPF labeled B. It then improves its science, engineering, and management technology and shifts outward to PPF labeled C. If it then improves its economic institutions, it moves further outward to D.

The succession of PPF increases artificially divides economic progress (the outward movement of the PPF) into different sources: extensive growth, intensive growth through technological progress, and then through improvements in institutions. It is difficult to separate technological progress from institutional improvements. In empirical analysis, we are only able to distinguish with some degree of accuracy between growth due to the increase in inputs and growth due to everything else, which we call the Solow residual. *The **Solow residual** measures the economic growth that is not explained by the growth of labor and capital inputs.*

We use growth accounting to study the sources of growth. ***Growth accounting** seeks to explain why growth has occurred by means of the expansion of inputs and technological progress.* The standard growth accounting formula is:

$$\dot{Y} = 2\dot{K} + (1 - 2)\dot{L} + \dot{T} \qquad (22.2)$$

where Y = real GDP, K = capital, L = labor input, and T = technological progress. The dots(˙) denote annual rates of growth. The 2 equals capital's share of output and $1 - 2$ equals labor's share.

Thus if $\dot{Y} = 3\%, \dot{K} = 4\%, \dot{L} = 1\%$ and $2 = .4$, we can calculate that $\dot{T}$ grew at .8% per year and accounts for 27% (.8/3) of the growth of GDP.

FIGURE 22.5   Shifts in the Production Possibilities Curve Due to Input Increases, Technological Progress, and Improvements in Economic Institutions

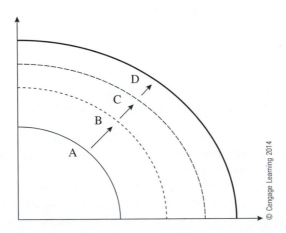

© Cengage Learning 2014

An even more important formula explains the growth of labor productivity, which equals $\dot{Y} - \dot{L}$. The formula is:

$$\dot{Y} - \dot{L} = 2(\dot{K} - \dot{L}) + \dot{T} \tag{22.3}$$

which says that labor productivity grows because of capital deepening (more capital per worker, or $\dot{K} - \dot{L}$) and because of technological progress.

In our numerical example, labor productivity grows 2 percent per year, capital per worker grows 3 percent per year, and technological progress is .8 percent per year, or explains 40 percent (.8/2) of the growth of labor productivity.

The most important marker for a society is its living standard. Is output per capita sufficient to give the average citizen a good or even affluent lifestyle? Or is it so low that the average person lives in poverty with the associated negative consequences of poor education, health, and shelter?

Equation 22.2 shows that labor productivity (the primary determinant of per capita GDP) is determined, in part, by the level of capital per worker. The average worker in India works with $10,000 worth of capital. The average American worker works with more than $200,000 worth of capital. Equation 22.2 shows that labor productivity also depends on technological progress, which includes the improvement of economic institutions. We can use this equation to calculate the Solow residual; in this case, the growth of labor productivity explained by things other than the rise in capital per worker.

Figure 22.6 shows the growth rates of technological progress (the Solow residual) in four affluent countries over long periods of time, starting in 1890. The data are divided into subperiods starting with 1890–1913 and ending with 1980–2006, before the onset of the most recent economic downturn.

Figure 22.6 shows that throughout the history of the affluent countries, labor productivity and hence living standards rose more due to technological progress than to the increase in capital per worker. Up until 1950, some three quarters of the increase in labor productivity was explained by the Solow residual, the only exception being Japan, which relied on increasing capital per worker. The early postwar period was characterized by enormous technological growth, spurred by the backlog of technology that built up during World War II between the United States and the rest of the world during World War I. The period 1980–2007 showed a more even distribution between capital per hour fo work and technological progress. The financial crisis of 2008-2001 caused a collapse of technological progress (which became negative) everywhere except the United States.

Figure 22.7 shows the sources of rising living standards in various regions of the world for the period 1960–1994. It covers a shorter period of time but a wider array of countries and experiences.

Figure 22.7 shows that during the 1960–1996 period—the early part of which many call a "golden age" of growth—labor productivity (and living standards, as an approximation) grew at roughly 3 percent per annum in the affluent (developed) world. Three percent growth over thirty-six years means almost a

FIGURE 22.6   Growth Rates of Labor Productivity, 1890–2006, Four Affluent Countries

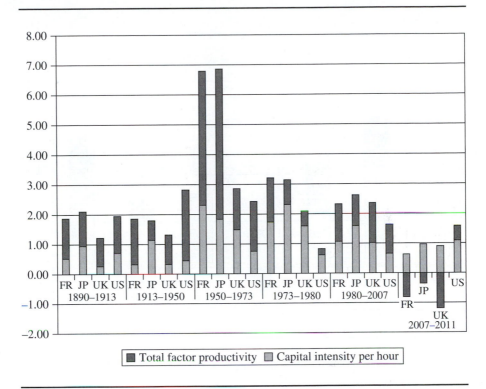

Source: Gilbert Cette, Yusuf Kocoglu, and Jacques Mairesse, "Productivity Growth and Levels in France, Japan, the United Kingdom and the United States," NBER Working Paper 15577, December 2009, http://www.nber.org/papers/w15577.pdf. Figure updated by the authors themselves. Used with permission.

tripling of living standards. The Asian miracle worked its magic during this same period as labor productivity increased more than 4 percent per annum, but a smaller percentage of its increase was explained by technological progress. Four percent growth over thirty-six years means more than a fourfold increase in living standards. Four of the Southeast Asian economies became affluent during this period. South Asia had lower rates of productivity growth, as did the Middle East and Latin America. Sub-Saharan Africa had negative rates of growth of technological progress.

The period 1960–1996 was largely one of progress for the developed world and Asia that was not shared by other lagging parts of the globe. The affluent world and Southeast Asia developed institutions that enabled them to take advantage of advances in technology and institutions to raise their living standards. Other areas of the world lacked such institutions. Their living standards have to lag behind until they develop the necessary institutions.

FIGURE 22.7   Sources of Increases in Labor Productivity, 1960–1994, Various Regions of the World

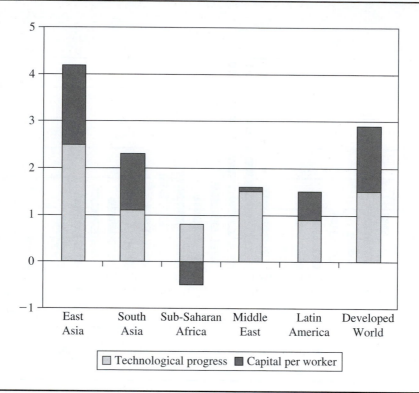

Source: Based on data from Jong-il Kim, "Total Factor Productivity Growth in East Asia: Implications for Future Growth," April 2001, http://www.cid.harvard.edu/events/papers/kim.pdf.

The Soviet Command Socialist Model

Figure 22.8 provides data on the sources of labor productivity growth in the USSR and its Eastern European satellites from 1950 to 1984. During the era of planned socialism, there was considerable skepticism concerning the reliability of real GDP growth estimates for these countries.

Figure 22.8 cites Western recalculations. Nevertheless, many observers feel that even these recalculations provide a too optimistic picture. It should be noted that authoritative sources suggest a much bleaker picture for the USSR over even a longer period of time.[15]

Figure 22.8 illustrates the reasons for earlier ambiguity about the merits of the planned socialist system. For the early postwar period, the planned socialist economies appeared to have high rates of labor productivity growth caused in large part by technological progress. The USSR was an outlier with labor productivity growth sustained in large part by rapid capital formation. Observers examining these results from the vantage

FIGURE 22.8   Sources of Labor Productivity Growth, Planned Socialist Economies, 1950–1984

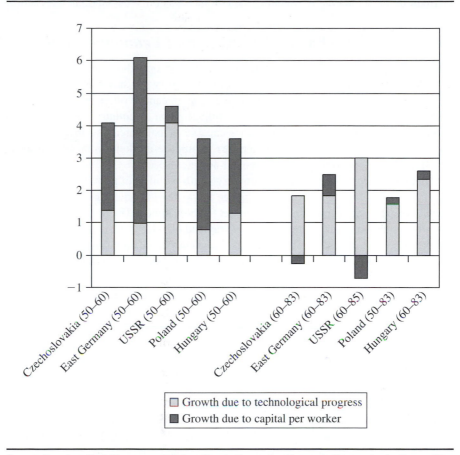

Source: Based on Paul Gregory and Robert Stuart, *Comparing Economic Systems in the Twenty-First Century* (Boston: Houghton Mifflin, 2004), 355.

point of 1960 were hard-pressed to judge which economic system—planned socialism or capitalism—outperformed the other with respect to labor productivity growth.

The 1960–1983 figures show the sharp reversal of the performance of the planned socialist economies. Labor productivity growth slumped. In two countries, the contribution of technological progress became negative, and in all cases labor productivity advanced only because of ambitious investment programs. The leaderships of these countries realized there were limits to which capital formation could be pushed. The slim increases in labor productivity did not translate into increases in consumer goods and services and higher standards of living.

Popular dissatisfaction arose as these countries became better informed about living standards in the West. Soviet citizens visiting Eastern Europe were surprised by its higher living standards. The relatively few Eastern Europeans allowed to travel to the West were doubly surprised. The East Germans could see the higher West German living standards by watching the commercials on West German television.

Science and Technical Advances and Economic Systems

Intelligence should be fairly normally distributed among the world's population. Therefore, the human potential for scientific discovery for any particular country or economic system would depend, in the first instance, on population size. If there is normally one genius for every million, then a country of 200 million would be expected to have 200 geniuses capable of path-breaking inventions and applications. Very small countries, therefore, would be unlikely to be among those in which the major scientific and technical advances occur.

People do move from country to country. With mobility of population, a country or economic system can contribute to science and technology disproportionately to its population, if it can disproportionally attract the best minds. The ability to attract the scientists, engineers, and technicians would depend on relative levels of affluence and opportunities and rewards for those who make scientific and entrepreneurial contributions. Clearly, a country's educational system is also a key determinant of scientific and technological contributions. In a large country with low literacy rates, potential geniuses or high contributors cannot be identified. A country whose education system encourages independent thinking is more likely to produce the best scientists and engineers than one that relies on memorization and rote learning.

Economic systems contribute to scientific and technological advances through institutions that encourage the exchange of ideas, attract scientists and engineers from other economic systems, and generously reward and protect those with high achievements.

We have no direct measurement of one country's or one economic system's contribution to the advancement of science and technology. We lack a single measure of "cumulated gross inventions and innovations." We could never agree how to add all inventions and innovations together in one unit of measurement.

Intellectual Property Rights

The stocks and flows of scientific and technical knowledge are most often measured in by one of the few empirical indicators: patents.[16] The economics of optimal patents addresses the tradeoff between the protection of intellectual property, which spurs invention, and the barriers to innovation a patent creates. *A **patent**, in effect, gives the patent holder a monopoly over the product for a specified period of time*. There is a substantial literature on patents and intellectual property rights that has not been well integrated into the study of economic systems. The fact that patents have been a fact of life in affluent countries for a very long period of time suggests that their benefits outweigh their costs.

Economic systems differ with respect to the granting or enforcement of intellectual property rights. ***Intellectual property rights** stand for property rights protected under law, including copyrightable works, ideas, discoveries, and inventions*. If patents spur innovation and invention, the economic system that best enforces them will have superior innovation and invention.

Insofar as intellectual property rights belong to a larger family of property rights, presumably those societies that weakly protect general property rights will also have weak protection of intellectual property rights. Countries lacking a rule of law offer poor protection of intellectual property.

Figure 22.9 ranks a sample of countries according to the degree of piracy of copyrights for business software. Only countries charged with violation of intellectual property rights are included, so the list is not comprehensive. The most affluent countries tend to have the strongest rules of law and will not show up in the chart because of the infrequency of violation of intellectual property rights.

Figure 22.9 shows that intellectual property piracy rankings are consistent with rule of law rankings. Finland and Canada have the highest rule of law ranking and low piracy, and Venezuela has the worst piracy record and the lowest rule of law ranking in the sample.[17]

On the basis of this limited information, we should conclude that economic systems that protect property rights, such as the Anglo-Saxon and European models, should have higher rates of invention and innovation than those who allow piracy and other infractions of intellectual property rights.

China and India both have weak rule of law and high piracy rates. In both countries, the owners of intellectual property will be reluctant to share new

FIGURE 22.9   Estimated Levels of Copyright Piracy, Selected Countries

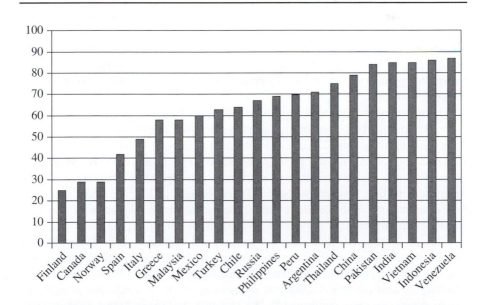

Source: Based on data from 2010 "Special 301" USTR Decisions, http://www.iipa.com/pdf/IIPA2010USTRDecisionsSpecial301TableofEstimatedTradeLossesandPiracyLevels061110.pdf.

technologies for fear they will be stolen. The high piracy rates of China and India can therefore retard technological progress by depriving these countries of the latest technologies. Local inventors will also lack motivation to invent if their ideas are stolen without punishment.[18] At a minimum, the unprotected innovator or inventor would try to emigrate to a country that does offer suitable protection.

Intellectual property holders can sue violators in Chinese courts. Court records show that most cases are brought by one Chinese firm against another. Western companies like Paramount Pictures, Adidas, and Nike are among the most frequent complainants against Chinese knock-off firms, but the Chinese courts award small settlements to successful plaintiffs. Seeking legal remedies is not worth the effort.[19] Western research firms have retaliated by relocating research parks to other countries that have better protection of intellectual property rights. In such cases, China is the loser.

Nobel Prizes   We can use other indirect measures to gauge which types of countries produce the world's geniuses and high contributors to science and technology. One is the list of Nobel Laureates by country and prize as shown in Figure 22.9, which shows the distribution of Nobel Prizes by country over time.

Figure 22.10 shows that Germany and France were the primary producers of Nobel Laureates before World War II. German, French, and English universities and scientific academies boasted legendary scientists like Wilhelm Roentgen, Max Planck, Marie Curie, Werner Heisenberg, James Chadwick, and Albert Einstein. U.S.-based scientists had only a smattering of prizes. The postwar era saw the dramatic shift away from Germany, France, and England and toward domination by American-based scientists.

The United States has attracted scientific minds to its shores on a huge scale. Of the 314 laureates who won their Nobel Prize while working in the United States, 32 percent were foreign born, including 15 Germans, 12 Canadians, 10 British, 6 Russians, and 6 Chinese. In Germany, only 6 of its 65 Nobel Laureates were born outside of Germany. Japan has no foreigners among its 9 Nobel Laureates.[20]

Large countries with well-educated populations have produced remarkably few Nobel Laureates. The most prominent example is the Soviet Union, with a larger population than the United States and a vaunted reputation in science and engineering education. The Soviet higher educational establishment was deliberately planned by the higher-education ministry and state planning commission to produce the scientific manpower needed by the economy. Yet the USSR produced just a smattering of Nobel Laureates, despite the apolitical nature of the hard sciences and engineering.

Joseph Berliner, in his study of science and engineering in Soviet Russia, blamed the Soviet planned system for not rewarding innovation and entrepreneurship both on the part of the individual and for the innovating enterprise. In fact, the planning system actively discouraged innovation on the grounds that it made the planning process too complicated.[21] The fact that the Soviet Union kept its engineers and scientists isolated from the outside world of science also retarded

FIGURE **22.10**   Nobel Prizes by Country

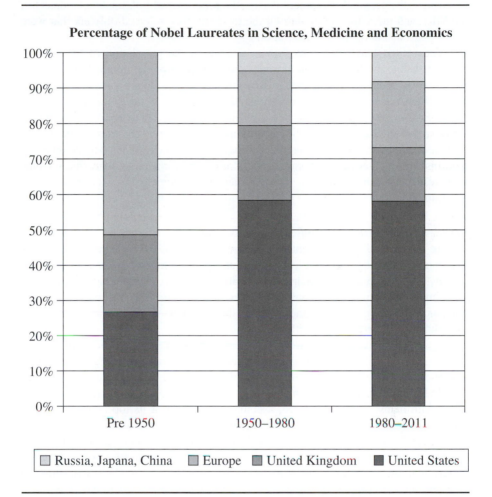

Percentage of Nobel Laureates in Science, Medicine and Economics

☐ Russia, Japana, China   ☐ Europe   ☐ United Kingdom   ■ United States

Source: Nobel Commission.

scientific achievements. The relative lack of Chinese Nobel Laureates may also be the result of isolation from the world scientific community.

Top Inventions   At a less elevated level, we can examine the distribution of top inventions and innovations that have changed the way we live from the hospital, to outer space, to the kitchen. Of course, there is no established method for determining what products and things belong on such a list. The magazine *Popular Mechanics* mounted such an effort by forming a panel of fifteen experts to rate the top fifty inventions of the past half century. Other panels likely would have chosen different products, but we imagine the geographic distribution would be roughly the same.

The *Popular Mechanics* panel chose products such as the microwave oven, the jet airliner, the personal computer, Velcro, the birth control pill, the smoke detector, the MRI, and the automated teller. Of the top fifty, they selected only six that were developed outside of the United States.[22]

The United States accounts for one quarter of the population of the affluent (OECD) countries. It is also the primary representative of the Anglo-Saxon model in the world today. The fact that it accounts for such a disproportionate share of Nobel Prizes and significant inventions does not prove the superiority of the Anglo-Saxon model in creating new useful knowledge. There are too few observations, but combined with U.S. institutions—rule of law, rewards for economic achievement, the ease of creating new companies, and so on—one possible interpretation is that the U.S. Anglo-Saxon model does outperform other economic systems with respect to the creation of scientific and technological knowledge and their dissemination.

Creation and Destruction of Companies   Another measure of technological change is the ability of a country or economic system to create new companies that evolve from small to large companies. Joseph Schumpeter referred to this process as creative destruction. Schumpeter felt that creative destruction held the key to technological progress. A country or an economic system that fails to create new companies and resists the decline of established companies should have lower rates of technological progress and infusion of new products.

If we examine data on the world's largest companies and their foundation dates, we see striking differences between the United States and the largest European countries. In the United States, one third of the top one hundred companies were founded after World War II. Their names are familiar: Apple, Microsoft, Costco, along with many others. In France, less than 20 percent of its top companies were founded after the war, and in Germany the percentage shrinks to 10 percent.

Figure 22.11 shows the reverse side of business creation; namely, business destruction or reorganization through bankruptcy. The countries are arrayed by the bankruptcy rate (the number of bankruptcies divided by the number of businesses) and arranged according to Anglo-Saxon countries (broadly defined), European countries, and Asian countries.

Although there are outliers for each economic system (Sweden for Europe and Singapore for Asia), the general pattern is a higher rate of bankruptcy in the Anglo-Saxon countries, lower rates in Europe, and even lower rates in Asia. This finding is supported by more sophisticated empirical analysis.[23]

If we wish to judge economic systems by Schumpeter's creative destruction, the Anglo-Saxon model appears to outperform the others. The explanation is, perhaps, that the European and Asian models rely on bank financing and family financing. In both cases, lenders and owners are reluctant to let the companies in which they have invested resources go under. In the impersonal Anglo-Saxon capital market, finance and management tend to be unrelated. If a company is not doing well, financial markets shift their resources to other companies.

FIGURE 22.11   Bankruptcy Rates by Countries in Different Economic Systems (figures represent averages from the 1990s)

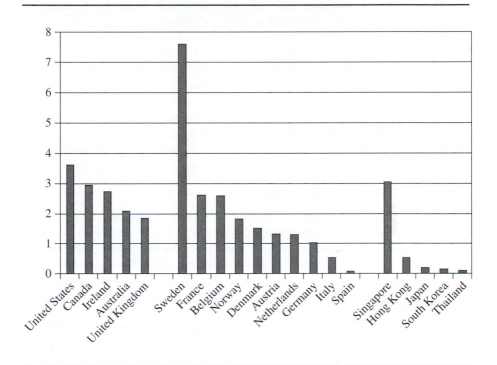

Source: Based on data from Stijn Claessens and Leonora Klapper, "Bankruptcy Around the World: Explanations of its Relative Use," The World Bank, June 2002, http://siteresources.worldbank.org/INTLAWJUSTINST/Resources/Bankruptcy.pdf.

Spillovers and Free Riding on Technological Advances   One lesson of Figure 22.6 is that the country that originates new technology is not necessarily the primary beneficiary. During World War II, technological advance continued and even accelerated in the United States while it ground to a halt in war-torn Europe and Japan. At the end of the war, Europe and Japan grew at "golden age" rates as they worked off the technological lag relative to the United States. The United States created the technology. Other countries benefited.

Likewise, China's remarkable growth has benefited from science, technology, and know-how brought in by its Western partners (or stolen from its Western partners). Again, we have one country benefiting from technology produced in another country.

New technologies spread of their own accord in this information age, even if fully protected by patents and intellectual property rights. Those occupying a lower position in the technology chain are the primary beneficiaries.

Economist William Nordhaus has studied the spread of technology and the distribution of its benefits between the creator of the knowledge and the ultimate beneficiaries of this knowledge who are able to free ride on the initial invention. His research shows that the creator of the new technology captures only 3.5 percent of the ultimate benefits from the innovation.[24]

An example would be the founders of Apple Computer, most notably its principal founder Steve Jobs, who created new products that change the way the world receives and exchanges information and entertainment. In 2012, Apple became the world's most valuable company with a market capitalization in excess of half a trillion dollars. The shares of the original founders constituted less than 10 percent of the total, which means Apple created almost a half trillion dollars of wealth for others.

The Distribution of Income

We can judge economic systems on the basis of how they distribute income. There is probably no more controversial subject in economics and politics than the distribution of income. We all agree on what constitutes a dysfunctional distribution of income. Distributions in which a few households have all the income and wealth or in which everyone receives the same are dysfunctional. The disagreement arises when we consider income distributions that are in between extremes.

The distribution of income is determined by two factors. The first is the distribution of factor income, namely what each household earns from labor income, capital income, and rental incomes. Earnings from capital and rental income depend on the distribution of financial and real wealth. Different economies in different economic systems might have different distributions of factor income. Our discussion of Sweden, for example, in Chapter 13, pointed out that Sweden experimented with a solidarity wage to equalize the distribution of income before taxes. The Soviet planned economy did not allow for earnings from capital, and it should have had a different distribution of factor income from countries that do have capital income.

The second factor determining the distribution of income is the amount of redistribution of factor income that the state carries out. State income redistribution occurs through transfers of financial and in-kind benefits.

The most relevant measure of income distribution is the distribution of income after all transfers. This distribution shows the distribution of command over goods and services among households. As noted in Chapter 2, we use the Gini coefficient to measure how evenly or unevenly income is distributed. Recall that a Gini coefficient of one represents an income distribution in which one household has all the income. A Gini of zero represents a distribution in which every household has the same income.

Figure 22.12 groups countries according to the economic systems we have identified. The first group represents the Anglo-Saxon world (defined as broadly as possible to include countries like Ireland, Switzerland, and Israel). The second group represents the European model; the third, the Asian model. At the far right, we have China as a standalone.

FIGURE 22.12   The Distribution of Income after Money and In-Kind Transfers
(Gini coefficients)

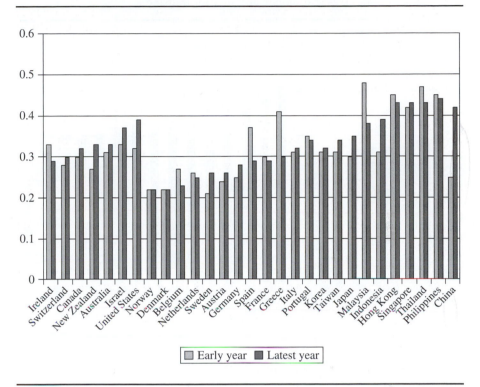

Sources: OECD statistical database, http://stats.oecd.org/Index.aspx?DataSetCode=INEQUALITY; Min-
quan Liu and Yimeng Yin, "Human Development in East and Southeast Asian Economies: 1990–2010,"
UNDP Human Development Research Paper, 17/2010, 2010/17 http://hdr.undp.org/en/reports/global/
hdr2010/papers/HDRP_2010_17.pdf.

Figure 22.12 gives Gini coefficients from an early year (usually the 1970s or
1980s) and from the latest year available (usually the mid-2000s). These two show
whether income has become more or less equally distributed. If we break the
results down by groups, we see that income is generally less equally distributed in
the Anglo-Saxon world and the distribution has become somewhat more unequal
with the passage of time. Income is distributed more equally in the European
model and, with the exception of Sweden, Austria, and Germany, the distribution
of income has become more equal. In Spain and Greece, the distribution of income
has become markedly more equal.

Are these differences in after-transfer income distributions the result of the distribution of factor income or redistribution by the state?

Figure 22.13 shows the amount of redistribution by the state, as measured as
the ratio of the Gini coefficient of factor income with the Gini coefficient after
income redistribution. In the Anglo-Saxon countries, there was less redistribution
than in Europe. In the two Asian countries for which we have data, Japan had
about the same redistribution as the Anglo-Saxon countries and Korea had less.

FIGURE 22.13   The Redistribution of Income by the State (The ratio of the
distribution of factor income to the distribution of income
after taxes and money and in-kind transfers)

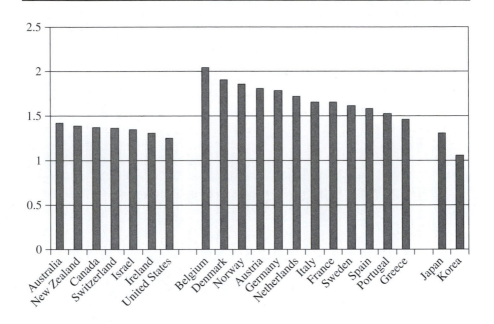

Source: OECD statistical database, http://stats.oecd.org/Index.aspx?DataSetCode=INEQUALITY. http://
stats.oecd.org/Index.aspx?QueryId=26067&Lang=en

The Welfare State

The state redistributed income by taxing one segment of the population and redistributing the tax revenues to another segment of the population through cash and
in-kind transfers. Insofar as state transfers make the distribution of income more
equal, a wealthier segment of the population is being taxed in order to transfer
income to a less wealthy segment of the population.

A state that commands a small share of the economy's resources is not in a
position to engage in large-scale redistribution. Therefore, we expect a larger state
(as a percentage of the economy) to be associated with a high degree of income
distribution. *The* **welfare state** *is one in which the state collects and redistributes
a large share of economic resources for the purpose of achieving economic and
political goals.* These goals can include diverse desiderata, such as income redistribution, social security, elimination of poverty, or promoting social and political
goals, such as nutrition, home ownership, or many other things.

The constitutional origins of the Anglo-Saxon model feature a limited role for
government. European history explains why the European model is based on the
notion of a larger, more intrusive state. The countries that make up the Asian
model are relative newcomers to affluence and industrialization. They began their

economic development without the tradition of a strong central government with vast powers of taxation and redistribution.

Figure 22.14 shows the dramatic differences in levels and trends in spending on social welfare across the different economic systems.

Figure 22.14 divides the world economies into Anglo-Saxon countries (again defined as broadly as possible to include Switzerland, Ireland, the United Kingdom, and Israel) and the European world, which consists of the countries of northern and southern Europe. The third group includes the Central European transition economies of Central Europe and the Baltic states. The fourth group captures Asia, including Southeast Asia, Japan, and China.

With the exception of the highly affluent Japan, the Asian countries have a very small welfare state. Individual citizens must look primarily to themselves and their families for health care, retirement, and other forms of security. The European countries rely heavily on the state to provide for health and income security. The Anglo-Saxon countries have a mixed system whereby the citizens of these countries combine private and public funds to provide for income and security. The transition countries combine features of both system and do not yield a clear pattern.

FIGURE 22.14   Shares of Spending on Social Welfare as a Percent of GDP, Various countries

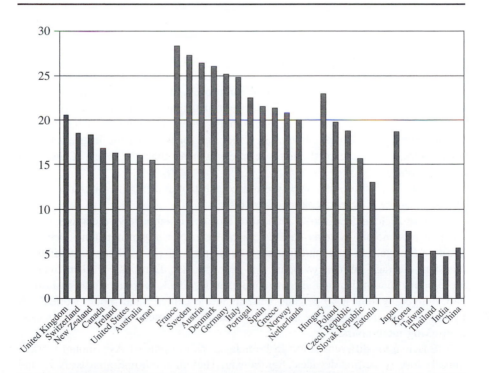

Sources: OPECD database, http://stats.oecd.org/Index.aspx?QueryId=4549; Asian Development Bank statistical database www.adb.org.

The European welfare state traces its origins to Bismarckian Germany in the 1880s. Despite opposition from his own party, the powerful German Chancellor, Otto von Bismarck, concluded that a welfare state offered the best protection against a socialist revolution. The United States was founded by hardy settlers, fearful of an intrusive state. The U.S. Constitution promised to protect American citizens from its own government under the motto: "That government is best which governs least."

Europeans seemed to have settled into their welfare state. The American electorate decides at each congressional or presidential election whether to expand the limits of government, with a Democratic party that favors a larger state and a Republican party that opposes. The battle over the size and power of the state, particularly the federal government, is the most important constant of American political life.

The Asian countries, with the exception of Japan, Hong Kong, and Singapore, are still relative newcomers to affluence. They began their industrialization with relatively small states and they continue to have relatively low levels of taxation and government spending today. As they become more affluent, they must decide whether to copy the European model of expansive government or the original U.S. model of limited government.

Effort and Leisure in Different Economic Systems

Among the decisions that people make are whether to work or study or stay at home, whether to negotiate for more pay or more leisure time. They may work harder and accept less leisure depending on the economic system in which they live. If they are affluent, they may demand more leisure. Or if the political system gives them more leisure through the political process, they support those who make them this offer at the ballot box. The system of taxation also affects labor-leisure choices. A 50 percent tax on labor means that workers take home only half of their gross earnings. At such take-home rates, they opt for more leisure instead of additional work. The value of the extra leisure is greater than the value of the extra market work.

Figure 22.15 shows that there are indeed substantial differences in labor-leisure outcomes in the different economic systems.

Figure 22.15 indeed shows marked differences in labor-leisure choices among the major economic systems covered in this text. North America (and Oceania), Western Europe, England, and Japan began the postwar era working approximately the same average number of hours per year. In fact, European workers worked more hours than in the United States or Japan. By 2011, working hours in Europe had plunged by almost 40 percent, whereas in the United States hours worked fell by less than a quarter. European workers increasingly opted for leisure as opposed to working more hours.

Asia is a far different story. In both Japan and Southeast Asia, hours worked initially rose in the first decades after the war. They then fell in Southeast Asia, and they fell even more in Japan. At the current time, Southeast Asian workers average more than 2,600 hours per year whereas Western European workers average about

FIGURE 22.15   Average Hours Worked Per Year, Various Countries, 1950–2011

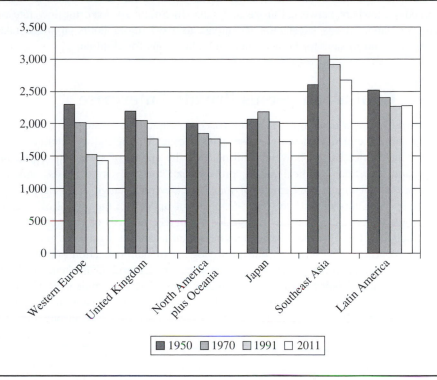

Source: Based on data from The Conference Board, Total Economy Database, "Output, Labor, and Labor Productivity Country Details, 1950–2011."

1,400 hours; U.S. workers fall somewhere in the middle. Latin American workers work less than Asians and more than Americans, but they have not yet experienced much of a fall in working hours.

Why do we have such different levels and trends in average hours worked? An easy answer is that European democratic states have legislated shorter working hours by legislating work hours per week and the duration of paid vacations. But legislated changes often have deeper economic explanations.

A notable difference between the European, Anglo-Saxon and Asian models is the level and the nature of taxation. Europe has a generally higher level of taxation and much higher taxes on labor. Asia has relatively low levels of taxation and lower payroll taxes. In some Asian countries, the wedge between what workers receive and what employees pay is minimal.

In Sweden, there was a time when it cost more in taxes to raise worker take-home pay than the worker actually took home. With such disincentives to work, employers and workers settled on increases in leisure rather than increases in pay and hours of work. In many cases, this appeared as a deal negotiated by labor and management, but the underlying cause was the high rate of taxation on labor.

Note that the United States and the Anglo-Saxon world occupy middle ground between Europe and Southeast Asia. Therefore, we see levels and trends in hours worked somewhere between Europe and Asia. In Southeast Asia, the low rate of taxes on labor means substantial incentives to work more hours, to raise take home pay, and to save for homes, cars, and educations for children.

State Capitalism versus Private Enterprise

Earlier debate over economic systems focused on capitalism versus socialism. That debate largely ended with the collapse of the Soviet Union and its satellites. The end of the Soviet Union, however, did not end the appeal of socialism. European and Latin American political parties proudly call themselves socialists, and the evils of capitalism and the benefits of socialism are freely taught in institutions of higher learning throughout the world. One cannot understate the appeal of slogans of fairness and equality and the distaste for the perceived evils of capitalism.

Socialists, however, have learned an important lesson: It is difficult to own and run an economy. It is better to put away slogans of nationalization and to allow enterprises to remain in private hands. They can be controlled through taxation, regulation, subsidization, and other indirect means. The government of François Mitterrand in France in the 1980s was the last major administration to preach nationalization. His nationalization program convinced socialists throughout the world not to nationalize. He convinced them that there are better ways of achieving desired goals.

This does not mean that nationalization is behind us. Currently in Latin America, nationalization, especially of foreign companies, is a convenient political tool in the hands of populists such as the Chávez regime in Venezuela and the Kirchner regime in Argentina. Nationalization of foreign companies has great appeal.

For those who distrust capitalist markets, there is a great wariness to allow private decision making to prevail in important industries and companies. For this reason, those who dislike private enterprise prefer state capitalism—the control or ownership of the commanding heights of the economy by the state or quasi-state bodies. State capitalism, its proponents argue, reacts more quickly to crises, and steers the economy through booms, busts, and bubbles. We should rely on technocrats to run things more effectively than chaotic markets.

State capitalism has been used, some argue, with great effectiveness in the BRICS (Brazil, Russia, India, China, and South Africa)—the rapidly growing large economies that rely on more pervasive state involvement and control of the economy. China is held up as exhibit number one due to its rapid growth. Russia, although a large country, is not featured because of the pervasive corruption.

State capitalism is not a new idea. It has been tried in a number of countries before the current state-capitalist-BRICS craze. France, Japan, Malaysia, and other countries have all experimented with state capitalism at one time or another.

Those who argue against state capitalism point out two basic flaws: One is the fatal conceit of the belief that human minds can better control an economy than the subtle signals of market forces. It is wishful thinking to believe that technocrats can better foresee the future than markets, or that they are able to avoid systemic risk. The second flaw is that state capitalism is prone to corruption and cronyism. Decisions are not made based on economics but rather on connections and politics.

The U.S. presidential election of 2012 will touch on the issue of state capitalism in that the Obama administration appears to have less faith in market resource allocation than his Republican opponent.

Summary

- Economic systems and their institutions affect economic performance over the long run. We should not judge systems based on cycles.
- We live in interesting times and times of surprises; for example, the rise of China, the European Union, the rapid growth of India, and the collapse of communism.
- There are no well-defined economic systems to describe the economies of Africa and Latin America. There is an established model of Islamic economics.
- We can measure the performance of economic systems by the quality of their institutions. There are now empirical measures of institutions. We can agree that some institutions are good, but there is disagreement on others, such as economic freedom versus regulation.
- The performance of economies is most frequently measured in terms of GDP growth and GDP growth per capita. The two can yield different results and comparison is complicated by the fact that population growth may depend on economic growth.
- It is difficult to capture the effect of the economic system on growth, but there are natural experiments, such as the divided Koreas, that give conclusive answers.
- We measure the efficiency of the economy in terms of the Solow residual. We use it to explain the sources of labor productivity growth.
- Various measures—such as Nobel Prizes, business formation and destruction, and practical inventions—shed light on the performance of economic systems.
- There is distinctive difference in the distribution of income among the basic models of economic systems. There are also distinctive differences with respect to the role of the welfare state.

Key Terms

fatwa—In the Islamic faith, a fatwa is a religious opinion concerning Islamic law issued by an Islamic scholar.

growth accounting—Seeks to explain why growth has occurred by means of the expansion of inputs and technological progress.

Institutional Possibilities Frontier (IPF)—Measures the social costs (losses) associated with different combinations of economic institutions.

intellectual property rights—Property rights protected under law, including copyrightable works, ideas, discoveries, and inventions.

mufti—A person who issues a fatwa.

patent—Gives the patent holder a monopoly over the product for a specified period of time

Solow residual—Measures the economic growth that is not explained by the growth of labor and capital inputs.

welfare state—The state collects and redistributes a large share of economic resources for the purpose of achieving economic and political goals.

Notes

1. Carmen M. Reinhart and Kenneth S. Rogoff, *This Time is Different: Eight Centuries of Financial Folly* (Princeton, N.J.: Princeton University Press, 2009), p. xlv.
2. "The Rise of State Capitalism," *The Economist*, January 21, 2012.
3. Josef Goldmann, "Fluctuations and Trends in the Rate of Economic Growth in Some Socialist Economies," *Economics of Planning* 4, no. 2 (1964), 89–98.
4. John Maynard Keynes, *The General Theory of Employment, Interest and Money* (London: Macmillan, 1936).
5. Kenneth Pomeranz, The Great Divergence: China, Europe and the Making of the Modern World Economy (Princeton: Princeton University Press, 2001).
6. "The Hopeful Continent: Africa Rising," *The Economist*, December 3, 2011.
7. Morgan Lorraine Roach, "The 2012 Index of Economic Freedom: Africa Still Rising," Heritage Foundation, 2012 Index of Economic Freedom, http://blog.heritage.org/2012/01/13/the-2012-index-of-economic-freedom-africa-still-rising/.
8. Freedom House, "Freedom in the World: 2012 Freedom in the World," http://www.freedomhouse.org/report-types/freedom-world.
9. Timur Kuran, "Islamic Economics and the Islamic Subeconomy," *Journal of Economic Perspectives* 9, no. 4 (Fall 1995), 155–174; Timur Kuran, "Why the Middle East Is Economically Underdeveloped: Historical Mechanisms of Institutional Stagnation," *The Journal of Economic Perspectives* 18, no. 3 (Summer 2004), 71–90.
10. Kuran, "Islamic Economics," p. 161.
11. Simeon Djankov, Edward Glaeser, Rafael La Porta, Florencio Lopez-de-Silanes, and Andrei Shleifer, "The New Comparative Economics," http://mba.tuck.dartmouth.edu/pages/faculty/rafael.laporta/docs/publications/LaPorta%20PDF%20Papers-ALL/New%20Comparative%20Economics.pdf.
12. Indexmundi, http://www.indexmundi.com/g/g.aspx?v=31&c=bc&l=en.
13. Historical Statistics of the United States, Millennial edition. Online edition, http://hsus.cambridge.org/HSUSWeb/toc/tableToc.do?id=Ca9-19.
14. Angus Maddison Home Page, http://www.ggdc.net/MADDISON/oriindex.htm.
15. William Easterly and Stanley Fischer, "The Soviet Historical Decline: Historical and Republican Data," NBER Working Papers, 4735, May 1994.
16. Patents and Innovation: Trends and Policy Challenges, OECD, http://www.oecd.org/dataoecd/48/12/24508541.pdf.
17. Center for Financial Stability, "The Global Competitiveness Report 2011-2012," Center for Financial Stability Rule of Law Index, http://www.centerforfinancialstability.org/rli.php.
18. Carsten Fink and Keith Maskus, *Intellectual Property and Development: Lessons from Recent Economic Research* (New York: Oxford University Press, 2006).

19. NERA Consulting, "China: Intellectual Property Rights Protection: Trends In Litigation And Economic Damages," February 17, 2009, http://www.mondaq.com/article.asp?articleid=74520.

20. Jon Bruner, "American Leadership in Science, Measured in Nobel Prizes," http://www.forbes.com/sites/jonbruner/2011/10/05/nobel-prizes-and-american-leadership-in-science-infographic/.

21. Joseph Berliner, *The Innovation Decision in Soviet Industry* (Cambridge, Mass.: MIT Press, 1976).

22. Alex Hutchinson, "The Top 50 Inventions of the Past 50 Years," *Popular Mechanics*, http://www.popularmechanics.com/technology/gadgets/news/2078467.

23. Stijn Claessens and Leonora Klapper, "Bankruptcy Around the World: Explanations of its Relative Use," The World Bank, June 2002.

24. William Nordhaus, *Invention, Growth and Welfare: A Theoretical Treatment of Technological Change* (Cambridge, Mass.: MIT Press, 1969).

Recommended Readings

Erik Berglof, Alexander Plekhanov Yevgeniya, and Jeromin Zettelmeyer, "Understanding the Crisis in Emerging Europe," EBRD, Working Paper No. 109, November 2009.

Simon Commander and Zlatko Nikoloski, "Institutions and Economic Performance: What Can be Explained?" EBRD Working Paper no. 121, December 2010.

Padma Desai, *Financial Crisis, Contagion, and Containment* (Princeton: Princeton University Press, 2003).

Simeon Djankov, Edward Glaeser, Rafael La Porta, Florencio Lopez-de-Silanes, and Andrei Shleifer, "The New Comparative Economics," http://mba.tuck.dartmouth.edu/pages/faculty/rafael.laporta/docs/publications/LaPorta%20PDF%20Papers-ALL/New%20Comparative%20Economics.pdf.

EBRD, *Regional Economic Prospects in EBRD Countries of Operations: May, 2011* (London: EBRD Office of the Chief Economist, 2011)

———, *Transition Report 2009: Transition in Crisis?* (London: EBRD, 2009).

———, *Transition Report 2010: Recovery and Reform* (London: EBRD, 2010).

Barry Eichengreen, "Crisis and Growth in the Advanced Economies: What We Know, What We Do Not, and What We Can Learn From the 1930s" *Comparative Economic Studies* 53 (2011), 383–406.

———, *European Monetary Unification: Theory, Practice, Analysis* (Cambridge, Mass.: MIT Press, 1997).

Carsten Fink and Keith Maskus, *Intellectual Property and Development: Lessons from Recent Economic Research* (New York: Oxford University Press, 2006).

Libor Krkoska and Katrin Robeck, "The Impact of Crime on the Enterprise Sector: Transition Versus Non-Transition Countries," EBRD Working Paper no. 97, May 2006.

Timur Kuran, "Islamic Economics and the Islamic Sub-economy," *Journal of Economic Perspectives* 9, no. 4 (Fall 1995), 155–174.

Ross Levine and David Renelt, "A Sensitovity Analysis of Cross-Country Growth Regressions" *The American Economic Review* 82, no. 4 (1992), 942–963.

Angus Maddison, *Economic Growth in the West* (London: George Allen & Unwin, 1964).

———, *Explaining the Economic Performance of Nations: Essays in Time and Space* (Brookfield, Vt.: E. Elgar, 1995).

Casey B. Mulligan, Ricard Gil, and Xavier Sala-i-Martin, "Do Democracies Have Different Public Policies Than Nondemocracies?" *Journal of Economic Perspectives* 18, no. 1 (Winter 2004), 51–74.

Larry Neal and Daniel Barbezat, *The Economics of the European Union and the Economies of Europe* (New York: Oxford University Press, 1998).

William Nordhaus, *Invention, Growth and Welfare: A Theoretical Treatment of Technological Change* (Cambridge, Mass.: MIT Press, 1969).

Kenneth Pomeranz, *The Great Divergence: China, Europe and the Making of the Modern World Economy* (Princeton: Princeton University Press, 2001).

Carmen Reinhart and Kenneth S. Rogoff, *This Time is Different: Eight Centuries of Financial Folly* (Princeton, N.J.: Princeton University Press, 2009).

Glossary

ABC of Communism   Nikolai Bukharin and Evgeny Preobrazhensky's book, describing an economy in which the workers collectively own the means of production, goods are kept in public warehouses, and people take what they need.

accession   Process through which states (countries) become members of the European Union.

administrators   Issue the orders and intervene when they feel necessary.

adverse selection   Agents conceal information from principals, making it impossible for their superiors to distinguish among them.

agency–managerial problems   Members of the organization pursue objectives differing from those established for the organization.

agent   Acts for, on behalf of, or as a representative of a principal.

Anglo-Saxon model   Historical origins in Great Britain; patterned after the classical liberal ideas of Adam Smith and the constitutional precepts of classical liberalism.

Asian model   High rates of capital formation and on other devices, often supported by the state, to overcome relative backwardness in as short a time as possible.

asset stripping   The acquisition of valuable assets during privatization with the intent of financial gain rather than eventual corporate restructuring.

association   Members make decisions in the absence of a superior–subordinate relationship.

Austrian School of Economics   The importance of individualism and free markets to create the information and incentives needed to manage the complex interactions of an economy.

average branch cost pricing   This term means that profits cannot be used to gauge managerial performance.

balanced plan   Availabilities of each good or service matches its planned uses.

balances of the national economy   Tallies of the availability and uses of commodities, such as grain or electricity.

barter   Exchange of goods and services between two parties when money is not involved as an intermediary.

board of directors   Elected by the stockholders, makes its major decisions, and appoints management to run the corporation.

bounded rationality   Decision makers have limited information and other constraints that force them to use rules of thumb.

broad and liquid stock market   A large number of shareholders, none of whom hold significant numbers of shares, and shareholders can sell their shares readily without affecting the share price.

cadres department   Appoints officials to elite positions in the party and state. The party uses promotions and other rewards to incentivize regional officials.

capital account convertibility   Exists when a currency can be purchased and sold in a market for the purpose of engaging in transactions pertaining to capital assets.

capital market   Market in which businesses raise investment finance through the issue of stocks and bonds and bank borrowing.

capital market inefficiency   Investment finance does not go to uses that yield the highest rates of return (adjusted for risk).

capitalism   Private ownership of the factors of production, decentralized decision making, coordinated by the market, material incentives, and public choices are made by democratic political institutions.

capitalist breakdown   Conditions occurring in the final stages of capitalism—overproduction, underconsumption, disproportions, and the alienation of the working class.

Central European Free Trade Area (CEFTA)   Free trade area (common market) formed in 1992.

central planning board (CPB)   Catchall phrase for the political and administrative committees in charge of planned resource allocation.

centralized   Most decisions are made at high levels.

ceteris paribus   A Latin term meaning all other things being equal.

China Puzzle   How China with its poor protection of private property, weak corporate governance, lack of democratic accountability, and absence of a rule of law can grow rapidly over more than three decade.

Chinese SOEs   State sole-funded corporations and enterprises with the state as the biggest share holder.

Chinese-style socialism   The state and private economies coexist, national planning is absent, and private property rights are supposed to be protected.

civil law   A legal system in which laws are written and codified and are not determined by judges based on custom or precedent.

clash of civilizations   The fundamental sources of future conflict will not be based on ideology or economics but on clashes of culture (Huntington).

cluster   If countries do not cluster according to their institutions, they cannot be treated as economic systems.

co-determination   Worker representatives serve on the boards of directors of corporations and workers participate in decision making at the shop floor level.

coefficient of relative effectiveness   An interest rate disguised using another technical term.

collective farms (*kolkhozy*)   Compulsory collectives of peasant households that delivered their products to the state at prices dictated by the state.

collective ownership   Property rights belong to the members of the collective.

command economy   An economic system where resources allocation is directed by a central planning agency, the function of which is to give directives to enterprises.

Commanding Heights   Notion that the entire economy could be controlled by centralized control of only its most important industries (Lenin).

common law   A legal system based on custom and precedents rather than a written legal code.

Commonwealth of Independent States (CIS)   Organization that comprises those states emerging from the former Soviet Union except the Baltic states of Latvia, Lithuania, and Estonia.

communism   The highest stage of social development, characterized by the absence of markets and money, abundance, and the withering away of the state.

Communist Manifesto   Invited the "workers of the world to unite" against their capitalist oppressors; they "have nothing to lose but their chains" (Marx and Engels).

comparative economics   The use of international data across countries and across time to study economic phenomena.

complex markets Require sophisticated institutional infrastructure that often deal in non-homogeneous goods and services that may be bought in one period of time and sold in another period of time or that involve a series of payments over time.

confucianism Emphasizes the qualities of loyalty, nationalism, social solidarity, collectivism, benevolence, faith, and bravery.

consistent plan Supplies and demands for the various planned commodities are in balance.

constitution Establishes the basic political, economic, and social rules of the game for a society.

consumer sovereignty The basic decision of what to produce is dominated by consumers in the marketplace.

contract responsibility system An agreement of a group of peasant households to collectively deliver quotas to the state while keeping the rest for their consumption or sale.

contracts An enforceable agreement between two or more individuals.

control figures Preliminary output targets of the national economic plan.

control owner Sufficient ownership shares to control the operation of the company.

convertible currency Currency for which there is a market (supply and demand), and thus a market determined rate of exchange, available to participants within and beyond the borders of an economy.

corporate bonds Corporation pays interest over the life of the bond and returns the principal at maturity.

corporate governance (1) Determines in whose interests a corporation, in which owners are not managers, will be run.

corporate governance (2) The manner in which the internal operations of an enterprise or business are organized and operated.

corporate raiders Mobilize substantial funds to mount hostile takeovers against underperforming corporations.

corporate transparency Companies supply the public with regular, accurate, and readily accessible information concerning their operations and prospects.

corporation Company owned by its stockholders, who have limited liability, and can act as a legal person.

Corporatization The creation of a corporate type of ownership with shares that can be traded.

Council for Mutual Economic Assistance (CMEA) Trade bloc established by the former administrative command economies in 1949 to provide integration of the command economies through coordinated economic planning and trade; abolished in 1989.

counterfactual information What would have happened in the absence of a particular event.

country fixed effects The use of dummy variables assigned to each country to hold constant the impact of the economic system so as to allow proper analysis of other variables.

creative destruction The driving force of capitalism according to Schumpeter in which innovation ensures the replacement of the old by the new.

crony capitalism An economic system in which the nation's wealth is siphoned off by insiders close to those in power and by those in power themselves.

cross holding Ownership of significant blocks of shares by one company in other companies.

Cultural Revolution Sought to restore socialist zeal and discipline by liquidating capitalist and traditional elements from Chinese society.

current-account convertibility   Exists when a currency can be purchased and sold in a market for the purpose of engaging in transactions pertaining to the current account.

customs union   One of a variety of forms of economic integration that eliminates the trade barriers among member countries and imposes a common external tariff on nonmember countries by Poland, Hungary, and Czechoslovakia.

de novo privatization   Expansion of the private sector by the creation of new and usually small firms.

deadweight loss   A measure of inefficiency caused by a variety of distortions that cause the economy to operate below its potential.

decentralization   Shifting decision-making authority and responsibility from higher levels to lower levels in the organizational hierarchy.

decentralized   Decisions made primarily at low levels of the organization.

democracy   Public choices are put to a majority vote.

democratic socialism   State ownership of the means of production combined with a democratic state.

deregulation (1)   Reduction in the amount of regulation a business or industry faces.

deregulation (2)   The reduction of government regulation and the return of decision making back to the private business.

dialectical materialism (1)   Marx's explanation of the pending triumph of socialism over capitalism.

dialectical materialism (2)   The philosophical foundations of change in the Marxian vision of change based on the writings of Hegel and Feuerbach.

dictatorship of the proletariat   Governs in the first stage of socialism and directly represents the interests of the proletariat.

direct sale   The transfer of ownership from one person or persons to others usually absent intermediate mechanisms, such as an auction.

directive planning   Targets set by planners to directly determine outcomes; plan targets legally binding on enterprises.

distortion   In the transition setting, usually refers to differences in structure and allocation of resources when, for example, command economic systems are compared to market economic systems at similar levels of economic development.

distributional coalition   A component of contemporary public choice theory—a vested-interest coalition that uses the political process to gain monopoly profits.

dynamic efficiency   The ability of an economic system to enhance its capacity to produce goods and services over time without an increase in capital and labor inputs.

economic freedom   The degree to which participants in the economy are free to make economic decisions unconstrained by state intervention or corruption.

economic growth   The increase in real GDP or real GDP per capita over a period of time.

economic institutions   The way we organize our economic activities, covering a broad range of economic, social, and political activities.

economic levers   Mechanisms such as prices and profits used to guide socialist managers.

economic managers   Responsible for fulfilling these orders and rewarded or penalized based on the level of fulfillment.

economic outcomes (EO)   The performance of the economy as measured by criteria such as economic growth, living standards, employment, and other measure that are deemed important.

economic reform (1)   An attempt to modify an existing system.

economic reform (2)   Changes in arrangements within an economic system; often applied to attempts to change command economies and to improve their performance.

economic regulation Government involvement in markets, such as setting prices, restricting corporate decision making, and controlling competition.

economic system (ES) (1) This is multidimensional and is defined in terms of its many institutions, such as how it manages information, its organizational structure, its provision for property rights, and how it makes public choices.

economic system (2) A set of institutions for decision making and for the implementation of decisions concerning production, income, and consumption within a given geographic area.

economic system (3) The organizational arrangements, institutions, and policies responsible for resource allocation in a given geographic (country) setting.

economically rational regulation Regulation that yields benefits in excess of its costs.

economics The study of how economic agents (households, firms, and governments) allocate scarce resources (land, labor, and capital) among competing ends according to the prevailing economic system.

economy of shortage A cornerstone of socialist economic systems according to Kornai, characterized by shortage as a perpetual and self-reproducing condition.

efficiency (1) Measures how effectively the factors of production are combined to produce output using available technology.

efficiency (2) The effectiveness with which a system utilizes its available resources (including knowledge) at a particular time (static efficiency) or through time (dynamic efficiency).

efficiency (3) The relationship between inputs and outputs.

emerging market economies Economies typically at a lower level of economic development pursuing economic growth through market institutions.

eminent domain The right of the state to take property under certain conditions in the public interest (such as buying land for the construction of railways or making way for an interstate highway).

enclosure Lands that had been tilled in open fields or used in common were assigned to specific users, such as the manor owner or more prosperous peasant families.

End of History Fukuyama's idea that Western liberalism had triumphed over socialism, leaving no competing alternatives.

endogenous variable In an economic model, a variable whose value is explained within the model being studied.

entitlement program Recipients are entitled to receive payments once they qualify under the rules of the program.

environmental factors (1) The economic setting in which the economic system operates.

environmental factors (2) Factors such as resource endowments arguably likely to influence resource allocation in economic systems.

equity Fairness.

EU accession countries Those countries that became members of the EU in recent years.

EU stability pact The agreement that no member country could run a public deficit of more than 3 percent of GDP.

European Central Bank Shares many features with the Federal Reserve Bank of the United States. Its board consists of representatives from the national banks of the various EU members, just as the Federal Reserve Board is comprised of representatives from the district banks. Each member has one vote, unlike other EU bodies that weight votes according to population.

European Common Market A precursor of the European Union. It created a common market of member countries by eliminating import duties and quotas.

European Marxist reformers People who abandoned the goal of socialist revolution to work within the political system to reform capitalism to make it better for workers.

European model   Economic ideas enunciated in France and Germany in the nineteenth century that place less faith in the invisible hand and call for more state intervention in economic affairs.

European Union (1)   Consists of twenty-seven member countries and a number of candidate countries that form a common market with common rules. It is governed by a multinational form of government, consisting of a Council of the European Union, an elected European Parliament, a European Commission, a European Central Bank, a European Court of Justice, and a European Council of Auditors.

European Union (EU) (2)   Group of European nations making up a single economic community.

European Union (3)   An economic and political association of twenty-seven European nations designed to create a single market.

European welfare state   Replaces families, private savings, and charity with state programs for economic security and welfare.

exogenous variable   In an economic model, a variable whose value is explained outside the model being studied.

export promotion   State policies to promote exports. Such policies range from subsidies of export industries to free-trade practices for the economy as a whole.

extensive growth   Growth through the expansion of inputs.

external balance   When the demand side for foreign exchange is equalized with the supply of foreign exchange; in other words, the market for foreign exchange is in equilibrium.

externalities   The actions of one producer or consumer directly affect the costs or utilities of others outside of the price system.

Fair Labor Standards Act of 1938   Established standards for minimum wages, overtime pay, record keeping, and child labor.

family-owned company   Families own and likely manage the company.

fatwa   In the Islamic faith, a fatwa is a religious opinion concerning Islamic law issued by an Islamic scholar.

feudal agriculture   Large estates, or manors, where peasants farmed strips of land in open fields and worked on the landlord's land in return.

fiduciary responsibility   A relationship in which one person has a responsibility to care for the assets or rights of other persons.

final demand   Output invested, consumed by households or government, or exported.

financial intermediaries   Link savers and borrowers in financial markets that include banks and other bank-like institutions.

fiscal policy   How the state collects taxes and spends revenue.

flexible labor markets   Give employers freedom to hire and fire employees and change conditions of work and pay with few restrictions.

foreign direct investment (FDI) (1)   Investment by foreign investors in the form of acquiring substantial shares in domestic companies or entering into partnerships with domestic companies through joint ventures.

foreign direct investment (FDI) (2)   Investment by investors in one country in companies in other countries by which the investors gain significant management control.

foreign direct investment (FDI) (3)   Investment flows from one country to another that occur directly—for example, through the construction of plant and equipment by a donor country in a host country—rather than through financial instruments such as stocks.

Soviet foreign-trade monopoly   Handled all international transaction between Soviet and foreign enterprises.

Four Tigers   Hong Kong, Singapore, South Korea, and Taiwan, which have grown rapidly since the 1970s and are now relatively affluent.

free riders, or nonpayers   Cannot be prevented from using a good, and one person's use does not prevent any other person from using the good.

free riding   Potential donors hold down their contributions and rely on others to solve the poverty problem.

full disclosure   The principle that the corporations listing stock must make available to potential buyers all relevant information, good and bad, about the company.

full-employment policy   A government policy whose objective is the ability to sustain jobs for all who want them.

full ownership (or full property rights)   Owner has the right to dispose of the property, use the property, and receive the income the property generates.

fund holders   Recipients of funded commodities.

funded commodities   Those whose "limits" were assigned to enterprises by the planning system.

General Agreement on Tariffs and Trade (GATT)   Predecessor to the World Trade Organization (WTO); established as a framework for the discussion of world trade policies and negotiations.

German civil law   An accessible written collection of laws to govern behavior as persons, workers, borrowers, lenders, lessors and lessees, and businesspeople.

Germany, Inc   Germany's extensive cross-ownership among corporations and directors serving on the boards of companies in which they own significant shares.

Gerschenkron's theory of substitutions   Backward countries could find innovative substitutions for missing preconditions.

Gini coefficient (1)   A numerical measure of the degree of inequality in the distribution of income or wealth. Its value ranges from zero, if everyone has the same income or wealth, to one, if one person has all the income or wealth.

Gini coefficient (2)   A standard measure of income equality that usually expresses the gap between low income earners (say the bottom 10 percent of income earners) and high income earners (say the top 10 percent of income earners).

globalization   Increasing interlocking of the world's economies via expanding trade in goods, services, and capital.

golden parachute   Provides for a limited number of top executives to receive generous severance bonuses if their company is taken over.

Gosplan   The Russian name for the State Planning Commission.

Great Leap Forward   Massive resurgence of radical ideology, which replaced rationality.

Great Moderation   The period from the 1980s to 2007 noted for its economic growth and economic stability.

Greater China   Vast numbers of Chinese both inside and outside of China proper.

gross value of output   The planned output of the ministry or enterprise expressed either in physical units or in value terms.

growth accounting   Seeks to explain why growth has occurred by means of the expansion of inputs and technological progress.

growth of factor productivity   Measures the rate of growth of output per unit of capital and labor input.

happiness research   A fairly young branch of economics that uses national and international surveys of households probing how content residents of different countries are with their lives.

hard budget constraint   Under capitalism, enterprises must cover costs or eventually be replaced, according to Kornai.

hierarchy (1)   Superiors (principals) establish objectives and issue orders to subordinates (agents) who are supposed to carry out assigned tasks to achieve organizational objectives.

hierarchy (2)   The division of an organization into superior and subordinate levels. The person in charge of a higher level in the organization is superior to subordinates at lower levels.

highly leveraged companies   Heavy debt burdens relative to equity, which must be serviced by regular interest and principal payments.

hire and fire labor market   A market in which workers and employees can be fired or laid off with few limits placed on it by the state.

horizontal transaction   Concluded by subordinates at the same level of the administrative structure without the approval of administrative superiors.

horizontal trust   Parties to horizontal transactions trust each other sufficiently to engage in unsanctioned transactions by superiors.

hostile merger or acquisition   Targeted company actively opposes the takeover.

hukou   Residence registration system, which registers households by place of urban or rural location.

human action   Spontaneous institutional change not the result of human action.

human design   Institutional changes resulting from deliberate, planned, or legislative activity.

impersonal capital market   Capital is supplied by entities outside of and unrelated to the enterprise on the basis of economic criteria.

implicit lifetime labor contract   An unwritten understanding that employees will keep their jobs over the entire course of their working years.

import substitution (1)   Policies that protect domestic industries from foreign competition via tariffs or other barriers.

import substitution (2)   Protection of the domestic economy from foreign competition by tariff barriers so as to reserve the domestic economy for domestic producers.

indicative plan   Planners project aggregate or sectoral trends and provide information beyond that normally supplied by the market.

indicative planning   Sets nonbinding targets for industries or sectors to provide information about the future to businesses.

industrial democracy   Requires management to consider workers' interests to achieve a consensus.

industrial policy   State attempts to preferentially promote and develop industries and branches that are particularly worthy or deemed important to growth and development.

industrial prices   Set to equal the average cost of the industrial branch plus a profit markup.

Industrial Revolution   The dramatic economic rise of Europe and North America in the nineteenth century that began in England and then spread to the European continent and to North America.

inefficient cooperatives   Occurs if two cooperative in equilibrium have different productivities. This result is inefficient because output could be increased by redistributing labor between the two firms.

inflexible labor markets   Require employers to follow strict rules and procedures in hiring and firing employees.

information economics   How markets cause specialization in the generation and utilization of information.

information, telecommunications, and transportation revolution   Technological changes that lower transactions costs in domestic and international trade.

informationally decentralized systems These systems generate, process, and utilize information at the lower levels in the organization that is not exchanged with higher levels in the organization.

initial conditions (1) Characteristics of economies observed at the beginning of transition; for example, the heavy industry bias typical of the command economies.

initial conditions (2) Conditions existing at the beginning of the transition era, for example institutional arrangements, industrial structure, and so on.

initial conditions (3) The starting point from which the growth and development of an economy begins.

insider privatization The sale of an enterprise to those who are employed by the enterprise.

insiders Board members or managers of the company who have more information about the corporation's performance than do public shareholders.

Institutional Possibilities Frontier (IPF) Measures the social costs (losses) associated with different combinations of economic institutions.

institutions The rules of the game of a society that shape economic decisions, or, more fundamentally, the humanly devised constraints that shape human interaction.

intellectual property rights Property rights protected under law, including copyrightable works, ideas, discoveries, and inventions.

intensive growth Growth that occurs through the increase in efficiency of resource use.

interindustry demand The output of one industry (for example, coal) used as the input for another industry (for example, steel).

internal balance Equilibrium of the domestic economy usually characterized by full employment and the absence of inflation.

internalization An action that makes the cost of the externality a private cost.

International Monetary Fund (IMF) World organization helping member nations manage international financial transactions.

invisible hand A highly efficient and harmonious economic system is the result if competitive markets are left to function freely without government intervention (Smith).

Islamic (Sharia) law Religious law based directly on the teachings of the Koran as interpreted by senior religious figures.

"J curve" A characterization of the pattern of output change observed in a number of transition economies; severe collapse followed by subsequent recovery.

Japan's economic miracle Exceptional growth in the first three decades after World War II.

Japan's Ministry of International Trade and Industry (MITI, renamed METI) Agency responsible for Japan's industrial policy.

job right constraint A policy, prevalent in command economies, in which full employment would in effect be guaranteed through limitations on the firing of unneeded workers and the provision of funds to finance unneeded workers.

job rights economy (1) Everyone guaranteed a job; no incentives to change jobs, and few incentives to work hard.

job rights economy (2) Workers are guaranteed a job by the state.

keiretsu Horizontal or vertical conglomerates with large banks at their center.

Keynesian revolution The general acceptance of Keynes's proposition that governments must actively counter economic downturns.

kibbutz Characterized by equal (or more equal) sharing in the distribution of income: no private property, a noncash economy, high provision of local public goods for use by kibbutz members, and separate residences for children.

kleptocracy The widespread theft of society's resources by the nation's rulers.

labor or trade union   An organization of employees and workers of a company, occupation, or branch that comes together for the purpose of affecting conditions of work and pay.

labor theory of value (Marx)   Value is determined by labor alone and therefore excludes interest and rent from allowable costs.

laissez-faire (French for "let it be")   A policy that says that the state should not intervene in private economic transactions except in strictly limited cases (Smith).

Lange's two rules   (1) Produce the level of output at which price is equal to marginal cost and (2) minimize the cost of production at that output.

law of the declining rate of profit   The profit rate of capitalists must inevitably fall and contribute to the general crisis of capitalism.

leading role of the party   The recognized status of the communist party as the primary decision-making body of the Soviet Union.

legal personhood   Corporation can enter into contracts and do business in its own name.

Lenin's Bolshevik Party   A small party of professional underground revolutionaries, the Bolsheviks, bent on a violent socialist revolution.

Leviathan   Hobbes's term to describe the all-powerful state that he advocated.

liberalization (1)   The reduction of state controls and the implementation of decentralized (usually market) forces to influence resource allocation.

liberalization (2)   The reduction of state controls over economic activity typical of the early stages of transition.

limited liability   Shareholders of a joint stock company (corporation) are not responsible for the debts of the company if it goes bankrupt.

Maastricht Treaty   A treaty that outlined the introduction of a common currency, the euro, for those countries that chose to join the euro zone.

macroeconomic balance   Supply of consumer goods at established prices equaled desired consumer spending.

managerial capitalism   A system of corporate governance that places the interests of stakeholders above those or equal to the shareholders, or owners.

Market (1)   Activities that are coordinated by the buying and selling of goods and services among organizations.

Market (2)   Any organizational arrangement that brings buyers and sellers together.

market-based contracting   An impersonal form of contracting based on formal contracts backed by a rule of law.

market capitalization   The market value of outstanding shares.

market economy (1)   An economic system where resource allocation is directed through market arrangements and the forces of supply and demand.

market economy (2)   Market provides signals that trigger organizations to make decisions on resource utilization and coordinates the activities of decision-making units.

market for corporate control   A rival management team has the opportunity to buy control of the corporation from its share owners.

market power   Business can affect the price at which it buys or sells.

market socialism (1)   An economic system that combines social ownership of capital with market allocation.

market socialism (2)   Public ownership; decentralized decision making; coordinated by the market; both material and moral incentives.

Marxist revisionists   Concluded that the goals of socialism—workers' rights, a fair distribution of income, and state control of the marketplace—could be achieved through the democratic political process. They worked for reform legislation as members of organized worker parties.

mass privatization Shifting the ownership of real property from the state to individuals on a wide scale rather than on a selective basis.

material balance Comparison of the planned supply of a particular product with the planned uses of that product.

material incentives Promote desirable behavior by giving the recipient a greater claim over material goods.

materialist conception of history Economic forces (called productive forces) determine how production relations, markets, and society itself (the superstructure) are organized.

median voter Separates the lower half of the voting population from the higher half.

Meiji Restoration in 1868 Replaced the military regime with a new government of progressive officials determined to embark on modernization.

Mercantilism (1) Advocates a strong state to regulate and control the domestic and international transactions of a national economy in order to promote its political and economic strength vis-à-vis its neighbors.

Mercantilism (2) Notion that the state must strictly regulate all forms of economic activity to limit the flow of imports and grounds of political and economic security.

merger or acquisition One corporation buys another either by purchase or through the exchange of stock, corporate debt, or borrowed money.

mergers and acquisitions The buying, selling, and merger of one company with another.

M-Form organization Organizes and manages economic tasks on a regional rather than a sectoral basis.

middle-income trap The inability of fast-growing poor countries to raise per capita income from middle-income to affluent status.

Mini Dragons Countries like Thailand, Indonesia, Malaysia and the Philippines that have begun to grow rapidly but remain relatively poor.

Mitterrand's socialist program Income and wealth redistribution, expansion of the welfare state, and nationalization of large companies in industry and finance.

monetarists The money supply should be expanded at a fairly constant rate rather than being manipulated to combat the business cycle.

monetary overhang Excess monetary emissions in an otherwise state-controlled economy.

monetary policy Conducted by a central bank, which determines the quantity of money and credit conditions.

monetary union One of a variety forms of integration in which member countries agree to use a common currency.

money illusion Economic agents base their decisions on nominal prices and wages rather than on relative prices and real wages.

monopolist The sole producer of a product for which there are no good substitutes. This gives the monopolist some power to set the price of the product.

monopoly rent seeking The expenditure of resources to gain preferences and advantages from the state.

moral hazard Agent exploits an information advantage to alter its behavior after entering into an agreement with the principal.

moral incentives Reward desirable behavior by appealing to the recipient's responsibility to society (or the company) and accordingly raising the recipient's social stature within the community.

mufti A person who issues a fatwa.

multinational corporation A corporation that manages and delivers production and services in a number of countries and employs managers and employees from a number of countries.

multinational enterprises Firms that function in two or more countries.

national champions Companies deemed of such national importance that they must be owned and managed by the state.

national economic plan Directs resource allocation for all (or the most important) sectors of the economy.

National Labor Relations Act of 1935 (NLRA, also called the Wagner Act) The union "bill of rights."

nationalization When privately owned property becomes publicly owned.

natural experiments Serendipitous situations in which persons, groups, or countries are assigned randomly to a treatment and a control group, and outcomes are analyzed for the purposes of testing hypotheses.

natural justice An income distribution based on marginal productivity.

net foreign investment When a country's national savings rate exceeds its domestic investment rate.

net wealth The accumulation of assets in excess of debts or other liabilities.

New Deal A series of public work, unemployment, and social legislation designed to pull the country out of the Great Depression and to help those harmed by it.

New Economic Policy (1) Restored private trade in agricultural goods, denationalized smaller enterprises, and kept larger enterprises under state ownership and control (March 1921 to 1928).

New Economic Policy (NEP) (2) Returned smaller enterprises to private ownership, legalized private trade, and introduced a tax on agriculture to replace grain requisitions.

New Institutional Economics The evolution of institutions and their effect on economic life as explained by economic rationality and self-interest.

New Soviet Person New breed of worker, expert, and manager sharing the idealistic goal of building socialism.

newly independent states (NIS) States (countries) emerging from the former Soviet Union sometimes known in Russia as the "near abroad."

nomenklatura A list of responsible positions that were to be filled by the personnel department of the party.

nonprice information Signals of scarcity and priority that agents in the planned economy send out that are unrelated to prices.

nontax compulsory payments Pension contributions, unemployment insurance, and health benefits.

objective function Summarizes the planners' economic objectives.

objective of the labor-managed enterprise Maximize net income per worker, where net income equals revenue minus costs including taxes.

open economies Economies engaged in international trade—the development of exports and imports and the expansion of direct foreign investment.

opportunistic behavior Agents act contrary to the goals of the principal.

optimal plan That plan from all the possible consistent plans that maximizes the planners' objectives.

organization The complex pattern of communications and other relations in a group of human beings. Or, organization consists of a set of participants (members) regularly interacting in the process of carrying on one or more activities.

organizational reform Changes in organizational arrangements that comprise an economic system.

output plan Tells the producers what to produce and in what assortments.

outsider privatization The sale of an enterprise to persons not connected in any way with the enterprise.

ownership   Amalgam of rights that individuals may have over objects or claims on objects or services; these rights may affect an object's disposition or its utilization.

participatory economy   Firms managed in participatory fashion, income sharing equal for labor of equal intensity and quality, capital owned by the state, and market allocation and freedom of choice of occupation (Vanek).

partnership   Company owned by two or more partners, who make all the business decisions and share in the profits and losses.

patent   Gives the patent holder a monopoly over the product for a specified period of time.

path dependence   Technology and institutional arrangements are not predetermined but depend on initial conditions.

perceptional measures   Measure quantitative measures of aspects of the economic system to study the performance of economic systems.

perfect centralization of information   Single decision maker possesses all information about all participants, their actions, and their environment and transmits only limited pieces of information to subunits.

period of stagnation   The declining growth of the Soviet economic starting in the early 1970s.

petty tutelage   The constant interventions in the affairs of enterprises by superiors.

plan   Activities that are carried out entirely within the organization without the use of market transactions with other organizations.

planned economy   Agents throughout the economy are coordinated by specific instructions or directives formulated by a superior agency (a planning board) and disseminated through a plan document.

planned socialism   Public ownership of the factors of production; centralized decision making; coordinated by a central plan; issuing binding directives; both material and moral incentives; public choices are made by a dictator.

planners' preferences (1)   The basic decision of what to produce is made by planners.

planners' preferences (2)   The setting of economic priorities by political authorities not by households acting as consumers.

planning from the achieved level (1)   Planners make few changes in their plans and repeat historical patterns to avoid major disruptions of the material balances.

planning from the achieved level (2)   The practice of planning based on last year's targets plus marginal changes.

policy (POL)   Trade policy, macroeconomic decision making, the regulatory setting, and other actions that can be changed without changing the economic system itself.

policy activism   The discretionary use of monetary and fiscal policy to try to prevent or ameliorate the business cycle.

policy measures   The framework of political directives designed to influence and direct patterns of resource allocation in an economic system.

politburo   Headed by the **General Secretary of the Party**—the most important position in China.

political economy   Applies economic analysis to the study of how we organize our political system and how politics impacts economic behavior and outcomes.

portfolio investment (1)   Foreign investors simply purchase shares or debt of domestic companies.

portfolio investment (2)   Investment flows from one country to another that occur through the purchase of financial instruments such as stocks and bonds rather than as direct investment (FDI).

poverty deficit   Amount of funding that would be necessary to raise all those below an established poverty line up to that line.

present value   The value on a given date of a future stream of monies usually discounted.

primary market Market in which, the corporation, sells (issues) new shares of stocks or bonds to buyers. Such sales of new shares are called initial public offerings (IPOs).

primary party organization supposedly represented the interests of the party at the local enterprise level.

primitive accumulation Means by which the capitalist class gained a monopoly ownership of capital.

primitive accumulation of capital Initial capital accumulation by the emerging capitalist class.

princelings The offspring of the older generation of party leaders who have profited from their family connections.

principal Party having controlling authority and engaging an agent to act subject to the principal's control and instruction.

principal–agent problem Exists when the agent has a different goal from the principal and when the agent has more information than the principal.

principle of judicial precedents Court decisions should be consistent with past decisions.

private ownership Ownership rights ultimately belongs to individuals, subject to limitations on disposition, use, and earnings.

private sector The business sector in which private ownership prevails and government regulation or intervention is limited.

privatization (1) Property that had been state-owned is transferred to private owners.

privatization (2) The conversion of enterprises owned by the state into enterprises at least partially owned by private owners.

privatization (3) The movement away from state ownership of economic activity and toward private ownership.

producer cooperatives Defined by three characteristics: worker control, profit sharing, and employee ownership.

production relations The arrangements for producing goods and services in an economic system.

productive forces The basic economic forces, for example labor and capital resources, of an economic system.

progressive tax Higher income earners pay a larger share of their incomes in taxation.

property rights Claims for the ownership and use of real property.

propping Financial and other support given by the more profitable units of the conglomerate to support sister units.

public choice The study of how the political system is organized to tax citizens and to spend public resources.

public-choice economics Studies the efficiency of public decision making in democratic societies.

public goods Nonpayers (called free riders) cannot be prevented from enjoying the benefits of the public good, and one person's use of the good does not generally prevent others from using it.

public ownership Ownership rights belong to the state.

qualitative changes Abrupt and violent changes caused by the conflict between old and new productive forces that create a new superstructure.

rational-expectations theory People and businesses tend to use all available information to try to anticipate the future, in particular the rate of inflation.

real business cycle The business cycle is caused by random shocks and cannot be controlled by factors other than the self-correcting mechanism.

reform Systemic changes designed to make the existing system work better.

regionally decentralized authoritarian regime (RDA)   Combination of political centralization and economic regional decentralization.

regressive tax   Higher income earners pay a smaller share of their incomes in taxation.

regulation   The setting of prices and product quality by an agency of the state.

regulatory capture   Regulators favor the interests of the monopolist rather than the interests of the public.

relational contracting   Based not on a formal rule of law but on personal relationships and trust.

relative valuations   Calculated ratios of equivalence substituting for market prices (Barone).

representative democracy   Voters elect representatives to make their public choices for them.

resource base   Typically a reference to natural resources (minerals, timber, agricultural land, favorable climate for agricultural production, etc.).

resource managers   The actors, not the plan itself, that made the actual resource allocation decisions for the economy in the course of plan implementation.

restitution   In transition economies, the compensation for property seized by the state when Communist governments assumed power.

restructuring (1)   Changing the manner in which an enterprise is organized and functions internally.

restructuring (2)   The change of corporate governance arrangements in enterprises as private economic activity replaces state economic activity.

reversibility   The possibility, during transition, that the process of moving from plan to market might be slowed or reversed.

revisionist debate   Argued whether social democrats should abandon Marx's goal of a socialist revolution and work for change within the existing political system.

ruble control   The monitoring of plan fulfillment by monitoring the financial transactions among enterprises.

rule of law   Participants in society and the economy agree on the legal rules concerning social and economic behavior; they behave according to these rules, and there is a punishment mechanism when the rule of law is violated.

rural people's commune   Chinese version of the Soviet collective farm, although on a scale of thousands of families rather than hundreds.

safety net   Policies designed to maintain a minimum standard of living for the population. Examples are unemployment insurance benefits and pensions for the elderly.

savings overhang   The accumulation of forced savings that resulted from having nothing to buy.

Say's Law   There can be no lasting deficiency of aggregate demand because the act of producing a given value of output creates an equivalent amount of income.

scale   The size of an enterprise.

second-economy   Activities that meet at least one of the following two criteria: (1) the activity is engaged in for private gain; (2) the person engaging in the activity knowingly contravenes existing law.

second-round effects   Effects of changing one output or input on other inputs and outputs elsewhere in the balance.

shadow economy   That part of an economy that is outside official channels often conducted in non-monetary terms but not necessarily in violation of laws.

share economy   Employee compensation is tied to company performance through profit sharing (Weitzman).

share economy   Employees share the risks of the company by having bonuses, based on profits, as a substantial component of their compensation.

shareholder value   The value of the corporation in stock markets as measured by its market capitalization.

simple markets   Markets that do not require sophisticated institutions.

social contract (1)   People contract together consensually to establish a limited government. Only such a government is legitimate (Locke).

social contract (2)   The relationship between people and government defined through institutions, laws, policies, etc.

social costs   Equal the private cost plus the unpriced cost of the externality.

Social Market Economy   The state should ensure the workability of the competitive market system but the market should allocate resources. The state should be prepared to intervene, however, to achieve necessary social goals.

social policies   A broad concept referring to policies adopted for preserving the well-being of a society, for example income maintenance programs, unemployment benefits, and the like.

social regulation   The regulation of health, safety, and environment.

socialism   An intermediate and transitory stage during which scarcity still exists and a strong state would be required.

socialism in one country   The argument about whether the Bolsheviks should set as their goal the building of socialism in the USSR or promote a world socialist revolution.

socialist controversy   Whether a planned socialist economy can work at all, and, if yes, whether it can work at a reasonable level of efficiency.

socialist critique   Socialism would not work because relative scarcities cannot be known without market prices and individuals not motivated without private property (Mises and Hayek).

soft budget constraint (1)   Enterprises in socialist economic systems can live beyond their means because they are automatically bailed out by a higher authority.

soft budget constraint (2)   Enterprises that failed to cover their costs received automatic subsidies from the ministry, which redistributed profits from profitable to unprofitable enterprises, or from the state budget.

soft budget constraint (3)   In command economies, the concept that enterprise budgets can be exceeded without consequences.

sole proprietorship   Company owned by one individual, who makes all the business decisions and absorbs the profits (or losses) that the business earns.

Solow residual   Measures the economic growth that is not explained by the growth of labor and capital inputs.

Soviet/Chinese collective farm   Delivers to the state obligatory agricultural products at prices set by the state, sharing what was left over after deliveries and without ownership rights.

special economic zones   Areas freed of trade restrictions and barriers that were allowed to operate under foreign legal regimes.

specification   The nature of an equation, for example, that has been designed to measure the impact of selected explanatory variables on a dependent variable.

spontaneous order   Spontaneous process in which institutions that "work" are sustained and improved while those that do not "work" are replaced.

stability   The absence of significant fluctuations in growth rates, the maintenance of relatively low rates of unemployment, and the avoidance of excessive inflation.

stabilization (1)   The adoption of policies designed to limit the downslide of economic activity as command economies replaced state mechanisms with market mechanisms.

stabilization (2)   The development of institutions and policies designed to limit the decrease of output exhibited during the early phases of transition.

stakeholders   Participate in the operation of the corporation as managers, employees, workers, suppliers, or buyers, but not as owners.

Stalin's Great Break   The policies Stalin put in place starting in 1929 to establish the administrative command economic and political system.

State Bank (Gosbank)   The monopoly bank that handled all enterprise transactions throughout the economy.

state capitalism   An economic model in which the state exercises considerable influence over the economy through its control of large enterprises and extensive regulation.

State Council   The executive branch of the central government.

state-owned company   Owned by the state, which must organize the management team for the company.

state-owned enterprises (SOEs) (1)   Firms or business enterprises owned by the state.

state-owned enterprises (SOEs) (2)   Owned by the state under the jurisdiction of a government entity and run by a state-appointed manager.

state privatization agency   In transition economies, a state agency responsible for organizing and executing privatization.

State Public Banks   Owned in large part by the German state governments (such as Bavaria, Berlin, Westphalia) and by local savings banks. They were founded to promote the regional economy.

static efficiency (1)   An economy operating on its production possibilities frontier.

static efficiency (2)   Takes a snapshot of an economy's efficiency at one point in time.

sterilization   Policy designed to prevent the loss of foreign exchange reserves from affecting the domestic money stock.

stock option   Grants executives the right to buy a designated number of shares of the company at a specified price (often the stock price on the day the stock options were granted).

structural distortion   Usually refers to differences in sectoral structures, for example an emphasis on heavy industry, when former command systems are compared to market economic systems.

success indicator problem   Managers' need to select which orders to fulfill among the multitude of orders they received.

superstructure   The organizational arrangements through which resources (productive forces) will be organized and utilized.

supply plan   Tells producers to whom to deliver their outputs.

surplus value   Profits under capitalism derived from the exploitation of labor.

takeoff into sustained growth   Initial spurt of industrial growth from the first effects of the Industrial Revolution (Rostow).

tax wedge   The difference between the wage received by the worker and the wage paid by the employer.

technical–administrative problems   Limits on decision making because of, for example, incomplete information.

technical coefficients   The inputs needed to produce one unit of output.

techpromfinplan (technical–industrial–financial plan)   The enterprises plan, including output, assortment, labor staffing, and financial plans.

theory of relative backwardness   Backward countries grossly underutilizing resources take steps to accelerate economic growth to catch up to more advanced rivals.

thesis versus antithesis   Evolutionary and inevitable qualitative change that occurs through the competition of opposing forces.

time lags   For example, the time that elapses between the development of a policy measure, the implementation of that measure, and changes in real-world outcomes resulting from this policy measure.

tournament competition   Players in the competition are judged by their relative performance (relative to other players).

township and village enterprises (TVEs)   Enterprises that are at least nominally owned by the township or village. They provided official cover for what were often purely private owners.

trade aversion   The deliberate underutilization of trade potential.

trade barriers   Tariffs, export subsidies, and other non-tariff barriers that are designed to reduce imports.

tradeoffs   The sacrifice of one thing (such as one economic goal) for another.

tragedy of the commons   The misuse and eventual destruction by individuals, acting in their own interests, of a commonly held asset.

transaction costs   Costs associated with searching for information, bargaining, and policing and enforcement.

transfer payments   Payments by the state out of revenues from taxpayers to recipients who have not provided a service in return.

transition   The replacement of one economic system by a fundamentally different economic system.

transition economics   Study of the process of converting the countries of the former Soviet Union and Eastern Europe from planned socialist economies into entirely different economic systems.

transparency   The openness of a process such that all aspects of the process can be observed and assessed.

trial and error pricing   The CPB sets prices arbitrarily and then adjusts them based on shortages and surpluses until equilibrium prices are reached (Lange).

tunneling   Awarding of contract to firms, individuals, or interests that are insiders to the conglomerate.

turnover tax   A differentiated tax on consumer good that depended on consumer demand for the product and is the difference between the wholesale and retail price.

two-tier labor market   Full-time employees enjoy full protection, but part-time workers and independent contractors are not protected by labor protection laws.

underemployment   The employment of individuals on a full-time basis at work in which they utilize their skills at well under their full potential.

underwriter   Organizes the initial sale of shares, sometimes buying stakes in the company themselves.

unfunded liability   The shortfall in funds that have been accumulated to meet the future obligations of an entitlement program.

unifying features of the Asian model   The high rates of savings and investment and the distinctive organization of capital markets and corporate governance.

universal banks   Perform not only traditional banking but also risk-sharing, stock sales, and merchant-banking functions.

U.S. exceptionalism   The notion that the United States is a unique social, economic, and political experiment made possible by a unique confluence of events in the late eighteenth century.

valuation   Assessing the worth of an enterprise for the purpose of sale.

veil of ignorance   A hypothetical situation in which people would be born without any clue of the advantages or disadvantages that lay before them in life.

venture capital (1)   Capital invested in new businesses in which there is a considerable amount of risk.

venture capital (2)   Financing through purchases of shares or loans to start up businesses.

venture capital fund   Provides start-up capital to new firms and takes a stake in them in return.

vertical transaction   An order from an administrative superior that is binding on the subordinate.

vertical trust   Subordinates obey orders given to them by superiors.

virtuous government   As taught by Confucianism suggested a significant and positive role for government in the economy.

vouchers   A document that represents an ownership claim that can be exercised to acquire the shares of an enterprise.

War Communism (1)   The nationalization of most of the economy, the attempt to eliminate market relationships in industry and trade, and the forced requisitioning of agricultural products from the peasants.

War Communism (2)   The Soviet economic system that existed from 1918 to March 1921; virtually all enterprises nationalized, private trade and money outlawed, and peasant crops confiscated.

Washington Consensus   Set of guidelines developed and implemented by the IMF to promote economic growth through macroeconomic stabilization and privatization.

weights   These measure how important each performance indicator is.

welfare state   The state collects and redistributes a large share of economic resources for the purpose of achieving economic and political goals.

"Western-style" tax system   The tax system used in market economies (sales, VAT, and so on) as opposed to command economies (turnover tax and the like).

widely held company   A large number of owners (shareholders), none of which own a controlling interest.

World Bank   An international organization making loans to member countries for the purpose of promoting economic growth and development. Founded in 1944 and located in Washington, D.C., it works closely with the International Monetary Fund.

World Trade Organization (WTO)   Successor to GATT; provides a forum for the discussion of world trade issues.

WTO membership   Obligated China to comply with WTO rules and regulations concerning international copyright laws, trademarks, visas, business licenses, and protection of domestic industries.

zaibatsu   Vertical or horizontal conglomerates that dominated Japanese industry and commerce before World War II.

Index

Note: Page numbers followed by an "e" indicates exhibits; a "f" indicates figures; a "t" indicates tables.